W9-ADM-567

STOCKS
BONDS
BILLS
AND
INFLATION

SBBI

1999
YEARBOOK

MARKET
RESULTS
FOR
1926-1998

IBBOTSON
ASSOCIATES

Stocks, Bonds, Bills, and Inflation 1999 Yearbook.

Published by:

Ibbotson Associates
225 North Michigan Avenue, Suite 700
Chicago, Illinois 60601-7676
Telephone (312) 616-1620
Fax (312) 616-0404
www.ibbotson.com

ISBN 1-882864-09-3
ISSN 1047-2436

Additional copies of this Yearbook may be obtained for $100, plus shipping and handling, by calling or writing to the address above. Order forms are provided inside the back cover. Information about volume discounts, companion publications and consulting services may also be obtained. The data in this *Yearbook* are also available with our Analyst software, a Microsoft Windows™ application. Statistics and graphs can be quickly accessed over any subperiod. Updates can be obtained annually, semi-annually, quarterly or monthly. For more information about Analyst, call (800) 758-3557 or write to the address listed above.

Table of Contents

Table of Contents

(continued)

Table of Contents
(continued)

Most Commonly Used References

Graph/Table/Equation

List of Tables
(Text)

List of Tables
(Text)

(continued)

List of Graphs
(Text)

List of Graphs
(Text)

(continued)

List of Graphs
(Image)

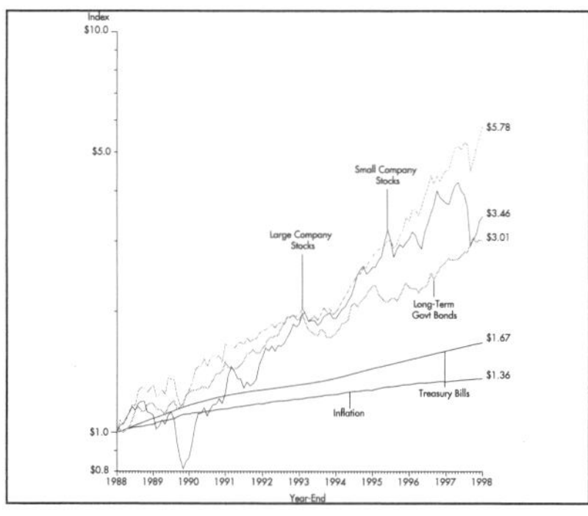

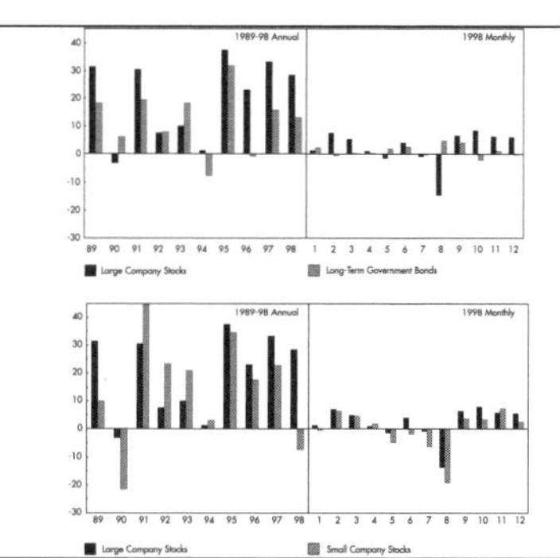

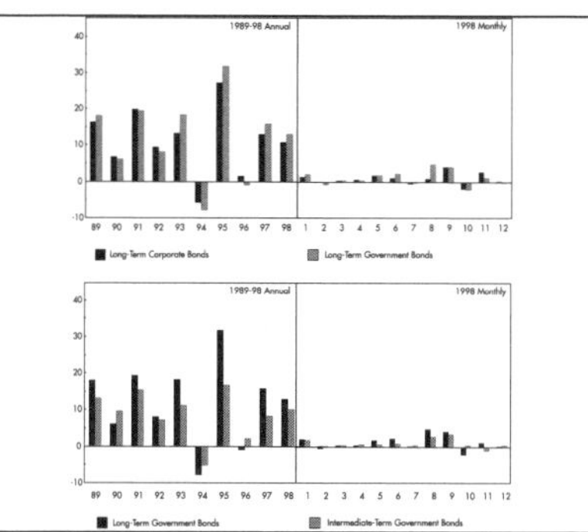

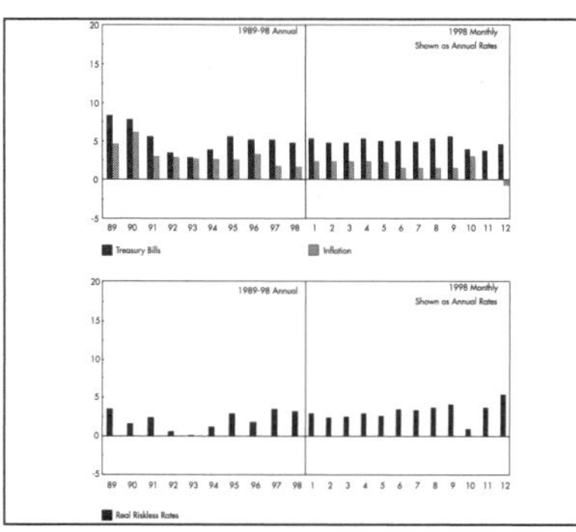

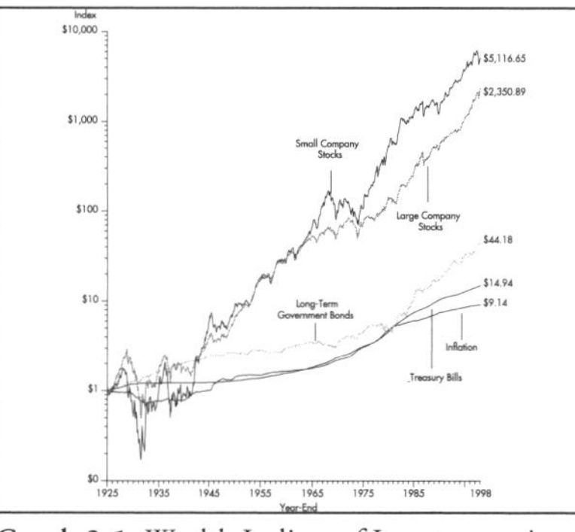

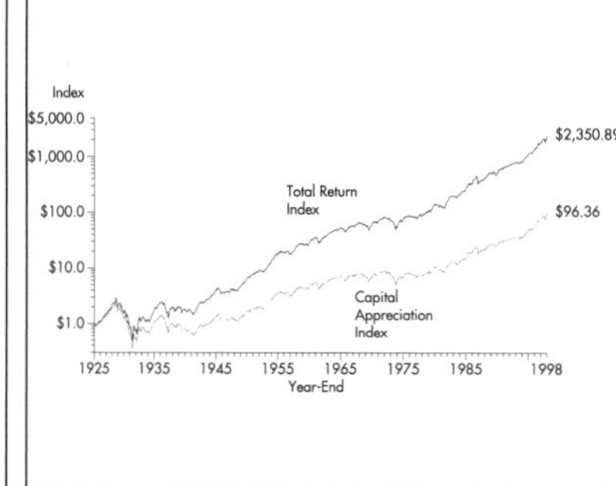

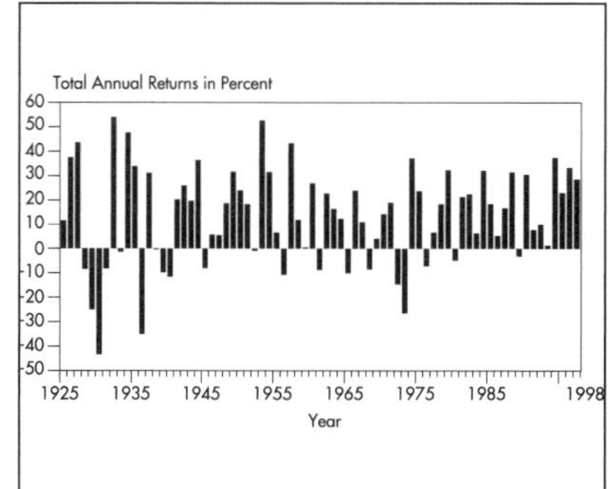

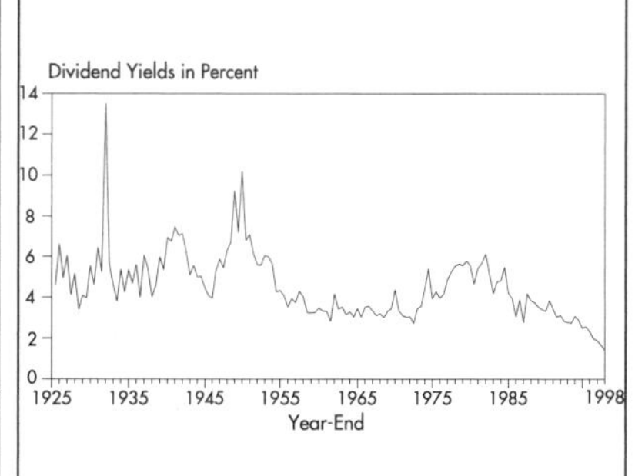

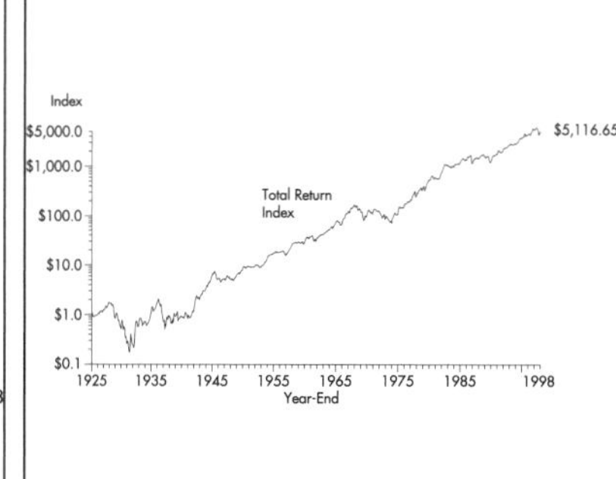

List of Graphs
(Image)

(continued)

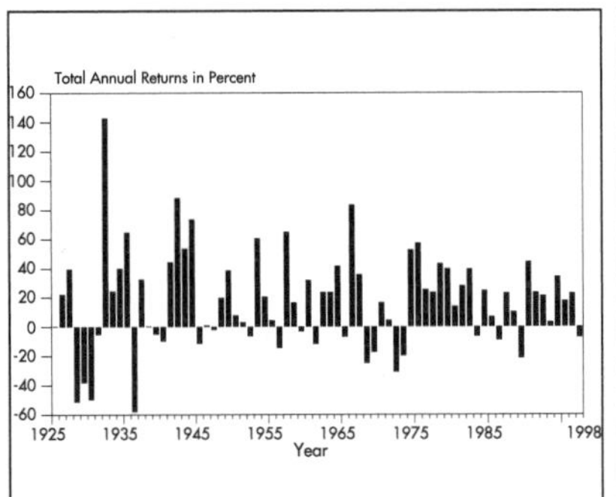

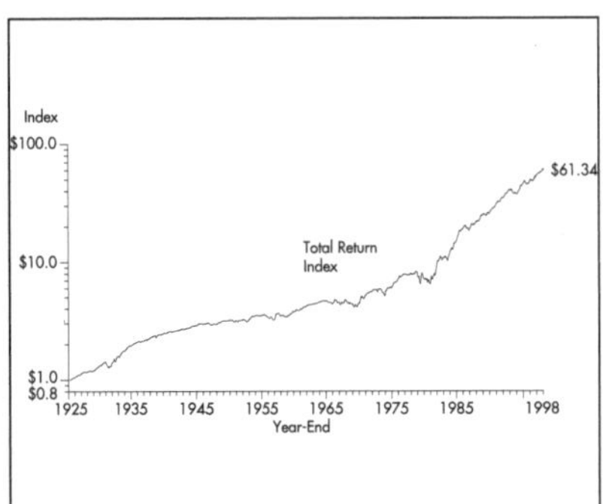

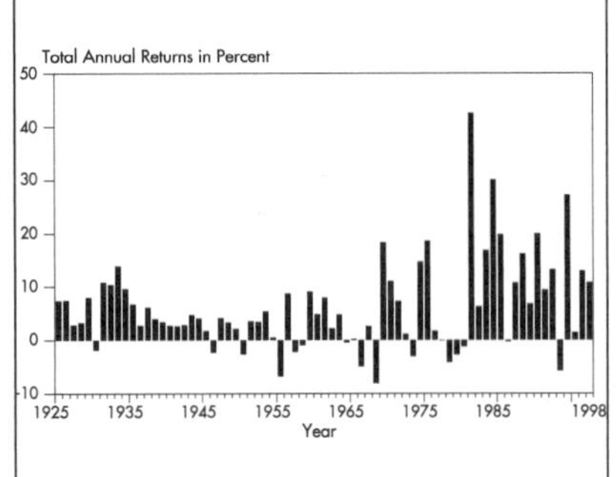

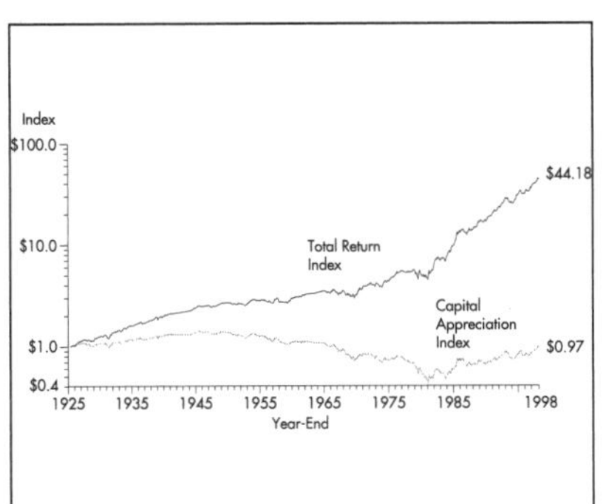

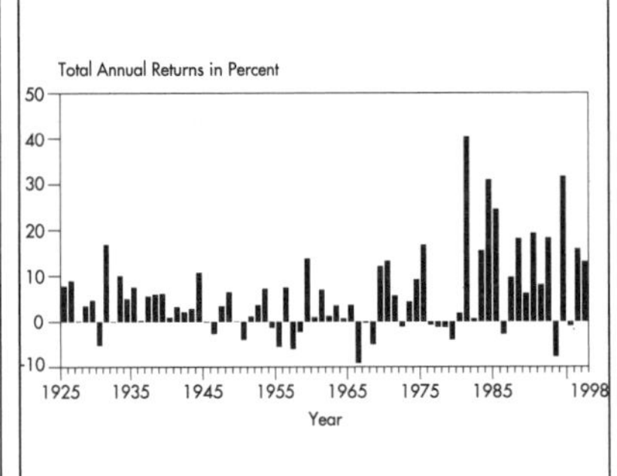

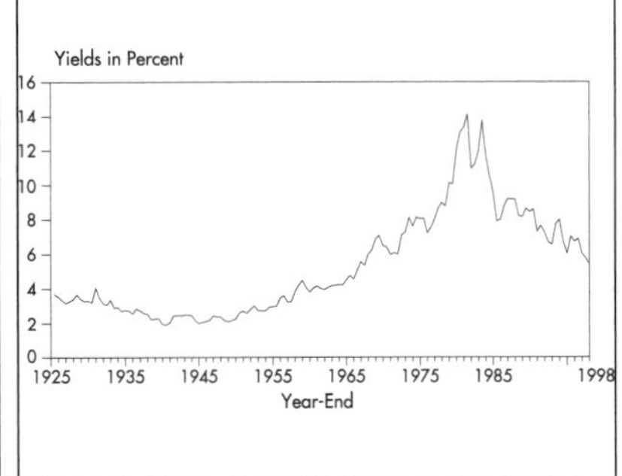

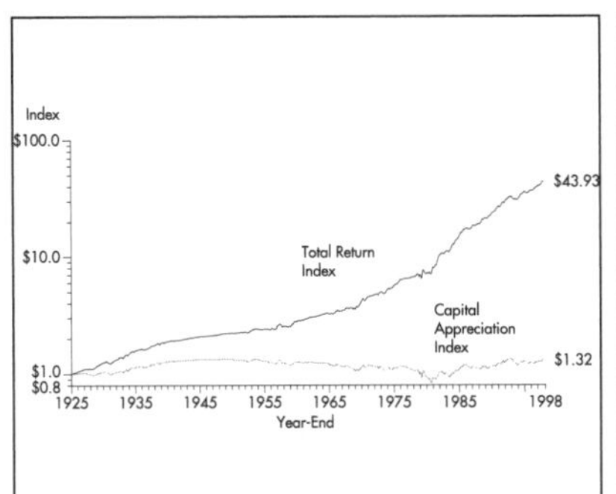

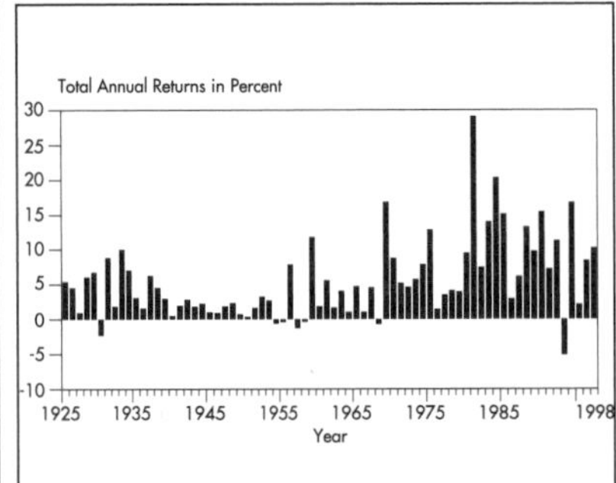

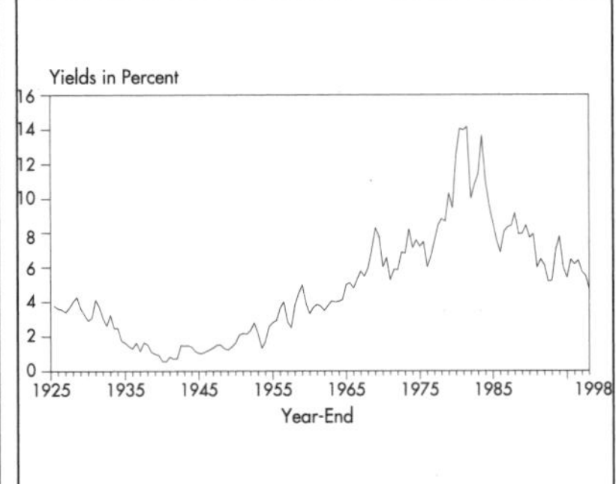

List of Graphs
(Image)

(continued)

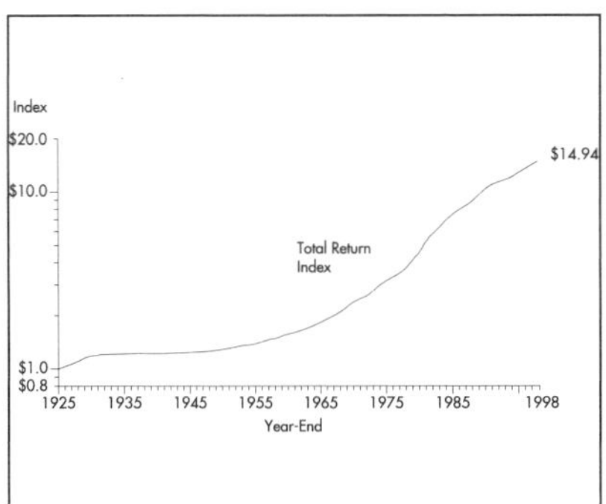

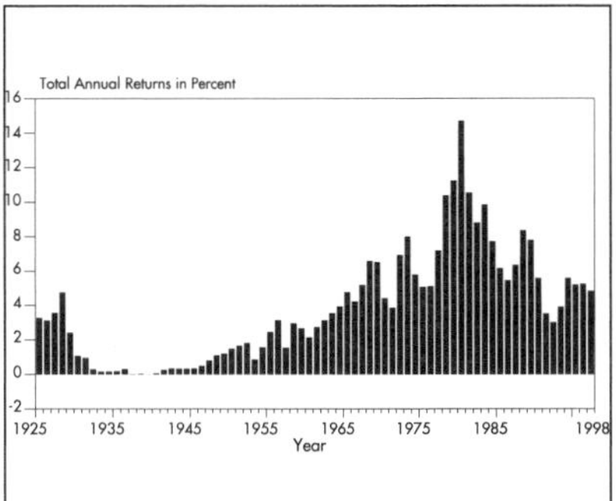

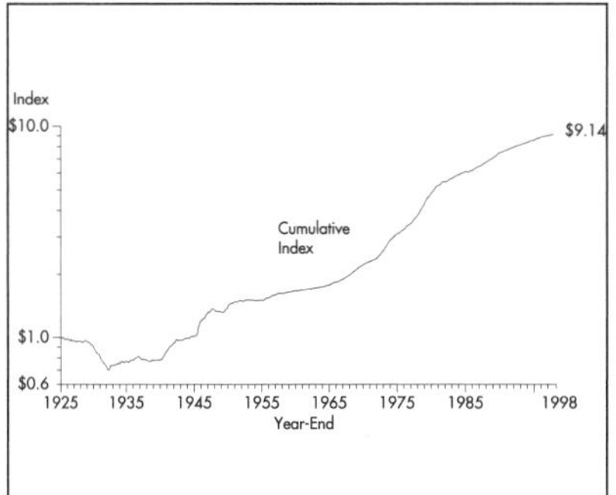

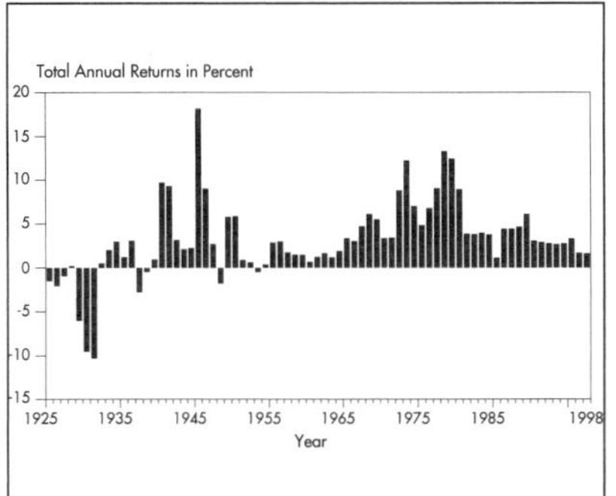

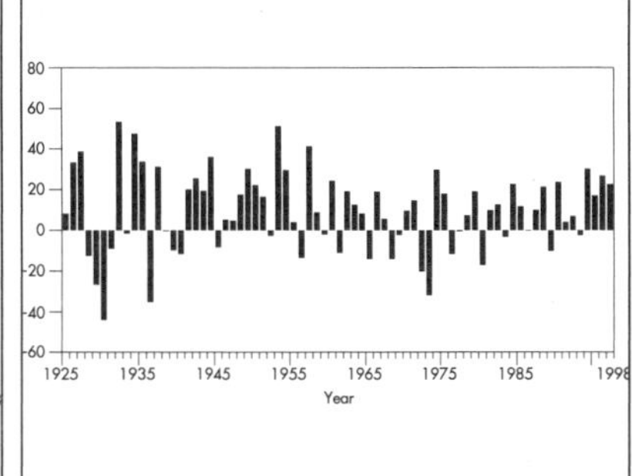

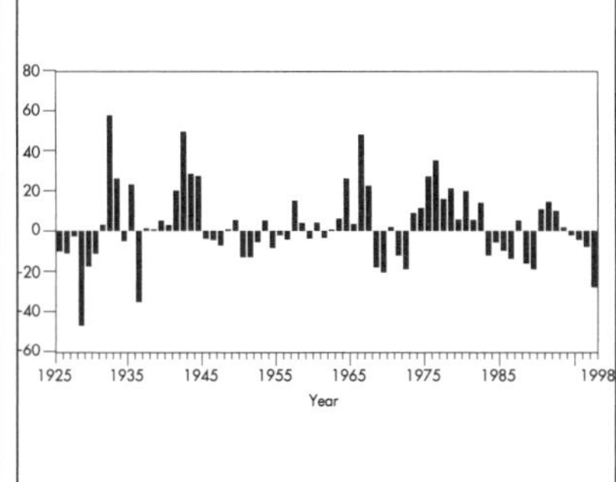

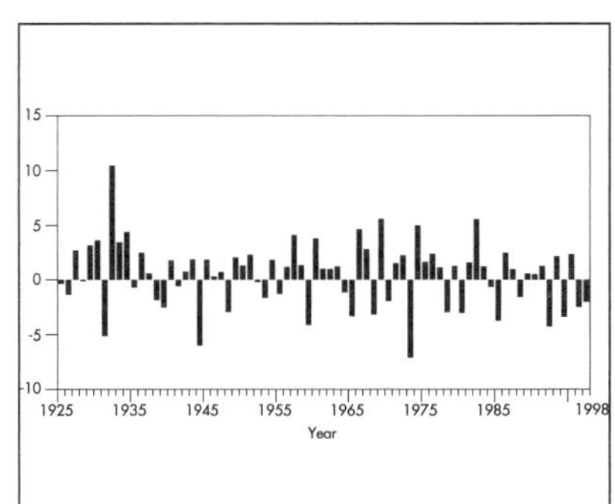

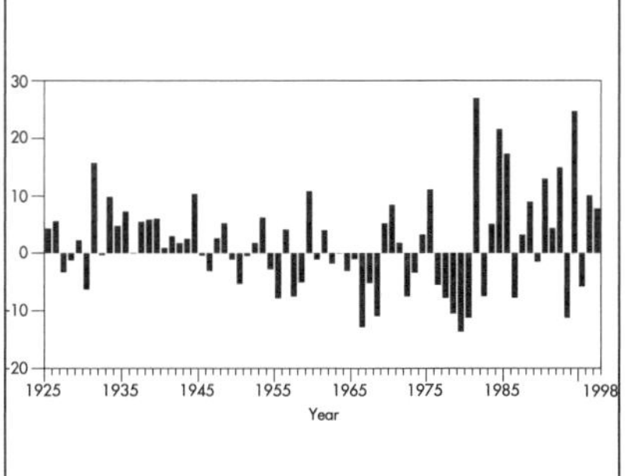

List of Graphs
(Image)

(continued)

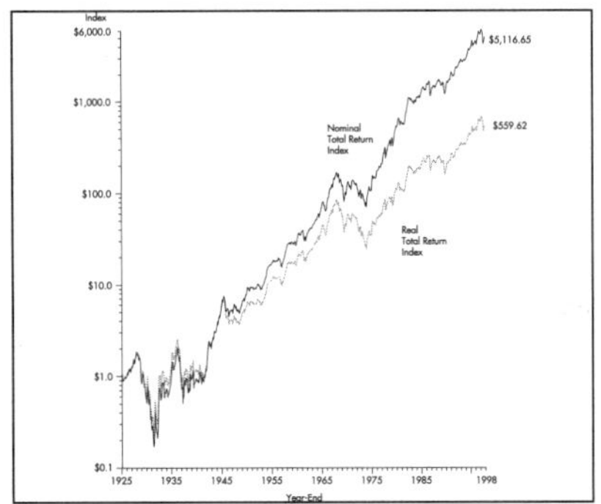

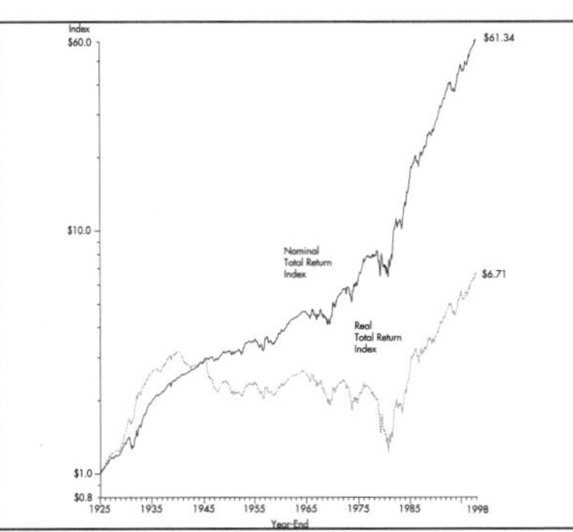

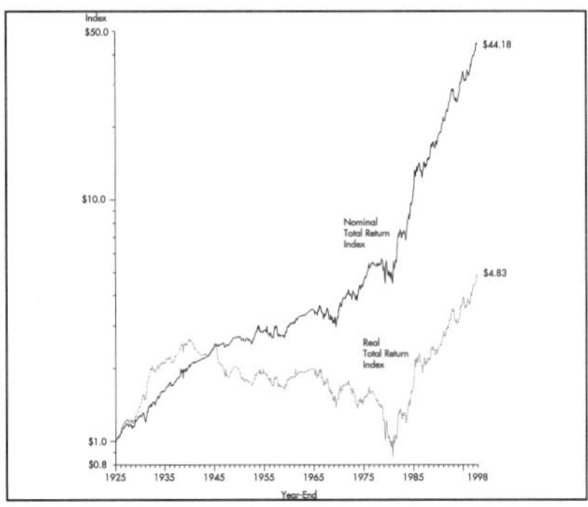

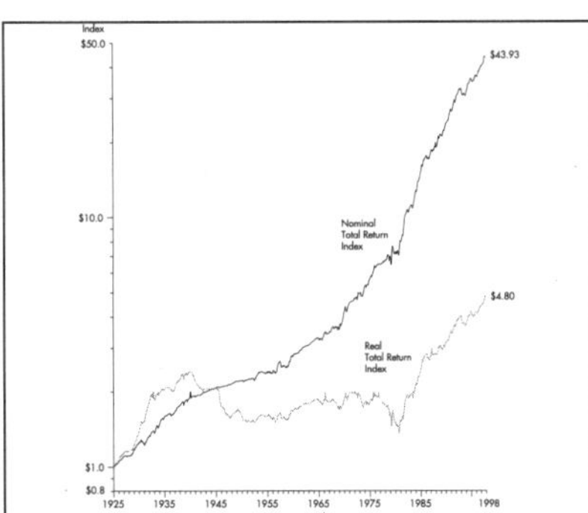

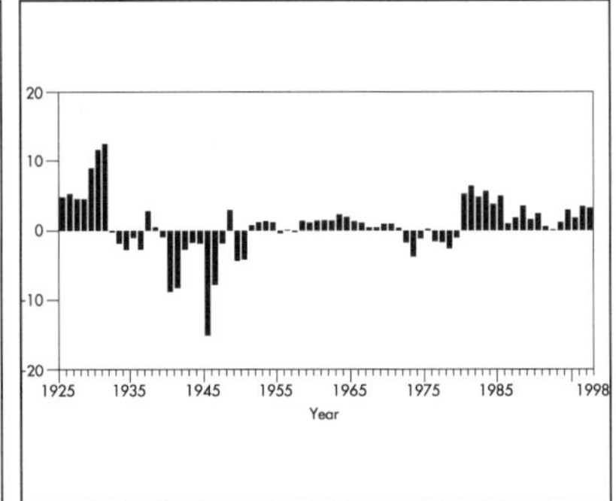

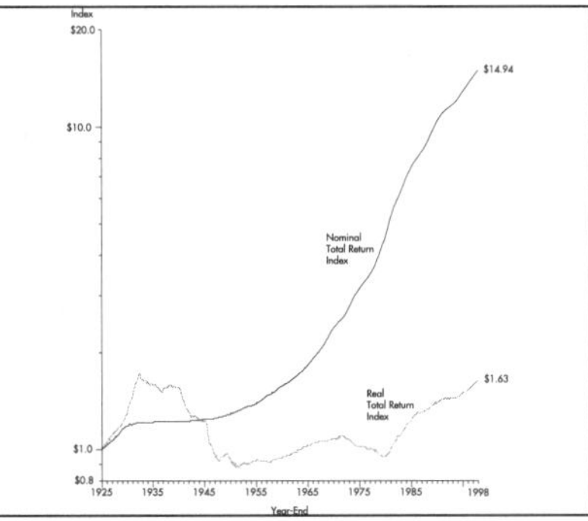

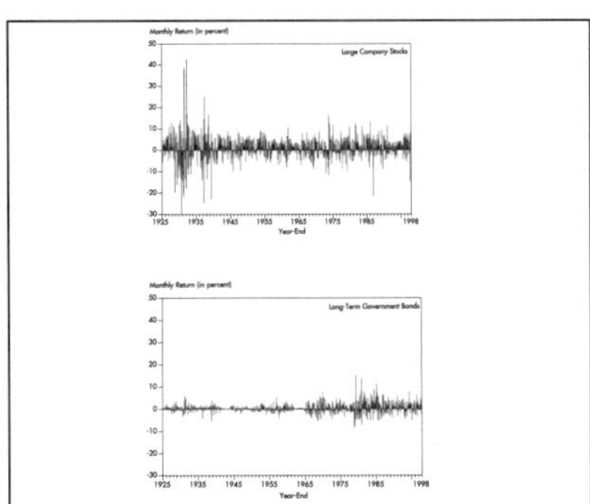

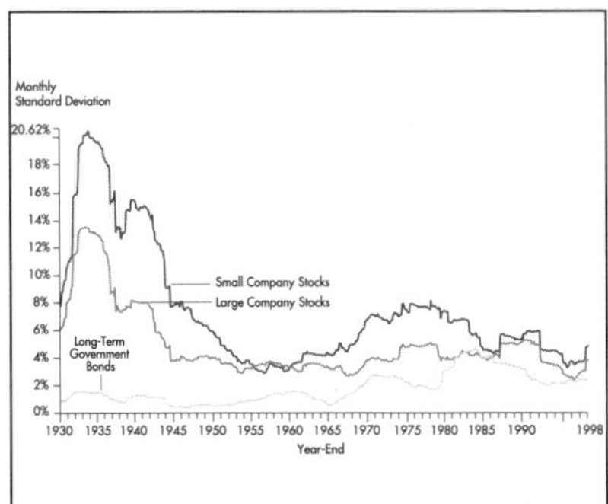

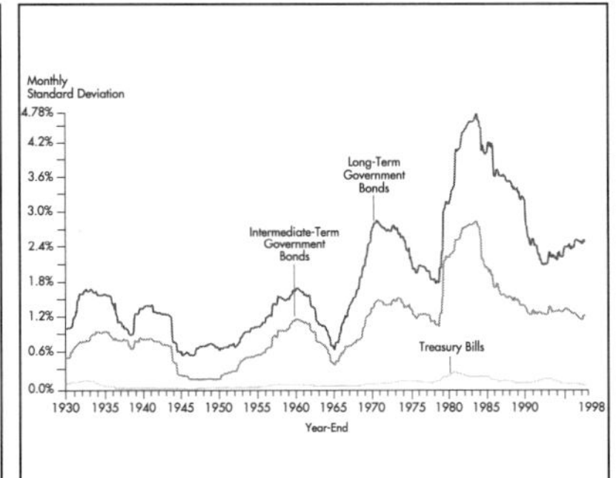

List of Graphs
(Image)

(continued)

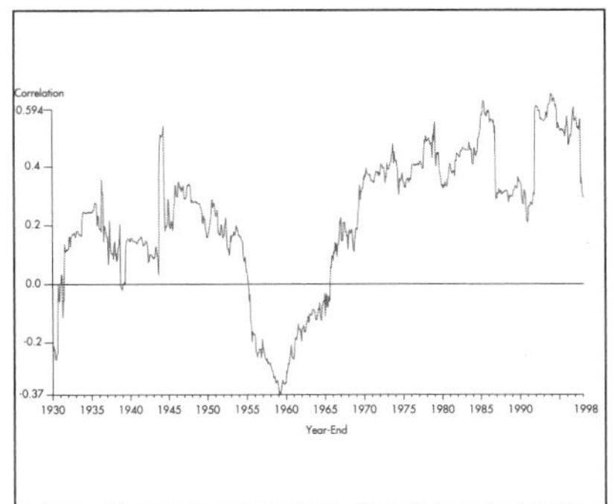

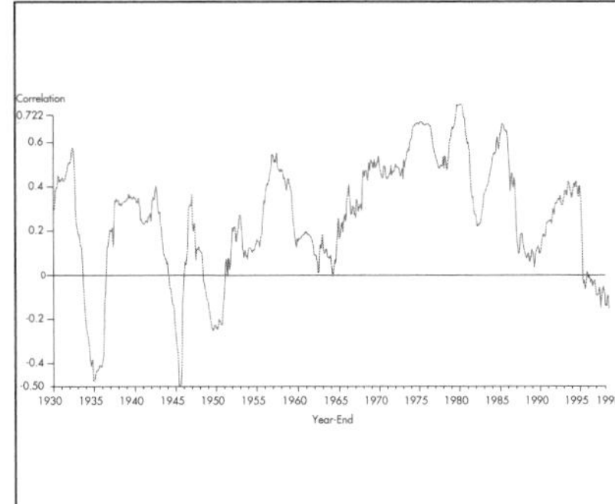

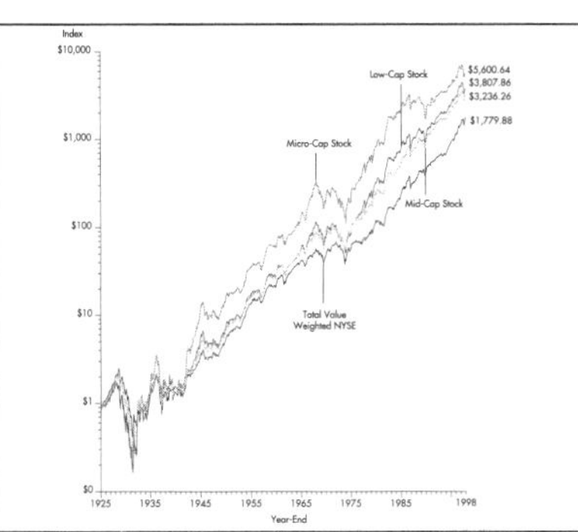

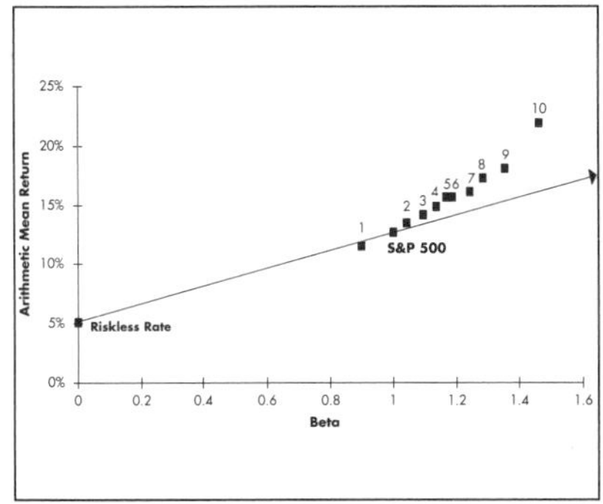

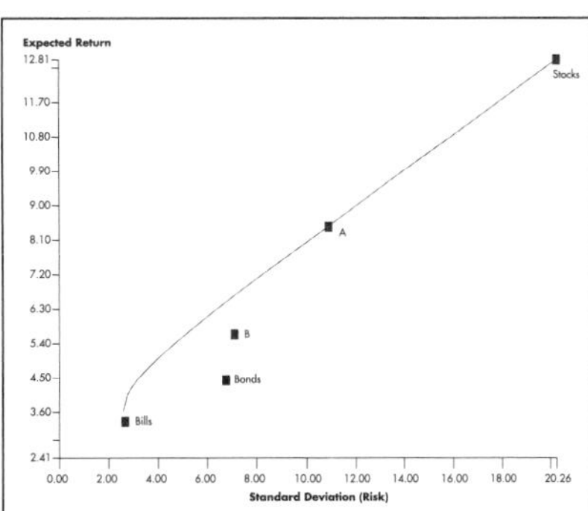

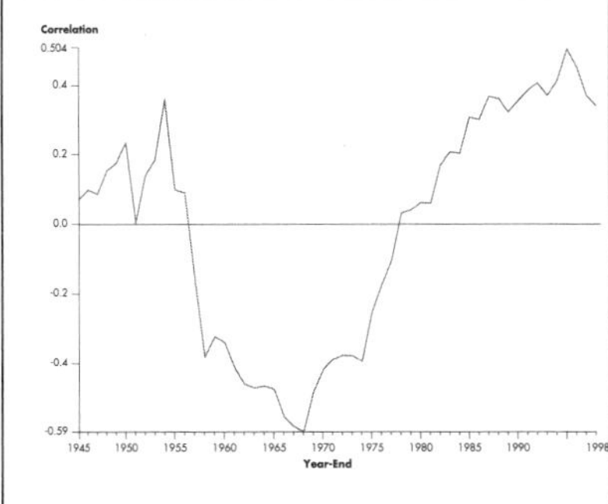

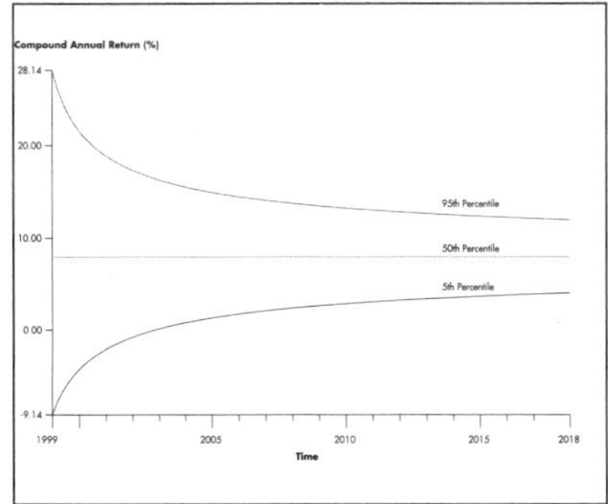

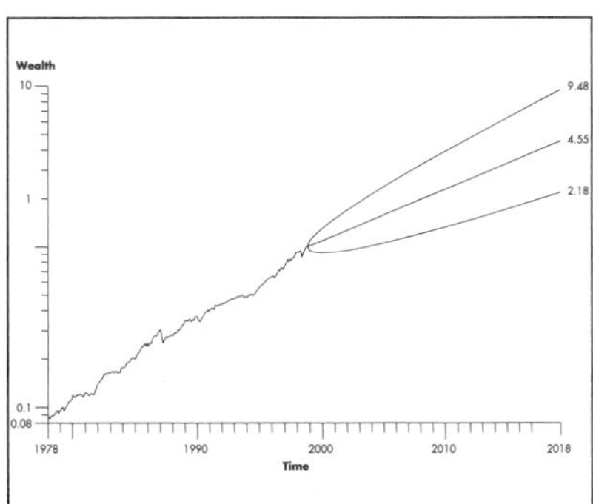

Acknowledgments

We thank, foremost, Roger G. Ibbotson, professor in the practice of finance at the Yale School of Management and chairman of Ibbotson Associates, for his contribution to this book. Professor Ibbotson and Rex A. Sinquefield, chairman of Dimensional Fund Advisors, Inc. (Santa Monica, CA), wrote the two journal articles and four books upon which this *Yearbook* is based and formulated much of the philosophy and methodology. Mr. Sinquefield also provides the small stock returns, as he has since 1982.

We thank others who contributed to this book. Rolf W. Banz provided the small stock returns for 1926–1981. Thomas S. Coleman (Greenwich, CT), Professor Lawrence Fisher of Rutgers University, and Roger Ibbotson constructed the model used to generate the intermediate-term government bond series for 1926–1933. The pioneering work of Professors Fisher and James H. Lorie of the University of Chicago inspired the original monograph. Stan V. Smith, President of the Corporate Financial Group, Ltd. and former Managing Director at Ibbotson Associates, originated the idea of the *Yearbook* and its companion update services. The Center for Research in Security Prices at the University of Chicago contributed the data and methodology for the returns on the NYSE by capitalization decile used in Chapter 7, *Firm Size and Return.* Michael J. Mattson, former Managing Director at Ibbotson Associates contributed Chapter 8, *Estimating the Cost of Capital or Discount Rate.* Paul D. Kaplan, *Vice President and Chief Economist* at Ibbotson Associates contributed Chapter 9, using historical data in optimization and forecasting.

We thank Laurence B. Siegel, Director of Quantitative Analysis at the Ford Foundation (New York) and former Managing Director at Ibbotson Associates, for his many creative contributions to the *Yearbook* over the years. We also thank David Montgomery, Managing Director of Ibbotson Associates, for his guidance and expertise. Finally, we would like to thank Dian D. Chesney for her dedication to the design of this publication from its inception.

Production Staff
Kevin Ryan, *Managing Editor*
Heather Alsum, *Desktop Publisher/Graphic Design*
Renée Lyn Altobelli, *Production Coordinator*
LaVonne Mikesh, *Graphic Design*

Contributing Editors
Devin Armstrong
Tom Hogan
Matt Kammerzell
Mary Nguyen
Kevin Wilson

Senior Editors
Michael Annin, CFA
Dominic Falaschetti, CFA

Introduction

Who Should Read This Book

This book is a history of the returns on the capital markets in the United States from 1926 to the present. It is useful to a wide variety of readers. Foremost, anyone serious about investments or investing needs an appreciation of capital market history. Such an appreciation, which can be gained from this book, is equally valuable to the individual and institutional investor. For students at both the graduate and undergraduate levels, this book is both a source of ideas and a reference. Other intended readers include teachers of these students; practitioners and scholars in finance, economics, and business; portfolio strategists; and security analysts.

Chief financial officers and, in some cases, chief executive officers of corporations will find this book useful. Persons concerned with the cost of capital can directly apply the findings. More generally, persons concerned with history may find it valuable to study the detail of economic history as revealed in more than six decades of capital market returns.

To these diverse readers, we provide two resources. One is the data. The other is a thinking person's guide to using historical data to understand the financial markets and make decisions. This historical record raises many questions. This book represents our way of appreciating the past—only one of the many possible ways—but one grounded in real theory. We provide a means for the reader to think about the past and the future of financial markets.

How to Read This Book

Intended Reader	Most Important Chapters	Other Related Chapters, Graphs, Tables, and Appendices
Persons Concerned with Data	Chapters 1, 2, and 3	➢ Chapters 4 and 7; Graph 2-1; Table 2-1; and Appendices A, B, and C
Financial Planners, Asset Allocators, and Investment Consultants	Chapters 1, 2, and 9	➢ Chapter 6; Graphs 2-1 and 9-1; and Tables 2-7 and 6-6
Individual Investors	Chapters 1 and 2	➢ Graph 2-1; and Table 2-1
Institutional Investors, Portfolio Managers, and Security Analysts	Chapters 1 through 9	➢ Tables 2-7, 6-6 and 7-1

Intended Reader	Most Important Chapters	Other Related Chapters, Graphs, Tables, and Appendices
Students, Faculty, and Economists	Chapters 2, 5, 7, 8, 9	➢ Tables 6-6 and 8-1
Brokers and Security Sales Representatives	Chapters 1 and 2	➢ Graph 2-1; and Tables 2-1 and 2-5
Investment Bankers, Security Sales Representatives, Appraisers, and Valuation Consultants	Chapters 2, 7, and 8	➢ Tables 2-1 and 8-1
Executives, Corporate Planners, Chief Financial Officers, Chief Executive Officers, and Treasurers	Chapters 1, 2, 8, and 9	➢ Chapters 1 and 2; Graph 9-1; and Table 8-1
Pension Plan Sponsors	Chapters 1, 2, and 9	➢ Graph 2-1; and Tables 2-1 and 2-4

The Journal of Business published Roger G. Ibbotson and Rex A. Sinquefield's two companion papers on security returns in January 1976 and July 1976. In the first paper, the authors collected historical data on the returns from stocks, government and corporate bonds, U.S. Treasury bills, and consumer goods (inflation). To uncover the risk/return and the real/nominal relationship in the historical data, they presented a framework in which the return on an asset class is the sum of two or more elemental parts. These elements, such as real returns (returns in excess of inflation) and risk premia (for example, the net return from investing in large company stocks rather than bills), are referred to throughout the book as derived series.

In the second paper, the authors analyzed the time series behavior of the derived series and the information contained in the U.S. government bond yield curve to obtain inputs for a simulation model of future security price behavior. Using the methods developed in the two papers, they forecast security returns through the year 2000.

The response to these works showed that historical data are fascinating in their own right. Both total and component historical returns have a wide range of applications in investment management, corporate finance, academic research, and industry regulation. Subsequent work—the 1977, 1979 and 1982 Institute of Chartered Financial Analysts (ICFA) monographs; the 1989 Dow Jones-Irwin book; and Ibbotson Associates' 1983 through 1998 *Stocks, Bonds, Bills, and Inflation*™ *Yearbooks*—updated and further developed the historical data and forecasts. (All references for previous works used in the development of Stocks, Bonds, Bills, and Inflation [SBBI] data appear at the end of this introduction in the References section.)

In 1981, Ibbotson and Sinquefield began tracking a new asset class: small company stocks. This class consists of issues listed on the New York Stock Exchange (NYSE) that rank in the ninth and tenth (lowest) deciles when sorted by capitalization (price times number of shares outstanding), plus non-NYSE issues of comparable capitalization. This asset class has been of interest to researchers and investors because of its high long-term returns. Intermediate-term (five years to maturity) government bonds were added in 1988. Monthly and annual total returns, income returns, capital appreciation returns, and yields are presented.

The Stocks, Bonds, Bills, and Inflation 1999 Yearbook

In the present volume the historical data are updated. The motivations are: 1) to document this history of security market returns; 2) to uncover the relationships between the various asset class returns as revealed by the derived series: inflation, real interest rates, risk premia, and other premia; 3) to encourage deeper understanding of the underlying economic history through the graphic presentation of data; and 4) to answer questions most frequently asked by subscribers.

In keeping with the spirit of the previous work, the asset classes contained in this edition highlight the differences between targeted segments of the financial markets in the United States. Our intent is to show historical trade-offs between risk and return.

In this book, the equity markets are segmented between large and small company stocks. Fixed income markets are segmented on two dimensions. Riskless U.S. government securities are differentiated by maturity or investment horizon. U.S. Treasury bills with approximately 30 days to maturity are used to describe the short end of the horizon; U.S. Treasury securities with approximately five years to maturity are used to describe the middle horizon segment; and U.S. Treasury securities with approximately 20 years to maturity are used to describe the long maturity end of the market. A corporate bond series with a long maturity is used to describe fixed income securities that contain risk of default.

Some indices of the stock and bond markets are broad, capturing most or all of the capitalization of the market. Our indices are intentionally narrow. The large company stock series captures the largest issues (those in the Standard & Poor's 500 Composite Index), while the small company stock series is composed of the smallest issues. By studying these polar cases, we identify the small stock premium (small minus large stock returns) and the premium of large stocks over bonds and bills. Neither series is intended to be representative of the entire stock market. Likewise, our long-term government bond and

U.S. Treasury bill indices show the returns for the longest and shortest ends of the yield curve, rather than the return for the entire Treasury float. Readers and investors should understand that our bond indices do not, and are not intended to, describe the experience of the typical bond investor who is diversified across maturities; rather, we present returns on carefully focused segments of the market for U.S. Treasury securities.

Recent Changes and Additions

In this most recent edition, the publication has been redesigned for easier readability. This includes expanding some tables from one to two pages and presenting data with larger fonts.

In previous editions, the two equity asset classes were described as common stocks and small company stocks. The returns for the S&P 500 aggregate were used to construct the common stock indices. While the S&P 500 is generally accepted as a benchmark of the U.S. equity market as a whole, it is composed of 500 of the largest companies in the U.S. equity markets. Therefore, we use large company stocks, or large stocks, to describe this asset class in this edition.

The data provider for the S&P 500 returns is now Standard and Poor's. Previously data was provided by the American National Bank and Trust Company. See Chapter 3, *Description of Basic Series*, for more details.

In Chapter 6, *Statistical Analysis of Returns*, the discussion of *Changes in the Risk of Assets Over Time* has been expanded to include a table of annualized monthly standard deviations by decade.

Chapter 7, *Firm Size and Return*, includes tables and a graph featuring mid-, low- and micro-cap total return and index values. In addition, Chapter 7 and 8 now refer to the expected size premia, or return in excess of risk, rather than the expected small stock premia. In Chapter 8, the expected risk premia for fixed income are now calculated from 1970 to present, reflecting the fundamental change in the U.S. bond market at that time.

Additional examples have been added to explain many of the calculations found within each chapter. The glossary of helpful terms and definitions has also been expanded and can be found on page 311.

In prior editions, a back-revision was made to the June 1992 large company stock total return resulting in a restatement of index values for that month and all subsequent months. The numerical impact of this revision is very small. Long-term corporate bond total returns for January 1980–September 1985 were revised in prior editions to reflect those published by our source, Salomon Brothers. This resulted in a restatement of the index values for those months and all subsequent months.

Throughout the 1996 edition, the December 1995 inflation rate was estimated due to delays from the U.S. Department of Labor, Bureau of Labor Statistics. Due to severe weather in Washington and the partial government shut down, an actual December 1995 inflation number was unavailable at the time of publication. All data and statistics affected by this estimate have been restated in the 1997 and current editions to reflect the figures reported by the U.S. Department of Labor.

The SBBI Data Series

The series presented here are total returns, and where applicable or available, capital appreciation returns and income returns for:

SBBI Data Series	Series Construction	Index Components	Approximate Maturity
1. Large Company Stocks	S&P 500 Composite with dividends reinvested. (S&P 500, 1957–Present; S&P 90, 1926–1956)	Total Return Income Return Capital Appreciation Return	n/a
2. Small Company Stocks	Fifth capitalization quintile of stocks on the NYSE for 1926–1981. Performance of the Dimensional Fund Advisors (DFA) Small Company Fund 1982–Present.	Total Return	n/a
3. Long-Term Corporate Bonds	Salomon Brothers Long-Term High Grade Corporate Bond Index	Total Return	20 Years
4. Long-Term Government Bonds	A One Bond Portfolio	Total Return Income Return Capital Appreciation Return Yield	20 Years
5. Intermediate-Term Government Bonds	A One Bond Portfolio	Total Return Income Return Capital Appreciation Return Yield	5 Years
6. U.S. Treasury Bills	A One Bill Portfolio	Total Return	30 Days
7. Consumer Price Index	CPI—All Urban Consumers, not seasonally adjusted	Inflation Rate	n/a

References

1. *Stocks, Bonds, Bills, and Inflation Yearbook,* annual. 1983, 1984, 1985, 1986, 1987, 1988, 1989, 1990, 1991, 1992, 1993, 1994, 1995, 1996, 1997, 1998. Ibbotson Associates, Chicago.

2. Banz, Rolf W., "The Relationship Between Return and Market Value of Common Stocks," *Journal of Financial Economics* 9:3-18, 1981.

3. Coleman, Thomas S., Lawrence Fisher, and Roger G. Ibbotson, *U.S. Treasury Yield Curves 1926–1988,* Moody's Investment Service, New York, 1990.

4. Coleman, Thomas S., Lawrence Fisher, and Roger G. Ibbotson, *Historical U.S. Treasury Yield Curves 1926–1992* with 1994 update, Ibbotson Associates, Chicago, 1994.

5. Ibbotson, Roger G., and Rex A. Sinquefield, *Stocks, Bonds, Bills, and Inflation: Historical Returns (1926–1987),* 1989 ed., Dow-Jones Irwin, Homewood, IL, 1989.

6. Ibbotson, Roger G., and Rex A. Sinquefield, (foreword by Laurence B. Siegel) *Stocks, Bonds, Bills, and Inflation: The Past and the Future,* 1982 ed., Institute of Chartered Financial Analysts, Charlottesville, VA, 1982.

7. Ibbotson, Roger G., and Rex A. Sinquefield, *Stocks, Bonds, Bills, and Inflation: Historical Returns (1926–1978),* Institute of Chartered Financial Analysts, Charlottesville, VA, 1979.

8. Ibbotson, Roger G., and Rex A. Sinquefield (foreword by Jack L. Treynor), *Stocks, Bonds, Bills, and Inflation: The Past (1926–1976) and the Future (1977–2000),* 1977 ed., Institute of Chartered Financial Analysts, Charlottesville, VA, 1977.

9. Ibbotson, Roger G., and Rex A. Sinquefield, "Stocks, Bonds, Bills, and Inflation: Simulations of the Future (1926–2000)," *The Journal of Business* 49, No. 3 (July 1976), pp. 313–338.

10. Ibbotson, Roger G., and Rex A. Sinquefield, "Stocks, Bonds, Bills, and Inflation: Year-By-Year Historical Returns (1926–1974)," *The Journal of Business* 49, No. 1 (January 1976), pp. 11–47.

STOCKS
BONDS
BILLS
AND
INFLATION

Part One: Results and Methods

1

Chapter 1 Highlights of the 1998 Markets and the Past Decade

Events of 1998

Despite considerable volatility, domestic large stocks continued to perform well in 1998. This is the fourth consecutive year of stock returns over twenty percent, marking the only four-year period of its kind over the past 73 years. Small stocks continued their uncharacteristic period of under-performing their larger counterparts. The margin of underperformance was much larger than it has been previously. Bond returns were also rather volatile throughout 1998. Yields dropped in the later part of the year as the Fed lowered its Federal Funds Rate on three separate occasions. The Fed's action was taken to alleviate credit concerns due to the economic crisis overseas. Since May of 1997 the rate had remained unchanged at 5.5 percent. Three consecutive 0.25 percent rate reductions were made in September, October, and November, ending at 4.75 percent. This benchmark for short-term interest rates has not been this low since 1994. The October rate cut was also the first time since 1994 that the Fed changed rates between regularly scheduled meetings.

Economic Growth Continues

In spite of economic uncertainty, the Gross Domestic Product (GDP), a measure of the market value of all goods and services produced within the U.S., grew at the same real (inflation-adjusted) rate as the prior year. Both the 1997 and 1998 growth rates were approximately 3.9 percent. However, quarterly growth was much more sporadic than in the prior year, with a significant slowdown in the second quarter.

In 1998, the U.S. civilian unemployment rate continued to fall. From a high of 4.7 percent at year end 1997, unemployment fell slightly to 4.3 percent by year end 1998. The jobless rate has not been this low since 1973. The tightening of the job market and steady growth were offset by other economic events, curbing inflationary pressures.

The Asian Crisis Spreads

Concerns regarding the spread of the Asian crisis to other emerging and developed markets continued in 1998. The main U.S. concern throughout the year was the impact on the demand for U.S. goods and services in foreign markets. The devaluation of many currencies and economic turmoil contributed to an increase in the U.S. trade deficit, which peaked in August. Uncertainty concerning the ultimate impact of the crisis fueled volatility in the U.S. markets. Increased integration of international markets contributed to the spread of the crisis, as more nations are dependent on each other as trade partners.

The International Monetary Fund (IMF) headed many rescue programs aimed at restoring stability to the affected nations. However, the effectiveness of these IMF bailouts came under strong criticism at the same time the IMF faced a shortage of funds due to the number and severity of each country's needs. Rather than improving, the crisis continued to spread from its beginnings in Asia to the emerging markets of Latin America, Russia, and finally the developed markets. Economic turmoil as well as other factors led ultimately to the resignation of Indonesia's longtime ruler, President Suharto. Japan's leader, Prime Minister Hashimoto also stepped down, having failed to resolve Japan's continued economic problems.

The full impact of the crisis was felt worldwide in August. The U.S. market dropped dramatically as Russia devalued the ruble and defaulted on its international loans. Preceding these events, political problems and corruption hindered IMF and foreign assistance. Though Russia is not a major trading partner with the U.S., the fear that other nations would follow Russia's example caused the U.S. markets to tumble. The U.S. economy also began to show mixed signals after a prolonged period of rapid growth; causing some to speculate about the possibility of global recession.

The Fed's action of lowering interest rates partially subdued the fears of recession and most sectors of the market fully recovered by the end of 1998. Reforms passed in Japan also eased these fears. In the past, Japan has been a stabilizing factor in the region, however, it too was severely impacted by the Asian crisis. The poor regional economy put a strain on an already ailing Japanese economy. The security of Japan's banking industry was a major concern. Late in the year, Japan passed legislation to aid the banking industry, also easing concerns in the region.

Impeachment Proceedings

Following a lengthy investigation of President William Jefferson Clinton headed by Independent Counsel Kenneth Starr, the House of Representatives approved two articles of impeachment; 1) lying under oath in front of a federal grand jury and 2) obstructing justice. The vote taken by the House followed along party lines. At the end of the year, the issue resided with the Senate, where a trial seemed inevitable. This marks the first time in 130 years that the U.S. Senate has considered removing a president from office. However, removal of the president seems unlikely as Senate Republicans do not have enough votes without bipartisan support—two-thirds of the Senate are necessary to remove a president from office. Alternatively, the Senate may consider some measure of presidential censure. In a period of global economic uncertainty, these proceedings added to an already volatile market. Concern that a full impeachment inquiry would reduce investor confidence in the U.S. markets, especially foreign investors, contributed to the volatility of the U.S. markets.

Surprise Mid-term Election Results

In an election year where Republicans expected to strengthen their majority control of both the House of Representatives and the Senate, the Democrats came out on top. Democrats picked up 5 seats in the House of Representatives and remained even in the Senate. Some viewed the results as a reaction to the Republicans' involvement in the impeachment proceedings, a role that appeared to be unpopular with the electorate. Following the results, Speaker of the House Newt Gingrich stepped down from his post. Controversy over the handling of the impeachment process, the recent federal budget debate, and a lack of a clear agenda may have contributed to Gingrich's fall from power.

Hedge Fund Debacle

The investment firm of Long-Term Capital Management nearly collapsed when the market turned in August. The firm, headed by a former head at Solomon Brothers and two Nobel Prize laureates, operated a hedge fund that took advantage of inefficiencies in various bond markets. The exposure of the firm amounted in the billions of dollars when their positions turned sour. Since so many financial institutions were involved in these trades, the effect of Long-Term Capital not being able to meet its obligations could have been enormous. The Fed arranged a bailout of the firm with the cooperation of several large Wall Street firms. This action helped keep the firm solvent and avoided the immediate threat of further financial crisis.

Budget surplus

Due to the growing economy and lower than expected spending, the U.S. government posted a budget surplus of $70 billion, the first surplus in three decades. The budget passed late in the year preserved most of the surplus to determine how it should be used at a later date. Tax cuts, repaying the national debt, and restructuring Social Security are among the chief items being considered. Speculation regarding how to use this year's and next year's projected surplus continues. Some of the surplus was used to fund new programs.

Mega Mergers

For the fourth year in a row, record breaking merger and acquisition activity was a key factor in shaping 1998 market. Low interest rates, savings from streamlined operations, and low inflation fueled these activities. The recent trend in mergers differs from that of the late 80s in that they favor equity transactions (as opposed to junk bonds) and are more strategic in nature. Companies looked to mergers to increase market share or enter new markets, thus becoming more competitive. Others hoped to gain access to new technologies and adapt to the new cost-conscious environment. This record year was highlighted by the size of the deals being conducted. One record sized deal after another reshaped the oil, banking, and telecommunications industries. It appeared that no firm was too large to be considered a target. Also notable was the number of deals that bridged international borders.

The low cost of oil contributed to the rapid growth of the economy for several years, but forced many oil companies to rethink the way they do business to survive. First, British Petroleum announced plans to acquire Amoco Corp. for approximately $48 billion. Then Exxon Corp. and Mobil Corp. announced a stock swap valued at nearly $80 billion. This deal would reunite two of the firms created when the Standard Oil monopoly was disolved. Other players in the industry are rumored to be considering deals in attempts to cut costs and enter new territories.

The consolidation in the telecommunications industry continued. Bell Atlantic Corp. announced plans to acquire GTE Corp. for stock valued at over $50 billion. The deal would add long distance capability as well as open other markets for Bell Atlantic's existing wireless and local services. AT&T plans to purchase Tele-Communications Inc. (TCI) in another deal valued at over $50 billion. In addition to entering the cable television industry, the deal will help AT&T enter the local telephone market and further develop its Internet presence. In another move to enter the local telephone market, AT&T had announced earlier in the year that it would acquire Teleport Communications for approximately $11 billion in stock. SBC Communications Inc. announced plans to buy Ameritech Corp. for approximately $60 billion in a step to become a national provider of local telephone service and extend its network for possible long-distance service. SBC had struck a deal earlier in the year to acquire New England Telecom for over $4 billion. All of these mergers were made possible in part to the deregulation of the telecommunications industry.

The financial services industry also continued its recent trend of consolidation. Deregulation of interstate banking initially created the opportunity for the merger and acquisition activity that we have seen over the past several years. The largest bank was created when Deutche Bank acquired Bankers Trust Corp. for nearly $10 billion. BankAmerica Corp. and NationsBank Corp. announced a deal valued at $60 billion that would merge these West Coast and Southeastern giants. Banc One Corp. and First Chicago NBD Corp. announced a stock swap worth $30 billion, creating the largest Midwest provider of retail and commercial banking services. In a move that would combine major banks from the West Coast and the Midwest, Wells Fargo and Norwest agreed to a merger valued at over $30 billion. In the insurance arena, American International Group announced plans to purchase SunAmerica for $18 billion. Finally, the largest financial services firm in the world was created with the merger of the Travelers Group Inc. and Citicorp. The deal was valued at over $70 billion.

Another important deal not related to the above three industries was the purchase of Chrysler Corp. by Dailmer-Benz in a $40 billion deal. The new entity will offer vehicles in all segments of the auto industry. A notable consequence of this acquisition is the removal of Chrysler Corp. from many of the U.S. market indices including the S&P 500®.

IPO Volume Down

Though the amount of money raised declined from prior years, some of the largest deals to date were completed in 1998. The number of deals declined in the later part of the year as economic uncertainty grew. Among the deals completed in 1998 were a number of Internet related offerings. Overall, IPOs did not perform well. In contrast, most Internet related offerings skyrocketed in their first days of trading. Although most of these Internet companies failed to show substantial profit, investors scrambled to participate in their potential growth. However, many shares fell dramatically after reaching incredible heights on their first days of trading. The volatility of these offerings was also tremendous. Investors who missed the opportunity to participate in the initial trading generally missed out on the incredible gains.

Unrest in the Middle East Continues

U.S. President Bill Clinton made a historic trip to Gaza to salvage some of the remnants of the Middle East Wye River Accord, the U.S. brokered land for security accords between the Israeli and Palestinian governments. The October conference was held between U.S. President Bill Clinton, Israeli Prime Minister Benjamin Netanyahu and Palestinian government leader Yasser Arafat. Some Israelis criticized Netanyahu for not following through with the Wye Accord, while Jewish settlers were incensed at the idea of handing over more West Bank land to the Palestinians. In December the prolonged controversy led Netanyahu to dissolve his government and leave office. The continued instability within this part of the world and the United States' commitment to maintaining the peace there comes at a high price. For U.S. financial markets already besieged by a great deal of volatility, the prospect of a protracted U.S. government involvement in another conflict in the Middle East may prove unsettling at the very least.

The beginning of 1998 brought with it renewed concern in Washington regarding Iraqi weapons inspections. U.N. Secretary-General Kofi Annan twice prevented air strikes against Iraq by personally visiting Baghdad and re-establishing full access to suspected weapons sites for U.N. Special Commission (UNSCOM) inspectors. Diplomacy on the part of Russia and a handful of Arab nations averted another round of U.S. and British air strikes in the 11th hour. The U.S. followed with a strong warning to Iraq that any further attempt to subvert the inspection process would result in immediate reprisals from the U.S. and its allies without advance notice. Despite this stern warning Iraq once again hampered the inspection process over access to documents requested by Richard Bulter, the chief U.N. weapons inspector. In December of 1998, combined American and British forces carried out four days of air strikes against Iraq. Weapons inspections are not likely to resume. The food for oil program, which allows Iraq to sell a limited amount of oil to buy food for the Iraqi people, is scheduled for renewal in May of 1999. Iraqi trade Minister Mohammed Mehdi Saleh retracted his earlier comments about removing some 400 workers who monitor the U.N. food for oil program. The possibility of unfettered Iraqi oil flowing into an already depressed oil marketplace has an ominous implication for many investors.

The European Monetary Union

The eleven countries participating in the Economic and Monetary Union (EMU), Austria, Belgium, Finland, France, Germany, Ireland, Italy, Luxembourg, Netherlands, Portugal and Spain, are poised to launch a uniform currency, the euro, on January 1, 1999. Britain and Denmark may choose to join at a later date. Greece and Sweden initially failed to meet the requirements to participate but may join when conditions permit. Local currencies will initially continue to be used for cash transactions. Legal tender of the new euro will not be introduced until January 2002. Other currencies will cease to be legal tender later that year. The EMU will be governed by a single central bank and will allow unrestricted movement of capital and goods within the region.

Results of 1998 Capital Markets

Despite a significant decline in the month of August, large company stocks performed well in 1998. Small stocks suffered their first negative year since 1990, which made this the fourth consecutive year they under-performed large company stocks. Despite considerable volatility, bond returns increased in 1998 as yields decreased. The Federal Reserve cut its fed funds rate by a quarter-point at meetings in September and November. It also cut the rate a quarter-point in October, the first time such action between meetings since 1994, ending at 4.75 percent. The rate cuts were viewed as a measure to block the economic slowdown overseas from spreading to the United States.

Large Company Stocks

The market for U.S. large company stocks is represented here by the total return on the S&P 500®. (The total return includes reinvestment of dividends). The year's large company stock return of 28.58 percent was substantially above the long-term average return (1926-1998) of 11.22 percent. Nine of the twelve months between January and December 1998 produced positive returns, while August led the negative months with a drop of 14.46 percent. The 1994-1998 period ranks as the best five-year period in the 73 years. Over just the past four years, the cumulative return on large company stocks was a staggering 190 percent.

Considering the market's impressive performance, an index of large company stock total returns, initialized at $1.00 on December 31, 1925, closed at an all-time high on an annual basis. The index grew to $2,350.89 by the end of 1998, compared with $1,828.33 a year earlier.

Small Company Stocks

Small company stocks again trailed the equities of larger companies, at -7.31 percent. This return ranks as the 15th worst of the 73 years in the 1926-1998 period. The small stock premium, or excess return of small over large stocks, was negative 35.89 percent, which is the lowest it has been since 1929 and considerably under the long-term average of 4.21 percent.

The cumulative wealth index, initialized at $1.00 at the end of 1925, fell to $5,116.65, moderately lower than its 1997 close of $5,519.97. Thus, 1998 will stand as only the third year this decade not to maintain returns in positive, double figures.

A Fall in Bond Yields

Bond prices rose as yields on all categories of bonds fell in 1998. Intermediate-term interest rates fell more than long-term rates. In contrast, short-term rates experienced relatively modest declines. Since long-term bonds are more interest-rate sensitive, they increased in value more than their intermediate-term counterparts.

Long-Term Government Bonds

Long-term government bonds (with maturity near 20 years) returned 13.06 percent in 1998, which is slightly lower than the previous year of 15.85 percent. This return ranks as the 14th largest annual gain on record over the past 73 years. The yield on long-term government bond issues rose slightly through the first third of the year, reaching a peak of 6.04 percent in April. The yield fell to a low of 5.17 percent in September, but rose back to 5.42 percent by year end.

An index of total returns, initialized at $1.00 at year-end 1925, rose to an all-time high of $44.18 at the end of December 1998. The capital appreciation index of long-term government bond returns closed at $0.97, which is significantly less than its all-time high of $1.42 reached in early 1945.

Intermediate-Term Government Bonds

The yield on intermediate-term government bonds (with maturity near 5 years) fluctuated considerably throughout 1998. Following the first quarter, the yield fell to a low of 4.34 percent in October 1998. By year-end 1998, the yield increased slightly to 4.68 percent. The total return on intermediate-term government bonds in 1998 was 10.21 percent, more than a 20 percent increase from the 1997 total return of 8.38 percent. This return ranks as the 12th largest annual gain for the 1926-1998 period.

The wealth index of intermediate-term government bonds, initialized at $1.00 at year-end 1925, reached an all-time high of $43.93 at the end of December 1998. The capital appreciation index closed at $1.32.

Long-Term Corporate Bonds

Long-term corporate bonds (with maturity near 20 years) also performed well for the second consecutive year, but not as well as their government counterparts. Their 1998 total return was 10.76 percent. Total returns were positive in nine of twelve months during the year, with negative returns occurring in February, July, and October. This return ranks as the 16th largest annual gain for the 1926-1998 period.

The bond default premium, or net return from investing in long-term corporate bonds rather than long-term government bonds of equal maturity, was negative 2.04 percent, significantly lower than that of its long-term (1926-1998) average of 0.45 percent. A dollar invested in long-term corporate bonds at year-end 1925, rose to an all-time high of $61.34 by the end of December 1998.

Treasury Bills

The yield on U.S. Treasury bills experienced a modest decline in 1998, falling from 5.1 percent at the end of 1997 to 4.5 percent at year-end 1998. An investment in bills with approximately 30 days to maturity had a total return of 4.86 percent, the 26th highest return over the past 73 years. The cumulative index of Treasury bill total returns ended the year at $14.94, compared with $14.25 a year earlier. Because monthly Treasury bill returns are nearly always positive, each monthly index value typically sets a new all-time high.

Inflation

Consumer prices rose 1.61 percent in 1998, a decrease from the 1997 rate of 1.70 percent. This is the second lowest inflation rate in the last 33 years. (Inflation was below 1.61 percent in 1986.) Thus inflation has remained below 5 percent for sixteen of the last seventeen years. (Inflation was above 5 percent in 1990.) The 1998 inflation rate was well below the long-term (1926-1998) average of 3.08 percent.

Graph 1-1 **The Decade: Wealth Indices of Investments in U.S. Stocks, Bonds, Bills, and Inflation**

Year-End 1988 = $1.00

From December 1988 to December 1998

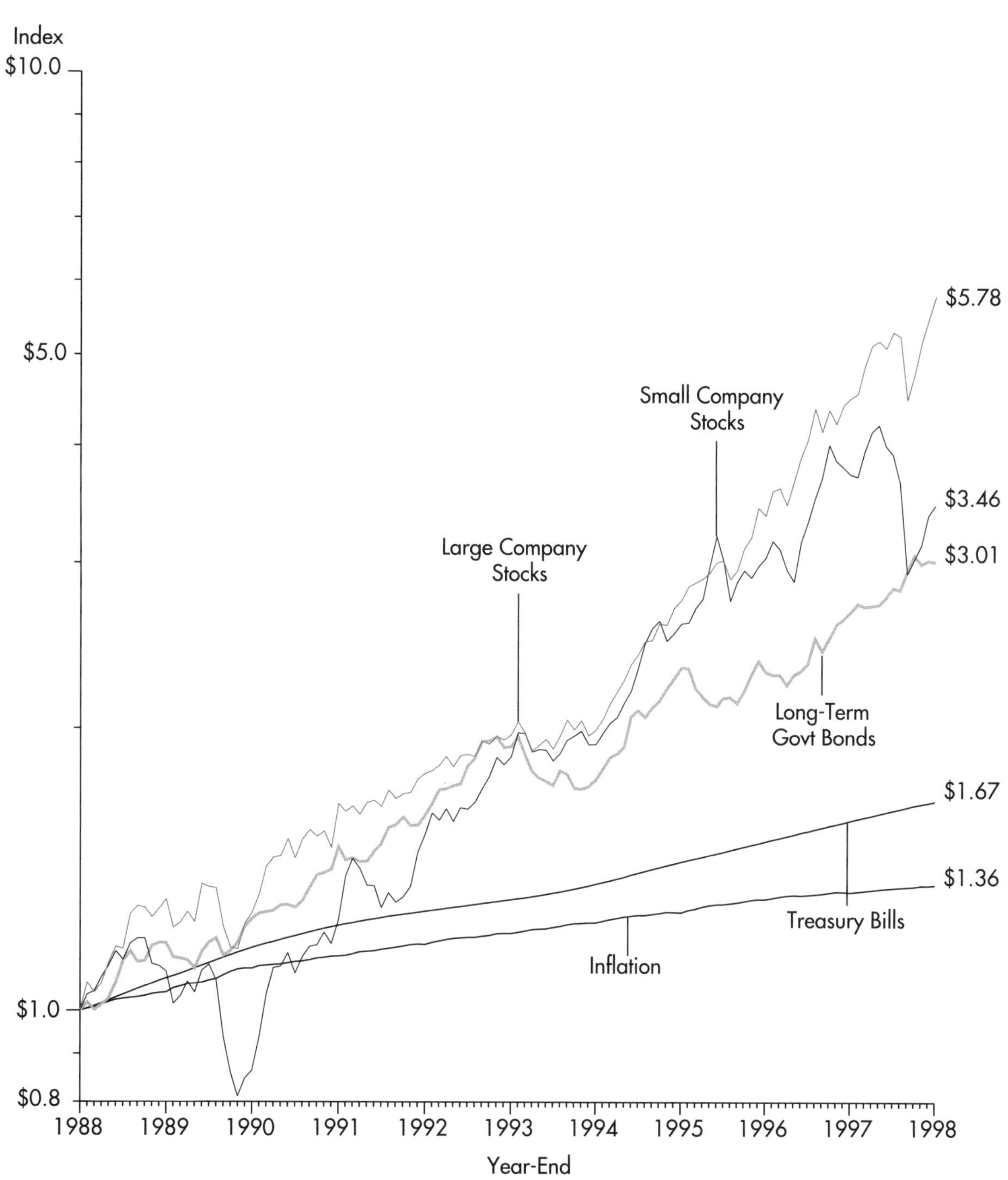

A cumulative inflation index, initialized at $1.00 at year-end 1925, finished 1998 at $9.14, up from $9.00 a year earlier. That is, a basket of consumer goods and services that cost $1.00 in 1925 would cost $9.14 today. The two baskets are not identical, but are intended to be comparable.

A Graphic View of the Decade

The past decade, 1989–1998, has been characterized by a robust rate of increase in stock prices, accompanied by long periods of stability. At first, in 1988–1990, the quiet was punctuated by bursts of volatility. Later, over 1991–1996, stock market volatility fell to levels not seen since the 1960s, as prices slowly climbed. Volatility increased again in 1997 and 1998.

The decade begins with the recovery from the stock market crash of 1987. The contraction began in August 1987, and culminated in October 1987, as the stock market fell by 34 percent in ten trading days. On October 19, 1987, stocks fell by more than 20 percent, marking the worst period of downside volatility since 1929, when the market fell by 44 percent from mid-October to mid-November. (October 19, 1987, was also nearly twice as bad as the worst day of 1929.) By the end of 1987, however, the savage bear market had run its course.

In 1929, the October/November crash presaged a decline that would, by the summer of 1932, wipe out 86 percent of the market capitalization of the New York Stock Exchange. Fortunately, this experience was not repeated in the aftermath of the 1987 crash. Stocks recouped their 1987 pre-crash losses within two years. The economy continued to grow until 1990, when a recession—not a depression—began.

Graph 1-1 shows the market results for the past decade—illustrating the growth of $1.00 invested on December 31, 1988 in stocks, bonds, and bills, along with an index of inflation. A review of the major themes of the past decade, as revealed in the capital markets, appears later in this chapter.

The Decade in Perspective

The great stock and bond market rise of the 1980s was one of the most unusual in the history of the capital markets. In terms of the magnitude of the rise, the decade most closely resembled the 1920s and 1950s. These three decades accounted for a majority of the market's cumulative total return over the past 73 years. While the importance of a long-term view of investing is noted consistently in this book and elsewhere, the counterpart of this observation is: To achieve high returns on your investments, you only need to participate in the few periods of truly outstanding return. The bull markets of 1922 to mid-1929, 1949–1961 (roughly speaking, the Fifties), mid-1982 to mid-1987, and 1991-1998 were such periods.

Table 1-1 Compound Annual Rates of Return by Decade

	1920s*	1930s	1940s	1950s	1960s	1970s	1980s	1990s**	1989-98
Large Company	19.2%	-0.1%	9.2%	19.4%	7.8%	5.9%	17.5%	17.9%	19.2%
Small Company	-4.5	1.4	20.7	16.9	15.5	11.5	15.8	13.6	13.2
Long-Term Corp	5.2	6.9	2.7	1.0	1.7	6.2	13.0	10.3	10.9
Long-Term Govt	5.0	4.9	3.2	-0.1	1.4	5.5	12.6	11.0	11.7
Inter-Term Govt	4.2	4.6	1.8	1.3	3.5	7.0	11.9	8.3	8.7
Treasury Bills	3.7	0.6	0.4	1.9	3.9	6.3	8.9	5.0	5.3
Inflation	-1.1	-2.0	5.4	2.2	2.5	7.4	5.1	3.0	3.1

* Based on the period 1926–1929.
** Based on the period 1990–1998.

Table 1-1 compares the returns by decade on all of the basic asset classes covered in this book. It is notable that either large company stocks or small company stocks were the best performing asset class in every full decade save one. In this table, the Twenties cover the period 1926–1929 and the Nineties cover the period 1990–1998.

It is interesting to place the decades of superior performance in historical context. The Twenties were preceded by mediocre returns and high inflation and were followed by the most devastating stock market crash and economic depression in American history. This sequence of events mitigated the impact of the Twenties bull market on investor wealth. Nevertheless, the stock market became a liquid secondary market in the Twenties, rendering that period important for reasons other than return. In contrast, the Fifties were preceded and followed by decades with roughly average equity returns. The Eighties were preceded by a decade of "stagflation" where modest stock price gains were seriously eroded by inflation and were followed by a period of stability in the Nineties.

The bond market performance of the Eighties and Nineties has no precedent. Bond yields, which had risen consistently since the 1940s, reached unprecedented levels in 1980–1981. (Other countries experiencing massive inflation have had correspondingly high interest rates.) Never before having had so far to fall, bond yields dropped further and faster than at any other time, producing what is indisputably the greatest bond bull market in history. Unfortunately, the boom came to an end in 1994. After falling to 21-year lows one year earlier, bond yields rose in 1994 to their highest level in over three years.

The historical themes of the past decade, as they relate to the capital markets, can be summarized in three observations. First, the past 16 1/2 years—that is, the period starting in mid-1982—comprised a rare span of time in which investors quickly accumulated wealth.

Second, the postwar aberration of ever-higher inflation rates ended with a dramatic disinflation in the early Eighties. In the Nineties to date, inflation remains low. However, the more deeply embedded aberration of consistently positive inflation rates—that is, ever-higher prices—has not ended.

Finally, participation in the returns of the capital markets reached levels not even approached in the Twenties, the Fifties, or the atypical boom period of 1967–1972. The vast size and importance of pension funds, as well as the rapidly increasing popularity of stock and bond mutual funds as a basic savings vehicle, have caused more individuals to experience the returns of the capital markets than ever before.

Graphic Depiction of Returns in the Decade

Graphs 1-2, 1-3 and 1-4 contain bar graphs of 1989–1998 annual and 1998 monthly total returns on the assets discussed above. The top part of Graph 1-2 compares large company stocks and long-term government bonds. The graph shows that stock and bond returns were quite closely correlated over the decade. [See Chapter 6.] The bottom half of Graph 1-2 compares large company stocks and small company stocks, showing that neither consistently outperformed the other over the past decade.

The top part of Graph 1-3 compares corporate and government bonds of like maturity (approximately 20 years). Clearly, returns of corporate bonds did not always outperform government bonds over the past decade, contradicting their historical trend. The bottom part of Graph 1-3 compares long-term and intermediate-term government bonds. Intermediate-term bonds are less volatile; and, as usual, tended to return less than long-term bonds in rising markets.

Graph 1-4 displays bar graphs of the 1989–1998 annual and 1998 monthly Treasury bill returns, inflation rates, and real riskless rates of return. The top part of Graph 1-4 compares Treasury bills and inflation. The bottom part of Graph 1-4 shows month-by-month real riskless rates of return, defined as Treasury bill returns in excess of inflation.

Tables of Market Results for 1989–1998

The 1989–1998 annual and 1998 quarterly and monthly total returns on the seven basic asset classes studied in this book are presented in Table 1-2. Table 1-3 displays cumulative indices of the returns shown in Table 1-2, based on a starting value of $1.00 on December 31, 1925.

For the decade, stocks had unusually high returns. Long-term government bonds had five of their ten best years ever. (The best year was 1982, with a long-term government bond return of 40.4 percent.) Treasury bill yields fell, but generally remained above their 73-year historical average. Inflation rates fell to levels below the 73-year average.

Graph 1-2

1989–1998 Annual and 1998 Monthly Total Returns

A Comparison of Large Company Stocks with Long-Term Government Bonds, and Large Company Stocks with Small Company Stocks

(in percent)

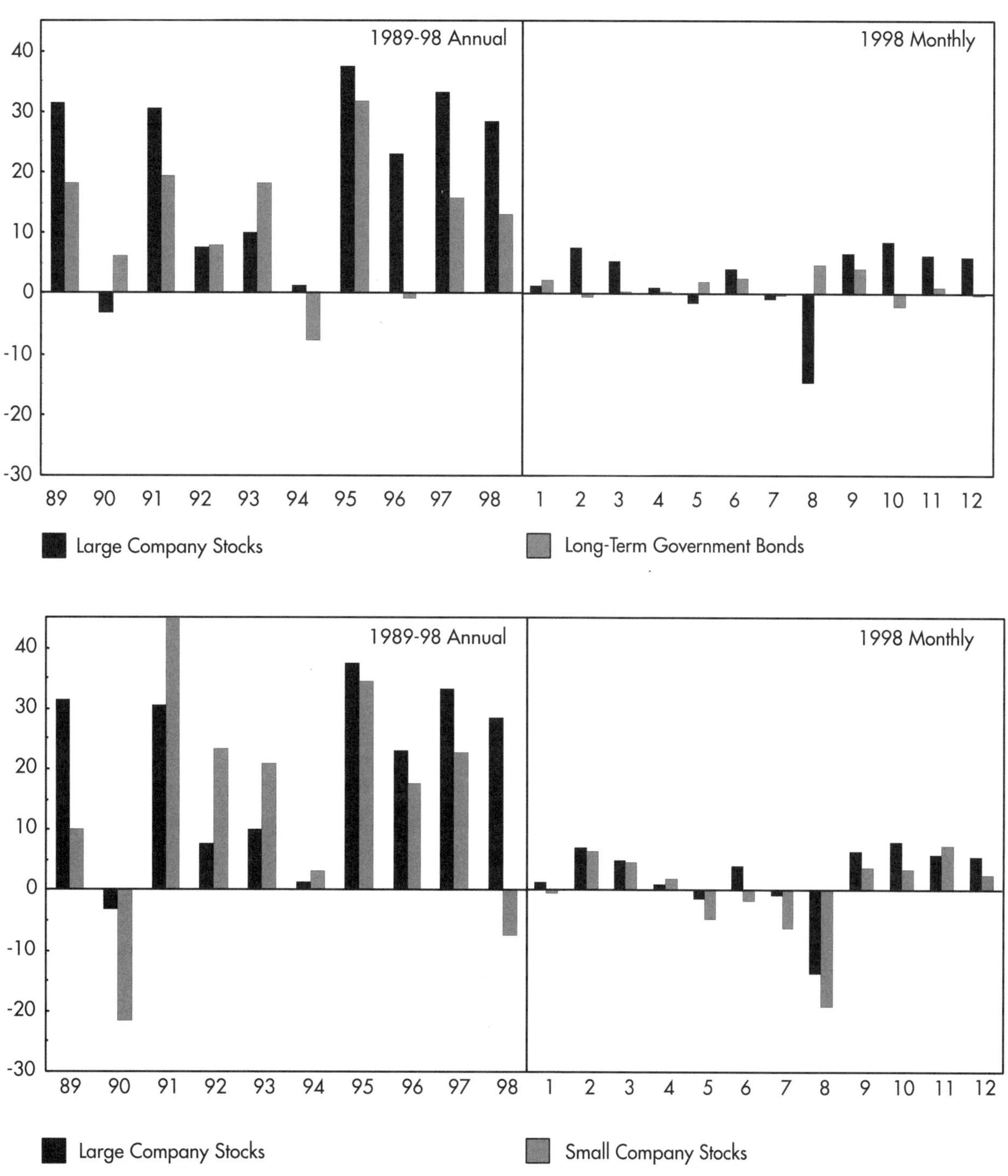

Graph 1–3 **1989–1998 Annual and 1998 Monthly Total Returns**

A Comparison of Long-Term Corporate Bonds with Long-Term Government Bonds, and Long-Term Governemnt Bonds with Intermediate-Term Government Bonds

(in percent)

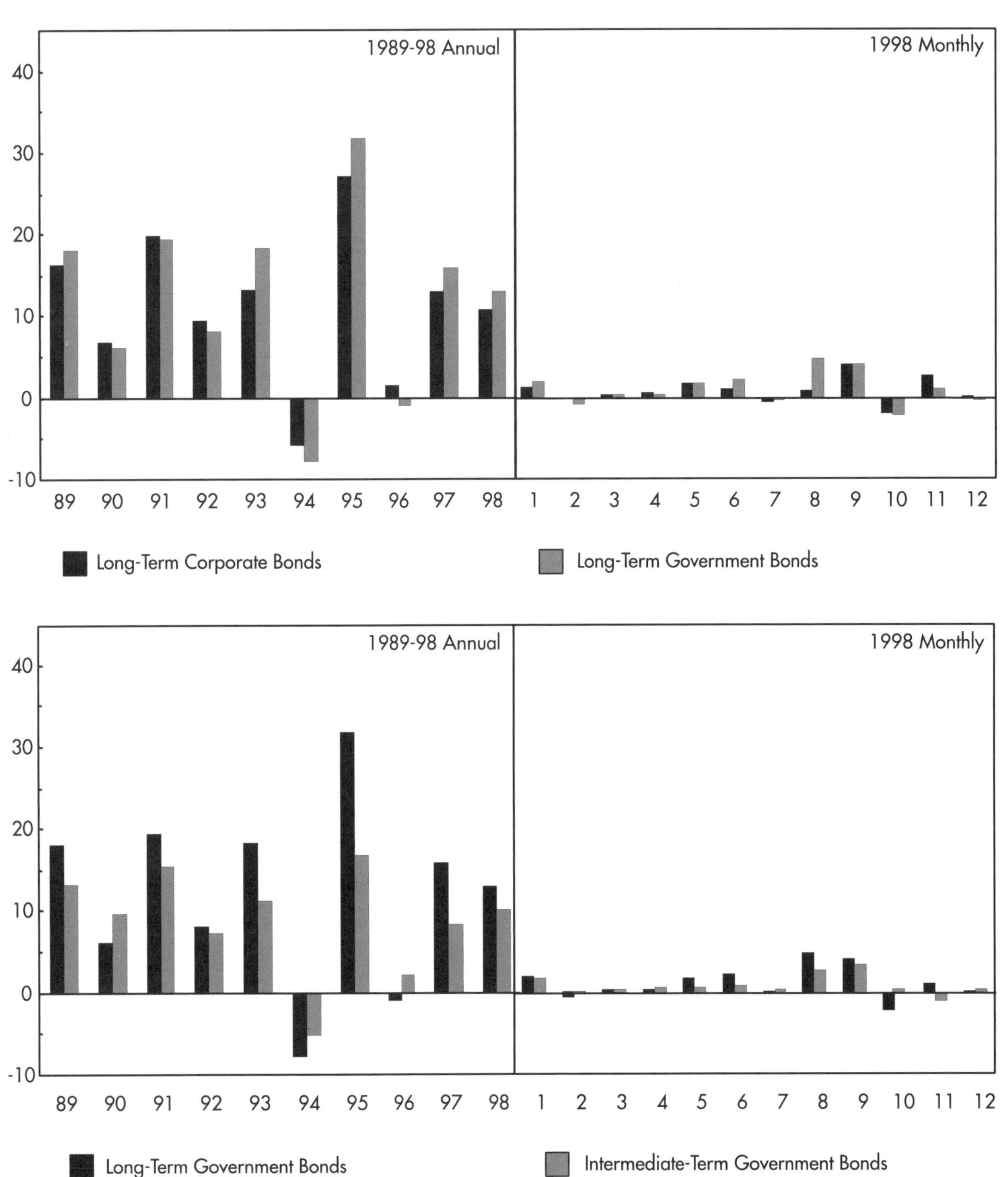

Graph 1–4 **1989–1998 Annual and 1998 Monthly Total Returns**

Treasury Bills, Inflation and Real Riskless Rates of Return

(in percent)

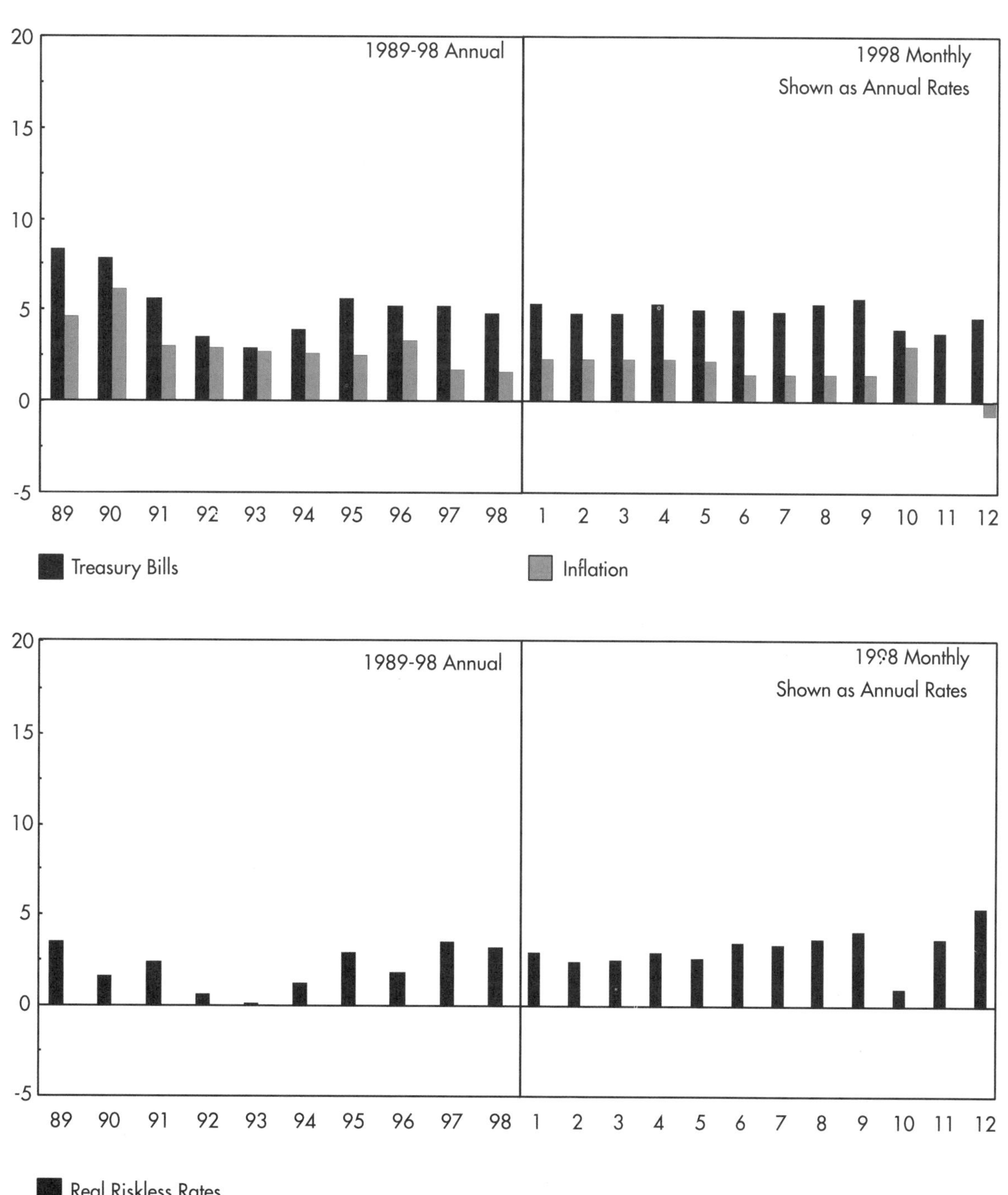

Table 1-2 **1989–1998 Annual and 1998 Quarterly and Monthly Market Results**

Returns on Stocks, Bonds, Bills, and Inflation

(in percent)

Year	Large Company Stocks	Small Company Stocks	Long-Term Corporate Bonds	Long-Term Government Bonds	Intermediate Government Bonds	U.S. Treasury Bills	Inflation
1989–1998 Annual Returns							
1989	31.49	10.18	16.23	18.11	13.29	8.37	4.65
1990	-3.17	-21.56	6.78	6.18	9.73	7.81	6.11
1991	30.55	44.63	19.89	19.30	15.46	5.60	3.06
1992	7.67	23.35	9.39	8.05	7.19	3.51	2.90
1993	9.99	20.98	13.19	18.24	11.24	2.90	2.75
1994	1.31	3.11	-5.76	-7.77	-5.14	3.90	2.67
1995	37.43	34.46	27.20	31.67	16.80	5.60	2.54
1996	23.07	17.62	1.40	-0.93	2.10	5.21	3.32
1997	33.36	22.78	12.95	15.85	8.38	5.26	1.70
1998	28.58	-7.31	10.76	13.06	10.21	4.86	1.61
1998 Quarterly Returns							
I-98	13.95	10.95	1.68	1.52	1.67	1.22	0.56
II-98	3.30	-5.36	3.38	4.42	2.11	1.25	0.49
III-98	-9.95	-22.71	4.47	8.34	6.37	1.29	0.37
IV-98	21.30	14.22	0.85	-1.56	-0.20	1.01	0.18
1998 Monthly Returns							
1-98	1.11	-0.59	1.37	2.00	1.80	0.43	0.19
2-98	7.21	6.49	-0.07	-0.72	-0.39	0.39	0.19
3-98	5.12	4.81	0.38	0.25	0.26	0.39	0.19
4-98	1.01	1.68	0.53	0.26	0.61	0.43	0.18
5-98	-1.72	-4.97	1.67	1.82	0.70	0.40	0.18
6-98	4.06	-2.06	1.15	2.28	0.79	0.41	0.12
7-98	-1.06	-6.71	-0.56	-0.40	0.27	0.40	0.12
8-98	-14.46	-20.10	0.89	4.65	2.71	0.43	0.12
9-98	6.41	3.69	4.13	3.95	3.30	0.46	0.12
10-98	8.13	3.56	-1.90	-2.18	0.41	0.32	0.24
11-98	6.06	7.58	2.70	0.97	-0.98	0.31	0.00
12-98	5.76	2.52	0.10	-0.32	0.37	0.38	-0.06

Table 1-3 **1989–1998 Annual and 1998 Monthly Market Results**

Indices of Returns on Stocks, Bonds, Bills, and Inflation

Year-End 1925 = $1.00

Year	Large Company Stocks	Small Company Stocks	Long-Term Corporate Bonds	Long-Term Government Bonds	Intermediate Government Bonds	U.S. Treasury Bills	Inflation
1989–1998 Annual Indices							
1989	534.455	1628.590	25.447	17.322	21.524	9.673	7.034
1990	517.499	1277.449	27.173	18.392	23.618	10.429	7.464
1991	675.592	1847.629	32.577	21.942	27.270	11.012	7.693
1992	727.412	2279.039	35.637	23.709	29.230	11.398	7.916
1993	800.078	2757.147	40.336	28.034	32.516	11.728	8.133
1994	810.538	2842.773	38.012	25.856	30.843	12.186	8.351
1995	1113.918	3822.398	48.353	34.044	36.025	12.868	8.563
1996	1370.946	4495.993	49.031	33.727	36.782	13.538	8.847
1997	1828.326	5519.969	55.380	39.074	39.864	14.250	8.998
1998	2350.892	5116.648	61.339	44.178	43.933	14.942	9.143
1998 Monthly Indices							
12-97	1828.326	5519.969	55.380	39.074	39.864	14.250	8.998
1-98	1848.621	5487.401	56.139	39.856	40.583	14.311	9.015
2-98	1981.943	5843.534	56.100	39.570	40.426	14.367	9.032
3-98	2083.439	6124.608	56.313	39.668	40.530	14.423	9.048
4-98	2104.398	6227.501	56.611	39.771	40.777	14.485	9.065
5-98	2068.223	5917.994	57.557	40.497	41.062	14.544	9.082
6-98	2152.235	5796.084	58.219	41.421	41.385	14.603	9.093
7-98	2129.313	5407.166	57.893	41.256	41.495	14.662	9.104
8-98	1821.457	4320.326	58.408	43.173	42.619	14.725	9.115
9-98	1938.140	4479.746	60.820	44.876	44.023	14.792	9.126
10-98	2095.788	4639.225	59.664	43.896	44.203	14.840	9.149
11-98	2222.814	4990.878	61.275	44.320	43.772	14.886	9.149
12-98	2350.892	5116.648	61.339	44.178	43.933	14.942	9.143

Chapter 2 The Long Run Perspective

Motivation

A long view of capital market history, exemplified by the 73-year period (1926–1998) examined here, uncovers the basic relationships between risk and return among the different asset classes and between nominal and real (inflation-adjusted) returns. The goal of this study of asset returns is to provide a period long enough to include most or all of the major types of events that investors have experienced and may experience in the future. Such events include war and peace, growth and decline, bull and bear markets, inflation and deflation, and other less dramatic events that affect asset returns.

By studying the past, one can make inferences about the future. While the actual events that occurred during 1926–1998 will not be repeated, the event-types (not specific events) of that period can be expected to recur. It is sometimes said that only a few periods are unusual, such as the crash of 1929–1932 and World War II. This logic is suspicious because all periods are unusual. Two of the most unusual events of the century—the stock market crash of 1987 and the equally remarkable inflation of the 1970s and early 1980s—took place over the last two decades. From the perspective that historical event-types tend to repeat themselves, a 73-year examination of past capital market returns reveals a great deal about what may be expected in the future. [See Chapters 8 and 9.]

Historical Returns on Stocks, Bonds, Bills, and Inflation

Graph 2-1 graphically depicts the growth of $1.00 invested in large company stocks, small company stocks, long-term government bonds, Treasury bills, and a hypothetical asset returning the inflation rate over the period from the end of 1925 to the end of 1998. All results assume reinvestment of dividends on stocks or coupons on bonds and no taxes. Transaction costs are not included, except in the small stock index starting in 1982.

Each of the cumulative index values is initialized at $1.00 at year-end 1925. The graph vividly illustrates that large company stocks and small company stocks were the big winners over the entire 73-year period: investments of $1.00 in these assets would have grown to $2,350.89 and $5,116.65, respectively, by year-end 1998. This phenomenal growth was earned by taking substantial risk. In contrast, long-term government bonds (with an approximate 20-year maturity), which exposed the holder to much less risk, grew to only $44.18.

The lowest-risk strategy over the past 73 years (for those with short-term time horizons) was to buy U.S. Treasury bills. Since Treasury bills tended to track inflation, the resulting real (inflation-adjusted) returns were just above zero for the entire 1926–1998 period.

Graph 2-1 **Wealth Indices of Investments in the U.S. Capital Markets**

Year-End 1925 = $1.00

From 1925 to 1998

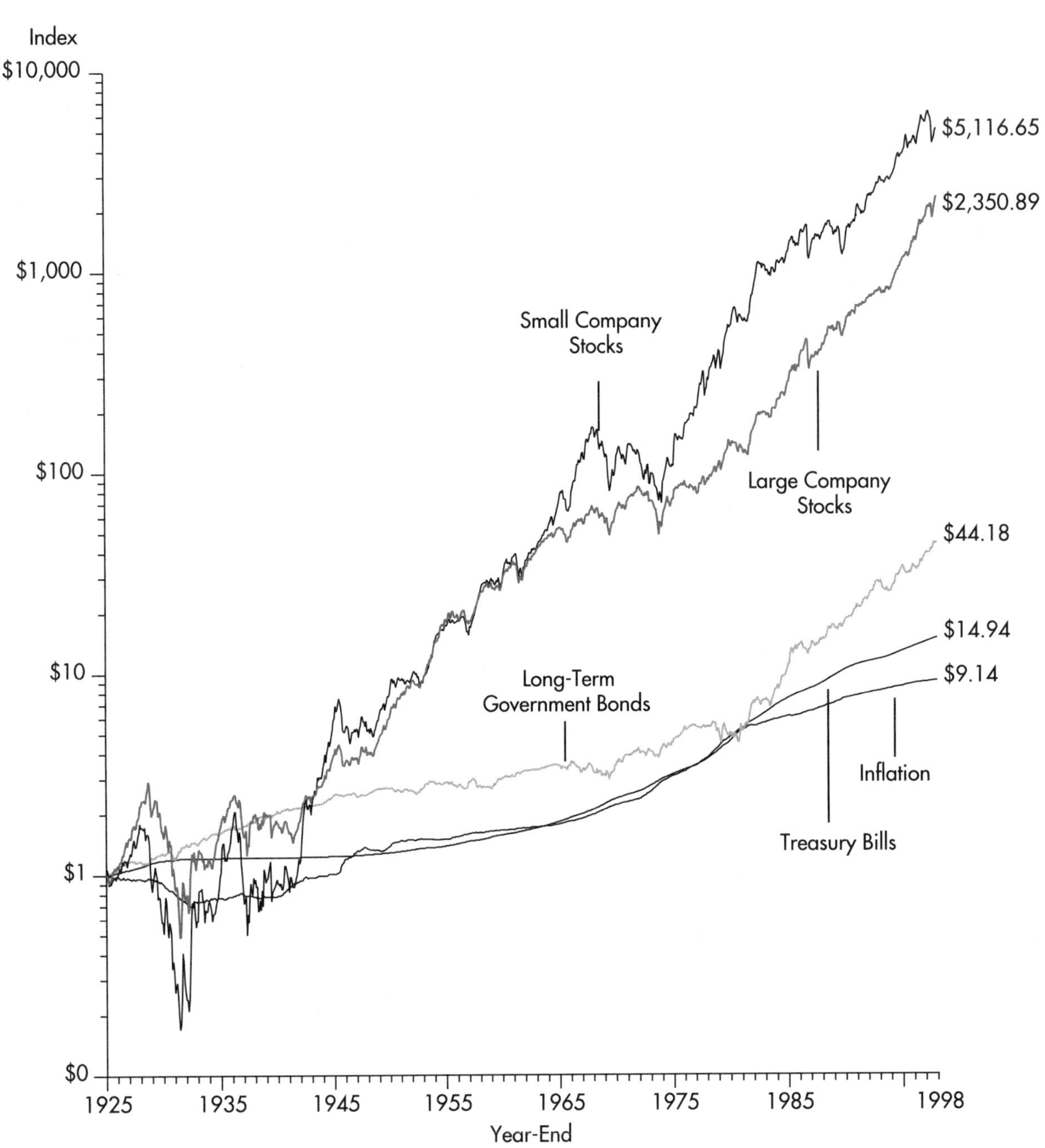

Logarithmic Scale on the Index Graphs

A logarithmic scale is used on the vertical axis of our index graphs. The date appears on the horizontal axis.

A logarithmic scale allows for the direct comparison of the series' behavior at different points in time. Specifically, the use of a logarithmic scale allows the following interpretation of the data: the same vertical distance, no matter where it is measured on the graph, represents the same percentage change in the series. On the log scale shown below, a 50 percent gain from $10 to $15 occupies the same vertical distance as a 50 percent gain from $100 to $150. On the linear scale, the same percentage gains look different.

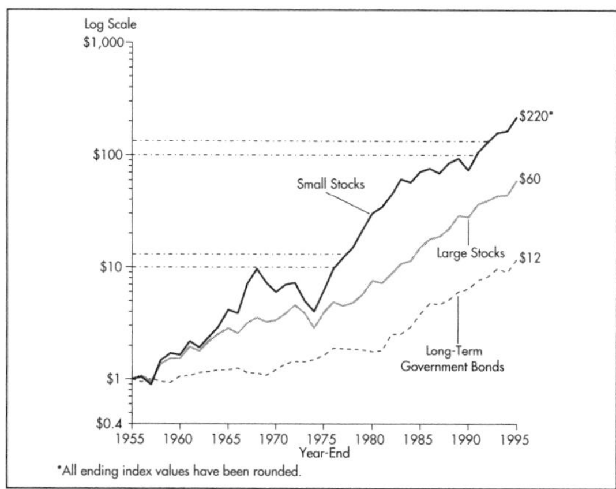

*All ending index values have been rounded.

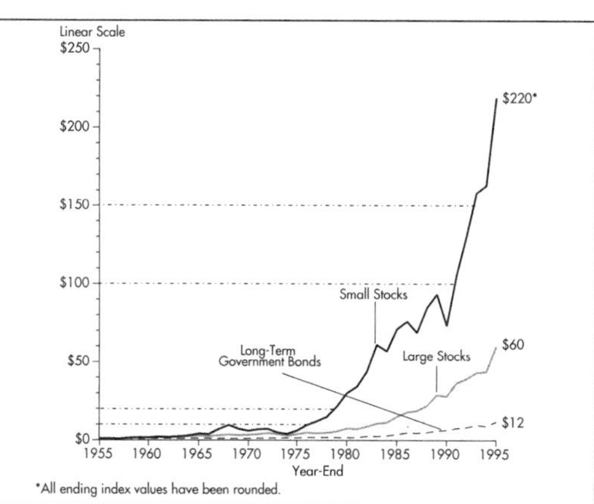

*All ending index values have been rounded.

A logarithmic scale allows the viewer to compare investment performance across different time periods; thus the viewer can concentrate on rates of return, without worrying about the number of dollars invested at any given time. An additional benefit of the logarithmic scale is the way the scale spreads the action out over time. This allows the viewer to more carefully examine the fluctuations of the individual time series in different periods.

Large Company Stocks

As noted above, an index of S&P 500 total returns, initialized on December 31, 1925 at $1.00, closed 1998 at $2,350.89, a compound annual growth rate of 11.2 percent. The inflation-adjusted S&P 500 total return index closed 1998 at a level of $257.12.

Small Company Stocks

Over the long run, small stock returns surpassed the S&P 500, with the small stock total return index ending 1998 at a level of $5,516.65. This represents a compound annual growth rate of 12.4 percent, the highest rate among the asset classes studied here.

Long-Term Government Bonds

The long-term government bond total return index, constructed with an approximate 20-year maturity, closed 1998 at a level of $44.18 (based on year-end 1925 equaling $1.00). Based on the capital appreciation component alone, the $1.00 index fell to a level of $0.97, a 3 percent capital loss over the period 1926–1998. This indicates that more than all of the positive historical return on long-term government bonds were due to income returns. The compound annual total return for long-term government bonds was 5.3 percent.

Intermediate-Term Government Bonds

Over the 1926–1998 period, intermediate-term government bonds outperformed long-term government bonds. One dollar invested in intermediate-term bonds at the end of 1925, with coupons reinvested, grew to $43.93 by year-end 1998. This compares with $44.18 for long-term government bonds. The compound annual total return for intermediate-term government bonds was 5.3 percent.

Capital appreciation caused $1.00 to increase to $1.32 over the 73-year period, representing a compound annual growth rate of 0.4 percent. This increase was unexpected: Since yields rose on average over the period, capital appreciation on a hypothetical intermediate-term government bond portfolio with a constant five-year maturity should have been negative.

Long-Term Corporate Bonds

Long-term corporate bonds outperformed both categories of government bonds with a compound annual total return of 5.8 percent. One dollar invested in the long-term corporate bond index at year-end 1925 was worth $61.34 by the end of 1998. This higher return reflected the risk premium that investors require for investing in corporate bonds, which are subject to the risk of default.

Treasury Bills

One dollar invested in Treasury bills at the end of 1925 was worth $14.94 by year-end 1998, with a compound annual growth rate of 3.8 percent. Treasury bill returns followed distinct patterns, described on the next page. Moreover, Treasury bills tended to track inflation; therefore, the average inflation-adjusted return on Treasury bills (or real riskless rate of return) was only 0.7 percent over the 73-year period. This real return also followed distinct patterns.

Patterns In Treasury Bill Returns

During the late 1920s and early 1930s, Treasury bill returns were just above zero. (These returns were observed during a largely deflationary period.) Beginning in late 1941, the yields on Treasury bills were pegged by the government at low rates while high inflation was experienced.

Treasury bills closely tracked inflation after March 1951, when Treasury bill yields were deregulated in the U.S. Treasury-Federal Reserve Accord. (Treasury bill returns after that date reflect free market rates.) This tracking relationship has weakened since 1973. From about 1974 to 1980, Treasury bill returns were consistently lower than inflation rates. Then, from about 1981 to 1986, Treasury bills outpaced inflation, yielding substantial positive real returns. Since 1987, real returns on Treasury bills have still been positive, but lower than before.

Federal Reserve Operating Procedure Changes

The disparity between performance and volatility for the periods prior to and after October 1979 can be attributed to the Federal Reserve's new operating procedures. Prior to this date, the Fed used the federal funds rate as an operating target. Subsequently, the Fed deemphasized this rate as an operating target and, instead, began to focus on the manipulation of the money supply (through nonborrowed reserves). As a result, the federal funds rate underwent much greater volatility, thereby bringing about greater volatility in Treasury returns.

In the fall of 1982, however, the Federal Reserve again changed the policy procedures regarding its monetary policy. The Fed abandoned its new monetary controls and returned to a strategy of preventing excessive volatility in interest rates. Volatility in Treasury bill returns from the fall of 1979 through the fall of 1982 was nearly 50 percent greater than that which has occurred since.

Inflation

The compound annual inflation rate over 1926–1998 was 3.1 percent. The inflation index, initiated at $1.00 at year-end 1925, grew to $9.14 by year-end 1998. The entire increase occurred during the postwar period. The years 1926–1933 were marked by deflation; inflation then raised consumer prices to their 1926 levels by the middle of 1945. After a brief postwar spurt of inflation, prices rose slowly over most of the 1950s and 1960s. Then, in the 1970s, inflation reached a pace unprecedented in peacetime, peaking at 13.3 percent in 1979. (On a month-by-month basis, the peak inflation rate was a breathtaking 24.0 percent, stated in annualized terms, in August 1973.) The 1980s saw a reversion to more moderate, though still substantial, inflation rates averaging about 5 percent. Inflation rates continued to decline in the 1990s with a compound annual rate of 3.0 percent.

Summary Statistics of Total Returns

Table 2-1 presents summary statistics of the annual total returns on each asset class over the entire 73-year period of 1926–1998. The data presented in these exhibits are described in detail in Chapters 3 and 6.

Note that in Table 2-1, the arithmetic mean returns are always higher than the geometric mean returns. (Where they appear the same, it is due to rounding.) The difference between these two means is related to the standard deviation, or variability, of the series. (See Chapter 6.)

The "skylines" or histograms to the right in Table 2-1 show the frequency distribution of returns on each asset class. The height of the common stock skyline in the range between +10 and +20 percent, for example, shows the number of years in 1926–1998 that large company stocks had a return in that range. The histograms are shown in 5 percent increments to fully display the spectrum of returns as seen over the last 73 years, especially in stocks.

Riskier assets, such as large company stocks and small company stocks, have low, spread-out skylines, reflecting the broad distribution of returns from very poor to very good. Less risky assets, such as bonds, have narrow skylines that resemble a single tall building, indicating the tightness of the distribution around the mean of the series. The histogram for Treasury bills is one-sided, lying almost entirely to the right of the vertical line representing a zero return; that is, Treasury bills rarely experienced negative returns on a yearly basis over the 1926–1998 period. The inflation skyline shows both positive and negative annual rates. Although a few deflationary months and quarters have occurred recently, the last negative annual inflation rate occurred in 1954.

The histograms in Tables 2-2 through 2-4 show the total return distributions on the basic series over the past 73 years. These histograms are useful in determining the years with similar returns. The stock histograms are shown in 10 percent increments while the bond, bill, and inflation histograms are in 2 percent increments. The increments are smaller for the assets with less widely distributed returns. Treasury bills are the most tightly clustered of any of the asset classes, confirming that this asset bears little risk; the annual return usually fell near zero.

Table 2-1 **Basic Series: Summary Statistics of Annual Total Returns**

From 1926 to 1998

Series	Geometric Mean	Arithmetic Mean	Standard Deviation	Distribution
Large Company Stocks	11.2%	13.2%	20.3%	
Small Company Stocks	12.4	17.4	33.8	*
Long-Term Corporate Bonds	5.8	6.1	8.6	
Long-Term Government	5.3	5.7	9.2	
Intermediate-Term Government	5.3	5.5	5.7	
U.S. Treasury Bills	3.8	3.8	3.2	
Inflation	3.1	3.2	4.5	

-90% 0% 90%

*The 1933 Small Company Stock Total Return was 142.9 percent.

Table 2-2 **Histogram**

Large Company Stock
and Small Company Stock
Total Returns

(in percent)

From 1926 to 1998

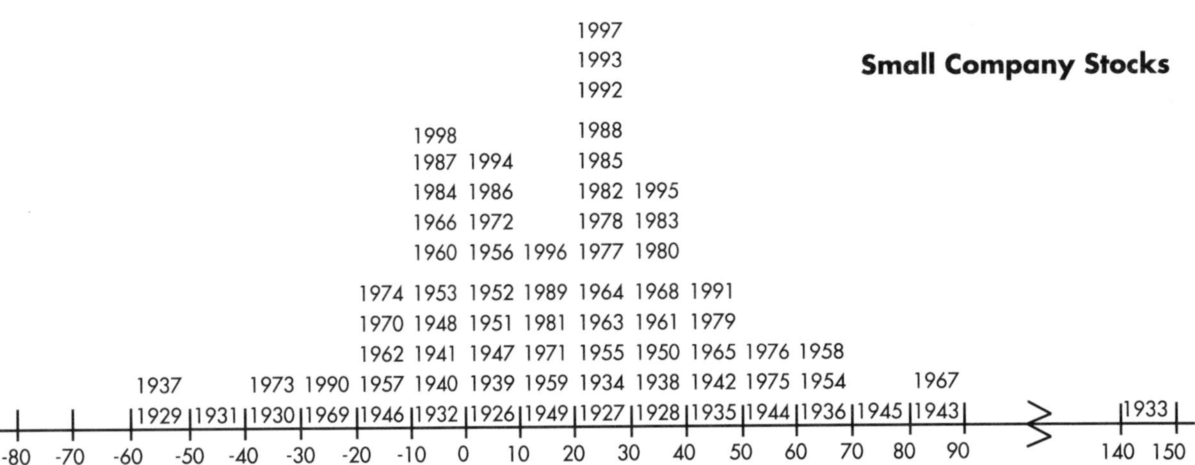

Table 2-3 **Histogram**

Long-Term Government Bond and Intermediate-Term Government Bond Total Returns

(in percent)

From 1926 to 1998

Long-Term Government Bonds

Return (%)	Years
-10 to -8	1967
-8 to -6	1958, 1994
-6 to -4	1931, 1956, 1969
-4 to -2	1947, 1951, 1959, 1980, 1987
-2 to 0	1933, 1946, 1955, 1968, 1973, 1977, 1978, 1979, 1996
0 to 2	1928, 1937, 1941, 1950, 1952, 1961, 1963, 1965, 1981, 1983
2 to 4	1929, 1942, 1943, 1944, 1948, 1953, 1964, 1966
4 to 6	1930, 1935, 1938, 1939, 1972, 1974
6 to 8	1926, 1936, 1940, 1949, 1954, 1957, 1962, 1990
8 to 10	1927, 1975, 1988, 1992
10 to 12	1934, 1945
12 to 14	1960, 1970, 1971, 1998
14 to 16	1984, 1997
16 to 18	1932, 1976
18 to 20	1989, 1991, 1993
24 to 26	1986
30 to 32	1985, 1995
40 to 42	1982

Intermediate-Term Government Bonds

Return (%)	Years
-6 to -4	1994
-4 to -2	1931
-2 to 0	1955, 1956, 1958, 1959, 1969
0 to 2	1928, 1933, 1937, 1941, 1942, 1944, 1946, 1947, 1948, 1950, 1951, 1952, 1961, 1963, 1965, 1967, 1977
2 to 4	1936, 1940, 1943, 1945, 1949, 1953, 1954, 1978, 1980, 1987, 1996
4 to 6	1926, 1927, 1939, 1962, 1964, 1966, 1968, 1972, 1973, 1974, 1979
6 to 8	1929, 1930, 1935, 1938, 1957, 1975, 1983, 1988, 1992
8 to 10	1932, 1934, 1971, 1981, 1990, 1997
10 to 12	1960, 1993, 1998
12 to 14	1976, 1989
14 to 16	1984, 1986, 1991
16 to 18	1970, 1995
20 to 22	1985
28 to 30	1982

Table 2-4 **Histogram**

U.S. Treasury Bill
Total Returns
and Inflation

(in percent)

From 1926 to 1998

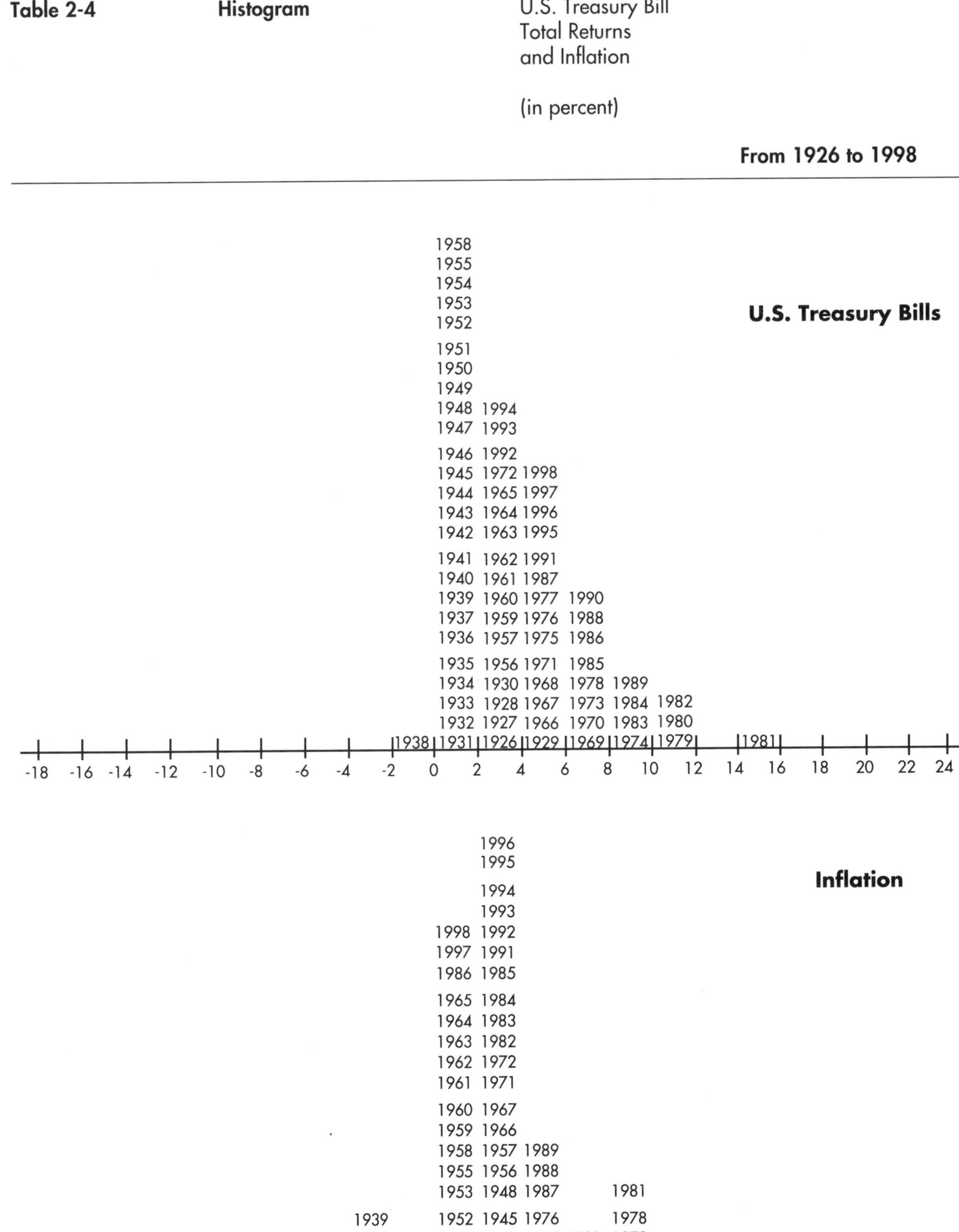

Annual Total Returns

Table 2-5 shows annual total returns for the seven basic asset classes for the full 73-year time period. This table can be used to compare the performance of each asset class for the same annual period. Monthly total returns for large company stocks, small company stocks, long-term corporate bonds, long-term government bonds, intermediate-term government bonds, Treasury bills and inflation rates are presented in Appendix A: Tables A-1, A-4, A-5, A-6, A-10, A-14, and A-15, respectively.

Capital Appreciation, Income, and Reinvestment Returns

Table 2-6 provides further detail on the returns of large company stocks, and long- and intermediate-term government bonds. Total annual returns are shown as the sum of three components: capital appreciation returns, income returns, and reinvestment returns. The capital appreciation and income components are explained in Chapter 3. The third component, reinvestment return, reflects monthly income reinvested in the total return index in subsequent months in the year. Thus, for a single month the reinvestment return is zero, but over a longer period of time it is non-zero. Since the returns in Table 2-6 are annual, reinvestment return is relevant.

The annual total return formed by compounding the monthly total returns does not equal the sum of the annual capital appreciation and income components; the difference is reinvestment return. A simple example illustrates this point. In 1995, an "up" year on a total return basis, the total annual return on large company stocks was 37.4 percent. The annual capital appreciation was 34.1 percent and the annual income return was 2.9 percent. These two components sum to 37.0 percent; the remaining 0.4 percent of the total 1995 return came from the reinvestment of dividends in the market. For more information on calculating annual total and income returns, see Chapter 5.

Monthly income and capital appreciation returns for large company stocks are presented in Appendix A: Tables A-2 and A-3 respectively. Monthly income and capital appreciation returns are presented for long-term government bonds in Appendix A: Tables A-7 and A-8; and for intermediate-term government bonds in Tables A-11 and A-12.

Table 2-5 **Basic Series** Annual Total Returns

(in percent)

From 1926 to 1970

Year	Large Company Stocks	Small Company Stocks	Long-Term Corporate Bonds	Long-Term Government Bonds	Intermediate-Term Government Bonds	U.S. Treasury Bills	Inflation
1926	11.62	0.28	7.37	7.77	5.38	3.27	-1.49
1927	37.49	22.10	7.44	8.93	4.52	3.12	-2.08
1928	43.61	39.69	2.84	0.10	0.92	3.56	-0.97
1929	-8.42	-51.36	3.27	3.42	6.01	4.75	0.20
1930	-24.90	-38.15	7.98	4.66	6.72	2.41	-6.03
1931	-43.34	-49.75	-1.85	-5.31	-2.32	1.07	-9.52
1932	-8.19	-5.39	10.82	16.84	8.81	0.96	-10.30
1933	53.99	142.87	10.38	-0.07	1.83	0.30	0.51
1934	-1.44	24.22	13.84	10.03	9.00	0.16	2.03
1935	47.67	40.19	9.61	4.98	7.01	0.17	2.99
1936	33.92	64.80	6.74	7.52	3.06	0.18	1.21
1937	-35.03	-58.01	2.75	0.23	1.56	0.31	3.10
1938	31.12	32.80	6.13	5.53	6.23	-0.02	-2.78
1939	-0.41	0.35	3.97	5.94	4.52	0.02	-0.48
1940	-9.78	-5.16	3.39	6.09	2.96	0.00	0.96
1941	-11.59	-9.00	2.73	0.93	0.50	0.06	9.72
1942	20.34	44.51	2.60	3.22	1.94	0.27	9.29
1943	25.90	88.37	2.83	2.08	2.81	0.35	3.16
1944	19.75	53.72	4.73	2.81	1.80	0.33	2.11
1945	36.44	73.61	4.08	10.73	2.22	0.33	2.25
1946	-8.07	-11.63	1.72	-0.10	1.00	0.35	18.16
1947	5.71	0.92	-2.34	-2.62	0.91	0.50	9.01
1948	5.50	-2.11	4.14	3.40	1.85	0.81	2.71
1949	18.79	19.75	3.31	6.45	2.32	1.10	-1.80
1950	31.71	38.75	2.12	0.06	0.70	1.20	5.79
1951	24.02	7.80	-2.69	-3.93	0.36	1.49	5.87
1952	18.37	3.03	3.52	1.16	1.63	1.66	0.88
1953	-0.99	-6.49	3.41	3.64	3.23	1.82	0.62
1954	52.62	60.58	5.39	7.19	2.68	0.86	-0.50
1955	31.56	20.44	0.48	-1.29	-0.65	1.57	0.37
1956	6.56	4.28	-6.81	-5.59	-0.42	2.46	2.86
1957	-10.78	-14.57	8.71	7.46	7.84	3.14	3.02
1958	43.36	64.89	-2.22	-6.09	-1.29	1.54	1.76
1959	11.96	16.40	-0.97	-2.26	-0.39	2.95	1.50
1960	0.47	-3.29	9.07	13.78	11.76	2.66	1.48
1961	26.89	32.09	4.82	0.97	1.85	2.13	0.67
1962	-8.73	-11.90	7.95	6.89	5.56	2.73	1.22
1963	22.80	23.57	2.19	1.21	1.64	3.12	1.65
1964	16.48	23.52	4.77	3.51	4.04	3.54	1.19
1965	12.45	41.75	-0.46	0.71	1.02	3.93	1.92
1966	-10.06	-7.01	0.20	3.65	4.69	4.76	3.35
1967	23.98	83.57	-4.95	-9.18	1.01	4.21	3.04
1968	11.06	35.97	2.57	-0.26	4.54	5.21	4.72
1969	-8.50	-25.05	-8.09	-5.07	-0.74	6.58	6.11
1970	4.01	-17.43	18.37	12.11	16.86	6.52	5.49

Table 2-5 **Basic Series** Annual Total Returns

(continued) (in percent)

From 1971 to 1998

Year	Large Company Stocks	Small Company Stocks	Long-Term Corporate Bonds	Long-Term Government Bonds	Intermediate-Term Government Bonds	U.S. Treasury Bills	Inflation
1971	14.31	16.50	11.01	13.23	8.72	4.39	3.36
1972	18.98	4.43	7.26	5.69	5.16	3.84	3.41
1973	-14.66	-30.90	1.14	-1.11	4.61	6.93	8.80
1974	-26.47	-19.95	-3.06	4.35	5.69	8.00	12.20
1975	37.20	52.82	14.64	9.20	7.83	5.80	7.01
1976	23.84	57.38	18.65	16.75	12.87	5.08	4.81
1977	-7.18	25.38	1.71	-0.69	1.41	5.12	6.77
1978	6.56	23.46	-0.07	-1.18	3.49	7.18	9.03
1979	18.44	43.46	-4.18	-1.23	4.09	10.38	13.31
1980	32.42	39.88	-2.76	-3.95	3.91	11.24	12.40
1981	-4.91	13.88	-1.24	1.86	9.45	14.71	8.94
1982	21.41	28.01	42.56	40.36	29.10	10.54	3.87
1983	22.51	39.67	6.26	0.65	7.41	8.80	3.80
1984	6.27	-6.67	16.86	15.48	14.02	9.85	3.95
1985	32.16	24.66	30.09	30.97	20.33	7.72	3.77
1986	18.47	6.85	19.85	24.53	15.14	6.16	1.13
1987	5.23	-9.30	-0.27	-2.71	2.90	5.47	4.41
1988	16.81	22.87	10.70	9.67	6.10	6.35	4.42
1989	31.49	10.18	16.23	18.11	13.29	8.37	4.65
1990	-3.17	-21.56	6.78	6.18	9.73	7.81	6.11
1991	30.55	44.63	19.89	19.30	15.46	5.60	3.06
1992	7.67	23.35	9.39	8.05	7.19	3.51	2.90
1993	9.99	20.98	13.19	18.24	11.24	2.90	2.75
1994	1.31	3.11	-5.76	-7.77	-5.14	3.90	2.67
1995	37.43	34.46	27.20	31.67	16.80	5.60	2.54
1996	23.07	17.62	1.40	-0.93	2.10	5.21	3.32
1997	33.36	22.78	12.95	15.85	8.38	5.26	1.70
1998	28.58	-7.31	10.76	13.06	10.21	4.86	1.61

Table 2-6 **Large Company Stocks, Long-Term Government Bonds, and Intermediate-Term Government Bonds**

Annual Total, Income, Capital Appreciation, and Reinvestment Returns

(in percent)

From 1926 to 1970

	Large Company Stocks				Long-Term Government Bonds					Intermediate-Term Government Bonds				
Year	Capital Apprec Return	Income Return	Rein-vest-ment Return	Total Return	Capital Apprec Return	Income Return	Rein-vest-ment Return	Total Return	Year-end Yield	Capital Apprec Return	Income Return	Rein-vest-ment Return	Total Return	Year-end Yield
1926	5.72	5.41	0.50	11.62	3.91	3.73	0.13	7.77	3.54	1.51	3.78	0.10	5.38	3.61
1927	30.91	5.71	0.87	37.49	5.40	3.41	0.12	8.93	3.16	0.96	3.49	0.07	4.52	3.40
1928	37.88	4.81	0.91	43.61	-3.12	3.22	0.01	0.10	3.40	-2.73	3.64	0.01	0.92	4.01
1929	-11.91	3.98	-0.49	-8.42	-0.20	3.47	0.15	3.42	3.40	1.77	4.07	0.18	6.01	3.62
1930	-28.48	4.57	-0.98	-24.90	1.28	3.32	0.05	4.66	3.30	3.30	3.30	0.11	6.72	2.91
1931	-47.07	5.35	-1.62	-43.34	-8.46	3.33	-0.17	-5.31	4.07	-5.40	3.16	-0.08	-2.32	4.12
1932	-15.15	6.16	0.80	-8.19	12.94	3.69	0.22	16.84	3.15	5.02	3.63	0.16	8.81	3.04
1933	46.59	6.39	1.01	53.99	-3.14	3.12	-0.05	-0.07	3.36	-0.99	2.83	-0.02	1.83	3.25
1934	-5.94	4.46	0.04	-1.44	6.76	3.18	0.09	10.03	2.93	5.97	2.93	0.09	9.00	2.49
1935	41.37	4.95	1.35	47.67	2.14	2.81	0.03	4.98	2.76	4.94	2.02	0.05	7.01	1.63
1936	27.92	5.36	0.64	33.92	4.64	2.77	0.10	7.52	2.55	1.60	1.44	0.02	3.06	1.29
1937	-38.59	4.66	-1.09	-35.03	-2.48	2.66	0.05	0.23	2.73	0.05	1.48	0.03	1.56	1.14
1938	25.21	4.83	1.07	31.12	2.83	2.64	0.06	5.53	2.52	4.37	1.82	0.04	6.23	1.52
1939	-5.45	4.69	0.35	-0.41	3.48	2.40	0.06	5.94	2.26	3.18	1.31	0.03	4.52	0.98
1940	-15.29	5.36	0.14	-9.78	3.77	2.23	0.09	6.09	1.94	2.04	0.90	0.02	2.96	0.57
1941	-17.86	6.71	-0.44	-11.59	-1.01	1.94	0.00	0.93	2.04	-0.17	0.67	0.00	0.50	0.82
1942	12.43	6.79	1.12	20.34	0.74	2.46	0.02	3.22	2.46	1.17	0.76	0.00	1.94	0.72
1943	19.45	6.24	0.21	25.90	-0.37	2.44	0.02	2.08	2.48	1.23	1.56	0.02	2.81	1.45
1944	13.80	5.48	0.47	19.75	0.32	2.46	0.03	2.81	2.46	0.35	1.44	0.01	1.80	1.40
1945	30.72	4.97	0.74	36.44	8.27	2.34	0.12	10.73	1.99	1.02	1.19	0.01	2.22	1.03
1946	-11.87	4.09	-0.29	-8.07	-2.15	2.04	0.01	-0.10	2.12	-0.08	1.08	0.00	1.00	1.12
1947	0.00	5.49	0.22	5.71	-4.70	2.13	-0.06	-2.62	2.43	-0.30	1.21	0.00	0.91	1.34
1948	-0.65	6.08	0.08	5.50	0.96	2.40	0.04	3.40	2.37	0.27	1.56	0.01	1.85	1.51
1949	10.26	7.50	1.03	18.79	4.15	2.25	0.06	6.45	2.09	0.95	1.36	0.01	2.32	1.23
1950	21.78	8.77	1.16	31.71	-2.06	2.12	0.00	0.06	2.24	-0.69	1.39	0.00	0.70	1.62
1951	16.46	6.91	0.65	24.02	-6.27	2.38	-0.04	-3.93	2.69	-1.63	1.98	0.01	0.36	2.17
1952	11.78	5.93	0.66	18.37	-1.48	2.66	-0.02	1.16	2.79	-0.57	2.19	0.01	1.63	2.35
1953	-6.62	5.46	0.18	-0.99	0.67	2.84	0.12	3.64	2.74	0.61	2.55	0.07	3.23	2.18
1954	45.02	6.21	1.39	52.62	4.35	2.79	0.05	7.19	2.72	1.08	1.60	0.01	2.68	1.72
1955	26.40	4.56	0.60	31.56	-4.07	2.75	0.03	-1.29	2.95	-3.10	2.45	0.00	-0.65	2.80
1956	2.62	3.83	0.11	6.56	-8.46	2.99	-0.12	-5.59	3.45	-3.45	3.05	-0.02	-0.42	3.63
1957	-14.31	3.84	-0.30	-10.78	3.82	3.44	0.20	7.46	3.23	4.05	3.59	0.20	7.84	2.84
1958	38.06	4.38	0.93	43.36	-9.23	3.27	-0.14	-6.09	3.82	-4.17	2.93	-0.05	-1.29	3.81
1959	8.48	3.31	0.16	11.96	-6.20	4.01	-0.07	-2.26	4.47	-4.56	4.18	-0.01	-0.39	4.98
1960	-2.97	3.26	0.19	0.47	9.29	4.26	0.23	13.78	3.80	7.42	4.15	0.19	11.76	3.31
1961	23.13	3.48	0.28	26.89	-2.86	3.83	0.00	0.97	4.15	-1.72	3.54	0.03	1.85	3.84
1962	-11.81	2.98	0.10	-8.73	2.78	4.00	0.11	6.89	3.95	1.73	3.73	0.10	5.56	3.50
1963	18.89	3.61	0.30	22.80	-2.70	3.89	0.02	1.21	4.17	-2.10	3.71	0.03	1.64	4.04
1964	12.97	3.33	0.18	16.48	-0.72	4.15	0.07	3.51	4.23	-0.03	4.00	0.07	4.04	4.03
1965	9.06	3.21	0.18	12.45	-3.45	4.19	-0.04	0.71	4.50	-3.10	4.15	-0.03	1.02	4.90
1966	-13.09	3.11	-0.08	-10.06	-1.06	4.49	0.22	3.65	4.55	-0.41	4.93	0.17	4.69	4.79
1967	20.09	3.64	0.25	23.98	-13.55	4.59	-0.23	-9.18	5.56	-3.85	4.88	-0.02	1.01	5.77
1968	7.66	3.18	0.22	11.06	-5.51	5.50	-0.25	-0.26	5.98	-0.99	5.49	0.03	4.54	5.96
1969	-11.42	3.04	-0.13	-8.50	-10.83	5.95	-0.19	-5.07	6.87	-7.27	6.65	-0.11	-0.74	8.29
1970	0.16	3.41	0.43	4.01	4.84	6.74	0.52	12.11	6.48	8.71	7.49	0.66	16.86	5.90

Table 2-6 **Large Company Stocks, Long-Term Government Bonds, and Intermediate-Term Government Bonds**

(continued)

Annual Total, Income, Capital Appreciation, and Reinvestment Returns

(in percent)

From 1971 to 1998

	Large Company Stocks				Long-Term Government Bonds					Intermediate-Term Government Bonds				
Year	Capital Apprec Return	Income Return	Rein-vest-ment Return	Total Return	Capital Apprec Return	Income Return	Rein-vest-ment Return	Total Return	Year-end Yield	Capital Apprec Return	Income Return	Rein-vest-ment Return	Total Return	Year-end Yield
1971	10.79	3.33	0.19	14.31	6.61	6.32	0.31	13.23	5.97	2.72	5.75	0.25	8.72	5.25
1972	15.63	3.09	0.26	18.98	-0.35	5.87	0.17	5.69	5.99	-0.75	5.75	0.16	5.16	5.85
1973	-17.37	2.86	-0.16	-14.66	-7.70	6.51	0.08	-1.11	7.26	-2.19	6.58	0.22	4.61	6.79
1974	-29.72	3.69	-0.44	-26.47	-3.45	7.27	0.54	4.35	7.60	-1.99	7.24	0.44	5.69	7.12
1975	31.55	5.37	0.29	37.20	0.73	7.99	0.47	9.20	8.05	0.12	7.35	0.36	7.83	7.19
1976	19.15	4.38	0.31	23.84	8.07	7.89	0.80	16.75	7.21	5.25	7.10	0.51	12.87	6.00
1977	-11.50	4.31	0.01	-7.18	-7.86	7.14	0.04	-0.69	8.03	-5.15	6.49	0.06	1.41	7.51
1978	1.06	5.33	0.17	6.56	-9.05	7.90	-0.03	-1.18	8.98	-4.49	7.83	0.14	3.49	8.83
1979	12.31	5.71	0.42	18.44	-9.84	8.86	-0.25	-1.23	10.12	-5.07	9.04	0.12	4.09	10.33
1980	25.77	5.73	0.92	32.42	-14.00	9.97	0.08	-3.95	11.99	-6.81	10.55	0.17	3.91	12.45
1981	-9.72	4.89	-0.08	-4.91	-10.33	11.55	0.64	1.86	13.34	-4.55	12.97	1.03	9.45	13.96
1982	14.76	5.50	1.15	21.41	23.95	13.50	2.91	40.36	10.95	14.23	12.81	2.06	29.10	9.90
1983	17.27	5.00	0.24	22.51	-9.82	10.38	0.09	0.65	11.97	-3.30	10.35	0.35	7.41	11.41
1984	1.39	4.56	0.31	6.27	2.32	11.74	1.42	15.48	11.70	1.22	11.68	1.12	14.02	11.04
1985	26.34	5.10	0.72	32.16	17.84	11.25	1.88	30.97	9.56	9.01	10.29	1.04	20.33	8.55
1986	14.63	3.74	0.10	18.47	14.99	8.98	0.56	24.53	7.89	6.99	7.72	0.43	15.14	6.85
1987	2.03	3.64	-0.44	5.23	-10.69	7.92	0.06	-2.71	9.20	-4.75	7.47	0.19	2.90	8.32
1988	12.41	4.17	0.24	16.81	0.36	8.97	0.34	9.67	9.18	-2.26	8.24	0.13	6.10	9.17
1989	27.26	3.85	0.38	31.49	8.62	8.81	0.68	18.11	8.16	4.34	8.46	0.49	13.29	7.94
1990	-6.56	3.36	0.03	-3.17	-2.61	8.19	0.61	6.18	8.44	1.02	8.15	0.56	9.73	7.70
1991	26.31	3.82	0.42	30.55	10.10	8.22	0.98	19.30	7.30	7.36	7.43	0.67	15.46	5.97
1992	4.46	3.03	0.18	7.67	0.34	7.26	0.45	8.05	7.26	0.64	6.27	0.28	7.19	6.11
1993	7.06	2.83	0.11	9.99	10.71	7.17	0.35	18.24	6.54	5.56	5.53	0.15	11.24	5.22
1994	-1.54	2.82	0.03	1.31	-14.29	6.59	-0.07	-7.77	7.99	-11.14	6.07	-0.07	-5.14	7.80
1995	34.11	2.91	0.41	37.43	23.04	7.60	1.03	31.67	6.03	9.66	6.69	0.45	16.80	5.38
1996	20.26	2.54	0.27	23.07	-7.37	6.18	0.26	-0.93	6.73	-3.90	5.82	0.18	2.10	6.16
1997	31.01	2.11	0.25	33.36	8.51	6.64	0.71	15.85	6.02	1.94	6.14	0.30	8.38	5.73
1998	26.67	1.68	0.24	28.58	6.89	5.83	0.34	13.06	5.42	4.66	5.29	0.25	10.21	4.68

Rolling Period Returns

The highest and lowest returns on the basic series, expressed as annual rates, are shown for 1-, 5-, 10-, 15-, and 20-year holding periods in Table 2-7. This exhibit also shows the number of times that an asset had a positive return, and the number of times that an asset's return was the highest among all those studied. The number of times positive (or times highest) is compared to the total number of observations—that is, 73 annual, 69 overlapping five-year, 64 overlapping 10-year, 59 overlapping 15-year, and 54 overlapping 20-year holding periods.

Tables 2-8, 2-9, 2-10 and 2-11 show the compound annual total returns for 5-, 10-, 15-, and 20-year holding periods. Often, these calculations are referred to as rolling period returns as they are obtained by rolling a data window of fixed length along each time series. They are useful for examining the behavior of returns for holding periods similar to those actually experienced by investors and show the effects of time diversification. Holding assets for long periods of time has the effect of lowering the risk of experiencing a loss in asset value.

Table 2-7 **Basic Series**

Maximum and Minimum Values of Returns for 1-, 5-, 10-, 15-, and 20-Year Holding Periods

(compound annual rates of return in percent)

Series	Maximum Value Return	Maximum Value Year(s)	Minimum Value Return	Minimum Value Year(s)	Times Positive (out of 73 Years)	Times Highest Returning Asset
Annual Returns						
Large Company Stocks	53.99	1933	-43.34	1931	53	16
Small Company Stocks	142.87	1933	-58.01	1937	51	31
Long-Term Corporate Bonds	42.56	1982	-8.09	1969	57	6
Long-Term Government Bonds	40.36	1982	-9.18	1967	53	6
Intermediate-Term Government Bonds	29.10	1982	-5.14	1994	66	2
U.S. Treasury Bills	14.71	1981	-0.02	1938	72	6
Inflation	18.16	1946	-10.30	1932	63	6
5-Year Rolling Period Returns					(out of 69 overlapping 5-year periods)	
Large Company Stocks	24.06	1994–98	-12.47	1928–32	62	21
Small Company Stocks	45.90	1941–45	-27.54	1928–32	60	37
Long-Term Corporate Bonds	22.51	1982–86	-2.22	1965–69	66	7
Long-Term Government Bonds	21.62	1982–86	-2.14	1965–69	63	1
Intermediate-Term Government Bonds	16.98	1982–86	0.96	1955–59	69	2
U.S. Treasury Bills	11.12	1979–83	0.07	1938–42	69	0
Inflation	10.06	1977–81	-5.42	1928–32	62	1
10-Year Rolling Period Returns					(out of 64 overlapping 10-year periods)	
Large Company Stocks	20.06	1949–58	-0.89	1929–38	62	19
Small Company Stocks	30.38	1975–84	-5.70	1929–38	62	35
Long-Term Corporate Bonds	16.32	1982–91	0.98	1947–56	64	6
Long-Term Government Bonds	15.56	1982–91	-0.07	1950–59	63	0
Intermediate-Term Government Bonds	13.13	1982–91	1.25	1947–56	64	2
U.S. Treasury Bills	9.17	1978–87	0.15	1933–42/1934–43	64	1
Inflation	8.67	1973–82	-2.57	1926–35	58	1
15-Year Rolling Period Returns					(out of 59 overlapping 15-year periods)	
Large Company Stocks	18.24	1942–56	0.64	1929–43	59	11
Small Company Stocks	23.33	1975–89	-1.30	1927–41	56	44
Long-Term Corporate Bonds	13.66	1982–96	1.02	1955–69	59	4
Long-Term Government Bonds	13.53	1981–95	0.40	1955–69	59	0
Intermediate-Term Government Bonds	11.27	1981–95	1.45	1945–59	59	0
U.S. Treasury Bills	8.32	1977–91	0.22	1933–47	59	0
Inflation	7.30	1968–82	-1.59	1926–40	56	0
20-Year Rolling Period Returns					(out of 54 overlapping 20-year periods)	
Large Company Stocks	17.75	1979–98	3.11	1929–48	54	4
Small Company Stocks	21.13	1942–61	5.74	1929–48	54	50
Long-Term Corporate Bonds	10.86	1979–98	1.34	1950–69	54	0
Long-Term Government Bonds	11.14	1979–98	0.69	1950–69	54	0
Intermediate-Term Government Bonds	9.85	1979–98	1.58	1940–59	54	0
U.S. Treasury Bills	7.72	1972–91	0.42	1931–50	54	0
Inflation	6.36	1966–85	0.07	1926–45	54	0

Table 2-8 **Basic Series**

Compound Annual Returns for 5-Year Holding Periods

(percent per annum)

From 1926 to 1970

Period	Large Company Stocks	Small Company Stocks	Long-Term Corporate Bonds	Long-Term Government Bonds	Intermediate Government Bonds	U.S. Treasury Bills	Inflation
1926–1930	8.68	-12.44	5.76	4.93	4.69	3.42	-2.10
1927–1931	-5.10	-23.74	3.87	2.25	3.11	2.98	-3.75
1928–1932	-12.47	-27.54	4.52	3.69	3.95	2.54	-5.42
1929–1933	-11.24	-19.06	6.01	3.66	4.13	1.89	-5.14
1930–1934	-9.93	-2.37	8.09	4.95	4.71	0.98	-4.80
1931–1935	3.12	14.99	8.42	5.01	4.77	0.53	-3.04
1932–1936	22.47	45.83	10.26	7.71	5.90	0.35	-0.84
1933–1937	14.29	23.96	8.60	4.46	4.45	0.22	1.96
1934–1938	10.67	9.86	7.75	5.61	5.33	0.16	1.29
1935–1939	10.91	5.27	5.81	4.81	4.46	0.13	0.78
1936–1940	0.50	-2.64	4.59	5.03	3.65	0.10	0.38
1937–1941	-7.51	-13.55	3.79	3.71	3.13	0.08	2.02
1938–1942	4.62	10.70	3.76	4.32	3.21	0.07	3.21
1939–1943	3.77	18.71	3.10	3.63	2.54	0.14	4.44
1940–1944	7.67	29.28	3.25	3.01	2.00	0.20	4.98
1941–1945	16.96	45.90	3.39	3.90	1.85	0.27	5.25
1942–1946	17.87	45.05	3.19	3.69	1.95	0.33	6.82
1943–1947	14.86	35.00	2.17	2.49	1.75	0.37	6.77
1944–1948	10.87	18.43	2.43	2.75	1.55	0.47	6.67
1945–1949	10.69	12.66	2.15	3.46	1.66	0.62	5.84
1946–1950	9.91	7.72	1.76	1.39	1.36	0.79	6.57
1947–1951	16.70	12.09	0.87	0.60	1.23	1.02	4.25
1948–1952	19.37	12.55	2.05	1.37	1.37	1.25	2.65
1949–1953	17.86	11.53	1.91	1.41	1.64	1.45	2.23
1950–1954	23.92	18.27	2.31	1.55	1.72	1.41	2.50
1951–1955	23.89	14.97	1.98	1.28	1.44	1.48	1.43
1952–1956	20.18	14.21	1.10	0.93	1.28	1.67	0.84
1953–1957	13.58	10.01	2.10	2.15	2.49	1.97	1.27
1954–1958	22.31	23.22	0.96	0.16	1.58	1.91	1.49
1955–1959	14.96	15.54	-0.29	-1.67	0.96	2.33	1.90
1956–1960	8.92	10.58	1.36	1.16	3.37	2.55	2.12
1957–1961	12.79	15.93	3.77	2.53	3.83	2.48	1.68
1958–1962	13.31	16.65	3.63	2.42	3.39	2.40	1.33
1959–1963	9.85	10.11	4.55	3.97	4.00	2.72	1.30
1960–1964	10.73	11.43	5.73	5.17	4.91	2.83	1.24
1961–1965	13.25	20.28	3.82	2.63	2.81	3.09	1.33
1962–1966	5.72	12.13	2.88	3.17	3.38	3.61	1.86
1963–1967	12.39	29.86	0.30	-0.14	2.47	3.91	2.23
1964–1968	10.16	32.37	0.37	-0.43	3.04	4.33	2.84
1965–1969	4.96	19.78	-2.22	-2.14	2.08	4.93	3.82
1966–1970	3.34	7.51	1.23	-0.02	5.10	5.45	4.54
1967–1971	8.42	12.47	3.32	1.77	5.90	5.38	4.54
1968–1972	7.53	0.47	5.85	4.90	6.75	5.30	4.61
1969–1973	2.01	-12.25	5.55	4.72	6.77	5.65	5.41
1970–1974	-2.36	-11.09	6.68	6.72	8.11	5.93	6.60

Table 2-8 **Basic Series** Compound Annual Returns for 5-Year Holding Periods

(continued) (percent per annum)

From 1971 to 1998

Period	Large Company Stocks	Small Company Stocks	Long-Term Corporate Bonds	Long-Term Government Bonds	Intermediate Government Bonds	U.S. Treasury Bills	Inflation
1971–1975	3.21	0.56	6.00	6.16	6.39	5.78	6.90
1972–1976	4.87	6.80	7.42	6.82	7.19	5.92	7.20
1973–1977	-0.21	10.77	6.29	5.50	6.41	6.18	7.89
1974–1978	4.32	24.41	6.03	5.48	6.18	6.23	7.94
1975–1979	14.76	39.80	5.78	4.33	5.86	6.69	8.15
1976–1980	13.95	37.35	2.36	1.68	5.08	7.77	9.21
1977–1981	8.08	28.75	-1.33	-1.05	4.44	9.67	10.06
1978–1982	14.05	29.28	5.57	6.03	9.60	10.78	9.46
1979–1983	17.27	32.51	6.87	6.42	10.42	11.12	8.39
1980–1984	14.76	21.59	11.20	9.80	12.45	11.01	6.53
1981–1985	14.71	18.82	17.86	16.83	15.80	10.30	4.85
1982–1986	19.87	17.32	22.51	21.62	16.98	8.60	3.30
1983–1987	16.49	9.51	14.06	13.02	11.79	7.59	3.41
1984–1988	15.38	6.74	15.00	14.98	11.52	7.10	3.53
1985–1989	20.40	10.34	14.88	15.50	11.38	6.81	3.67
1986–1990	13.14	0.58	10.43	10.75	9.34	6.83	4.13
1987–1991	15.36	6.86	10.44	9.81	9.40	6.71	4.52
1988–1992	15.89	13.63	12.50	12.14	10.30	6.31	4.22
1989–1993	14.50	13.28	13.00	13.84	11.35	5.61	3.89
1990–1994	8.69	11.79	8.36	8.34	7.46	4.73	3.49
1991–1995	16.57	24.51	12.22	13.10	8.81	4.29	2.79
1992–1996	15.20	19.47	8.52	8.98	6.17	4.22	2.84
1993–1997	20.24	19.35	9.22	10.51	6.40	4.57	2.60
1994–1998	24.06	13.16	8.74	9.52	6.20	4.96	2.37

Table 2-9 **Basic Series** Compound Annual Returns for 10-Year Holding Periods

(percent per annum)

From 1926 to 1970

Period	Large Company Stocks	Small Company Stocks	Long-Term Corporate Bonds	Long-Term Government Bonds	Intermediate Government Bonds	U.S. Treasury Bills	Inflation
1926–1935	5.86	0.34	7.08	4.97	4.73	1.97	-2.57
1927–1936	7.81	5.45	7.02	4.95	4.50	1.66	-2.30
1928–1937	0.02	-5.22	6.54	4.08	4.20	1.37	-1.80
1929–1938	-0.89	-5.70	6.88	4.63	4.73	1.02	-1.98
1930–1939	-0.05	1.38	6.95	4.88	4.58	0.55	-2.05
1931–1940	1.80	5.81	6.49	5.02	4.21	0.32	-1.34
1932–1941	6.43	12.28	6.97	5.69	4.51	0.21	0.58
1933–1942	9.35	17.14	6.15	4.39	3.83	0.15	2.59
1934–1943	7.17	14.20	5.40	4.62	3.93	0.15	2.85
1935–1944	9.28	16.66	4.53	3.91	3.22	0.17	2.86
1936–1945	8.42	19.18	3.99	4.46	2.75	0.18	2.79
1937–1946	4.41	11.98	3.49	3.70	2.54	0.20	4.39
1938–1947	9.62	22.24	2.96	3.40	2.48	0.22	4.97
1939–1948	7.26	18.57	2.77	3.19	2.04	0.30	5.55
1940–1949	9.17	20.69	2.70	3.24	1.83	0.41	5.41
1941–1950	13.38	25.37	2.57	2.64	1.60	0.53	5.91
1942–1951	17.28	27.51	2.02	2.13	1.59	0.67	5.53
1943–1952	17.09	23.27	2.11	1.93	1.56	0.81	4.69
1944–1953	14.31	14.93	2.17	2.08	1.60	0.96	4.43
1945–1954	17.12	15.43	2.23	2.51	1.69	1.01	4.16
1946–1955	16.69	11.29	1.87	1.33	1.40	1.14	3.96
1947–1956	18.43	13.14	0.98	0.76	1.25	1.35	2.53
1948–1957	16.44	11.27	2.07	1.76	1.93	1.61	1.96
1949–1958	20.06	17.23	1.43	0.79	1.61	1.68	1.86
1950–1959	19.35	16.90	1.00	-0.07	1.34	1.87	2.20
1951–1960	16.16	12.75	1.67	1.22	2.40	2.01	1.77
1952–1961	16.43	15.07	2.43	1.73	2.55	2.08	1.26
1953–1962	13.44	13.28	2.86	2.29	2.94	2.19	1.30
1954–1963	15.91	16.48	2.74	2.05	2.78	2.31	1.40
1955–1964	12.82	13.47	2.68	1.69	2.92	2.58	1.57
1956–1965	11.06	15.33	2.58	1.89	3.09	2.82	1.73
1957–1966	9.20	14.02	3.33	2.85	3.60	3.05	1.77
1958–1967	12.85	23.08	1.95	1.13	2.93	3.15	1.78
1959–1968	10.00	20.73	2.44	1.75	3.52	3.52	2.07
1960–1969	7.81	15.53	1.68	1.45	3.48	3.88	2.52
1961–1970	8.18	13.72	2.51	1.30	3.95	4.26	2.92
1962–1971	7.06	12.30	3.10	2.47	4.63	4.49	3.19
1963–1972	9.93	14.22	3.04	2.35	4.59	4.60	3.41
1964–1973	6.00	7.77	2.93	2.11	4.89	4.98	4.12
1965–1974	1.24	3.20	2.13	2.20	5.05	5.43	5.20
1966–1975	3.27	3.98	3.59	3.03	5.74	5.62	5.71
1967–1976	6.63	9.60	5.35	4.26	6.54	5.65	5.86
1968–1977	3.59	5.50	6.07	5.20	6.58	5.74	6.24
1969–1978	3.16	4.48	5.79	5.10	6.47	5.94	6.67
1970–1979	5.86	11.49	6.23	5.52	6.98	6.31	7.37

Table 2-9 **Basic Series** Compound Annual Returns for 10-Year Holding Periods

(continued) (percent per annum)

From 1971 to 1998

Period	Large Company Stocks	Small Company Stocks	Long-Term Corporate Bonds	Long-Term Government Bonds	Intermediate Government Bonds	U.S. Treasury Bills	Inflation
1971–1980	8.44	17.53	4.16	3.90	5.73	6.77	8.05
1972–1981	6.47	17.26	2.95	2.81	5.80	7.78	8.62
1973–1982	6.68	19.67	5.93	5.76	8.00	8.46	8.67
1974–1983	10.61	28.40	6.45	5.95	8.28	8.65	8.16
1975–1984	14.76	30.38	8.46	7.03	9.11	8.83	7.34
1976–1985	14.33	27.75	9.84	8.99	10.31	9.03	7.01
1977–1986	13.82	22.90	9.95	9.70	10.53	9.14	6.63
1978–1987	15.26	18.99	9.73	9.47	10.69	9.17	6.39
1979–1988	16.33	18.93	10.86	10.62	10.97	9.09	5.93
1980–1989	17.55	15.83	13.02	12.62	11.91	8.89	5.09
1981–1990	13.93	9.32	14.09	13.75	12.52	8.55	4.49
1982–1991	17.59	11.97	16.32	15.56	13.13	7.65	3.91
1983–1992	16.19	11.55	13.28	12.58	11.04	6.95	3.81
1984–1993	14.94	9.96	14.00	14.41	11.43	6.35	3.71
1985–1994	14.40	11.06	11.57	11.86	9.40	5.76	3.58
1986–1995	14.84	11.90	11.32	11.92	9.08	5.55	3.46
1987–1996	15.28	12.98	9.48	9.39	7.77	5.46	3.68
1988–1997	18.05	16.46	10.85	11.32	8.33	5.44	3.41
1989–1998	19.19	13.22	10.85	11.66	8.74	5.29	3.12

Table 2-10 **Basic Series**

Compound Annual Returns for 15-Year Holding Periods

(percent per annum)

From 1926 to 1970

Period	Large Company Stocks	Small Company Stocks	Long-Term Corporate Bonds	Long-Term Government Bonds	Intermediate Government Bonds	U.S. Treasury Bills	Inflation
1926–1940	4.04	-0.66	6.24	4.99	4.37	1.34	-1.59
1927–1941	2.44	-1.30	5.93	4.53	4.04	1.13	-0.88
1928–1942	1.53	-0.19	5.60	4.16	3.87	0.94	-0.16
1929–1943	0.64	1.82	5.60	4.29	4.00	0.73	0.12
1930–1944	2.46	9.94	5.70	4.25	3.71	0.44	0.24
1931–1945	6.62	17.77	5.44	4.65	3.42	0.30	0.81
1932–1946	10.11	22.29	5.70	5.02	3.65	0.25	2.62
1933–1947	11.15	22.81	4.81	3.75	3.13	0.22	3.96
1934–1948	8.39	15.59	4.40	3.99	3.13	0.26	4.11
1935–1949	9.75	15.31	3.73	3.76	2.70	0.32	3.85
1936–1950	8.91	15.23	3.24	3.43	2.28	0.39	4.03
1937–1951	8.36	12.02	2.61	2.66	2.10	0.47	4.34
1938–1952	12.78	18.92	2.66	2.72	2.11	0.56	4.19
1939–1953	10.68	16.18	2.48	2.59	1.91	0.68	4.43
1940–1954	13.88	19.88	2.57	2.67	1.79	0.74	4.43
1941–1955	16.78	21.80	2.38	2.18	1.55	0.85	4.39
1942–1956	18.24	22.91	1.71	1.73	1.49	1.01	3.94
1943–1957	15.91	18.68	2.11	2.00	1.87	1.20	3.53
1944–1958	16.92	17.63	1.76	1.44	1.59	1.28	3.44
1945–1959	16.39	15.47	1.39	1.09	1.45	1.45	3.40
1946–1960	14.04	11.05	1.70	1.28	2.05	1.61	3.35
1947–1961	16.52	14.07	1.91	1.35	2.11	1.72	2.25
1948–1962	15.38	13.04	2.59	1.98	2.41	1.87	1.75
1949–1963	16.56	14.81	2.46	1.84	2.40	2.03	1.67
1950–1964	16.40	15.05	2.56	1.65	2.51	2.19	1.88
1951–1965	15.18	15.21	2.38	1.69	2.54	2.37	1.63
1952–1966	12.74	14.08	2.58	2.21	2.82	2.59	1.46
1953–1967	13.09	18.56	2.00	1.47	2.78	2.76	1.61
1954–1968	13.96	21.55	1.94	1.21	2.87	2.98	1.88
1955–1969	10.14	15.53	1.02	0.40	2.64	3.36	2.31
1956–1970	8.43	12.66	2.13	1.25	3.75	3.69	2.65
1957–1971	8.94	13.50	3.33	2.49	4.36	3.82	2.69
1958–1972	11.05	15.03	3.23	2.37	4.19	3.86	2.71
1959–1973	7.27	8.55	3.47	2.73	4.59	4.22	3.17
1960–1974	4.31	5.87	3.32	3.18	5.00	4.56	3.86
1961–1975	6.50	9.15	3.66	2.89	4.75	4.77	4.23
1962–1976	6.32	10.43	4.52	3.90	5.47	4.97	4.51
1963–1977	6.44	13.06	4.11	3.39	5.19	5.13	4.89
1964–1978	5.44	13.06	3.95	3.22	5.32	5.40	5.38
1965–1979	5.56	14.19	3.34	2.90	5.32	5.85	6.17
1966–1980	6.71	14.09	3.18	2.58	5.52	6.33	6.87
1967–1981	7.11	15.64	3.08	2.46	5.83	6.97	7.24
1968–1982	6.96	12.89	5.90	5.47	7.58	7.40	7.30
1969–1983	7.66	13.10	6.15	5.54	7.77	7.64	7.24
1970–1984	8.74	14.76	7.86	6.93	8.77	7.85	7.09

Table 2-10 **Basic Series** (continued)

Compound Annual Returns for 15-Year Holding Periods

(percent per annum)

From 1971 to 1998

Period	Large Company Stocks	Small Company Stocks	Long-Term Corporate Bonds	Long-Term Government Bonds	Intermediate Government Bonds	U.S. Treasury Bills	Inflation
1971–1985	10.50	17.96	8.54	8.04	8.99	7.93	6.97
1972–1986	10.76	17.28	9.10	8.73	9.40	8.06	6.82
1973–1987	9.86	16.18	8.57	8.13	9.25	8.17	6.89
1974–1988	12.18	20.73	9.23	8.88	9.35	8.13	6.59
1975–1989	16.61	23.33	10.56	9.78	9.86	8.15	6.10
1976–1990	13.93	17.96	10.03	9.58	9.99	8.29	6.04
1977–1991	14.33	17.30	10.11	9.73	10.15	8.32	5.92
1978–1992	15.47	17.17	10.65	10.35	10.56	8.21	5.66
1979–1993	15.72	17.01	11.57	11.68	11.09	7.92	5.24
1980–1994	14.52	14.47	11.45	11.17	10.41	7.48	4.55
1981–1995	14.80	14.17	13.46	13.53	11.27	7.11	3.92
1982–1996	16.79	14.41	13.66	13.32	10.76	6.50	3.55
1983–1997	17.52	14.09	11.91	11.88	9.47	6.15	3.41
1984–1998	17.90	11.02	12.22	12.75	9.66	5.89	3.26

Table 2-11 **Basic Series**

Compound Annual Returns for 20-Year Holding Periods

(percent per annum)

From 1926 to 1970

Period	Large Company Stocks	Small Company Stocks	Long-Term Corporate Bonds	Long-Term Government Bonds	Intermediate Government Bonds	U.S. Treasury Bills	Inflation
1926–1945	7.13	9.36	5.52	4.72	3.73	1.07	0.07
1927–1946	6.10	8.67	5.24	4.32	3.51	0.93	0.99
1928–1947	4.71	7.64	4.74	3.74	3.33	0.80	1.53
1929–1948	3.11	5.74	4.80	3.91	3.38	0.66	1.72
1930–1949	4.46	10.61	4.80	4.06	3.20	0.48	1.61
1931–1950	7.43	15.17	4.51	3.82	2.90	0.42	2.22
1932–1951	11.72	19.65	4.47	3.90	3.04	0.44	3.02
1933–1952	13.15	20.16	4.11	3.15	2.69	0.48	3.63
1934–1953	10.68	14.56	3.77	3.34	2.76	0.55	3.64
1935–1954	13.13	16.04	3.37	3.20	2.45	0.59	3.51
1936–1955	12.48	15.17	2.92	2.89	2.07	0.66	3.37
1937–1956	11.20	12.56	2.23	2.22	1.90	0.77	3.46
1938–1957	12.98	16.63	2.52	2.58	2.20	0.91	3.45
1939–1958	13.48	17.90	2.10	1.98	1.83	0.99	3.69
1940–1959	14.15	18.78	1.85	1.57	1.58	1.14	3.79
1941–1960	14.76	18.89	2.12	1.93	2.00	1.27	3.82
1942–1961	16.86	21.13	2.22	1.93	2.07	1.37	3.37
1943–1962	15.25	18.17	2.48	2.11	2.25	1.50	2.98
1944–1963	15.11	15.70	2.45	2.06	2.19	1.63	2.90
1945–1964	14.95	14.44	2.45	2.10	2.30	1.79	2.86
1946–1965	13.84	13.29	2.23	1.61	2.24	1.97	2.84
1947–1966	13.72	13.58	2.15	1.80	2.42	2.19	2.15
1948–1967	14.63	17.03	2.01	1.45	2.43	2.38	1.87
1949–1968	14.92	18.97	1.93	1.26	2.56	2.60	1.96
1950–1969	13.43	16.21	1.34	0.69	2.41	2.87	2.36
1951–1970	12.10	13.23	2.09	1.26	3.17	3.13	2.35
1952–1971	11.65	13.67	2.77	2.10	3.58	3.28	2.22
1953–1972	11.67	13.75	2.95	2.32	3.76	3.39	2.35
1954–1973	10.85	12.04	2.83	2.08	3.83	3.64	2.75
1955–1974	6.87	8.21	2.41	1.94	3.98	4.00	3.37
1956–1975	7.10	9.51	3.08	2.46	4.41	4.21	3.70
1957–1976	7.91	11.78	4.34	3.55	5.06	4.34	3.80
1958–1977	8.12	13.95	3.99	3.15	4.74	4.44	3.98
1959–1978	6.53	12.31	4.10	3.41	4.99	4.72	4.34
1960–1979	6.83	13.49	3.93	3.46	5.22	5.09	4.92
1961–1980	8.31	15.61	3.34	2.59	4.84	5.51	5.46
1962–1981	6.76	14.75	3.03	2.64	5.21	6.12	5.87
1963–1982	8.30	16.92	4.47	4.04	6.28	6.51	6.01
1964–1983	8.28	17.63	4.68	4.01	6.57	6.80	6.12
1965–1984	7.79	16.00	5.25	4.58	7.06	7.12	6.26
1966–1985	8.66	15.25	6.67	5.97	8.00	7.31	6.36
1967–1986	10.17	16.06	7.63	6.94	8.52	7.38	6.24
1968–1987	9.27	12.04	7.88	7.31	8.62	7.44	6.31
1969–1988	9.54	11.47	8.30	7.82	8.70	7.50	6.30
1970–1989	11.55	13.64	9.58	9.01	9.42	7.59	6.22

Table 2-11 **Basic Series** (continued)

Compound Annual Returns for 20-Year Holding Periods (percent per annum)

From 1971 to 1998

Period	Large Company Stocks	Small Company Stocks	Long-Term Corporate Bonds	Long-Term Government Bonds	Intermediate Government Bonds	U.S. Treasury Bills	Inflation
1971–1990	11.15	13.35	9.01	8.71	9.08	7.66	6.26
1972–1991	11.89	14.58	9.43	9.00	9.40	7.72	6.24
1973–1992	11.33	15.54	9.54	9.12	9.51	7.70	6.21
1974–1993	12.76	18.82	10.16	10.10	9.85	7.49	5.91
1975–1994	14.58	20.33	10.00	9.42	9.25	7.29	5.44
1976–1995	14.59	19.57	10.58	10.45	9.69	7.28	5.22
1977–1996	14.55	17.84	9.71	9.54	9.14	7.28	5.14
1978–1997	16.65	17.71	10.29	10.39	9.51	7.29	4.89
1979–1998	17.75	16.04	10.86	11.14	9.85	7.17	4.52

Chapter 3 Description of the Basic Series

This chapter presents the returns for the seven basic asset classes and describes the construction of these returns. More detail on the construction of some series can be found in the January 1976 *Journal of Business* article, referenced at the end of the Introduction. Annual total returns and capital appreciation returns for each asset class are formed by compounding the monthly returns that appear in Appendix A. Annual income returns are formed by summing the monthly income payments and dividing this sum by the beginning-of-year price. Returns are formed assuming no taxes or transaction costs, except for returns on small company stocks that show the performance of an actual, tax-exempt investment fund including transaction and management costs, starting in 1982.

Large Company Stocks

Overview

One dollar invested in large company stocks at year-end 1925, with dividends reinvested, grew to $2,350.89 by year-end 1998; this represents a compound annual growth rate of 11.2 percent. [See Graph 3-1.] Capital appreciation alone caused $1.00 to grow to $96.36 over the 73-year period, a compound annual growth rate of 6.5 percent. Annual total returns ranged from a high of 54.0 percent in 1933 to a low of -43.3 percent in 1931. The 73-year average annual dividend yield was 4.5 percent.

Total Returns

From September 1997 to the present, the large company stock total return is provided by Standard and Poor's, which calculates the total return based on the daily reinvestment of dividends on the ex-dividend date. Standard and Poor's uses closing pricing (usually from the New York Stock Exchange) in their calculation. From 1977 to August 1997, the total return was provided by the American National Bank and Trust Company of Chicago, which modified monthly income numbers provided by Wilshire Associates, Santa Monica, CA. Dividends (measured as of the ex-dividend date) are accumulated over the month and invested on the last trading day of the month in the S&P 500 index at the day's closing level. Wilshire uses the last trading price of the day for the stocks, usually from the Pacific Stock Exchange. Prior to 1977, the total return for a given month was calculated by summing the capital appreciation return and the income return as described on the following pages.

The large company stock total return index is based upon the S&P Composite Index. This index is a readily available, carefully constructed, market-value-weighted benchmark of large company stock performance. Market-value-weighted means that the weight of each stock in the index, for a given month, is proportionate to its market capitalization (price times the number of shares outstanding) at the beginning of that month. Currently, the S&P Composite includes 500 of the largest stocks

Graph 3-1 **Large Company Stocks** Return Indices, Returns, and Dividend Yields

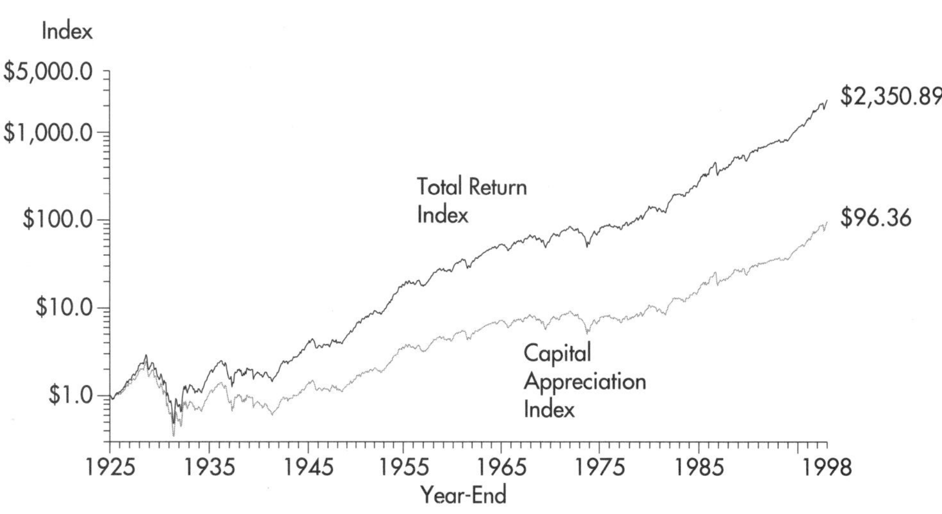

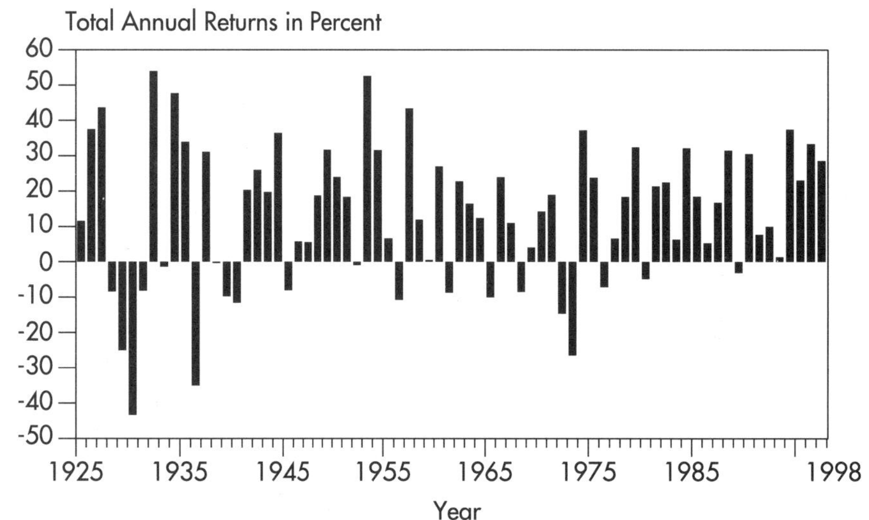

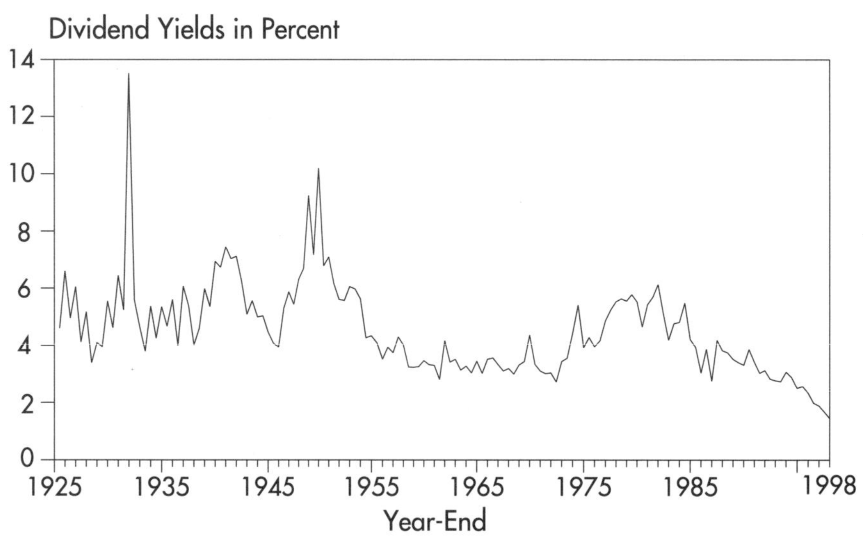

(in terms of stock market value) in the United States; prior to March 1957 it consisted of 90 of the largest stocks.

Capital Appreciation Return

The capital appreciation component of the large company stock total return is the change in the S&P 500-stock index (or 90-stock index) as reported in *The Wall Street Journal* for the period 1977–1998, and in Standard & Poor's *Trade and Securities Statistics* from 1926–1976.

Income Return

For 1977–1998, the income return was calculated as the difference between the total return and the capital appreciation return. For 1926–1976, quarterly dividends were extracted from rolling yearly dividends reported quarterly in S&P's *Trade and Securities Statistics*, then allocated to months within each quarter using proportions taken from the 1974 actual distribution of monthly dividends within quarters.

The dividend yields depicted in the bottom graph of Graph 3-1 were derived by annualizing the semi-annual income return.

Small Company Stocks

Overview

One dollar invested in small company stocks at year-end 1925 grew to $5,116.65 by year-end 1998. [See Graph 3-2.] This represents a compound annual growth rate of 12.4 percent over the past 73 years. Total annual returns ranged from a high of 142.9 percent in 1933 to a low of -58.0 percent in 1937.

DFA Small Company Fund (1982–1998)

For 1982–1998, the small company stock return series is the total return achieved by the Dimensional Fund Advisors (DFA) Small Company 9/10 (for ninth and tenth deciles) Fund. The fund is a market-value-weighted index of the ninth and tenth deciles of the New York Stock Exchange (NYSE), plus stocks listed on the American Stock Exchange (AMEX) and over-the-counter (OTC) with the same or less capitalization as the upper bound of the NYSE ninth decile. The weight of each stock within the fund is proportionate to its market capitalization; therefore, those stocks with a higher market capitalization value will be weighted more than those with a lower market capitalization value. Since the lower bound of the tenth decile is near zero, stocks are not purchased if they are smaller than $10 million in market capitalization (although they are held if they fall below that level). A company's

Graph 3-2 **Small Company Stocks** Return Index and Returns

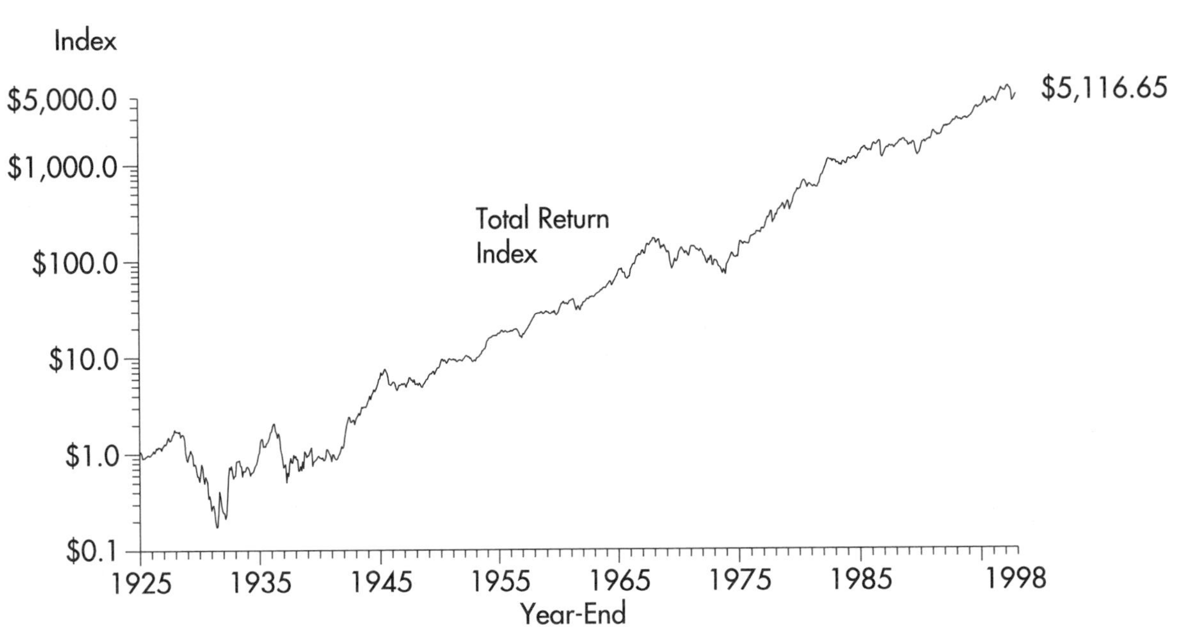

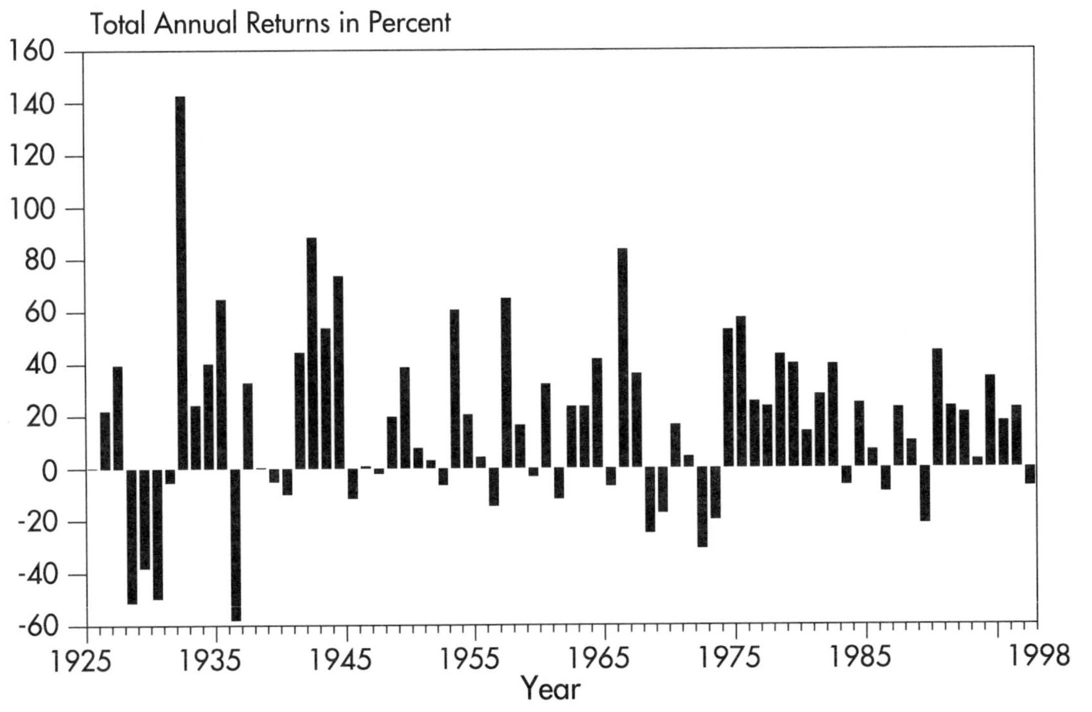

stock is not purchased if it is in bankruptcy; however, a stock already held is retained if the company becomes bankrupt.

Stocks remain in the portfolio if they rise into the eighth NYSE decile, but they are sold when they rise into the seventh NYSE decile or higher. The returns for the DFA Small Company 9/10 Fund represent after-transaction-cost returns, while the returns for the other asset classes and for pre-1982 small company stocks are before-transaction-cost returns.

At year-end 1998, the DFA Small Company Fund contained approximately 2,769 stocks, with a weighted average market capitalization of $164 million. The unweighted average market capitalization was $97 million, while the median was $64 million. See Table 7-5 for decile size, bounds, and composition.

NYSE Fifth Quintile Returns (1926–1981)

The equities of smaller companies from 1926 to 1980 are represented by the historical series developed by Professor Rolf W. Banz (see reference on page 6). This is composed of stocks making up the fifth quintile (*i.e.*, the ninth and tenth deciles) of the New York Stock Exchange (NYSE); the stocks on the NYSE are ranked by capitalization (price times number of shares outstanding), and each decile contains an equal number of stocks at the beginning of each formation period. The ninth and tenth decile portfolio was first ranked and formed as of December 31, 1925. This portfolio was "held" for five years, with value-weighted portfolio returns computed monthly. Every five years the portfolio was rebalanced (*i.e.*, all of the stocks on the NYSE were re-ranked, and a new portfolio of those falling in the ninth and tenth deciles was formed) as of December 31, 1930 and every five years thereafter through December 31, 1980. This method avoided survivorship bias by including the return after the delisting or failure of a stock in constructing the portfolio returns. (Survivorship bias is caused by studying only stocks that have survived events such as bankruptcy and acquisition.)

For 1981, Dimensional Fund Advisors, Inc. updated the returns using Professor Banz' methods. The data for 1981 are significant to only three decimal places (in decimal form) or one decimal place when returns are expressed in percent.

Long-Term Corporate Bonds

Overview

One dollar invested in long-term high-grade corporate bonds at the end of 1925 was worth $61.34 by year-end 1998. [See Graph 3-3.] The compound annual growth rate over the 73-year period was

5.8 percent. Total annual returns ranged from a high of 42.6 percent in 1982 to a low of -8.1 percent in 1969.

Total Returns

For 1969–1998, corporate bond total returns are represented by the Salomon Brothers Long-Term High-Grade Corporate Bond Index. Since most large corporate bond transactions take place over the counter, a major dealer is the natural source of these data. The index includes nearly all Aaa- and Aa-rated bonds. If a bond is downgraded during a particular month, its return for the month is included in the index before removing the bond from future portfolios.

Over 1926–1968 total returns were calculated by summing the capital appreciation returns and the income returns. For the period 1946–1968, Ibbotson and Sinquefield backdated the Salomon Brothers' index, using Salomon Brothers' monthly yield data with a methodology similar to that used by Salomon for 1969–1998. Capital appreciation returns were calculated from yields assuming (at the beginning of each monthly holding period) a 20-year maturity, a bond price equal to par, and a coupon equal to the beginning-of-period yield.

For the period 1926–1945, Standard & Poor's monthly High-Grade Corporate Composite yield data were used, assuming a 4 percent coupon and a 20-year maturity. The conventional present-value formula for bond price was used for the beginning and end-of-month prices. (This formula is presented in Ross, Stephen A., and Randolph W. Westerfield, *Corporate Finance*, Times Mirror/Mosby, St. Louis, 1990, p. 97 ["Level-Coupon Bonds"]). The monthly income return was assumed to be one-twelfth the coupon.

Long-Term Government Bonds

Overview

One dollar invested in long-term government bonds at year-end 1925, with coupons reinvested, grew to $44.18 by year-end 1998; this represents a compound annual growth rate of 5.3 percent. [See Graph 3-4.] However, returns from the capital appreciation component alone caused $1.00 to *decrease* to $0.97 over the 73-year period, representing a compound annual growth rate of -0.04 percent. Total annual returns ranged from a high of 40.4 percent in 1982 to a low of -9.2 percent in 1967. The 73-year compounded yield-to-maturity (or yield-to-first-call, where applicable) was 5.2 percent.

Graph 3-3 **Long-Term Corporate Bonds** Return Index and Returns

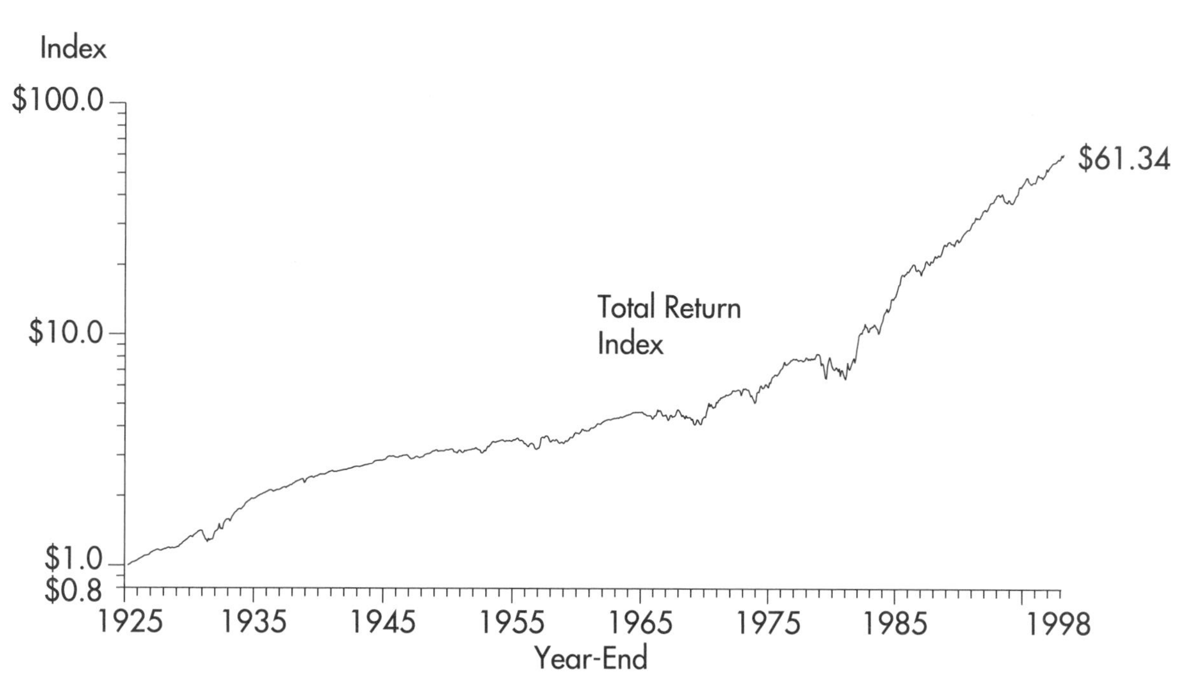

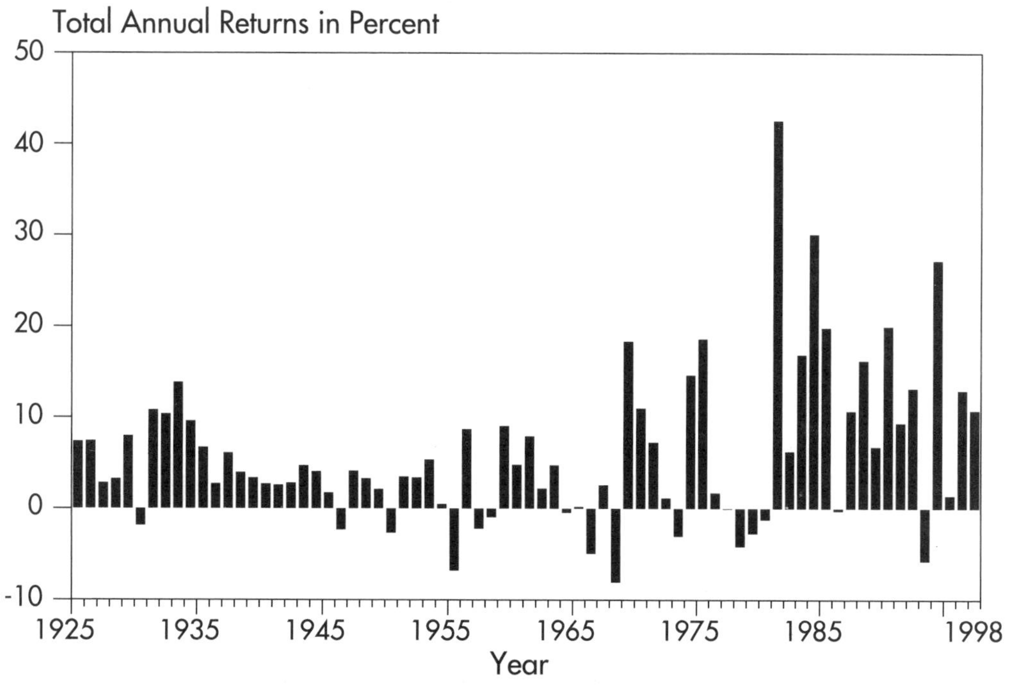

Graph 3-4 **Long-Term Government Bonds** Return Indices, Returns, and Yields

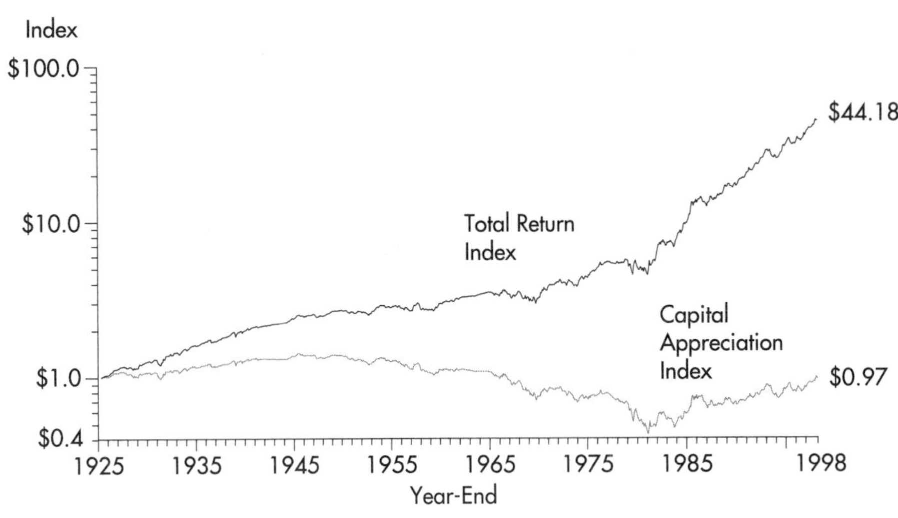

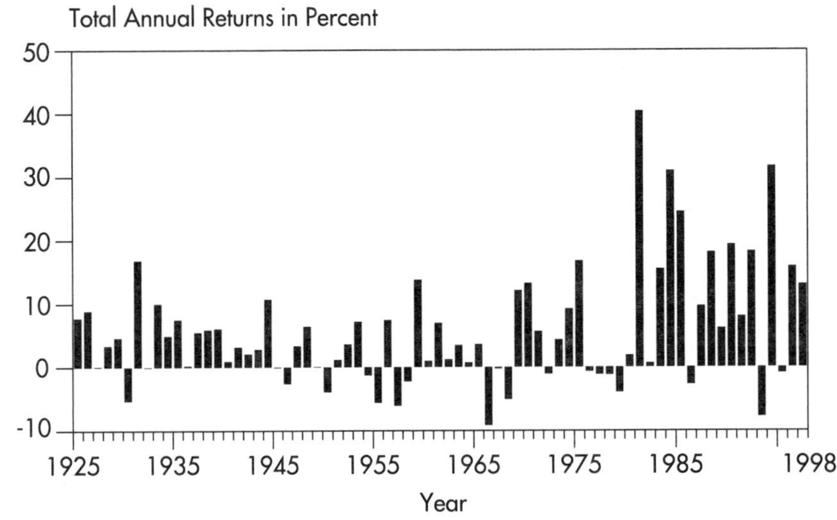

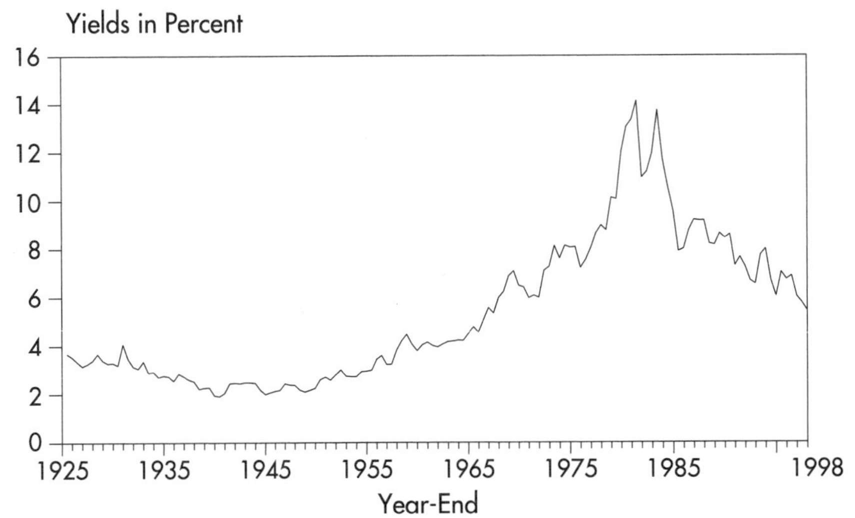

Total Returns

The total returns on long-term government bonds from 1977 to 1998 are constructed with data from *The Wall Street Journal.* The bond used in 1998 is the 8.125 percent issue that matures on August 15, 2019. The data from 1926–1976 are obtained from the Government Bond File at the Center for Research in Security Prices (CRSP) at the University of Chicago Graduate School of Business. The bonds used to construct the index are shown in Table 3-1. To the greatest extent possible, a one-bond portfolio with a term of approximately 20 years and a reasonably current coupon—whose returns did not reflect potential tax benefits, impaired negotiability, or special redemption or call privileges—was used each year. Where "flower" bonds (tenderable to the Treasury at par in payment of estate taxes) had to be used, we chose the bond with the smallest potential tax benefit. Where callable bonds had to be used, the term of the bond was assumed to be a simple average of the maturity and first call dates minus the current date. The bond was "held" for the calendar year and returns were computed.

Total returns for 1977–1998 are calculated as the change in the flat or and-interest price.[1] The flat price is the average of the bond's bid and ask prices, plus the accrued coupon.[2] The accrued coupon is equal to zero on the day a coupon is paid, and increases over time until the next coupon payment according to this formula:

$$A = fC \tag{1}$$

where,

A = accrued coupon;

C = semiannual coupon rate; and

$$f = \frac{\text{number of days since last coupon payment}}{\text{number of days from last coupon payment to next coupon payment}}$$

Income Return

For 1977–1998, the income return is calculated as the change in flat price plus any coupon actually paid from one period to the next, holding the yield constant over the period. As in the total return series, the exact number of days comprising the period is used. For 1926–1976, the income return for a given month is calculated as the total return minus the capital appreciation return (see below).

1 "Flat price" is used here to mean the unmodified economic value of the bond, *i.e.*, the and-interest price, or quoted price plus accrued interest. In contrast, some sources use *flat price* to mean the quoted price.

2 For the purpose of calculating the return in months when a coupon payment is made, the change in the flat price includes the coupon.

Capital Appreciation or Return in Excess of Yield

For 1977–1998, capital appreciation is taken as the total return minus the income return for each month. For 1926–1976, the capital appreciation return (also known as the return in excess of yield) is obtained from the CRSP Government Bond File.

A bond's *capital appreciation* is defined as the total return minus the income return; that is, the return in excess of yield. This definition omits the capital gain or loss that comes from the movement of a bond's price toward par (in the absence of interest rate change) as it matures. Capital appreciation, as defined here, captures changes in bond prices caused by changes in the interest rate.

Yields

The yield on the long-term government bond series is defined as the internal rate of return that equates the bond's price (the average of bid and ask, plus the accrued coupon) with the stream of cash flows (coupons and principal) promised to the bondholder. The yields reported for 1977–1998 were calculated from *The Wall Street Journal* prices for the bonds listed in Table 3-1. For noncallable bonds, the maturity date is shown. For callable bonds, the first call date and the maturity dates are shown as in the following example: 10/15/47–52 refers to a bond that is first callable on 10/15/1947 and matures on 10/15/1952. Dates from 47–99 refer to 1947–1999; 00-16 refers to 2000–2016. For callable bonds trading below par, the yield to maturity is used; above par, the yield to call is used. The yields for 1926–1976 were obtained from the CRSP Government Bond File.

Intermediate-Term Government Bonds

Overview

One dollar invested in intermediate-term government bonds at year-end 1925, with coupons reinvested, grew to $43.93 by year-end 1998. [See Graph 3-5.] This represents a 73-year compound annual growth rate of 5.3 percent. Total annual returns ranged from a high of 29.1 percent in 1982 to a low of -5.1 percent in 1994. The compound yield-to-maturity (or yield-to-first-call, where applicable) was 4.7 percent.

Capital appreciation caused $1.00 to increase to $1.32 over the 73-year period, representing a compound annual growth rate of 0.4 percent. This increase was unexpected: Since yields rose on average over the period, capital appreciation on a hypothetical intermediate-term government bond portfolio with a constant five-year maturity should have been negative. An explanation of the positive average return is given at the end of this chapter.

Graph 3-5 **Intermediate-Term Government Bonds** Return Indices, Returns, and Yields

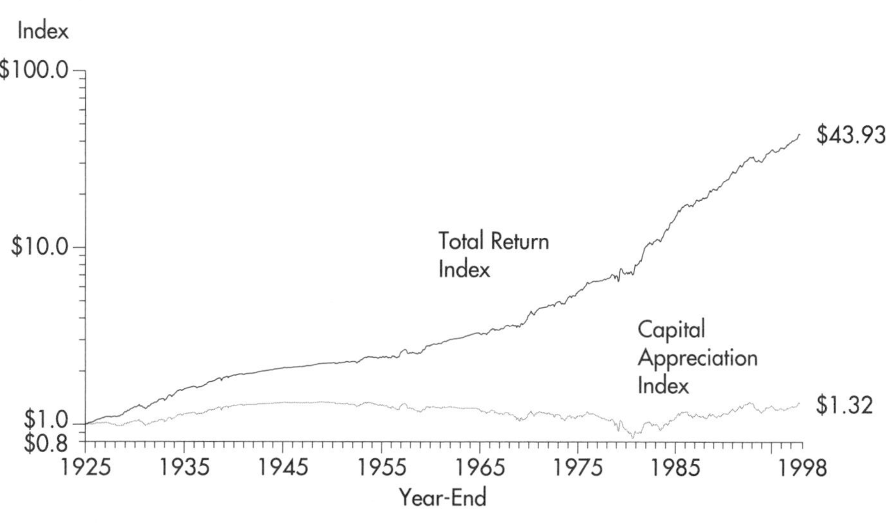

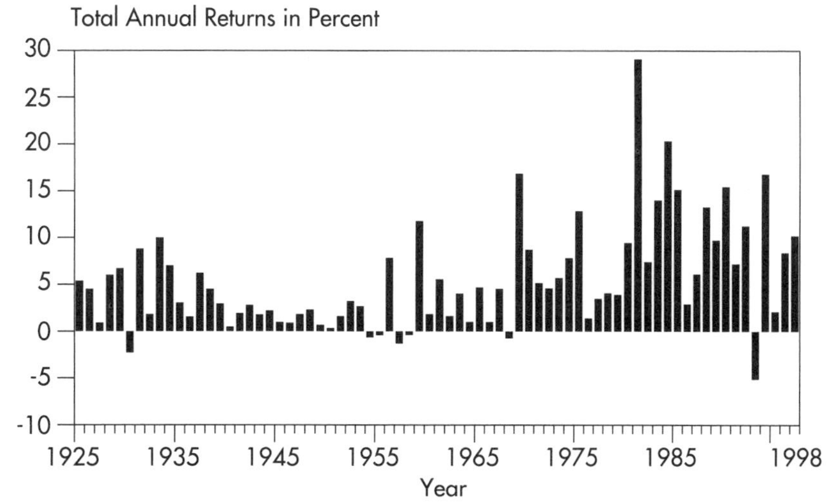

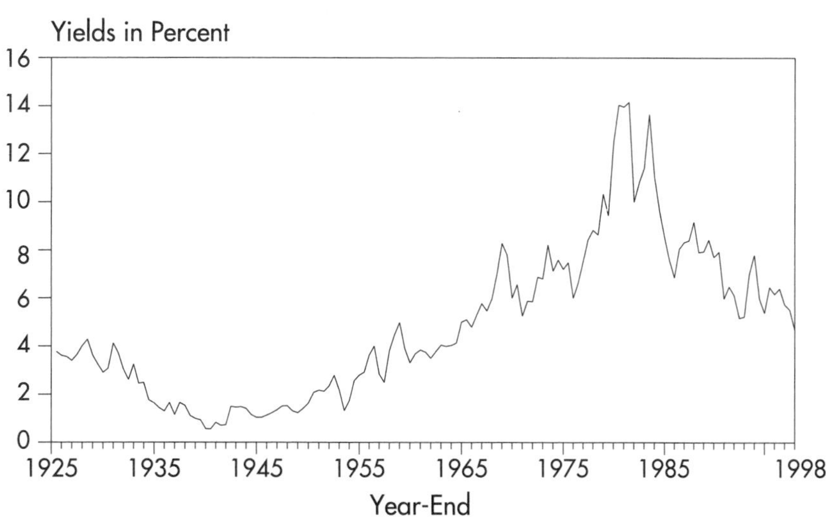

Total Returns

Total returns of the intermediate-term government bonds for 1987–1998 are calculated from *The Wall Street Journal* prices, using the coupon accrual method described above for long-term government bonds. [See equation (1).] The bond used in 1998 is the 5.75 percent issue maturing on August 15, 2003. Returns over 1934–1986 are obtained from the CRSP Government Bond File. The bonds used to construct the index over 1934–1998 are shown in Table 3-1.

As with long-term government bonds, one-bond portfolios are used to construct the intermediate-term government bond index. The bond chosen each year is the shortest noncallable bond with a maturity not less than five years, and it is "held" for the calendar year. Monthly returns are computed. (Bonds with impaired negotiability or special redemption privileges are omitted, as are partially or fully tax-exempt bonds starting with 1943.)

Over 1934–1942, almost all bonds with maturities near five years were partially or fully tax-exempt and selected using the rules described above. Personal tax rates were generally low in that period, so that yields on tax-exempt bonds were similar to yields on taxable bonds.

Over 1926–1933, there are few bonds suitable for construction of a series with a five-year maturity. For this period, five-year bond yield estimates are used. These estimates are obtained from Thomas S. Coleman, Lawrence Fisher, and Roger G. Ibbotson, *Historical U.S. Treasury Yield Curves: 1926–1992* with 1995 update (Ibbotson Associates, Chicago, 1995).[3] The estimates reflect what a "pure play" five-year Treasury bond, selling at par and with no special redemption or call provisions, would have yielded had one existed. Estimates are for partially tax-exempt bonds for 1926–1932 and for fully tax-exempt bonds for 1933. Monthly yields are converted to monthly total returns by calculating the beginning and end-of-month flat prices for the hypothetical bonds. The bond is "bought" at the beginning of the month at par (*i.e.*, the coupon equals the previous month-end yield), assuming a maturity of five years. It is "sold" at the end of the month, with the flat price calculated by discounting the coupons and principal at the end-of-month yield, assuming a maturity of 4 years and 11 months. The flat price is the price of the bond including coupon accruals, so that the change in flat price represents total return. Monthly income returns are assumed to be equal to the previous end-of-month yield, stated in monthly terms. Monthly capital appreciation returns are formed as total returns minus income returns.

[3] For additional information regarding *Historical U.S. Treasury Yield Curves*, refer to the Product Information page at the back of this book.

Table 3-1 **Long-Term and Intermediate-Term Government Bond Issues**

Long-Term Government Bonds

Period Bond is Held in Index	Coupon (%)	Call/Maturity Date
1926–1931	4.25	10/15/47-52
1932–1935	3.00	9/15/51–55
1936–1941	2.875	3/15/55–60
1942–1953	2.50	9/15/67–72
1954–1958	3.25	6/15/78–83
1959–1960	4.00	2/15/80
1961–1965	4.25	5/15/75–85
1966–1972	4.25	8/15/87–92
1973–1974	6.75	2/15/93
1975–1976	8.50	5/15/94–99
1977–1980	7.875	2/15/95–00
1981	8.00	8/15/96–01
1982	13.375	8/15/01
1983	10.75	2/15/03
1984	11.875	11/15/03
1985	11.75	2/15/05–10
1986–1989	10.00	5/15/05–10
1990–1992	10.375	11/15/07–12
1993–1996	7.25	5/15/16
1997–1998	8.125	8/15/19

Intermediate-Term Government Bonds

Period Bond is Held in Index	Coupon (%)	Call/Maturity Date
1934–1936	3.25	8/01/41
1937	3.375	3/15/43
1938–1940	2.50	12/15/45
1941	3.00	1/01/46
1942	3.00	1/01/47
1943	1.75	6/15/48
1944–1945	2.00	3/15/50
1946	2.00	6/15/51
1947	2.00	3/15/52
1948	2.00	9/15/53
1949	2.50	3/15/54
1950	2.25	6/15/55
1951–1952	2.50	3/15/58
1953	2.375	6/15/58
1954	2.375	3/15/59
1955	2.125	11/15/60
1956	2.75	9/15/61
1957–1958	2.50	8/15/63
1959	3.00	2/15/64
1960	2.625	2/15/65
1961	3.75	5/15/66
1962	3.625	11/15/67
1963	3.875	5/15/68
1964	4.00	2/15/69
1965	4.00	8/15/70
1966	4.00	8/15/71
1967	4.00	2/15/72
1968	4.00	8/15/73
1969	5.625	8/15/74
1970	5.75	2/15/75
1971	6.25	2/15/76
1972	1.50	10/01/76
1973	6.25	2/15/78
1974	6.25	8/15/79
1975	6.875	5/15/80
1976	7.00	2/15/81
1977	6.375	2/15/82
1978	8.00	2/15/83
1979	7.25	2/15/84
1980	8.00	2/15/85
1981	13.50	2/15/86
1982	9.00	2/15/87
1983	12.375	1/01/88
1984	14.625	1/15/89
1985	10.50	1/15/90
1986	11.75	1/15/91
1987	11.625	1/15/92
1988	8.75	1/15/93
1989	9.00	2/15/94
1990	8.625	10/15/95
1991–1992	7.875	7/15/96
1993	6.375	1/15/99
1994	5.50	4/15/00
1995	8.50	2/15/00
1996	7.75	2/15/01
1997	6.375	8/15/02
1998	5.75	8/15/03

Income Return and Capital Appreciation

For the period 1987–1998, the income return is calculated according to the methodology stated under "Long-Term Government Bonds." Monthly capital appreciation (return in excess of yield) over this same period is the difference between total return and income return.

For 1934–1986, capital appreciation (return in excess of yield) is taken directly from the CRSP Government Bond File. The income return is calculated as the total return minus the capital appreciation return. Prior to 1934, the income and capital appreciation components of total return are generated from yield estimates as described earlier under *Total Returns.*

Yields

The yield on an intermediate-term government bond is the internal rate of return that equates the bond's price with the stream of cash flows (coupons and principal) promised to the bondholder. The yields reported for 1987–1998 are calculated from *The Wall Street Journal* bond prices listed in Table 3-1. For 1934–1986, yields were obtained from the CRSP Government Bond File. Yields for 1926–1933 are estimates from Coleman, Fisher, and Ibbotson, *Historical U.S. Treasury Yield Curves: 1926–1992* with 1995 update.

U.S. Treasury Bills

Overview

One dollar invested in U.S. Treasury bills at year-end 1925 grew to $14.94 by year-end 1998; this represents a compound annual growth rate of 3.8 percent. [See Graph 3-6.] Total annual returns ranged from a high of 14.7 percent in 1981 to a low of 0.0 percent for the period 1938 to 1940.

Total Returns

For the U.S. Treasury bill index, data from *The Wall Street Journal* are used for 1977–1998; the CRSP U.S. Government Bond File is the source until 1976. Each month a one-bill portfolio containing the shortest-term bill having not less than one month to maturity is constructed. (The bill's original term to maturity is not relevant.) To measure holding period returns for the one-bill portfolio, the bill is priced as of the last trading day of the previous month-end and as of the last trading day of the current month.

Graph 3-6 **U.S. Treasury Bills** Return Index and Returns

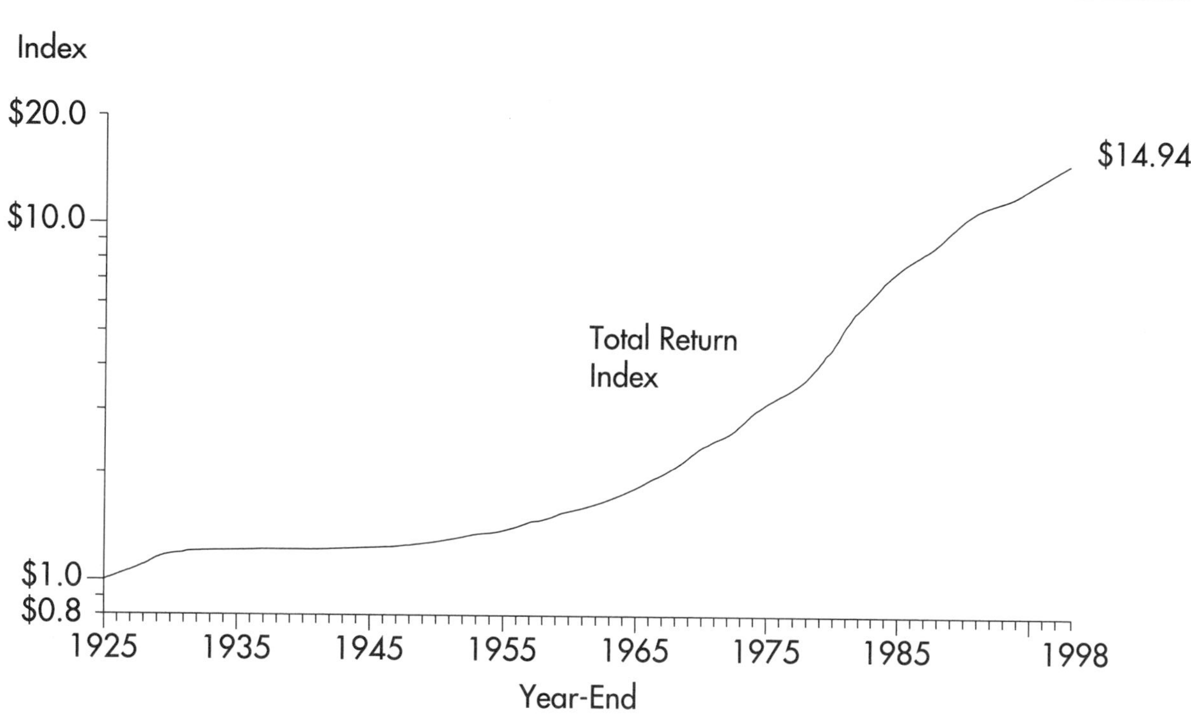

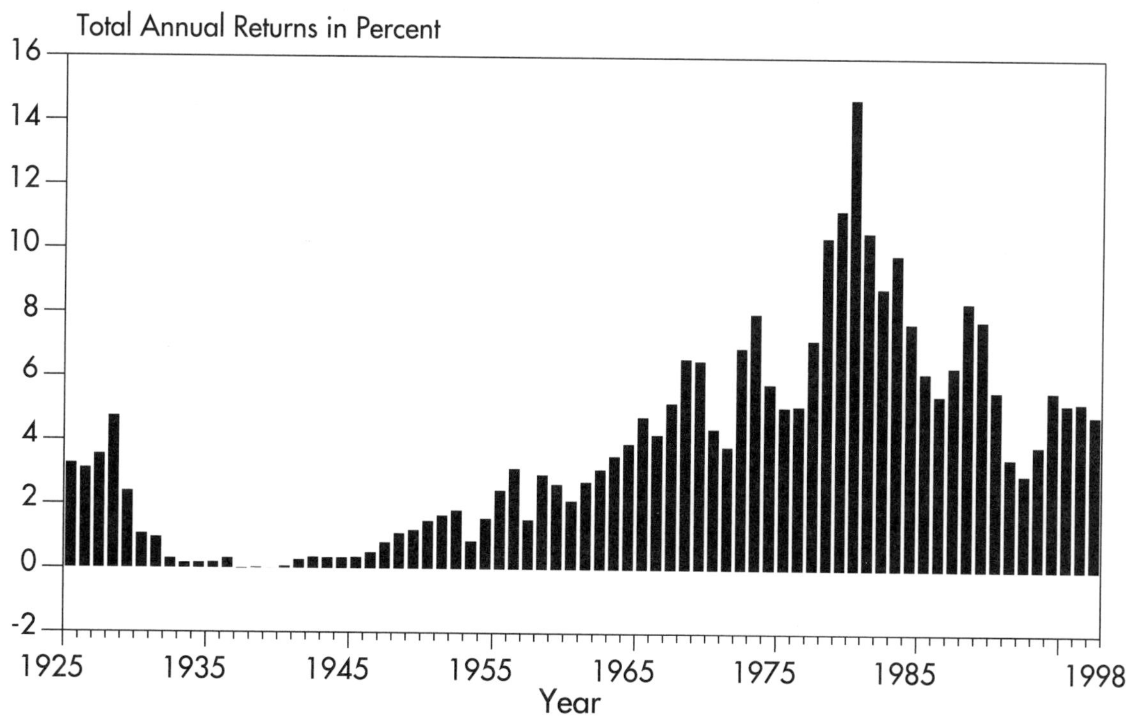

The price of the bill (**P**) at each time (**t**) is given as:

$$P_t = \left[1 - \frac{rd}{360}\right] \qquad (2)$$

where,

r = decimal yield (the average of bid and ask quotes) on the bill at time **t**; and,

d = number of days to maturity as of time **t**.

The total return on the bill is the month-end price divided by the previous month-end price, minus one.

Negative Returns on Treasury Bills

Monthly Treasury bill returns (as reported in Appendix A-14) were negative in February 1933, and in 12 months during the 1938–1941 period. Also, the annual Treasury bill return was negative for 1938. Since negative Treasury bill returns contradict logic, an explanation is in order.

Negative yields observed in the data do not imply that investors purchased Treasury bills with a guaranteed negative return. Rather, Treasury bills of that era were exempt from personal property taxes in some states, while cash was not. Further, for a bank to hold U.S. government deposits, Treasury securities were required as collateral. These circumstances created excessive demand for the security, and thus bills were sold at a premium. Given the low interest rates during the period, owners of the bills experienced negative returns.

Inflation

Overview

A basket of consumer goods purchased for $1.00 at year-end 1925 would cost $9.14 by year-end 1998. [See Graph 3-7.] Of course, the exact contents of the basket changed over time. This increase represents a compound annual rate of inflation of 3.1 percent over the past 73 years. Inflation rates ranged from a high of 18.2 percent in 1946 to a low of -10.3 percent in 1932.

Inflation

The Consumer Price Index for All Urban Consumers (CPI-U), not seasonally adjusted, is used to measure inflation, which is the rate of change of consumer goods prices. Unfortunately, the CPI is not

Graph 3-7 **Inflation** Cumulative Index and Rates of Change

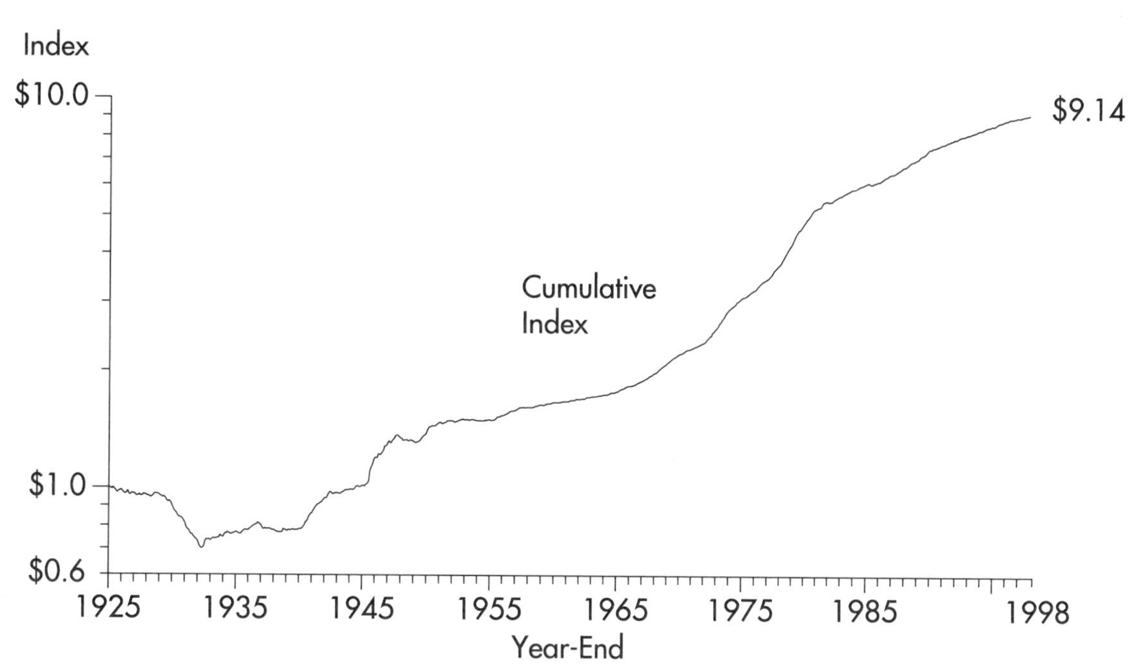

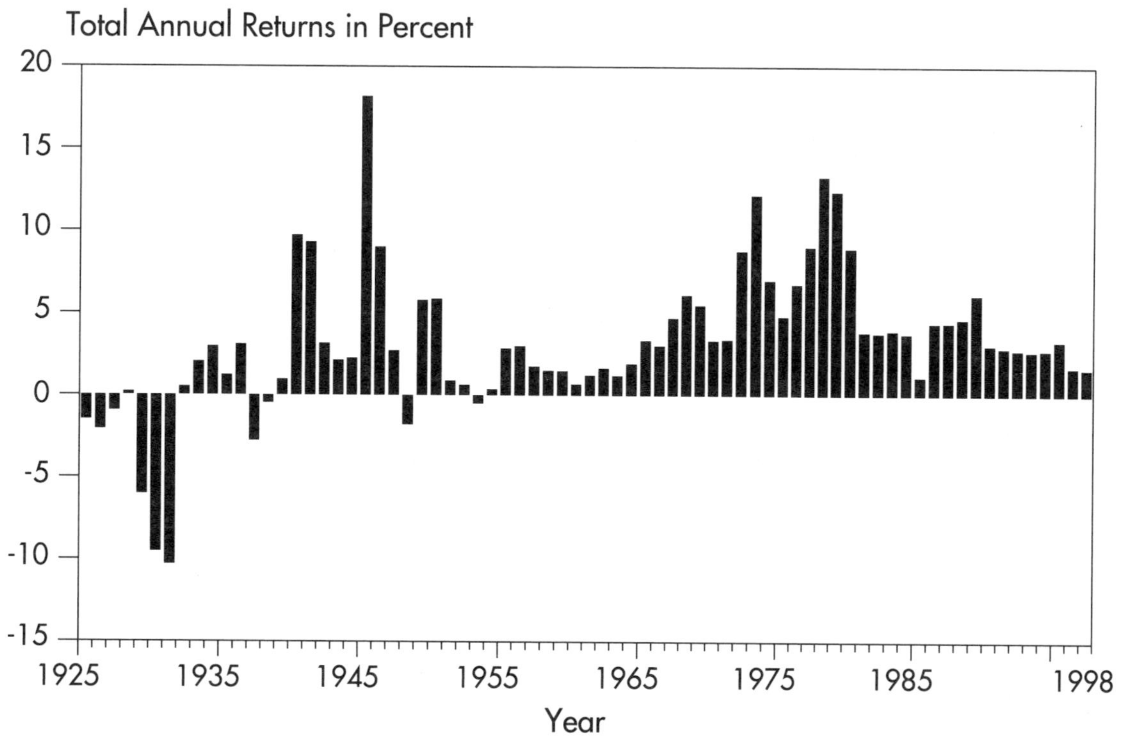

measured over the same period as the other asset returns. All of the security returns are measured from one month-end to the next month-end. CPI commodity prices are collected during the month. Thus, measured inflation rates lag the other series by about one-half month. Prior to January 1978, the CPI (as compared with CPI-U) was used. For the period 1978 through 1987, the index uses the year 1967 in determining the items compromising the basket of goods. Following 1987, a three-year period, 1982 through 1984, was used to determine the items making up the basket of goods. All inflation measures are constructed by the U.S. Department of Labor, Bureau of Labor Statistics, Washington.

Positive Capital Appreciation on Intermediate-Term Government Bonds

The capital appreciation component of intermediate-term government bond returns caused $1.00 invested at year-end 1925 to grow to $1.32 by the end of 1998, representing a compound annual rate of 0.4 percent. This is surprising because yields, on average, rose over the period.

An investor in a hypothetical five-year constant maturity portfolio, with continuous rebalancing, suffered a capital *loss* (that is, excluding coupon income) over 1926–1998. An investor who rebalanced yearly, choosing bonds according to the method set forth above, fared better. This investor would have earned the 0.4 percent per year capital *gain* recorded here.

This performance relates to the construction of the intermediate-term bond series. For 1926–1933, the one-bond portfolio was rebalanced monthly to maintain a constant maturity of five years. For the period 1934–1998, one bond (the shortest bond not less than five years to maturity) was chosen at the beginning of each year and priced monthly. New bonds were not picked each month to maintain a constant five years to maturity intra-year.

There are several possible reasons for the positive capital appreciation return. Chief among these reasons are convexity of the bond portfolio and the substitution of one bond for another at each year-end.

Convexity

Each year, we "bought" a bond with approximately five years to maturity and held it for one year. During this period, the market yield on the bond fluctuates. Because the duration of the bond shortens (the bond becomes less interest-rate sensitive) as yields rise and the duration lengthens as yields fall, more is gained from a fall in yield than is lost from a rise in yield. This characteristic of a bond is known as convexity.

For example, suppose an 8 percent coupon bond is bought at par at the beginning of a year; the yield fluctuates (but the portfolio is not rebalanced) during the year; and the bond is sold at par at the end of the year. The price of the bond at both the beginning and end of the year is $100; the change in bond price is zero. However, the fluctuations will have caused the gains during periods of falling yields to exceed the losses during periods of rising yields. Thus the total return for the year exceeds 8 percent. Since our measure of capital appreciation is the return in excess of yield, rather than the change in bond price, capital appreciation for this bond (as measured) will be greater than zero.

In 1992, the yield for intermediate-term government bonds started the year at 5.97 percent, rose, fell, and finally rose again to end at 6.11 percent, slightly higher than the starting point. In the absence of convexity, the capital appreciation return for 1992 would be negative. Because of the fluctuation of yields during the year, however, the capital appreciation return on the intermediate-term government bond index was positive 0.64 percent.

It should be noted that the return in excess of yield, or capital gain, from convexity is caused by holding, over the year, a bond whose yield at purchase is different than the current market yield. If the portfolio were rebalanced each time the data were sampled (in this case, monthly), by selling the old bond and buying a new five-year bond selling at par, the portfolio would have no convexity. That is, over a period where yields ended where they started, the measured capital appreciation would be zero. However, this is neither a practical way to construct an index of actual bonds nor to manage a bond portfolio.

Bond Substitution

Another reason why the intermediate-term government bond series displays positive capital appreciation even though yields rose is the way in which bonds were removed from the portfolio and replaced with other bonds. In general, it was not possible to replace a bond "sold" by buying one with exactly the same yield. This produces a spurious change in the yield of the series—one that should not be associated with a capital gain or loss.

For example: Suppose a five-year bond yielding 8 percent is bought at par at the beginning of the year; at that time, four-year bonds yield 7 percent. Over the year, the yield curve rises in parallel by one percentage point so that when it comes time to sell the bond at year-end, it yields 8 percent and has four years to maturity. Therefore, at both the beginning and end of the year, the price of the bond is $100.

The proceeds from the sale are used to buy a new five-year bond yielding 9 percent. While the bond price change was zero over the year, the yield of the series has risen from 8 percent to 9 percent. Thus it is possible, because of the process of substituting one bond for another, for the yield series to contain a spurious rise that is not, and should not be expected to be, associated with a decline in the price of any particular bond. This phenomenon is likely to be the source of some of the positive capital appreciation in our intermediate-term government bond series.

Other Issues

While convexity and bond substitution may explain the anomaly of positive capital appreciation in a bond series with rising yields, there are other incomplete-market problems that may also help explain the capital gain. For example, intermediate-term government bonds were scarce in the 1930s and 1940s. As a result, the bonds chosen for this series occasionally had maturities longer than five years, ranging as high as eight years when bought. The 1930s and the first half of the 1940s were bullish for the bond market. Longer bonds included in this series had higher yields and substantially higher capital gain returns than bonds with exactly five years to maturity might have had if any existed. This upward bias is particularly noticeable in 1934, 1937, and 1938.

In addition, callable and fully or partially tax-exempt bonds were used when necessary to obtain a bond for some years. The conversion of the Treasury bond market from tax-exempt to taxable status produced a one-time upward jump in *stated* yields, but not a capital loss on any given bond. Therefore, part of the increase in stated yields over 1926–1998 was a tax effect that did not cause a capital loss on the intermediate-term bond index. Further, the callable bonds used in the early part of the period may have commanded a return premium for taking this extra risk.

Chapter 4 Description of the Derived Series

Historical data suggests that investors are rewarded for taking risks and that returns are related to inflation rates. The risk/return and the real/nominal relationships in the historical data are revealed by looking at the risk premium and inflation-adjusted series derived from the basic asset series. Monthly total returns for the four risk premia are presented in Appendix A: Tables A-16 through A-19. Monthly inflation-adjusted total returns for the six asset classes are presented in Appendix A: Tables A-20 through A-25.

Geometric Differences Used to Calculate Derived Series

Derived series are calculated as the geometric differences between two basic asset classes. Returns on basic series **A** and **B** and derived series **C** are related as follows:

$$(1+C) = \left[\frac{1+A}{1+B}\right] \tag{3}$$

where the series **A**, **B** and **C** are in decimal form (*i.e.*, 5 percent is indicated by 0.05). Thus **C** is given by:

$$C = \left[\frac{1+A}{1+B}\right] - 1 \approx A - B \tag{4}$$

As an example, suppose return **A** equals 15%, or 0.15; and return **B** is 5%, or 0.05. Then **C** equals (1.15 / 1.05) - 1 = 0.0952, or 9.52 percent. This result, while slightly different from the simple arithmetic difference of 10 percent, is conceptually the same.

Definitions of the Derived Series

From the seven basic asset classes—large company stocks, small company stocks, long-term corporate bonds, long-term government bonds, intermediate-term government bonds, U.S. Treasury bills, and consumer goods (inflation)—10 additional series are derived representing the component or elemental parts of the asset returns.

Two Categories of Derived Series

The 10 derived series are categorized as risk premia, or payoffs for taking various types of risk; and as inflation-adjusted asset returns. The risk premia series are the bond horizon premium, the bond default premium, the equity risk premium, and the small stock premium. The inflation-adjusted asset return series are constructed by geometrically subtracting inflation from each of the six asset total return series.

These 10 derived series are:

Series	Derivation
Risk Premia	
Equity Risk Premium	$\frac{(1+\text{Large Stock TR})}{(1+\text{Treasury Bill TR})}-1$
Small Stock Premium	$\frac{(1+\text{Small Stock TR})}{(1+\text{Large Stock TR})}-1$
Bond Default Premium	$\frac{(1+\text{LT Corp Bond TR})}{(1+\text{LT Govt Bond TR})}-1$
Bond Horizon Premium	$\frac{(1+\text{LT Govt Bond TR})}{(1+\text{Treasury Bill TR})}-1$
Inflation-Adjusted	
Large Company Stock Returns	$\frac{(1+\text{Large Stock TR})}{(1+\text{Inflation})}-1$
Small Company Stock Returns	$\frac{(1+\text{Small Stock TR})}{(1+\text{Inflation})}-1$
Corporate Bond Returns	$\frac{(1+\text{Corp Bond TR})}{(1+\text{Inflation})}-1$
Long-Term Government Bond Returns	$\frac{(1+\text{LT Govt Bond TR})}{(1+\text{Inflation})}-1$
Intermediate-Term Government Bond Returns	$\frac{(1+\text{IT Govt Bond TR})}{(1+\text{Inflation})}-1$
Treasury Bill Returns (Real Riskless Rate of Return)	$\frac{(1+\text{Treasury Bill TR})}{(1+\text{Inflation})}-1$

TR= Total Return

Equity Risk Premium

Large company stock returns are composed of inflation, the real riskless rate, and the equity risk premium. The equity risk premium is the geometric difference between large company stock total returns and U.S. Treasury bill total returns.

Because large company stocks are not strictly comparable with bonds, horizon and default premia are not used to analyze the components of equity returns. (Large company stocks have characteristics that are analogous to horizon and default risk, but they are not equivalent.)

The monthly equity risk premium is given by:

$$\frac{(1+\text{Large Stock TR})}{(1+\text{Treasury Bill TR})}-1 \qquad (5)$$

Graph 4-1 shows equity risk premium volatility over the last 73 years.

Graph 4-1 Equity Risk Premium Annual Returns (in percent)

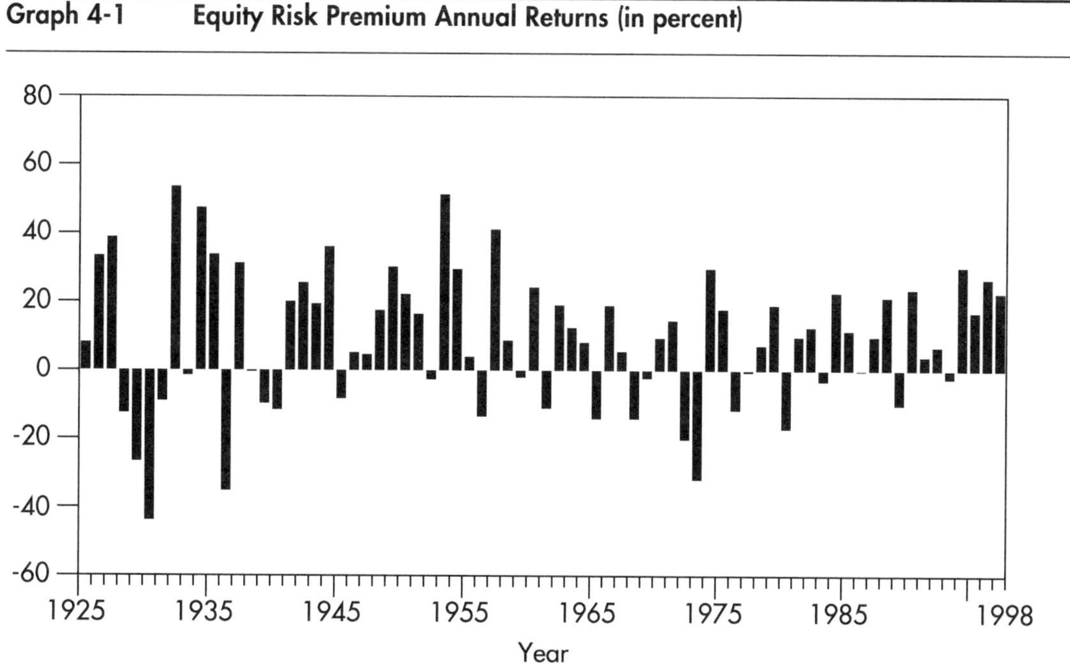

Small Stock Premium

The small stock premium is the geometric difference between small company stock total returns and large company stock total returns. The monthly small stock premium is given by:

$$\frac{(1+\text{Small Stock TR})}{(1+\text{Large Stock TR})}-1 \qquad (6)$$

Graph 4-2 shows small stock premium volatility over the last 73 years.

Graph 4-2 Small Stock Premium Annual Returns (in percent)

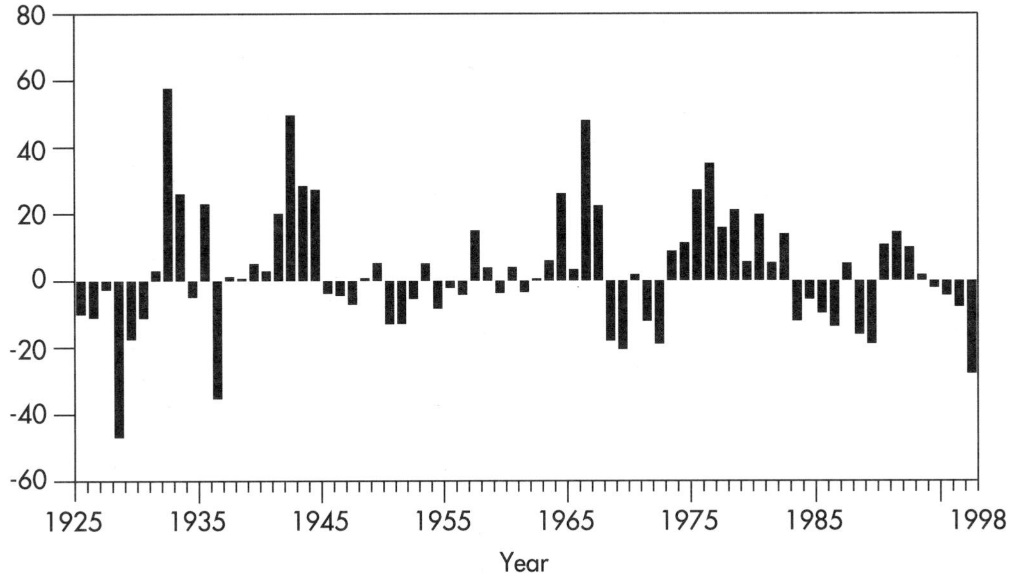

Bond Default Premium

The bond default premium is defined as the net return from investing in long-term corporate bonds rather than long-term government bonds of equal maturity. Since there is a possibility of default on a corporate bond, bondholders receive a premium that reflects this possibility, in addition to inflation, the real riskless rate, and the horizon premium.

The monthly bond default premium is given by:

$$\frac{(1+\text{LT Corp Bond TR})}{(1+\text{LT Govt Bond TR})}-1 \qquad (7)$$

Components of the Default Premium

Bonds susceptible to default have higher returns (when they do not default) than riskless bonds. Default on a bond may be a small loss, such as a late or skipped interest payment; it may be a larger loss, such as the loss of any or all principal as well as interest. In any case, part of the default premium on a portfolio of bonds is consumed by the losses on those bonds that do default.

The remainder of the default premium—over and above the portion consumed by defaults—is a pure risk premium, which the investor demands and, over the long run, receives for taking the risk of default. The expected return on a corporate bond, or portfolio of corporate bonds, is less than the bond's yield. The portion of the yield that is expected to be consumed by defaults must be subtracted. The expected return on a corporate bond is equal to the expected return on a government bond of like maturity, plus the pure *risk premium portion* of the bond default premium.

Callability Risk is Captured in the Default Premium

Callability risk is the risk that a bond will be redeemed (at or near par) by its issuer before maturity, at a time when market interest rates are lower than the bond's coupon rate. The possibility of redemption is risky because it would prevent the bondholder of the redeemed issue from reinvesting the proceeds at the original (higher) interest rate. The bond default premium, as measured here, also inadvertently captures any premium investors may demand or receive for this risk.

Graph 4-3 shows bond default premium volatility over the last 73 years.

Graph 4-3 Bond Default Premium Annual Returns (in percent)

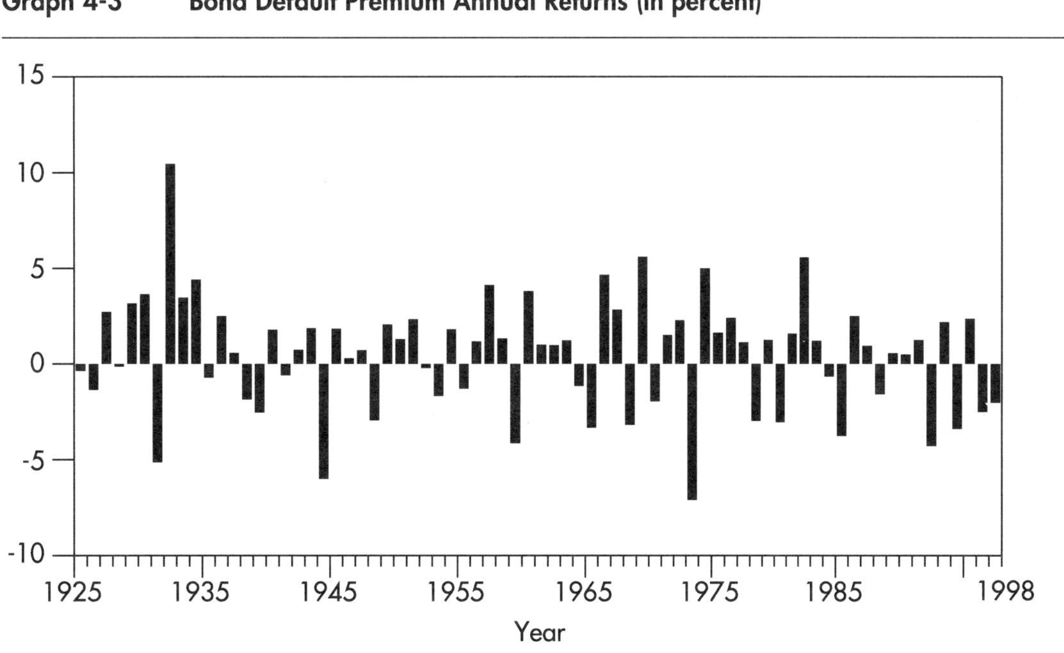

Bond Horizon Premium

Long-term government bonds behave differently than short-term bills in that their prices (and hence returns) are more sensitive to interest rate fluctuations. The bond horizon premium is the premium investors demand for holding long-term bonds instead of U.S. Treasury bills.

The monthly bond horizon premium is given by:

$$\frac{(1+\text{LT Govt Bond TR})}{(1+\text{Treasury Bill TR})}-1 \qquad (8)$$

Long-term rather than intermediate-term government bonds are used to derive the bond horizon premium so as to capture a "full unit" of price fluctuation risk. Intermediate-term government bonds may display a partial horizon premium, which is smaller than the difference between long-term bonds and short-term bills.

Does Maturity or Duration Determine the Bond Premium?

Duration is the present-value-weighted average time to receipt of cash flows (coupons and principal) from holding a bond, and can be calculated from the bond's yield, coupon rate, and term to maturity. The *duration* of a given bond determines the amount of return premium arising from differences in bond life. The bond horizon premium is also referred to as the "maturity premium," based on the observation that bonds with longer maturities command a return premium over shorter-maturity bonds. Duration, not term to maturity, however, is the bond characteristic that determines this return premium.

Why a "Horizon" Premium?

Investors often strive to match the duration of their bond holdings (cash inflows) with the estimated duration of their obligations or cash outflows. Consequently, investors with short time horizons regard long-duration bonds as risky (due to price fluctuation risk), and short-term bills as riskless. Conversely, investors with long time horizons regard short-term bills as risky (due to the uncertainty about the yield at which bills can be reinvested), and long-duration bonds as riskless or less risky.

Empirically, long-duration bonds bear higher yields and greater returns than short-term bills; that is, the yield curve slopes upward on average over time. This observation indicates that investors are more averse to the price fluctuation risk of long-duration bonds than to the reinvestment risk of bills.

Bond-duration risk is thus in the eye of the beholder, or bondholder. Therefore, rather than identifying the premium as a payoff for long-bond risk (which implies a judgment that short-horizon investors are "right" in their risk perceptions), it is better to go directly to the source of the return differential (the differing time horizons of investors) and use the label "horizon premium".

Graph 4-4 shows the bond horizon premium over the last 73 years.

Graph 4-4 Bond Horizon Premium Annual Returns (in percent)

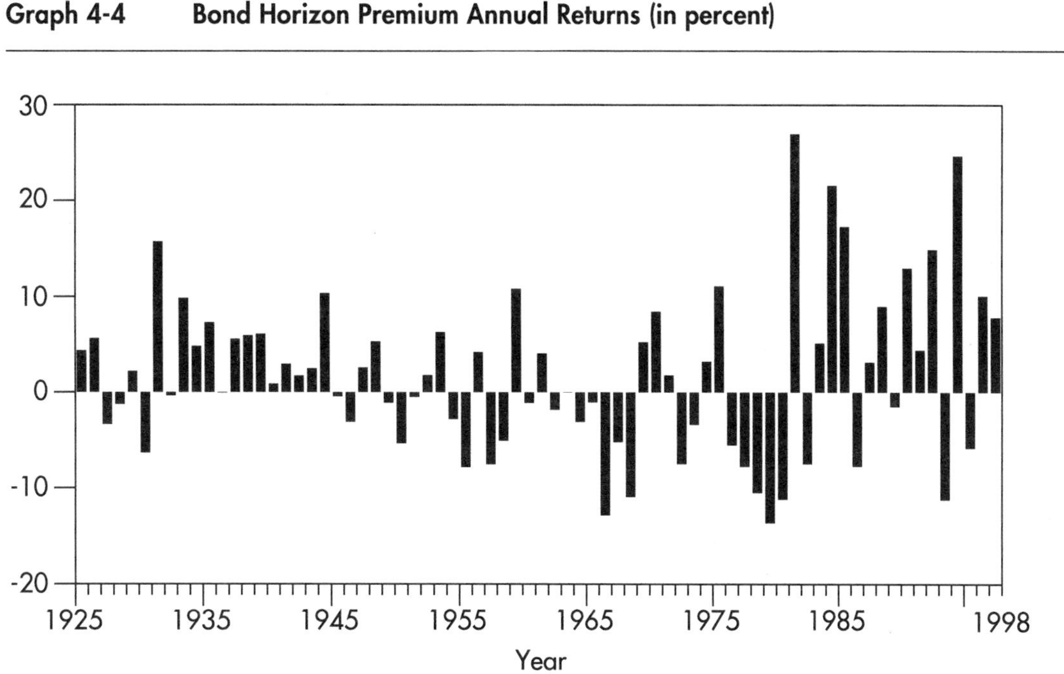

Inflation-Adjusted Large Company Stock Returns

Overview

Large company stock total returns were 11.2 percent compounded annually over the period 1926–1998 in nominal terms. [See Graph 4-5.] In real (inflation- adjusted) terms, stocks provided a 7.9 percent compound annual return. Thus, a large company stock investor would have experienced a substantial increase in real wealth, or purchasing power, over the 73-year period.

Graph 4-5 **Large Company Stocks**

Real and Nominal Return Indices

Year-End 1925 = $1.00

From 1925 to 1998

Construction

The inflation-adjusted return is a geometric difference and is approximately equal to the arithmetic difference between the large company stock total return and the inflation rate. The monthly inflation-adjusted large company stock return is given by:

$$\frac{(1+\text{Large Stock TR})}{(1+\text{Inflation})}-1 \quad (9)$$

The inflation-adjusted large company stock return may also be expressed as the geometric sum of the real riskless rate and the equity risk premium:

$$[(1 + \text{Real Riskless Rate}) \times (1 + \text{Equity Risk Premium})] - 1 \quad (10)$$

Inflation-Adjusted Small Company Stock Returns

Overview

Small company stock total returns were 12.4 percent compounded annually over the period 1926–1998 in nominal terms. [See Graph 4-6.] In real terms, small company stocks provided an 9.1 percent compound annual return. Thus, long-term a small company stock investor would have experienced a substantial increase in real wealth, or purchasing power, over the 73-year period.

Construction

The inflation-adjusted return is a geometric difference and is approximately equal to the arithmetic difference between the small company stock total return and the inflation rate. The monthly inflation-adjusted small company stock return is given by:

$$\frac{(1+\text{Small Stock TR})}{(1+\text{Inflation})}-1 \quad (11)$$

Inflation-Adjusted Long-Term Corporate Bond Returns

Overview

Corporate bonds returned 5.8 percent compounded annually over the period 1926–1998 in nominal terms, and a 2.6 percent compound annual return in real (inflation-adjusted) terms. [See Graph 4-7.] Thus, corporate bonds have outpaced inflation over the past 73 years.

Graph 4-6 **Small Company Stocks**

Real and Nominal Return Indices

Year-End 1925 = $1.00

From 1925 to 1998

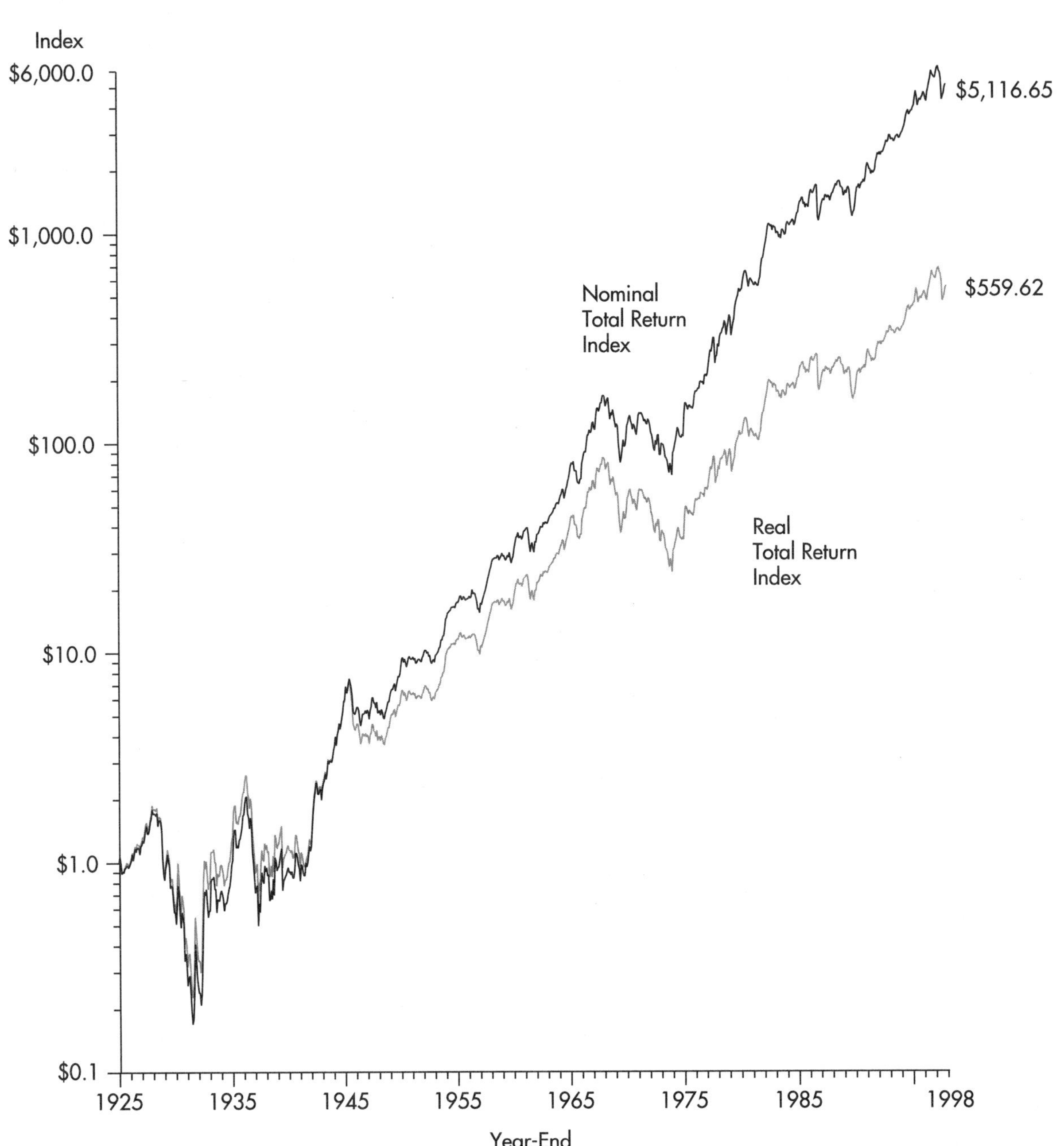

Graph 4-7 **Long-Term Corporate Bonds**

Real and Nominal Return Indices

Year-End 1925 = $1.00

From 1925 to 1998

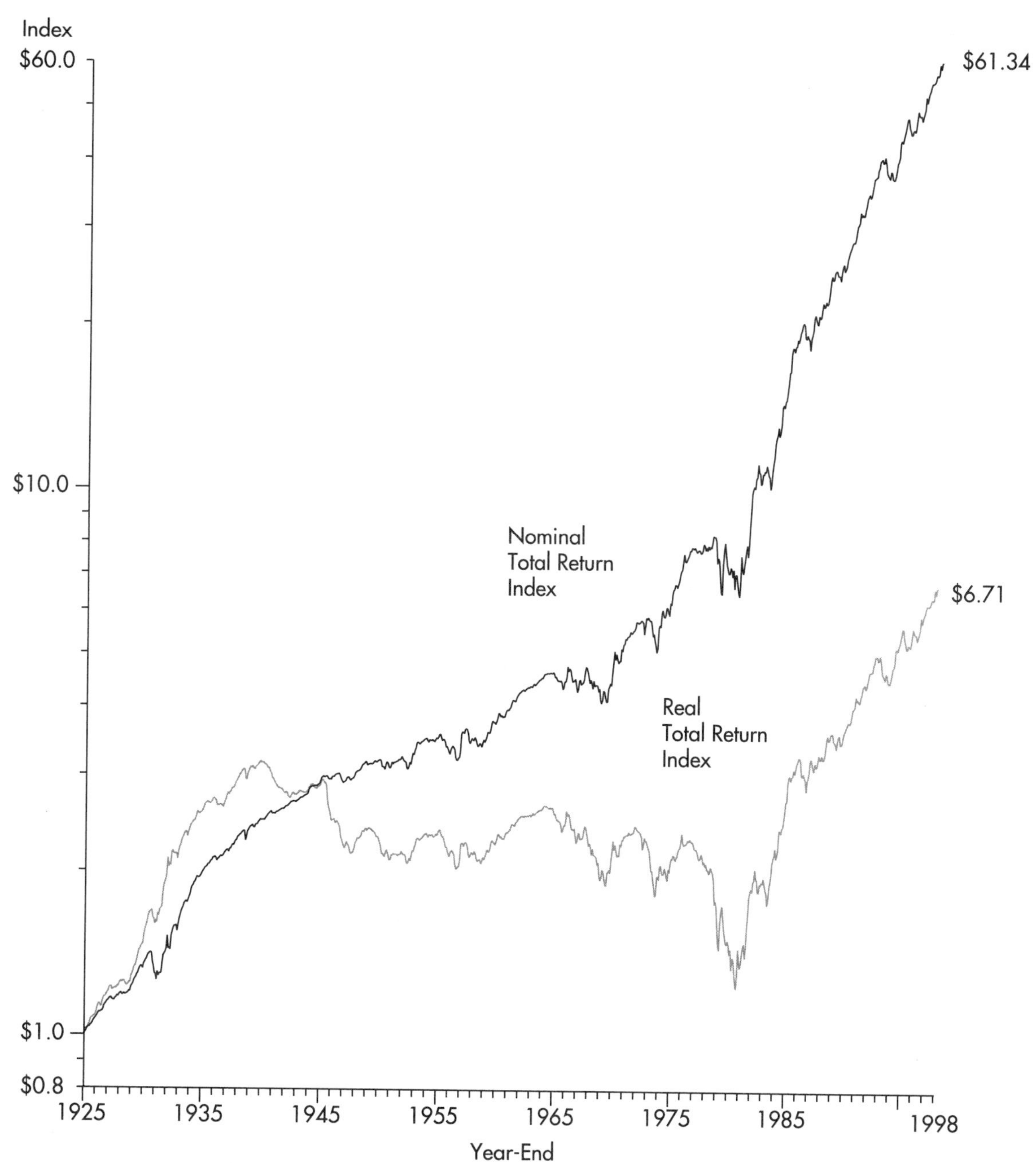

Construction

The inflation-adjusted return is a geometric difference and is approximately equal to the arithmetic difference between the long-term corporate bond total return and the inflation rate. The monthly inflation-adjusted corporate bond total return is given by:

$$\frac{(1+\text{Corp Bond TR})}{(1+\text{Inflation})}-1 \qquad (12)$$

Inflation-Adjusted Long-Term Government Bond Returns

Overview

Long-term government bonds returned 5.3 percent compounded annually over the period 1926–1998 in nominal terms, and a 2.2 percent compound annual return in real (inflation-adjusted) terms. [See Graph 4-8.] Thus, long-term government bonds have outpaced inflation over the past 73 years despite falling bond prices over most of the period.

Construction

The inflation-adjusted return is a geometric difference and is approximately equal to the arithmetic difference between the long-term government bond total return and the inflation rate. The monthly inflation-adjusted long-term government bond total return is given by:

$$\frac{(1+\text{LT Govt Bond TR})}{(1+\text{Inflation})}-1 \qquad (13)$$

Since government bond returns are composed of inflation, the real riskless rate and the horizon premium, the inflation-adjusted government bond returns may also be expressed as:

$$[(1+\text{Real Riskless Rate})\times(1+\text{Horizon Premium})]-1 \qquad (14)$$

Graph 4-8 **Long-Term Government Bonds**

Real and Nominal Return Indices

Year-End 1925 = $1.00

From 1925 to 1998

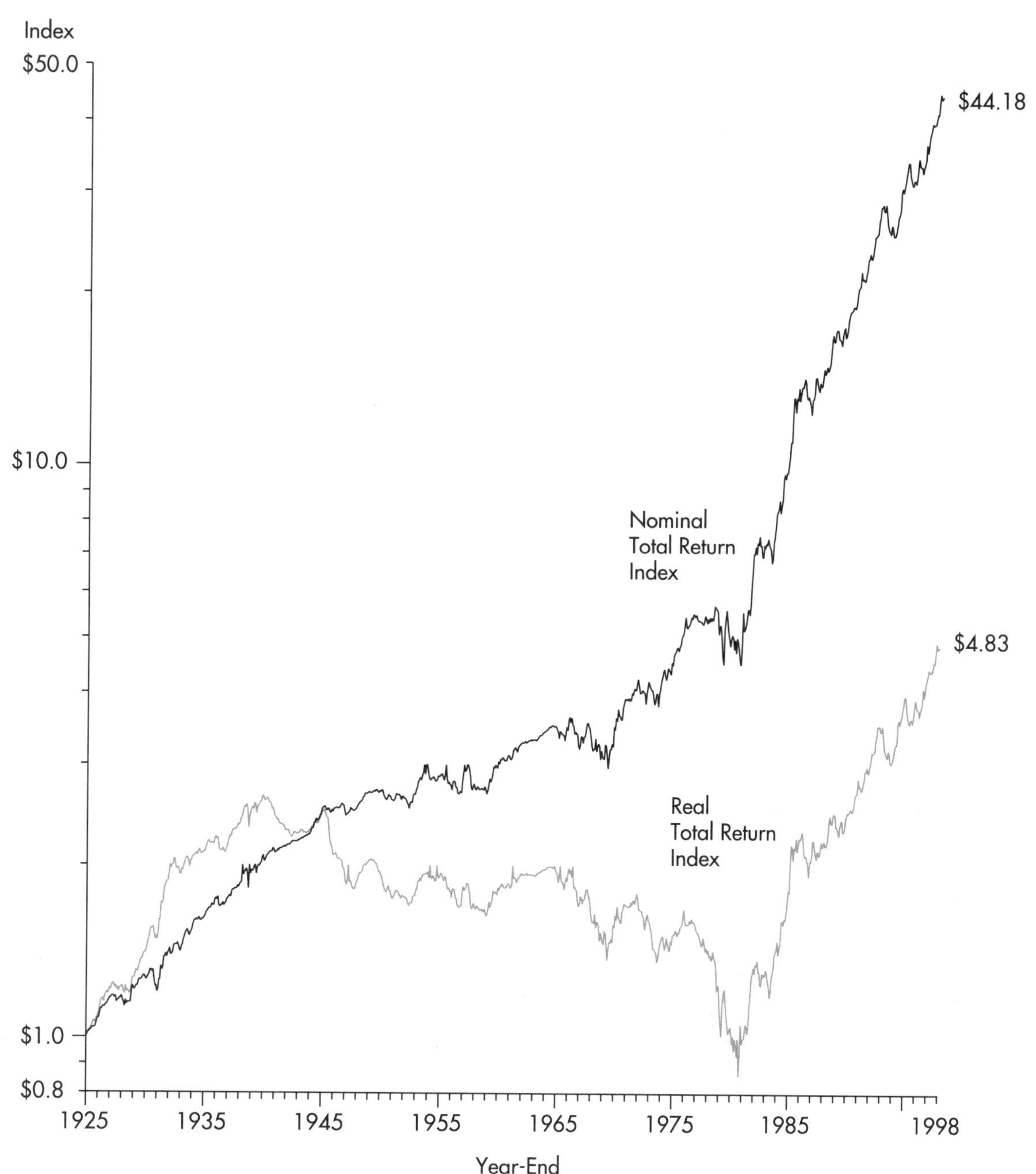

Inflation-Adjusted Intermediate-Term Government Bond Returns

Overview

Intermediate-term government bonds returned 5.3 percent compounded annually in nominal terms, and 2.2 percent in real (inflation-adjusted) terms. [See Graph 4-9.]

Construction

The inflation-adjusted return is a geometric difference and is approximately equal to the arithmetic difference between the intermediate-term government bond total return and the inflation rate. The monthly inflation-adjusted intermediate-term government bond return is given by:

$$\frac{(1+\text{IT Govt Bond TR})}{(1+\text{Inflation})}-1 \qquad (15)$$

Inflation-Adjusted U.S. Treasury Bill Returns (Real Riskless Rates of Return)

Overview

Treasury bills returned 3.8 percent compounded annually over 1926 to 1998, in nominal terms, but only a 0.7 percent compound annual return in real (inflation-adjusted) terms. [See Graph 4-11.] Thus, an investor in Treasury bills would have barely beaten inflation over the 73-year period.

Construction

The real riskless rate of return is the difference in returns between riskless U.S. Treasury bills and inflation. This is given by:

$$\frac{(1+\text{Treasury Bill TR})}{(1+\text{Inflation})}-1 \qquad (16)$$

Graph 4-9 **Intermediate-Term Government Bonds**

Real and Nominal Return Indices

Year-End 1925 = $1.00

From 1925 to 1998

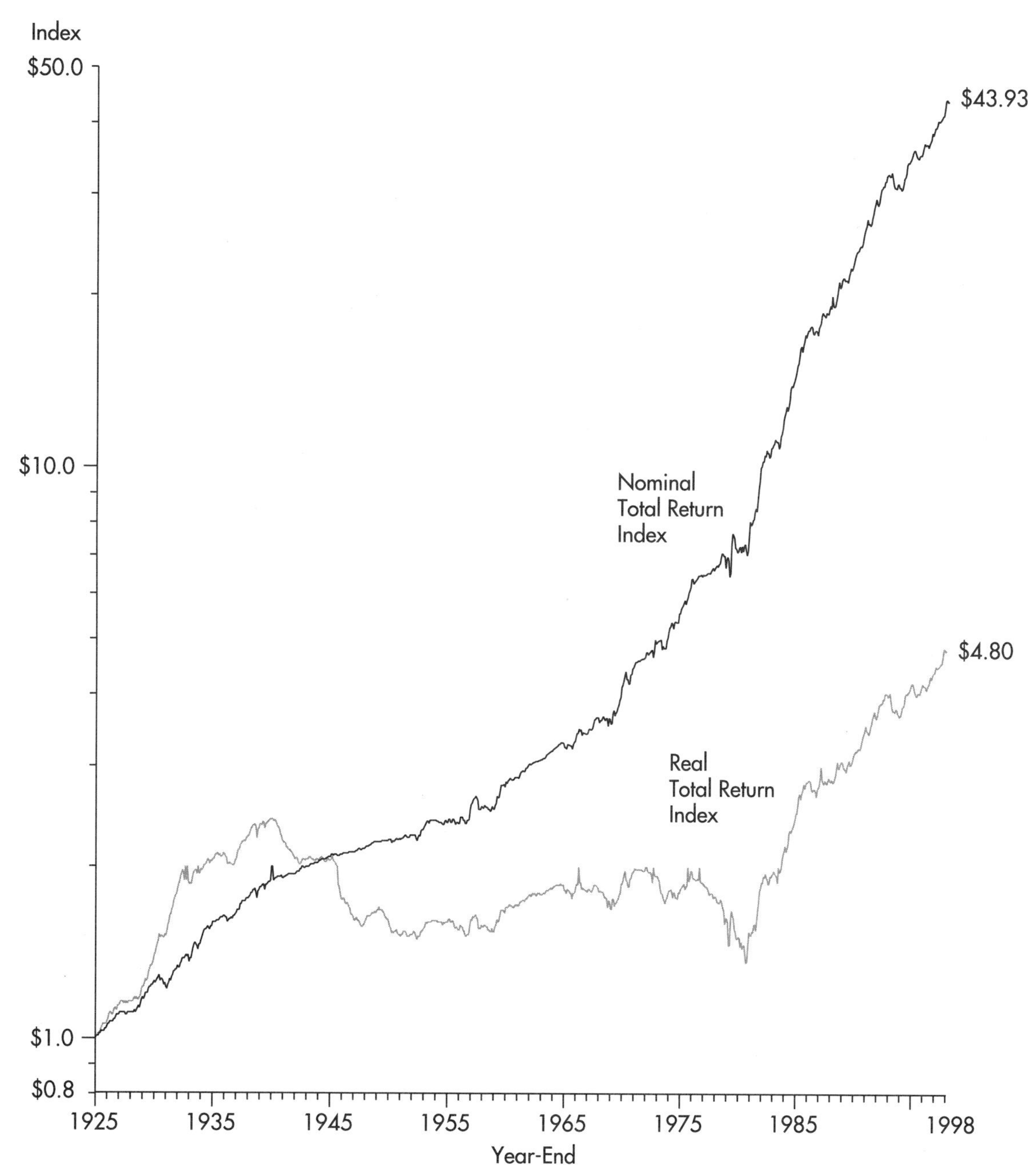

Graph 4-10 shows the levels, volatility, and patterns of real interest rates over the last 73 years.

Graph 4-10 Annual Real Riskless Rates of Return (in percent)

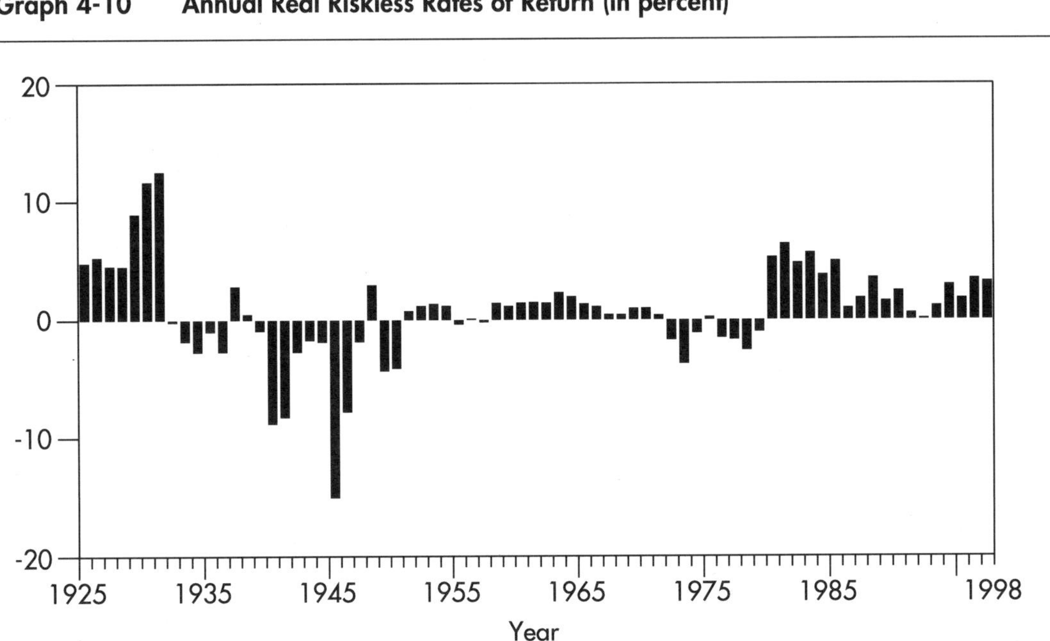

Returns on the Derived Series

Annual returns for the 10 derived series are calculated from monthly returns in the same manner as the annual basic series. Table 4-1 presents annual returns for each of the 10 derived series. Four of the derived series are risk premia and six are inflation-adjusted total returns on asset classes.

Graph 4-11 **U.S. Treasury Bills**

Real and Nominal Return Indices

Year-End 1925 = $1.00

From 1925 to 1998

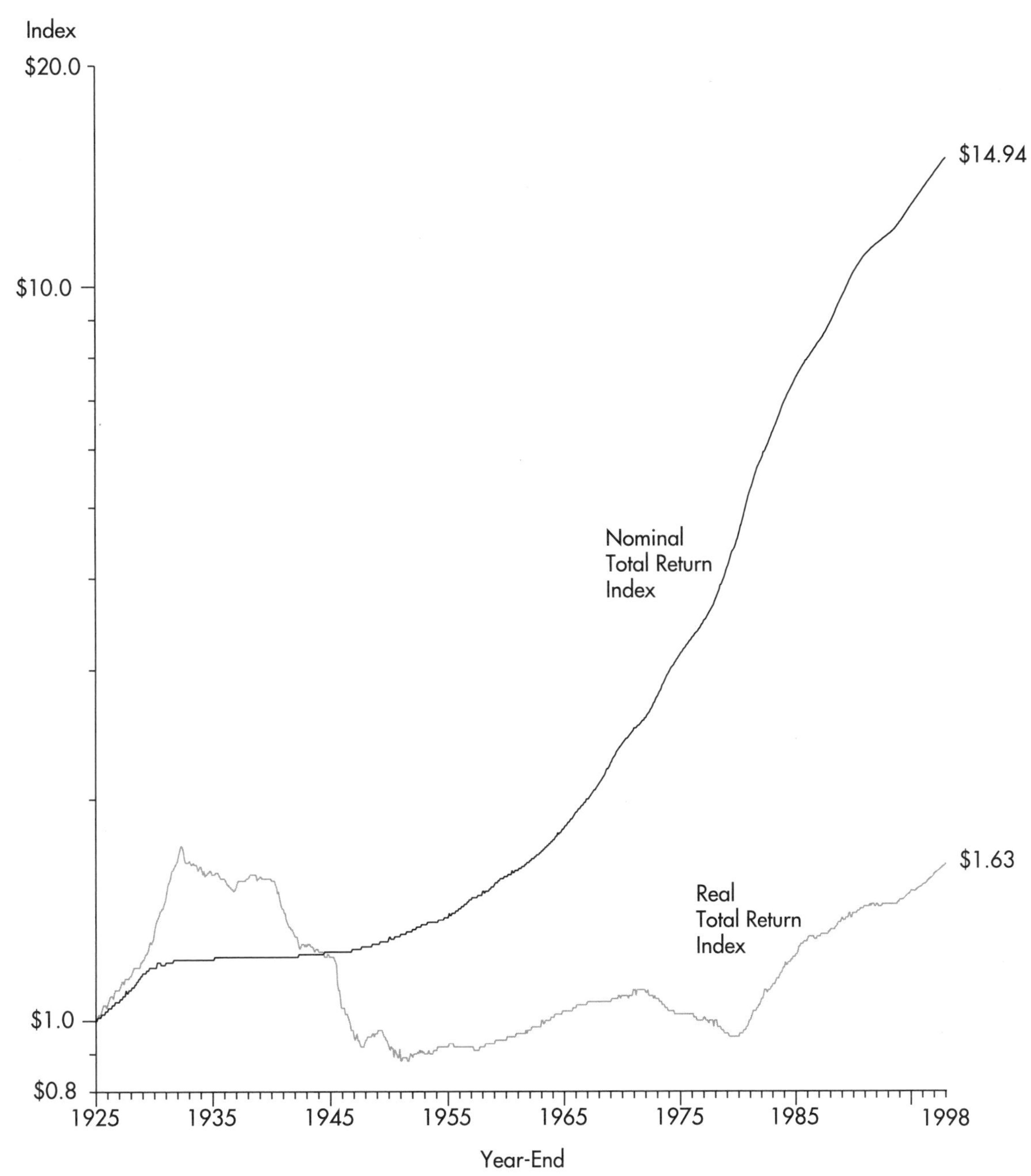

Table 4-1 **Derived Series** Annual Returns

(in percent)

From 1926 to 1970

					Inflation-Adjusted					
Year	Equity Risk Premia	Small Stock Premia	Default Premia	Horizon Premia	Large Company Stocks	Small Company Stocks	Long-Term Corporate Bonds	Long-Term Government Bonds	Intermediate Government Bonds	U.S. Treasury Bills
1926	8.09	-10.17	-0.37	4.36	13.31	1.79	9.00	9.40	6.97	4.83
1927	33.32	-11.19	-1.36	5.63	40.41	24.69	9.73	11.24	6.74	5.31
1928	38.67	-2.73	2.73	-3.34	45.01	41.06	3.84	1.08	1.90	4.57
1929	-12.57	-46.89	-0.14	-1.27	-8.59	-51.45	3.07	3.22	5.81	4.54
1930	-26.66	-17.64	3.17	2.20	-20.08	-34.18	14.90	11.38	13.56	8.98
1931	-43.94	-11.33	3.65	-6.31	-37.37	-44.46	8.48	4.66	7.96	11.71
1932	-9.07	3.05	-5.15	15.73	2.35	5.47	23.54	30.26	21.30	12.55
1933	53.53	57.72	10.46	-0.37	53.21	141.63	9.82	-0.58	1.31	-0.21
1934	-1.60	26.04	3.47	9.85	-3.40	21.75	11.58	7.84	6.83	-1.83
1935	47.42	-5.06	4.41	4.81	43.39	36.13	6.44	1.94	3.91	-2.73
1936	33.68	23.06	-0.72	7.32	32.32	62.83	5.47	6.23	1.83	-1.02
1937	-35.23	-35.37	2.51	-0.08	-36.98	-59.27	-0.35	-2.78	-1.50	-2.71
1938	31.14	1.28	0.57	5.55	34.87	36.59	9.16	8.55	9.27	2.84
1939	-0.43	0.76	-1.86	5.92	0.07	0.83	4.46	6.45	5.02	0.50
1940	-9.79	5.13	-2.54	6.08	-10.64	-6.05	2.41	5.08	1.99	-0.94
1941	-11.64	2.93	1.78	0.87	-19.42	-17.06	-6.37	-8.01	-8.40	-8.80
1942	20.02	20.08	-0.60	2.94	10.11	32.23	-6.12	-5.55	-6.73	-8.25
1943	25.46	49.62	0.73	1.73	22.04	82.60	-0.32	-1.04	-0.34	-2.73
1944	19.36	28.37	1.87	2.48	17.28	50.55	2.57	0.69	-0.31	-1.74
1945	35.99	27.25	-6.01	10.37	33.43	69.79	1.78	8.30	-0.03	-1.88
1946	-8.39	-3.87	1.83	-0.45	-22.20	-25.21	-13.91	-15.46	-14.52	-15.07
1947	5.18	-4.53	0.29	-3.11	-3.03	-7.42	-10.41	-10.67	-7.43	-7.80
1948	4.65	-7.22	0.71	2.57	2.72	-4.69	1.39	0.67	-0.84	-1.85
1949	17.50	0.80	-2.95	5.29	20.97	21.95	5.21	8.40	4.20	2.96
1950	30.16	5.34	2.05	-1.12	24.50	31.15	-3.47	-5.42	-4.81	-4.34
1951	22.19	-13.07	1.29	-5.34	17.14	1.82	-8.09	-9.26	-5.21	-4.14
1952	16.44	-12.96	2.33	-0.49	17.33	2.13	2.62	0.27	0.74	0.77
1953	-2.76	-5.55	-0.22	1.78	-1.60	-7.07	2.77	2.99	2.59	1.19
1954	51.32	5.21	-1.68	6.27	53.39	61.38	5.91	7.72	3.20	1.37
1955	29.52	-8.45	1.80	-2.82	31.07	19.99	0.10	-1.66	-1.02	1.19
1956	4.00	-2.13	-1.30	-7.85	3.59	1.38	-9.41	-8.21	-3.19	-0.39
1957	-13.50	-4.25	1.17	4.19	-13.40	-17.08	5.52	4.31	4.67	0.11
1958	41.19	15.01	4.13	-7.52	40.88	62.03	-3.91	-7.72	-3.00	-0.22
1959	8.75	3.97	1.32	-5.06	10.30	14.68	-2.43	-3.70	-1.86	1.43
1960	-2.14	-3.74	-4.14	10.83	-0.99	-4.70	7.48	12.12	10.13	1.17
1961	24.25	4.10	3.81	-1.13	26.04	31.21	4.12	0.30	1.17	1.44
1962	-11.16	-3.48	0.99	4.04	-9.83	-12.97	6.64	5.59	4.29	1.49
1963	19.09	0.62	0.97	-1.85	20.81	21.56	0.54	-0.43	-0.01	1.44
1964	12.50	6.04	1.22	-0.03	15.11	22.07	3.54	2.29	2.82	2.32
1965	8.20	26.06	-1.16	-3.10	10.33	39.08	-2.33	-1.19	-0.89	1.97
1966	-14.15	3.39	-3.33	-1.06	-12.98	-10.03	-3.06	0.29	1.29	1.36
1967	18.97	48.07	4.66	-12.85	20.32	78.15	-7.76	-11.86	-1.97	1.13
1968	5.57	22.43	2.84	-5.20	6.05	29.84	-2.05	-4.76	-0.18	0.46
1969	-14.16	-18.09	-3.18	-10.94	-13.77	-29.37	-13.38	-10.54	-6.45	0.45
1970	-2.36	-20.61	5.59	5.24	-1.41	-21.73	12.21	6.27	10.78	0.98

Table 4-1 **Derived Series** (continued) Annual Returns (in percent)

From 1971 to 1998

					Inflation-Adjusted					
Year	Equity Risk Premia	Small Stock Premia	Default Premia	Horizon Premia	Large Company Stocks	Small Company Stocks	Long-Term Corporate Bonds	Long-Term Government Bonds	Intermediate Government Bonds	U.S. Treasury Bills
1971	9.51	1.91	-1.96	8.47	10.60	12.71	7.41	9.55	5.19	0.99
1972	14.58	-12.22	1.49	1.78	15.05	0.99	3.72	2.20	1.69	0.41
1973	-20.19	-19.03	2.27	-7.52	-21.56	-36.49	-7.04	-9.10	-3.85	-1.72
1974	-31.92	8.87	-7.11	-3.38	-34.46	-28.65	-13.60	-6.99	-5.80	-3.74
1975	29.68	11.38	4.99	3.21	28.21	42.80	7.13	2.04	0.76	-1.13
1976	17.85	27.08	1.62	11.11	18.16	50.15	13.20	11.40	7.69	0.26
1977	-11.70	35.08	2.41	-5.53	-13.07	17.43	-4.74	-6.99	-5.02	-1.55
1978	-0.58	15.86	1.12	-7.80	-2.26	13.24	-8.34	-9.36	-5.08	-1.69
1979	7.31	21.13	-2.98	-10.52	4.53	26.62	-15.43	-12.83	-8.13	-2.59
1980	19.04	5.63	1.24	-13.65	17.81	24.45	-13.48	-14.54	-7.55	-1.03
1981	-17.10	19.76	-3.04	-11.20	-12.71	4.53	-9.34	-6.50	0.47	5.30
1982	9.83	5.43	1.57	26.97	16.88	23.23	37.25	35.13	24.28	6.42
1983	12.61	14.00	5.57	-7.49	18.03	34.56	2.37	-3.03	3.48	4.82
1984	-3.26	-12.17	1.20	5.12	2.22	-10.22	12.42	11.08	9.68	5.67
1985	22.68	-5.67	-0.67	21.58	27.36	20.13	25.36	26.21	15.96	3.81
1986	11.59	-9.81	-3.76	17.30	17.15	5.66	18.51	23.14	13.85	4.98
1987	-0.22	-13.81	2.51	-7.76	0.79	-13.13	-4.48	-6.82	-1.44	1.01
1988	9.84	5.19	0.94	3.13	11.87	17.67	6.02	5.03	1.61	1.85
1989	21.33	-16.21	-1.59	8.99	25.65	5.29	11.07	12.87	8.26	3.56
1990	-10.19	-18.99	0.57	-1.51	-8.74	-26.08	0.64	0.07	3.42	1.61
1991	23.63	10.79	0.49	12.98	26.67	40.33	16.32	15.75	12.03	2.46
1992	4.02	14.56	1.24	4.39	4.64	19.87	6.31	5.01	4.17	0.59
1993	6.89	9.99	-4.28	14.91	7.05	17.74	10.16	15.08	8.26	0.14
1994	-2.50	1.78	2.18	-11.24	-1.33	0.42	-8.22	-10.17	-7.62	1.20
1995	30.15	-2.16	-3.39	24.69	34.03	31.13	24.06	28.41	13.91	2.98
1996	16.98	-4.43	2.35	-5.83	19.12	13.84	-1.86	-4.12	-1.18	1.82
1997	26.70	-7.94	-2.51	10.07	31.13	20.72	11.06	13.91	6.57	3.49
1998	22.63	-27.91	-2.04	7.83	26.54	-8.78	9.00	11.27	8.46	3.19

STOCKS
BONDS
BILLS
AND
INFLATION

Part Two: Presentation of the Data

Chapter 5 Annual Returns and Indices

Returns and indices are used to measure the rewards investors earn for holding an asset class. Indices represent levels of wealth or prices, while returns represent changes in levels of wealth. Total returns for specific asset classes consist of component returns that are defined by the nature of the rewards being measured. For example: The total return on a security can be divided into income and capital appreciation components. The income return measures the cash income stream earned by holding the security, such as coupon interest or dividend payments. In contrast, the capital appreciation return results from a change in the price of the security. The method for computing a return varies with the nature of the payment (income or capital appreciation) and the time period of measure (monthly or annual frequency). Indices are computed by establishing a base period and base value and increasing that value by the successive returns. Indices are used to illustrate the cumulative growth of wealth from holding an asset class. This chapter describes the computation of the annual returns and indices.

Annual and Monthly Returns

Returns on the Basic Asset Classes

Annual total returns on each of the seven basic asset classes are presented in Table 2-5 in Chapter 2. The monthly total returns on the asset classes appear in Appendix A: Tables A-1, A-4, A-5, A-6, A-10, A-14, and A-15.

Calculating Annual Returns

Annual returns are formed by compounding the 12 monthly returns. Compounding, or linking, monthly returns is multiplying together the return relatives, or one plus the return, then subtracting one from the result. The equation is denoted as the geometric sum as follows:

$$\mathbf{r}_{\text{year}} = \left[(1+\mathbf{r}_{\text{Jan}})(1+\mathbf{r}_{\text{Feb}})\ldots(1+\mathbf{r}_{\text{Dec}})\right]-1 \qquad (17)$$

where,

$\mathbf{r}_{\text{year}}$ = the compound total return for the year; and,

$\mathbf{r}_{\text{Jan}}, \mathbf{r}_{\text{Feb}},\ldots,\mathbf{r}_{\text{Dec}}$ = the returns for the 12 months of the year.

The compound return reflects the growth of funds invested in an asset. The following example illustrates the compounding method for a hypothetical year:

Month	Return (Percent)	Return (Decimal)	Return Relative
Jan	1%	0.01	1.01
Feb	6	0.06	1.06
Mar	2	0.02	1.02
Apr	1	0.01	1.01
May	-3	-0.03	0.97
Jun	2	0.02	1.02
Jul	-4	-0.04	0.96
Aug	-2	-0.02	0.98
Sep	3	0.03	1.03
Oct	-3	-0.03	0.97
Nov	2	0.02	1.02
Dec	1	0.01	1.01

The return for this hypothetical year is the geometric sum:

$$(1.01 \times 1.06 \times 1.02 \times 1.01 \times 0.97 \times 1.02 \times 0.96 \times 0.98 \times 1.03 \times 0.97 \times 1.02 \times 1.01) - 1 = 1.0567 - 1 = 0.0567$$

or a gain of 5.67 percent. Note that this is different than the simple addition result, (1 + 6 + 2 + 1 – 3 + 2 – 4 – 2 + 3 – 3 + 2 + 1) = 6 percent. One dollar invested in this hypothetical asset at the beginning of the year would have grown to slightly less than $1.06.

Calculation of Returns from Index Values

Equivalently, annual returns, r_t, can be formed by dividing index values according to:

$$r_t = \left[\frac{V_t}{V_{t-1}}\right] - 1 \qquad (18)$$

where,

r_t = the annual return in period **t**;
V_t = the index value as of year-end **t**; and,
V_{t-1} = the index value as of the previous year-end, **t** – 1.

The construction of index values is discussed later in this chapter.

Calculation of Annual Income Returns

The conversion of monthly income returns to annual income returns is calculated by adding all the cash flows (income payments) for the period, then dividing the sum by the beginning period price:

$$r_I = \frac{(I_{Jan} + I_{Feb} + \ldots + I_{Dec})}{P_0} \tag{19}$$

where,

r_I = the income return for the year;

$I_{Jan}, I_{Feb}, \ldots, I_{Dec}$ = the income payments for the 12 months of the year; and,

P_0 = the price of the security at the beginning of the year.

The following example illustrates the method for a hypothetical year:

Month	Beginning of Month Price	Income Return (Decimal)	Income Payment
Jan	$100	0.006	$0.60
Feb	102	0.004	0.41
Mar	105	0.002	0.21
Apr	101	0.001	0.10
May	99	0.005	0.50
Jun	103	0.004	0.41
Jul	105	0.003	0.32
Aug	103	0.002	0.21
Sep	105	0.003	0.32
Oct	103	0.004	0.41
Nov	106	0.001	0.11
Dec	105	0.002	0.21

Sum the income payments (not the returns), and divide by the price at the beginning of the year:

$$(0.60 + 0.41 + 0.21 + 0.10 + 0.50 + 0.41 + 0.32 + 0.21 + 0.32 + 0.41 + 0.11 + 0.21) / 100 = 0.0381,$$

or an annual income return of 3.81 percent.

Annual income and capital appreciation returns do not sum to the annual total return. The difference may be viewed as a reinvestment return, which is the return from investing income from a given month into the same asset class in subsequent months within the year.

Index Values

Index values, or indices, represent the cumulative effect of returns on a dollar invested. For example: One dollar invested in large company stocks (with dividends reinvested) as of December 31, 1925 grew to $1.12 by December 1926, reflecting the 12 percent total return in 1926. [See Table 5-1.] Over the year 1927, the $1.12 grew to $1.53 by December, reflecting the 37.5 percent total return for that year.

By the end of 1998, the \$1.00 invested at year-end 1925 grew to \$2,350.89. Such growth reveals the power of compounding (reinvesting) one's investment returns.

Year-end indices of total returns for all seven basic asset classes are displayed in Table 5-1. This table also shows indices of capital appreciation for large company stocks as well as long- and intermediate-term government bonds. Indices of the inflation-adjusted return series are presented in Table 5-2. Monthly indices of total returns and, where applicable, capital appreciation returns on the basic asset classes are presented in Appendix B: Tables B-1 through B-10. Monthly indices of returns on the inflation-adjusted series are presented in Appendix B: Tables B-11 through B-16.

Graphs of index values, such as Graph 2-1 "Wealth Indices of Investments in the U.S. Capital Markets," depict the growth of wealth. The vertical scale is logarithmic so that equal distances represent equal percentage changes anywhere along the axis.

The inflation-adjusted indices in Table 5-2 are notable in that they show the growth of each asset class in *constant dollars*, or (synonymously) in *real* terms. Thus an investor in large company stocks, with dividends reinvested, would have multiplied his or her wealth in real terms, or purchasing power, by a factor of 257.1 between the end of 1925 and the end of 1998.

Calculation of Index Values

It is possible to mathematically describe the nature of the indices in Tables 5-1 and 5-2 precisely. At the end of each month, a cumulative wealth index (V_n) for each of the monthly return series (basic and derived) is formed. This index is initialized as of December 1925 at \$1.00 (represented by $V_0 = 1.00$). This index is formed for month n by taking the product of one plus the returns each period, as in the following manner:

$$V_n = V_0\left[\prod_{t=1}^{n}(1+r_t)\right] \tag{20}$$

where,

V_n = the index value at end of period **n**;
V_0 = the initial index value at time **0**; and,
r_t = the return in period **t**.

Using Index Values for Performance Measurement

Index values can be used to determine whether an investment portfolio accumulated more wealth for the investor over a period of time than another portfolio, or whether the investment performed as well as an industry benchmark. In the following example, which produced more wealth—the "investor portfolio" or a hypothetical S&P 500 index fund returning exactly the S&P total return? Each index measures total return and assumes monthly reinvestment of dividends.

	Investor Portfolio	S&P 500
Jan 1990	-5.35%	-6.71%
Feb 1990	0.65	1.29
Mar 1990	0.23	2.63
Accumulated Wealth of $1	$0.955	$0.970

Taking December 1989 as the base period, and using the computation method described above, the S&P 500 outperformed the investor portfolio.

Computing Returns for Non-Calendar Periods

Index values are also useful for computing returns for non-calendar time periods. To compute the capital appreciation return for long-term government bonds from the end of June 1987 through the end of June 1988, divide the index value in June 1988, 0.661, by the index value in June 1987, 0.683, and subtract 1. [Refer to Table B-6 in Appendix B.]

This yields: (0.661/ 0.683) – 1 = –0.0322, or –3.22 percent.

Table 5-1 **Basic Series**

Indices of Year-End Cumulative Wealth

Year-End 1925 = $1.00

From 1925 to 1970

Year	Large Stocks Total Returns	Large Stocks Capital Apprec	Small Stocks Total Returns	Long-Term Corp Bonds Total Returns	Long-Term Government Bonds Total Returns	Long-Term Government Bonds Capital Apprec	Intermediate-Term Government Bonds Total Returns	Intermediate-Term Government Bonds Capital Apprec	U.S. T-Bills Total Returns	Inflation
1925	1.000	1.000	1.000	1.000	1.000	1.000	1.000	1.000	1.000	1.000
1926	1.116	1.057	1.003	1.074	1.078	1.039	1.054	1.015	1.033	0.985
1927	1.535	1.384	1.224	1.154	1.174	1.095	1.101	1.025	1.065	0.965
1928	2.204	1.908	1.710	1.186	1.175	1.061	1.112	0.997	1.103	0.955
1929	2.018	1.681	0.832	1.225	1.215	1.059	1.178	1.014	1.155	0.957
1930	1.516	1.202	0.515	1.323	1.272	1.072	1.258	1.048	1.183	0.899
1931	0.859	0.636	0.259	1.299	1.204	0.982	1.228	0.991	1.196	0.814
1932	0.789	0.540	0.245	1.439	1.407	1.109	1.337	1.041	1.207	0.730
1933	1.214	0.792	0.594	1.588	1.406	1.074	1.361	1.031	1.211	0.734
1934	1.197	0.745	0.738	1.808	1.547	1.146	1.483	1.092	1.213	0.749
1935	1.767	1.053	1.035	1.982	1.624	1.171	1.587	1.146	1.215	0.771
1936	2.367	1.346	1.705	2.116	1.746	1.225	1.636	1.165	1.217	0.780
1937	1.538	0.827	0.716	2.174	1.750	1.195	1.661	1.165	1.221	0.804
1938	2.016	1.035	0.951	2.307	1.847	1.229	1.765	1.216	1.221	0.782
1939	2.008	0.979	0.954	2.399	1.957	1.272	1.845	1.255	1.221	0.778
1940	1.812	0.829	0.905	2.480	2.076	1.319	1.899	1.280	1.221	0.786
1941	1.602	0.681	0.823	2.548	2.096	1.306	1.909	1.278	1.222	0.862
1942	1.927	0.766	1.190	2.614	2.163	1.316	1.946	1.293	1.225	0.942
1943	2.427	0.915	2.242	2.688	2.208	1.311	2.000	1.309	1.229	0.972
1944	2.906	1.041	3.446	2.815	2.270	1.315	2.036	1.314	1.233	0.993
1945	3.965	1.361	5.983	2.930	2.514	1.424	2.082	1.327	1.237	1.015
1946	3.645	1.199	5.287	2.980	2.511	1.393	2.102	1.326	1.242	1.199
1947	3.853	1.199	5.335	2.911	2.445	1.328	2.122	1.322	1.248	1.307
1948	4.065	1.191	5.223	3.031	2.529	1.341	2.161	1.326	1.258	1.343
1949	4.829	1.313	6.254	3.132	2.692	1.396	2.211	1.338	1.272	1.318
1950	6.360	1.600	8.677	3.198	2.693	1.367	2.227	1.329	1.287	1.395
1951	7.888	1.863	9.355	3.112	2.587	1.282	2.235	1.307	1.306	1.477
1952	9.336	2.082	9.638	3.221	2.617	1.263	2.271	1.300	1.328	1.490
1953	9.244	1.944	9.013	3.331	2.713	1.271	2.345	1.308	1.352	1.499
1954	14.108	2.820	14.473	3.511	2.907	1.326	2.407	1.322	1.364	1.492
1955	18.561	3.564	17.431	3.527	2.870	1.272	2.392	1.281	1.385	1.497
1956	19.778	3.658	18.177	3.287	2.710	1.165	2.382	1.237	1.419	1.540
1957	17.646	3.134	15.529	3.573	2.912	1.209	2.568	1.287	1.464	1.587
1958	25.298	4.327	25.605	3.494	2.734	1.098	2.535	1.233	1.486	1.615
1959	28.322	4.694	29.804	3.460	2.673	1.030	2.525	1.177	1.530	1.639
1960	28.455	4.554	28.823	3.774	3.041	1.125	2.822	1.264	1.571	1.663
1961	36.106	5.607	38.072	3.956	3.070	1.093	2.874	1.243	1.604	1.674
1962	32.954	4.945	33.540	4.270	3.282	1.124	3.034	1.264	1.648	1.695
1963	40.469	5.879	41.444	4.364	3.322	1.093	3.084	1.237	1.700	1.723
1964	47.139	6.642	51.193	4.572	3.438	1.085	3.209	1.237	1.760	1.743
1965	53.008	7.244	72.567	4.552	3.462	1.048	3.242	1.199	1.829	1.777
1966	47.674	6.295	67.479	4.560	3.589	1.037	3.394	1.194	1.916	1.836
1967	59.104	7.560	123.870	4.335	3.259	0.896	3.428	1.148	1.997	1.892
1968	65.642	8.139	168.429	4.446	3.251	0.847	3.583	1.136	2.101	1.981
1969	60.059	7.210	126.233	4.086	3.086	0.755	3.557	1.054	2.239	2.102
1970	62.465	7.222	104.226	4.837	3.460	0.792	4.156	1.145	2.385	2.218

Table 5-1 **Basic Series** Indices of Year-End Cumulative Wealth

(continued) Year-End 1925 = $1.00

From 1971 to 1998

Year	Large Stocks Total Returns	Large Stocks Capital Apprec	Small Stocks Total Returns	Long-Term Corp Bonds Total Returns	Long-Term Government Bonds Total Returns	Long-Term Government Bonds Capital Apprec	Intermediate-Term Government Bonds Total Returns	Intermediate-Term Government Bonds Capital Apprec	U.S. T-Bills Total Returns	Inflation
1971	71.406	8.001	121.423	5.370	3.917	0.844	4.519	1.177	2.490	2.292
1972	84.956	9.252	126.807	5.760	4.140	0.841	4.752	1.168	2.585	2.371
1973	72.500	7.645	87.618	5.825	4.094	0.777	4.971	1.142	2.764	2.579
1974	53.311	5.373	70.142	5.647	4.272	0.750	5.254	1.120	2.986	2.894
1975	73.144	7.068	107.189	6.474	4.665	0.755	5.665	1.121	3.159	3.097
1976	90.584	8.422	168.691	7.681	5.447	0.816	6.394	1.180	3.319	3.246
1977	84.077	7.453	211.500	7.813	5.410	0.752	6.484	1.119	3.489	3.466
1978	89.592	7.532	261.120	7.807	5.346	0.684	6.710	1.069	3.740	3.778
1979	106.113	8.459	374.614	7.481	5.280	0.617	6.985	1.015	4.128	4.281
1980	140.514	10.639	523.992	7.274	5.071	0.530	7.258	0.946	4.592	4.812
1981	133.616	9.605	596.717	7.185	5.166	0.476	7.944	0.903	5.267	5.242
1982	162.223	11.023	763.829	10.242	7.251	0.589	10.256	1.031	5.822	5.445
1983	198.745	12.926	1066.828	10.883	7.298	0.532	11.015	0.997	6.335	5.652
1984	211.199	13.106	995.680	12.718	8.427	0.544	12.560	1.009	6.959	5.875
1985	279.117	16.559	1241.234	16.546	11.037	0.641	15.113	1.100	7.496	6.097
1986	330.671	18.981	1326.275	19.829	13.745	0.737	17.401	1.177	7.958	6.166
1987	347.967	19.366	1202.966	19.776	13.372	0.658	17.906	1.121	8.393	6.438
1988	406.458	21.769	1478.135	21.893	14.665	0.661	18.999	1.096	8.926	6.722
1989	534.455	27.703	1628.590	25.447	17.322	0.718	21.524	1.143	9.673	7.034
1990	517.499	25.886	1277.449	27.173	18.392	0.699	23.618	1.155	10.429	7.464
1991	675.592	32.695	1847.629	32.577	21.942	0.769	27.270	1.240	11.012	7.693
1992	727.412	34.155	2279.039	35.637	23.709	0.772	29.230	1.248	11.398	7.916
1993	800.078	36.565	2757.147	40.336	28.034	0.855	32.516	1.317	11.728	8.133
1994	810.538	36.002	2842.773	38.012	25.856	0.733	30.843	1.170	12.186	8.351
1995	1113.918	48.282	3822.398	48.353	34.044	0.901	36.025	1.283	12.868	8.563
1996	1370.946	58.066	4495.993	49.031	33.727	0.835	36.782	1.233	13.538	8.847
1997	1828.326	76.071	5519.969	55.380	39.074	0.906	39.864	1.257	14.250	8.998
1998	2350.892	96.359	5116.648	61.339	44.178	0.968	43.933	1.316	14.942	9.143

Table 5-2 **Inflation-Adjusted Series**

Indices of Year-End Cumulative Wealth

Year-End 1925 = $1.00

From 1925 to 1970

	Inflation-Adjusted					
	Large Company Stocks	Small Company Stocks	Long-Term Corporate Bonds	Long-Term Government Bonds	Intermediate Government Bonds	U.S. Treasury Bills
1925	1.000	1.000	1.000	1.000	1.000	1.000
1926	1.133	1.018	1.090	1.094	1.070	1.048
1927	1.591	1.269	1.196	1.217	1.142	1.104
1928	2.307	1.790	1.242	1.230	1.164	1.154
1929	2.109	0.869	1.280	1.270	1.231	1.207
1930	1.685	0.572	1.471	1.414	1.398	1.315
1931	1.056	0.318	1.596	1.480	1.509	1.469
1932	1.080	0.335	1.971	1.928	1.831	1.654
1933	1.655	0.810	2.165	1.917	1.855	1.650
1934	1.599	0.986	2.415	2.067	1.982	1.620
1935	2.292	1.342	2.571	2.107	2.059	1.576
1936	3.033	2.185	2.712	2.238	2.097	1.560
1937	1.912	0.890	2.702	2.176	2.065	1.517
1938	2.578	1.216	2.950	2.362	2.257	1.561
1939	2.580	1.226	3.082	2.514	2.370	1.568
1940	2.305	1.152	3.156	2.642	2.417	1.554
1941	1.858	0.955	2.955	2.430	2.214	1.417
1942	2.046	1.263	2.774	2.295	2.065	1.300
1943	2.496	2.306	2.765	2.271	2.058	1.264
1944	2.928	3.472	2.836	2.287	2.052	1.242
1945	3.907	5.895	2.887	2.477	2.051	1.219
1946	3.039	4.409	2.485	2.094	1.753	1.035
1947	2.947	4.081	2.227	1.871	1.623	0.955
1948	3.027	3.890	2.258	1.883	1.609	0.937
1949	3.662	4.744	2.375	2.042	1.677	0.965
1950	4.560	6.221	2.293	1.931	1.596	0.923
1951	5.341	6.335	2.107	1.752	1.513	0.885
1952	6.267	6.469	2.162	1.757	1.524	0.891
1953	6.166	6.012	2.222	1.809	1.564	0.902
1954	9.458	9.703	2.354	1.949	1.614	0.914
1955	12.397	11.642	2.356	1.917	1.597	0.925
1956	12.843	11.803	2.134	1.759	1.547	0.922
1957	11.122	9.788	2.252	1.835	1.619	0.923
1958	15.669	15.859	2.164	1.694	1.570	0.921
1959	17.283	18.187	2.112	1.631	1.541	0.934
1960	17.111	17.333	2.270	1.829	1.697	0.945
1961	21.567	22.741	2.363	1.834	1.717	0.958
1962	19.447	19.792	2.520	1.937	1.791	0.973
1963	23.494	24.060	2.534	1.928	1.790	0.987
1964	27.044	29.370	2.623	1.972	1.841	1.010
1965	29.838	40.848	2.562	1.949	1.825	1.029
1966	25.964	36.751	2.484	1.955	1.848	1.043
1967	31.239	65.471	2.291	1.723	1.812	1.055
1968	33.129	85.005	2.244	1.641	1.808	1.060
1969	28.567	60.042	1.944	1.468	1.692	1.065
1970	28.164	46.993	2.181	1.560	1.874	1.075

Table 5-2 **Inflation-Adjusted Series** (continued)

Indices of Year-End Cumulative Wealth

Year-End 1925 = $1.00

From 1971 to 1998

	Inflation-Adjusted					
	Large Company Stocks	Small Company Stocks	Long-Term Corporate Bonds	Long-Term Government Bonds	Intermediate Government Bonds	U.S. Treasury Bills
1971	31.149	52.968	2.343	1.709	1.971	1.086
1972	35.837	53.492	2.430	1.746	2.005	1.091
1973	28.110	33.971	2.259	1.587	1.927	1.072
1974	18.422	24.238	1.951	1.476	1.815	1.032
1975	23.619	34.612	2.091	1.506	1.829	1.020
1976	27.908	51.971	2.366	1.678	1.970	1.023
1977	24.260	61.029	2.254	1.561	1.871	1.007
1978	23.712	69.108	2.066	1.415	1.776	0.990
1979	24.786	87.502	1.747	1.233	1.632	0.964
1980	29.201	108.894	1.512	1.054	1.508	0.954
1981	25.489	113.831	1.371	0.985	1.515	1.005
1982	29.792	140.278	1.881	1.332	1.884	1.069
1983	35.165	188.759	1.926	1.291	1.949	1.121
1984	35.947	169.470	2.165	1.434	2.138	1.184
1985	45.781	203.588	2.714	1.810	2.479	1.230
1986	53.631	215.106	3.216	2.229	2.822	1.291
1987	54.053	186.867	3.072	2.077	2.782	1.304
1988	60.466	219.893	3.257	2.182	2.826	1.328
1989	75.977	231.516	3.617	2.462	3.060	1.375
1990	69.333	171.148	3.641	2.464	3.164	1.397
1991	87.822	240.179	4.235	2.852	3.545	1.431
1992	91.893	287.908	4.502	2.995	3.693	1.440
1993	98.369	338.990	4.959	3.447	3.998	1.442
1994	97.059	340.412	4.552	3.096	3.693	1.459
1995	130.085	446.387	5.647	3.976	4.207	1.503
1996	154.953	508.167	5.542	3.812	4.157	1.530
1997	203.190	613.460	6.155	4.342	4.430	1.584
1998	257.121	559.616	6.709	4.832	4.805	1.634

STOCKS
BONDS
BILLS
AND
INFLATION

Part Three: Interpretation of the Data

Chapter 6 Statistical Analysis of Returns

Statistical analysis of historical asset returns can reveal the growth rate of wealth invested in an asset or portfolio, the riskiness or volatility of asset classes, the comovement of assets, and the random or cyclical behavior of asset returns. This chapter focuses on arithmetic and geometric mean returns, standard deviations, and serial and cross-correlation coefficients, and discusses the use of each statistic to characterize the various asset classes by growth rate, variability, and safety.

Calculating Arithmetic Mean Returns

The arithmetic mean of a series is the simple average of the elements in the series. The arithmetic mean return equation is:

$$r_A = \frac{1}{n}\sum_{t=1}^{n} r_t \qquad (21)$$

where,

r_A = the arithmetic mean return;

r_t = the series return in period **t**, that is, from time **t–1** to time **t**; and,

n = the inclusive number of periods.

Calculating Geometric Mean Returns

The geometric mean of a return series over a period is the compound rate of return over the period. The geometric mean return equation is:

$$r_G = \left[\prod_{t=1}^{n}(1+r_t)\right]^{\frac{1}{n}} - 1 \qquad (22)$$

where,

r_G = the geometric mean return;

r_t = the series return in period **t**; and,

n = the inclusive number of periods.

The geometric mean return can be restated using beginning and ending period index values. The equation is:

$$r_G = \left[\frac{V_n}{V_0}\right]^{\frac{1}{n}} - 1 \tag{23}$$

where,

r_G = the geometric mean return;

V_n = the ending period index value at time **n**;

V_0 = the initial index value at time **0**; and,

n = the inclusive number of periods.

The annualized geometric mean return over any period of months can also be computed by expressing n as a fraction. For example: Starting at the beginning of 1996 to the end of May 1996 is equivalent to five-twelfths of a year, or 0.4167. V_n would be the index value at the end of May 1996, V_0 would be the index value at the beginning of 1996, and n would be 0.4167.

Geometric Mean Versus Arithmetic Mean

A simple example illustrates the difference between geometric and arithmetic means. Suppose $1.00 was invested in a large company stock portfolio that experiences successive annual returns of +50 percent and -50 percent. At the end of the first year, the portfolio is worth $1.50. At the end of the second year, the portfolio is worth $0.75. The annual arithmetic mean is 0.0 percent, whereas the annual geometric mean is -13.4 percent. Both are calculated as follows:

$$r_A = \frac{1}{2}(0.50 - 0.50) = 0.0\text{, and}$$

$$r_G = \left[\frac{0.75}{1.00}\right]^{\frac{1}{2}} - 1 = -0.134.$$

The geometric mean is backward-looking, measuring the change in wealth over more than one period. On the other hand, the arithmetic mean better represents a typical performance over single periods and serves as the correct rate for forecasting, discounting, and estimating the cost of capital. [See Chapters 8 and 9.]

In general, the geometric mean for any time period is less than or equal to the arithmetic mean. The two means are equal only for a return series that is constant (*i.e.*, the same return in every period). For a non-constant series, the difference between the two is positively related to the variability or standard deviation of the returns. For example, in Table 6-7, the difference between the arithmetic and geometric mean is much larger for risky large company stocks than it is for nearly riskless Treasury bills.

Calculating Standard Deviations

The standard deviation of a series is a measure of the extent to which observations in the series differ from the arithmetic mean of the series. For a series of asset returns, the standard deviation is a measure of the volatility, or risk, of the asset. The standard deviation is a measure of the variation around an average or mean.

In a normally distributed series, about two-thirds of the observations lie within one standard deviation of the arithmetic mean; about 95 percent of the observations lie within two standard deviations; and more than 99 percent lie within three standard deviations.

For example, the standard deviation for large company stocks over the period 1926–1998 was 20.3 percent with an annual arithmetic mean of 13.2 percent. Therefore, roughly two-thirds of the observations have annual returns between -7.1 percent and 33.5 percent (13.2 ± 20.3); approximately 95 percent of the observations are between -27.4 percent and 53.8 percent (13.2 ± 40.6).

The equation for the standard deviation of a series of returns (σ_r) is:

$$\sigma_r = \sqrt{\frac{1}{n-1}\sum_{t=1}^{n}(r_t - r_A)^2} \qquad (24)$$

where,

r_t = the return in period **t**;

r_A = the arithmetic mean of the return series **r**; and,

n = the number of periods.

The scaling of the standard deviation depends on the frequency of the data; therefore, a series of monthly returns produces a monthly standard deviation. For example; Using the monthly returns for the hypothetical year on page 96, a monthly standard deviation of 2.94 percent is calculated following equation (24):

$$\begin{aligned}&[\tfrac{1}{12-1}((0.01-0.005)^2+(0.06-0.005)^2+(0.02-0.005)^2+(0.01-0.005)^2\\&+(-0.03-0.005)^2+(0.02-0.005)^2+(-0.04-0.005)^2+(0.02-0.005)^2\\&+(0.03-0.005)^2+(-0.03-0.005)^2+(0.02-0.005)^2+(0.01-0.005)^2)]^{\frac{1}{2}}=0.0294\end{aligned}$$

It is sometimes useful to express the standard deviation of the series in another time scale. To calculate the annualized monthly standard deviations (σ_n), one uses equation (25).[4]

$$\sigma_n = \sqrt{\left[\sigma_1^2 + (1+\mu_1)^2\right]^n - (1+\mu_1)^{2n}} \quad (25)$$

where,

n = the number of periods per year, e.g. 12 for monthly, 4 for quarterly, etc.;

σ_1 = the monthly standard deviation; and,

μ_1 = the monthly arithmetic mean.

Applying this formula to the prior monthly standard deviation of 2.94 percent results in an annualized monthly standard deviation of 10.78 percent. The annualized monthly standard deviation is calculated with equation (25) as follows:

$$\sqrt{[0.0294^2 + (1+0.005)^2]^{12} - (1+0.005)^{2(12)}} = 0.1078$$

This equation is the exact form of the common approximation:

$$\sigma_n \approx \sqrt{n}\sigma_1$$

The approximation treats an annual return as if it were the sum of 12 independent monthly returns, whereas equation (25) treats an annual return as the compound return of 12 independent monthly returns. [See Equation (17) on page 95.] While the approximation can be used for "back of the envelope" calculations, the exact formula should be used in applications of quantitative analysis. For example, when forming inputs for mean-variance optimization. Note that both the exact formula and the approximation assume that there is no monthly autocorrelation.

Volatility of the Markets

The volatility of stocks and long-term government bonds is shown by the bar graphs of monthly returns in Graph 6-1. The stock market was tremendously volatile in the first few years studied; this period was marked by the 1920s boom, the crash of 1929–1932, and the Great Depression years. The market settled after World War II and provided more stable returns in the postwar period. In the 1970s and 1980s, stock market volatility increased, but not to the extreme levels of the 1920s and 1930s, with the exception of October 1987. In the 1990s to date, volatility has been moderate.

[4] The equation appears in Haim Levy and Deborah Gunthorpe, "Optimal Investment Proportions in Senior Securities and Equities Under Alternative Holding Periods," *Journal of Portfolio Management*, Summer 1993, page 33.

Graph 6-1 **Month-by-Month Returns on Stocks**

From 1925 to 1998

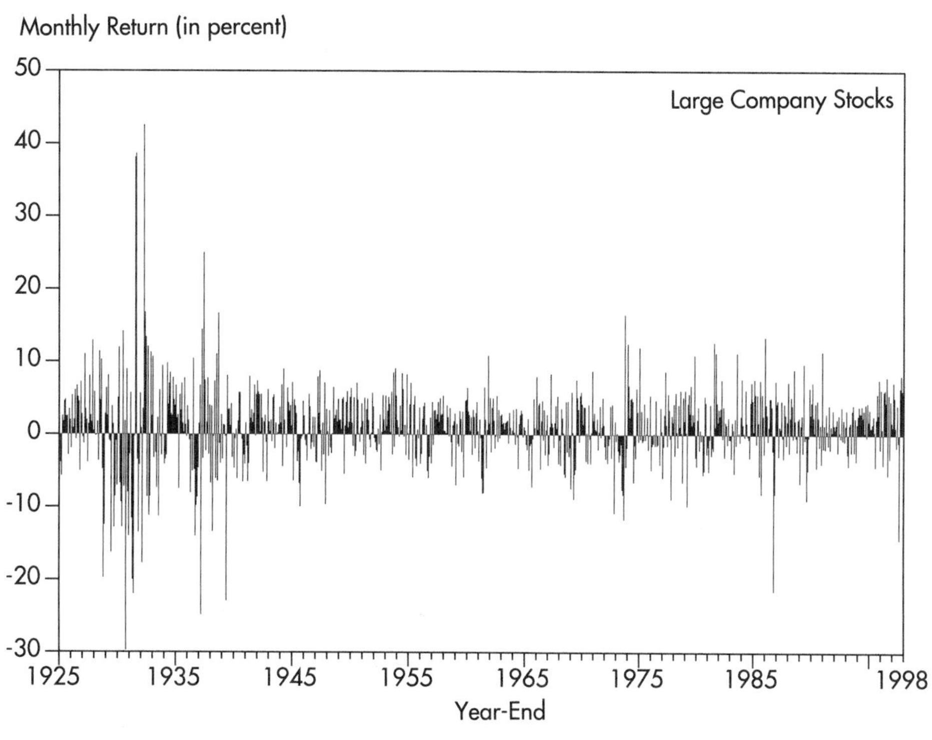

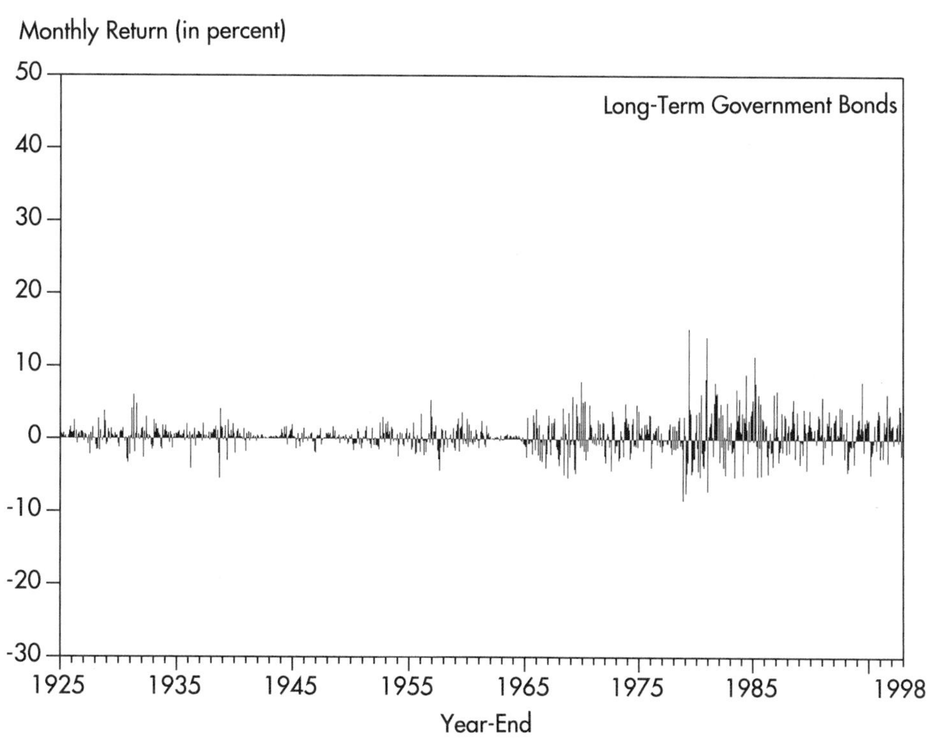

Bonds present a mirror image. Long-term government bonds were extremely stable in the 1920s and remained so through the crisis years of the 1930s, providing shelter from the storms of the stock markets. Starting in the late 1960s and early 1970s, however, bond volatility soared; in the 1973–1974 stock market decline, bonds did not provide the shelter they once did. Bond pessimism (*i.e.*, high yields) peaked in 1981 and subsequent returns were sharply positive. While the astronomical interest rates of the 1979–1981 period have passed, the volatility of the bond market remains higher.

Changes in the Risk of Assets Over Time

Table 6-1 Annualized Monthly Standard Deviations by Decade

	1920s*	1930s	1940s	1950s	1960s	1970s	1980s	1990s**	1989-98
Large Company	23.9%	41.6%	17.5%	14.1%	13.1%	17.1%	19.4%	15.9%	15.9%
Small Company	24.7	78.6	34.5	14.4	21.5	30.8	22.5	19.6	18.9
Long-Term Corp	1.8	5.3	1.8	4.4	4.9	8.7	14.1	7.0	7.0
Long-Term Govt	4.1	5.3	2.8	4.6	6.0	8.7	16.0	9.1	9.1
Inter-Term Govt	1.7	3.3	1.2	2.9	3.3	5.2	8.8	4.7	4.8
Treasury Bills	0.3	0.2	0.1	0.2	0.4	0.6	0.9	0.4	0.5
Inflation	2.0	2.5	3.1	1.2	0.7	1.2	1.3	0.7	0.7

* Based on the period 1926–1929.
** Based on the period 1990–1998.

Another time series property of great interest is change in volatility or riskiness over time. Such change is indicated by the standard deviation of the series over different subperiods. Table 6-1 shows the annualized monthly standard deviations of the basic data series by decade beginning in 1926 and illustrates differences and changes in return volatility. In this table, the '20s cover the period 1926–1929 and the '90s cover the period 1990–1998. Equity returns have been the most volatile of the basic series, with volatility peaking in the 1930s due to the instability of the market following the 1929 market crash. The significant bond yield fluctuations of the '80s caused the fixed income series' volatility to soar compared to prior decades.

The standard deviation of a series for a particular year is the standard deviation of the 12 monthly returns for that year (around that year's arithmetic mean). This monthly estimate is then annualized according to equation (25). Table 6-2 displays the annualized standard deviation of the monthly returns on each of the basic and derived series from 1926 to 1998. The estimates in this table and in Table 6-1 are not strictly comparable to Table 2-1 and Table 6-7 and 6-8, where the 73-year period standard deviation of *annual* returns (around the 73-year annual arithmetic mean) was reported. The arithmetic mean drifts for a series that does not follow a random pattern. A series with a drifting mean will have much higher deviations around its long-term mean than it has around the mean during a particular calendar year.

As shown in Table 6-2, large company stocks and equity risk premia have virtually the same annualized monthly standard deviations because there is very little deviation in the U.S. Treasury bill series. These two series also have much higher variability in the pre-World War II period than in the postwar period. On the other hand, the various bond series (long- and intermediate-term government bonds, long-term corporate bonds, horizon premia, and default premia) were quite volatile in the Great Depression and then more so recently.

The series with drifting means (U.S. Treasury bills, inflation rates, and inflation-adjusted U.S. Treasury bills) all tend to have very low annualized monthly standard deviations, since these series are quite predictable from month to month. As seen in Tables 6-7 and 6-8, however, there is much less predictability for these series over the long term. Since it is difficult to forecast the direction and magnitude of the drift in the long-term mean, these series have higher standard deviations over the long term in comparison to their annualized monthly standard deviations.

Correlation Coefficients: Serial and Cross-Correlations

The behavior of an asset return series over time reveals its predictability. For example, a series may be random or unpredictable; or it may be subject to trends, cycles, or other patterns, making the series predictable to some degree. The serial correlation coefficient of a series determines its predictability given knowledge of the last observation. The cross-correlation coefficient (often shortened to "correlation") between two series determines the predictability of one series, conditional on knowledge of the other.

Serial Correlations

The serial correlation, also known as the first-order autocorrelation, of a return series describes the extent to which the return in one period is related to the return in the next period. A return series with a high (near one) serial correlation is very predictable from one period to the next, while one with a low (near zero) serial correlation is random and unpredictable.

Table 6-2 **Basic and Derived Series**

Annualized Monthly Standard Deviations

(in percent)

From 1926 to 1970

	Basic Series							Derived Series				
Year	Large Company Stocks	Small Company Stocks	Long-Term Corp Bonds	Long-Term Govt Bonds	Inter-mediate Term-Govt Bonds	U.S. Treasury Bills	Inflation	Equity Risk Premia	Small Stock Premia	Bond Default Premia	Bond Horizon Premia	Inflation-Adjusted T-Bills
1926	13.10	16.89	0.96	1.88	1.02	0.32	2.03	12.73	9.74	1.63	1.68	2.06
1927	17.90	21.19	1.49	2.88	1.05	0.11	2.78	17.35	11.13	2.90	2.76	3.03
1928	24.62	28.68	1.87	3.21	1.27	0.32	1.72	23.65	14.48	2.74	3.06	1.84
1929	30.55	18.35	2.42	6.56	2.82	0.21	1.62	29.16	7.76	6.79	6.20	1.62
1930	21.19	25.55	2.38	2.34	2.43	0.30	2.03	20.65	11.68	2.45	2.12	2.31
1931	30.04	45.35	5.91	5.24	3.72	0.16	1.35	29.72	27.44	5.25	5.18	1.75
1932	83.36	147.23	7.71	9.50	2.94	0.29	1.74	82.72	41.92	12.69	9.35	2.40
1933	99.82	286.56	11.74	5.11	3.70	0.10	4.24	99.27	72.06	7.67	5.06	4.15
1934	22.64	73.85	3.10	4.50	4.07	0.04	2.03	22.59	42.03	2.52	4.46	1.94
1935	23.73	36.09	2.53	2.88	2.78	0.01	2.18	23.69	15.08	1.36	2.88	2.05
1936	19.06	66.23	1.18	2.25	1.27	0.02	1.55	19.02	37.72	1.78	2.25	1.51
1937	16.33	21.81	1.99	5.04	2.44	0.05	1.74	16.28	16.46	3.93	5.01	1.63
1938	58.87	114.31	2.38	2.35	2.48	0.07	1.78	58.85	30.94	1.89	2.31	1.89
1939	31.09	95.06	5.36	8.59	5.06	0.02	2.26	31.07	43.55	8.40	8.59	2.24
1940	25.56	46.88	2.02	5.20	3.25	0.02	1.09	25.55	25.68	3.92	5.19	1.07
1941	12.95	29.10	1.67	3.71	1.50	0.03	2.30	12.92	20.75	3.59	3.70	1.90
1942	17.67	37.55	0.73	1.42	0.79	0.03	1.39	17.60	25.78	1.16	1.42	1.17
1943	19.59	71.56	0.90	0.65	0.51	0.01	2.35	19.53	33.94	0.58	0.65	2.21
1944	9.30	28.75	1.34	0.37	0.29	0.01	0.97	9.27	15.14	1.11	0.37	0.94
1945	17.64	37.50	1.42	2.97	0.50	0.01	1.32	17.59	16.92	1.92	2.96	1.26
1946	17.72	27.25	2.15	2.73	0.94	0.00	6.65	17.65	12.20	1.74	2.72	4.66
1947	10.15	18.24	2.13	2.86	0.52	0.07	3.34	10.09	10.58	3.26	2.90	2.79
1948	21.49	24.11	2.20	1.95	0.59	0.07	2.90	21.30	6.44	1.92	1.96	2.73
1949	12.02	18.75	2.17	1.83	0.47	0.02	1.63	11.89	6.72	2.44	1.80	1.71
1950	13.99	20.58	1.07	1.45	0.34	0.03	1.81	13.83	8.82	1.35	1.44	1.62
1951	15.04	16.02	3.92	3.03	1.91	0.05	1.79	14.80	6.12	2.67	2.95	1.63
1952	13.32	9.66	2.85	3.24	1.32	0.08	1.15	13.11	3.78	3.82	3.23	1.14
1953	9.32	10.90	5.53	5.16	3.26	0.11	1.01	9.21	8.74	3.50	5.07	0.95
1954	19.27	20.02	2.35	3.47	1.93	0.06	0.74	19.08	10.08	2.32	3.42	0.77
1955	16.11	7.70	2.17	3.60	1.65	0.14	0.67	15.91	8.83	2.36	3.47	0.71
1956	15.86	8.39	3.00	4.28	2.64	0.10	1.08	15.50	7.87	2.60	4.15	1.00
1957	11.48	10.42	9.40	8.26	5.57	0.07	0.66	11.13	9.98	5.48	8.00	0.65
1958	8.74	15.44	4.56	6.29	4.50	0.27	0.90	8.47	7.99	3.73	6.16	0.88
1959	8.91	10.34	3.91	3.25	2.72	0.18	0.65	8.67	7.31	3.35	3.18	0.59
1960	13.63	13.37	3.93	6.45	4.99	0.27	0.71	13.36	7.07	3.85	6.22	0.80
1961	11.16	19.02	3.63	3.55	1.57	0.07	0.51	10.94	7.72	3.93	3.51	0.50
1962	18.97	21.58	2.27	3.70	2.15	0.08	0.67	18.46	8.38	2.17	3.63	0.70
1963	11.91	13.47	1.25	0.72	0.60	0.08	0.55	11.54	7.26	1.28	0.72	0.55
1964	4.63	7.05	1.46	0.91	0.78	0.06	0.41	4.47	3.78	1.84	0.87	0.38
1965	9.56	20.55	1.96	1.51	1.83	0.08	0.67	9.26	11.19	1.09	1.47	0.64
1966	9.96	17.80	4.80	8.08	4.13	0.11	0.71	9.50	13.76	5.39	7.66	0.73
1967	14.89	36.96	7.33	6.58	3.81	0.16	0.44	14.24	17.30	5.14	6.27	0.54
1968	14.49	28.29	7.39	7.93	3.50	0.09	0.42	13.76	16.40	3.57	7.52	0.40
1969	12.10	18.71	6.93	9.95	5.54	0.22	0.62	11.35	9.73	7.39	9.34	0.63
1970	21.60	27.68	11.28	15.07	7.05	0.22	0.44	20.33	13.19	9.22	14.11	0.47

Table 6-2 **Basic and Derived Series** (continued)

Annualized Monthly Standard Deviations (in percent)

From 1971 to 1998

	Basic Series							Derived Series				
Year	Large Company Stocks	Small Company Stocks	Long-Term Corp Bonds	Long-Term Govt Bonds	Intermediate Term-Govt Bonds	U.S. Treasury Bills	Inflation	Equity Risk Premia	Small Stock Premia	Bond Default Premia	Bond Horizon Premia	Inflation-Adjusted T-Bills
1971	15.64	29.73	11.12	10.67	6.98	0.19	0.57	14.97	14.61	6.12	10.15	0.63
1972	7.80	16.60	3.21	5.85	1.97	0.17	0.41	7.51	11.39	3.97	5.61	0.42
1973	12.15	21.94	7.57	8.38	4.99	0.37	1.53	11.27	14.21	5.12	7.71	1.34
1974	18.74	20.15	11.45	8.64	5.73	0.36	0.91	17.52	22.03	5.76	8.05	0.89
1975	24.38	46.28	11.49	9.13	5.68	0.21	0.78	23.00	19.98	4.43	8.55	0.77
1976	16.89	50.83	5.21	5.43	4.24	0.13	0.48	16.00	27.53	1.55	5.15	0.45
1977	8.97	17.05	4.57	5.69	2.73	0.19	0.77	8.49	13.33	1.56	5.41	0.85
1978	17.92	42.56	4.45	4.45	2.07	0.36	0.67	16.75	26.56	1.66	4.21	0.78
1979	15.79	34.71	10.43	10.81	7.31	0.29	0.53	14.28	15.64	2.16	9.77	0.60
1980	24.19	39.80	20.12	21.16	16.77	0.98	1.45	22.26	14.54	4.57	18.60	1.18
1981	12.44	21.37	20.21	23.25	11.84	0.51	1.15	10.85	16.03	5.23	20.23	1.00
1982	23.38	21.97	17.80	14.40	8.91	0.78	1.64	21.57	7.84	5.37	13.37	1.42
1983	12.02	21.83	10.86	11.43	5.72	0.18	0.73	11.13	14.33	3.98	10.52	0.67
1984	15.00	14.57	12.97	13.34	7.17	0.34	0.61	13.63	4.37	1.92	11.97	0.61
1985	15.85	18.10	13.28	15.78	6.69	0.18	0.33	14.66	6.42	2.56	14.56	0.35
1986	21.39	15.49	9.71	21.58	6.53	0.20	1.03	20.12	6.61	9.54	20.26	1.17
1987	34.04	34.45	9.67	10.09	4.93	0.23	0.68	32.38	11.21	3.03	9.49	0.64
1988	11.69	16.08	9.10	11.03	5.00	0.36	0.57	11.07	11.14	2.45	10.45	0.64
1989	16.03	11.65	7.13	9.53	6.07	0.23	0.63	14.80	6.87	2.36	8.73	0.67
1990	18.25	16.85	7.55	9.89	4.75	0.18	1.16	16.92	6.83	2.67	9.18	1.16
1991	20.49	22.50	5.08	7.33	3.49	0.17	0.54	19.40	9.75	2.13	6.99	0.51
1992	7.91	21.58	5.77	7.62	5.83	0.14	0.54	7.68	19.95	2.32	7.38	0.53
1993	6.69	11.43	5.53	8.38	4.44	0.05	0.57	6.52	8.37	2.38	8.15	0.57
1994	10.74	10.38	6.70	8.12	4.50	0.24	0.47	10.31	6.35	2.27	7.77	0.62
1995	6.95	12.65	7.37	9.70	3.94	0.13	0.60	6.63	8.39	1.88	9.11	0.64
1996	13.29	21.06	7.62	9.33	3.89	0.09	0.61	12.67	15.16	2.14	8.87	0.62
1997	21.08	22.13	8.00	10.44	4.10	0.13	0.53	19.99	16.40	2.30	9.91	0.60
1998	27.90	25.76	5.91	7.70	4.63	0.16	0.30	26.69	6.81	4.35	7.24	0.31

The serial correlation of a series is closely approximated by the equation for the cross-correlation between two series, which is given in equation (26) below. The data, however, are the series and its "lagged" self. For example, the lagged series is the series of one-period-old returns:

Return Year	Return Series (X)	Lagge Series (Y)
1	0.10	undefined
2	-0.10	0.10
3	0.15	-0.10
4	0.00	0.15

Cross-Correlations

The cross-correlation between two series measures the extent to which they are linearly related.[5] The correlation coefficient measures the sensitivity of returns on one asset class or portfolio to the returns of another. The correlation equation between return series X and Y is:

$$\rho_{X,Y} = \left[\frac{\text{Cov}(X,Y)}{\sigma_X \sigma_Y}\right] \quad (26)$$

where,

Cov (X,Y) = the covariance of X and Y, defined below;

σ_X = the standard deviation of X; and,

σ_Y = the standard deviation of Y.

The covariance equation is:

$$\textbf{Cov (X, Y)} = \frac{1}{n-1}\sum_{t=1}^{n}(r_{X,t} - r_{X,A})(r_{Y,t} - r_{Y,A}) \quad (27)$$

where,

$r_{X,t}$ = the return for series X in period t;

$r_{Y,t}$ = the return for series Y in period t;

$r_{X,A}$ = the arithmetic mean of series X;

$r_{Y,A}$ = the arithmetic mean of series Y; and,

n = the number of periods.

[5] Two series can be related in a non-linear way and have a correlation coefficient of zero. An example is the function $y = x^2$, for which $\rho_{x,y} = 0$.

Correlations of the Basic Series

Table 6-3 presents the annual cross-correlations and serial correlations for the seven basic series. Long-term government and long-term corporate bond returns are highly correlated with each other but negatively correlated with inflation. Since the inflation was largely unanticipated, it had a negative effect on fixed income securities. In addition, U.S. Treasury bills and inflation are reasonably highly correlated, a result of the post-1951 "tracking" described in Chapter 2. Lastly, both the U.S. Treasury bills and inflation series display high serial correlations.

Correlations of the Derived Series

The annual cross-correlations and serial correlations for the four risk premium series and inflation are presented in Table 6-4. These correlations reveal that the small stock premia and bond default premia (each of which is a premium for "economy" risk) are significantly correlated with equity risk premia. With one exception, the remaining series are independent of one another, having cross-correlations that do not differ from zero at the 5 percent statistical significance level. The exception is inflation that is negatively correlated with the horizon premium. Increasing inflation causes long-term bond yields to rise and prices to fall; therefore, a negative horizon premium is observed in times of rising inflation.

Table 6-5 presents annual cross-correlations and serial correlations for the inflation-adjusted asset return series. It is interesting to observe how the relationship between the asset returns are substantially different when these returns are expressed in inflation-adjusted terms (as compared with nominal terms). In general, the cross-correlations between asset classes are *higher* when one accounts for inflation (*i.e.*, subtracts inflation from the nominal returns).

Serial Correlation in the Derived Series: Trends or Random Behavior?

The risk/return relationships in the historical data are represented in the equity risk premia, the small stock premia, the bond horizon premia, and the bond default premia. The real/nominal historical relationships are represented in the inflation rates and the real interest rates. The objective is to uncover whether each series is random or is subject to any trends, cycles, or other patterns.

The one-year serial correlation coefficients measure the degree of correlation between returns from each year and the previous year for the same series. Highly positive (near 1) serial correlations indicate trends, while highly negative (near - 1) serial correlations indicate cycles. There is strong evidence that both inflation rates and real riskless rates follow trends. Serial correlations near zero suggest no patterns (*i.e.*, random behavior); equity risk premia and bond horizon premia are random variables. Small stock premia and bond default premia fall into a middle range where it cannot be determined that they either

Table 6-3 **Basic Series**

Serial and Cross Correlations of Historical Annual Returns

From 1926 to 1998

Series	Large Company Stocks	Small Company Stocks	Long-Term Corp. Bonds	Long-Term Gov't Bonds	Inter-mediate Gov't Bonds	U.S. Treasury Bills	Inflation
Large Company Stocks	1.00						
Small company Stocks	0.79	1.00					
Long-Term Corporate Bonds	0.26	0.11	1.00				
Long-Term Government Bonds	0.20	0.03	0.94	1.00			
Intermediate-Term Government Bonds	0.11	-0.03	0.90	0.90	1.00		
U.S. Treasury Bills	-0.03	-0.10	0.22	0.25	0.50	1.00	
Inflation	-0.03	0.05	-0.16	-0.15	0.01	0.41	1.00
Serial Correlations*	0.01	0.09	0.10	-0.01	0.18	0.92	0.65

* The standard error for all estimates is 0.12

Table 6-4 **Risk Premia and Inflation**

Serial and Cross Correlations of Historical Annual Returns

From 1926 to 1998

Series	**Equity Risk Premia**	**Small Stock Premia**	**Default Premia**	**Horizon Premia**	**Inflation**
Equity Risk Premia	1.00				
Small Stock Premia	0.33	1.00			
Default Premia	0.16	0.15	1.00		
Horizon Premia	0.22	-0.08	-0.33	1.00	
Inflation	-0.09	0.13	0.00	-0.30	1.00
Serial Correlations*	0.01	0.39	-0.29	-0.07	0.65

* The standard error for all estimates is 0.12

Table 6-5 **Inflation-Adjusted Series**

Serial and Cross Correlations of Historical Annual Returns

From 1926 to 1998

	Inflation-Adjusted						
Series	Large Company Stocks	Small Company Stocks	Long-Term Corp. Bonds	Long-Term Gov't Bonds	Inter-mediate Gov't Bonds	T-Bills (Real Interest Rates)	Inflation
Inflation-Adjusted Large Company Stocks	1.00						
Inflation-Adjusted Small Company Stocks	0.79	1.00					
Inflation-Adjusted Long-Term Corporate Bonds	0.32	0.13	1.00				
Inflation-Adjusted Long-Term Government Bonds	0.27	0.06	0.96	1.00			
Inflation-Adjusted Intermediate-Term Government Bonds	0.21	0.01	0.94	0.94	1.00		
Inflation-Adjusted Treasury Bills (Real interest Rates)	0.12	-0.06	0.60	0.60	0.74	1.00	
Inflation	-0.23	-0.08	-0.54	-0.54	-0.62	-0.75	1.00
Serial Correlations*	0.00	0.05	0.21	0.07	0.25	0.67	0.65

* The standard error for all estimates is 0.12

follow a trend or behave randomly, although the serial correlation of annual small stock premia is high enough to suggest a trend.

Each of the component series' serial correlations can be interpreted as following a random pattern, trend or uncertain path, as given in Table 6-6.

Table 6-6 Interpretation of the Annual Serial Correlations

Series	Serial Correlation	Interpretation
Equity Risk Premia	.01	Random
Small Stock Premia	.39	Likely Trend
Bond Default Premia	-.29	Possible Cycle
Bond Horizon Premia	-.07	Random
Inflation Rates	.65	Trend
Real Interest Rates	.67	Trend

Summary Statistics for Basic and Inflation-Adjusted Series

Table 6-7 presents summary statistics of annual total returns, and where applicable, income and capital appreciation, for each asset class. The summary statistics presented here are arithmetic mean, geometric mean, standard deviation, and serial correlation. Table 6-8 presents summary statistics for the six inflation-adjusted total return series.

Highlights of the Summary Statistics

Table 6-7 shows that over 1926–1998 small company stocks were the riskiest asset class with a standard deviation of 33.8 percent, but provide the greatest rewards to long-term investors, with an arithmetic mean annual return of 17.4 percent. The geometric mean of the small stock series is 12.4 percent. Large company stocks, long-term government bonds, long-term corporate bonds, and intermediate-term government bonds are progressively less risky, and have correspondingly lower average returns. An exception to this general pattern are intermediate-term government bonds, which outreturned long-term government bonds due to the rise in bond yields over the period. Treasury bills were nearly riskless and had the lowest return. In general, risk is rewarded by a higher return over the long term.

Inflation-adjusted basic series summary statistics are presented in Table 6-8. Note that the real rate of interest is close to zero (0.7 percent) on average. For the 73-year period, the geometric and arithmetic means are lower by the amount of inflation than those of the nominal series.

Table 6-7 **Total Returns, Income Returns, and Capital Appreciation of the Basic Asset Classes**

Summary Statistics of Annual Returns

From 1926 to 1998

Series	Geometric Mean	Arithmetic Mean	Standard Deviation	Serial Correlation
Large Company Stocks				
Total Returns	11.2%	13.2%	20.3%	0.01
Income	4.5	4.5	1.4	0.84
Capital Appreciation	6.5	8.4	19.6	0.01
Small Company Stocks				
Total Returns	12.4	17.4	33.8	0.09
Long-Term Corporate Bonds				
Total Returns	5.8	6.1	8.6	0.10
Long-Term Government Bonds				
Total Returns	5.3	5.7	9.2	-0.01
Income	5.2	5.2	2.9	0.97
Capital Appreciation	0.0	0.3	8.0	-0.17
Intermediate-Term Government Bonds				
Total Returns	5.3	5.5	5.7	0.18
Income	4.8	4.8	3.0	0.96
Capital Appreciation	0.4	0.5	4.4	-0.19
Treasury Bills				
Total Returns	3.8	3.8	3.2	0.92
Inflation	3.1	3.2	4.5	0.65

Total return is equal to the sum of three component returns; income return, capital appreciation return, and reinvestment return. Annual reinvestment returns for select asset classes are provided in Table 2-6.

Table 6-8 **Inflation-Adjusted Series** Summary Statistics of Annual Returns

From 1926 to 1998

Series	Geometric Mean	Arithmetic Mean	Standard Deviation	Serial Correlation
Inflation-Adjusted Large Company Stocks	7.9%	9.9%	20.4%	0.00
Inflation-Adjusted Small Company Stocks	9.1	13.9	33.1	0.05
Inflation-Adjusted Long-Term Corporate Bonds	2.6	3.1	9.9	0.21
Inflation-Adjusted Long-Term-Government Bonds	2.2	2.7	10.5	0.07
Inflation-Adjusted Intermediate-Term Government Bonds	2.2	2.4	7.0	0.25
Inflation-Adjusted U.S. Treasury Bills (Real Riskless Rates of Returns)	0.7	0.8	4.1	0.67

The standard deviations of large company stock and small company stock returns remain approximately the same after adjusting for inflation, while inflation-adjusted bonds and bills are more volatile (*i.e.*, have higher standard deviations).

Rolling Period Standard Deviations

Rolling period standard deviations are obtained by rolling a view window of fixed length along each time series and computing the standard deviation for the asset class for each window of time. They are useful for examining the volatility or riskiness of returns for holding periods similar to those actually experienced by investors. Graph 6-2 graphically depicts the volatility. Monthly data are used to maximize the number of data points included in the standard deviation computation.

The upper graph places the five-year rolling standard deviation for large company stocks, small company stocks, and long-term government bonds on the same scale. It is interesting to see the relatively high standard deviation for small company stocks and large company stocks in the 1930s, with an apparent lessening of volatility for five year holding periods during the 1980s. Note also how the standard deviation for long-term government bonds increases and exceeds that for both common stock asset classes during part of the 1980s.

The lower graph places the five-year rolling standard deviation for long- and intermediate-term government bonds, and Treasury bills on the same scale.

Rolling Period Correlations

Rolling period correlations are obtained by moving a view window of fixed length along time series for two asset classes and computing the cross-correlation between the two asset classes for each window of time. They are useful for examining how asset class returns vary together for holding periods similar to those actually experienced by investors. Monthly data are used to maximize the number of data points included in the correlation computation.

Graph 6-3 shows cross correlations between two asset classes for five year (60 months of monthly data) holding periods. The first rolling period covered is January 1926-December 1930 so the graphs begin at December 1930. The top graph shows the volatility of the correlations between large company stocks and long-term government bonds. There are wide fluctuations between strong positive and strong negative correlations over the past 73 years.

The lower graph shows the correlation between Treasury bills and inflation. While there were seom wide fluctuations during the 1930s and 1940s, the correlation has generally been positive since the mid-1960s.

Graph 6-2 **Rolling 60-Month Standard Deviation**

Small Company Stocks,
Large Company Stocks,
Long-Term Government Bonds, and
Treasury Bills

From January 1926-December 1930 to January 1992-December 1998

Small Company Stocks, Large Company Stocks, Long-Term Government Bonds

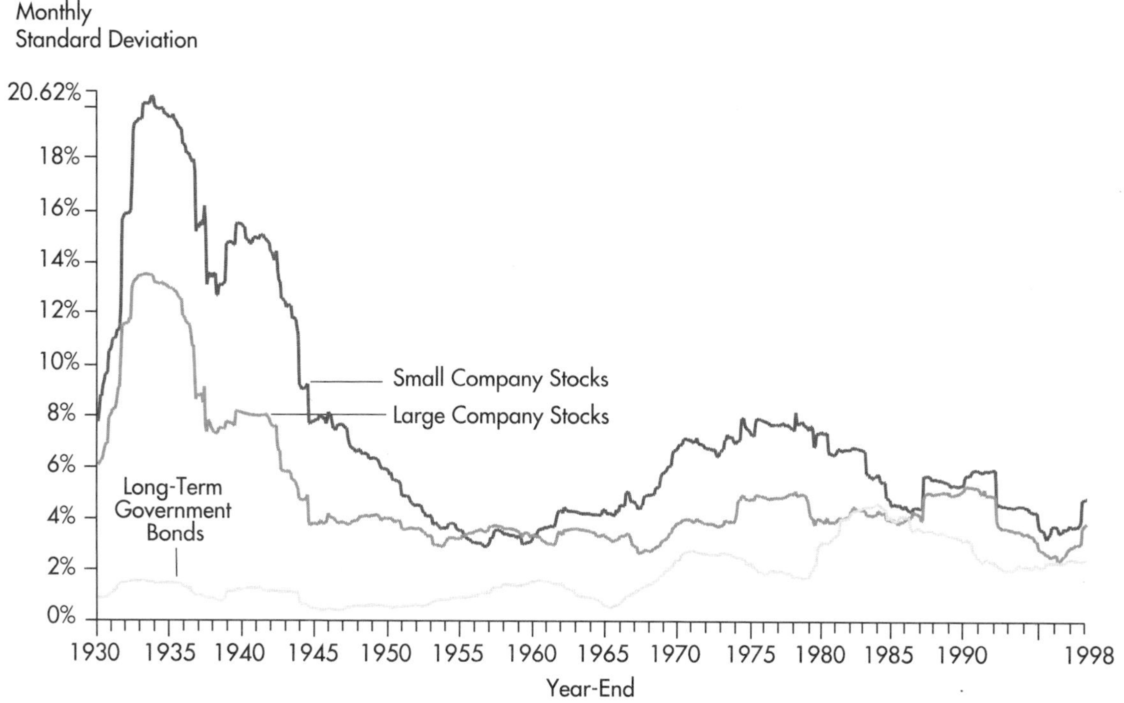

Long-Term Gov't Bonds, Intermediate-Term Gov't Bonds, Treasury Bills

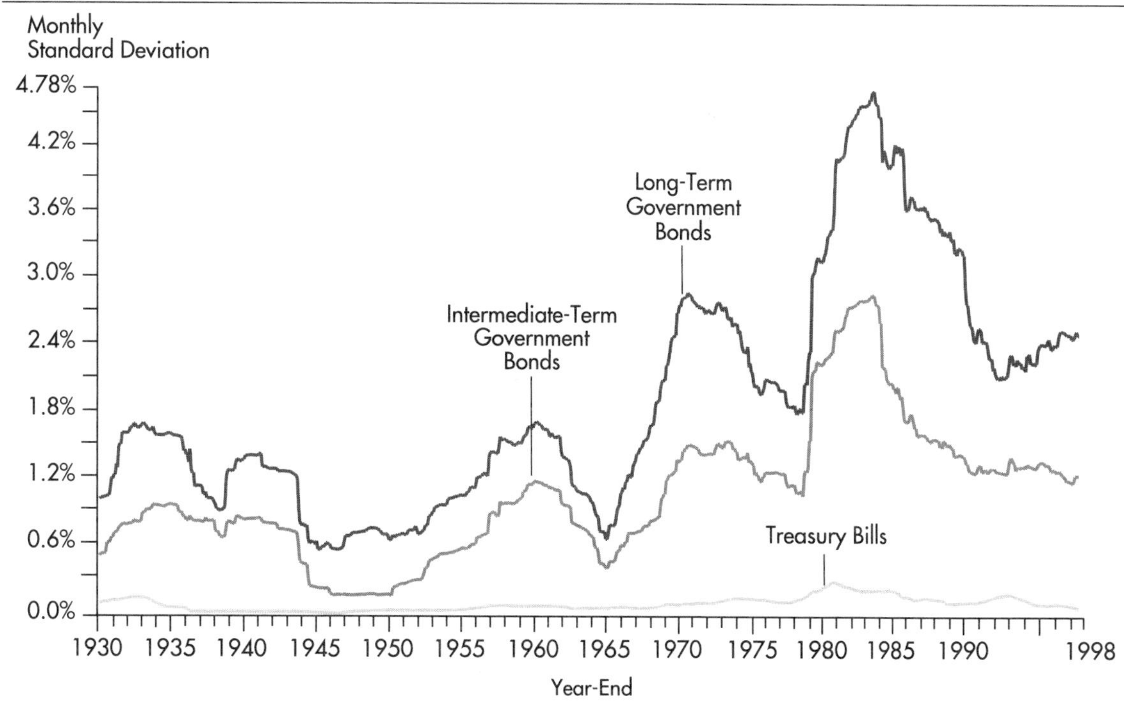

Graph 6-3 **Rolling 60-Month Correlations**

Large Company Stocks and Long-Term Government Bonds, and Treasury Bills and Inflation

From January 1926-December 1930 to January 1992-December 1998

Large Company Stocks and Long-Term Government Bonds

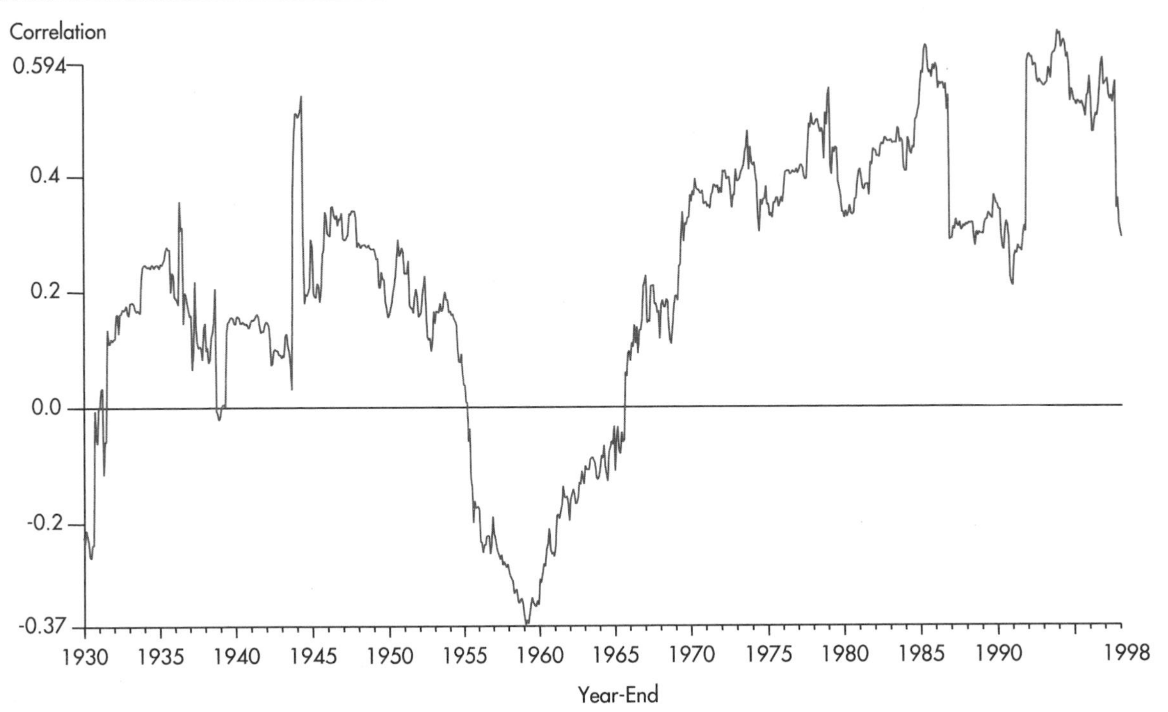

Treasury Bills and Inflation

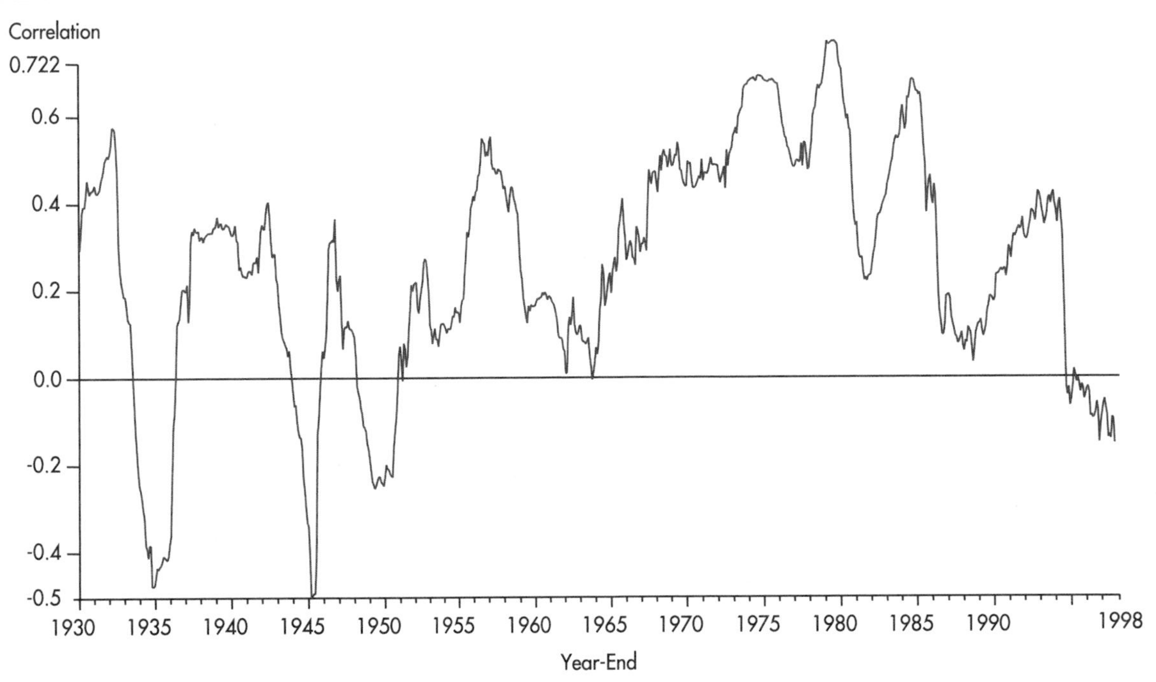

Chapter 7 Firm Size and Return

The Firm Size Phenomenon

One of the most remarkable discoveries of modern finance is the finding of a relationship between firm size and return.[6] On average, small companies have higher returns than large ones. Earlier chapters document this phenomenon for the smallest stocks on the New York Stock Exchange (NYSE). The relationship between firm size and return cuts across the entire size spectrum; it is not restricted to the smallest stocks. In this chapter, the returns across the entire range of firm size are examined.

Construction of the Decile Portfolios

The portfolios used in this chapter are those created by the Center for Research in Security Prices (CRSP) at the University of Chicago's Graduate School of Business. CRSP has refined the methodology of creating size-based portfolios and has applied this methodology to the entire universe of NYSE listed securities going back to 1926.

In 1993, CRSP changed the method used to construct these portfolios, thereby causing the return and index values in Table 7-2 and 7-3 to be significantly different from those reported in previous editions of the *Yearbook*. Previously, some eligible companies had been excluded or delayed from inclusion when the portfolios were reformed at the end of each calendar quarter.

The New York Stock Exchange universe is restricted by excluding closed-end mutual funds, real estate investment trusts, foreign stocks, American Depository Receipts, unit investment trusts, and Americus Trusts. All companies on the NYSE are ranked by the combined market capitalization of all their eligible equity securities. The companies are then split into 10 equally populated groups or deciles. The portfolios are rebalanced using closing prices for the last trading day of March, June, September, and December. Securities added during the quarter are assigned to the appropriate portfolio when two consecutive month-end prices are available. For securities that become delisted, when the last NYSE price is a month-end price, that month's return is included in the portfolio's quarterly return. When a month-end NYSE price is missing, the month-end value is derived from merger terms, quotations on regional exchanges, and other sources. If a month-end value is not available, the last available daily price is used.

Base security returns are monthly holding period returns. All distributions are added to the month-end prices. Appropriate adjustments are made to prices to account for stock splits and dividends. The return on a portfolio for one month is calculated as the weighted average of the returns for the

[6] Rolf W. Banz was the first to document this phenomenon. See Banz, Rolf W., "The Relationship Between Returns and Market Value of Common Stocks," *Journal of Financial Economics*, Vol. 9 (1981), pp. 3–18.

individual stocks in the portfolio. Annual portfolio returns are calculated by compounding the monthly portfolio returns.

Aspects of the Firm Size Effect

The firm size phenomenon is remarkable in several ways. First, the greater risk of small stocks does not, in the context of the Capital Asset Pricing Model, fully account for their higher returns over the long term. In the CAPM, only systematic or beta risk is rewarded. Small company stocks have had returns in excess of those implied by the betas of small stocks. Secondly, the calendar annual return differences between small and large companies are serially correlated. This suggests that past annual returns may be of some value in predicting future annual returns. Such serial correlation, or autocorrelation, is practically unknown in the market for large stocks and in most other capital markets.

In addition, the firm size effect is seasonal. For example, small company stocks outperformed large company stocks in the month of January in a large majority of the years. Again, such predictability is surprising and suspicious in the light of modern capital market theory. These three aspects of the firm size effect (long-term returns in excess of risk, serial correlation and seasonality) will be analyzed after the data are presented.

Presentation of the Decile Data

Summary statistics of annual returns of the 10 deciles over 1926–1998 are presented in Table 7-1. Note from this exhibit that the average return tends to increase as one moves from the largest decile to the smallest. (Because securities are ranked quarterly, returns on the ninth and tenth deciles are different than those suggested by the small company stock index presented in earlier chapters. The inclusion of American Stock Exchange and over-the-counter data in the small company stock index beginning in 1982 is also partly responsible for these differences. A detailed methodology for the small company stock index is included in Chapter 3.) The total risk, or standard deviation of annual returns, also increases with decreasing firm size. The serial correlations of returns are near zero for all but the smallest three deciles.

Table 7-2 gives the year-by-year history of the returns for the different size categories. Table 7-3 shows the growth of $1.00 invested in each of the categories as of year-end 1925.

The sheer magnitude of the size effect in some years is noteworthy. While the largest stocks actually declined in 1977, the smallest stocks rose more than 15 percent. A more extreme case occurred in the depression-recovery year of 1933, when the difference between the first and tenth decile returns was

Table 7-1 **Size-Decile Portfolios of the NYSE** Summary Statistics of Annual Returns

From 1926 to 1998

Decile	Geometric Mean	Arithmetic Mean	Standard Deviation	Serial Correlation
1-Largest	10.4%	12.1%	18.9%	0.05
2	11.3	13.7	22.2	0.03
3	11.5	14.1	23.9	-0.01
4	11.7	14.8	26.4	-0.01
5	12.1	15.5	27.2	-0.01
6	11.9	15.6	28.2	0.07
7	11.8	16.0	30.6	0.03
8	12.0	17.0	34.4	0.09
9	12.2	17.9	37.0	0.09
10-Smallest	13.1	21.0	45.8	0.18
Mid-Cap 3-5	11.7	14.6	25.1	-0.01
Low-Cap 6-8	12.0	16.0	30.0	0.06
Micro-Cap 9-10	12.6	18.7	39.2	0.12
NYSE Total Value Weighted Index	10.8	12.7	20.1	0.02

Results are for *quarterly* re-ranking for the deciles. The small company stock summary statistics presented in earlier chapters comprise a re-ranking of the portfolios every five years prior to 1982. Moreover, starting in 1982, the small company stock series presented in earlier chapters includes NASDAQ and AMEX stocks; the deciles presented here are constructed entirely from NYSE stocks.

Table 7-2 **Size-Decile Portfolios of the NYSE** Year-by-Year Returns

From 1926 to 1970

	Decile 1	Decile 2	Decile 3	Decile 4	Decile 5	Decile 6	Decile 7	Decile 8	Decile 9	Decile 10
1926	0.1438	0.0545	0.0355	0.0085	0.0033	0.0335	-0.0250	-0.0932	-0.0997	-0.0605
1927	0.3400	0.2957	0.3116	0.4134	0.3467	0.2312	0.3025	0.2553	0.3190	0.3126
1928	0.3889	0.3777	0.3982	0.3736	0.4965	0.2809	0.3530	0.3212	0.3740	0.6974
1929	-0.1056	-0.0793	-0.2569	-0.3177	-0.2448	-0.4044	-0.3769	-0.4082	-0.4993	-0.5359
1930	-0.2422	-0.3747	-0.3465	-0.3418	-0.3627	-0.3781	-0.3661	-0.4951	-0.4570	-0.4567
1931	-0.4215	-0.5011	-0.4600	-0.4569	-0.4865	-0.5102	-0.4787	-0.4907	-0.4908	-0.5010
1932	-0.1196	-0.0100	-0.0137	-0.1333	-0.1144	0.0660	-0.1648	0.0129	-0.0029	0.3843
1933	0.4655	0.7467	1.0331	1.1220	0.9497	1.0972	1.1784	1.5880	1.7361	2.2160
1934	0.0223	0.0569	0.0894	0.1782	0.0753	0.2185	0.1480	0.2776	0.2253	0.3185
1935	0.4078	0.5846	0.3689	0.3702	0.6401	0.5537	0.6466	0.6423	0.6201	0.8212
1936	0.2961	0.3553	0.2857	0.4341	0.4612	0.4999	0.5213	0.4931	0.8344	0.8600
1937	-0.3185	-0.3662	-0.3827	-0.4352	-0.4867	-0.4763	-0.4918	-0.5275	-0.5165	-0.5562
1938	0.2507	0.3455	0.3536	0.3387	0.5054	0.4339	0.3505	0.4541	0.3040	0.0900
1939	0.0472	-0.0346	-0.0253	0.0025	0.0146	0.0386	0.0770	-0.0426	-0.0627	0.1908
1940	-0.0709	-0.0906	-0.0873	-0.0388	-0.0113	-0.0607	-0.0617	-0.0583	-0.0446	-0.3104
1941	-0.1065	-0.0650	-0.0614	-0.0973	-0.1207	-0.1024	-0.0915	-0.0933	-0.1226	-0.1684
1942	0.1308	0.2419	0.1969	0.2056	0.2117	0.2466	0.2892	0.3063	0.4354	0.7740
1943	0.2353	0.3465	0.3449	0.3967	0.4822	0.4254	0.7373	0.7034	0.8559	1.4216
1944	0.1696	0.2627	0.2411	0.3261	0.3951	0.4469	0.3730	0.4935	0.5675	0.6994
1945	0.2914	0.4890	0.5354	0.6345	0.5455	0.6075	0.6412	0.6954	0.7647	0.9507
1946	-0.0448	-0.0459	-0.0748	-0.1312	-0.0974	-0.0669	-0.1563	-0.1463	-0.0995	-0.1837
1947	0.0559	0.0064	-0.0009	0.0188	0.0343	-0.0339	-0.0226	-0.0291	-0.0342	-0.0246
1948	0.0370	0.0057	0.0208	-0.0188	-0.0145	-0.0370	-0.0294	-0.0725	-0.0670	-0.0522
1949	0.1870	0.2517	0.2628	0.1999	0.1872	0.2309	0.2202	0.1615	0.1992	0.2485
1950	0.2864	0.2851	0.2643	0.3172	0.3700	0.3451	0.3700	0.4076	0.4037	0.5571
1951	0.2147	0.2256	0.2187	0.1687	0.1446	0.1414	0.1801	0.1515	0.1128	0.0584
1952	0.1429	0.1303	0.1168	0.1240	0.1108	0.1022	0.0984	0.0839	0.0865	0.0180
1953	0.0110	0.0157	0.0016	-0.0203	-0.0258	-0.0081	-0.0251	-0.0780	-0.0437	-0.0841
1954	0.4844	0.4844	0.5839	0.5101	0.5793	0.5945	0.5725	0.5341	0.6359	0.6853
1955	0.2838	0.1873	0.1893	0.1897	0.1819	0.2304	0.1794	0.2076	0.1972	0.2648
1956	0.0779	0.1160	0.0782	0.0869	0.0845	0.0590	0.0854	0.0478	0.0589	-0.0149
1957	-0.0955	-0.0883	-0.1342	-0.1105	-0.1347	-0.1831	-0.1725	-0.1824	-0.1448	-0.1618
1958	0.4078	0.4959	0.5432	0.5889	0.5616	0.5627	0.6697	0.6648	0.7102	0.6963
1959	0.1322	0.0967	0.1297	0.1505	0.1885	0.1483	0.2103	0.1719	0.1927	0.1552
1960	-0.0007	0.0558	0.0455	0.0085	-0.0115	-0.0147	-0.0552	-0.0428	-0.0377	-0.0824
1961	0.2699	0.2690	0.2919	0.2955	0.2878	0.2733	0.3034	0.3416	0.2988	0.3183
1962	-0.0880	-0.0945	-0.1166	-0.1217	-0.1626	-0.1705	-0.1673	-0.1131	-0.1428	-0.0827
1963	0.2279	0.2100	0.1752	0.1715	0.1294	0.1858	0.1783	0.2152	0.1938	0.1661
1964	0.1605	0.1426	0.2020	0.1768	0.1677	0.1767	0.1587	0.1974	0.1749	0.2576
1965	0.0915	0.1975	0.2477	0.2538	0.2895	0.3597	0.3364	0.3156	0.3452	0.4062
1966	-0.1038	-0.0540	-0.0548	-0.0561	-0.0703	-0.0655	-0.1021	-0.1034	-0.0334	-0.1486
1967	0.2203	0.2154	0.3139	0.4491	0.5366	0.4903	0.6309	0.7364	0.7408	0.8359
1968	0.0738	0.1694	0.1903	0.1824	0.2833	0.3092	0.2728	0.4184	0.3954	0.6610
1969	-0.0575	-0.1316	-0.1085	-0.1676	-0.1710	-0.2040	-0.2573	-0.2486	-0.3323	-0.3112
1970	0.0244	0.0164	0.0343	-0.0446	-0.0462	-0.0157	-0.0484	-0.0742	-0.0341	-0.0657

Source: Center for Research in Security Prices, University of Chicago.

Table 7-2 **Size-Decile Portfolios of the NYSE** Year-by-Year Returns

(continued)

From 1971 to 1998

	Decile 1	Decile 2	Decile 3	Decile 4	Decile 5	Decile 6	Decile 7	Decile 8	Decile 9	Decile 10
1971	0.1495	0.1387	0.1909	0.2470	0.1789	0.2195	0.2015	0.1843	0.1336	0.2087
1972	0.2219	0.1334	0.0940	0.0787	0.0649	0.0454	0.0555	0.0221	0.0347	0.0638
1973	-0.1293	-0.2220	-0.2439	-0.2552	-0.3201	-0.3241	-0.3667	-0.3517	-0.3600	-0.3553
1974	-0.2789	-0.2436	-0.2339	-0.2656	-0.2212	-0.2736	-0.2603	-0.2651	-0.3182	-0.3463
1975	0.3169	0.4627	0.5297	0.6652	0.5883	0.6147	0.6292	0.7526	0.7425	0.7863
1976	0.2088	0.3035	0.3787	0.3977	0.4632	0.4852	0.5393	0.6183	0.5649	0.6036
1977	-0.0867	-0.0445	0.0009	0.0416	0.1051	0.1551	0.1871	0.2084	0.2017	0.2005
1978	0.0633	0.0262	0.1116	0.0807	0.1131	0.1569	0.1539	0.2037	0.1622	0.2618
1979	0.1477	0.2808	0.3140	0.3448	0.3531	0.4183	0.3925	0.4290	0.3992	0.4221
1980	0.3291	0.3250	0.3085	0.3067	0.2998	0.2823	0.3325	0.2568	0.3021	0.2873
1981	-0.0845	0.0140	0.0369	0.0513	0.0707	0.0813	0.0298	0.0807	0.1564	0.1046
1982	0.1977	0.1793	0.2154	0.2694	0.3471	0.3331	0.3565	0.3648	0.3279	0.3335
1983	0.2095	0.1767	0.2709	0.2784	0.3032	0.2962	0.3382	0.4333	0.4658	0.5121
1984	0.0868	0.0854	0.0272	-0.0219	-0.0349	0.0672	-0.0051	-0.0295	0.0134	-0.1145
1985	0.3181	0.3797	0.2924	0.3393	0.3095	0.2802	0.2414	0.2833	0.2882	0.2985
1986	0.1813	0.1971	0.1651	0.1881	0.1711	0.1303	0.0672	0.0983	0.0657	0.0564
1987	0.0503	-0.0197	0.0478	0.0398	-0.0206	-0.0542	-0.1054	-0.0775	-0.0714	-0.1393
1988	0.1468	0.2075	0.2106	0.2577	0.2385	0.2930	0.3235	0.3086	0.1969	0.1733
1989	0.3276	0.3007	0.2615	0.2054	0.2006	0.2295	0.1684	0.0859	0.0817	-0.1351
1990	-0.0054	-0.0799	-0.1094	-0.1005	-0.1171	-0.1896	-0.1536	-0.2348	-0.3249	-0.4705
1991	0.2925	0.3211	0.3674	0.3391	0.4515	0.4691	0.3391	0.3219	0.4469	0.3568
1992	0.0447	0.1599	0.1772	0.1463	0.2659	0.1650	0.1901	0.1369	0.1847	0.3041
1993	0.0708	0.1389	0.1783	0.1633	0.1771	0.1546	0.2280	0.2385	0.1621	0.1772
1994	0.0146	-0.0016	-0.0389	-0.0302	-0.0260	-0.0031	0.0002	0.0017	-0.0273	0.0562
1995	0.3922	0.3481	0.3091	0.2646	0.2779	0.2045	0.2746	0.2598	0.1891	0.2556
1996	0.2150	0.1989	0.1878	0.2461	0.1818	0.1948	0.2656	0.2907	0.2447	0.1435
1997	0.3553	0.3017	0.2528	0.2975	0.2408	0.3234	0.3441	0.3017	0.3558	0.1986
1998	0.2845	0.1075	0.0190	-0.0048	-0.0392	-0.0263	-0.0852	-0.0765	-0.1032	-0.1544

Source: Center for Research in Security Prices, University of Chicago.

Table 7-3 **Size-Decile Portfolios of the NYSE** Year-End Index Values

From 1925 to 1970

	Decile 1	Decile 2	Decile 3	Decile 4	Decile 5	Decile 6	Decile 7	Decile 8	Decile 9	Decile 10
1925	1.000	1.000	1.000	1.000	1.000	1.000	1.000	1.000	1.000	1.000
1926	1.144	1.055	1.036	1.008	1.003	1.033	0.975	0.907	0.900	0.940
1927	1.533	1.366	1.358	1.425	1.351	1.272	1.270	1.138	1.187	1.233
1928	2.129	1.882	1.899	1.958	2.022	1.630	1.718	1.504	1.632	2.093
1929	1.904	1.733	1.411	1.336	1.527	0.971	1.071	0.890	0.817	0.972
1930	1.443	1.084	0.922	0.879	0.973	0.604	0.679	0.449	0.444	0.528
1931	0.835	0.541	0.498	0.478	0.500	0.296	0.354	0.229	0.226	0.263
1932	0.735	0.535	0.491	0.414	0.443	0.315	0.295	0.232	0.225	0.365
1933	1.077	0.935	0.999	0.878	0.863	0.661	0.644	0.600	0.616	1.173
1934	1.101	0.988	1.088	1.035	0.928	0.805	0.739	0.766	0.755	1.546
1935	1.550	1.566	1.489	1.418	1.522	1.251	1.217	1.259	1.223	2.816
1936	2.009	2.122	1.915	2.034	2.223	1.877	1.851	1.879	2.244	5.237
1937	1.369	1.345	1.182	1.149	1.141	0.983	0.941	0.888	1.085	2.324
1938	1.712	1.810	1.600	1.538	1.718	1.409	1.270	1.291	1.415	2.533
1939	1.793	1.747	1.559	1.542	1.743	1.464	1.368	1.236	1.326	3.017
1940	1.666	1.589	1.423	1.482	1.723	1.375	1.284	1.164	1.267	2.081
1941	1.488	1.486	1.336	1.338	1.515	1.234	1.166	1.056	1.112	1.730
1942	1.683	1.845	1.599	1.613	1.836	1.538	1.503	1.379	1.596	3.069
1943	2.079	2.484	2.150	2.252	2.722	2.193	2.612	2.349	2.962	7.432
1944	2.432	3.137	2.669	2.987	3.797	3.173	3.586	3.508	4.642	12.631
1945	3.141	4.671	4.098	4.882	5.868	5.100	5.885	5.947	8.192	24.638
1946	3.000	4.457	3.791	4.241	5.297	4.759	4.965	5.077	7.378	20.112
1947	3.167	4.485	3.787	4.321	5.478	4.597	4.853	4.930	7.126	19.619
1948	3.285	4.511	3.866	4.240	5.399	4.427	4.711	4.572	6.648	18.594
1949	3.899	5.646	4.882	5.087	6.410	5.449	5.748	5.311	7.972	23.214
1950	5.016	7.256	6.173	6.701	8.781	7.330	7.874	7.476	11.191	36.145
1951	6.093	8.893	7.522	7.832	10.051	8.366	9.292	8.608	12.453	38.255
1952	6.963	10.052	8.401	8.804	11.165	9.221	10.207	9.330	13.530	38.944
1953	7.040	10.210	8.414	8.625	10.876	9.147	9.951	8.602	12.938	35.669
1954	10.449	15.155	13.328	13.025	17.177	14.584	15.647	13.197	21.166	60.112
1955	13.415	17.994	15.851	15.496	20.301	17.944	18.455	15.937	25.340	76.032
1956	14.461	20.081	17.091	16.843	22.016	19.002	20.030	16.698	26.832	74.902
1957	13.080	18.308	14.798	14.982	19.051	15.524	16.575	13.653	22.947	62.781
1958	18.413	27.387	22.837	23.804	29.749	24.258	27.675	22.730	39.243	106.497
1959	20.848	30.036	25.799	27.386	35.356	27.856	33.494	26.637	46.805	123.020
1960	20.834	31.712	26.972	27.618	34.951	27.446	31.645	25.497	45.042	112.881
1961	26.456	40.242	34.845	35.778	45.011	34.947	41.245	34.206	58.498	148.816
1962	24.128	36.438	30.784	31.424	37.694	28.989	34.345	30.338	50.147	136.508
1963	29.627	44.090	36.178	36.814	42.573	34.374	40.467	36.867	59.868	159.183
1964	34.384	50.376	43.486	43.322	49.712	40.448	46.890	44.144	70.337	200.197
1965	37.530	60.327	54.259	54.318	64.102	54.997	62.666	58.076	94.620	281.509
1966	33.633	57.069	51.288	51.271	59.595	51.394	56.270	52.072	91.455	239.665
1967	41.041	69.361	67.387	74.297	91.576	76.592	91.772	90.419	159.203	439.997
1968	44.072	81.113	80.212	87.846	117.522	100.277	116.804	128.249	222.149	730.848
1969	41.538	70.441	71.509	73.128	97.422	79.825	86.746	96.366	148.323	503.410
1970	42.551	71.598	73.963	69.864	92.924	78.570	82.543	89.219	143.267	470.324

Source: Center for Research in Security Prices, University of Chicago.

Table 7-3 **Size-Decile Portfolios of the NYSE** Year-End Index Values

(continued)

From 1971 to 1998

	Decile 1	Decile 2	Decile 3	Decile 4	Decile 5	Decile 6	Decile 7	Decile 8	Decile 9	Decile 10
1971	48.910	81.526	88.082	87.118	109.544	95.814	99.180	105.660	162.402	568.466
1972	59.765	92.402	96.365	93.972	116.651	100.168	104.687	107.996	168.036	604.762
1973	52.040	71.889	72.866	69.994	79.307	67.706	66.294	70.015	107.536	389.872
1974	37.527	54.376	55.821	51.402	61.768	49.182	49.036	51.454	73.314	254.854
1975	49.419	79.538	85.391	85.596	98.108	79.414	79.889	90.175	127.750	455.257
1976	59.738	103.677	117.725	119.638	143.550	117.947	122.975	145.931	199.918	730.045
1977	54.562	99.064	117.831	124.611	158.641	136.239	145.982	176.340	240.239	876.430
1978	58.017	101.660	130.987	134.671	176.583	157.610	168.445	212.262	279.217	1105.847
1979	66.583	130.209	172.117	181.105	238.931	223.544	234.567	303.313	390.675	1572.655
1980	88.496	172.531	225.212	236.642	310.573	286.652	312.570	381.199	508.697	2024.528
1981	81.021	174.950	233.524	248.771	332.518	309.945	321.872	411.963	588.244	2236.249
1982	97.042	206.323	283.821	315.801	447.919	413.192	436.633	562.246	781.152	2981.957
1983	117.377	242.785	360.700	403.730	583.713	535.564	584.322	805.884	1145.029	4508.959
1984	127.570	263.511	370.516	394.900	563.317	571.581	581.352	782.097	1160.319	3992.493
1985	168.155	363.561	478.852	528.883	737.674	731.745	721.691	1003.692	1494.702	5184.219
1986	198.649	435.209	557.914	628.363	863.911	827.102	770.197	1102.386	1592.870	5476.636
1987	208.645	426.647	584.605	653.397	846.090	782.285	689.030	1016.931	1479.163	4713.774
1988	239.270	515.186	707.751	821.772	1047.874	1011.459	911.922	1330.752	1770.397	5530.484
1989	317.650	670.081	892.857	990.538	1258.119	1243.565	1065.481	1445.061	1914.950	4783.302
1990	315.929	616.518	795.188	890.951	1110.838	1007.728	901.809	1105.822	1292.711	2532.903
1991	408.326	814.492	1087.344	1193.072	1612.369	1480.421	1207.640	1461.764	1870.372	3436.688
1992	426.568	944.734	1280.054	1367.589	2041.142	1724.664	1437.263	1661.939	2215.789	4481.909
1993	456.750	1075.956	1508.309	1590.923	2402.616	1991.252	1764.914	2058.335	2575.052	5276.304
1994	463.405	1074.231	1449.698	1542.842	2340.158	1985.095	1765.294	2061.766	2504.850	5572.592
1995	645.162	1448.159	1897.833	1951.008	2990.372	2391.060	2249.999	2597.313	2978.482	6996.764
1996	783.889	1736.206	2254.237	2431.224	3534.129	2856.796	2847.509	3352.346	3707.263	8000.911
1997	1062.373	2260.095	2824.204	3154.593	4385.152	3780.609	3827.196	4363.832	5026.410	9589.858
1998	1364.666	2503.097	2877.999	3139.608	4213.438	3681.201	3500.958	4029.863	4507.880	8108.865

Source: Center for Research in Security Prices, University of Chicago.

Table 7-4 **Size-Decile Portfolios of the NYSE**

Mid-, Low-, Micro-, and Total Capitalization Returns and Index Values

From 1926 to 1970

	Total Return				Index Value			
Year	Mid-Cap Stocks	Low-Cap Stocks	Micro-Cap Stocks	Total Value Weighted NYSE	Mid-Cap Stocks	Low-Cap Stocks	Micro-Cap Stocks	Total Value Weighted NYSE
1925					1.000	1.000	1.000	1.000
1926	0.0217	-0.0129	-0.0891	0.0952	1.022	0.987	0.911	1.095
1927	0.3471	0.2591	0.3151	0.3301	1.376	1.243	1.198	1.457
1928	0.4100	0.3121	0.4502	0.3872	1.941	1.631	1.737	2.021
1929	-0.2714	-0.3967	-0.5081	-0.1452	1.414	0.984	0.854	1.728
1930	-0.3476	-0.3979	-0.4569	-0.2827	0.922	0.592	0.464	1.239
1931	-0.4637	-0.4968	-0.4960	-0.4392	0.495	0.298	0.234	0.695
1932	-0.0653	-0.0223	0.0908	-0.0975	0.462	0.291	0.255	0.627
1933	1.0415	1.2177	1.8718	0.5753	0.944	0.646	0.733	0.988
1934	0.1137	0.2056	0.2513	0.0435	1.051	0.779	0.917	1.031
1935	0.4145	0.6020	0.6754	0.4398	1.487	1.248	1.536	1.484
1936	0.3641	0.5064	0.8447	0.3226	2.028	1.880	2.834	1.963
1937	-0.4207	-0.4916	-0.5271	-0.3465	1.175	0.956	1.340	1.283
1938	0.3774	0.4110	0.2466	0.2824	1.619	1.349	1.670	1.645
1939	-0.0085	0.0350	-0.0015	0.0283	1.605	1.396	1.668	1.692
1940	-0.0574	-0.0605	-0.1213	-0.0717	1.513	1.312	1.466	1.571
1941	-0.0844	-0.0968	-0.1322	-0.0986	1.385	1.185	1.272	1.416
1942	0.2023	0.2715	0.5126	0.1591	1.665	1.506	1.924	1.641
1943	0.3869	0.5799	0.9979	0.2836	2.309	2.380	3.843	2.106
1944	0.2977	0.4325	0.6053	0.2133	2.997	3.409	6.170	2.555
1945	0.5678	0.6386	0.8224	0.3798	4.699	5.586	11.244	3.526
1946	-0.0975	-0.1154	-0.1280	-0.0592	4.241	4.941	9.805	3.317
1947	0.0127	-0.0293	-0.0309	0.0356	4.295	4.797	9.503	3.436
1948	0.0008	-0.0428	-0.0615	0.0217	4.298	4.592	8.918	3.510
1949	0.2272	0.2117	0.2156	0.2034	5.275	5.564	10.840	4.224
1950	0.3026	0.3675	0.4548	0.2945	6.871	7.608	15.771	5.468
1951	0.1870	0.1562	0.0941	0.2075	8.156	8.797	17.254	6.602
1952	0.1179	0.0970	0.0636	0.1342	9.117	9.650	18.352	7.489
1953	-0.0106	-0.0288	-0.0568	0.0059	9.020	9.372	17.310	7.533
1954	0.5607	0.5749	0.6513	0.5009	14.078	14.759	28.584	11.306
1955	0.1876	0.2093	0.2184	0.2521	16.720	17.848	34.826	14.156
1956	0.0822	0.0649	0.0353	0.0824	18.093	19.007	36.054	15.323
1957	-0.1270	-0.1796	-0.1503	-0.1027	15.796	15.592	30.634	13.749
1958	0.5607	0.6177	0.7058	0.4500	24.652	25.224	52.256	19.936
1959	0.1477	0.1729	0.1811	0.1315	28.294	29.586	61.722	22.558
1960	0.0227	-0.0337	-0.0511	0.0084	28.935	28.588	58.565	22.748
1961	0.2922	0.2972	0.3048	0.2743	37.391	37.085	76.413	28.988
1962	-0.1273	-0.1574	-0.1244	-0.0981	32.631	31.250	66.910	26.146
1963	0.1652	0.1902	0.1850	0.2146	38.021	37.193	79.287	31.758
1964	0.1880	0.1758	0.2009	0.1627	45.168	43.730	95.218	36.924
1965	0.2575	0.3422	0.3648	0.1408	56.798	58.694	129.957	42.123
1966	-0.0582	-0.0856	-0.0726	-0.0888	53.492	53.671	120.523	38.383
1967	0.3976	0.5888	0.7717	0.2687	74.761	85.271	213.528	48.696
1968	0.2070	0.3229	0.4844	0.1282	90.235	112.807	316.958	54.938
1969	-0.1403	-0.2316	-0.3246	-0.0990	77.577	86.685	214.072	49.499
1970	-0.0064	-0.0388	-0.0454	0.0134	77.082	83.324	204.361	50.161

Source: Center for Research in Security Prices, University of Chicago.

Table 7-4 **Size-Decile Portfolios of the NYSE**

(continued)

Mid-, Low-, Micro-, and Total Capitalization Returns and Index Values

From 1971 to 1998

	Total Return				**Index Value**			
Year	Mid-Cap Stocks	Low-Cap Stocks	Micro-Cap Stocks	Total Value Weighted NYSE	Mid-Cap Stocks	Low-Cap Stocks	Micro-Cap Stocks	Total Value Weighted NYSE
1971	0.2050	0.2065	0.1601	0.1604	92.882	100.531	237.085	58.206
1972	0.0838	0.0437	0.0447	0.1746	100.661	104.920	247.686	68.370
1973	-0.2622	-0.3439	-0.3580	-0.1745	74.268	68.839	159.009	56.442
1974	-0.2409	-0.2676	-0.3278	-0.2691	56.376	50.417	106.889	41.255
1975	0.5795	0.6484	0.7582	0.3831	89.044	83.108	187.926	57.059
1976	0.3997	0.5301	0.5775	0.2633	124.637	127.162	296.462	72.080
1977	0.0327	0.1763	0.2015	-0.0491	128.710	149.578	356.205	68.543
1978	0.1023	0.1664	0.1940	0.0707	141.874	174.468	425.308	73.386
1979	0.3312	0.4125	0.4072	0.2143	188.868	246.444	598.497	89.110
1980	0.3064	0.2929	0.2974	0.3220	246.729	318.619	776.493	117.803
1981	0.0483	0.0645	0.1403	-0.0354	258.641	339.162	885.443	113.629
1982	0.2577	0.3468	0.3295	0.2152	325.296	456.788	1177.236	138.083
1983	0.2801	0.3371	0.4804	0.2277	416.406	610.767	1742.783	169.522
1984	-0.0009	0.0241	-0.0260	0.0643	416.016	625.495	1697.479	180.418
1985	0.3104	0.2685	0.2911	0.3240	545.130	793.443	2191.551	238.866
1986	0.1737	0.1043	0.0626	0.1781	639.807	876.182	2328.826	281.404
1987	0.0321	-0.0743	-0.0925	0.0286	660.357	811.057	2113.426	289.464
1988	0.2301	0.3056	0.1903	0.1777	812.304	1058.907	2515.612	340.915
1989	0.2331	0.1837	0.0218	0.2981	1001.664	1253.432	2570.535	442.531
1990	-0.1079	-0.1867	-0.3613	-0.0437	893.589	1019.473	1641.726	423.181
1991	0.3737	0.4018	0.4272	0.3131	1227.560	1429.100	2343.115	555.672
1992	0.1842	0.1677	0.2098	0.0887	1453.667	1668.770	2834.760	604.988
1993	0.1736	0.1931	0.1659	0.1041	1706.079	1991.036	3304.975	667.979
1994	-0.0336	-0.0013	-0.0062	0.0031	1648.726	1988.509	3284.593	670.034
1995	0.2893	0.2372	0.2079	0.3608	2125.624	2460.217	3967.493	911.765
1996	0.2041	0.2363	0.2171	0.2120	2559.359	3041.482	4828.783	1105.088
1997	0.2638	0.3256	0.3139	0.3327	3234.551	4031.772	6344.467	1472.731
1998	0.0005	-0.0555	-0.1172	0.2086	3236.260	3807.862	5600.638	1779.881

Source: Center for Research in Security Prices, University of Chicago.

Graph 7-1 **Size-Decile Portfolios of the NYSE: Wealth Indices of Investments in Mid-, Low-, Micro-, and Total Capitalization Stocks**

Year-End 1925 = $1.00

From 1925 to 1998

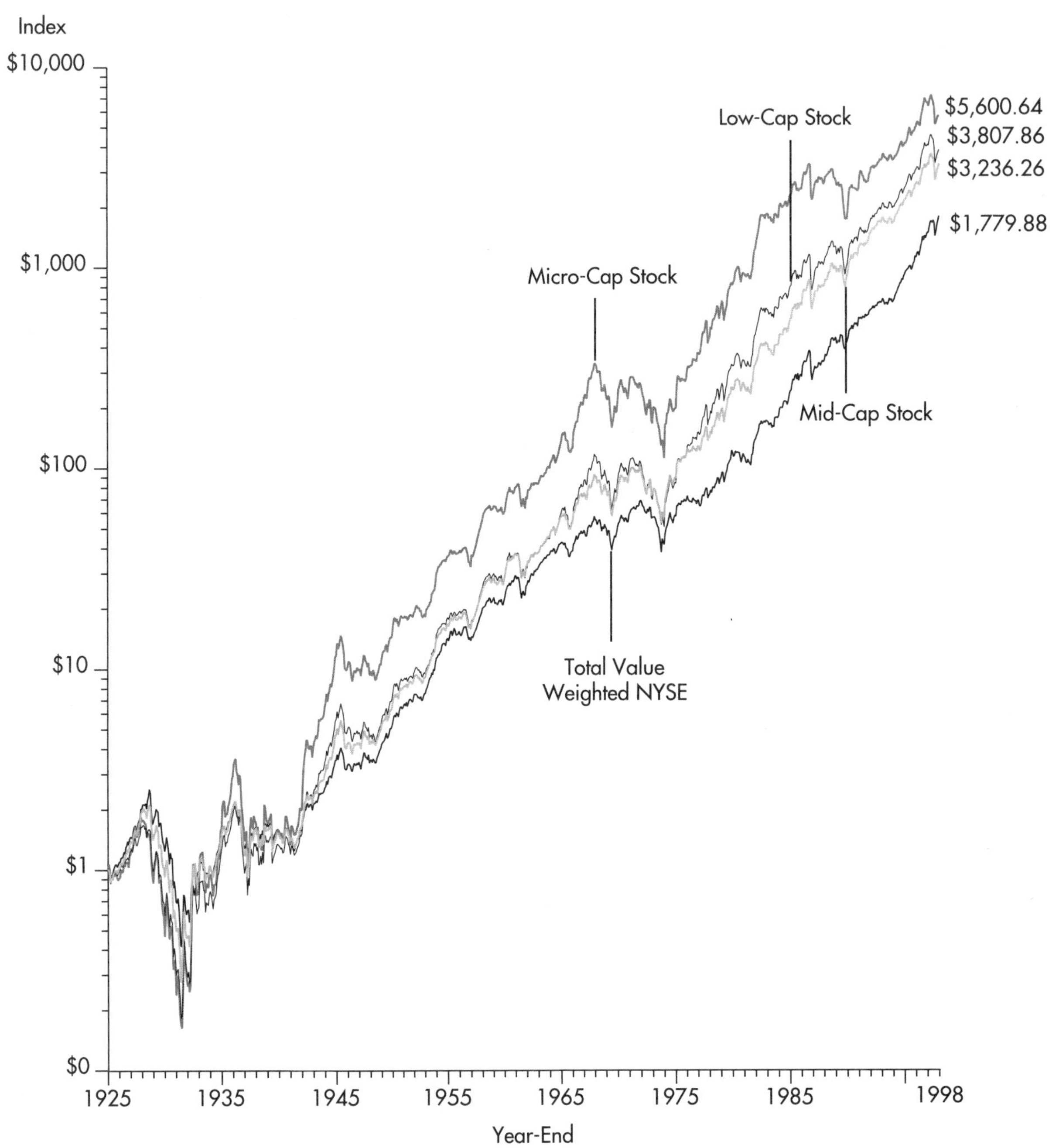

far more substantial. The divergence in the performance of small and large company stocks is a common occurrence.

In Table 7-4, the decile returns and index values of the NYSE are broken down into mid-cap, low-cap, and micro-cap stocks. Mid-cap stocks are defined here as the aggregate of *deciles 3–5*. Based on the most recent data, companies within this mid-cap range have market capitalizations at or below $4,199,948,000, but greater than $918,323,000. Low-cap stocks include *deciles 6–8*, and currently include all companies in the NYSE with market capitalizations at or below $918,323,000 but greater than $252,109,000. Micro-cap stocks include *deciles 9–10*, and include companies with market capitalizations at or below $252,109,000. The returns and index values of the entire NYSE are also included. All returns presented are value-weighted based on the market capitalizations of the deciles contained in each sub-group. Graph 7-1 graphically depicts the growth of $1.00 invested in each of these capitalization groups.

Size of the Deciles

Table 7-5 reveals that most of the market value of the stocks listed on the NYSE is represented by the top three deciles. Approximately two-thirds of the value is represented by the first decile, which currently consists of 189 stocks. The smallest decile represents less than one-quarter of one percent of the market value of the NYSE. The data in the second column of Table 7-5 are averages across all 73 years. Of course, the proportions represented by the various deciles vary from year to year.

In columns three and four are the number of companies and market capitalization. These present a snapshot of the structure of the deciles near the end of 1998. It is important to note that these proportions are not representative of the American Stock Exchange (AMEX) or the over-the-counter (OTC) market. Small firms, as defined by NYSE rankings, make up far higher proportions of value in the AMEX and OTC markets. The aggregate market value of small firms in the AMEX and OTC markets is much larger than the corresponding value on the NYSE. Thus, one cannot assume that findings that hold for NYSE firms will hold for firms traded elsewhere.

The lower portion of Table 7-5 shows the largest firm in each decile and its market capitalization.

Table 7-5 **Size-Decile Portfolios of the NYSE** Bounds, Size, and Composition

From 1926 to 1998

Decile	Historical Average Percentage of Total Capitalization	Recent Number of Companies	Recent Decile Market Capitalization (in thousands)	Recent Percentage of Total Capitalization
1-Largest	65.15%	189	$5,985,553,146	72.60%
2	14.48%	189	1,052,131,226	12.76%
3	7.63%	190	476,920,534	5.78%
4	4.61%	189	273,895,749	3.32%
5	3.01%	189	170,846,605	2.07%
6	2.03%	189	114,517,587	1.39%
7	1.37%	190	78,601,405	0.95%
8	0.90%	189	53,218,441	0.65%
9	0.55%	189	27,647,937	0.34%
10-Smallest	0.25%	190	10,764,268	0.13%
Mid-Cap 3-5	15.25%	568	921,662,888	11.18%
Low-Cap 6-8	4.31%	568	246,337,434	2.99%
Micro-Cap 9-10	0.80%	379	38,412,205	0.47%

Source: Center for Research in Security Prices, University of Chicago.

Historical average percentage of total capitalization shows the average, over the last 73 years, of the decile market values as a percentage of the total NYSE calculated each year. Number of companies in deciles, recent market capitalization of deciles and recent percentage of total capitalization are as of September 30, 1998.

Decile	Recent Market Capitalization (in thousands)	Company Name
1-Largest	$296,072,749	General Electric Co.
2	9,835,796	Fort James Corp.
3	4,199,948	Century Telephone Entrprs Inc.
4	2,266,156	Darden Restaurants Inc.
5	1,396,666	Commerce Group Inc. Mass
6	918,323	Downey Financial Corp.
7	632,639	Central Maine Power Co.
8	416,435	Suburban Propane Partners L.P.
9	252,109	Gray Communications Systems Inc.
10-Smallest	123,872	Rowe Furniture Corp.

Source: Center for Research in Security Prices, University of Chicago.

Market capitalization and name of largest company in each decile as of September 30, 1998.

Long-Term Returns in Excess of Risk

The Capital Asset Pricing Model (CAPM) does not fully account for the higher returns of small company stocks. Table 7-6 shows the returns in excess of risk over the past 73 years for each decile of the NYSE. The beta of each decile indicates the degree to which an asset's return moves with that of the overall market. For a more detailed description of CAPM and beta, see Chapter 8, equations (31) and (32).

The CAPM is used here to calculate the *CAPM return in excess of the riskless rate* based on historical performance. According to the CAPM, the return on a security should consist of the riskless rate, in this case 5.2 percent, plus an additional return to compensate for the risk of the security. Table 7-6 uses the 73-year arithmetic mean income return component of 20-year government bonds as the historical riskless rate. (However, it is appropriate to match the maturity, or duration, of the riskless asset with the investment horizon.) *This CAPM return in excess of the historical riskless rate* is β (beta) multiplied by the realized equity risk premium. The realized equity risk premium is the return that compensates investors for taking on risk equal to the risk of the market as a whole (estimated by the 73-year arithmetic mean return on large company stocks, 13.2 percent, less the historical riskless rate, 5.2 percent).

A beta greater than 1 indicates that the security is riskier than the market, and according to the CAPM equation, investors are compensated for taking on this additional risk. However, based on historical return data on the NYSE decile portfolios, the smaller deciles have had returns that are not fully explainable by the CAPM. This *return in excess of CAPM*, grows larger as one moves from the largest companies in decile 1 to the smallest in decile 10. The excess return is especially pronounced for micro-cap stocks (deciles 9–10). This size related phenomenon has prompted a revision to the CAPM, which includes a size premium. Chapter 8 presents the modified CAPM theory in more detail.

This phenomenon can also be viewed graphically, as depicted in the Graph 7-2. The security market line is based on the pure CAPM without adjusting for the size premium. Based on the risk (or beta) of a security, the expected return should fluctuate along the security market line. However, the expected returns for the smaller deciles of the NYSE lie above the line, indicating that these deciles have had returns in excess of their risk.

Table 7-6 Size-Decile Portfolios of the NYSE:
Long-Term Returns in Excess of CAPM

From 1926 to 1998

Decile	Beta*	Arithmetic Mean Return	Actual Return in Excess of Riskless Rate**	CAPM Return in Excess of Riskless Rate**	Size Premium (Return in Excess of CAPM)
1	0.90	12.12%	6.91%	7.19%	-0.28%
2	1.04	13.66	8.46	8.28	0.18
3	1.09	14.11	8.91	8.67	0.25
4	1.13	14.76	9.56	8.98	0.57
5	1.16	15.52	10.31	9.22	1.09
6	1.18	15.60	10.40	9.41	0.99
7	1.23	15.99	10.79	9.81	0.98
8	1.27	17.05	11.85	10.13	1.72
9	1.34	17.85	12.65	10.68	1.96
10	1.44	21.03	15.83	11.48	4.35
Mid-Cap, 3-5	1.11	14.56	9.35	8.86	0.49
Low-Cap, 6-8	1.21	16.01	10.81	9.68	1.13
Micro-Cap, 9-10	1.37	18.70	13.49	10.90	2.60

Graph 7-2 Size-Decile Portfolios of the NYSE:
Security Market Line

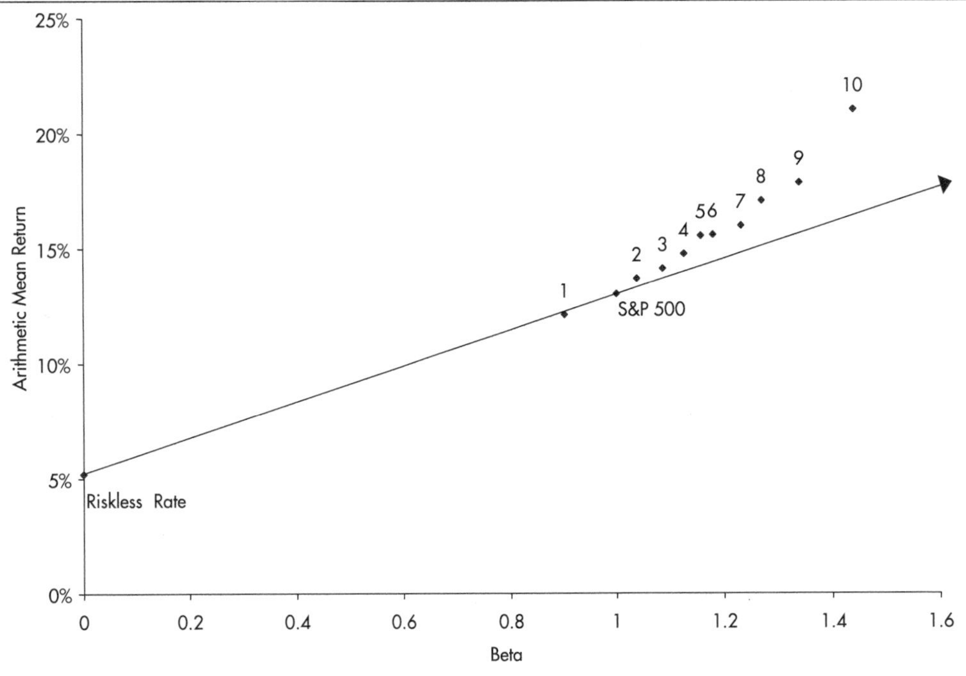

* Betas are estimated from monthly returns in excess of the 30-day U.S. Treasury bill total return, January 1926–December 1998.

** Historical riskless rate measured by the 73-year arithmetic mean income return component of 20-year government bonds (5.20).

Serial Correlation in Small Company Stock Returns

The serial correlation, or first-order autocorrelation, of returns on large capitalization stocks is near zero. [See Table 7-1.] If stock returns are serially correlated, then one can gain some information about future performance based on past returns. For the smallest deciles of stocks, the serial correlation is near or above 0.1. This observation bears further examination.

Table 7-7 Size-Decile Portfolios of the NYSE:
Serial Correlations of Annual Returns in Excess of Decile 1 Returns

Decile	Serial Correlations of Annual Returns in Excess of Decile 1 Return
Decile 2	0.20
Decile 3	0.31
Decile 4	0.21
Decile 5	0.25
Decile 6	0.37
Decile 7	0.29
Decile 8	0.38
Decile 9	0.35
Decile 10	0.41

To remove the randomizing effect of the market as a whole, the returns for decile 1 are geometrically subtracted from the returns for deciles 2 through 10. The result illustrates that these series differences exhibit greater serial correlation than the decile series themselves. Table 7-7 above presents the serial correlations of the excess returns for deciles 2 through 10. These serial correlations suggest some predictability of smaller company excess returns. However, caution is necessary. The serial correlation of small company excess returns for non-calendar years (February through January, etc.) do not always confirm the results shown here for calendar (January through December) years. The results for the non-calendar years (not shown in this book) suggest that predicting small company excess returns may not be easy.

Seasonality

Unlike the returns on large company stocks, the returns on small company stocks appear to be seasonal. In January, small company stocks often outperform larger stocks by amounts far greater than in any other month.

Table 7-8 shows the returns of capitalization deciles 2 through 10 in excess of the return on decile 1. This table segregates excess returns into months. For each decile and for each month, the exhibit shows both the average excess return as well as the number of times the excess return is positive. These two statistics measure the seasonality of the excess return in different ways. The average excess return illustrates the size of the effect, while the number of positive excess returns shows the reliability of the effect.

Virtually all of the small stock effect occurs in January. The excess outcomes of the other months are on net, mostly negative for small company stocks. Excess returns in January relate to size in a precisely rank-ordered fashion. This "January effect" seems to pervade all size groups.

Table 7-8 **Size-Decile Portfolios of the NYSE** Returns in Excess of the First Decile

(in percent)

From 1926 to 1998

First row: average excess return in percent
Second row: number of times excess return was positive (in 73 years)

Decile	Jan	Feb	Mar	Apr	May	Jun	Jul	Aug	Sep	Oct	Nov	Dec	Total (Jan–Dec)
2	0.94%	0.37%	-0.03%	-0.47%	-0.08%	-0.07%	0.05%	0.24%	0.02%	-0.26%	0.06%	0.26%	1.08%
	53	46	32	26	34	36	33	41	38	33	38	38	
3	1.30%	0.29%	0.12%	-0.30%	-0.36%	-0.21%	0.07%	0.35%	0.07%	-0.42%	0.36%	0.07%	1.43%
	54	48	37	23	28	31	36	44	38	32	39	41	
4	1.54%	0.50%	-0.02%	-0.34%	-0.11%	-0.14%	0.01%	0.41%	0.09%	-0.82%	0.20%	0.30%	1.75%
	52	47	37	30	34	36	34	45	34	25	40	40	
5	2.49%	0.55%	-0.04%	-0.43%	-0.30%	-0.19%	0.07%	0.34%	0.05%	-0.74%	0.21%	0.15%	2.31%
	55	45	37	25	28	31	35	41	39	28	40	37	
6	2.96%	0.61%	-0.14%	-0.28%	0.14%	-0.39%	0.09%	0.58%	0.13%	-1.34%	-0.07%	-0.17%	2.36%
	57	46	40	30	34	28	39	42	35	28	35	34	
7	3.46%	0.71%	0.06%	-0.30%	-0.07%	-0.66%	0.06%	0.24%	0.21%	-1.05%	-0.10%	-0.24%	2.48%
	56	49	40	33	31	29	32	37	36	26	35	30	
8	4.79%	0.92%	-0.26%	-0.58%	0.19%	-0.80%	0.26%	0.08%	-0.04%	-1.16%	-0.01%	-0.57%	3.24%
	59	47	35	30	30	32	35	30	37	27	30	34	
9	6.36%	1.09%	0.10%	-0.47%	-0.09%	-0.66%	0.27%	0.19%	-0.30%	-1.30%	-0.22%	-1.43%	3.76%
	60	41	42	28	30	29	34	34	33	25	28	32	
10	9.63%	1.05%	-0.54%	-0.22%	0.27%	-1.01%	0.68%	-0.24%	0.41%	-1.59%	-0.70%	-2.05%	6.23%
	64	37	34	30	31	24	33	24	34	25	25	24	

Part Four: Uses of the Data

Chapter 8 Estimating the Cost of Capital or Discount Rate

Introduction

The SBBI historical data can be used, along with other inputs, to make forecasts of the future, including estimates of the cost of capital. A cost of capital estimate is a forecast because it seeks to discern the expected return, or forecast mean return, on an investment in a security, firm, project, or division. This chapter focuses on forecasting issues related to cost of capital estimation;[7] Chapter 9 addresses the uses of SBBI data in forming optimization inputs and probabilistic forecasts of asset returns in general.

The cost of capital (sometimes called the expected or required rate of return or the discount rate) can be viewed from three different perspectives. On the asset side of a firm's balance sheet, it is the discount rate that should be used to reduce the future value of cash flows to be derived from the assets to a present value. On the liability side, it is the economic cost to the firm of attracting and retaining capital in a competitive environment where investors (capital providers) carefully analyze and compare all return-generating opportunities. To the investor, it is the return one *expects* and requires from his/her investment in a firm's debt or equity.[8] While each of these perspectives might view the cost of capital differently, they are all viewing *the same number*.

The cost of capital is always an expectational or forward-looking concept. While the past performance of an investment and other historical information can be a good guide and is often used to estimate the required rate of return on capital, the expectations of future events are the only factors that actually determine the cost of capital. (An investor contributes capital to a firm with the expectation that the business' future performance will provide a fair return on the investment. If past performance were the criterion most important to investors, no one would invest in startup ventures.) It should be noted that the cost of capital is a function of the *investment*, not the investor.

The cost of capital is an opportunity cost. Some persons consider the phrase "opportunity cost of capital" to be the correct term. The opportunity cost of an investment is the expected return that

---

[7] For additional information regarding the cost of capital, see the *Cost of Capital Quarterly* (CCQ)™ described on the product information page at the back of this book.

[8] The expected return on an asset equals the market-required rate of return on that asset if the asset is fairly priced, *i.e.*, in an equilibrium. In a disequilibrium, where the expected return is not equal to the market-required return, an arbitrage profit can be earned. The discussion in this chapter assumes equilibrium pricing. It is also important to note that the cost of capital equals the expected return only in a world without taxes or transaction costs. Franco Modigliani and Merton H. Miller showed that corporate taxes can cause the cost of debt capital to differ from the debtholder's expected return; see "Corporate Income Taxes and the Cost of Capital: A Correction," *American Economic Review*, Vol. 53, No. 3 (June 1963), pp. 433–43.

would be earned on the next best investment. In a competitive world with many investment choices, a given investment and the next best investment have practically identical expected returns.

The cost of capital has many different applications in investment management, corporate finance, and regulatory and tax issues. Three applications that merit special mention are the valuation of business entities, regulatory proceedings, and project selection.

Valuation

The cost of capital is a critical factor in valuation analyses performed using the discounted cash flow method (or income approach). In this context, the cost of capital is used to discount the *expected* future cash flows, or income, from a business or asset to present value.[9] A common error in estimating the cash flows is to use the "realistic best case" or some other measure that is not the statistically expected value. It is important to calculate the future cash flows as expected values, weighting all favorable and unfavorable scenarios. It is likewise important to ensure that certain factors, such as lack of marketability or a minority position, are accounted for in either the cost of capital or in the cash flows, but *not in both.*

While the cost of capital explicitly enters into valuations performed using the income approach, it is also a crucial factor in valuations relying on price/earnings ratios (or multiples) of comparable companies. The P/E multiple is simply the reciprocal of the capitalization rate; and the latter is the discount rate less the expected perpetual growth rate (this is discussed later in this chapter under the section entitled "*The Discounted Cash Flow Model.*"

Regulatory Proceedings

Most utilities are regulated by local government bodies—usually a commission appointed to ensure that the utility, because of its alleged monopolistic power, does not take advantage of its customers *and* that the investors in the utility receive a fair rate of return on their invested capital. One of the most important functions of the commission is to determine an appropriate (often called the "allowed") rate of return. The procedures for setting rates of return for regulated utilities often specify or suggest that the required rate of return for a regulated firm is that which would allow the firm to attract and retain debt and equity capital over the long term.

[9] A liability can be similarly valued as an asset held short (owed to someone). Every liability is someone else's asset.

Although the cost of capital estimation techniques set forth later in this chapter are applicable to rate setting, certain additional adjustments may be necessary. One such adjustment is for flotation costs (amounts that must be paid by the issuer to underwriters to attract and retain capital). In addition, certain regulatory environments may require that the shareholder not earn more then the allowed rate of return. If the shareholder does earn more, future returns may be reduced by the regulating body. Under this condition, the allowed rate of return must be higher than the cost of capital for the investor to earn the market-required rate of return on average over time. Still, other regulatory conditions may require that the allowed rate of return be different from the cost of capital.

The Cost of Capital for Project Selection

In a situation where there is no significant budget constraint (capital rationing), a firm should accept every project that has a positive net present value (NPV). The NPV of a project is calculated by discounting all of the cash flows to and from the project—including the initial and subsequent investment amounts—at the project's cost of capital. The cost of capital for a project is typically estimated by studying capital costs (including debt and equity) for existing projects deemed to be comparable in risk to the one being contemplated. The cost of capital for a project is related to the risk of the project, not to the risk or credit worthiness of the firm contemplating undertaking the project. Thus, if different firms have the same expectations about the cash flows and risks of a project, each firm will perceive the project as having the same NPV. This illustrates the point made earlier that the cost of capital is specific to the investment, not the investor.

Overall Cost of Capital for the Firm

Most firms use both debt and equity capital to fund their operations. The overall cost of capital for the firm must be such that, over the long run, there is sufficient compensation to distribute to the providers of both debt and equity capital. Thus, the cost of capital for the firm is the weighted average of the debt and equity costs of capital, where the weights are determined by some reasonable method. Market value weights are theoretically the best to use, but they are not always readily observable.

As suggested by the following formula, the overall cost of capital is determined by estimating the required rates of return on each type of instrument composing the firm's long-term capital structure:[10]

[10] This formula yields the before-tax cost of capital for the firm where $\mathbf{k}_e$ and $\mathbf{k}_d$ are estimated before tax; and it yields the after-tax cost of capital for the firm where $\mathbf{k}_e$ and $\mathbf{k}_d$ are estimated after tax.

$$k = \frac{(k_e \times w_e) + (k_d \times w_d)}{w_e + w_d} \quad (28)$$

where,

k = the overall cost of capital of the firm;

k_e and k_d = the expected rates of return on equity and debt, respectively; and,

w_e and w_d = the appropriate weights (usually the *market value* of equity and the book value of debt, respectively).[11]

In the late 1950s, Merton Miller and Franco Modigliani demonstrated that the overall cost of capital of a firm was *not* a function of how the firm was financed; rather, the costs of equity and debt varied such that the weighted average of the two did not change, assuming no taxes, transaction costs, or market imperfections.[12] Later, Miller argued that even *with taxes, under certain conditions*, a firm's overall cost of capital is not dependent on how it is financed.[13] While Miller and Modigliani's theory, in the absence of taxes and bankruptcy costs, is well accepted, Miller's later contention is still somewhat controversial.

Debt Cost of Capital

The debt cost of capital, or the expected return on debt, is relatively simple to estimate. Unlike the cost of equity, the required return on debt is directly observable in the market. It is best approximated by the current yield-to-maturity (or yield) on the applicable debt. Sometimes an average of recent yields is also used. The yield embodies the market's expectation of future returns; if the market's expectations of future debt returns were different from those implicit in the price, the market price of the debt would be bid up or down so that the market's expectations were, again, reflected by the price.

However, for debt instruments that are subject to default risk, such as corporate bonds, this approximation of expected return contains an upward bias because the yield-to-maturity is a *promised* yield; that is, it includes both a risk premium (which the investor receives) and compensation for the expected loss from default. (The probability of default depends upon the quality of the debt.) Because of this default risk, the debt cost of capital is actually the yield-to-maturity minus the expected default loss.

---

[11] The market values of both debt and equity are always preferred, if available. Since the book value of debt is usually close to market value, book value is usually used for the debt weight. This is not true of the equity.

[12] Franco Modigliani and Merton H. Miller, "The Cost of Capital, Corporation Finance and the Theory of Investment," *American Economic Review*, June 1958, pp. 261–297.

[13] Merton H. Miller, "Debt and Taxes," *Journal of Finance*, May 1977, pp. 261–276.

The methods used in this book do not produce an independent estimate of the expected loss from defaults on bonds. Our measure of the corporate bond total return, it is hoped, is already reduced by the losses from default; or, in instances where it is not, such losses can be ignored (considering the high credit quality of the corporate bond portfolio measured). Thus, rather than subtract an estimate of default losses (which we do not have) from corporate bond yields, we add the corporate bond default premium in Table 8-1 to the yield on a government bond of the desired maturity to arrive at the expected return on corporate bonds, or cost of capital for risky debt.

Equity Cost of Capital

Estimating the equity cost of capital is a much more difficult task, to which much of modern financial theory is devoted. As mentioned earlier, the equity cost of capital is equal to the expected rate of return (forecast mean return) for a firm's equity; this return includes all dividends plus any capital gains or losses. A properly specified cost of equity must include, if appropriate, provisions for flotation costs and certain market inefficiencies that might not be captured by standard methods for estimating equity rates of return.

There are several widely used and effective methods to estimate the equity cost of capital. The most common of these are 1) the Capital Asset Pricing Model (CAPM), 2) the Discounted Cash Flow (DCF) method, and 3) Arbitrage Pricing Theory (APT). Of these, the CAPM is directly related to the information presented in this book. A key variable in the CAPM, the expected equity risk premium, is best estimated by studying the historical returns on stocks, bonds, and bills.

The Capital Asset Pricing Model

The CAPM is a simple and elegant model that describes the expected (future) rate of return on any security or portfolio of securities. It is among the most widely used techniques to estimate the cost of equity. The CAPM is the product of the efforts of three recipients of the Nobel Memorial Prize in Economic Science: Harry M.Markowitz, James Tobin, and William F. Sharpe. Sharpe received the Nobel Prize primarily for his work related to the CAPM. When awarding the prizes to Tobin and Markowitz, the Nobel committee cited the contributions of these men to the CAPM.

The principal insight of the CAPM is that the expected return on an asset is related to its risk; that is, risk-taking is rewarded. In fact, the CAPM predicts what the expected return will be for any asset. Assume there is a riskless rate of return that can be earned on a hypothetical investment whose returns do not vary. A risky investment (one whose returns vary from one period to the next) will provide the investor with a reward in the form of a *risk premium*—an expected return higher than the riskless rate.

For a particular risky investment, the CAPM says the size of the risk premium is proportionate, in a linear fashion, to the amount of risk taken. More specifically, the CAPM breaks up the *total risk* (the variability of returns) of an investment into two parts: *systematic* risk and *unsystematic* risk.

Systematic risk is unavoidable; it pervades (to a greater or lesser degree) every asset in the real economy and every claim (such as a stock) on those assets. Systematic risk generally springs from external, macroeconomic factors that affect all companies in a particular fashion, albeit with different magnitudes. For example, a sharp interest rate rise would generally have a negative effect on all stock returns. The CAPM concludes that taking systematic risk is rewarded with a risk premium; the size of the risk premium is proportionate to the degree of co-movement (called *beta*) with the market portfolio consisting of all risky assets. In contrast, unsystematic risk is that portion of total risk that can be avoided by diversifying; the CAPM concludes that unsystematic risk is not rewarded with a risk premium. For example, the possibility that a firm will lose market share to a competitor is a source of unsystematic risk for the stock of a particular company.

The CAPM describes the cost of equity for any company's stock as equaling the riskless rate plus an amount proportionate to the amount of systematic risk an investor assumes.

$$k_s = r_f + (\beta_s \times ERP) \tag{29}$$

where,

k_s = the cost of equity for company s;
r_f = the expected return of the riskless asset;
β_s = the beta of the stock of company s; and,
ERP = the expected equity risk premium, or the amount by which investors expect the future return on equities to exceed that on the riskless asset.

Beta

The amount of an asset's systematic risk is measured by its *beta*. The beta of an asset indicates the degree to which an asset's return moves with that of the overall market. Beta for the stock of company s is defined as:

$$\beta_s = \frac{cov(r_s, r_m)}{var(r_m)} \tag{30}$$

where,

β_s = the beta of the stock of company s;

$cov(r_s, r_m)$ = the *expected* covariance between the return on portfolio or security s and the market return; and,

$var(r_m)$ = the *expected* variance of the return on the overall stock market.

The covariance measures the degree to which the return on a particular security and the overall market's return move together. A positive (negative) covariance indicates that these variables tend to move in the same (opposite) direction. The variance measures the extent to which the return in each period differs from the average return.

A company whose stock has a beta of 1.0 is as risky as the overall stock market and, therefore, will provide expected returns to investors equal to those of the market. The return on a stock with a beta of 2.0 will, on average, rise approximately twice as much as the overall stock market during periods of rising stock prices, and fall approximately twice as much as the market in periods of declining stock prices. Stocks with betas less than 1.0 have risk levels and, consequently, expected returns that are lower than that of the overall stock market.

In the context of the CAPM, β_s is actually an expected future value; that is, one would ideally *forecast* the beta of the security under consideration. Because this expected beta is not observable in the market, however, β_s is often estimated using historical data. A typical approach is to obtain β_s by performing the following regression analysis:[14]

$$(r_s - r_f) = \alpha_s + \beta_s \times (r_m - r_f) + \varepsilon_s \tag{31}$$

where,

r_m = the return on the market;

r_f = the expected return of the riskless asset;

r_s = the return on portfolio or security s;

α_s = regression constant term; and,

ε_s = regression error term.

[14] Descriptions of the regression analysis can be found in most statistics textbooks.

The regression is usually performed using monthly data for the most recent five years. The return on the S&P 500, which is a readily available series, is a good proxy for the return on the overall stock market. A good proxy for the riskless asset would be one whose horizon matches the frequency of the portfolio or security data. For example, when using monthly return data, the 30-day U.S. Treasury bill would be an appropriate proxy for the riskless asset. Some analysts adjust the calculated β_s towards 1.00 because it is their belief that the betas of most stocks converge to 1.00 over time.

Riskless Rate

The CAPM implicitly assumes the presence of a single riskless asset, that is, an asset perceived by all investors as having no risk. Common choices for the nominal riskless rate are the U.S. Treasury bill yield, the yield on intermediate U.S. Treasury bonds, or long-term U.S. Treasury bonds. These obligations are practically default-free because of the ability of the U.S. government to create money to fulfill its debt obligations under virtually any scenario. While interest rate changes cause government obligations to fluctuate in price, investors face essentially no default risk as to either coupon payment or return of principal.

Table 8-1 gives 1998 year-end values of the long-term, intermediate-term, and short-term riskless rates.

Expected Equity Risk Premium

Unlike the yield on a bond, the expected equity risk premium is unobservable in the market and must be estimated, typically by using historical data.[15] It can be calculated by subtracting the long-term average of the income return on the riskless asset from the long-term average stock market return (measured over the same period as for the riskless asset). The maturity (or duration) of the riskless asset from which $\mathbf{r_f}$ is taken must be the same as that used to estimate **ERP**. When calculating the equity risk premium, some analysts subtract a long-term Treasury bond's *total return*—rather than its income return—from the total return on the overall stock market. The income return is the better measure of return to be subtracted from the stock market total return for two reasons:

1. It is the completely riskless portion of the issues' returns (Treasury securities are subject to price risk).

[15] It should be noted that from a valuation specialist's point of view, the stock market returns presented in this book are after corporate taxes but before personal taxes, and should be applied to cash flows calculated on the same basis.

2. Bond yields have risen historically, causing capital losses in fixed-income securities (including U.S. Treasury issues). These capital losses caused bonds' total returns to be lower than the returns that investors expected. In other words, had the investor held the bond to maturity, the investor would have realized the yield on the bond as the total return; but in a constant maturity portfolio such as those used to measure bond returns in this book, bonds are sold before maturity (at a capital loss if the market yield has risen since the time of purchase). There is no evidence that investors expect bond capital losses to be repeated in the future (otherwise bond prices would be adjusted accordingly), so that historical total returns are biased downward as indicators of future expectations. Historical income returns, in contrast, are unbiased estimators of the returns that investors expected.

Since the market provides a clear measure of what investors in Treasury obligations expected—the bonds' yields or income returns—this information should be used to estimate the riskless rate for the purpose of calculating the expected equity risk premium.

As with β_s, the expected equity risk premium is usually estimated using historical information. Implicit in using history to forecast the future is the assumption that investors' expectations conform to that which is actually realizable. This method assumes that the price of taking on risk changes only slowly, if at all, over time. The "future equals past" assumption is applicable to a random time-series variable.

A time-series variable is random if its value in one period is independent of its value in other periods. This is important because empirical research suggests that the yearly difference between the stock market total return and the U.S. Treasury income return in any particular year is random. (The actual, observed difference between the return on the stock market and the riskless rate is known as the *realized* equity risk premium.) This means that the realized equity risk premium next year will not be dependent on the realized risk premium from this or any previous year. For example, if this year's difference between the riskless rate and the return on the stock market is higher than last year's, that does not imply that next year's will be higher than this year's. It is as likely to be higher as it is lower.[16] The best estimate of the expected value of a variable that has behaved randomly in the past is the average (or arithmetic mean) of its past values.

The short-horizon, intermediate-horizon and long-horizon equity risk premia shown in Table 8-1 are computed over the period from 1926 to 1998 (using annual data). The estimate of the expected risk

[16] The serial correlation coefficient for the total return on the overall stock market less long-term government bond income returns over the 73-year period 1926 to 1998 is nearly zero, based on yearly returns. (That is, there is no discernible pattern in the realized risk premium—implying that it is virtually impossible to forecast next year's realized risk premium based on the premia in previous years.) This result is powerful evidence in favor of treating the equity risk premium as a random variable. These results have been independently confirmed by a number of other academic studies.

premium depends on the length of the data series studied. A proper estimate of the expected risk premium requires a long data series, long enough to give a reliable average without being unduly influenced by very good and very poor short-term returns. When calculated using a long data series, the historical risk premium is relatively stable.[17] Furthermore, because an average of the realized equity risk premia is quite volatile when calculated using a short series, using a long series makes it less likely that the analyst can justify any number he or she wants.

Some analysts calculate the expected equity risk premium over a shorter, more recent time period on the basis that more recent events are more likely to be repeated in the near future; furthermore, the 1920s, 1930s, and 1940s contain too many unusual events. This view is suspect because all periods contain unusual events. Some of the most "unusual" events of this century took place quite recently. These events include the inflation of the late 1970s and early 1980s, the October 1987 stock market crash, the collapse of the high yield bond market, the major contraction and consolidation of the thrift industry, and the collapse of the Soviet Union—all of which happened in the past 20 years. Without an appreciation of the 1920s and 1930s, no one would believe that such events could happen. More generally, the 73-year period starting with 1926 is representative of what can happen: it includes high and low returns, volatile and quiet markets, war and peace, inflation and deflation, and prosperity and depression. Restricting attention to a shorter historical period underestimates the amount of change that could occur in a long future period. Finally, because historical event-types (not specific events) tend to repeat themselves, long-run capital market return studies can reveal a great deal about the future. Investors probably expect "unusual" events to occur from time to time and their return expectations reflect this.

The equity risk premium data presented in this publication are derived from data on publicly traded companies, a majority of whom are minority held. There is no evidence to suggest that the equity risk premium represents a minority interest risk premium. The equity risk premium data make no distinction between majority or minority ownership interests.

[17] This assertion is further corroborated by data presented in *Global Investing: The Professional's Guide to the World Capital Markets* (by Roger G. Ibbotson and Gary P. Brinson and published by McGraw-Hill, New York). Ibbotson and Brinson constructed a stock market total return series back to 1790. Even with some uncertainty about the accuracy of the data before the mid-19th century, the results are remarkable in that the real (adjusted for inflation) returns that investors received during the three 50-year periods and one 51-year period between 1790 and 1990 did not differ greatly (that is, in a statistically significant amount) from one another, nor did they differ greatly from the overall 201-year average. This finding implies that because real stock market returns have been reasonably consistent over time, investors can use these past returns as reasonable bases for forming their expectations of future returns.

Calculating the Expected Equity Risk Premium

Arithmetic Versus Geometric Differences

For use as the expected equity risk premium in the CAPM, the *arithmetic* or *simple difference* of the *arithmetic means* of stock market returns and riskless rates is the relevant number. This is because the CAPM is an additive model where the cost of capital is the sum of its parts. Therefore, the CAPM expected equity risk premium must be derived by arithmetic, *not geometric*, subtraction.

Arithmetic Versus Geometric Means

The expected equity risk premium should always be calculated using the arithmetic mean. The arithmetic mean is the rate of return which, when compounded over multiple periods, gives the mean of the probability distribution of ending wealth values. (A simple example given below shows that this is true.) This makes the arithmetic mean return appropriate for computing the cost of capital. The discount rate that equates expected (mean) future values with the present value of an investment is that investment's cost of capital. The logic of using the discount rate as the cost of capital is reinforced by noting that investors will discount their expected (mean) ending wealth values from an investment back to the present using the arithmetic mean, for the reason given above. They will, therefore, require such an expected (mean) return prospectively (that is, in the present looking toward the future) to commit their capital to the investment.

For example, assume a stock has an expected return of +10 percent in each year and a standard deviation of 20 percent. Assume further that only two outcomes are possible each year— +30 percent and -10 percent (that is, the mean plus or minus one standard deviation), and that these outcomes are equally likely. (The arithmetic mean of these returns is 10 percent, and the geometric mean is 8.2 percent.) Then the growth of wealth over a two-year period occurs as shown below:

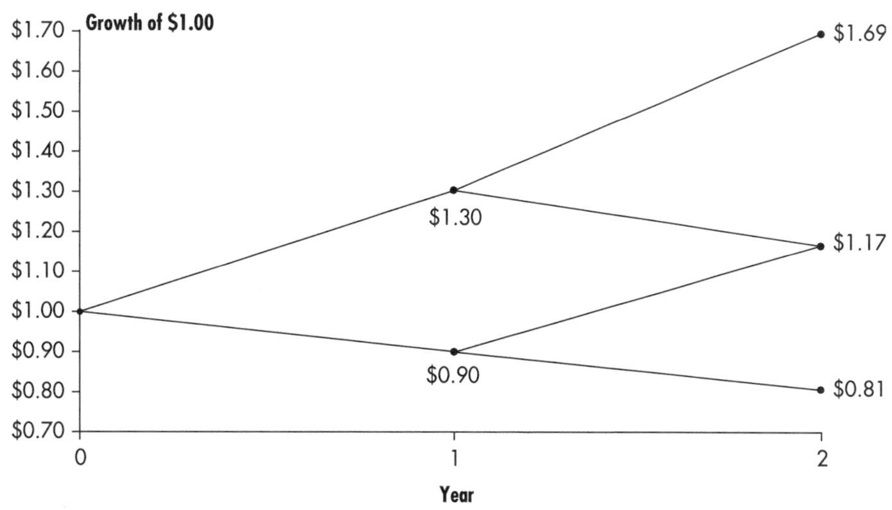

Note that the median (middle outcome) and mode (most common outcome) are given by the geometric mean, 8.2 percent, which compounds up to 17 percent over a 2-year period (hence a terminal wealth of $1.17). However, the *expected value*, or probability-weighted average of all possible outcomes, is equal to:

	(.25	x	1.69)	=	0.4225
+	(.50	x	1.17)	=	0.5850
+	(.25	x	0.81)	=	0.2025
TOTAL					1.2100

Now, the rate that must be compounded up to achieve a terminal wealth of $1.21 after 2 years is 10 percent; that is, the expected value of the terminal wealth is given by compounding up the *arithmetic*, not the geometric mean. Since the arithmetic mean equates the expected future value with the present value, it is the discount rate.

Stated another way, the arithmetic mean is correct because an investment with uncertain returns will have a higher expected ending wealth value than an investment that earns, with certainty, its compound or geometric rate of return every year. In the above example, compounding at the rate of 8.2 percent for two years yields a terminal wealth of $1.17, based on $1.00 invested. But holding the uncertain investment, with a possibility of high returns (two +30 percent years in a row) as well as low returns (two -10 percent years in a row), yields a higher expected terminal wealth, $1.21. In other words, more money is gained by higher-than-expected returns than is lost by lower-than-expected returns. Therefore, in the investment markets, where returns are described by a probability distribution, the arithmetic mean is the measure that accounts for uncertainty, and is the appropriate one for estimating discount rates and the cost of capital.

Arbitrage Pricing Theory

APT is a model of the expected return on a security. It was originated by Stephen A. Ross, and elaborated by Richard Roll. APT treats the expected return on a security (*i.e.*, its cost of capital) as the sum of the payoffs for an indeterminate number of risk factors, where the amount of each risk factor inherent in a given security is estimated. Like the CAPM, APT is a model that is consistent with equilibrium and does not attempt to outguess the market. APT may be viewed as an extended CAPM with multiple "betas" and multiple risk premia.

Nai-fu Chen, with Roll and Ross, conducted an empirical investigation of APT relating stock returns to macroeconomic factors. They found five factors to be important: 1) changes in industrial production, 2) changes in anticipated inflation, 3) unanticipated inflation, 4) the return differential between low-grade corporate bonds and government bonds (both with long maturities), and 5) the return differential between long-term government bonds and short-term Treasury bills. APT risk premia are additive, as in the CAPM; therefore, differences of arithmetic means, such as those in Table 8-1, should be used as estimates of future risk premia.

The cost of capital for a stock, bond, or company can be estimated using APT. Generally, this is accomplished by estimating the size of the payoffs for each risk factor and the amount of each risk factor inherent in the given security.

A standard APT formulation is:

$$\mathbf{k}_s = \mathbf{r}_f + \gamma_{s1}\lambda_1 + \gamma_{s2}\lambda_2 + \ldots + \gamma_{sn}\lambda_n + \varepsilon_s \qquad (32)$$

where,

$\mathbf{k}_s$ = the cost of equity for company **s**;

$\mathbf{r}_f$ = the riskless rate;

$\lambda_1, \lambda_2, \ldots, \lambda_n$ = the various risk premia;

$\gamma_{s1}, \gamma_{s2}, \ldots, \gamma_{sn}$ = the risk premia weights (or exposure of the security to each of the risks); and,

ε_s = the error term.

While APT may seem complicated, various software tools make it usable for cost of capital estimation. Due to the flexibility of APT, it is reasonable to expect that this model will become more prominent in the future, as more is learned about its explanatory and predictive power.

The Discounted Cash Flow Model

The DCF model, or dividend growth model, was originated by John Burr Williams and elaborated by Myron J. Gordon and Eli Shapiro. In its simplest form, this model describes the cost of equity capital for a dividend-paying stock that has a constant expected dividend growth rate in perpetuity. It specifies the equity cost of capital as equal to:

$$k_s = y_s + g_s \tag{33}$$

where,

k_s = the cost of equity for company s;

y_s = the dividend, earnings, or cash flow yield expected to be earned in the next period by shareholders in company s;[18] and,

g_s = the expected dividend or cash flow growth rate into perpetuity.

The DCF in this form is simple to use. The dividend (or cash flow or income) in the next period is easily forecast since it is closely related to the most recent dividend payment. The value of a stock is directly observable as its price in the market. But the difficulty with this model is obtaining an accurate dividend growth forecast. One way of obtaining such a forecast is to use a consensus of security analysts' estimates.

The reason it is difficult to estimate the perpetual growth rate of dividends, earnings, or cash flows is that these quantities do not in fact grow at stable rates forever. Typically it is easier to forecast a company-specific or project-specific growth rate over the short run than over the long run. To produce a better estimate of the equity cost of capital, one can use a two stage DCF model:

$$V_s = \sum_{t=1}^{n} \frac{d_0(1+g_1)^t}{(1+k_s)^t} + \sum_{t=n+1}^{\infty} \frac{d_n(1+g_2)^{t-n}}{(1+k_s)^t} \tag{34}$$

where,

k_s = the cost of equity for company s;

V_s = the current market value of the stock (sometimes an average of recent market prices is used);

t = a measure of time, in this example the unit of measure is a year;

n = the number of years in the first stage of growth;

d_0 = the dividend amount (in \$) in year **0**;

d_n = the dividend amount (in \$) in year **n**;

g_1 = the dividend growth rate from year **1** to year **n**; and,

g_2 = the perpetual dividend growth rate starting in year **n+1**.

[18] As discussed earlier in this chapter, y_s which is the capitalization rate (also called the cap rate) is the reciprocal of the price/earnings ratio. Mathematically this can be seen as: $PE_s = 1/y_s = 1/(r_s - g_s)$.

The equity cost of capital is given by the value of $\mathbf{k}_s$ that makes the right-hand side of the above equation equal to the current stock price (V_s). The first summation term denotes the present value of dividends expected over the first **n** years (deemed to be the readily forecastable short run), and the second summation term denotes the present value of dividends expected over all years thereafter. For the resulting cost of capital estimate to be useful, the growth rate over the latter period should be sustainable indefinitely. An example of an indefinitely sustainable growth rate is the expected long-run growth rate of the economy.

Additional growth stages can be used, but, in practice, usually only one-, two-, or three-stage DCF models are employed.

Other Methods for Computing Costs of Equity

There are other models for computing the cost of equity capital. Some such models rely on "anomalies," or apparent violations of the CAPM or other equilibrium models. The size effect, described below, is one such anomaly. A recent (and controversial) study by Professors Eugene Fama and Kenneth French finds that the returns on stocks are better explained as a function of the company's size (capturing the size effect) and its book-to-market ratio than by the single-factor CAPM.[19] Specifically, they found that the return on a firm's equity is negatively related to its size (*i.e.*, the smaller the company, the higher its expected cost of equity) and positively related to its book-to-market ratio (*i.e.*, the higher the book value relative to the market value, the more "distressed" the company and the greater the compensation required by the investors). This finding suggests a predictive model in which these variables—size and book-to-market ratio—are used (in conjunction with or instead of beta) to estimate the expected return or cost of equity capital.

The Size Effect

One of the important characteristics not necessarily captured by the methods discussed above is what is known as the size effect.[20] This is discussed in detail in Chapter 7. The need for this premium when using the CAPM arises due to the fact that even after adjusting for the systematic (beta) risk of small stocks, small stocks outperform large stocks. The betas for small companies tend to be larger than those for larger companies; however, they do not account for all of the risks faced by investors in small companies. This premium can be added directly to the results obtained using the CAPM:

[19] A more detailed discussion of this can be found in "The Cross-Section of Expected Stock Returns." *Journal of Finance*, 47 (1992a), pp. 427–465 by Professors Fama and French.

[20] It is not captured in the standard CAPM. It may or may not be included in a DCF or APT estimate. It is explicitly counted in the model discussed by Professors Fama and French.

$$k_s = r_f + (\beta_s \times \text{ERP}) + \text{SP} \qquad (35)$$

where all of the variables are as given in equation (29) and **SP** is the appropriate size premium shown in Table 8-1. The market capitalization of company **s** will determine the relevant size premium, whether mid-cap, low-cap, or micro-cap.

For example: Suppose one is trying to find the cost of equity for company XYZ. Assume that the beta of company XYZ is 1.2, the company's market capitalization is $350 million, and the time horizon is long-term. From Table 8-1, one can obtain the key variables for the risk-free rate (5.2), the expected equity risk premium (8.0), and the appropriate size premium (1.1). Using equation (35), the cost of equity for company XYZ is:

$$k_s = 5.2 + (1.2 \times 8.0) + 1.1 = 15.9 \text{ percent.}$$

The size premia given in this chapter and in Chapter 7 are different from the small stock premium shown earlier in this yearbook and in previous editions of the *Stocks, Bonds, Bills, and Inflation Yearbook* (prior to the 1995 *Yearbook*).

The small stock premium is the difference in long-term average returns between the large company stock total return series (currently represented by the S&P 500) and the small company stock total return series (currently represented by the Dimensional Fund Advisors Small Company 9/10 Fund). The size premia given here are based on slightly different baskets of stocks from the CRSP (Center for Research on Securities Pricing) data set and, more importantly, they are adjusted for beta. That is, small stocks do have higher betas than large stocks; the return, above what might be expected because of the higher betas, is the size premia. These size premia increase as the capitalization of the company decreases. Chapter 7 describes the development of these premia in more detail.

A Note on Inflation

The methodologies presented here suggest that anticipated future inflation is included in both stock and bond expected returns. That is, when inflation rates are higher, expected returns on both stocks and bonds should be correspondingly higher. Yet in inflationary times, such as during 1973 to 1974 and 1981 to 1982, investors suffered severe losses in the stock market. This observation leads one to question whether inflation rates are really included in stock returns.

The apparent paradox is resolved by noting that when high inflation rates are anticipated—that is, reflected in bond yields—these higher rates also tend to be impounded in the returns of equities. Unanticipated inflation, however, is detrimental to stock returns since it generally happens during periods of great uncertainty. Inversely, there is also some evidence that unanticipated disinflation is beneficial to stock returns. Thus in a cycle of increasing, followed by decreasing inflation, investors may have to wait for the disinflationary part of the cycle to realize high returns, as occurred in 1975 to 1976 and 1983 to 1987.

None of the methodologies presented above are really able to capture these unexpected inflationary/disinflationary shocks (although some versions of the APT include an inflation "surprise" factor). All of them, however, capture the market's expectation of future inflation. The CAPM and many formulations of the APT do this explicitly through their inclusion of bond market yields/factors. The DCF only captures future inflation to the extent that it is appropriately factored into the growth rate(s) and the current stock price.

Conclusion

Estimating the cost of capital is one of the most important and difficult tasks performed by financial analysts. There is no clear consensus on the best way to approach this problem. Because of the impact that the cost of capital can have on valuation and financial decision making, the analyst should typically use at least two methods to derive the cost of equity.

Ibbotson Associates has begun to offer a publication whose purpose is to assist analysts in estimating the cost of equity for a company. The publication, called the *Cost of Capital Quarterly (CCQ)*, provides a variety of financial and valuation measures, including multiple estimates (using the methodologies covered in this section) for the cost of equity on approximately 300 industries (where companies are classified in industries according to their SICs or Standard Industrial Classification codes).

Table 8-1 **Key Variables in Estimating the Cost of Capital**

	Value
Yields (Riskless Rates)*	
Long-term (20-year) U.S. Treasury Coupon Bond Yield	5.4%
Intermediate-term (5-year) U.S. Treasury Coupon Note Yield	4.7
Short-term (30-day) U.S. Treasury Bill Yield	4.5
Risk Premia**	
Long-horizon expected equity risk premium: large company stock total returns minus long-term government bond income returns	8.0
Intermediate-horizon expected equity risk premium: large company stock total returns minus intermediate-term government bond income returns	8.4
Short-horizon expected equity risk premium: large company stock total returns minus U.S. Treasury bill total returns†	9.4
Expected default premium: long-term corporate bond total returns minus long-term government bond total returns	0.4
Expected long-term horizon premium: long-term government bond income returns minus U.S. Treasury bill total returns†	1.4
Expected intermediate-term horizon premium: intermediate-term government bond income returns minus U.S. Treasury bill total returns†	1.0
Size Premia***	
Expected mid-capitalization equity size premium: capitalization between $918 and $4,200 million	0.5
Expected low-capitalization equity size premium: capitalization between $252 and $918 million	1.1
Expected micro-capitalization equity size premium: capitalization below $252 million	2.6

* As of December 31, 1998. Maturities are approximate.

** Expected risk premia for equities are based on the differences of historical arithmetic mean returns from 1926–1998. Expected risk premia for fixed income are based on the differences of historical arithmetic mean returns from 1970–1998.

***See Chapter 7 for complete methodology.

† For U.S. Treasury bills, the income return and total return are the same.

Note: An example of how these variables can be used is found with equation (35).

Chapter 9 Using Historical Data in Optimization and Forecasting

Introduction

In Chapter 8, the uses of SBBI historical data to estimate the cost of capital are discussed. Cost of capital estimation is a special case of the more general problem of forecasting. This chapter addresses the general problem.

When forecasting the return on an asset or a portfolio, investors are (or should be) interested in the entire probability distribution of future outcomes, not just the mean or "point estimate." An example of a point estimate forecast is that large company stocks will have a return of 13 percent in 1999. It is more helpful to know the uncertainty surrounding this point estimate than to know the point estimate itself. One measure of uncertainty is standard deviation. The large company stock return forecast can be expressed as 13 x 20 percent, where 20 percent is the standard deviation of large company stock annual returns.

If the returns on large company stocks are normally distributed, the mean (expected return) and the standard deviation provide enough information to forecast the likelihood of any return. Suppose one wants to ascertain the likelihood that large company stocks will have a return of -25 percent or lower in 1999. Given the above example, a return of -25 percent is [13 - (-25)]/20 = 1.9 standard deviations below the mean. The likelihood of an observation 1.9 or more standard deviations below the mean is 2.9 percent. (This can be looked up in any statistics textbook, in the table showing values of the probability density function for a normal distribution.) Thus, the likelihood that the stock market will fall by 25 percent or more in 1999 is 2.9 percent. This is valuable information, both to the investor who believes that stocks are a sure thing and to the investor who is certain that they will crash tomorrow.

In fact, the historical returns of large company stocks are not exactly normally distributed, and a slightly different method needs to be used to make probabilistic forecasts. The actual model used to forecast the distribution of stock returns is described later in this chapter.

Some people are wary of probabilistic forecasts because they seem too wide to be useful, or because they lack punch. (The most widely quoted forecasters, after all, make very specific predictions.) However, the forecast of a probability distribution actually reveals much more than the point estimate. The point estimate reflects what statisticians call an "expected value"—but one does not actually expect this particular outcome to happen. The actual return will likely be higher or lower than the point estimate. By knowing the extent to which actual returns are likely to deviate from the point estimate, the investor can assess the *risk* of every asset, and thus compare investment opportunities in terms of their risks as well as their expected returns. As Harry Markowitz showed nearly a half-century ago in his Nobel Prize-winning work on portfolio theory, investors care about avoiding risk as well as seeking return. Probabilistic forecasts enable investors to quantify these concepts.

Uses of Probabilistic Forecasts

Probabilistic forecasts of asset returns have two principal applications: 1) optimization and 2) simulation. This chapter first introduces optimization and simulation; then, because the forecasts needed to conduct optimization and simulation are practically identical, the methods of constructing inputs for both are addressed in a single section.

Mean-Variance Optimization

Optimization is the process of identifying portfolios that have the highest possible expected return for a given level of risk, or the lowest possible risk for a given expected return. Such a portfolio is considered "efficient," and the locus of all efficient portfolios is called the efficient frontier. An efficient frontier constructed from large company stocks, intermediate-term government bonds, and Treasury bills is shown in Graph 9-1. All investors should hold portfolios that are efficient with respect to the assets in their opportunity set.

The most widely accepted framework for optimization is Markowitz or mean-variance optimization (MVO), which makes the following assumptions: 1) the forecast mean, or expected return, describes the attribute that investors consider to be desirable about an asset; 2) the risk of the asset is measured by its expected standard deviation of returns; and 3) the interaction between one asset and another is captured by the expected correlation coefficient of the two assets' returns. MVO thus requires forecasts of the return and standard deviation of each asset, and the correlation of each asset with every other asset.[21]

In the 1950s, Harry Markowitz developed both the concept of the efficient frontier and the mathematical means of constructing it (mean-variance optimization)[22]. Currently, there are a number of commercially available mean-variance optimization software packages, including Ibbotson Associates' Portfolio Strategist™ and EnCorr Optimizer.™ [23]

[21] The standard deviation is the square root of the variance; hence the term "mean-variance" in describing this form of the optimization problem.

[22] Markowitz, Harry M., Portfolio Selection: Efficient Diversification of Investments, New York: John Wiley & Sons, 1959.

[23] For additional information regarding Portfolio Strategist and EnCorr software, refer to the Product Information page at the back of this book.

Graph 9-1 **Efficient Frontier**

Large Company Stocks,
Intermediate-Term
Government Bonds, and
U.S. Treasury Bills

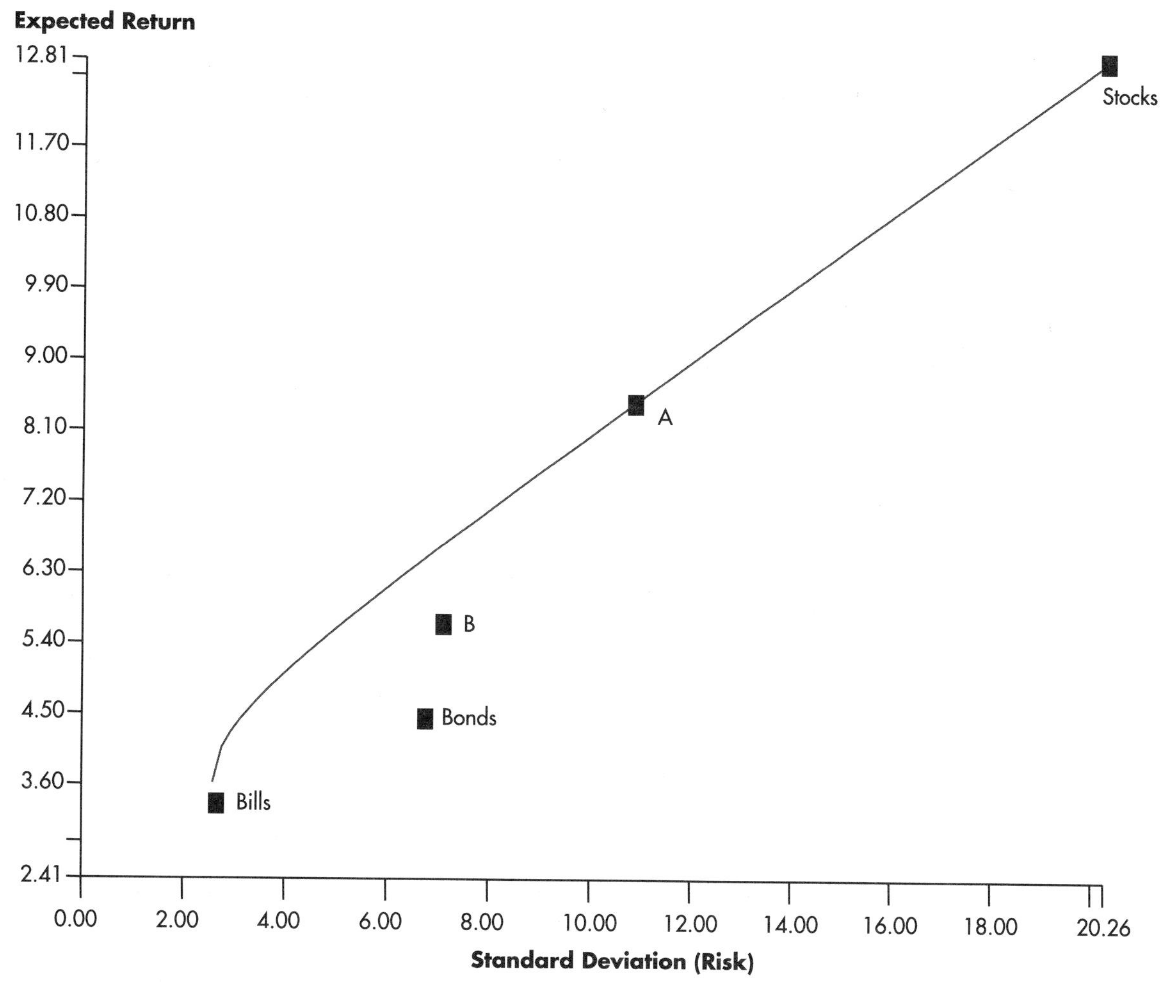

Simulation

In its most general sense, simulation is concerned with creating fictitious stories based on factual knowledge of what can happen. The fictitious event may be in the past or the future, or it may have no specific place on the time line. Thus, it is meaningful to talk about using a computer to simulate a thunderstorm, or a random number generator (a tossed coin will do) to simulate returns in the stock market. The kind of simulation with which this chapter is concerned is creating future probability distributions of asset and portfolio returns based on historical and current data.

Unlike optimization, which is a single-period technique for dealing with the future, simulation can be extended to as many time periods as one wants. Thus, simulation of the future probability distributions of asset or portfolio returns is sometimes called multi-period planning. An example of multi-period planning is shown in Table 9-1, which shows (in the top panel) the probability distribution of compound annual returns on large company stocks over the next 20 years. The top line shows the 95th percentile or optimistic case, the middle line the 50th percentile or median case, and the bottom line the 5th percentile or pessimistic case. The bottom panel shows the same projections, redrawn as cumulative values of $1.00 invested at the beginning of the period simulated. Simulations such as these are used for asset allocation, funding of liabilities, and other portfolio management-related applications; Ibbotson Associates' *Portfolio Strategist* and *EnCorr Optimizer* can produce these forecasts.

Table 9-1 Forecast Distributions of Compound Annual Returns and End of Period Wealth
Large Company Stocks: Year-End 1998

	Compound Annual Return (in percent)				
Percentile	1999	2000	2003	2008	2018
95th	50.8%	37.2%	26.7%	21.9%	18.6%
90th	40.9	30.9	23.1	19.4	16.9
75th	25.9	21.1	17.2	15.4	14.1
50th	11.0	11.0	11.0	11.0	11.0
25th	-2.1	1.8	5.2	6.9	8.1
10th	-12.5	-5.8	0.2	3.3	5.5
5th	-18.2	-10.1	-2.7	1.2	4.0

	End of Period Wealth ($1 Invested on 12/31/98)				
Percentile	1999	2000	2003	2008	2018
95th	$1.46	$1.83	$3.20	$7.11	$29.75
90th	1.37	1.68	2.78	5.80	22.29
75th	1.23	1.44	2.18	4.12	13.76
50th	1.10	1.22	1.67	2.82	8.05
25th	0.98	1.03	1.28	1.93	4.71
10th	0.88	0.89	1.01	1.38	2.90
5th	0.83	0.81	0.87	1.12	2.18

To simulate future probability distributions of asset and portfolio returns, one typically estimates parameters of the historical return data. The parameters that are required to simulate returns on an asset are its mean and standard deviation. To simulate returns on portfolios of assets, one must also estimate the correlation of each asset in the portfolio with every other asset. Thus, the parameters required to conduct a simulation are the same as those required as inputs into an optimizer.[24]

Estimating the Means, Standard Deviations, and Correlations of Asset Returns

To illustrate how to estimate the parameters of asset class returns relevant to optimization and forecasting, we construct an example using large company stocks, intermediate-term government bonds, and Treasury bills. The techniques used to estimate these parameters are described below. They are the same techniques as those used in Ibbotson Associates' *Optimizer Inputs*™ data product and EnCorr InputsGenerator™ software product.

Means, or Expected Returns

The mean return (forecast mean, or expected return) on an asset is the probability-weighted average of all possible returns on the asset over a future period. Estimates of expected returns are based on *models* of asset returns. While many models of asset returns incorporate estimates of GNP, the money supply, and other macroeconomic variables, ours do not. This is because we assume (for the present purpose) that asset markets are informationally efficient, with all relevant and available information fully incorporated in asset prices. If our assumption holds, investor expectations (forecasts) can be discerned from market-observable data. Such forecasts are not attempts to outguess, or beat, the market. They are attempts to discern the market's expectations, *i.e.*, to read what the market itself is forecasting.

For some assets, expected returns can be estimated using current market data alone. For example, the yield on a riskless bond is an estimate of its expected return. For other assets, current data are not sufficient. Stocks, for example, have no exact analogue to the yield on a bond. In such cases, we use the statistical time series properties of historical data in forming the estimates.

To know which data to use in estimating expected returns, we need to know the rebalancing frequency of the portfolios and the planning horizon. In our example, we will assume an annual rebalancing frequency and a five-year planning horizon. The rebalancing frequency gives the time units in which returns are measured.

---

[24] It is also possible to conduct a simulation using entire data sets, that is, without estimating the statistical parameters of the data sets. Typically, in such a nonparametric simulation, the frequency of an event occurring in the simulated history is equal to the frequency of the event occurring in the actual history used to construct the data set.

With a fixed five-year planning horizon, the relevant riskless rate is the yield on a zero-coupon, five-year bond. At the end of 1998, the yield on a five-year "zero" was 4.4 percent. This riskless rate is the baseline, from which the expected return on every other asset class is derived by adding or subtracting risk premia.

Large Company Stocks

The expected return on large company stocks is the riskless rate, plus the expected risk premium of large company stocks over bonds that are riskless over the planning horizon. With a five-year planning horizon, this risk premium is 8.4 percent, shown as the intermediate-horizon expected equity risk premium in Table 8-1. Hence, the expected return on large company stocks is 4.4 (the riskless rate) plus 8.4 (the risk premium) for a total of 12.8 percent (due to rounding).

Bonds and Bills

For default-free bonds with a maturity equal to the planning horizon, the expected return is the yield on the bond; that is, the expected return is the riskless rate of 4.4 percent. For bonds with other maturities, the expected bond horizon premium should be added to the riskless rate (for longer maturities) or subtracted from the riskless rate (for shorter maturities). Since expected capital gains on a bond are zero, the expected horizon premium is estimated by the historical average difference of the *income returns* on the bonds.[25]

For Treasury bills, the expected return over a given time horizon is equal to the expected return on a Treasury bond of a similar horizon, less the *expected* horizon premium of bonds over bills. This premium is estimated by the historical average of the difference of the income return on bonds and the return on bills. From Table 8-1, this is 1.0 percent. Subtracting this from the riskless rate gives us an expected return on bills of 3.4 percent. Of course, this forecast typically differs from the current yield on a Treasury bill, since a portfolio of Treasury bills is rolled over (the proceeds of maturing bills are invested in new bills, at yields not yet known) during the time horizon described.

Standard Deviations

Standard deviations are estimated from historical data as described in Chapter 6. Since there is no evidence of a major change in the variability of returns on large company stocks, we use the entire

[25] The expected capital gain on a par bond is self-evidently zero. For a zero-coupon (or other discount) bond, investors expect the price to rise as the bond ages, but the expected portion of this price increase should not be considered a capital gain. It is a form of income return.

period 1926–1998 to estimate the standard deviation of these asset classes. For bonds and bills, we use the period 1970–1998. The use of this more recent period reflects the fact that the volatility of bonds has increased over time.

Correlations

Correlations between the asset classes are estimated from historical data as described in Chapter 6. We use the period 1926–1998 to form the estimates for stocks, the same period over which standard deviations are calculated. Correlation coefficients for bonds and bills are derived from 1970–1998. Correlations between major asset classes change over time. Graph 9-2 shows the historical correlation of annual returns on large company stocks and intermediate bonds over 20 year rolling periods from 1926–1945 through 1978–1998.

Constructing Efficient Portfolios

A mean-variance optimizer uses the complete set of optimizer inputs (the expected return and standard deviation of each asset class and the correlation of returns for each pair of asset classes) to generate an efficient frontier. The efficient frontier shown in Graph 9-1 was generated from the inputs described above and summarized in Table 9-2. Each point on the frontier represents a portfolio mix that is mean-variance efficient. The point labeled A represents a portfolio with a level of risk typical of portfolios that are well diversified among asset classes; it contains 53 percent in large company stocks, 7 percent in intermediate-term bonds, and 40 percent in Treasury bills. (Recall that other asset classes were not considered in this example.) From the location of point A on the grid, we can find its expected return (8.4 percent) and standard deviation (10.9 percent).

Table 9-2 Optimizer Inputs: Year-End 1998
Large Company Stocks, Intermediate-Term Government Bonds, and U.S. Treasury Bills

	Expected Return	Standard Deviation	Correlation with		
			Stocks	Bonds	Bills
Stocks	12.8%	20.3%	1.00		
Bonds	4.4	6.8	0.36	1.00	
Bills	3.4	2.7	-0.10	0.23	1.00

Graph 9-2 **Twenty Year Rolling Period Correlations of Annual Returns**

Large Company Stocks and Intermediate-Term Government Bonds

From 1926–1945 through 1978–1998

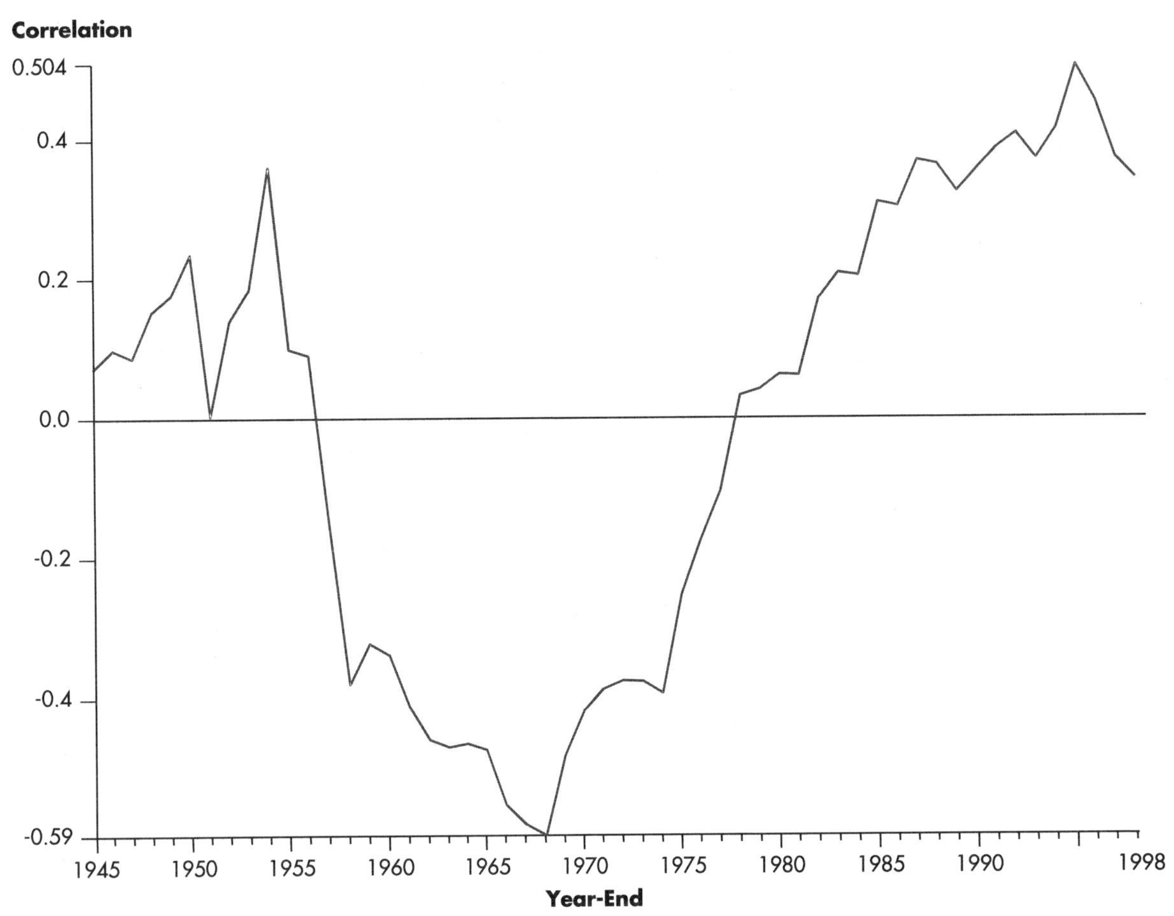

Using Inputs to Form Other Portfolios

Given a complete set of inputs, the expected return and standard deviation of any portfolio (efficient or other) of the asset classes can be calculated. The expected return of a portfolio is the weighted average of the expected returns of the asset classes:

$$r_p = \sum_{i=1}^{n} x_i r_i \qquad (36)$$

where,

r_p = the expected return of the portfolio **p**;

n = the number of asset classes;

x_i = the portfolio weight of asset class **i**, scaled such that

$\sum_{i=1}^{n} x_i = 1$; and,

r_i = the expected return of asset class **i**.

The point labeled B in Graph 9-1 represents a portfolio that contains 15 percent in large company stocks (asset class 1), 80 percent in intermediate-term bonds (asset class 2), and 5 percent in Treasury bills (asset class 3). Applying the above formula to this portfolio using the inputs in Table 9-2, we calculate the expected return to be 5.6 percent as follows:

$$(0.15 \times 0.128) + (0.80 \times 0.044) + (0.05 \times 0.034) = 0.056$$

The standard deviation of the portfolio depends not only on the standard deviations of the asset classes, but on all of the correlations as well. It is given by:

$$\sigma_p = \sqrt{\sum_{i=1}^{n} \sum_{j=1}^{n} x_i x_j \sigma_i \sigma_j \rho_{ij}} \qquad (37)$$

where,

σ_p = the standard deviation of the portfolio;

x_i and x_j = the portfolio weights of asset classes **i** and **j**;

σ_i and σ_j = the standard deviations of returns on asset classes **i** and **j**; and,

ρ_{ij} = the correlation between returns on asset classes **i** and **j**.
Note that ρ_{ii} equals one and that ρ_{ij} is equal to ρ_{ji}.

The standard deviation for point B in Graph 9-1 (containing three asset classes) would be calculated as follows:

	Stocks (asset class 1)	Bonds (asset class 2)	Bills (asset class 3)
Stocks	$x_1^2 \sigma_1^2 \rho_{1,1}$ = (0.15)²(0.203)²(1)= 0.00093	$x_1 x_2 \sigma_1 \sigma_2 \rho_{1,2}$ = (0.15)(0.8)(0.203)(0.068)(0.36)= 0.00060	$x_1 x_3 \sigma_1 \sigma_3 \rho_{1,3}$ = (0.15)(0.05)(0.203)(0.027)(-0.10) = 0.00000
Bonds	$x_1 x_2 \sigma_1 \sigma_2 \rho_{1,2}$ = (0.15)(0.8)(0.203)(0.068)(0.36)= 0.00060	$x_2^2 \sigma_2^2 \rho_{2,2}$ = (0.8)²(0.068)²(1)= 0.00296	$x_2 x_3 \sigma_2 \sigma_3 \rho_{2,3}$ = (0.8)(0.05)(0.068)(0.027)(0.23) = 0.00002
Bills	$x_1 x_3 \sigma_1 \sigma_3 \rho_{1,3}$ = (0.15)(0.05)(0.203)(0.027)(-0.10)= 0.00000	$x_2 x_3 \sigma_2 \sigma_3 \rho_{2,3}$ = (0.8)(0.05)(0.068)(0.027)(0.23)= 0.00002	$x_3^2 \sigma_3^2 \rho_{3,3}$ = (0.05)²(0.027)²(1) = 0.00000

By summing these terms and taking the square root of the total, the result is a standard deviation of 7.2 percent.

Generating Probabilistic Forecasts

Ibbotson and Sinquefield used a simulation, or random drawing, method of making probabilistic forecasts of asset returns in their 1977 *Stocks, Bonds, Bills, and Inflation* book. Their method, known as a Monte Carlo simulation, relied on drawings from the actual historical data sets. Later, other researchers showed that Ibbotson and Sinquefield's forecasts could be closely replicated by a lognormal distribution with parameters derived from summary statistics of historical returns and current bond yields.[26] This latter, *parametric* method based on the lognormal distribution was first adopted by Ibbotson and Sinquefield in the 1982 edition of their book to produce probabilistic forecasts. It has since been incorporated into Ibbotson Associates' software products.

The Lognormal Distribution

In the lognormal model, the natural logarithms of asset *return relatives* are assumed to be normally distributed. (A return relative is one plus the return. That is, if an asset has a return of 15 percent in a given period, its return relative is 1.15.)

The lognormal distribution is skewed to the right. That is, the expected value, or mean, is greater than the median. Furthermore, if return relatives are lognormally distributed, returns cannot fall below

26 Lewis, Alan L., Sheen T. Kassouf, R. Dennis Brehm, and Jack Johnston, "The Ibbotson-Sinquefield Simulation Made Easy," Journal of Business, vol. 53 (1980), pp. 205–214.

negative 100 percent. These properties of the lognormal distribution make it a more accurate characterization of the behavior of market returns than does the normal distribution.

In all normal distributions, moreover, the probability of an observation falling below the mean by as much as one standard deviation equals the probability of falling above the mean by as much as one standard deviation; both probabilities are about 34 percent. In a lognormal distribution, these probabilities differ and depend on the parameters of the distribution.

Forecasting Wealth Values and Rates of Return

Using the lognormal model, it is fairly simple to form probabilistic forecasts of both compound rates of return and ending period wealth values. Wealth at time **n** (assuming reinvestment of all income and no taxes) is:

$$W_n = W_0(1+r_1)(1+r_2)\ldots(1+r_n) \tag{38}$$

where,

W_n = the wealth value at time **n**;
W_0 = the initial investment at time **0**; and,
r_1, r_2, etc. = the total returns on the portfolio for the rebalancing period ending at times 1, 2, and so forth.

The compound rate of return or geometric mean return over the same period, r_G, is:

$$r_G = \left(\frac{W_n}{W_0}\right)^{\frac{1}{n}} - 1 \tag{39}$$

where,

r_G = the geometric mean return;
W_n = the ending period wealth value at time **n**;
W_0 = the initial wealth value at time 0; and,
n = the inclusive number of periods.

By assuming that all of the $(1+ r_n)$s are lognormally distributed with the same expected value and standard deviation and are all statistically independent of each other, it follows that W_n and $(1+ r_G)$ are lognormally distributed. In fact, even if the $(1+ r_n)$s are not themselves lognormally distributed but are independent and identically distributed, W_n and $(1+ r_G)$ are approximately lognormal for large enough values of n. This "central-limit theorem" means that the lognormal model can be useful in long-term forecasting even if short-term returns are not well described by a lognormal distribution.

Calculating Parameters of the Lognormal Model

To use the lognormal model, we must first calculate the expected value and standard deviation of the natural logarithm of the return relative of the portfolio. These parameters, denoted m and s respectively, can be calculated from the expected return (μ) and standard deviation (σ) of the portfolio as follows:

$$m = \ln(1+\mu) - \left(\frac{s^2}{2}\right) \tag{40}$$

$$s = \sqrt{\ln\left[1+\left(\frac{\sigma}{1+\mu}\right)^2\right]} \tag{41}$$

where,
ln = the natural logarithm function.

To calculate a particular percentile of wealth or return for a given time horizon, the only remaining parameter needed is the z-score of the percentile. The z-score of a percentile ranking is that percentile ranking expressed as the number of standard deviations that it is above or below the mean of a normal distribution. For example, the z-score of the 95th percentile is 1.645 because in a *normal distribution*, the 95th percentile is 1.645 standard deviations above the 50th percentile or median, which is also the mean. Z-scores can be obtained from a table of cumulative values of the standard normal distribution or from software that produces such values.

Given the logarithmic parameters of a portfolio (**m** and **s**), a time horizon (**n**), and the z-score of a percentile (**z**), the percentile in question in terms of cumulative wealth at the end of the time horizon (W_n) is:

$$e^{\left(mn+zs\sqrt{n}\right)} \tag{42}$$

Similarly, the percentile in question in terms of the compound rate of return for the period (r_G) is:

$$e^{\left(m+z\frac{s}{\sqrt{n}}\right)}-1 \tag{43}$$

Probabilistic Forecast Results

For portfolio A in Graph 9-1, the logarithmic parameters are m = 0.0761 and **s** = 0.1004. The z-scores of the 95th, 50th, and 5th percentile are 1.645, 0, and -1.645, respectively. Using these parameters, we can calculate the 95th, 50th, and 5th percentiles of cumulative wealth and compound returns over various time horizons. Graph 9-3 shows percentiles of compound returns over the entire range of one to twenty year horizons in graphical form. This type of graph is sometimes called a "trumpet" graph because the high and low percentile curves taken together make the shape of a trumpet. The "mouthpiece" of the trumpet is on the right side of the graph because for long time horizons, all percentiles converge to the median (50th percentile).

Graph 9-4 is a graph showing percentiles of cumulative wealth over the entire range of zero to twenty year time horizons, along with the back history of the portfolio's performance. The past and forecasted (future) values on the graph are connected by setting the wealth index to $1.00 at the end of 1998. The past index values show how much wealth one would have had to hold in Portfolio A to have $1.00 at the end of 1998; the percentiles of future value show the probability distribution of future growth of $1.00 invested in Portfolio A. This type of graph is sometimes called a "tulip" graph because of its overall shape.

All tables and graphs presented in this chapter were prepared using Ibbotson Associates' *Portfolio Strategist*™ and *EnCorr*™ suite of asset allocation software and data products. Using these tools, similar analyses can be performed for a wide variety of asset classes, historical time periods, percentiles, and planning horizons. Additionally, Ibbotson Associates offers returns based style analysis products to aid in the evaluation of mutual funds for use in implementing an optimal asset mix. These products include EnCorr Attribution software and the new Fund Strategist CD-Rom tool.

Graph 9-3 **Forecast Total Return Distribution**

53 Percent Stocks,
7 Percent Bonds, and
40 Percent Bills

From 1999 to 2018

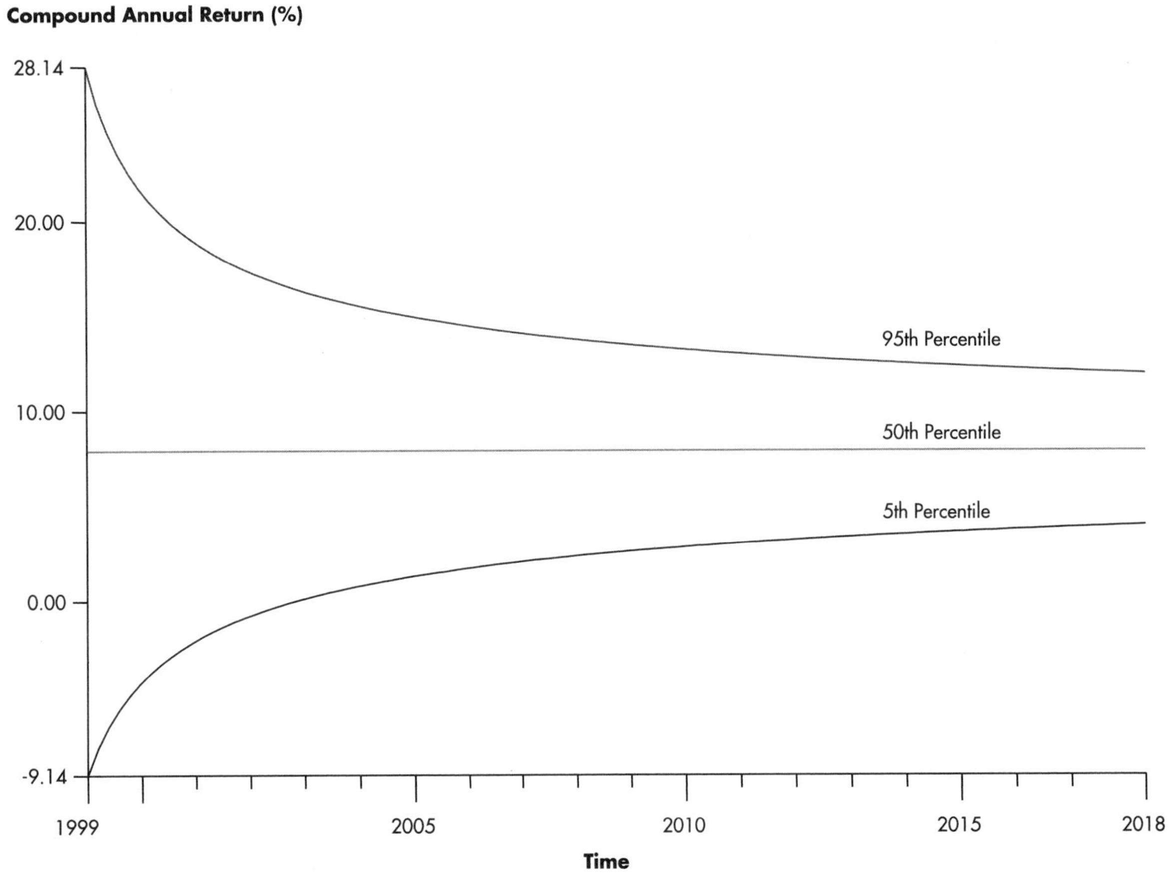

Compound Annual Return (%)

28.14
20.00
10.00
0.00
-9.14

95th Percentile
50th Percentile
5th Percentile

1999 2005 2010 2015 2018

Time

Graph 9-4 **Forecast Distribution of Wealth Index Value**

53 Percent Stocks,
7 Percent Bonds, and
40 Percent Bills

Year-End 1998 $1.00

From 1999 to 2018

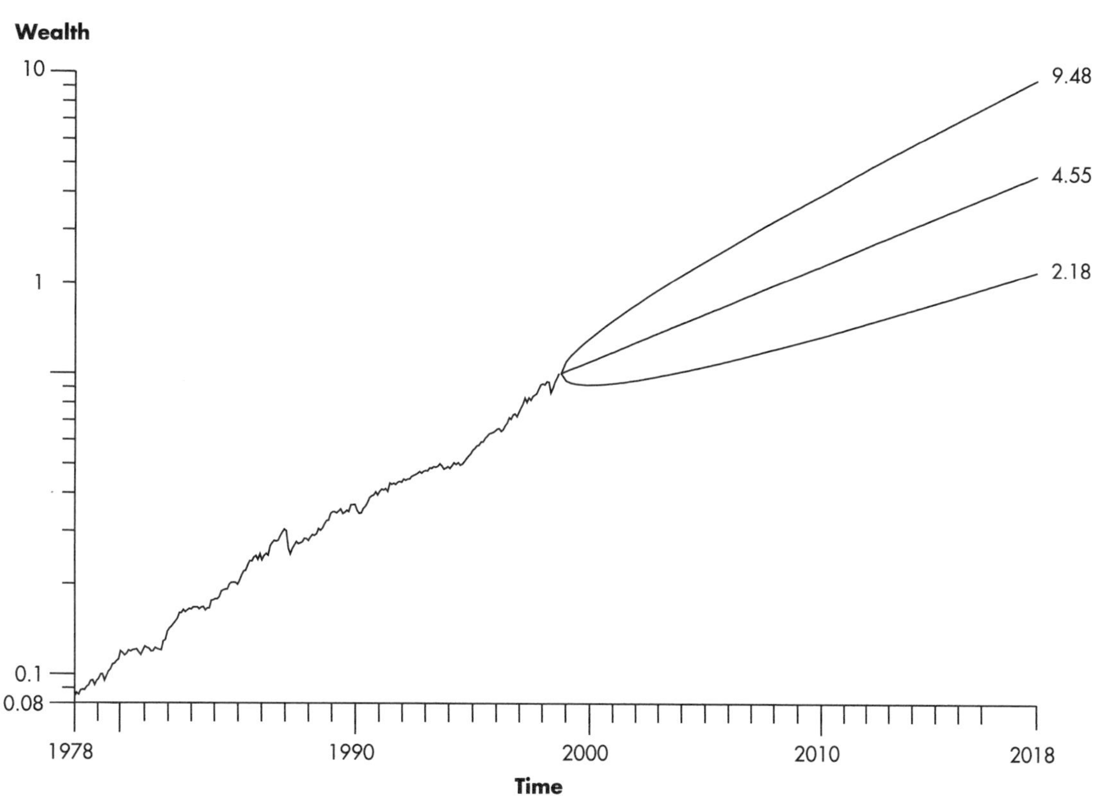

STOCKS
BONDS
BILLS
AND
INFLATION

Appendix A: Monthly Returns of Basic and Derived Series

January 1926
to
December 1998

Appendix A Monthly Returns on Basic and Derived Series

Basic Series

Risk Premia

Inflation-Adjusted Returns

Table A-1 **Large Company Stocks: Total Returns**

From January 1926 to December 1970

YEAR	JAN	FEB	MAR	APR	MAY	JUN	JUL	AUG	SEP	OCT	NOV	DEC	YEAR	JAN-DEC*
1926	0.0000	-0.0385	-0.0575	0.0253	0.0179	0.0457	0.0479	0.0248	0.0252	-0.0284	0.0347	0.0196	1926	0.1162
1927	-0.0193	0.0537	0.0087	0.0201	0.0607	-0.0067	0.0670	0.0515	0.0450	-0.0502	0.0721	0.0279	1927	0.3749
1928	-0.0040	-0.0125	0.1101	0.0345	0.0197	-0.0385	0.0141	0.0803	0.0259	0.0168	0.1292	0.0049	1928	0.4361
1929	0.0583	-0.0019	-0.0012	0.0176	-0.0362	0.1140	0.0471	0.1028	-0.0476	-0.1973	-0.1246	0.0282	1929	-0.0842
1930	0.0639	0.0259	0.0812	-0.0080	-0.0096	-0.1625	0.0386	0.0141	-0.1282	-0.0855	-0.0089	-0.0706	1930	-0.2490
1931	0.0502	0.1193	-0.0675	-0.0935	-0.1279	0.1421	-0.0722	0.0182	-0.2973	0.0896	-0.0798	-0.1400	1931	-0.4334
1932	-0.0271	0.0570	-0.1158	-0.1997	-0.2196	-0.0022	0.3815	0.3869	-0.0346	-0.1349	-0.0417	0.0565	1932	-0.0819
1933	0.0087	-0.1772	0.0353	0.4256	0.1683	0.1338	-0.0862	0.1206	-0.1118	-0.0855	0.1127	0.0253	1933	0.5399
1934	0.1069	-0.0322	0.0000	-0.0251	-0.0736	0.0229	-0.1132	0.0611	-0.0033	-0.0286	0.0942	-0.0010	1934	-0.0144
1935	-0.0411	-0.0341	-0.0286	0.0980	0.0409	0.0699	0.0850	0.0280	0.0256	0.0777	0.0474	0.0394	1935	0.4767
1936	0.0670	0.0224	0.0268	-0.0751	0.0545	0.0333	0.0701	0.0151	0.0031	0.0775	0.0134	-0.0029	1936	0.3392
1937	0.0390	0.0191	-0.0077	-0.0809	-0.0024	-0.0504	0.1045	-0.0483	-0.1403	-0.0981	-0.0866	-0.0459	1937	-0.3503
1938	0.0152	0.0674	-0.2487	0.1447	-0.0330	0.2503	0.0744	-0.0226	0.0166	0.0776	-0.0273	0.0401	1938	0.3112
1939	-0.0674	0.0390	-0.1339	-0.0027	0.0733	-0.0612	0.1105	-0.0648	0.1673	-0.0123	-0.0398	0.0270	1939	-0.0041
1940	-0.0336	0.0133	0.0124	-0.0024	-0.2289	0.0809	0.0341	0.0350	0.0123	0.0422	-0.0316	0.0009	1940	-0.0978
1941	-0.0463	-0.0060	0.0071	-0.0612	0.0183	0.0578	0.0579	0.0010	-0.0068	-0.0657	-0.0284	-0.0407	1941	-0.1159
1942	0.0161	-0.0159	-0.0652	-0.0399	0.0796	0.0221	0.0337	0.0164	0.0290	0.0678	-0.0021	0.0549	1942	0.2034
1943	0.0737	0.0583	0.0545	0.0035	0.0552	0.0223	-0.0526	0.0171	0.0263	-0.0108	-0.0654	0.0617	1943	0.2590
1944	0.0171	0.0042	0.0195	-0.0100	0.0505	0.0543	-0.0193	0.0157	-0.0008	0.0023	0.0133	0.0374	1944	0.1975
1945	0.0158	0.0683	-0.0441	0.0902	0.0195	-0.0007	-0.0180	0.0641	0.0438	0.0322	0.0396	0.0116	1945	0.3644
1946	0.0714	-0.0641	0.0480	0.0393	0.0288	-0.0370	-0.0239	-0.0674	-0.0997	-0.0060	-0.0027	0.0457	1946	-0.0807
1947	0.0255	-0.0077	-0.0149	-0.0363	0.0014	0.0554	0.0381	-0.0203	-0.0111	0.0238	-0.0175	0.0233	1947	0.0571
1948	-0.0379	-0.0388	0.0793	0.0292	0.0879	0.0054	-0.0508	0.0158	-0.0276	0.0710	-0.0961	0.0346	1948	0.0550
1949	0.0039	-0.0296	0.0328	-0.0179	-0.0258	0.0014	0.0650	0.0219	0.0263	0.0340	0.0175	0.0486	1949	0.1879
1950	0.0197	0.0199	0.0070	0.0486	0.0509	-0.0548	0.0119	0.0443	0.0592	0.0093	0.0169	0.0513	1950	0.3171
1951	0.0637	0.0157	-0.0156	0.0509	-0.0299	-0.0228	0.0711	0.0478	0.0013	-0.0103	0.0096	0.0424	1951	0.2402
1952	0.0181	-0.0282	0.0503	-0.0402	0.0343	0.0490	0.0196	-0.0071	-0.0176	0.0020	0.0571	0.0382	1952	0.1837
1953	-0.0049	-0.0106	-0.0212	-0.0237	0.0077	-0.0134	0.0273	-0.0501	0.0034	0.0540	0.0204	0.0052	1953	-0.0099
1954	0.0536	0.0111	0.0325	0.0516	0.0418	0.0031	0.0589	-0.0275	0.0851	-0.0167	0.0909	0.0534	1954	0.5262
1955	0.0197	0.0098	-0.0030	0.0396	0.0055	0.0841	0.0622	-0.0025	0.0130	-0.0284	0.0827	0.0015	1955	0.3156
1956	-0.0347	0.0413	0.0710	-0.0004	-0.0593	0.0409	0.0530	-0.0328	-0.0440	0.0066	-0.0050	0.0370	1956	0.0656
1957	-0.0401	-0.0264	0.0215	0.0388	0.0437	0.0004	0.0131	-0.0505	-0.0602	-0.0302	0.0231	-0.0395	1957	-0.1078
1958	0.0445	-0.0141	0.0328	0.0337	0.0212	0.0279	0.0449	0.0176	0.0501	0.0270	0.0284	0.0535	1958	0.4336
1959	0.0053	0.0049	0.0020	0.0402	0.0240	-0.0022	0.0363	-0.0102	-0.0443	0.0128	0.0186	0.0292	1959	0.1196
1960	-0.0700	0.0147	-0.0123	-0.0161	0.0326	0.0211	-0.0234	0.0317	-0.0590	-0.0007	0.0465	0.0479	1960	0.0047
1961	0.0645	0.0319	0.0270	0.0051	0.0239	-0.0275	0.0342	0.0243	-0.0184	0.0298	0.0447	0.0046	1961	0.2689
1962	-0.0366	0.0209	-0.0046	-0.0607	-0.0811	-0.0803	0.0652	0.0208	-0.0465	0.0064	0.1086	0.0153	1962	-0.0873
1963	0.0506	-0.0239	0.0370	0.0500	0.0193	-0.0188	-0.0022	0.0535	-0.0097	0.0339	-0.0046	0.0262	1963	0.2280
1964	0.0283	0.0147	0.0165	0.0075	0.0162	0.0178	0.0195	-0.0118	0.0301	0.0096	0.0005	0.0056	1964	0.1648
1965	0.0345	0.0031	-0.0133	0.0356	-0.0030	-0.0473	0.0147	0.0272	0.0334	0.0289	-0.0031	0.0106	1965	0.1245
1966	0.0062	-0.0131	-0.0205	0.0220	-0.0492	-0.0146	-0.0120	-0.0725	-0.0053	0.0494	0.0095	0.0002	1966	-0.1006
1967	0.0798	0.0072	0.0409	0.0437	-0.0477	0.0190	0.0468	-0.0070	0.0342	-0.0276	0.0065	0.0278	1967	0.2398
1968	-0.0425	-0.0261	0.0110	0.0834	0.0161	0.0105	-0.0172	0.0164	0.0400	0.0087	0.0531	-0.0402	1968	0.1106
1969	-0.0068	-0.0426	0.0359	0.0229	0.0026	-0.0542	-0.0587	0.0454	-0.0236	0.0459	-0.0297	-0.0177	1969	-0.0850
1970	-0.0743	0.0586	0.0030	-0.0889	-0.0547	-0.0482	0.0752	0.0509	0.0347	-0.0097	0.0536	0.0584	1970	0.0401

* Compound annual return

Table A-1 **Large Company Stocks: Total Returns**

(continued)

From January 1971 to December 1998

YEAR	JAN	FEB	MAR	APR	MAY	JUN	JUL	AUG	SEP	OCT	NOV	DEC	YEAR	JAN–DEC*
1971	0.0419	0.0141	0.0382	0.0377	-0.0367	0.0021	-0.0399	0.0412	-0.0056	-0.0404	0.0027	0.0877	1971	0.1431
1972	0.0194	0.0299	0.0072	0.0057	0.0219	-0.0205	0.0036	0.0391	-0.0036	0.0107	0.0505	0.0131	1972	0.1898
1973	-0.0159	-0.0333	-0.0002	-0.0395	-0.0139	-0.0051	0.0394	-0.0318	0.0415	0.0003	-0.1082	0.0183	1973	-0.1466
1974	-0.0085	0.0019	-0.0217	-0.0373	-0.0272	-0.0128	-0.0759	-0.0828	-0.1170	0.1657	-0.0448	-0.0177	1974	-0.2647
1975	0.1251	0.0674	0.0237	0.0493	0.0509	0.0462	-0.0659	-0.0144	-0.0328	0.0637	0.0313	-0.0096	1975	0.3720
1976	0.1199	-0.0058	0.0326	-0.0099	-0.0073	0.0427	-0.0068	0.0014	0.0247	-0.0206	-0.0009	0.0540	1976	0.2384
1977	-0.0489	-0.0151	-0.0119	0.0014	-0.0150	0.0475	-0.0151	-0.0133	0.0000	-0.0415	0.0370	0.0048	1977	-0.0718
1978	-0.0596	-0.0161	0.0276	0.0870	0.0136	-0.0152	0.0560	0.0340	-0.0048	-0.0891	0.0260	0.0172	1978	0.0656
1979	0.0421	-0.0284	0.0575	0.0036	-0.0168	0.0410	0.0110	0.0611	0.0025	-0.0656	0.0514	0.0192	1979	0.1844
1980	0.0610	0.0031	-0.0987	0.0429	0.0562	0.0296	0.0676	0.0131	0.0281	0.0187	0.1095	-0.0315	1980	0.3242
1981	-0.0438	0.0208	0.0380	-0.0213	0.0062	-0.0080	0.0007	-0.0554	-0.0502	0.0528	0.0441	-0.0265	1981	-0.0491
1982	-0.0163	-0.0512	-0.0060	0.0414	-0.0288	-0.0174	-0.0215	0.1267	0.0110	0.1126	0.0438	0.0173	1982	0.2141
1983	0.0348	0.0260	0.0365	0.0758	-0.0052	0.0382	-0.0313	0.0170	0.0136	-0.0134	0.0233	-0.0061	1983	0.2251
1984	-0.0065	-0.0328	0.0171	0.0069	-0.0534	0.0221	-0.0143	0.1125	0.0002	0.0026	-0.0101	0.0253	1984	0.0627
1985	0.0768	0.0137	0.0018	-0.0032	0.0615	0.0159	-0.0026	-0.0061	-0.0321	0.0447	0.0716	0.0467	1985	0.3216
1986	0.0044	0.0761	0.0554	-0.0124	0.0549	0.0166	-0.0569	0.0748	-0.0822	0.0556	0.0256	-0.0264	1986	0.1847
1987	0.1343	0.0413	0.0272	-0.0088	0.0103	0.0499	0.0498	0.0385	-0.0220	-0.2152	-0.0819	0.0738	1987	0.0523
1988	0.0427	0.0470	-0.0302	0.0108	0.0078	0.0464	-0.0040	-0.0331	0.0424	0.0273	-0.0142	0.0181	1988	0.1681
1989	0.0723	-0.0249	0.0236	0.0516	0.0402	-0.0054	0.0898	0.0193	-0.0039	-0.0233	0.0208	0.0236	1989	0.3149
1990	-0.0671	0.0129	0.0263	-0.0247	0.0975	-0.0070	-0.0032	-0.0903	-0.0492	-0.0037	0.0644	0.0274	1990	-0.0317
1991	0.0442	0.0716	0.0238	0.0028	0.0428	-0.0457	0.0468	0.0235	-0.0164	0.0134	-0.0404	0.1143	1991	0.3055
1992	-0.0186	0.0128	-0.0196	0.0291	0.0054	-0.0145	0.0403	-0.0202	0.0115	0.0036	0.0337	0.0131	1992	0.0767
1993	0.0073	0.0135	0.0215	-0.0245	0.0270	0.0033	-0.0047	0.0381	-0.0074	0.0203	-0.0094	0.0123	1993	0.0999
1994	0.0335	-0.0270	-0.0435	0.0130	0.0163	-0.0247	0.0331	0.0407	-0.0241	0.0229	-0.0367	0.0146	1994	0.0131
1995	0.0260	0.0388	0.0296	0.0291	0.0395	0.0235	0.0333	0.0027	0.0419	-0.0035	0.0440	0.0185	1995	0.3743
1996	0.0344	0.0096	0.0096	0.0147	0.0258	0.0041	-0.0445	0.0212	0.0562	0.0274	0.0759	-0.0196	1996	0.2307
1997	0.0621	0.0081	-0.0416	0.0597	0.0614	0.0446	0.0794	-0.0556	0.0548	-0.0334	0.0463	0.0172	1997	0.3336
1998	0.0111	0.0721	0.0512	0.0101	-0.0172	0.0406	-0.0107	-0.1446	0.0641	0.0813	0.0606	0.0576	1998	0.2858

* Compound annual return

Table A-2 Large Company Stocks: Income Returns

From January 1926 to December 1970

YEAR	JAN	FEB	MAR	APR	MAY	JUN	JUL	AUG	SEP	OCT	NOV	DEC	YEAR	JAN–DEC*
1926	0.0016	0.0055	0.0016	0.0026	0.0102	0.0025	0.0024	0.0078	0.0023	0.0030	0.0123	0.0030	1926	0.0541
1927	0.0015	0.0061	0.0022	0.0029	0.0085	0.0027	0.0020	0.0070	0.0018	0.0029	0.0105	0.0029	1927	0.0571
1928	0.0011	0.0051	0.0017	0.0021	0.0071	0.0020	0.0016	0.0062	0.0019	0.0023	0.0092	0.0021	1928	0.0481
1929	0.0012	0.0039	0.0012	0.0016	0.0066	0.0016	0.0014	0.0048	0.0013	0.0020	0.0091	0.0029	1929	0.0398
1930	0.0014	0.0044	0.0013	0.0016	0.0068	0.0020	0.0020	0.0066	0.0019	0.0032	0.0130	0.0036	1930	0.0457
1931	0.0013	0.0050	0.0017	0.0024	0.0093	0.0031	0.0020	0.0087	0.0022	0.0051	0.0180	0.0053	1931	0.0535
1932	0.0012	0.0063	0.0024	0.0027	0.0137	0.0067	0.0045	0.0115	0.0024	0.0037	0.0172	0.0046	1932	0.0616
1933	0.0015	0.0072	0.0018	0.0034	0.0096	0.0021	0.0018	0.0060	0.0018	0.0031	0.0100	0.0030	1933	0.0639
1934	0.0010	0.0045	0.0009	0.0019	0.0076	0.0021	0.0020	0.0069	0.0022	0.0033	0.0114	0.0031	1934	0.0446
1935	0.0011	0.0055	0.0023	0.0024	0.0086	0.0021	0.0020	0.0063	0.0018	0.0026	0.0080	0.0023	1935	0.0495
1936	0.0015	0.0056	0.0014	0.0020	0.0087	0.0028	0.0020	0.0063	0.0019	0.0025	0.0093	0.0029	1936	0.0536
1937	0.0012	0.0045	0.0017	0.0022	0.0079	0.0025	0.0019	0.0071	0.0019	0.0036	0.0146	0.0045	1937	0.0466
1938	0.0019	0.0065	0.0018	0.0035	0.0113	0.0032	0.0017	0.0048	0.0017	0.0016	0.0061	0.0024	1938	0.0483
1939	0.0015	0.0065	0.0016	0.0027	0.0110	0.0026	0.0018	0.0066	0.0027	0.0023	0.0094	0.0033	1939	0.0469
1940	0.0016	0.0066	0.0025	0.0024	0.0107	0.0043	0.0030	0.0087	0.0028	0.0028	0.0108	0.0038	1940	0.0536
1941	0.0019	0.0089	0.0030	0.0040	0.0140	0.0043	0.0030	0.0096	0.0029	0.0029	0.0137	0.0044	1941	0.0671
1942	0.0023	0.0091	0.0023	0.0037	0.0157	0.0037	0.0024	0.0093	0.0023	0.0034	0.0117	0.0032	1942	0.0679
1943	0.0020	0.0076	0.0018	0.0026	0.0104	0.0025	0.0016	0.0068	0.0025	0.0025	0.0101	0.0027	1943	0.0624
1944	0.0017	0.0068	0.0025	0.0025	0.0101	0.0032	0.0015	0.0071	0.0023	0.0023	0.0094	0.0023	1944	0.0548
1945	0.0015	0.0067	0.0021	0.0022	0.0081	0.0027	0.0020	0.0061	0.0019	0.0019	0.0072	0.0017	1945	0.0497
1946	0.0017	0.0054	0.0017	0.0017	0.0064	0.0021	0.0016	0.0056	0.0018	0.0020	0.0088	0.0027	1946	0.0409
1947	0.0020	0.0070	0.0019	0.0026	0.0103	0.0028	0.0020	0.0076	0.0026	0.0026	0.0110	0.0027	1947	0.0549
1948	0.0020	0.0082	0.0021	0.0027	0.0097	0.0024	0.0024	0.0082	0.0025	0.0032	0.0121	0.0041	1948	0.0608
1949	0.0026	0.0099	0.0027	0.0033	0.0115	0.0035	0.0028	0.0100	0.0026	0.0045	0.0162	0.0050	1949	0.0750
1950	0.0024	0.0100	0.0029	0.0035	0.0116	0.0032	0.0034	0.0118	0.0033	0.0051	0.0179	0.0051	1950	0.0877
1951	0.0025	0.0092	0.0028	0.0028	0.0107	0.0033	0.0024	0.0085	0.0021	0.0034	0.0122	0.0035	1951	0.0691
1952	0.0025	0.0083	0.0026	0.0029	0.0111	0.0029	0.0020	0.0075	0.0020	0.0029	0.0106	0.0027	1952	0.0593
1953	0.0023	0.0076	0.0023	0.0028	0.0110	0.0029	0.0021	0.0077	0.0021	0.0030	0.0114	0.0032	1953	0.0546
1954	0.0024	0.0084	0.0023	0.0026	0.0088	0.0024	0.0017	0.0065	0.0020	0.0028	0.0101	0.0026	1954	0.0621
1955	0.0017	0.0063	0.0019	0.0019	0.0068	0.0018	0.0015	0.0053	0.0016	0.0021	0.0078	0.0022	1955	0.0456
1956	0.0018	0.0066	0.0018	0.0017	0.0064	0.0018	0.0015	0.0053	0.0015	0.0015	0.0059	0.0018	1956	0.0383
1957	0.0017	0.0063	0.0018	0.0018	0.0068	0.0017	0.0017	0.0056	0.0018	0.0019	0.0071	0.0019	1957	0.0384
1958	0.0017	0.0065	0.0020	0.0019	0.0062	0.0018	0.0018	0.0057	0.0017	0.0016	0.0060	0.0015	1958	0.0438
1959	0.0014	0.0051	0.0014	0.0014	0.0050	0.0014	0.0014	0.0048	0.0013	0.0016	0.0054	0.0015	1959	0.0331
1960	0.0015	0.0056	0.0016	0.0014	0.0057	0.0016	0.0014	0.0056	0.0014	0.0017	0.0062	0.0016	1960	0.0326
1961	0.0014	0.0050	0.0014	0.0012	0.0047	0.0014	0.0014	0.0046	0.0013	0.0015	0.0054	0.0014	1961	0.0348
1962	0.0013	0.0046	0.0013	0.0013	0.0049	0.0015	0.0016	0.0055	0.0017	0.0020	0.0071	0.0018	1962	0.0298
1963	0.0014	0.0050	0.0016	0.0015	0.0050	0.0014	0.0013	0.0048	0.0014	0.0017	0.0059	0.0018	1963	0.0361
1964	0.0013	0.0048	0.0013	0.0014	0.0048	0.0014	0.0012	0.0044	0.0013	0.0015	0.0057	0.0017	1964	0.0333
1965	0.0013	0.0046	0.0013	0.0014	0.0047	0.0014	0.0013	0.0047	0.0014	0.0016	0.0056	0.0016	1965	0.0321
1966	0.0013	0.0047	0.0013	0.0015	0.0049	0.0015	0.0014	0.0053	0.0017	0.0018	0.0064	0.0017	1966	0.0311
1967	0.0016	0.0052	0.0015	0.0014	0.0048	0.0015	0.0014	0.0047	0.0014	0.0014	0.0054	0.0015	1967	0.0364
1968	0.0013	0.0051	0.0016	0.0014	0.0049	0.0014	0.0013	0.0049	0.0014	0.0015	0.0051	0.0014	1968	0.0318
1969	0.0013	0.0048	0.0014	0.0014	0.0048	0.0014	0.0014	0.0053	0.0015	0.0016	0.0056	0.0016	1969	0.0304
1970	0.0015	0.0059	0.0016	0.0016	0.0063	0.0018	0.0019	0.0064	0.0017	0.0017	0.0061	0.0016	1970	0.0341

* Compound annual return

Table A-2 **Large Company Stocks: Income Returns**

(continued)

From January 1971 to December 1998

YEAR	JAN	FEB	MAR	APR	MAY	JUN	JUL	AUG	SEP	OCT	NOV	DEC	YEAR	JAN–DEC*
1971	0.0014	0.0050	0.0014	0.0014	0.0048	0.0014	0.0014	0.0051	0.0014	0.0014	0.0052	0.0015	1971	0.0333
1972	0.0013	0.0046	0.0013	0.0013	0.0046	0.0013	0.0013	0.0047	0.0013	0.0014	0.0048	0.0013	1972	0.0309
1973	0.0012	0.0042	0.0013	0.0013	0.0050	0.0014	0.0014	0.0049	0.0014	0.0016	0.0056	0.0018	1973	0.0286
1974	0.0015	0.0055	0.0016	0.0017	0.0063	0.0018	0.0019	0.0074	0.0024	0.0027	0.0084	0.0024	1974	0.0369
1975	0.0023	0.0075	0.0020	0.0020	0.0068	0.0019	0.0018	0.0066	0.0018	0.0020	0.0066	0.0019	1975	0.0537
1976	0.0016	0.0056	0.0019	0.0011	0.0071	0.0018	0.0012	0.0065	0.0020	0.0017	0.0069	0.0015	1976	0.0438
1977	0.0016	0.0065	0.0021	0.0012	0.0086	0.0021	0.0011	0.0078	0.0025	0.0019	0.0100	0.0020	1977	0.0431
1978	0.0019	0.0086	0.0027	0.0016	0.0094	0.0023	0.0020	0.0081	0.0024	0.0025	0.0093	0.0023	1978	0.0533
1979	0.0024	0.0081	0.0024	0.0020	0.0095	0.0023	0.0022	0.0080	0.0025	0.0030	0.0088	0.0024	1979	0.0571
1980	0.0034	0.0075	0.0031	0.0018	0.0096	0.0026	0.0026	0.0073	0.0029	0.0026	0.0072	0.0024	1980	0.0573
1981	0.0019	0.0075	0.0020	0.0022	0.0079	0.0021	0.0032	0.0066	0.0036	0.0036	0.0075	0.0036	1981	0.0489
1982	0.0012	0.0093	0.0042	0.0014	0.0104	0.0029	0.0015	0.0107	0.0034	0.0022	0.0077	0.0021	1982	0.0550
1983	0.0017	0.0070	0.0034	0.0009	0.0071	0.0030	0.0017	0.0057	0.0034	0.0018	0.0059	0.0027	1983	0.0500
1984	0.0027	0.0061	0.0036	0.0014	0.0060	0.0046	0.0022	0.0062	0.0037	0.0027	0.0050	0.0029	1984	0.0456
1985	0.0027	0.0051	0.0047	0.0014	0.0074	0.0038	0.0022	0.0059	0.0026	0.0022	0.0065	0.0016	1985	0.0510
1986	0.0020	0.0046	0.0026	0.0017	0.0047	0.0025	0.0018	0.0036	0.0032	0.0009	0.0041	0.0019	1986	0.0374
1987	0.0025	0.0044	0.0008	0.0027	0.0043	0.0020	0.0016	0.0035	0.0022	0.0024	0.0034	0.0009	1987	0.0364
1988	0.0023	0.0052	0.0031	0.0014	0.0046	0.0031	0.0014	0.0055	0.0027	0.0013	0.0047	0.0034	1988	0.0417
1989	0.0012	0.0040	0.0028	0.0015	0.0051	0.0025	0.0014	0.0038	0.0026	0.0019	0.0043	0.0022	1989	0.0385
1990	0.0017	0.0044	0.0020	0.0022	0.0055	0.0019	0.0020	0.0040	0.0020	0.0030	0.0045	0.0026	1990	0.0336
1991	0.0027	0.0043	0.0016	0.0025	0.0042	0.0022	0.0019	0.0039	0.0027	0.0015	0.0035	0.0027	1991	0.0382
1992	0.0013	0.0032	0.0022	0.0012	0.0044	0.0028	0.0009	0.0038	0.0024	0.0015	0.0034	0.0030	1992	0.0303
1993	0.0003	0.0030	0.0028	0.0009	0.0043	0.0025	0.0006	0.0037	0.0026	0.0009	0.0035	0.0022	1993	0.0283
1994	0.0010	0.0030	0.0022	0.0015	0.0039	0.0021	0.0016	0.0031	0.0028	0.0020	0.0028	0.0023	1994	0.0282
1995	0.0017	0.0027	0.0023	0.0011	0.0032	0.0022	0.0015	0.0030	0.0018	0.0015	0.0030	0.0011	1995	0.0291
1996	0.0018	0.0027	0.0017	0.0013	0.0029	0.0018	0.0012	0.0024	0.0020	0.0013	0.0025	0.0019	1996	0.0254
1997	0.0008	0.0022	0.0010	0.0013	0.0028	0.0011	0.0013	0.0018	0.0016	0.0011	0.0017	0.0014	1997	0.0211
1998	0.0009	0.0017	0.0013	0.0010	0.0016	0.0012	0.0010	0.0012	0.0017	0.0010	0.0015	0.0012	1998	0.0168

* Compound annual return

Table A-3

Large Company Stocks: Capital Appreciation Returns

From January 1926 to December 1970

YEAR	JAN	FEB	MAR	APR	MAY	JUN	JUL	AUG	SEP	OCT	NOV	DEC	YEAR	JAN–DEC*
1926	-0.0016	-0.0440	-0.0591	0.0227	0.0077	0.0432	0.0455	0.0171	0.0229	-0.0313	0.0223	0.0166	1926	0.0572
1927	-0.0208	0.0477	0.0065	0.0172	0.0522	-0.0094	0.0650	0.0445	0.0432	-0.0531	0.0616	0.0250	1927	0.3091
1928	-0.0051	-0.0176	0.1083	0.0324	0.0127	-0.0405	0.0125	0.0741	0.0240	0.0145	0.1199	0.0029	1928	0.3788
1929	0.0571	-0.0058	-0.0023	0.0161	-0.0428	0.1124	0.0456	0.0980	-0.0489	-0.1993	-0.1337	0.0253	1929	-0.1191
1930	0.0625	0.0215	0.0799	-0.0095	-0.0165	-0.1646	0.0367	0.0075	-0.1301	-0.0888	-0.0218	-0.0742	1930	-0.2848
1931	0.0489	0.1144	-0.0692	-0.0959	-0.1372	0.1390	-0.0742	0.0095	-0.2994	0.0844	-0.0978	-0.1453	1931	-0.4707
1932	-0.0283	0.0507	-0.1182	-0.2025	-0.2333	-0.0089	0.3770	0.3754	-0.0369	-0.1386	-0.0589	0.0519	1932	-0.1515
1933	0.0073	-0.1844	0.0336	0.4222	0.1587	0.1317	-0.0880	0.1146	-0.1136	-0.0885	0.1027	0.0223	1933	0.4659
1934	0.1059	-0.0367	-0.0009	-0.0270	-0.0813	0.0208	-0.1152	0.0541	-0.0055	-0.0319	0.0829	-0.0042	1934	-0.0594
1935	-0.0421	-0.0396	-0.0309	0.0956	0.0323	0.0679	0.0831	0.0217	0.0239	0.0751	0.0393	0.0371	1935	0.4137
1936	0.0655	0.0168	0.0254	-0.0771	0.0458	0.0306	0.0681	0.0088	0.0013	0.0750	0.0041	-0.0058	1936	0.2792
1937	0.0378	0.0146	-0.0094	-0.0831	-0.0103	-0.0529	0.1026	-0.0554	-0.1421	-0.1017	-0.1011	-0.0504	1937	-0.3859
1938	0.0133	0.0608	-0.2504	0.1412	-0.0443	0.2470	0.0727	-0.0274	0.0149	0.0760	-0.0334	0.0377	1938	0.2521
1939	-0.0689	0.0325	-0.1354	-0.0055	0.0623	-0.0638	0.1087	-0.0714	0.1646	-0.0146	-0.0491	0.0238	1939	-0.0545
1940	-0.0352	0.0066	0.0099	-0.0049	-0.2395	0.0766	0.0311	0.0262	0.0095	0.0394	-0.0424	-0.0028	1940	-0.1529
1941	-0.0482	-0.0149	0.0040	-0.0653	0.0043	0.0535	0.0548	-0.0087	-0.0097	-0.0686	-0.0421	-0.0451	1941	-0.1786
1942	0.0138	-0.0250	-0.0675	-0.0437	0.0640	0.0184	0.0313	0.0070	0.0267	0.0644	-0.0138	0.0517	1942	0.1243
1943	0.0716	0.0506	0.0527	0.0009	0.0449	0.0198	-0.0543	0.0103	0.0237	-0.0132	-0.0755	0.0590	1943	0.1945
1944	0.0154	-0.0025	0.0169	-0.0125	0.0404	0.0510	-0.0208	0.0087	-0.0031	0.0000	0.0039	0.0351	1944	0.1380
1945	0.0143	0.0616	-0.0462	0.0880	0.0115	-0.0033	-0.0201	0.0580	0.0419	0.0303	0.0324	0.0099	1945	0.3072
1946	0.0697	-0.0695	0.0463	0.0376	0.0224	-0.0391	-0.0255	-0.0729	-0.1015	-0.0080	-0.0115	0.0429	1946	-0.1187
1947	0.0235	-0.0147	-0.0169	-0.0389	-0.0089	0.0526	0.0362	-0.0279	-0.0137	0.0212	-0.0285	0.0207	1947	0.0000
1948	-0.0399	-0.0470	0.0771	0.0265	0.0782	0.0030	-0.0532	0.0076	-0.0301	0.0678	-0.1082	0.0305	1948	-0.0065
1949	0.0013	-0.0394	0.0301	-0.0212	-0.0373	-0.0021	0.0621	0.0120	0.0237	0.0295	0.0012	0.0436	1949	0.1026
1950	0.0173	0.0100	0.0041	0.0451	0.0393	-0.0580	0.0085	0.0325	0.0559	0.0041	-0.0010	0.0461	1950	0.2178
1951	0.0612	0.0065	-0.0183	0.0481	-0.0406	-0.0260	0.0687	0.0393	-0.0009	-0.0138	-0.0026	0.0389	1951	0.1646
1952	0.0156	-0.0365	0.0477	-0.0431	0.0232	0.0461	0.0176	-0.0146	-0.0196	-0.0008	0.0465	0.0355	1952	0.1178
1953	-0.0072	-0.0182	-0.0236	-0.0265	-0.0032	-0.0163	0.0253	-0.0578	0.0013	0.0510	0.0090	0.0020	1953	-0.0662
1954	0.0512	0.0027	0.0302	0.0490	0.0329	0.0007	0.0572	-0.0340	0.0831	-0.0195	0.0808	0.0508	1954	0.4502
1955	0.0181	0.0035	-0.0049	0.0377	-0.0013	0.0823	0.0607	-0.0078	0.0113	-0.0305	0.0749	-0.0007	1955	0.2640
1956	-0.0365	0.0347	0.0693	-0.0021	-0.0657	0.0392	0.0515	-0.0381	-0.0455	0.0051	-0.0110	0.0353	1956	0.0262
1957	-0.0418	-0.0326	0.0196	0.0370	0.0369	-0.0013	0.0114	-0.0561	-0.0619	-0.0321	0.0161	-0.0415	1957	-0.1431
1958	0.0428	-0.0206	0.0309	0.0318	0.0150	0.0261	0.0431	0.0119	0.0484	0.0254	0.0224	0.0520	1958	0.3806
1959	0.0038	-0.0002	0.0005	0.0388	0.0189	-0.0036	0.0349	-0.0150	-0.0456	0.0113	0.0132	0.0276	1959	0.0848
1960	-0.0715	0.0092	-0.0139	-0.0175	0.0269	0.0195	-0.0248	0.0261	-0.0604	-0.0024	0.0403	0.0463	1960	-0.0297
1961	0.0632	0.0269	0.0255	0.0038	0.0191	-0.0288	0.0328	0.0196	-0.0197	0.0283	0.0393	0.0032	1961	0.2313
1962	-0.0379	0.0163	-0.0059	-0.0620	-0.0860	-0.0818	0.0636	0.0153	-0.0482	0.0044	0.1016	0.0135	1962	-0.1181
1963	0.0491	-0.0289	0.0355	0.0485	0.0143	-0.0202	-0.0035	0.0487	-0.0110	0.0322	-0.0105	0.0244	1963	0.1889
1964	0.0269	0.0099	0.0152	0.0061	0.0115	0.0164	0.0182	-0.0162	0.0287	0.0081	-0.0052	0.0039	1964	0.1297
1965	0.0332	-0.0015	-0.0145	0.0342	-0.0077	-0.0486	0.0134	0.0225	0.0320	0.0273	-0.0088	0.0090	1965	0.0906
1966	0.0049	-0.0179	-0.0218	0.0205	-0.0541	-0.0161	-0.0135	-0.0778	-0.0070	0.0475	0.0031	-0.0015	1966	-0.1309
1967	0.0782	0.0020	0.0394	0.0422	-0.0524	0.0175	0.0453	-0.0117	0.0328	-0.0291	0.0011	0.0263	1967	0.2009
1968	-0.0438	-0.0312	0.0094	0.0819	0.0112	0.0091	-0.0185	0.0115	0.0385	0.0072	0.0480	-0.0416	1968	0.0766
1969	-0.0082	-0.0474	0.0344	0.0215	-0.0022	-0.0556	-0.0602	0.0401	-0.0250	0.0442	-0.0353	-0.0193	1969	-0.1142
1970	-0.0759	0.0527	0.0015	-0.0905	-0.0610	-0.0500	0.0733	0.0445	0.0330	-0.0114	0.0474	0.0568	1970	0.0016

* Compound annual return

Table A-3 **Large Company Stocks: Capital Appreciation Returns**

(continued)

From January 1971 to December 1998

YEAR	JAN	FEB	MAR	APR	MAY	JUN	JUL	AUG	SEP	OCT	NOV	DEC	YEAR	JAN–DEC*
1971	0.0405	0.0091	0.0368	0.0363	-0.0416	0.0007	-0.0413	0.0361	-0.0070	-0.0418	-0.0025	0.0862	1971	0.1079
1972	0.0181	0.0253	0.0059	0.0044	0.0173	-0.0218	0.0023	0.0345	-0.0049	0.0093	0.0456	0.0118	1972	0.1563
1973	-0.0171	-0.0375	-0.0014	-0.0408	-0.0189	-0.0066	0.0380	-0.0367	0.0401	-0.0013	-0.1139	0.0166	1973	-0.1737
1974	-0.0100	-0.0036	-0.0233	-0.0391	-0.0336	-0.0147	-0.0778	-0.0903	-0.1193	0.1630	-0.0532	-0.0202	1974	-0.2972
1975	0.1228	0.0599	0.0217	0.0473	0.0441	0.0443	-0.0677	-0.0211	-0.0346	0.0616	0.0247	-0.0115	1975	0.3155
1976	0.1183	-0.0114	0.0307	-0.0110	-0.0144	0.0409	-0.0081	-0.0051	0.0226	-0.0222	-0.0078	0.0525	1976	0.1915
1977	-0.0505	-0.0217	-0.0140	0.0002	-0.0236	0.0454	-0.0162	-0.0210	-0.0025	-0.0434	0.0270	0.0028	1977	-0.1150
1978	-0.0615	-0.0248	0.0249	0.0854	0.0042	-0.0176	0.0539	0.0259	-0.0073	-0.0916	0.0166	0.0149	1978	0.0106
1979	0.0397	-0.0365	0.0551	0.0017	-0.0263	0.0387	0.0088	0.0531	0.0000	-0.0686	0.0426	0.0168	1979	0.1231
1980	0.0576	-0.0044	-0.1018	0.0411	0.0466	0.0270	0.0650	0.0058	0.0252	0.0160	0.1023	-0.0339	1980	0.2577
1981	-0.0457	0.0133	0.0360	-0.0235	-0.0017	-0.0101	-0.0025	-0.0620	-0.0538	0.0492	0.0366	-0.0301	1981	-0.0972
1982	-0.0175	-0.0605	-0.0102	0.0400	-0.0392	-0.0203	-0.0230	0.1160	0.0076	0.1104	0.0361	0.0152	1982	0.1476
1983	0.0331	0.0190	0.0331	0.0749	-0.0123	0.0352	-0.0330	0.0113	0.0102	-0.0152	0.0174	-0.0088	1983	0.1727
1984	-0.0092	-0.0389	0.0135	0.0055	-0.0594	0.0175	-0.0165	0.1063	-0.0035	-0.0001	-0.0151	0.0224	1984	0.0139
1985	0.0741	0.0086	-0.0029	-0.0046	0.0541	0.0121	-0.0048	-0.0120	-0.0347	0.0425	0.0651	0.0451	1985	0.2634
1986	0.0024	0.0715	0.0528	-0.0141	0.0502	0.0141	-0.0587	0.0712	-0.0854	0.0547	0.0215	-0.0283	1986	0.1463
1987	0.1318	0.0369	0.0264	-0.0115	0.0060	0.0479	0.0482	0.0350	-0.0242	-0.2176	-0.0853	0.0729	1987	0.0203
1988	0.0404	0.0418	-0.0333	0.0094	0.0032	0.0433	-0.0054	-0.0386	0.0397	0.0260	-0.0189	0.0147	1988	0.1241
1989	0.0711	-0.0289	0.0208	0.0501	0.0351	-0.0079	0.0884	0.0155	-0.0065	-0.0252	0.0165	0.0214	1989	0.2726
1990	-0.0688	0.0085	0.0243	-0.0269	0.0920	-0.0089	-0.0052	-0.0943	-0.0512	-0.0067	0.0599	0.0248	1990	-0.0656
1991	0.0415	0.0673	0.0222	0.0003	0.0386	-0.0479	0.0449	0.0196	-0.0191	0.0119	-0.0439	0.1116	1991	0.2631
1992	-0.0199	0.0096	-0.0218	0.0279	0.0010	-0.0174	0.0394	-0.0240	0.0091	0.0021	0.0303	0.0101	1992	0.0446
1993	0.0070	0.0105	0.0187	-0.0254	0.0227	0.0008	-0.0053	0.0344	-0.0100	0.0194	-0.0129	0.0101	1993	0.0706
1994	0.0325	-0.0300	-0.0457	0.0115	0.0124	-0.0268	0.0315	0.0376	-0.0269	0.0209	-0.0395	0.0123	1994	-0.0154
1995	0.0243	0.0361	0.0273	0.0280	0.0363	0.0213	0.0318	-0.0003	0.0401	-0.0050	0.0410	0.0174	1995	0.3411
1996	0.0326	0.0069	0.0079	0.0134	0.0229	0.0023	-0.0457	0.0188	0.0542	0.0261	0.0734	-0.0215	1996	0.2026
1997	0.0613	0.0059	-0.0426	0.0584	0.0586	0.0435	0.0781	-0.0574	0.0532	-0.0345	0.0446	0.0157	1997	0.3101
1998	0.0102	0.0704	0.0499	0.0091	-0.0188	0.0394	-0.0116	-0.1458	0.0624	0.0803	0.0591	0.0564	1998	0.2667

* Compound annual return

Table A-4 Small Company Stocks: Total Returns

From January 1926 to December 1970

YEAR	JAN	FEB	MAR	APR	MAY	JUN	JUL	AUG	SEP	OCT	NOV	DEC	YEAR	JAN-DEC*
1926	0.0699	-0.0639	-0.1073	0.0179	-0.0066	0.0378	0.0112	0.0256	-0.0001	-0.0227	0.0207	0.0332	1926	0.0028
1927	0.0296	0.0547	-0.0548	0.0573	0.0734	-0.0303	0.0516	-0.0178	0.0047	-0.0659	0.0808	0.0316	1927	0.2210
1928	0.0482	-0.0236	0.0531	0.0910	0.0438	-0.0842	0.0059	0.0442	0.0890	0.0276	0.1147	-0.0513	1928	0.3969
1929	0.0035	-0.0026	-0.0200	0.0306	-0.1336	0.0533	0.0114	-0.0164	-0.0922	-0.2768	-0.1500	-0.0501	1929	-0.5136
1930	0.1293	0.0643	0.1007	-0.0698	-0.0542	-0.2168	0.0301	-0.0166	-0.1459	-0.1097	-0.0028	-0.1166	1930	-0.3815
1931	0.2103	0.2566	-0.0708	-0.2164	-0.1379	0.1819	-0.0557	-0.0763	-0.3246	0.0770	-0.1008	-0.2195	1931	-0.4975
1932	0.1019	0.0291	-0.1311	-0.2220	-0.1193	0.0033	0.3523	0.7346	-0.1320	-0.1775	-0.1227	-0.0492	1932	-0.0539
1933	-0.0083	-0.1278	0.1118	0.5038	0.6339	0.2617	-0.0550	0.0924	-0.1595	-0.1236	0.0654	0.0055	1933	1.4287
1934	0.3891	0.0166	-0.0012	0.0240	-0.1275	-0.0024	-0.2259	0.1546	-0.0167	0.0097	0.0948	0.0172	1934	0.2422
1935	-0.0328	-0.0592	-0.1189	0.0791	-0.0024	0.0305	0.0855	0.0545	0.0357	0.0994	0.1412	0.0598	1935	0.4019
1936	0.3009	0.0602	0.0066	-0.1795	0.0272	-0.0231	0.0873	0.0210	0.0542	0.0635	0.1400	0.0160	1936	0.6480
1937	0.1267	0.0658	0.0120	-0.1679	-0.0408	-0.1183	0.1235	-0.0736	-0.2539	-0.1093	-0.1453	-0.1694	1937	-0.5801
1938	0.0534	0.0343	-0.3600	0.2776	-0.0849	0.3498	0.1499	-0.1001	-0.0157	0.2136	-0.0689	0.0487	1938	0.3280
1939	-0.0848	0.0107	-0.2466	0.0142	0.1088	-0.1042	0.2535	-0.1590	0.5145	-0.0397	-0.1053	0.0422	1939	0.0035
1940	0.0009	0.0821	0.0632	0.0654	-0.3674	0.1051	0.0231	0.0255	0.0213	0.0545	0.0245	-0.0447	1940	-0.0516
1941	0.0025	-0.0288	0.0319	-0.0669	0.0044	0.0753	0.2165	-0.0060	-0.0469	-0.0672	-0.0495	-0.1204	1941	-0.0900
1942	0.1894	-0.0073	-0.0709	-0.0353	-0.0032	0.0336	0.0737	0.0325	0.0912	0.1087	-0.0511	0.0413	1942	0.4451
1943	0.2132	0.1931	0.1445	0.0933	0.1156	-0.0083	-0.1083	-0.0002	0.0428	0.0123	-0.1113	0.1241	1943	0.8837
1944	0.0641	0.0295	0.0749	-0.0532	0.0740	0.1384	-0.0299	0.0318	-0.0020	-0.0108	0.0499	0.0869	1944	0.5372
1945	0.0482	0.1009	-0.0861	0.1157	0.0500	0.0855	-0.0556	0.0557	0.0679	0.0701	0.1172	0.0171	1945	0.7361
1946	0.1562	-0.0637	0.0273	0.0696	0.0591	-0.0462	-0.0530	-0.0849	-0.1603	-0.0118	-0.0141	0.0373	1946	-0.1163
1947	0.0421	-0.0041	-0.0336	-0.1031	-0.0534	0.0552	0.0789	-0.0037	0.0115	0.0282	-0.0303	0.0359	1947	0.0092
1948	-0.0154	-0.0783	0.0986	0.0368	0.1059	0.0048	-0.0578	0.0006	-0.0526	0.0647	-0.1116	0.0088	1948	-0.0211
1949	0.0182	-0.0481	0.0629	-0.0336	-0.0564	-0.0096	0.0671	0.0256	0.0489	0.0472	0.0016	0.0690	1949	0.1975
1950	0.0492	0.0221	-0.0037	0.0411	0.0255	-0.0777	0.0591	0.0530	0.0521	-0.0059	0.0322	0.0953	1950	0.3875
1951	0.0830	0.0061	-0.0477	0.0367	-0.0331	-0.0529	0.0373	0.0605	0.0215	-0.0222	-0.0083	0.0044	1951	0.0780
1952	0.0191	-0.0300	0.0175	-0.0519	0.0032	0.0272	0.0112	-0.0006	-0.0161	-0.0103	0.0485	0.0160	1952	0.0303
1953	0.0409	0.0269	-0.0067	-0.0287	0.0141	-0.0486	0.0152	-0.0628	-0.0262	0.0292	0.0126	-0.0266	1953	-0.0649
1954	0.0756	0.0094	0.0183	0.0140	0.0451	0.0086	0.0808	0.0014	0.0410	0.0068	0.0779	0.1112	1954	0.6058
1955	0.0201	0.0479	0.0085	0.0150	0.0078	0.0293	0.0064	-0.0028	0.0109	-0.0170	0.0468	0.0163	1955	0.2044
1956	-0.0047	0.0278	0.0431	0.0047	-0.0398	0.0056	0.0283	-0.0134	-0.0260	0.0104	0.0053	0.0038	1956	0.0428
1957	0.0236	-0.0200	0.0167	0.0248	0.0075	0.0073	-0.0060	-0.0386	-0.0452	-0.0832	0.0113	-0.0481	1957	-0.1457
1958	0.1105	-0.0170	0.0471	0.0376	0.0387	0.0324	0.0492	0.0428	0.0518	0.0407	0.0496	0.0313	1958	0.6489
1959	0.0575	0.0295	0.0027	0.0117	0.0014	-0.0042	0.0327	-0.0088	-0.0431	0.0227	0.0222	0.0322	1959	0.1640
1960	-0.0306	0.0050	-0.0315	-0.0187	0.0204	0.0340	-0.0189	0.0525	-0.0738	-0.0401	0.0437	0.0332	1960	-0.0329
1961	0.0915	0.0589	0.0619	0.0127	0.0427	-0.0543	0.0031	0.0130	-0.0339	0.0262	0.0613	0.0079	1961	0.3209
1962	0.0136	0.0187	0.0057	-0.0777	-0.1009	-0.0785	0.0763	0.0289	-0.0659	-0.0373	0.1248	-0.0089	1962	-0.1190
1963	0.0906	0.0034	0.0149	0.0312	0.0436	-0.0118	0.0033	0.0517	-0.0163	0.0236	-0.0106	-0.0048	1963	0.2357
1964	0.0274	0.0365	0.0219	0.0093	0.0157	0.0163	0.0398	-0.0029	0.0402	0.0205	0.0011	-0.0112	1964	0.2352
1965	0.0529	0.0390	0.0238	0.0509	-0.0078	-0.0901	0.0449	0.0595	0.0347	0.0572	0.0371	0.0622	1965	0.4175
1966	0.0756	0.0311	-0.0192	0.0343	-0.0961	-0.0012	-0.0012	-0.1080	-0.0164	-0.0107	0.0491	0.0065	1966	-0.0701
1967	0.1838	0.0450	0.0615	0.0271	-0.0085	0.1017	0.0951	0.0020	0.0565	-0.0311	0.0117	0.0965	1967	0.8357
1968	0.0154	-0.0709	-0.0109	0.1461	0.0999	0.0030	-0.0345	0.0367	0.0599	0.0030	0.0764	0.0062	1968	0.3597
1969	-0.0166	-0.0990	0.0396	0.0395	0.0173	-0.1165	-0.1070	0.0732	-0.0261	0.0610	-0.0557	-0.0687	1969	-0.2505
1970	-0.0608	0.0387	-0.0285	-0.1728	-0.1031	-0.0929	0.0554	0.0949	0.1086	-0.0706	0.0137	0.0726	1970	-0.1743

* Compound annual return

Table A-4 **Small Company Stocks: Total Returns**

(continued)

From January 1971 to December 1998

YEAR	JAN	FEB	MAR	APR	MAY	JUN	JUL	AUG	SEP	OCT	NOV	DEC	YEAR	JAN–DEC*
1971	0.1592	0.0317	0.0564	0.0247	-0.0605	-0.0319	-0.0563	0.0583	-0.0226	-0.0551	-0.0373	0.1144	1971	0.1650
1972	0.1130	0.0296	-0.0143	0.0129	-0.0191	-0.0305	-0.0413	0.0186	-0.0349	-0.0175	0.0592	-0.0214	1972	0.0443
1973	-0.0432	-0.0799	-0.0208	-0.0621	-0.0811	-0.0290	0.1194	-0.0445	0.1064	0.0084	-0.1962	-0.0014	1973	-0.3090
1974	0.1326	-0.0085	-0.0074	-0.0464	-0.0793	-0.0147	-0.0219	-0.0681	-0.0653	0.1063	-0.0438	-0.0788	1974	-0.1995
1975	0.2767	0.0285	0.0618	0.0531	0.0663	0.0750	-0.0254	-0.0574	-0.0182	-0.0050	0.0320	-0.0197	1975	0.5282
1976	0.2684	0.1390	-0.0015	-0.0359	-0.0361	0.0459	0.0045	-0.0290	0.0104	-0.0209	0.0404	0.1180	1976	0.5738
1977	0.0450	-0.0039	0.0131	0.0228	-0.0028	0.0772	0.0030	-0.0107	0.0092	-0.0330	0.1086	0.0081	1977	0.2538
1978	-0.0189	0.0347	0.1032	0.0788	0.0820	-0.0189	0.0684	0.0939	-0.0032	-0.2427	0.0732	0.0168	1978	0.2346
1979	0.1321	-0.0282	0.1120	0.0387	0.0035	0.0472	0.0171	0.0756	-0.0344	-0.1154	0.0858	0.0588	1979	0.4346
1980	0.0836	-0.0284	-0.1778	0.0694	0.0750	0.0452	0.1323	0.0604	0.0418	0.0333	0.0766	-0.0338	1980	0.3988
1981	0.0207	0.0094	0.0943	0.0657	0.0422	0.0076	-0.0316	-0.0684	-0.0733	0.0742	0.0276	-0.0220	1981	0.1388
1982	-0.0196	-0.0296	-0.0086	0.0383	-0.0248	-0.0159	-0.0015	0.0698	0.0327	0.1305	0.0779	0.0132	1982	0.2801
1983	0.0628	0.0712	0.0525	0.0767	0.0870	0.0348	-0.0088	-0.0197	0.0133	-0.0568	0.0516	-0.0145	1983	0.3967
1984	-0.0008	-0.0645	0.0174	-0.0085	-0.0521	0.0300	-0.0420	0.0998	0.0027	-0.0217	-0.0336	0.0150	1984	-0.0667
1985	0.1059	0.0272	-0.0214	-0.0174	0.0276	0.0106	0.0260	-0.0072	-0.0544	0.0261	0.0620	0.0470	1985	0.2466
1986	0.0112	0.0719	0.0477	0.0064	0.0360	0.0026	-0.0710	0.0218	-0.0559	0.0346	-0.0031	-0.0262	1986	0.0685
1987	0.0943	0.0809	0.0233	-0.0313	-0.0039	0.0266	0.0364	0.0287	-0.0081	-0.2919	-0.0397	0.0520	1987	-0.0930
1988	0.0556	0.0760	0.0408	0.0209	-0.0179	0.0612	-0.0025	-0.0246	0.0227	-0.0123	-0.0437	0.0394	1988	0.2287
1989	0.0404	0.0083	0.0358	0.0279	0.0362	-0.0201	0.0407	0.0122	0.0000	-0.0604	-0.0051	-0.0134	1989	0.1018
1990	-0.0764	0.0187	0.0368	-0.0266	0.0561	0.0144	-0.0382	-0.1296	-0.0829	-0.0572	0.0450	0.0194	1990	-0.2156
1991	0.0841	0.1113	0.0680	0.0034	0.0334	-0.0485	0.0407	0.0261	0.0032	0.0317	-0.0276	0.0601	1991	0.4463
1992	0.1128	0.0452	-0.0249	-0.0403	-0.0014	-0.0519	0.0370	-0.0228	0.0131	0.0259	0.0885	0.0441	1992	0.2335
1993	0.0543	-0.0180	0.0289	-0.0306	0.0342	-0.0038	0.0166	0.0339	0.0316	0.0471	-0.0175	0.0194	1993	0.2098
1994	0.0618	-0.0023	-0.0446	0.0060	-0.0012	-0.0262	0.0184	0.0337	0.0105	0.0115	-0.0326	0.0002	1994	0.0311
1995	0.0283	0.0252	0.0145	0.0352	0.0298	0.0568	0.0645	0.0358	0.0195	-0.0487	0.0192	0.0239	1995	0.3446
1996	0.0028	0.0369	0.0228	0.0848	0.0749	-0.0582	-0.0943	0.0476	0.0291	-0.0175	0.0288	0.0204	1996	0.1762
1997	0.0420	-0.0206	-0.0490	-0.0276	0.1022	0.0498	0.0605	0.0509	0.0844	-0.0386	-0.0155	-0.0171	1997	0.2278
1998	-0.0059	0.0649	0.0481	0.0168	-0.0497	-0.0206	-0.0671	-0.2010	0.0369	0.0356	0.0758	0.0252	1998	-0.0731

* Compound annual return

Table A-5 Long-Term Corporate Bonds: Total Returns

From January 1926 to December 1970

YEAR	JAN	FEB	MAR	APR	MAY	JUN	JUL	AUG	SEP	OCT	NOV	DEC	YEAR	JAN–DEC*
1926	0.0072	0.0045	0.0084	0.0097	0.0044	0.0004	0.0057	0.0044	0.0057	0.0097	0.0057	0.0056	1926	0.0737
1927	0.0056	0.0069	0.0083	0.0055	-0.0011	0.0043	0.0003	0.0083	0.0149	0.0055	0.0068	0.0068	1927	0.0744
1928	0.0027	0.0068	0.0041	0.0014	-0.0078	-0.0024	-0.0010	0.0083	0.0030	0.0083	-0.0036	0.0084	1928	0.0284
1929	0.0043	0.0030	-0.0087	0.0019	0.0045	-0.0046	0.0020	0.0020	0.0034	0.0073	-0.0018	0.0192	1929	0.0327
1930	0.0059	0.0072	0.0138	0.0084	0.0057	0.0110	0.0056	0.0136	0.0108	0.0054	-0.0012	-0.0090	1930	0.0798
1931	0.0203	0.0068	0.0094	0.0067	0.0134	0.0052	0.0052	0.0012	-0.0014	-0.0363	-0.0189	-0.0286	1931	-0.0185
1932	-0.0052	-0.0238	0.0356	-0.0176	0.0107	-0.0009	0.0043	0.0436	0.0301	0.0074	0.0073	0.0139	1932	0.1082
1933	0.0547	-0.0523	0.0047	-0.0095	0.0588	0.0190	0.0161	0.0093	-0.0014	0.0040	-0.0248	0.0257	1933	0.1038
1934	0.0257	0.0146	0.0187	0.0104	0.0090	0.0158	0.0047	0.0047	-0.0061	0.0102	0.0129	0.0101	1934	0.1384
1935	0.0211	0.0141	0.0043	0.0112	0.0042	0.0112	0.0111	-0.0042	0.0000	0.0042	0.0069	0.0083	1935	0.0961
1936	0.0082	0.0054	0.0082	0.0026	0.0040	0.0082	0.0011	0.0067	0.0067	0.0025	0.0109	0.0010	1936	0.0674
1937	0.0024	-0.0046	-0.0114	0.0068	0.0040	0.0053	0.0039	-0.0017	0.0025	0.0067	0.0067	0.0067	1937	0.0275
1938	0.0038	0.0010	-0.0087	0.0138	0.0010	0.0095	0.0066	-0.0019	0.0109	0.0080	0.0037	0.0122	1938	0.0613
1939	0.0022	0.0064	0.0022	0.0064	0.0049	0.0035	-0.0007	-0.0392	0.0151	0.0237	0.0079	0.0078	1939	0.0397
1940	0.0049	0.0021	0.0049	-0.0092	-0.0021	0.0121	0.0021	0.0007	0.0092	0.0049	0.0063	-0.0023	1940	0.0339
1941	0.0006	0.0006	-0.0022	0.0078	0.0049	0.0063	0.0063	0.0034	0.0048	0.0034	-0.0094	0.0006	1941	0.0273
1942	0.0006	-0.0008	0.0063	0.0006	0.0020	0.0034	0.0020	0.0035	0.0020	0.0006	0.0006	0.0049	1942	0.0260
1943	0.0049	0.0006	0.0020	0.0049	0.0048	0.0048	0.0019	0.0019	0.0005	-0.0009	-0.0023	0.0049	1943	0.0283
1944	0.0020	0.0034	0.0048	0.0034	0.0005	0.0020	0.0034	0.0034	0.0019	0.0019	0.0048	0.0149	1944	0.0473
1945	0.0076	0.0046	0.0018	0.0018	-0.0011	0.0032	-0.0011	0.0004	0.0032	0.0032	0.0032	0.0133	1945	0.0408
1946	0.0128	0.0034	0.0034	-0.0043	0.0019	0.0019	-0.0012	-0.0088	-0.0026	0.0020	-0.0025	0.0113	1946	0.0172
1947	0.0005	0.0005	0.0067	0.0020	0.0020	0.0004	0.0020	-0.0071	-0.0131	-0.0099	-0.0098	0.0024	1947	-0.0234
1948	0.0024	0.0039	0.0115	0.0038	0.0008	-0.0083	-0.0052	0.0055	0.0024	0.0024	0.0085	0.0131	1948	0.0414
1949	0.0038	0.0038	0.0007	0.0023	0.0038	0.0084	0.0099	0.0037	0.0021	0.0067	0.0021	-0.0145	1949	0.0331
1950	0.0037	0.0007	0.0022	-0.0008	-0.0008	0.0023	0.0069	0.0038	-0.0039	-0.0008	0.0054	0.0023	1950	0.0212
1951	0.0019	-0.0044	-0.0237	-0.0009	-0.0015	-0.0093	0.0205	0.0114	-0.0057	-0.0145	-0.0061	0.0058	1951	-0.0269
1952	0.0199	-0.0085	0.0076	-0.0004	0.0031	0.0016	0.0016	0.0063	-0.0018	0.0039	0.0108	-0.0091	1952	0.0352
1953	-0.0080	-0.0040	-0.0033	-0.0248	-0.0030	0.0109	0.0177	-0.0085	0.0253	0.0227	-0.0073	0.0172	1953	0.0341
1954	0.0124	0.0198	0.0039	-0.0034	-0.0042	0.0063	0.0040	0.0018	0.0040	0.0040	0.0025	0.0017	1954	0.0539
1955	-0.0097	-0.0063	0.0092	-0.0001	-0.0018	0.0029	-0.0041	-0.0038	0.0076	0.0078	-0.0030	0.0063	1955	0.0048
1956	0.0104	0.0026	-0.0146	-0.0115	0.0052	-0.0018	-0.0093	-0.0208	0.0012	-0.0105	-0.0126	-0.0082	1956	-0.0681
1957	0.0197	0.0093	0.0050	-0.0066	-0.0075	-0.0322	-0.0110	-0.0009	0.0095	0.0023	0.0311	0.0685	1957	0.0871
1958	0.0099	-0.0008	-0.0046	0.0163	0.0031	-0.0038	-0.0153	-0.0320	-0.0096	0.0107	0.0105	-0.0058	1958	-0.0222
1959	-0.0028	0.0126	-0.0083	-0.0172	-0.0114	0.0044	0.0089	-0.0068	-0.0088	0.0165	0.0135	-0.0096	1959	-0.0097
1960	0.0107	0.0128	0.0191	-0.0022	-0.0021	0.0141	0.0257	0.0117	-0.0063	0.0008	-0.0070	0.0104	1960	0.0907
1961	0.0148	0.0210	-0.0029	-0.0116	0.0049	-0.0080	0.0040	-0.0018	0.0144	0.0127	0.0028	-0.0026	1961	0.0482
1962	0.0080	0.0052	0.0151	0.0142	0.0000	-0.0026	-0.0015	0.0143	0.0089	0.0068	0.0062	0.0023	1962	0.0795
1963	0.0059	0.0023	0.0026	-0.0051	0.0048	0.0043	0.0028	0.0035	-0.0023	0.0049	0.0015	-0.0034	1963	0.0219
1964	0.0087	0.0054	-0.0062	0.0040	0.0057	0.0048	0.0052	0.0037	0.0021	0.0050	-0.0004	0.0088	1964	0.0477
1965	0.0081	0.0009	0.0012	0.0021	-0.0008	0.0003	0.0019	-0.0006	-0.0015	0.0046	-0.0057	-0.0149	1965	-0.0046
1966	0.0022	-0.0113	-0.0059	0.0013	-0.0026	0.0030	-0.0098	-0.0259	0.0078	0.0261	-0.0020	0.0201	1966	0.0020
1967	0.0450	-0.0201	0.0117	-0.0071	-0.0254	-0.0223	0.0041	-0.0007	0.0094	-0.0281	-0.0272	0.0127	1967	-0.0495
1968	0.0361	0.0037	-0.0197	0.0048	0.0032	0.0122	0.0341	0.0206	-0.0053	-0.0160	-0.0226	-0.0233	1968	0.0257
1969	0.0139	-0.0160	-0.0200	0.0335	-0.0227	0.0035	0.0005	-0.0020	-0.0244	0.0127	-0.0471	-0.0134	1969	-0.0809
1970	0.0141	0.0401	-0.0045	-0.0250	-0.0163	0.0001	0.0556	0.0100	0.0139	-0.0096	0.0584	0.0372	1970	0.1837

* Compound annual return

Table A-5 **Long-Term Corporate Bonds: Total Returns**

(continued)

From January 1971 to December 1998

YEAR	JAN	FEB	MAR	APR	MAY	JUN	JUL	AUG	SEP	OCT	NOV	DEC	YEAR	JAN–DEC*
1971	0.0532	-0.0366	0.0258	-0.0236	-0.0161	0.0107	-0.0025	0.0554	-0.0102	0.0282	0.0029	0.0223	1971	0.1101
1972	-0.0033	0.0107	0.0024	0.0035	0.0163	-0.0068	0.0030	0.0072	0.0031	0.0101	0.0249	-0.0004	1972	0.0726
1973	-0.0054	0.0023	0.0045	0.0061	-0.0039	-0.0056	-0.0476	0.0356	0.0356	-0.0066	0.0078	-0.0089	1973	0.0114
1974	-0.0053	0.0009	-0.0307	-0.0341	0.0105	-0.0285	-0.0211	-0.0268	0.0174	0.0885	0.0117	-0.0075	1974	-0.0306
1975	0.0596	0.0137	-0.0247	-0.0052	0.0106	0.0304	-0.0030	-0.0175	-0.0126	0.0553	-0.0088	0.0442	1975	0.1464
1976	0.0188	0.0061	0.0167	-0.0015	-0.0103	0.0150	0.0149	0.0231	0.0167	0.0070	0.0319	0.0347	1976	0.1865
1977	-0.0303	-0.0020	0.0094	0.0100	0.0106	0.0175	-0.0005	0.0136	-0.0022	-0.0038	0.0061	-0.0105	1977	0.0171
1978	-0.0089	0.0051	0.0042	-0.0023	-0.0108	0.0023	0.0101	0.0257	-0.0048	-0.0205	0.0134	-0.0133	1978	-0.0007
1979	0.0184	-0.0128	0.0106	-0.0052	0.0228	0.0269	-0.0031	0.0006	-0.0179	-0.0890	0.0222	-0.0108	1979	-0.0418
1980	-0.0645	-0.0665	-0.0062	0.1376	0.0560	0.0341	-0.0429	-0.0445	-0.0237	-0.0159	0.0017	0.0248	1980	-0.0276
1981	-0.0130	-0.0269	0.0311	-0.0769	0.0595	0.0023	-0.0372	-0.0345	-0.0199	0.0521	0.1267	-0.0580	1981	-0.0124
1982	-0.0129	0.0312	0.0306	0.0338	0.0245	-0.0468	0.0540	0.0837	0.0623	0.0759	0.0201	0.0108	1982	0.4256
1983	-0.0094	0.0428	0.0072	0.0548	-0.0324	-0.0046	-0.0455	0.0051	0.0392	-0.0025	0.0142	-0.0033	1983	0.0626
1984	0.0270	-0.0172	-0.0235	-0.0073	-0.0483	0.0199	0.0586	0.0307	0.0314	0.0572	0.0212	0.0128	1984	0.1686
1985	0.0325	-0.0373	0.0179	0.0296	0.0820	0.0083	-0.0121	0.0260	0.0071	0.0329	0.0370	0.0469	1985	0.3009
1986	0.0045	0.0752	0.0256	0.0016	-0.0164	0.0218	0.0031	0.0275	-0.0114	0.0189	0.0233	0.0117	1986	0.1985
1987	0.0216	0.0058	-0.0087	-0.0502	-0.0052	0.0155	-0.0119	-0.0075	-0.0422	0.0507	0.0125	0.0212	1987	-0.0027
1988	0.0517	0.0138	-0.0188	-0.0149	-0.0057	0.0379	-0.0111	0.0054	0.0326	0.0273	-0.0169	0.0039	1988	0.1070
1989	0.0202	-0.0129	0.0064	0.0213	0.0379	0.0395	0.0178	-0.0163	0.0040	0.0276	0.0070	0.0006	1989	0.1623
1990	-0.0191	-0.0012	-0.0011	-0.0191	0.0385	0.0216	0.0102	-0.0292	0.0091	0.0132	0.0285	0.0167	1990	0.0678
1991	0.0150	0.0121	0.0108	0.0138	0.0039	-0.0018	0.0167	0.0275	0.0271	0.0043	0.0106	0.0436	1991	0.1989
1992	-0.0173	0.0096	-0.0073	0.0016	0.0254	0.0156	0.0308	0.0090	0.0099	-0.0156	0.0069	0.0228	1992	0.0939
1993	0.0250	0.0256	0.0025	0.0052	0.0020	0.0293	0.0100	0.0287	0.0043	0.0051	-0.0188	0.0067	1993	0.1319
1994	0.0202	-0.0286	-0.0383	-0.0097	-0.0062	-0.0081	0.0309	-0.0031	-0.0265	-0.0050	0.0018	0.0157	1994	-0.0576
1995	0.0256	0.0289	0.0095	0.0175	0.0631	0.0079	-0.0101	0.0214	0.0153	0.0185	0.0242	0.0228	1995	0.2720
1996	0.0014	-0.0373	-0.0130	-0.0160	0.0005	0.0172	0.0010	-0.0070	0.0259	0.0361	0.0263	-0.0186	1996	0.0140
1997	-0.0028	0.0028	-0.0221	0.0184	0.0128	0.0187	0.0528	-0.0240	0.0226	0.0191	0.0101	0.0163	1997	0.1295
1998	0.0137	-0.0007	0.0038	0.0053	0.0167	0.0115	-0.0056	0.0089	0.0413	-0.0190	0.0270	0.0010	1998	0.1076

* Compound annual return

Table A-6 **Long-Term Government Bonds: Total Returns**

From January 1926 to December 1970

YEAR	JAN	FEB	MAR	APR	MAY	JUN	JUL	AUG	SEP	OCT	NOV	DEC	YEAR	JAN–DEC*
1926	0.0138	0.0063	0.0041	0.0076	0.0014	0.0038	0.0004	0.0000	0.0038	0.0102	0.0160	0.0078	1926	0.0777
1927	0.0075	0.0088	0.0253	-0.0005	0.0109	-0.0069	0.0050	0.0076	0.0018	0.0099	0.0097	0.0072	1927	0.0893
1928	-0.0036	0.0061	0.0045	-0.0004	-0.0077	0.0041	-0.0217	0.0076	-0.0041	0.0158	0.0003	0.0004	1928	0.0010
1929	-0.0090	-0.0157	-0.0144	0.0275	-0.0162	0.0110	0.0000	-0.0034	0.0027	0.0382	0.0236	-0.0089	1929	0.0342
1930	-0.0057	0.0129	0.0083	-0.0016	0.0139	0.0051	0.0034	0.0013	0.0074	0.0035	0.0042	-0.0070	1930	0.0466
1931	-0.0121	0.0085	0.0104	0.0086	0.0145	0.0004	-0.0042	0.0012	-0.0281	-0.0330	0.0027	-0.0220	1931	-0.0531
1932	0.0034	0.0413	-0.0018	0.0604	-0.0188	0.0065	0.0481	0.0003	0.0057	-0.0017	0.0032	0.0131	1932	0.1684
1933	0.0148	-0.0258	0.0097	-0.0032	0.0303	0.0050	-0.0017	0.0044	0.0023	-0.0091	-0.0149	-0.0113	1933	-0.0007
1934	0.0257	0.0081	0.0197	0.0126	0.0131	0.0067	0.0040	-0.0118	-0.0146	0.0182	0.0037	0.0112	1934	0.1003
1935	0.0182	0.0092	0.0041	0.0079	-0.0057	0.0092	0.0046	-0.0133	0.0009	0.0061	0.0010	0.0070	1935	0.0498
1936	0.0055	0.0081	0.0106	0.0035	0.0040	0.0021	0.0060	0.0111	-0.0031	0.0006	0.0205	0.0038	1936	0.0752
1937	-0.0013	0.0086	-0.0411	0.0039	0.0053	-0.0018	0.0138	-0.0104	0.0045	0.0042	0.0096	0.0082	1937	0.0023
1938	0.0057	0.0052	-0.0037	0.0210	0.0044	0.0004	0.0043	0.0000	0.0022	0.0087	-0.0022	0.0080	1938	0.0553
1939	0.0059	0.0080	0.0125	0.0118	0.0171	-0.0027	0.0113	-0.0201	-0.0545	0.0410	0.0162	0.0145	1939	0.0594
1940	-0.0017	0.0027	0.0177	-0.0035	-0.0299	0.0258	0.0052	0.0028	0.0110	0.0031	0.0205	0.0067	1940	0.0609
1941	-0.0201	0.0020	0.0096	0.0129	0.0027	0.0066	0.0022	0.0018	-0.0012	0.0140	-0.0029	-0.0177	1941	0.0093
1942	0.0069	0.0011	0.0092	-0.0029	0.0075	0.0003	0.0018	0.0038	0.0003	0.0024	-0.0035	0.0049	1942	0.0322
1943	0.0033	-0.0005	0.0009	0.0048	0.0050	0.0018	-0.0001	0.0021	0.0011	0.0005	0.0000	0.0018	1943	0.0208
1944	0.0021	0.0032	0.0021	0.0013	0.0028	0.0008	0.0036	0.0027	0.0014	0.0012	0.0024	0.0042	1944	0.0281
1945	0.0127	0.0077	0.0021	0.0160	0.0056	0.0169	-0.0086	0.0026	0.0054	0.0104	0.0125	0.0194	1945	0.1073
1946	0.0025	0.0032	0.0010	-0.0135	-0.0012	0.0070	-0.0040	-0.0111	-0.0009	0.0074	-0.0054	0.0145	1946	-0.0010
1947	-0.0006	0.0021	0.0020	-0.0037	0.0033	0.0010	0.0063	0.0081	-0.0044	-0.0037	-0.0174	-0.0192	1947	-0.0262
1948	0.0020	0.0046	0.0034	0.0045	0.0141	-0.0084	-0.0021	0.0001	0.0014	0.0007	0.0076	0.0056	1948	0.0340
1949	0.0082	0.0049	0.0074	0.0011	0.0019	0.0167	0.0033	0.0111	-0.0011	0.0019	0.0021	0.0052	1949	0.0645
1950	-0.0061	0.0021	0.0008	0.0030	0.0033	-0.0025	0.0055	0.0014	-0.0072	-0.0048	0.0035	0.0016	1950	0.0006
1951	0.0058	-0.0074	-0.0157	-0.0063	-0.0069	-0.0062	0.0138	0.0099	-0.0080	0.0010	-0.0136	-0.0061	1951	-0.0393
1952	0.0028	0.0014	0.0111	0.0171	-0.0033	0.0003	-0.0020	-0.0070	-0.0130	0.0148	-0.0015	-0.0086	1952	0.0116
1953	0.0012	-0.0087	-0.0088	-0.0105	-0.0148	0.0223	0.0039	-0.0008	0.0299	0.0074	-0.0049	0.0206	1953	0.0364
1954	0.0089	0.0240	0.0058	0.0104	-0.0087	0.0163	0.0134	-0.0036	-0.0010	0.0006	-0.0025	0.0064	1954	0.0719
1955	-0.0241	-0.0078	0.0087	0.0001	0.0073	-0.0076	-0.0102	0.0004	0.0073	0.0144	-0.0045	0.0037	1955	-0.0129
1956	0.0083	-0.0002	-0.0149	-0.0113	0.0225	0.0027	-0.0209	-0.0187	0.0050	-0.0054	-0.0057	-0.0179	1956	-0.0559
1957	0.0346	0.0025	-0.0024	-0.0222	-0.0023	-0.0180	-0.0041	0.0002	0.0076	-0.0050	0.0533	0.0307	1957	0.0746
1958	-0.0084	0.0100	0.0102	0.0186	0.0001	-0.0160	-0.0278	-0.0435	-0.0117	0.0138	0.0120	-0.0181	1958	-0.0609
1959	-0.0080	0.0117	0.0017	-0.0117	-0.0005	0.0010	0.0060	-0.0041	-0.0057	0.0150	-0.0119	-0.0159	1959	-0.0226
1960	0.0112	0.0204	0.0282	-0.0170	0.0152	0.0173	0.0368	-0.0067	0.0075	-0.0028	-0.0066	0.0279	1960	0.1378
1961	-0.0107	0.0200	-0.0037	0.0115	-0.0046	-0.0075	0.0035	-0.0038	0.0129	0.0071	-0.0020	-0.0125	1961	0.0097
1962	-0.0014	0.0103	0.0253	0.0082	0.0046	-0.0076	-0.0109	0.0187	0.0061	0.0084	0.0021	0.0035	1962	0.0689
1963	-0.0001	0.0008	0.0009	-0.0012	0.0023	0.0019	0.0031	0.0021	0.0004	-0.0026	0.0051	-0.0006	1963	0.0121
1964	-0.0014	-0.0011	0.0037	0.0047	0.0050	0.0069	0.0008	0.0020	0.0050	0.0043	0.0017	0.0030	1964	0.0351
1965	0.0040	0.0014	0.0054	0.0036	0.0018	0.0047	0.0022	-0.0013	-0.0034	0.0027	-0.0062	-0.0078	1965	0.0071
1966	-0.0104	-0.0250	0.0296	-0.0063	-0.0059	-0.0016	-0.0037	-0.0206	0.0332	0.0228	-0.0148	0.0413	1966	0.0365
1967	0.0154	-0.0221	0.0198	-0.0291	-0.0039	-0.0312	0.0068	-0.0084	-0.0004	-0.0400	-0.0196	0.0192	1967	-0.0918
1968	0.0328	-0.0033	-0.0212	0.0227	0.0043	0.0230	0.0289	-0.0003	-0.0102	-0.0132	-0.0269	-0.0363	1968	-0.0026
1969	-0.0206	0.0042	0.0010	0.0427	-0.0490	0.0214	0.0079	-0.0069	-0.0531	0.0365	-0.0243	-0.0068	1969	-0.0507
1970	-0.0021	0.0587	-0.0068	-0.0413	-0.0468	0.0486	0.0319	-0.0019	0.0228	-0.0109	0.0791	-0.0084	1970	0.1211

* Compound annual return

Table A-6

Long-Term Government Bonds: Total Returns

(continued)

From January 1971 to December 1998

YEAR	JAN	FEB	MAR	APR	MAY	JUN	JUL	AUG	SEP	OCT	NOV	DEC	YEAR	JAN–DEC*
1971	0.0506	-0.0163	0.0526	-0.0283	-0.0006	-0.0159	0.0030	0.0471	0.0204	0.0167	-0.0047	0.0044	1971	0.1323
1972	-0.0063	0.0088	-0.0082	0.0027	0.0270	-0.0065	0.0216	0.0029	-0.0083	0.0234	0.0226	-0.0229	1972	0.0569
1973	-0.0321	0.0014	0.0082	0.0046	-0.0105	-0.0021	-0.0433	0.0391	0.0318	0.0215	-0.0183	-0.0082	1973	-0.0111
1974	-0.0083	-0.0024	-0.0292	-0.0253	0.0123	0.0045	-0.0029	-0.0232	0.0247	0.0489	0.0295	0.0171	1974	0.0435
1975	0.0225	0.0131	-0.0267	-0.0182	0.0212	0.0292	-0.0087	-0.0068	-0.0098	0.0475	-0.0109	0.0390	1975	0.0920
1976	0.0090	0.0062	0.0166	0.0018	-0.0158	0.0208	0.0078	0.0211	0.0145	0.0084	0.0339	0.0327	1976	0.1675
1977	-0.0388	-0.0049	0.0091	0.0071	0.0125	0.0164	-0.0070	0.0198	-0.0029	-0.0093	0.0093	-0.0168	1977	-0.0069
1978	-0.0080	0.0004	-0.0021	-0.0005	-0.0058	-0.0062	0.0143	0.0218	-0.0106	-0.0200	0.0189	-0.0130	1978	-0.0118
1979	0.0191	-0.0135	0.0129	-0.0112	0.0261	0.0311	-0.0085	-0.0035	-0.0122	-0.0841	0.0311	0.0057	1979	-0.0123
1980	-0.0741	-0.0467	-0.0315	0.1523	0.0419	0.0359	-0.0476	-0.0432	-0.0262	-0.0263	0.0100	0.0352	1980	-0.0395
1981	-0.0115	-0.0435	0.0384	-0.0518	0.0622	-0.0179	-0.0353	-0.0386	-0.0145	0.0829	0.1410	-0.0713	1981	0.0186
1982	0.0046	0.0182	0.0231	0.0373	0.0034	-0.0223	0.0501	0.0781	0.0618	0.0634	-0.0002	0.0312	1982	0.4036
1983	-0.0309	0.0492	-0.0094	0.0350	-0.0386	0.0039	-0.0486	0.0020	0.0505	-0.0132	0.0183	-0.0059	1983	0.0065
1984	0.0244	-0.0178	-0.0156	-0.0105	-0.0516	0.0150	0.0693	0.0266	0.0342	0.0561	0.0118	0.0091	1984	0.1548
1985	0.0364	-0.0493	0.0307	0.0242	0.0896	0.0142	-0.0180	0.0259	-0.0021	0.0338	0.0401	0.0541	1985	0.3097
1986	-0.0025	0.1145	0.0770	-0.0080	-0.0505	0.0613	-0.0108	0.0499	-0.0500	0.0289	0.0267	-0.0018	1986	0.2453
1987	0.0161	0.0202	-0.0223	-0.0473	-0.0105	0.0098	-0.0178	-0.0165	-0.0369	0.0623	0.0037	0.0165	1987	-0.0271
1988	0.0666	0.0052	-0.0307	-0.0160	-0.0102	0.0368	-0.0170	0.0058	0.0345	0.0308	-0.0196	0.0110	1988	0.0967
1989	0.0203	-0.0179	0.0122	0.0159	0.0401	0.0550	0.0238	-0.0259	0.0019	0.0379	0.0078	-0.0006	1989	0.1811
1990	-0.0343	-0.0025	-0.0044	-0.0202	0.0415	0.0230	0.0107	-0.0419	0.0117	0.0215	0.0402	0.0187	1990	0.0618
1991	0.0130	0.0030	0.0038	0.0140	0.0000	-0.0063	0.0157	0.0340	0.0303	0.0054	0.0082	0.0581	1991	0.1930
1992	-0.0324	0.0051	-0.0094	0.0016	0.0243	0.0200	0.0398	0.0067	0.0185	-0.0198	0.0010	0.0246	1992	0.0805
1993	0.0280	0.0354	0.0021	0.0072	0.0047	0.0449	0.0191	0.0434	0.0005	0.0096	-0.0259	0.0020	1993	0.1824
1994	0.0257	-0.0450	-0.0395	-0.0150	-0.0082	-0.0100	0.0363	-0.0086	-0.0331	-0.0025	0.0066	0.0161	1994	-0.0777
1995	0.0273	0.0287	0.0091	0.0169	0.0790	0.0139	-0.0168	0.0236	0.0175	0.0294	0.0249	0.0272	1995	0.3167
1996	-0.0011	-0.0483	-0.0210	-0.0165	-0.0054	0.0203	0.0018	-0.0139	0.0290	0.0404	0.0351	-0.0256	1996	-0.0093
1997	-0.0079	0.0005	-0.0252	0.0255	0.0097	0.0195	0.0626	-0.0317	0.0316	0.0341	0.0148	0.0184	1997	0.1585
1998	0.0200	-0.0072	0.0025	0.0026	0.0182	0.0228	-0.0040	0.0465	0.0395	-0.0218	0.0097	-0.0032	1998	0.1306

* Compound annual return

Table A-7 **Long-Term Government Bonds: Income Returns**

From January 1926 to December 1970

YEAR	JAN	FEB	MAR	APR	MAY	JUN	JUL	AUG	SEP	OCT	NOV	DEC	YEAR	JAN–DEC*
1926	0.0031	0.0028	0.0032	0.0030	0.0028	0.0033	0.0031	0.0031	0.0030	0.0030	0.0031	0.0030	1926	0.0373
1927	0.0030	0.0027	0.0029	0.0027	0.0028	0.0027	0.0027	0.0029	0.0027	0.0028	0.0027	0.0027	1927	0.0341
1928	0.0027	0.0025	0.0027	0.0026	0.0027	0.0027	0.0027	0.0029	0.0027	0.0030	0.0027	0.0029	1928	0.0322
1929	0.0029	0.0027	0.0028	0.0034	0.0030	0.0029	0.0032	0.0030	0.0032	0.0031	0.0026	0.0031	1929	0.0347
1930	0.0029	0.0026	0.0029	0.0027	0.0027	0.0029	0.0028	0.0026	0.0029	0.0027	0.0026	0.0028	1930	0.0332
1931	0.0028	0.0026	0.0029	0.0027	0.0026	0.0028	0.0027	0.0027	0.0027	0.0029	0.0031	0.0032	1931	0.0333
1932	0.0032	0.0032	0.0031	0.0030	0.0028	0.0028	0.0028	0.0028	0.0026	0.0027	0.0026	0.0027	1932	0.0369
1933	0.0027	0.0023	0.0027	0.0025	0.0028	0.0025	0.0026	0.0026	0.0025	0.0026	0.0025	0.0028	1933	0.0312
1934	0.0029	0.0024	0.0027	0.0025	0.0025	0.0024	0.0024	0.0024	0.0023	0.0027	0.0025	0.0025	1934	0.0318
1935	0.0025	0.0021	0.0022	0.0023	0.0023	0.0022	0.0024	0.0023	0.0023	0.0023	0.0024	0.0024	1935	0.0281
1936	0.0024	0.0023	0.0024	0.0022	0.0022	0.0024	0.0023	0.0023	0.0021	0.0023	0.0022	0.0022	1936	0.0277
1937	0.0021	0.0020	0.0022	0.0023	0.0022	0.0025	0.0024	0.0023	0.0023	0.0023	0.0024	0.0023	1937	0.0266
1938	0.0023	0.0021	0.0023	0.0022	0.0022	0.0021	0.0021	0.0022	0.0021	0.0022	0.0021	0.0022	1938	0.0264
1939	0.0021	0.0019	0.0021	0.0019	0.0020	0.0018	0.0019	0.0018	0.0019	0.0023	0.0020	0.0019	1939	0.0240
1940	0.0020	0.0018	0.0019	0.0018	0.0019	0.0019	0.0020	0.0019	0.0018	0.0018	0.0018	0.0017	1940	0.0223
1941	0.0016	0.0016	0.0018	0.0017	0.0017	0.0016	0.0016	0.0016	0.0016	0.0016	0.0014	0.0016	1941	0.0194
1942	0.0021	0.0019	0.0021	0.0020	0.0019	0.0021	0.0021	0.0021	0.0020	0.0021	0.0020	0.0021	1942	0.0246
1943	0.0020	0.0019	0.0021	0.0020	0.0019	0.0021	0.0021	0.0021	0.0020	0.0020	0.0021	0.0021	1943	0.0244
1944	0.0021	0.0020	0.0021	0.0020	0.0022	0.0020	0.0021	0.0021	0.0020	0.0021	0.0020	0.0020	1944	0.0246
1945	0.0021	0.0018	0.0020	0.0019	0.0019	0.0019	0.0018	0.0019	0.0018	0.0019	0.0018	0.0018	1945	0.0234
1946	0.0017	0.0015	0.0016	0.0017	0.0018	0.0016	0.0019	0.0017	0.0018	0.0019	0.0018	0.0019	1946	0.0204
1947	0.0018	0.0016	0.0018	0.0017	0.0017	0.0019	0.0018	0.0017	0.0018	0.0018	0.0017	0.0021	1947	0.0213
1948	0.0020	0.0019	0.0022	0.0020	0.0018	0.0021	0.0019	0.0021	0.0020	0.0019	0.0021	0.0020	1948	0.0240
1949	0.0020	0.0018	0.0019	0.0018	0.0020	0.0019	0.0017	0.0019	0.0017	0.0018	0.0017	0.0017	1949	0.0225
1950	0.0018	0.0016	0.0018	0.0016	0.0019	0.0017	0.0018	0.0018	0.0017	0.0019	0.0018	0.0018	1950	0.0212
1951	0.0020	0.0017	0.0019	0.0020	0.0021	0.0020	0.0023	0.0021	0.0019	0.0023	0.0021	0.0022	1951	0.0238
1952	0.0023	0.0021	0.0023	0.0022	0.0020	0.0022	0.0022	0.0021	0.0023	0.0023	0.0021	0.0024	1952	0.0266
1953	0.0023	0.0021	0.0025	0.0024	0.0024	0.0027	0.0025	0.0025	0.0025	0.0023	0.0024	0.0024	1953	0.0284
1954	0.0023	0.0022	0.0025	0.0022	0.0020	0.0025	0.0022	0.0023	0.0022	0.0021	0.0023	0.0023	1954	0.0279
1955	0.0022	0.0022	0.0024	0.0022	0.0025	0.0023	0.0023	0.0027	0.0024	0.0025	0.0024	0.0024	1955	0.0275
1956	0.0025	0.0023	0.0023	0.0026	0.0026	0.0023	0.0026	0.0026	0.0025	0.0029	0.0027	0.0028	1956	0.0299
1957	0.0029	0.0025	0.0026	0.0029	0.0029	0.0025	0.0033	0.0030	0.0031	0.0031	0.0029	0.0029	1957	0.0344
1958	0.0027	0.0025	0.0027	0.0026	0.0024	0.0027	0.0027	0.0027	0.0032	0.0032	0.0028	0.0033	1958	0.0327
1959	0.0031	0.0031	0.0035	0.0033	0.0033	0.0036	0.0035	0.0035	0.0034	0.0035	0.0035	0.0036	1959	0.0401
1960	0.0035	0.0037	0.0036	0.0032	0.0037	0.0034	0.0032	0.0034	0.0032	0.0033	0.0032	0.0033	1960	0.0426
1961	0.0033	0.0030	0.0031	0.0031	0.0034	0.0032	0.0033	0.0033	0.0032	0.0034	0.0032	0.0031	1961	0.0383
1962	0.0037	0.0032	0.0033	0.0033	0.0032	0.0030	0.0034	0.0034	0.0030	0.0035	0.0031	0.0032	1962	0.0400
1963	0.0032	0.0029	0.0031	0.0034	0.0033	0.0030	0.0036	0.0033	0.0034	0.0034	0.0032	0.0036	1963	0.0389
1964	0.0035	0.0032	0.0037	0.0035	0.0032	0.0038	0.0035	0.0035	0.0034	0.0034	0.0035	0.0035	1964	0.0415
1965	0.0033	0.0032	0.0038	0.0033	0.0033	0.0038	0.0034	0.0037	0.0035	0.0034	0.0037	0.0037	1965	0.0419
1966	0.0038	0.0034	0.0040	0.0036	0.0041	0.0039	0.0038	0.0043	0.0041	0.0040	0.0038	0.0039	1966	0.0449
1967	0.0040	0.0034	0.0039	0.0035	0.0043	0.0039	0.0043	0.0042	0.0040	0.0045	0.0045	0.0044	1967	0.0459
1968	0.0050	0.0042	0.0043	0.0049	0.0046	0.0042	0.0048	0.0042	0.0044	0.0045	0.0043	0.0049	1968	0.0550
1969	0.0050	0.0046	0.0047	0.0055	0.0047	0.0055	0.0052	0.0048	0.0055	0.0057	0.0049	0.0060	1969	0.0595
1970	0.0056	0.0052	0.0056	0.0054	0.0055	0.0064	0.0059	0.0057	0.0056	0.0055	0.0058	0.0053	1970	0.0674

* Compound annual return

Table A-7

Long-Term Government Bonds: Income Returns

(continued)

From January 1971 to December 1998

YEAR	JAN	FEB	MAR	APR	MAY	JUN	JUL	AUG	SEP	OCT	NOV	DEC	YEAR	JAN–DEC*
1971	0.0051	0.0046	0.0056	0.0048	0.0047	0.0056	0.0052	0.0055	0.0049	0.0047	0.0051	0.0050	1971	0.0632
1972	0.0050	0.0047	0.0049	0.0048	0.0055	0.0049	0.0051	0.0049	0.0047	0.0052	0.0048	0.0045	1972	0.0587
1973	0.0054	0.0051	0.0056	0.0057	0.0058	0.0055	0.0061	0.0062	0.0055	0.0063	0.0056	0.0060	1973	0.0651
1974	0.0061	0.0055	0.0058	0.0068	0.0068	0.0061	0.0072	0.0065	0.0071	0.0070	0.0062	0.0067	1974	0.0727
1975	0.0068	0.0060	0.0066	0.0067	0.0067	0.0070	0.0068	0.0065	0.0073	0.0072	0.0061	0.0074	1975	0.0799
1976	0.0065	0.0060	0.0071	0.0064	0.0059	0.0073	0.0065	0.0069	0.0064	0.0061	0.0066	0.0063	1976	0.0789
1977	0.0059	0.0057	0.0065	0.0061	0.0067	0.0062	0.0059	0.0067	0.0061	0.0063	0.0063	0.0062	1977	0.0714
1978	0.0069	0.0060	0.0069	0.0063	0.0075	0.0069	0.0073	0.0070	0.0065	0.0073	0.0071	0.0068	1978	0.0790
1979	0.0079	0.0065	0.0074	0.0076	0.0077	0.0071	0.0076	0.0073	0.0068	0.0082	0.0083	0.0083	1979	0.0886
1980	0.0083	0.0084	0.0099	0.0100	0.0087	0.0086	0.0084	0.0081	0.0097	0.0097	0.0091	0.0108	1980	0.0997
1981	0.0094	0.0088	0.0111	0.0101	0.0104	0.0109	0.0109	0.0110	0.0114	0.0117	0.0113	0.0100	1981	0.1155
1982	0.0108	0.0103	0.0124	0.0112	0.0101	0.0120	0.0114	0.0112	0.0100	0.0091	0.0094	0.0093	1982	0.1350
1983	0.0087	0.0081	0.0089	0.0085	0.0091	0.0090	0.0088	0.0103	0.0096	0.0095	0.0094	0.0094	1983	0.1038
1984	0.0103	0.0092	0.0098	0.0104	0.0103	0.0106	0.0116	0.0106	0.0094	0.0108	0.0091	0.0098	1984	0.1174
1985	0.0096	0.0082	0.0094	0.0102	0.0097	0.0080	0.0094	0.0085	0.0088	0.0089	0.0081	0.0086	1985	0.1125
1986	0.0079	0.0073	0.0071	0.0063	0.0062	0.0070	0.0066	0.0063	0.0065	0.0069	0.0059	0.0070	1986	0.0898
1987	0.0064	0.0059	0.0066	0.0065	0.0066	0.0075	0.0073	0.0075	0.0075	0.0079	0.0075	0.0078	1987	0.0792
1988	0.0072	0.0071	0.0072	0.0070	0.0078	0.0076	0.0071	0.0083	0.0076	0.0076	0.0070	0.0075	1988	0.0897
1989	0.0080	0.0069	0.0079	0.0070	0.0080	0.0070	0.0068	0.0066	0.0065	0.0072	0.0064	0.0064	1989	0.0881
1990	0.0073	0.0066	0.0071	0.0075	0.0075	0.0068	0.0074	0.0071	0.0069	0.0081	0.0071	0.0072	1990	0.0819
1991	0.0071	0.0064	0.0064	0.0076	0.0068	0.0063	0.0076	0.0068	0.0068	0.0065	0.0060	0.0068	1991	0.0822
1992	0.0061	0.0059	0.0067	0.0065	0.0061	0.0067	0.0063	0.0060	0.0058	0.0057	0.0061	0.0063	1992	0.0726
1993	0.0059	0.0055	0.0063	0.0057	0.0052	0.0062	0.0054	0.0056	0.0050	0.0049	0.0053	0.0055	1993	0.0717
1994	0.0055	0.0049	0.0058	0.0057	0.0063	0.0061	0.0060	0.0066	0.0061	0.0066	0.0064	0.0066	1994	0.0659
1995	0.0070	0.0059	0.0064	0.0058	0.0065	0.0054	0.0056	0.0057	0.0052	0.0057	0.0051	0.0049	1995	0.0760
1996	0.0054	0.0048	0.0052	0.0059	0.0058	0.0054	0.0062	0.0057	0.0060	0.0058	0.0052	0.0056	1996	0.0618
1997	0.0056	0.0051	0.0059	0.0059	0.0059	0.0057	0.0058	0.0049	0.0058	0.0054	0.0047	0.0054	1997	0.0664
1998	0.0048	0.0044	0.0052	0.0049	0.0048	0.0052	0.0049	0.0048	0.0044	0.0042	0.0045	0.0045	1998	0.0583

* Compound annual return

Table A-8 **Long-Term Government Bonds: Capital Appreciation Returns**

From January 1926 to December 1970

YEAR	JAN	FEB	MAR	APR	MAY	JUN	JUL	AUG	SEP	OCT	NOV	DEC	YEAR	JAN–DEC*
1926	0.0106	0.0035	0.0009	0.0046	-0.0014	0.0005	-0.0027	-0.0031	0.0007	0.0072	0.0129	0.0048	1926	0.0391
1927	0.0045	0.0061	0.0224	-0.0032	0.0081	-0.0096	0.0022	0.0047	-0.0009	0.0071	0.0071	0.0045	1927	0.0540
1928	-0.0063	0.0036	0.0019	-0.0029	-0.0104	0.0015	-0.0245	0.0047	-0.0067	0.0128	-0.0024	-0.0024	1928	-0.0312
1929	-0.0119	-0.0183	-0.0171	0.0242	-0.0192	0.0081	-0.0032	-0.0064	-0.0004	0.0351	0.0211	-0.0120	1929	-0.0020
1930	-0.0086	0.0102	0.0055	-0.0043	0.0113	0.0022	0.0007	-0.0013	0.0045	0.0008	0.0017	-0.0098	1930	0.0128
1931	-0.0149	0.0059	0.0076	0.0059	0.0119	-0.0024	-0.0069	-0.0015	-0.0307	-0.0360	-0.0004	-0.0252	1931	-0.0846
1932	0.0002	0.0382	-0.0049	0.0574	-0.0216	0.0037	0.0453	-0.0025	0.0031	-0.0044	0.0006	0.0104	1932	0.1294
1933	0.0122	-0.0282	0.0070	-0.0057	0.0274	0.0025	-0.0043	0.0018	-0.0002	-0.0117	-0.0174	-0.0140	1933	-0.0314
1934	0.0228	0.0057	0.0170	0.0101	0.0106	0.0043	0.0016	-0.0143	-0.0169	0.0155	0.0013	0.0087	1934	0.0676
1935	0.0157	0.0070	0.0019	0.0056	-0.0079	0.0070	0.0022	-0.0156	-0.0014	0.0038	-0.0014	0.0047	1935	0.0214
1936	0.0031	0.0059	0.0083	0.0013	0.0019	-0.0003	0.0037	0.0088	-0.0053	-0.0017	0.0183	0.0017	1936	0.0464
1937	-0.0034	0.0067	-0.0433	0.0016	0.0031	-0.0043	0.0114	-0.0128	0.0022	0.0019	0.0072	0.0059	1937	-0.0248
1938	0.0034	0.0031	-0.0059	0.0187	0.0022	-0.0016	0.0022	-0.0022	0.0001	0.0065	-0.0043	0.0059	1938	0.0283
1939	0.0038	0.0061	0.0105	0.0099	0.0151	-0.0045	0.0095	-0.0219	-0.0564	0.0386	0.0142	0.0125	1939	0.0348
1940	-0.0037	0.0009	0.0158	-0.0053	-0.0318	0.0239	0.0032	0.0009	0.0092	0.0013	0.0187	0.0050	1940	0.0377
1941	-0.0217	0.0004	0.0078	0.0112	0.0011	0.0050	0.0005	0.0002	-0.0028	0.0124	-0.0044	-0.0194	1941	-0.0101
1942	0.0048	-0.0008	0.0071	-0.0049	0.0056	-0.0018	-0.0003	0.0017	-0.0016	0.0004	-0.0055	0.0028	1942	0.0074
1943	0.0013	-0.0024	-0.0012	0.0028	0.0031	-0.0003	-0.0021	0.0000	-0.0009	-0.0015	-0.0021	-0.0003	1943	-0.0037
1944	0.0000	0.0012	0.0000	-0.0006	0.0006	-0.0012	0.0015	0.0006	-0.0006	-0.0009	0.0003	0.0022	1944	0.0032
1945	0.0105	0.0058	0.0001	0.0141	0.0037	0.0150	-0.0104	0.0007	0.0037	0.0085	0.0108	0.0177	1945	0.0827
1946	0.0008	0.0017	-0.0006	-0.0152	-0.0030	0.0054	-0.0058	-0.0129	-0.0028	0.0055	-0.0072	0.0126	1946	-0.0215
1947	-0.0024	0.0005	0.0002	-0.0054	0.0016	-0.0009	0.0044	0.0064	-0.0062	-0.0055	-0.0191	-0.0213	1947	-0.0470
1948	0.0000	0.0028	0.0013	0.0025	0.0123	-0.0105	-0.0041	-0.0019	-0.0006	-0.0012	0.0055	0.0036	1948	0.0096
1949	0.0062	0.0031	0.0055	-0.0006	0.0000	0.0148	0.0016	0.0092	-0.0029	0.0001	0.0004	0.0035	1949	0.0415
1950	-0.0080	0.0005	-0.0010	0.0014	0.0014	-0.0042	0.0037	-0.0004	-0.0089	-0.0067	0.0017	-0.0001	1950	-0.0206
1951	0.0038	-0.0091	-0.0176	-0.0083	-0.0090	-0.0082	0.0116	0.0077	-0.0098	-0.0012	-0.0157	-0.0083	1951	-0.0627
1952	0.0005	-0.0007	0.0088	0.0149	-0.0054	-0.0019	-0.0041	-0.0091	-0.0153	0.0124	-0.0036	-0.0110	1952	-0.0148
1953	-0.0011	-0.0108	-0.0113	-0.0129	-0.0171	0.0195	0.0014	-0.0033	0.0275	0.0051	-0.0073	0.0182	1953	0.0067
1954	0.0066	0.0218	0.0034	0.0081	-0.0107	0.0138	0.0113	-0.0059	-0.0031	-0.0015	-0.0048	0.0042	1954	0.0435
1955	-0.0264	-0.0100	0.0063	-0.0022	0.0048	-0.0099	-0.0125	-0.0022	0.0049	0.0119	-0.0069	0.0013	1955	-0.0407
1956	0.0058	-0.0025	-0.0172	-0.0139	0.0199	0.0004	-0.0234	-0.0213	0.0025	-0.0083	-0.0084	-0.0206	1956	-0.0846
1957	0.0317	0.0000	-0.0050	-0.0250	-0.0052	-0.0206	-0.0074	-0.0028	0.0045	-0.0081	0.0504	0.0277	1957	0.0382
1958	-0.0112	0.0075	0.0075	0.0160	-0.0023	-0.0187	-0.0305	-0.0463	-0.0149	0.0106	0.0092	-0.0213	1958	-0.0923
1959	-0.0111	0.0087	-0.0018	-0.0150	-0.0038	-0.0026	0.0025	-0.0076	-0.0091	0.0115	-0.0154	-0.0195	1959	-0.0620
1960	0.0077	0.0167	0.0246	-0.0202	0.0115	0.0139	0.0335	-0.0101	0.0043	-0.0061	-0.0098	0.0247	1960	0.0929
1961	-0.0140	0.0170	-0.0069	0.0085	-0.0080	-0.0106	0.0001	-0.0071	0.0097	0.0037	-0.0052	-0.0156	1961	-0.0286
1962	-0.0051	0.0071	0.0220	0.0049	0.0014	-0.0106	-0.0143	0.0153	0.0031	0.0049	-0.0010	0.0003	1962	0.0278
1963	-0.0033	-0.0022	-0.0022	-0.0046	-0.0010	-0.0011	-0.0005	-0.0011	-0.0029	-0.0060	0.0019	-0.0042	1963	-0.0270
1964	-0.0048	-0.0043	0.0000	0.0012	0.0018	0.0031	-0.0027	-0.0015	0.0015	0.0009	-0.0018	-0.0005	1964	-0.0072
1965	0.0007	-0.0018	0.0016	0.0003	-0.0015	0.0009	-0.0012	-0.0050	-0.0069	-0.0007	-0.0099	-0.0115	1965	-0.0345
1966	-0.0142	-0.0284	0.0256	-0.0099	-0.0100	-0.0054	-0.0074	-0.0249	0.0292	0.0188	-0.0187	0.0374	1966	-0.0106
1967	0.0115	-0.0255	0.0159	-0.0326	-0.0082	-0.0351	0.0026	-0.0126	-0.0045	-0.0445	-0.0241	0.0148	1967	-0.1355
1968	0.0278	-0.0075	-0.0254	0.0178	-0.0003	0.0188	0.0241	-0.0044	-0.0146	-0.0177	-0.0312	-0.0412	1968	-0.0551
1969	-0.0256	-0.0004	-0.0036	0.0371	-0.0537	0.0159	0.0027	-0.0117	-0.0586	0.0309	-0.0293	-0.0129	1969	-0.1083
1970	-0.0077	0.0535	-0.0124	-0.0467	-0.0523	0.0422	0.0260	-0.0076	0.0172	-0.0164	0.0733	-0.0137	1970	0.0484

* Compound annual return

Table A-8 **Long-Term Government Bonds: Capital Appreciation Returns**

(continued)

From January 1971 to December 1998

YEAR	JAN	FEB	MAR	APR	MAY	JUN	JUL	AUG	SEP	OCT	NOV	DEC	YEAR	JAN–DEC*
1971	0.0455	-0.0209	0.0470	-0.0331	-0.0053	-0.0214	-0.0022	0.0416	0.0154	0.0120	-0.0098	-0.0006	1971	0.0661
1972	-0.0114	0.0041	-0.0131	-0.0021	0.0215	-0.0113	0.0165	-0.0021	-0.0129	0.0182	0.0178	-0.0275	1972	-0.0035
1973	-0.0375	-0.0037	0.0026	-0.0012	-0.0162	-0.0076	-0.0495	0.0329	0.0263	0.0153	-0.0238	-0.0142	1973	-0.0770
1974	-0.0144	-0.0079	-0.0350	-0.0320	0.0055	-0.0016	-0.0101	-0.0298	0.0176	0.0419	0.0233	0.0105	1974	-0.0345
1975	0.0157	0.0071	-0.0333	-0.0248	0.0145	0.0222	-0.0155	-0.0133	-0.0171	0.0403	-0.0170	0.0316	1975	0.0073
1976	0.0025	0.0001	0.0094	-0.0046	-0.0217	0.0135	0.0013	0.0142	0.0081	0.0023	0.0273	0.0265	1976	0.0807
1977	-0.0447	-0.0106	0.0026	0.0010	0.0058	0.0102	-0.0130	0.0131	-0.0089	-0.0156	0.0031	-0.0230	1977	-0.0786
1978	-0.0149	-0.0056	-0.0090	-0.0068	-0.0133	-0.0132	0.0070	0.0148	-0.0171	-0.0273	0.0117	-0.0198	1978	-0.0905
1979	0.0112	-0.0200	0.0056	-0.0188	0.0184	0.0240	-0.0161	-0.0108	-0.0190	-0.0922	0.0229	-0.0026	1979	-0.0984
1980	-0.0824	-0.0551	-0.0413	0.1424	0.0332	0.0272	-0.0560	-0.0513	-0.0358	-0.0360	0.0009	0.0244	1980	-0.1400
1981	-0.0209	-0.0524	0.0274	-0.0618	0.0518	-0.0288	-0.0462	-0.0496	-0.0259	0.0712	0.1297	-0.0813	1981	-0.1033
1982	-0.0062	0.0079	0.0107	0.0262	-0.0067	-0.0343	0.0387	0.0669	0.0519	0.0543	-0.0097	0.0219	1982	0.2395
1983	-0.0396	0.0410	-0.0183	0.0265	-0.0477	-0.0051	-0.0574	-0.0083	0.0408	-0.0227	0.0089	-0.0152	1983	-0.0982
1984	0.0141	-0.0270	-0.0254	-0.0210	-0.0619	0.0044	0.0577	0.0160	0.0248	0.0453	0.0027	-0.0007	1984	0.0232
1985	0.0268	-0.0575	0.0212	0.0140	0.0798	0.0061	-0.0274	0.0173	-0.0109	0.0248	0.0320	0.0455	1985	0.1784
1986	-0.0105	0.1073	0.0699	-0.0142	-0.0567	0.0543	-0.0173	0.0437	-0.0565	0.0220	0.0208	-0.0087	1986	0.1499
1987	0.0096	0.0143	-0.0289	-0.0538	-0.0171	0.0023	-0.0251	-0.0239	-0.0443	0.0544	-0.0038	0.0088	1987	-0.1069
1988	0.0595	-0.0019	-0.0378	-0.0230	-0.0180	0.0292	-0.0241	-0.0025	0.0269	0.0232	-0.0266	0.0035	1988	0.0036
1989	0.0124	-0.0248	0.0044	0.0088	0.0321	0.0480	0.0170	-0.0325	-0.0046	0.0307	0.0014	-0.0070	1989	0.0862
1990	-0.0416	-0.0090	-0.0115	-0.0277	0.0340	0.0162	0.0033	-0.0490	0.0048	0.0135	0.0331	0.0114	1990	-0.0261
1991	0.0059	-0.0033	-0.0026	0.0065	-0.0068	-0.0126	0.0082	0.0272	0.0236	-0.0011	0.0022	0.0513	1991	0.1010
1992	-0.0385	-0.0008	-0.0161	-0.0049	0.0181	0.0133	0.0334	0.0007	0.0127	-0.0255	-0.0051	0.0183	1992	0.0034
1993	0.0222	0.0299	-0.0042	0.0015	-0.0006	0.0387	0.0138	0.0378	-0.0045	0.0048	-0.0312	-0.0035	1993	0.1071
1994	0.0202	-0.0498	-0.0453	-0.0208	-0.0146	-0.0161	0.0303	-0.0152	-0.0392	-0.0091	0.0002	0.0095	1994	-0.1429
1995	0.0203	0.0227	0.0028	0.0112	0.0725	0.0084	-0.0223	0.0179	0.0122	0.0237	0.0198	0.0223	1995	0.2304
1996	-0.0065	-0.0530	-0.0262	-0.0224	-0.0112	0.0149	-0.0045	-0.0196	0.0230	0.0345	0.0299	-0.0312	1996	-0.0737
1997	-0.0135	-0.0046	-0.0311	0.0196	0.0037	0.0138	0.0567	-0.0367	0.0258	0.0287	0.0101	0.0130	1997	0.0851
1998	0.0152	-0.0116	-0.0028	-0.0023	0.0135	0.0176	-0.0088	0.0416	0.0350	-0.0260	0.0052	-0.0077	1998	0.0689

* Compound annual return

Table A-9 **Long-Term Government Bonds: Yields**

From January 1926 to December 1970

YEAR	JAN	FEB	MAR	APR	MAY	JUN	JUL	AUG	SEP	OCT	NOV	DEC	YR-END	YIELD
1926	0.0374	0.0372	0.0371	0.0368	0.0369	0.0368	0.0370	0.0373	0.0372	0.0367	0.0358	0.0354	1926	0.0354
1927	0.0351	0.0347	0.0331	0.0333	0.0327	0.0334	0.0333	0.0329	0.0330	0.0325	0.0320	0.0316	1927	0.0316
1928	0.0321	0.0318	0.0317	0.0319	0.0327	0.0326	0.0344	0.0341	0.0346	0.0336	0.0338	0.0340	1928	0.0340
1929	0.0349	0.0363	0.0377	0.0358	0.0373	0.0367	0.0369	0.0375	0.0375	0.0347	0.0331	0.0340	1929	0.0340
1930	0.0347	0.0339	0.0335	0.0338	0.0329	0.0328	0.0327	0.0328	0.0324	0.0324	0.0322	0.0330	1930	0.0330
1931	0.0343	0.0338	0.0332	0.0327	0.0317	0.0319	0.0325	0.0326	0.0353	0.0385	0.0385	0.0407	1931	0.0407
1932	0.0390	0.0367	0.0370	0.0336	0.0349	0.0347	0.0320	0.0321	0.0319	0.0322	0.0322	0.0315	1932	0.0315
1933	0.0308	0.0325	0.0321	0.0325	0.0308	0.0306	0.0309	0.0308	0.0308	0.0315	0.0327	0.0336	1933	0.0336
1934	0.0321	0.0317	0.0307	0.0300	0.0292	0.0289	0.0288	0.0299	0.0310	0.0300	0.0299	0.0293	1934	0.0293
1935	0.0281	0.0275	0.0274	0.0269	0.0276	0.0270	0.0268	0.0281	0.0282	0.0279	0.0280	0.0276	1935	0.0276
1936	0.0285	0.0281	0.0275	0.0274	0.0273	0.0273	0.0271	0.0264	0.0268	0.0269	0.0257	0.0255	1936	0.0255
1937	0.0258	0.0253	0.0285	0.0284	0.0282	0.0285	0.0277	0.0286	0.0284	0.0283	0.0278	0.0273	1937	0.0273
1938	0.0271	0.0268	0.0273	0.0259	0.0257	0.0259	0.0257	0.0259	0.0259	0.0254	0.0257	0.0252	1938	0.0252
1939	0.0249	0.0245	0.0237	0.0229	0.0217	0.0221	0.0213	0.0231	0.0278	0.0247	0.0236	0.0226	1939	0.0226
1940	0.0229	0.0228	0.0215	0.0220	0.0246	0.0227	0.0224	0.0223	0.0215	0.0214	0.0199	0.0194	1940	0.0194
1941	0.0213	0.0213	0.0206	0.0196	0.0195	0.0191	0.0191	0.0190	0.0193	0.0182	0.0186	0.0204	1941	0.0204
1942	0.0247	0.0247	0.0244	0.0246	0.0243	0.0244	0.0244	0.0244	0.0244	0.0244	0.0247	0.0246	1942	0.0246
1943	0.0245	0.0246	0.0247	0.0246	0.0244	0.0244	0.0245	0.0245	0.0246	0.0247	0.0248	0.0248	1943	0.0248
1944	0.0248	0.0247	0.0247	0.0248	0.0247	0.0248	0.0247	0.0247	0.0247	0.0247	0.0247	0.0246	1944	0.0246
1945	0.0240	0.0236	0.0236	0.0228	0.0226	0.0217	0.0224	0.0223	0.0221	0.0216	0.0210	0.0199	1945	0.0199
1946	0.0199	0.0198	0.0198	0.0207	0.0209	0.0206	0.0209	0.0217	0.0219	0.0216	0.0220	0.0212	1946	0.0212
1947	0.0214	0.0214	0.0213	0.0217	0.0216	0.0216	0.0214	0.0210	0.0213	0.0217	0.0229	0.0243	1947	0.0243
1948	0.0243	0.0241	0.0241	0.0239	0.0231	0.0238	0.0241	0.0242	0.0242	0.0243	0.0239	0.0237	1948	0.0237
1949	0.0233	0.0231	0.0227	0.0227	0.0227	0.0217	0.0216	0.0210	0.0212	0.0212	0.0212	0.0209	1949	0.0209
1950	0.0215	0.0214	0.0215	0.0214	0.0213	0.0216	0.0214	0.0214	0.0220	0.0225	0.0224	0.0224	1950	0.0224
1951	0.0221	0.0228	0.0241	0.0248	0.0254	0.0259	0.0252	0.0246	0.0253	0.0254	0.0264	0.0269	1951	0.0269
1952	0.0268	0.0269	0.0263	0.0254	0.0257	0.0259	0.0261	0.0267	0.0277	0.0269	0.0272	0.0279	1952	0.0279
1953	0.0279	0.0287	0.0294	0.0303	0.0314	0.0301	0.0301	0.0303	0.0284	0.0281	0.0286	0.0274	1953	0.0274
1954	0.0291	0.0279	0.0278	0.0273	0.0279	0.0272	0.0266	0.0269	0.0271	0.0271	0.0274	0.0272	1954	0.0272
1955	0.0286	0.0292	0.0288	0.0290	0.0287	0.0293	0.0300	0.0301	0.0298	0.0292	0.0295	0.0295	1955	0.0295
1956	0.0292	0.0293	0.0303	0.0311	0.0299	0.0299	0.0313	0.0325	0.0324	0.0329	0.0333	0.0345	1956	0.0345
1957	0.0328	0.0328	0.0331	0.0345	0.0348	0.0361	0.0365	0.0367	0.0364	0.0369	0.0340	0.0323	1957	0.0323
1958	0.0330	0.0325	0.0321	0.0311	0.0313	0.0324	0.0343	0.0371	0.0380	0.0374	0.0368	0.0382	1958	0.0382
1959	0.0408	0.0402	0.0403	0.0414	0.0417	0.0419	0.0417	0.0423	0.0429	0.0421	0.0432	0.0447	1959	0.0447
1960	0.0441	0.0429	0.0411	0.0426	0.0417	0.0407	0.0382	0.0390	0.0387	0.0391	0.0399	0.0380	1960	0.0380
1961	0.0404	0.0392	0.0397	0.0391	0.0397	0.0404	0.0404	0.0410	0.0403	0.0400	0.0404	0.0415	1961	0.0415
1962	0.0419	0.0414	0.0398	0.0394	0.0393	0.0401	0.0412	0.0401	0.0398	0.0395	0.0396	0.0395	1962	0.0395
1963	0.0398	0.0400	0.0401	0.0405	0.0406	0.0407	0.0407	0.0408	0.0410	0.0415	0.0414	0.0417	1963	0.0417
1964	0.0421	0.0424	0.0424	0.0423	0.0422	0.0419	0.0421	0.0423	0.0421	0.0421	0.0422	0.0423	1964	0.0423
1965	0.0422	0.0424	0.0422	0.0422	0.0423	0.0423	0.0424	0.0428	0.0433	0.0433	0.0441	0.0450	1965	0.0450
1966	0.0457	0.0477	0.0460	0.0467	0.0473	0.0477	0.0482	0.0499	0.0480	0.0467	0.0480	0.0455	1966	0.0455
1967	0.0448	0.0465	0.0455	0.0477	0.0482	0.0507	0.0505	0.0514	0.0517	0.0549	0.0567	0.0556	1967	0.0556
1968	0.0536	0.0542	0.0560	0.0547	0.0547	0.0534	0.0517	0.0520	0.0531	0.0543	0.0566	0.0598	1968	0.0598
1969	0.0617	0.0618	0.0620	0.0593	0.0635	0.0623	0.0621	0.0630	0.0677	0.0653	0.0676	0.0687	1969	0.0687
1970	0.0693	0.0651	0.0661	0.0699	0.0743	0.0709	0.0687	0.0694	0.0680	0.0693	0.0637	0.0648	1970	0.0648

Table A-9

Long-Term Government Bonds: Yields

(continued)

From January 1971 to December 1998

YEAR	JAN	FEB	MAR	APR	MAY	JUN	JUL	AUG	SEP	OCT	NOV	DEC	YR-END	YIELD
1971	0.0612	0.0629	0.0593	0.0619	0.0624	0.0641	0.0643	0.0610	0.0598	0.0588	0.0596	0.0597	1971	0.0597
1972	0.0606	0.0602	0.0613	0.0615	0.0597	0.0607	0.0593	0.0595	0.0606	0.0591	0.0577	0.0599	1972	0.0599
1973	0.0685	0.0688	0.0686	0.0687	0.0703	0.0710	0.0760	0.0728	0.0703	0.0689	0.0712	0.0726	1973	0.0726
1974	0.0740	0.0748	0.0783	0.0816	0.0810	0.0812	0.0823	0.0855	0.0837	0.0795	0.0771	0.0760	1974	0.0760
1975	0.0796	0.0788	0.0824	0.0852	0.0836	0.0813	0.0829	0.0844	0.0862	0.0819	0.0838	0.0805	1975	0.0805
1976	0.0802	0.0802	0.0792	0.0797	0.0821	0.0807	0.0805	0.0790	0.0781	0.0779	0.0749	0.0721	1976	0.0721
1977	0.0764	0.0775	0.0772	0.0771	0.0765	0.0754	0.0768	0.0754	0.0764	0.0781	0.0777	0.0803	1977	0.0803
1978	0.0816	0.0822	0.0831	0.0838	0.0852	0.0865	0.0858	0.0843	0.0860	0.0889	0.0877	0.0898	1978	0.0898
1979	0.0886	0.0908	0.0902	0.0922	0.0903	0.0877	0.0895	0.0907	0.0927	0.1034	0.1009	0.1012	1979	0.1012
1980	0.1114	0.1186	0.1239	0.1076	0.1037	0.1006	0.1074	0.1140	0.1185	0.1231	0.1230	0.1199	1980	0.1199
1981	0.1211	0.1283	0.1248	0.1332	0.1265	0.1304	0.1370	0.1445	0.1482	0.1384	0.1220	0.1334	1981	0.1334
1982	0.1415	0.1402	0.1387	0.1348	0.1358	0.1412	0.1352	0.1254	0.1183	0.1112	0.1125	0.1095	1982	0.1095
1983	0.1113	0.1060	0.1083	0.1051	0.1112	0.1119	0.1198	0.1210	0.1157	0.1188	0.1176	0.1197	1983	0.1197
1984	0.1180	0.1217	0.1253	0.1284	0.1381	0.1374	0.1293	0.1270	0.1235	0.1173	0.1169	0.1170	1984	0.1170
1985	0.1127	0.1209	0.1181	0.1162	0.1062	0.1055	0.1091	0.1068	0.1082	0.1051	0.1011	0.0956	1985	0.0956
1986	0.0958	0.0841	0.0766	0.0782	0.0848	0.0790	0.0809	0.0763	0.0827	0.0803	0.0779	0.0789	1986	0.0789
1987	0.0778	0.0763	0.0795	0.0859	0.0880	0.0877	0.0907	0.0936	0.0992	0.0926	0.0931	0.0920	1987	0.0920
1988	0.0852	0.0854	0.0901	0.0929	0.0952	0.0917	0.0947	0.0950	0.0917	0.0889	0.0923	0.0918	1988	0.0918
1989	0.0903	0.0935	0.0929	0.0918	0.0878	0.0821	0.0801	0.0841	0.0847	0.0810	0.0808	0.0816	1989	0.0816
1990	0.0865	0.0876	0.0889	0.0924	0.0883	0.0864	0.0860	0.0920	0.0914	0.0898	0.0858	0.0844	1990	0.0844
1991	0.0837	0.0841	0.0844	0.0837	0.0845	0.0860	0.0850	0.0818	0.0790	0.0791	0.0789	0.0730	1991	0.0730
1992	0.0776	0.0777	0.0797	0.0803	0.0781	0.0765	0.0726	0.0725	0.0710	0.0741	0.0748	0.0726	1992	0.0726
1993	0.0725	0.0698	0.0702	0.0701	0.0701	0.0668	0.0656	0.0623	0.0627	0.0623	0.0651	0.0654	1993	0.0654
1994	0.0637	0.0682	0.0725	0.0745	0.0759	0.0774	0.0746	0.0761	0.0800	0.0809	0.0808	0.0799	1994	0.0799
1995	0.0780	0.0758	0.0755	0.0745	0.0677	0.0670	0.0691	0.0674	0.0663	0.0641	0.0623	0.0603	1995	0.0603
1996	0.0609	0.0659	0.0684	0.0706	0.0717	0.0703	0.0707	0.0726	0.0704	0.0671	0.0643	0.0673	1996	0.0673
1997	0.0689	0.0694	0.0723	0.0705	0.0701	0.0688	0.0637	0.0672	0.0649	0.0623	0.0614	0.0602	1997	0.0602
1998	0.0589	0.0599	0.0602	0.0604	0.0592	0.0576	0.0584	0.0547	0.0517	0.0540	0.0535	0.0542	1998	0.0542

Table A-10 **Intermediate-Term Government Bonds: Total Returns**

From January 1926 to December 1970

YEAR	JAN	FEB	MAR	APR	MAY	JUN	JUL	AUG	SEP	OCT	NOV	DEC	YEAR	JAN–DEC*
1926	0.0068	0.0032	0.0041	0.0090	0.0008	0.0027	0.0013	0.0009	0.0050	0.0054	0.0045	0.0089	1926	0.0538
1927	0.0057	0.0038	0.0038	0.0016	0.0020	0.0029	0.0043	0.0056	0.0060	-0.0034	0.0083	0.0037	1927	0.0452
1928	0.0046	-0.0004	0.0010	-0.0003	-0.0006	0.0017	-0.0089	0.0050	0.0028	0.0032	0.0019	-0.0007	1928	0.0092
1929	-0.0029	-0.0018	0.0005	0.0089	-0.0061	0.0107	0.0066	0.0052	-0.0014	0.0168	0.0180	0.0044	1929	0.0601
1930	-0.0041	0.0094	0.0161	-0.0071	0.0061	0.0142	0.0054	0.0022	0.0063	0.0076	0.0070	0.0024	1930	0.0672
1931	-0.0071	0.0099	0.0052	0.0083	0.0119	-0.0214	0.0016	0.0017	-0.0113	-0.0105	0.0049	-0.0159	1931	-0.0232
1932	-0.0032	0.0128	0.0078	0.0194	-0.0090	0.0108	0.0120	0.0124	0.0027	0.0045	0.0031	0.0118	1932	0.0881
1933	-0.0016	-0.0001	0.0099	0.0057	0.0199	0.0008	-0.0006	0.0073	0.0026	-0.0025	0.0027	-0.0253	1933	0.0183
1934	0.0130	0.0052	0.0189	0.0182	0.0120	0.0091	-0.0024	-0.0092	-0.0138	0.0190	0.0046	0.0125	1934	0.0900
1935	0.0114	0.0105	0.0125	0.0107	-0.0035	0.0113	0.0037	-0.0071	-0.0057	0.0109	0.0014	0.0120	1935	0.0701
1936	-0.0003	0.0069	0.0031	0.0024	0.0038	0.0012	0.0022	0.0050	0.0010	0.0025	0.0081	-0.0057	1936	0.0306
1937	-0.0031	0.0007	-0.0164	0.0047	0.0080	-0.0012	0.0059	-0.0043	0.0081	0.0032	0.0042	0.0062	1937	0.0156
1938	0.0085	0.0052	-0.0012	0.0230	0.0023	0.0075	0.0010	0.0015	-0.0013	0.0093	-0.0001	0.0052	1938	0.0623
1939	0.0029	0.0082	0.0081	0.0038	0.0095	0.0002	0.0040	-0.0147	-0.0262	0.0315	0.0074	0.0108	1939	0.0452
1940	-0.0014	0.0035	0.0088	0.0002	-0.0214	0.0187	0.0003	0.0043	0.0047	0.0036	0.0056	0.0028	1940	0.0296
1941	0.0001	-0.0047	0.0069	0.0033	0.0012	0.0056	0.0000	0.0011	0.0000	0.0023	-0.0092	-0.0016	1941	0.0050
1942	0.0074	0.0015	0.0023	0.0022	0.0016	0.0013	0.0000	0.0017	-0.0023	0.0017	0.0017	0.0000	1942	0.0194
1943	0.0039	0.0013	0.0021	0.0024	0.0057	0.0033	0.0021	0.0002	0.0014	0.0017	0.0015	0.0021	1943	0.0281
1944	0.0011	0.0016	0.0019	0.0028	0.0005	0.0007	0.0029	0.0024	0.0011	0.0011	0.0009	0.0010	1944	0.0180
1945	0.0052	0.0038	0.0004	0.0014	0.0012	0.0019	0.0000	0.0016	0.0017	0.0016	0.0010	0.0021	1945	0.0222
1946	0.0039	0.0048	-0.0038	-0.0020	0.0006	0.0033	-0.0010	0.0004	-0.0011	0.0026	-0.0008	0.0032	1946	0.0100
1947	0.0023	0.0006	0.0024	-0.0013	0.0008	0.0008	0.0006	0.0026	0.0000	-0.0023	0.0006	0.0021	1947	0.0091
1948	0.0015	0.0018	0.0018	0.0019	0.0053	-0.0008	-0.0002	-0.0004	0.0010	0.0013	0.0021	0.0032	1948	0.0185
1949	0.0028	0.0011	0.0025	0.0015	0.0023	0.0050	0.0020	0.0031	0.0008	0.0006	0.0002	0.0012	1949	0.0232
1950	-0.0005	0.0008	0.0000	0.0008	0.0020	0.0003	0.0020	-0.0007	-0.0004	0.0001	0.0018	0.0008	1950	0.0070
1951	0.0022	0.0007	-0.0127	0.0057	-0.0040	0.0050	0.0058	0.0036	-0.0057	0.0016	0.0032	-0.0016	1951	0.0036
1952	0.0038	-0.0020	0.0067	0.0054	0.0019	-0.0035	-0.0034	-0.0024	0.0019	0.0066	-0.0006	0.0019	1952	0.0163
1953	-0.0002	0.0003	-0.0017	-0.0096	-0.0117	0.0155	0.0056	-0.0008	0.0194	0.0038	0.0014	0.0103	1953	0.0323
1954	0.0065	0.0100	0.0027	0.0043	-0.0073	0.0125	-0.0005	0.0011	-0.0020	-0.0009	-0.0001	0.0005	1954	0.0268
1955	-0.0032	-0.0052	0.0024	0.0004	0.0001	-0.0036	-0.0071	0.0007	0.0082	0.0072	-0.0053	-0.0011	1955	-0.0065
1956	0.0105	0.0003	-0.0100	-0.0001	0.0112	0.0003	-0.0095	-0.0103	0.0092	-0.0019	-0.0047	0.0011	1956	-0.0042
1957	0.0237	-0.0012	0.0018	-0.0101	-0.0017	-0.0106	-0.0015	0.0109	0.0002	0.0043	0.0396	0.0215	1957	0.0784
1958	0.0034	0.0139	0.0053	0.0052	0.0060	-0.0068	-0.0091	-0.0356	-0.0017	0.0002	0.0132	-0.0061	1958	-0.0129
1959	-0.0013	0.0107	-0.0037	-0.0052	-0.0001	-0.0077	0.0034	-0.0078	0.0020	0.0174	-0.0092	-0.0020	1959	-0.0039
1960	0.0154	0.0072	0.0292	-0.0064	0.0031	0.0217	0.0267	-0.0004	0.0029	0.0016	-0.0094	0.0210	1960	0.1176
1961	-0.0059	0.0090	0.0037	0.0054	-0.0028	-0.0025	0.0007	0.0019	0.0079	0.0014	-0.0019	0.0018	1961	0.0185
1962	-0.0045	0.0155	0.0089	0.0025	0.0049	-0.0028	-0.0012	0.0125	0.0021	0.0051	0.0060	0.0056	1962	0.0556
1963	-0.0029	0.0017	0.0027	0.0030	0.0014	0.0014	0.0003	0.0019	0.0014	0.0011	0.0040	0.0003	1963	0.0164
1964	0.0033	0.0012	0.0016	0.0033	0.0081	0.0036	0.0027	0.0027	0.0045	0.0032	-0.0004	0.0058	1964	0.0404
1965	0.0042	0.0018	0.0043	0.0026	0.0035	0.0049	0.0017	0.0019	-0.0005	0.0000	0.0007	-0.0149	1965	0.0102
1966	0.0003	-0.0083	0.0187	-0.0019	0.0011	-0.0024	-0.0025	-0.0125	0.0216	0.0075	0.0027	0.0223	1966	0.0469
1967	0.0118	-0.0013	0.0183	-0.0089	0.0044	-0.0227	0.0133	-0.0036	0.0007	-0.0049	0.0028	0.0007	1967	0.0101
1968	0.0145	0.0040	-0.0026	-0.0016	0.0064	0.0167	0.0176	0.0021	0.0055	0.0009	-0.0013	-0.0173	1968	0.0454
1969	0.0086	-0.0013	0.0097	0.0079	-0.0082	-0.0084	0.0082	-0.0018	-0.0300	0.0333	-0.0047	-0.0193	1969	-0.0074
1970	0.0030	0.0439	0.0087	-0.0207	0.0110	0.0061	0.0152	0.0116	0.0196	0.0095	0.0451	0.0054	1970	0.1686

* Compound annual return

Table A-10 **Intermediate-Term Government Bonds: Total Returns**

(continued)

From January 1971 to December 1998

YEAR	JAN	FEB	MAR	APR	MAY	JUN	JUL	AUG	SEP	OCT	NOV	DEC	YEAR	JAN–DEC*
1971	0.0168	0.0224	0.0186	-0.0327	0.0011	-0.0187	0.0027	0.0350	0.0026	0.0220	0.0052	0.0110	1971	0.0872
1972	0.0106	0.0014	0.0015	0.0014	0.0016	0.0045	0.0015	0.0015	0.0014	0.0016	0.0045	0.0192	1972	0.0516
1973	-0.0006	-0.0075	0.0046	0.0064	0.0057	-0.0006	-0.0276	0.0254	0.0250	0.0050	0.0064	0.0040	1973	0.0461
1974	0.0009	0.0035	-0.0212	-0.0152	0.0130	-0.0087	0.0007	-0.0012	0.0319	0.0109	0.0236	0.0185	1974	0.0569
1975	0.0053	0.0148	-0.0059	-0.0186	0.0260	0.0027	-0.0030	-0.0009	0.0010	0.0366	-0.0010	0.0198	1975	0.0783
1976	0.0057	0.0084	0.0075	0.0116	-0.0145	0.0159	0.0119	0.0189	0.0076	0.0147	0.0321	0.0026	1976	0.1287
1977	-0.0190	0.0048	0.0055	0.0051	0.0056	0.0102	0.0001	0.0008	0.0015	-0.0060	0.0079	-0.0023	1977	0.0141
1978	0.0013	0.0017	0.0037	0.0024	-0.0002	-0.0021	0.0098	0.0079	0.0057	-0.0112	0.0092	0.0063	1978	0.0349
1979	0.0055	-0.0059	0.0112	0.0033	0.0193	0.0205	-0.0011	-0.0091	0.0006	-0.0468	0.0363	0.0087	1979	0.0409
1980	-0.0135	-0.0641	0.0143	0.1198	0.0490	-0.0077	-0.0106	-0.0387	-0.0038	-0.0152	0.0029	0.0171	1980	0.0391
1981	0.0032	-0.0235	0.0263	-0.0216	0.0245	0.0060	-0.0270	-0.0178	0.0164	0.0611	0.0624	-0.0142	1981	0.0945
1982	0.0050	0.0148	0.0042	0.0299	0.0146	-0.0135	0.0464	0.0469	0.0325	0.0531	0.0080	0.0185	1982	0.2910
1983	0.0007	0.0252	-0.0049	0.0259	-0.0122	0.0016	-0.0198	0.0081	0.0315	0.0019	0.0103	0.0047	1983	0.0741
1984	0.0177	-0.0064	-0.0035	-0.0003	-0.0250	0.0099	0.0393	0.0101	0.0202	0.0383	0.0192	0.0143	1984	0.1402
1985	0.0206	-0.0179	0.0166	0.0264	0.0485	0.0108	-0.0045	0.0148	0.0113	0.0162	0.0195	0.0257	1985	0.2033
1986	0.0082	0.0275	0.0338	0.0081	-0.0215	0.0276	0.0157	0.0266	-0.0110	0.0162	0.0113	0.0007	1986	0.1514
1987	0.0107	0.0059	-0.0031	-0.0244	-0.0038	0.0122	0.0025	-0.0038	-0.0141	0.0299	0.0083	0.0093	1987	0.0290
1988	0.0316	0.0123	-0.0086	-0.0044	-0.0049	0.0181	-0.0047	-0.0009	0.0196	0.0148	-0.0115	-0.0010	1988	0.0610
1989	0.0121	-0.0051	0.0049	0.0220	0.0212	0.0324	0.0235	-0.0246	0.0069	0.0237	0.0084	0.0012	1989	0.1329
1990	-0.0104	0.0007	0.0002	-0.0077	0.0261	0.0151	0.0174	-0.0092	0.0094	0.0171	0.0193	0.0161	1990	0.0973
1991	0.0107	0.0048	0.0023	0.0117	0.0059	-0.0023	0.0129	0.0247	0.0216	0.0134	0.0128	0.0265	1991	0.1546
1992	-0.0195	0.0022	-0.0079	0.0098	0.0222	0.0177	0.0242	0.0150	0.0194	-0.0182	-0.0084	0.0146	1992	0.0719
1993	0.0270	0.0243	0.0043	0.0088	-0.0009	0.0201	0.0005	0.0223	0.0056	0.0018	-0.0093	0.0032	1993	0.1124
1994	0.0138	-0.0258	-0.0257	-0.0105	-0.0002	-0.0028	0.0169	0.0026	-0.0158	-0.0023	-0.0070	0.0053	1994	-0.0514
1995	0.0182	0.0234	0.0063	0.0143	0.0369	0.0079	-0.0016	0.0086	0.0064	0.0121	0.0149	0.0095	1995	0.1680
1996	0.0006	-0.0138	-0.0118	-0.0050	-0.0032	0.0117	0.0025	-0.0005	0.0155	0.0183	0.0149	-0.0078	1996	0.0210
1997	0.0025	0.0002	-0.0114	0.0148	0.0079	0.0102	0.0264	-0.0098	0.0151	0.0150	-0.0001	0.0106	1997	0.0838
1998	0.0180	-0.0039	0.0026	0.0061	0.0070	0.0079	0.0027	0.0271	0.0330	0.0041	-0.0098	0.0037	1998	0.1021

* Compound annual return

Table A-11 Intermediate-Term Government Bonds: Income Returns

From January 1926 to December 1970

YEAR	JAN	FEB	MAR	APR	MAY	JUN	JUL	AUG	SEP	OCT	NOV	DEC	YEAR	JAN–DEC*
1926	0.0032	0.0032	0.0032	0.0031	0.0031	0.0031	0.0032	0.0032	0.0032	0.0031	0.0031	0.0030	1926	0.0378
1927	0.0029	0.0029	0.0029	0.0029	0.0029	0.0029	0.0029	0.0029	0.0028	0.0029	0.0028	0.0028	1927	0.0349
1928	0.0028	0.0028	0.0029	0.0029	0.0030	0.0030	0.0032	0.0032	0.0032	0.0032	0.0032	0.0033	1928	0.0364
1929	0.0034	0.0035	0.0036	0.0035	0.0037	0.0035	0.0035	0.0034	0.0035	0.0033	0.0030	0.0030	1929	0.0407
1930	0.0031	0.0030	0.0028	0.0030	0.0029	0.0027	0.0026	0.0026	0.0026	0.0025	0.0024	0.0024	1930	0.0330
1931	0.0026	0.0025	0.0024	0.0023	0.0021	0.0026	0.0026	0.0026	0.0028	0.0031	0.0031	0.0034	1931	0.0316
1932	0.0035	0.0034	0.0033	0.0030	0.0032	0.0031	0.0029	0.0027	0.0027	0.0027	0.0027	0.0025	1932	0.0363
1933	0.0026	0.0026	0.0025	0.0025	0.0021	0.0022	0.0022	0.0021	0.0021	0.0022	0.0022	0.0027	1933	0.0283
1934	0.0030	0.0024	0.0027	0.0024	0.0023	0.0021	0.0021	0.0021	0.0021	0.0026	0.0022	0.0023	1934	0.0293
1935	0.0021	0.0018	0.0018	0.0017	0.0016	0.0015	0.0015	0.0014	0.0015	0.0016	0.0015	0.0016	1935	0.0202
1936	0.0014	0.0013	0.0013	0.0012	0.0012	0.0013	0.0012	0.0012	0.0011	0.0011	0.0011	0.0010	1936	0.0144
1937	0.0010	0.0010	0.0012	0.0015	0.0013	0.0014	0.0014	0.0013	0.0014	0.0012	0.0012	0.0011	1937	0.0148
1938	0.0018	0.0016	0.0017	0.0017	0.0015	0.0014	0.0013	0.0014	0.0013	0.0014	0.0013	0.0013	1938	0.0182
1939	0.0013	0.0011	0.0012	0.0010	0.0011	0.0009	0.0009	0.0009	0.0011	0.0015	0.0010	0.0009	1939	0.0131
1940	0.0009	0.0008	0.0008	0.0007	0.0007	0.0010	0.0008	0.0008	0.0007	0.0007	0.0006	0.0005	1940	0.0090
1941	0.0006	0.0006	0.0008	0.0006	0.0006	0.0006	0.0005	0.0005	0.0005	0.0005	0.0004	0.0007	1941	0.0067
1942	0.0008	0.0006	0.0007	0.0006	0.0006	0.0006	0.0006	0.0006	0.0006	0.0006	0.0006	0.0006	1942	0.0076
1943	0.0014	0.0013	0.0014	0.0013	0.0013	0.0013	0.0013	0.0012	0.0012	0.0012	0.0012	0.0012	1943	0.0156
1944	0.0013	0.0012	0.0013	0.0012	0.0013	0.0012	0.0012	0.0012	0.0011	0.0012	0.0011	0.0011	1944	0.0144
1945	0.0012	0.0010	0.0010	0.0010	0.0010	0.0010	0.0010	0.0010	0.0009	0.0010	0.0009	0.0009	1945	0.0119
1946	0.0009	0.0008	0.0007	0.0009	0.0009	0.0009	0.0009	0.0009	0.0010	0.0010	0.0009	0.0010	1946	0.0108
1947	0.0010	0.0009	0.0010	0.0009	0.0010	0.0011	0.0010	0.0010	0.0010	0.0010	0.0010	0.0012	1947	0.0121
1948	0.0013	0.0012	0.0014	0.0013	0.0012	0.0013	0.0012	0.0013	0.0013	0.0013	0.0014	0.0013	1948	0.0156
1949	0.0013	0.0012	0.0013	0.0012	0.0013	0.0012	0.0010	0.0011	0.0010	0.0010	0.0010	0.0010	1949	0.0136
1950	0.0011	0.0010	0.0011	0.0010	0.0012	0.0011	0.0012	0.0011	0.0011	0.0013	0.0013	0.0013	1950	0.0139
1951	0.0016	0.0014	0.0015	0.0018	0.0017	0.0017	0.0018	0.0017	0.0015	0.0019	0.0017	0.0018	1951	0.0198
1952	0.0018	0.0017	0.0019	0.0017	0.0016	0.0017	0.0018	0.0018	0.0021	0.0020	0.0017	0.0021	1952	0.0219
1953	0.0019	0.0018	0.0021	0.0021	0.0022	0.0027	0.0024	0.0023	0.0023	0.0020	0.0020	0.0020	1953	0.0255
1954	0.0016	0.0014	0.0014	0.0013	0.0011	0.0016	0.0011	0.0012	0.0011	0.0012	0.0014	0.0014	1954	0.0160
1955	0.0018	0.0017	0.0020	0.0019	0.0021	0.0020	0.0020	0.0025	0.0023	0.0023	0.0021	0.0022	1955	0.0245
1956	0.0025	0.0021	0.0022	0.0026	0.0026	0.0023	0.0025	0.0027	0.0026	0.0030	0.0028	0.0030	1956	0.0305
1957	0.0030	0.0025	0.0026	0.0029	0.0030	0.0027	0.0036	0.0032	0.0032	0.0033	0.0031	0.0028	1957	0.0359
1958	0.0024	0.0021	0.0022	0.0021	0.0019	0.0021	0.0021	0.0022	0.0032	0.0032	0.0029	0.0032	1958	0.0293
1959	0.0031	0.0030	0.0033	0.0032	0.0033	0.0037	0.0038	0.0037	0.0039	0.0039	0.0038	0.0041	1959	0.0418
1960	0.0039	0.0039	0.0039	0.0032	0.0037	0.0035	0.0031	0.0030	0.0028	0.0029	0.0028	0.0031	1960	0.0415
1961	0.0030	0.0028	0.0029	0.0027	0.0030	0.0029	0.0031	0.0031	0.0030	0.0032	0.0030	0.0030	1961	0.0354
1962	0.0035	0.0031	0.0031	0.0031	0.0031	0.0029	0.0033	0.0032	0.0028	0.0033	0.0029	0.0030	1962	0.0373
1963	0.0030	0.0028	0.0029	0.0032	0.0031	0.0029	0.0034	0.0031	0.0033	0.0033	0.0031	0.0034	1963	0.0371
1964	0.0034	0.0030	0.0035	0.0033	0.0031	0.0036	0.0034	0.0033	0.0033	0.0033	0.0034	0.0034	1964	0.0400
1965	0.0033	0.0031	0.0037	0.0033	0.0033	0.0037	0.0034	0.0036	0.0034	0.0034	0.0038	0.0037	1965	0.0415
1966	0.0040	0.0036	0.0043	0.0038	0.0042	0.0040	0.0040	0.0047	0.0046	0.0044	0.0042	0.0042	1966	0.0493
1967	0.0041	0.0035	0.0039	0.0033	0.0042	0.0038	0.0045	0.0042	0.0041	0.0047	0.0046	0.0044	1967	0.0488
1968	0.0051	0.0043	0.0043	0.0049	0.0048	0.0043	0.0049	0.0042	0.0044	0.0044	0.0041	0.0047	1968	0.0549
1969	0.0054	0.0048	0.0049	0.0057	0.0050	0.0058	0.0059	0.0054	0.0061	0.0067	0.0056	0.0068	1969	0.0665
1970	0.0066	0.0061	0.0063	0.0059	0.0062	0.0067	0.0065	0.0062	0.0060	0.0057	0.0058	0.0050	1970	0.0749

* Compound annual return

Table A-11 **Intermediate-Term Government Bonds: Income Returns**

(continued)

From January 1971 to December 1998

YEAR	JAN	FEB	MAR	APR	MAY	JUN	JUL	AUG	SEP	OCT	NOV	DEC	YEAR	JAN–DEC*
1971	0.0047	0.0043	0.0047	0.0040	0.0044	0.0053	0.0053	0.0056	0.0048	0.0046	0.0047	0.0046	1971	0.0575
1972	0.0048	0.0044	0.0046	0.0044	0.0052	0.0048	0.0049	0.0050	0.0047	0.0053	0.0051	0.0049	1972	0.0575
1973	0.0056	0.0048	0.0054	0.0056	0.0056	0.0053	0.0059	0.0064	0.0055	0.0060	0.0055	0.0056	1973	0.0658
1974	0.0057	0.0051	0.0054	0.0065	0.0067	0.0059	0.0073	0.0067	0.0072	0.0067	0.0061	0.0064	1974	0.0724
1975	0.0061	0.0055	0.0059	0.0060	0.0063	0.0063	0.0063	0.0061	0.0069	0.0068	0.0055	0.0067	1975	0.0735
1976	0.0060	0.0055	0.0066	0.0059	0.0054	0.0069	0.0060	0.0062	0.0056	0.0054	0.0058	0.0050	1976	0.0710
1977	0.0051	0.0050	0.0056	0.0053	0.0058	0.0055	0.0052	0.0059	0.0056	0.0059	0.0059	0.0059	1977	0.0649
1978	0.0066	0.0057	0.0066	0.0060	0.0071	0.0066	0.0070	0.0068	0.0065	0.0072	0.0072	0.0069	1978	0.0783
1979	0.0079	0.0066	0.0075	0.0077	0.0077	0.0070	0.0074	0.0073	0.0070	0.0084	0.0089	0.0086	1979	0.0904
1980	0.0086	0.0083	0.0107	0.0103	0.0081	0.0075	0.0079	0.0076	0.0097	0.0094	0.0096	0.0111	1980	0.1055
1981	0.0101	0.0095	0.0117	0.0106	0.0110	0.0118	0.0116	0.0120	0.0130	0.0129	0.0121	0.0108	1981	0.1297
1982	0.0107	0.0102	0.0122	0.0112	0.0101	0.0118	0.0113	0.0109	0.0097	0.0089	0.0087	0.0085	1982	0.1281
1983	0.0084	0.0079	0.0084	0.0081	0.0086	0.0085	0.0082	0.0103	0.0094	0.0092	0.0091	0.0091	1983	0.1035
1984	0.0096	0.0088	0.0095	0.0101	0.0104	0.0105	0.0113	0.0105	0.0095	0.0110	0.0093	0.0093	1984	0.1168
1985	0.0090	0.0081	0.0089	0.0097	0.0090	0.0073	0.0083	0.0081	0.0082	0.0081	0.0074	0.0078	1985	0.1029
1986	0.0071	0.0066	0.0068	0.0060	0.0060	0.0068	0.0062	0.0057	0.0058	0.0060	0.0052	0.0060	1986	0.0772
1987	0.0055	0.0052	0.0060	0.0058	0.0062	0.0071	0.0066	0.0068	0.0068	0.0073	0.0070	0.0070	1987	0.0747
1988	0.0065	0.0066	0.0064	0.0063	0.0072	0.0070	0.0064	0.0077	0.0072	0.0071	0.0067	0.0071	1988	0.0824
1989	0.0077	0.0066	0.0078	0.0071	0.0080	0.0070	0.0067	0.0061	0.0065	0.0071	0.0063	0.0060	1989	0.0846
1990	0.0071	0.0064	0.0069	0.0071	0.0075	0.0067	0.0072	0.0068	0.0065	0.0074	0.0067	0.0067	1990	0.0815
1991	0.0064	0.0059	0.0059	0.0070	0.0065	0.0059	0.0069	0.0062	0.0061	0.0058	0.0052	0.0056	1991	0.0743
1992	0.0052	0.0052	0.0060	0.0058	0.0056	0.0058	0.0053	0.0050	0.0047	0.0044	0.0050	0.0053	1992	0.0627
1993	0.0049	0.0045	0.0049	0.0045	0.0041	0.0050	0.0041	0.0044	0.0041	0.0038	0.0042	0.0043	1993	0.0553
1994	0.0045	0.0039	0.0048	0.0049	0.0058	0.0055	0.0055	0.0060	0.0055	0.0060	0.0061	0.0063	1994	0.0607
1995	0.0067	0.0056	0.0060	0.0054	0.0062	0.0050	0.0051	0.0051	0.0047	0.0052	0.0047	0.0043	1995	0.0669
1996	0.0046	0.0041	0.0045	0.0053	0.0054	0.0050	0.0058	0.0052	0.0056	0.0053	0.0047	0.0050	1996	0.0582
1997	0.0052	0.0047	0.0054	0.0055	0.0055	0.0053	0.0054	0.0046	0.0054	0.0050	0.0043	0.0052	1997	0.0614
1998	0.0046	0.0041	0.0049	0.0046	0.0045	0.0049	0.0047	0.0046	0.0041	0.0035	0.0036	0.0039	1998	0.0529

* Compound annual return

Table A-12

Intermediate-Term Government Bonds: Capital Appreciation Returns

From January 1926 to December 1970

YEAR	JAN	FEB	MAR	APR	MAY	JUN	JUL	AUG	SEP	OCT	NOV	DEC	YEAR	JAN–DEC*
1926	0.0036	0.0000	0.0009	0.0059	-0.0023	-0.0004	-0.0018	-0.0023	0.0018	0.0023	0.0014	0.0059	1926	0.0151
1927	0.0027	0.0009	0.0009	-0.0014	-0.0009	0.0000	0.0014	0.0027	0.0032	-0.0064	0.0055	0.0009	1927	0.0096
1928	0.0018	-0.0032	-0.0018	-0.0032	-0.0036	-0.0014	-0.0122	0.0018	-0.0004	0.0000	-0.0014	-0.0041	1928	-0.0273
1929	-0.0063	-0.0054	-0.0031	0.0054	-0.0098	0.0072	0.0031	0.0018	-0.0049	0.0135	0.0150	0.0014	1929	0.0177
1930	-0.0072	0.0064	0.0133	-0.0100	0.0032	0.0115	0.0028	-0.0005	0.0037	0.0051	0.0046	0.0000	1930	0.0330
1931	-0.0097	0.0074	0.0028	0.0060	0.0098	-0.0240	-0.0009	-0.0009	-0.0142	-0.0136	0.0018	-0.0193	1931	-0.0540
1932	-0.0067	0.0094	0.0045	0.0164	-0.0122	0.0077	0.0091	0.0096	0.0000	0.0018	0.0005	0.0092	1932	0.0502
1933	-0.0041	-0.0028	0.0074	0.0032	0.0178	-0.0014	-0.0028	0.0051	0.0005	-0.0047	0.0005	-0.0280	1933	-0.0099
1934	0.0100	0.0028	0.0162	0.0158	0.0097	0.0070	-0.0044	-0.0113	-0.0160	0.0164	0.0024	0.0102	1934	0.0597
1935	0.0093	0.0088	0.0107	0.0090	-0.0050	0.0098	0.0022	-0.0086	-0.0072	0.0093	-0.0002	0.0105	1935	0.0494
1936	-0.0017	0.0056	0.0018	0.0012	0.0026	-0.0001	0.0010	0.0038	-0.0001	0.0014	0.0070	-0.0067	1936	0.0160
1937	-0.0041	-0.0003	-0.0176	0.0032	0.0067	-0.0027	0.0045	-0.0056	0.0068	0.0020	0.0030	0.0051	1937	0.0005
1938	0.0067	0.0036	-0.0030	0.0214	0.0008	0.0061	-0.0003	0.0000	-0.0026	0.0079	-0.0014	0.0039	1938	0.0437
1939	0.0016	0.0071	0.0069	0.0028	0.0084	-0.0007	0.0030	-0.0155	-0.0273	0.0300	0.0063	0.0098	1939	0.0318
1940	-0.0023	0.0027	0.0080	-0.0005	-0.0221	0.0177	-0.0005	0.0035	0.0040	0.0030	0.0050	0.0023	1940	0.0204
1941	-0.0006	-0.0052	0.0061	0.0027	0.0006	0.0051	-0.0004	0.0006	-0.0004	0.0018	-0.0096	-0.0023	1941	-0.0017
1942	0.0066	0.0009	0.0016	0.0016	0.0010	0.0006	-0.0006	0.0011	-0.0029	0.0011	0.0011	-0.0006	1942	0.0117
1943	0.0025	0.0001	0.0007	0.0010	0.0044	0.0020	0.0008	-0.0010	0.0002	0.0005	0.0002	0.0008	1943	0.0123
1944	-0.0002	0.0004	0.0007	0.0016	-0.0008	-0.0005	0.0016	0.0012	0.0000	-0.0001	-0.0003	-0.0001	1944	0.0035
1945	0.0040	0.0028	-0.0005	0.0005	0.0002	0.0009	-0.0010	0.0006	0.0008	0.0006	0.0001	0.0012	1945	0.0102
1946	0.0030	0.0040	-0.0045	-0.0028	-0.0003	0.0024	-0.0019	-0.0005	-0.0020	0.0015	-0.0018	0.0022	1946	-0.0008
1947	0.0012	-0.0003	0.0014	-0.0022	-0.0002	-0.0003	-0.0004	0.0016	-0.0010	-0.0033	-0.0004	0.0008	1947	-0.0030
1948	0.0002	0.0006	0.0003	0.0006	0.0042	-0.0021	-0.0014	-0.0018	-0.0003	0.0000	0.0006	0.0019	1948	0.0027
1949	0.0015	0.0000	0.0012	0.0003	0.0010	0.0038	0.0010	0.0019	-0.0002	-0.0004	-0.0008	0.0002	1949	0.0095
1950	-0.0016	-0.0002	-0.0011	-0.0003	0.0007	-0.0008	0.0009	-0.0019	-0.0015	-0.0012	0.0005	-0.0004	1950	-0.0069
1951	0.0006	-0.0007	-0.0142	0.0040	-0.0058	0.0033	0.0040	0.0019	-0.0072	-0.0003	0.0015	-0.0033	1951	-0.0163
1952	0.0019	-0.0037	0.0048	0.0037	0.0004	-0.0052	-0.0052	-0.0042	-0.0002	0.0046	-0.0023	-0.0002	1952	-0.0057
1953	-0.0022	-0.0016	-0.0038	-0.0117	-0.0138	0.0129	0.0032	-0.0031	0.0171	0.0018	-0.0006	0.0083	1953	0.0061
1954	0.0049	0.0086	0.0013	0.0031	-0.0084	0.0109	-0.0016	-0.0001	-0.0032	-0.0021	-0.0015	-0.0010	1954	0.0108
1955	-0.0050	-0.0070	0.0004	-0.0014	-0.0019	-0.0057	-0.0091	-0.0018	0.0059	0.0050	-0.0074	-0.0033	1955	-0.0310
1956	0.0080	-0.0018	-0.0122	-0.0027	0.0086	-0.0020	-0.0120	-0.0130	0.0066	-0.0049	-0.0075	-0.0019	1956	-0.0345
1957	0.0207	-0.0037	-0.0009	-0.0130	-0.0047	-0.0133	-0.0051	0.0077	-0.0030	0.0010	0.0365	0.0188	1957	0.0405
1958	0.0010	0.0117	0.0031	0.0031	0.0041	-0.0088	-0.0112	-0.0378	-0.0048	-0.0029	0.0103	-0.0093	1958	-0.0417
1959	-0.0045	0.0078	-0.0070	-0.0084	-0.0033	-0.0113	-0.0004	-0.0116	-0.0019	0.0134	-0.0130	-0.0060	1959	-0.0456
1960	0.0115	0.0032	0.0253	-0.0096	-0.0006	0.0182	0.0236	-0.0034	0.0001	-0.0012	-0.0122	0.0180	1960	0.0742
1961	-0.0089	0.0063	0.0008	0.0026	-0.0058	-0.0054	-0.0024	-0.0012	0.0049	-0.0018	-0.0049	-0.0012	1961	-0.0172
1962	-0.0080	0.0124	0.0058	-0.0006	0.0018	-0.0056	-0.0045	0.0092	-0.0007	0.0018	0.0031	0.0026	1962	0.0173
1963	-0.0059	-0.0011	-0.0002	-0.0002	-0.0017	-0.0015	-0.0030	-0.0012	-0.0019	-0.0022	0.0008	-0.0032	1963	-0.0210
1964	-0.0001	-0.0019	-0.0019	0.0000	0.0049	0.0000	-0.0006	-0.0006	0.0012	0.0000	-0.0037	0.0024	1964	-0.0003
1965	0.0009	-0.0013	0.0006	-0.0007	0.0002	0.0012	-0.0016	-0.0017	-0.0039	-0.0033	-0.0031	-0.0186	1965	-0.0310
1966	-0.0037	-0.0120	0.0145	-0.0056	-0.0032	-0.0064	-0.0065	-0.0171	0.0170	0.0031	-0.0015	0.0180	1966	-0.0041
1967	0.0077	-0.0048	0.0144	-0.0122	0.0002	-0.0265	0.0089	-0.0078	-0.0035	-0.0095	-0.0018	-0.0038	1967	-0.0385
1968	0.0095	-0.0003	-0.0069	-0.0065	0.0015	0.0123	0.0128	-0.0021	0.0011	-0.0034	-0.0054	-0.0220	1968	-0.0099
1969	0.0032	-0.0061	0.0048	0.0021	-0.0131	-0.0142	0.0024	-0.0072	-0.0361	0.0266	-0.0103	-0.0260	1969	-0.0727
1970	-0.0035	0.0378	0.0024	-0.0266	0.0049	-0.0006	0.0087	0.0054	0.0136	0.0037	0.0393	0.0005	1970	0.0871

* Compound annual return

Table A-12 **Intermediate-Term Government Bonds: Capital Appreciation Returns**

(continued)

From January 1971 to December 1998

YEAR	JAN	FEB	MAR	APR	MAY	JUN	JUL	AUG	SEP	OCT	NOV	DEC	YEAR	JAN–DEC*
1971	0.0121	0.0181	0.0139	-0.0367	-0.0034	-0.0240	-0.0027	0.0294	-0.0022	0.0173	0.0005	0.0064	1971	0.0272
1972	0.0058	-0.0030	-0.0031	-0.0030	-0.0035	-0.0003	-0.0034	-0.0035	-0.0033	-0.0037	-0.0006	0.0143	1972	-0.0075
1973	-0.0062	-0.0123	-0.0008	0.0007	0.0001	-0.0059	-0.0336	0.0190	0.0195	-0.0010	0.0009	-0.0016	1973	-0.0219
1974	-0.0048	-0.0016	-0.0266	-0.0217	0.0063	-0.0147	-0.0066	-0.0078	0.0247	0.0043	0.0175	0.0120	1974	-0.0199
1975	-0.0008	0.0092	-0.0119	-0.0246	0.0197	-0.0035	-0.0093	-0.0070	-0.0059	0.0298	-0.0065	0.0131	1975	0.0012
1976	-0.0003	0.0028	0.0010	0.0057	-0.0200	0.0090	0.0059	0.0127	0.0019	0.0093	0.0264	-0.0024	1976	0.0525
1977	-0.0241	-0.0002	-0.0001	-0.0001	-0.0002	0.0048	-0.0051	-0.0052	-0.0041	-0.0118	0.0019	-0.0082	1977	-0.0515
1978	-0.0053	-0.0041	-0.0029	-0.0036	-0.0073	-0.0087	0.0028	0.0010	-0.0008	-0.0184	0.0020	-0.0005	1978	-0.0449
1979	-0.0024	-0.0125	0.0038	-0.0044	0.0116	0.0135	-0.0086	-0.0163	-0.0065	-0.0553	0.0274	0.0001	1979	-0.0507
1980	-0.0221	-0.0724	0.0036	0.1095	0.0409	-0.0152	-0.0185	-0.0463	-0.0135	-0.0246	-0.0067	0.0060	1980	-0.0681
1981	-0.0069	-0.0331	0.0146	-0.0322	0.0135	-0.0058	-0.0386	-0.0298	0.0034	0.0482	0.0502	-0.0250	1981	-0.0455
1982	-0.0057	0.0046	-0.0080	0.0186	0.0045	-0.0253	0.0351	0.0359	0.0228	0.0442	-0.0007	0.0100	1982	0.1423
1983	-0.0076	0.0173	-0.0133	0.0177	-0.0208	-0.0069	-0.0280	-0.0022	0.0220	-0.0073	0.0012	-0.0043	1983	-0.0330
1984	0.0081	-0.0153	-0.0129	-0.0104	-0.0353	-0.0007	0.0280	-0.0005	0.0106	0.0274	0.0099	0.0050	1984	0.0122
1985	0.0116	-0.0260	0.0077	0.0167	0.0395	0.0035	-0.0129	0.0067	0.0031	0.0081	0.0121	0.0178	1985	0.0901
1986	0.0011	0.0210	0.0270	0.0021	-0.0274	0.0208	0.0095	0.0209	-0.0168	0.0102	0.0061	-0.0053	1986	0.0699
1987	0.0051	0.0007	-0.0091	-0.0302	-0.0100	0.0051	-0.0040	-0.0105	-0.0209	0.0226	0.0013	0.0023	1987	-0.0475
1988	0.0251	0.0057	-0.0151	-0.0107	-0.0121	0.0111	-0.0111	-0.0086	0.0124	0.0077	-0.0182	-0.0081	1988	-0.0226
1989	0.0044	-0.0117	-0.0029	0.0149	0.0132	0.0254	0.0168	-0.0307	0.0004	0.0166	0.0021	-0.0048	1989	0.0434
1990	-0.0176	-0.0057	-0.0067	-0.0148	0.0186	0.0084	0.0102	-0.0160	0.0030	0.0096	0.0126	0.0095	1990	0.0102
1991	0.0042	-0.0011	-0.0036	0.0046	-0.0006	-0.0081	0.0060	0.0184	0.0155	0.0077	0.0076	0.0209	1991	0.0736
1992	-0.0247	-0.0030	-0.0139	0.0039	0.0166	0.0118	0.0189	0.0100	0.0147	-0.0226	-0.0134	0.0093	1992	0.0064
1993	0.0221	0.0198	-0.0006	0.0043	-0.0051	0.0152	-0.0036	0.0179	0.0015	-0.0020	-0.0135	-0.0011	1993	0.0556
1994	0.0093	-0.0297	-0.0306	-0.0154	-0.0060	-0.0084	0.0115	-0.0034	-0.0213	-0.0084	-0.0131	-0.0010	1994	-0.1114
1995	0.0115	0.0178	0.0003	0.0090	0.0307	0.0030	-0.0066	0.0035	0.0017	0.0069	0.0102	0.0052	1995	0.0966
1996	-0.0040	-0.0178	-0.0164	-0.0103	-0.0086	0.0067	-0.0033	-0.0057	0.0100	0.0129	0.0102	-0.0128	1996	-0.0390
1997	-0.0027	-0.0045	-0.0168	0.0093	0.0024	0.0048	0.0210	-0.0143	0.0098	0.0100	-0.0045	0.0054	1997	0.0194
1998	0.0134	-0.0080	-0.0024	0.0015	0.0025	0.0030	-0.0020	0.0225	0.0289	0.0006	-0.0134	-0.0002	1998	0.0466

* Compound annual return

Table A-13 Intermediate-Term Government Bonds: Yields

From January 1926 to December 1970

YEAR	JAN	FEB	MAR	APR	MAY	JUN	JUL	AUG	SEP	OCT	NOV	DEC	YR-END	YIELD
1926	0.0386	0.0386	0.0384	0.0371	0.0376	0.0377	0.0381	0.0386	0.0382	0.0377	0.0374	0.0361	1926	0.0361
1927	0.0355	0.0353	0.0351	0.0354	0.0356	0.0356	0.0353	0.0347	0.0340	0.0354	0.0342	0.0340	1927	0.0340
1928	0.0336	0.0343	0.0347	0.0354	0.0362	0.0365	0.0392	0.0388	0.0389	0.0389	0.0392	0.0401	1928	0.0401
1929	0.0415	0.0427	0.0434	0.0422	0.0444	0.0428	0.0421	0.0417	0.0428	0.0398	0.0365	0.0362	1929	0.0362
1930	0.0378	0.0364	0.0335	0.0357	0.0350	0.0325	0.0319	0.0320	0.0312	0.0301	0.0291	0.0291	1930	0.0291
1931	0.0312	0.0296	0.0290	0.0277	0.0256	0.0308	0.0310	0.0312	0.0343	0.0373	0.0369	0.0412	1931	0.0412
1932	0.0427	0.0406	0.0396	0.0360	0.0387	0.0370	0.0350	0.0329	0.0329	0.0325	0.0324	0.0304	1932	0.0304
1933	0.0313	0.0319	0.0303	0.0296	0.0258	0.0261	0.0267	0.0256	0.0255	0.0265	0.0264	0.0325	1933	0.0325
1934	0.0325	0.0321	0.0296	0.0272	0.0257	0.0246	0.0253	0.0271	0.0298	0.0271	0.0267	0.0249	1934	0.0249
1935	0.0233	0.0218	0.0199	0.0184	0.0193	0.0175	0.0171	0.0187	0.0201	0.0183	0.0183	0.0163	1935	0.0163
1936	0.0166	0.0155	0.0151	0.0149	0.0143	0.0143	0.0141	0.0133	0.0133	0.0130	0.0114	0.0129	1936	0.0129
1937	0.0134	0.0135	0.0184	0.0175	0.0156	0.0164	0.0151	0.0168	0.0147	0.0141	0.0131	0.0114	1937	0.0114
1938	0.0205	0.0200	0.0204	0.0174	0.0173	0.0164	0.0164	0.0164	0.0168	0.0156	0.0158	0.0152	1938	0.0152
1939	0.0149	0.0138	0.0127	0.0122	0.0108	0.0110	0.0105	0.0131	0.0180	0.0127	0.0116	0.0098	1939	0.0098
1940	0.0103	0.0098	0.0083	0.0084	0.0127	0.0092	0.0093	0.0086	0.0078	0.0072	0.0061	0.0057	1940	0.0057
1941	0.0077	0.0089	0.0075	0.0069	0.0067	0.0055	0.0056	0.0055	0.0056	0.0051	0.0076	0.0082	1941	0.0082
1942	0.0083	0.0081	0.0077	0.0074	0.0071	0.0070	0.0071	0.0069	0.0076	0.0073	0.0070	0.0072	1942	0.0072
1943	0.0166	0.0166	0.0164	0.0162	0.0153	0.0149	0.0147	0.0149	0.0149	0.0147	0.0147	0.0145	1943	0.0145
1944	0.0150	0.0150	0.0148	0.0143	0.0146	0.0147	0.0142	0.0139	0.0139	0.0139	0.0140	0.0140	1944	0.0140
1945	0.0127	0.0118	0.0120	0.0118	0.0117	0.0114	0.0118	0.0115	0.0112	0.0109	0.0109	0.0103	1945	0.0103
1946	0.0099	0.0087	0.0101	0.0111	0.0112	0.0103	0.0110	0.0112	0.0120	0.0114	0.0121	0.0112	1946	0.0112
1947	0.0116	0.0117	0.0112	0.0120	0.0121	0.0122	0.0124	0.0117	0.0121	0.0136	0.0138	0.0134	1947	0.0134
1948	0.0160	0.0158	0.0157	0.0155	0.0142	0.0149	0.0154	0.0160	0.0161	0.0161	0.0158	0.0151	1948	0.0151
1949	0.0153	0.0153	0.0148	0.0147	0.0144	0.0129	0.0125	0.0117	0.0118	0.0120	0.0124	0.0123	1949	0.0123
1950	0.0131	0.0132	0.0137	0.0138	0.0134	0.0139	0.0134	0.0145	0.0154	0.0162	0.0159	0.0162	1950	0.0162
1951	0.0179	0.0180	0.0211	0.0202	0.0215	0.0208	0.0199	0.0194	0.0212	0.0212	0.0209	0.0217	1951	0.0217
1952	0.0212	0.0222	0.0209	0.0199	0.0198	0.0213	0.0228	0.0241	0.0242	0.0227	0.0235	0.0235	1952	0.0235
1953	0.0242	0.0245	0.0253	0.0277	0.0307	0.0279	0.0272	0.0279	0.0241	0.0237	0.0238	0.0218	1953	0.0218
1954	0.0187	0.0157	0.0153	0.0142	0.0173	0.0131	0.0138	0.0138	0.0152	0.0161	0.0168	0.0172	1954	0.0172
1955	0.0227	0.0240	0.0240	0.0242	0.0246	0.0257	0.0276	0.0280	0.0267	0.0257	0.0273	0.0280	1955	0.0280
1956	0.0271	0.0275	0.0300	0.0305	0.0287	0.0292	0.0317	0.0346	0.0331	0.0342	0.0359	0.0363	1956	0.0363
1957	0.0326	0.0333	0.0334	0.0357	0.0366	0.0390	0.0399	0.0385	0.0390	0.0388	0.0320	0.0284	1957	0.0284
1958	0.0282	0.0259	0.0253	0.0246	0.0238	0.0250	0.0281	0.0365	0.0376	0.0382	0.0359	0.0381	1958	0.0381
1959	0.0395	0.0378	0.0393	0.0413	0.0420	0.0447	0.0448	0.0477	0.0482	0.0448	0.0482	0.0498	1959	0.0498
1960	0.0471	0.0464	0.0409	0.0431	0.0432	0.0390	0.0334	0.0343	0.0343	0.0346	0.0377	0.0331	1960	0.0331
1961	0.0363	0.0350	0.0348	0.0342	0.0355	0.0368	0.0373	0.0376	0.0365	0.0369	0.0381	0.0384	1961	0.0384
1962	0.0402	0.0377	0.0366	0.0367	0.0363	0.0375	0.0384	0.0365	0.0366	0.0362	0.0355	0.0350	1962	0.0350
1963	0.0368	0.0370	0.0370	0.0371	0.0374	0.0378	0.0385	0.0388	0.0392	0.0398	0.0396	0.0404	1963	0.0404
1964	0.0402	0.0407	0.0411	0.0411	0.0399	0.0399	0.0401	0.0402	0.0399	0.0399	0.0409	0.0403	1964	0.0403
1965	0.0413	0.0416	0.0414	0.0416	0.0415	0.0413	0.0416	0.0420	0.0429	0.0437	0.0444	0.0490	1965	0.0490
1966	0.0482	0.0507	0.0477	0.0489	0.0496	0.0510	0.0525	0.0565	0.0526	0.0519	0.0522	0.0479	1966	0.0479
1967	0.0459	0.0470	0.0437	0.0466	0.0465	0.0530	0.0508	0.0528	0.0537	0.0562	0.0566	0.0577	1967	0.0577
1968	0.0548	0.0549	0.0563	0.0577	0.0574	0.0547	0.0518	0.0523	0.0520	0.0528	0.0541	0.0596	1968	0.0596
1969	0.0637	0.0651	0.0640	0.0636	0.0666	0.0699	0.0693	0.0711	0.0799	0.0735	0.0761	0.0829	1969	0.0829
1970	0.0820	0.0730	0.0724	0.0790	0.0778	0.0780	0.0757	0.0743	0.0707	0.0697	0.0591	0.0590	1970	0.0590

Table A-13 **Intermediate-Term Government Bonds: Yields**

(continued)

From January 1971 to December 1998

YEAR	JAN	FEB	MAR	APR	MAY	JUN	JUL	AUG	SEP	OCT	NOV	DEC	YR-END	YIELD
1971	0.0570	0.0526	0.0493	0.0585	0.0593	0.0656	0.0663	0.0585	0.0591	0.0545	0.0543	0.0525	1971	0.0525
1972	0.0556	0.0563	0.0570	0.0577	0.0586	0.0587	0.0595	0.0604	0.0613	0.0623	0.0625	0.0585	1972	0.0585
1973	0.0641	0.0671	0.0673	0.0671	0.0671	0.0686	0.0776	0.0725	0.0674	0.0677	0.0674	0.0679	1973	0.0679
1974	0.0687	0.0691	0.0751	0.0801	0.0786	0.0822	0.0838	0.0857	0.0797	0.0787	0.0743	0.0712	1974	0.0712
1975	0.0730	0.0709	0.0737	0.0798	0.0749	0.0758	0.0782	0.0800	0.0815	0.0736	0.0754	0.0719	1975	0.0719
1976	0.0743	0.0736	0.0733	0.0719	0.0771	0.0747	0.0732	0.0697	0.0692	0.0667	0.0594	0.0600	1976	0.0600
1977	0.0673	0.0673	0.0673	0.0674	0.0674	0.0662	0.0675	0.0689	0.0700	0.0733	0.0727	0.0751	1977	0.0751
1978	0.0773	0.0784	0.0791	0.0800	0.0820	0.0843	0.0836	0.0833	0.0835	0.0887	0.0882	0.0883	1978	0.0883
1979	0.0895	0.0928	0.0918	0.0929	0.0899	0.0864	0.0887	0.0933	0.0951	0.1112	0.1033	0.1033	1979	0.1033
1980	0.1093	0.1294	0.1285	0.1009	0.0903	0.0944	0.0996	0.1133	0.1171	0.1244	0.1264	0.1245	1980	0.1245
1981	0.1275	0.1371	0.1328	0.1427	0.1385	0.1404	0.1533	0.1636	0.1625	0.1472	0.1311	0.1396	1981	0.1396
1982	0.1397	0.1385	0.1406	0.1355	0.1343	0.1417	0.1315	0.1209	0.1144	0.1018	0.1020	0.0990	1982	0.0990
1983	0.1057	0.1010	0.1048	0.0997	0.1059	0.1080	0.1168	0.1175	0.1108	0.1131	0.1127	0.1141	1983	0.1141
1984	0.1137	0.1181	0.1219	0.1251	0.1363	0.1365	0.1274	0.1276	0.1242	0.1154	0.1121	0.1104	1984	0.1104
1985	0.1081	0.1152	0.1131	0.1084	0.0974	0.0963	0.1002	0.0982	0.0973	0.0949	0.0911	0.0855	1985	0.0855
1986	0.0870	0.0815	0.0743	0.0737	0.0816	0.0756	0.0728	0.0668	0.0718	0.0687	0.0669	0.0685	1986	0.0685
1987	0.0685	0.0683	0.0708	0.0793	0.0821	0.0806	0.0818	0.0849	0.0912	0.0844	0.0840	0.0832	1987	0.0832
1988	0.0782	0.0768	0.0807	0.0836	0.0870	0.0839	0.0871	0.0895	0.0859	0.0837	0.0892	0.0917	1988	0.0917
1989	0.0896	0.0927	0.0934	0.0895	0.0860	0.0791	0.0745	0.0834	0.0833	0.0786	0.0779	0.0794	1989	0.0794
1990	0.0842	0.0855	0.0871	0.0907	0.0864	0.0843	0.0819	0.0859	0.0851	0.0826	0.0795	0.0770	1990	0.0770
1991	0.0772	0.0774	0.0783	0.0772	0.0773	0.0793	0.0778	0.0732	0.0693	0.0673	0.0653	0.0597	1991	0.0597
1992	0.0683	0.0690	0.0720	0.0711	0.0674	0.0647	0.0604	0.0581	0.0547	0.0601	0.0634	0.0611	1992	0.0611
1993	0.0588	0.0547	0.0549	0.0540	0.0551	0.0517	0.0526	0.0486	0.0483	0.0488	0.0519	0.0522	1993	0.0522
1994	0.0515	0.0575	0.0638	0.0670	0.0682	0.0699	0.0675	0.0683	0.0730	0.0749	0.0778	0.0780	1994	0.0780
1995	0.0754	0.0708	0.0707	0.0685	0.0606	0.0598	0.0616	0.0606	0.0601	0.0582	0.0553	0.0538	1995	0.0538
1996	0.0528	0.0573	0.0614	0.0640	0.0663	0.0645	0.0654	0.0670	0.0643	0.0607	0.0578	0.0616	1996	0.0616
1997	0.0629	0.0639	0.0677	0.0656	0.0650	0.0639	0.0589	0.0624	0.0601	0.0576	0.0587	0.0573	1997	0.0573
1998	0.0545	0.0562	0.0567	0.0564	0.0558	0.0551	0.0556	0.0503	0.0435	0.0434	0.0467	0.0468	1998	0.0468

Table A-14 **U.S. Treasury Bills: Total Returns**

From January 1926 to December 1970

YEAR	JAN	FEB	MAR	APR	MAY	JUN	JUL	AUG	SEP	OCT	NOV	DEC	YEAR	JAN-DEC*
1926	0.0034	0.0027	0.0030	0.0034	0.0001	0.0035	0.0022	0.0025	0.0023	0.0032	0.0031	0.0028	1926	0.0327
1927	0.0025	0.0026	0.0030	0.0025	0.0030	0.0026	0.0030	0.0028	0.0021	0.0025	0.0021	0.0022	1927	0.0312
1928	0.0025	0.0033	0.0029	0.0022	0.0032	0.0031	0.0032	0.0032	0.0027	0.0041	0.0038	0.0006	1928	0.0356
1929	0.0034	0.0036	0.0034	0.0036	0.0044	0.0052	0.0033	0.0040	0.0035	0.0046	0.0037	0.0037	1929	0.0475
1930	0.0014	0.0030	0.0035	0.0021	0.0026	0.0027	0.0020	0.0009	0.0022	0.0009	0.0013	0.0014	1930	0.0241
1931	0.0015	0.0004	0.0013	0.0008	0.0009	0.0008	0.0006	0.0003	0.0003	0.0010	0.0017	0.0012	1931	0.0107
1932	0.0023	0.0023	0.0016	0.0011	0.0006	0.0002	0.0003	0.0003	0.0003	0.0002	0.0002	0.0001	1932	0.0096
1933	0.0001	-0.0003	0.0004	0.0010	0.0004	0.0002	0.0002	0.0003	0.0002	0.0001	0.0002	0.0002	1933	0.0030
1934	0.0005	0.0002	0.0002	0.0001	0.0001	0.0001	0.0001	0.0001	0.0001	0.0001	0.0001	0.0001	1934	0.0016
1935	0.0001	0.0002	0.0001	0.0001	0.0001	0.0001	0.0001	0.0001	0.0001	0.0001	0.0002	0.0001	1935	0.0017
1936	0.0001	0.0001	0.0002	0.0002	0.0002	0.0003	0.0001	0.0002	0.0001	0.0002	0.0001	0.0000	1936	0.0018
1937	0.0001	0.0002	0.0001	0.0003	0.0006	0.0003	0.0003	0.0002	0.0004	0.0002	0.0002	0.0000	1937	0.0031
1938	0.0000	0.0000	-0.0001	0.0001	0.0000	0.0000	-0.0001	0.0000	0.0002	0.0001	-0.0006	0.0000	1938	-0.0002
1939	-0.0001	0.0001	-0.0001	0.0000	0.0001	0.0001	0.0000	-0.0001	0.0001	0.0000	0.0000	0.0000	1939	0.0002
1940	0.0000	0.0000	0.0000	0.0000	-0.0002	0.0000	0.0001	-0.0001	0.0000	0.0000	0.0000	0.0000	1940	0.0000
1941	-0.0001	-0.0001	0.0001	-0.0001	0.0000	0.0000	0.0003	0.0001	0.0001	0.0000	0.0000	0.0001	1941	0.0006
1942	0.0002	0.0001	0.0001	0.0001	0.0003	0.0002	0.0003	0.0003	0.0003	0.0003	0.0003	0.0003	1942	0.0027
1943	0.0003	0.0003	0.0003	0.0003	0.0003	0.0003	0.0003	0.0003	0.0003	0.0003	0.0003	0.0003	1943	0.0035
1944	0.0003	0.0003	0.0002	0.0003	0.0003	0.0003	0.0003	0.0003	0.0002	0.0003	0.0003	0.0002	1944	0.0033
1945	0.0003	0.0002	0.0002	0.0003	0.0003	0.0002	0.0003	0.0003	0.0003	0.0003	0.0002	0.0003	1945	0.0033
1946	0.0003	0.0003	0.0003	0.0003	0.0003	0.0003	0.0003	0.0003	0.0003	0.0003	0.0003	0.0003	1946	0.0035
1947	0.0003	0.0003	0.0003	0.0003	0.0003	0.0003	0.0003	0.0003	0.0006	0.0006	0.0006	0.0008	1947	0.0050
1948	0.0007	0.0007	0.0009	0.0008	0.0008	0.0009	0.0008	0.0009	0.0004	0.0004	0.0004	0.0004	1948	0.0081
1949	0.0010	0.0009	0.0010	0.0009	0.0010	0.0010	0.0009	0.0009	0.0009	0.0009	0.0008	0.0009	1949	0.0110
1950	0.0009	0.0009	0.0010	0.0009	0.0010	0.0010	0.0010	0.0010	0.0010	0.0012	0.0011	0.0011	1950	0.0120
1951	0.0013	0.0010	0.0011	0.0013	0.0012	0.0012	0.0013	0.0013	0.0012	0.0016	0.0011	0.0012	1951	0.0149
1952	0.0015	0.0012	0.0011	0.0012	0.0013	0.0015	0.0015	0.0015	0.0016	0.0014	0.0010	0.0016	1952	0.0166
1953	0.0016	0.0014	0.0018	0.0016	0.0017	0.0018	0.0015	0.0017	0.0016	0.0013	0.0008	0.0013	1953	0.0182
1954	0.0011	0.0007	0.0008	0.0009	0.0005	0.0006	0.0005	0.0005	0.0009	0.0007	0.0006	0.0008	1954	0.0086
1955	0.0008	0.0009	0.0010	0.0010	0.0014	0.0010	0.0010	0.0016	0.0016	0.0018	0.0017	0.0018	1955	0.0157
1956	0.0022	0.0019	0.0015	0.0019	0.0023	0.0020	0.0022	0.0017	0.0018	0.0025	0.0020	0.0024	1956	0.0246
1957	0.0027	0.0024	0.0023	0.0025	0.0026	0.0024	0.0030	0.0025	0.0026	0.0029	0.0028	0.0024	1957	0.0314
1958	0.0028	0.0012	0.0009	0.0008	0.0011	0.0003	0.0007	0.0004	0.0019	0.0018	0.0011	0.0022	1958	0.0154
1959	0.0021	0.0019	0.0022	0.0020	0.0022	0.0025	0.0025	0.0019	0.0031	0.0030	0.0026	0.0034	1959	0.0295
1960	0.0033	0.0029	0.0035	0.0019	0.0027	0.0024	0.0013	0.0017	0.0016	0.0022	0.0013	0.0016	1960	0.0266
1961	0.0019	0.0014	0.0020	0.0017	0.0018	0.0020	0.0018	0.0014	0.0017	0.0019	0.0015	0.0019	1961	0.0213
1962	0.0024	0.0020	0.0020	0.0022	0.0024	0.0020	0.0027	0.0023	0.0021	0.0026	0.0020	0.0023	1962	0.0273
1963	0.0025	0.0023	0.0023	0.0025	0.0024	0.0023	0.0027	0.0025	0.0027	0.0029	0.0027	0.0029	1963	0.0312
1964	0.0030	0.0026	0.0031	0.0029	0.0026	0.0030	0.0030	0.0028	0.0028	0.0029	0.0029	0.0031	1964	0.0354
1965	0.0028	0.0030	0.0036	0.0031	0.0031	0.0035	0.0031	0.0033	0.0031	0.0031	0.0035	0.0033	1965	0.0393
1966	0.0038	0.0035	0.0038	0.0034	0.0041	0.0038	0.0035	0.0041	0.0040	0.0045	0.0040	0.0040	1966	0.0476
1967	0.0043	0.0036	0.0039	0.0032	0.0033	0.0027	0.0032	0.0031	0.0032	0.0039	0.0036	0.0033	1967	0.0421
1968	0.0040	0.0039	0.0038	0.0043	0.0045	0.0043	0.0048	0.0042	0.0043	0.0044	0.0042	0.0043	1968	0.0521
1969	0.0053	0.0046	0.0046	0.0053	0.0048	0.0051	0.0053	0.0050	0.0062	0.0060	0.0052	0.0064	1969	0.0658
1970	0.0060	0.0062	0.0057	0.0050	0.0053	0.0058	0.0052	0.0053	0.0054	0.0046	0.0046	0.0042	1970	0.0652

* Compound annual return

Table A-14 **U.S. Treasury Bills: Total Returns**

(continued)

From January 1971 to December 1998

YEAR	JAN	FEB	MAR	APR	MAY	JUN	JUL	AUG	SEP	OCT	NOV	DEC	YEAR	JAN–DEC*
1971	0.0038	0.0033	0.0030	0.0028	0.0029	0.0037	0.0040	0.0047	0.0037	0.0037	0.0037	0.0037	1971	0.0439
1972	0.0029	0.0025	0.0027	0.0029	0.0030	0.0029	0.0031	0.0029	0.0034	0.0040	0.0037	0.0037	1972	0.0384
1973	0.0044	0.0041	0.0046	0.0052	0.0051	0.0051	0.0064	0.0070	0.0068	0.0065	0.0056	0.0064	1973	0.0693
1974	0.0063	0.0058	0.0056	0.0075	0.0075	0.0060	0.0070	0.0060	0.0081	0.0051	0.0054	0.0070	1974	0.0800
1975	0.0058	0.0043	0.0041	0.0044	0.0044	0.0041	0.0048	0.0048	0.0053	0.0056	0.0041	0.0048	1975	0.0580
1976	0.0047	0.0034	0.0040	0.0042	0.0037	0.0043	0.0047	0.0042	0.0044	0.0041	0.0040	0.0040	1976	0.0508
1977	0.0036	0.0035	0.0038	0.0038	0.0037	0.0040	0.0042	0.0044	0.0043	0.0049	0.0050	0.0049	1977	0.0512
1978	0.0049	0.0046	0.0053	0.0054	0.0051	0.0054	0.0056	0.0055	0.0062	0.0068	0.0070	0.0078	1978	0.0718
1979	0.0077	0.0073	0.0081	0.0080	0.0082	0.0081	0.0077	0.0077	0.0083	0.0087	0.0099	0.0095	1979	0.1038
1980	0.0080	0.0089	0.0121	0.0126	0.0081	0.0061	0.0053	0.0064	0.0075	0.0095	0.0096	0.0131	1980	0.1124
1981	0.0104	0.0107	0.0121	0.0108	0.0115	0.0135	0.0124	0.0128	0.0124	0.0121	0.0107	0.0087	1981	0.1471
1982	0.0080	0.0092	0.0098	0.0113	0.0106	0.0096	0.0105	0.0076	0.0051	0.0059	0.0063	0.0067	1982	0.1054
1983	0.0069	0.0062	0.0063	0.0071	0.0069	0.0067	0.0074	0.0076	0.0076	0.0076	0.0070	0.0073	1983	0.0880
1984	0.0076	0.0071	0.0073	0.0081	0.0078	0.0075	0.0082	0.0083	0.0086	0.0100	0.0073	0.0064	1984	0.0985
1985	0.0065	0.0058	0.0062	0.0072	0.0066	0.0055	0.0062	0.0055	0.0060	0.0065	0.0061	0.0065	1985	0.0772
1986	0.0056	0.0053	0.0060	0.0052	0.0049	0.0052	0.0052	0.0046	0.0045	0.0046	0.0039	0.0049	1986	0.0616
1987	0.0042	0.0043	0.0047	0.0044	0.0038	0.0048	0.0046	0.0047	0.0045	0.0060	0.0035	0.0039	1987	0.0547
1988	0.0029	0.0046	0.0044	0.0046	0.0051	0.0049	0.0051	0.0059	0.0062	0.0061	0.0057	0.0063	1988	0.0635
1989	0.0055	0.0061	0.0067	0.0067	0.0079	0.0071	0.0070	0.0074	0.0065	0.0068	0.0069	0.0061	1989	0.0837
1990	0.0057	0.0057	0.0064	0.0069	0.0068	0.0063	0.0068	0.0066	0.0060	0.0068	0.0057	0.0060	1990	0.0781
1991	0.0052	0.0048	0.0044	0.0053	0.0047	0.0042	0.0049	0.0046	0.0046	0.0042	0.0039	0.0038	1991	0.0560
1992	0.0034	0.0028	0.0034	0.0032	0.0028	0.0032	0.0031	0.0026	0.0026	0.0023	0.0023	0.0028	1992	0.0351
1993	0.0023	0.0022	0.0025	0.0024	0.0022	0.0025	0.0024	0.0025	0.0026	0.0022	0.0025	0.0023	1993	0.0290
1994	0.0025	0.0021	0.0027	0.0027	0.0032	0.0031	0.0028	0.0037	0.0037	0.0038	0.0037	0.0044	1994	0.0390
1995	0.0042	0.0040	0.0046	0.0044	0.0054	0.0047	0.0045	0.0047	0.0043	0.0047	0.0042	0.0049	1995	0.0560
1996	0.0043	0.0039	0.0039	0.0046	0.0042	0.0040	0.0045	0.0041	0.0044	0.0042	0.0041	0.0046	1996	0.0521
1997	0.0045	0.0039	0.0043	0.0043	0.0049	0.0037	0.0043	0.0041	0.0044	0.0042	0.0039	0.0048	1997	0.0526
1998	0.0043	0.0039	0.0039	0.0043	0.0040	0.0041	0.0040	0.0043	0.0046	0.0032	0.0031	0.0038	1998	0.0486

* Compound annual return

Table A-15 **Inflation**

From January 1926 to December 1970

YEAR	JAN	FEB	MAR	APR	MAY	JUN	JUL	AUG	SEP	OCT	NOV	DEC	YEAR	JAN–DEC*
1926	0.0000	-0.0037	-0.0056	0.0094	-0.0056	-0.0075	-0.0094	-0.0057	0.0057	0.0038	0.0038	0.0000	1926	-0.0149
1927	-0.0076	-0.0076	-0.0058	0.0000	0.0077	0.0096	-0.0190	-0.0058	0.0058	0.0058	-0.0019	-0.0019	1927	-0.0208
1928	-0.0019	-0.0097	0.0000	0.0020	0.0058	-0.0078	0.0000	0.0020	0.0078	-0.0019	-0.0019	-0.0039	1928	-0.0097
1929	-0.0019	-0.0020	-0.0039	-0.0039	0.0059	0.0039	0.0098	0.0039	-0.0019	0.0000	-0.0019	-0.0058	1929	0.0020
1930	-0.0039	-0.0039	-0.0059	0.0059	-0.0059	-0.0059	-0.0139	-0.0060	0.0061	-0.0060	-0.0081	-0.0143	1930	-0.0603
1931	-0.0145	-0.0147	-0.0064	-0.0064	-0.0108	-0.0109	-0.0022	-0.0022	-0.0044	-0.0067	-0.0112	-0.0091	1931	-0.0952
1932	-0.0206	-0.0140	-0.0047	-0.0071	-0.0144	-0.0073	0.0000	-0.0123	-0.0050	-0.0075	-0.0050	-0.0101	1932	-0.1030
1933	-0.0153	-0.0155	-0.0079	-0.0027	0.0027	0.0106	0.0289	0.0102	0.0000	0.0000	0.0000	-0.0051	1933	0.0051
1934	0.0051	0.0076	0.0000	-0.0025	0.0025	0.0025	0.0000	0.0025	0.0150	-0.0074	-0.0025	-0.0025	1934	0.0203
1935	0.0149	0.0074	-0.0024	0.0098	-0.0048	-0.0024	-0.0049	0.0000	0.0049	0.0000	0.0049	0.0024	1935	0.0299
1936	0.0000	-0.0048	-0.0049	0.0000	0.0000	0.0098	0.0048	0.0072	0.0024	-0.0024	0.0000	0.0000	1936	0.0121
1937	0.0072	0.0024	0.0071	0.0047	0.0047	0.0023	0.0046	0.0023	0.0092	-0.0046	-0.0069	-0.0023	1937	0.0310
1938	-0.0139	-0.0094	0.0000	0.0047	-0.0047	0.0000	0.0024	-0.0024	0.0000	-0.0047	-0.0024	0.0024	1938	-0.0278
1939	-0.0048	-0.0048	-0.0024	-0.0024	0.0000	0.0000	0.0000	0.0000	0.0193	-0.0047	0.0000	-0.0048	1939	-0.0048
1940	-0.0024	0.0072	-0.0024	0.0000	0.0024	0.0024	-0.0024	-0.0024	0.0024	0.0000	0.0000	0.0048	1940	0.0096
1941	0.0000	0.0000	0.0047	0.0094	0.0070	0.0186	0.0046	0.0091	0.0180	0.0110	0.0087	0.0022	1941	0.0972
1942	0.0130	0.0085	0.0127	0.0063	0.0104	0.0021	0.0041	0.0061	0.0020	0.0101	0.0060	0.0080	1942	0.0929
1943	0.0000	0.0020	0.0158	0.0116	0.0077	-0.0019	-0.0076	-0.0038	0.0039	0.0038	-0.0019	0.0019	1943	0.0316
1944	-0.0019	-0.0019	0.0000	0.0058	0.0038	0.0019	0.0057	0.0038	0.0000	0.0000	0.0000	0.0038	1944	0.0211
1945	0.0000	-0.0019	0.0000	0.0019	0.0075	0.0093	0.0018	0.0000	-0.0037	0.0000	0.0037	0.0037	1945	0.0225
1946	0.0000	-0.0037	0.0074	0.0055	0.0055	0.0109	0.0590	0.0220	0.0116	0.0196	0.0240	0.0078	1946	0.1816
1947	0.0000	-0.0016	0.0218	0.0000	-0.0030	0.0076	0.0091	0.0105	0.0238	0.0000	0.0058	0.0130	1947	0.0901
1948	0.0114	-0.0085	-0.0028	0.0142	0.0070	0.0070	0.0125	0.0041	0.0000	-0.0041	-0.0068	-0.0069	1948	0.0271
1949	-0.0014	-0.0111	0.0028	0.0014	-0.0014	0.0014	-0.0070	0.0028	0.0042	-0.0056	0.0014	-0.0056	1949	-0.0180
1950	-0.0042	-0.0028	0.0043	0.0014	0.0042	0.0056	0.0098	0.0083	0.0069	0.0055	0.0041	0.0135	1950	0.0579
1951	0.0160	0.0118	0.0039	0.0013	0.0039	-0.0013	0.0013	0.0000	0.0064	0.0051	0.0051	0.0038	1951	0.0587
1952	0.0000	-0.0063	0.0000	0.0038	0.0013	0.0025	0.0076	0.0012	-0.0012	0.0012	0.0000	-0.0012	1952	0.0088
1953	-0.0025	-0.0050	0.0025	0.0013	0.0025	0.0038	0.0025	0.0025	0.0012	0.0025	-0.0037	-0.0012	1953	0.0062
1954	0.0025	-0.0012	-0.0012	-0.0025	0.0037	0.0012	0.0000	-0.0012	-0.0025	-0.0025	0.0012	-0.0025	1954	-0.0050
1955	0.0000	0.0000	0.0000	0.0000	0.0000	0.0000	0.0037	-0.0025	0.0037	0.0000	0.0012	-0.0025	1955	0.0037
1956	-0.0012	0.0000	0.0012	0.0012	0.0050	0.0062	0.0074	-0.0012	0.0012	0.0061	0.0000	0.0024	1956	0.0286
1957	0.0012	0.0036	0.0024	0.0036	0.0024	0.0060	0.0047	0.0012	0.0012	0.0000	0.0035	0.0000	1957	0.0302
1958	0.0059	0.0012	0.0070	0.0023	0.0000	0.0012	0.0012	-0.0012	0.0000	0.0000	0.0012	-0.0012	1958	0.0176
1959	0.0012	-0.0012	0.0000	0.0012	0.0012	0.0046	0.0023	-0.0011	0.0034	0.0034	0.0000	0.0000	1959	0.0150
1960	-0.0011	0.0011	0.0000	0.0057	0.0000	0.0023	0.0000	0.0000	0.0011	0.0045	0.0011	0.0000	1960	0.0148
1961	0.0000	0.0000	0.0000	0.0000	0.0000	0.0011	0.0045	-0.0011	0.0022	0.0000	0.0000	0.0000	1961	0.0067
1962	0.0000	0.0022	0.0022	0.0022	0.0000	0.0000	0.0022	0.0000	0.0055	-0.0011	0.0000	-0.0011	1962	0.0122
1963	0.0011	0.0011	0.0011	0.0000	0.0000	0.0044	0.0044	0.0000	0.0000	0.0011	0.0011	0.0022	1963	0.0165
1964	0.0011	-0.0011	0.0011	0.0011	0.0000	0.0022	0.0022	-0.0011	0.0022	0.0011	0.0021	0.0011	1964	0.0119
1965	0.0000	0.0000	0.0011	0.0032	0.0021	0.0053	0.0011	-0.0021	0.0021	0.0011	0.0021	0.0032	1965	0.0192
1966	0.0000	0.0063	0.0031	0.0042	0.0010	0.0031	0.0031	0.0051	0.0020	0.0041	0.0000	0.0010	1966	0.0335
1967	0.0000	0.0010	0.0020	0.0020	0.0030	0.0030	0.0050	0.0030	0.0020	0.0030	0.0030	0.0030	1967	0.0304
1968	0.0039	0.0029	0.0049	0.0029	0.0029	0.0058	0.0048	0.0029	0.0029	0.0057	0.0038	0.0028	1968	0.0472
1969	0.0028	0.0037	0.0084	0.0065	0.0028	0.0064	0.0046	0.0045	0.0045	0.0036	0.0054	0.0062	1969	0.0611
1970	0.0035	0.0053	0.0053	0.0061	0.0043	0.0052	0.0034	0.0017	0.0051	0.0051	0.0034	0.0051	1970	0.0549

* Compound annual return

Table A-15 **Inflation**

(continued)

From January 1971 to December 1998

YEAR	JAN	FEB	MAR	APR	MAY	JUN	JUL	AUG	SEP	OCT	NOV	DEC	YEAR	JAN–DEC*
1971	0.0008	0.0017	0.0033	0.0033	0.0050	0.0058	0.0025	0.0025	0.0008	0.0016	0.0016	0.0041	1971	0.0336
1972	0.0008	0.0049	0.0016	0.0024	0.0032	0.0024	0.0040	0.0016	0.0040	0.0032	0.0024	0.0032	1972	0.0341
1973	0.0031	0.0070	0.0093	0.0069	0.0061	0.0068	0.0023	0.0181	0.0030	0.0081	0.0073	0.0065	1973	0.0880
1974	0.0087	0.0129	0.0113	0.0056	0.0111	0.0096	0.0075	0.0128	0.0120	0.0086	0.0085	0.0071	1974	0.1220
1975	0.0045	0.0070	0.0038	0.0051	0.0044	0.0082	0.0106	0.0031	0.0049	0.0061	0.0061	0.0042	1975	0.0701
1976	0.0024	0.0024	0.0024	0.0042	0.0059	0.0053	0.0059	0.0047	0.0041	0.0041	0.0029	0.0029	1976	0.0481
1977	0.0057	0.0103	0.0062	0.0079	0.0056	0.0066	0.0044	0.0038	0.0038	0.0027	0.0049	0.0038	1977	0.0677
1978	0.0054	0.0069	0.0069	0.0090	0.0099	0.0103	0.0072	0.0051	0.0071	0.0080	0.0055	0.0055	1978	0.0903
1979	0.0089	0.0117	0.0097	0.0115	0.0123	0.0093	0.0130	0.0100	0.0104	0.0090	0.0093	0.0105	1979	0.1331
1980	0.0144	0.0137	0.0144	0.0113	0.0099	0.0110	0.0008	0.0065	0.0092	0.0087	0.0091	0.0086	1980	0.1240
1981	0.0081	0.0104	0.0072	0.0064	0.0082	0.0086	0.0114	0.0077	0.0101	0.0021	0.0029	0.0029	1981	0.0894
1982	0.0036	0.0032	-0.0011	0.0042	0.0098	0.0122	0.0055	0.0021	0.0017	0.0027	-0.0017	-0.0041	1982	0.0387
1983	0.0024	0.0003	0.0007	0.0072	0.0054	0.0034	0.0040	0.0033	0.0050	0.0027	0.0017	0.0013	1983	0.0380
1984	0.0056	0.0046	0.0023	0.0049	0.0029	0.0032	0.0032	0.0042	0.0048	0.0025	0.0000	0.0006	1984	0.0395
1985	0.0019	0.0041	0.0044	0.0041	0.0037	0.0031	0.0016	0.0022	0.0031	0.0031	0.0034	0.0025	1985	0.0377
1986	0.0031	-0.0027	-0.0046	-0.0021	0.0031	0.0049	0.0003	0.0018	0.0049	0.0009	0.0009	0.0009	1986	0.0113
1987	0.0060	0.0039	0.0045	0.0054	0.0030	0.0041	0.0021	0.0056	0.0050	0.0026	0.0014	-0.0003	1987	0.0441
1988	0.0026	0.0026	0.0043	0.0052	0.0034	0.0043	0.0042	0.0042	0.0067	0.0033	0.0008	0.0017	1988	0.0442
1989	0.0050	0.0041	0.0058	0.0065	0.0057	0.0024	0.0024	0.0016	0.0032	0.0048	0.0024	0.0016	1989	0.0465
1990	0.0103	0.0047	0.0055	0.0016	0.0023	0.0054	0.0038	0.0092	0.0084	0.0060	0.0022	0.0000	1990	0.0611
1991	0.0060	0.0015	0.0015	0.0015	0.0030	0.0029	0.0015	0.0029	0.0044	0.0015	0.0029	0.0007	1991	0.0306
1992	0.0015	0.0036	0.0051	0.0014	0.0014	0.0036	0.0021	0.0028	0.0028	0.0035	0.0014	-0.0007	1992	0.0290
1993	0.0049	0.0035	0.0035	0.0028	0.0014	0.0014	0.0000	0.0028	0.0021	0.0041	0.0007	0.0000	1993	0.0275
1994	0.0027	0.0034	0.0034	0.0014	0.0007	0.0034	0.0027	0.0040	0.0027	0.0007	0.0013	0.0000	1994	0.0267
1995	0.0040	0.0040	0.0033	0.0033	0.0020	0.0020	0.0000	0.0026	0.0020	0.0033	-0.0007	-0.0007	1995	0.0254
1996	0.0059	0.0032	0.0052	0.0039	0.0019	0.0006	0.0019	0.0019	0.0032	0.0032	0.0019	0.0000	1996	0.0332
1997	0.0032	0.0031	0.0025	0.0013	-0.0006	0.0012	0.0012	0.0019	0.0025	0.0025	-0.0006	-0.0012	1997	0.0170
1998	0.0019	0.0019	0.0019	0.0018	0.0018	0.0012	0.0012	0.0012	0.0012	0.0024	0.0000	-0.0006	1998	0.0161

* Compound annual return

Table A-16 **Equity Risk Premia**

From January 1926 to December 1970

YEAR	JAN	FEB	MAR	APR	MAY	JUN	JUL	AUG	SEP	OCT	NOV	DEC	YEAR	JAN–DEC*
1926	-0.0034	-0.0410	-0.0603	0.0218	0.0178	0.0421	0.0455	0.0223	0.0229	-0.0315	0.0315	0.0168	1926	0.0809
1927	-0.0217	0.0510	0.0057	0.0175	0.0575	-0.0093	0.0638	0.0486	0.0429	-0.0526	0.0699	0.0256	1927	0.3332
1928	-0.0065	-0.0158	0.1068	0.0322	0.0165	-0.0415	0.0108	0.0768	0.0231	0.0127	0.1248	0.0043	1928	0.3867
1929	0.0547	-0.0055	-0.0046	0.0140	-0.0404	0.1082	0.0436	0.0984	-0.0510	-0.2009	-0.1279	0.0245	1929	-0.1257
1930	0.0624	0.0229	0.0774	-0.0100	-0.0122	-0.1648	0.0366	0.0132	-0.1301	-0.0863	-0.0101	-0.0719	1930	-0.2666
1931	0.0487	0.1189	-0.0687	-0.0942	-0.1287	0.1412	-0.0727	0.0179	-0.2974	0.0885	-0.0813	-0.1411	1931	-0.4394
1932	-0.0293	0.0546	-0.1172	-0.2006	-0.2200	-0.0025	0.3811	0.3864	-0.0349	-0.1351	-0.0418	0.0564	1932	-0.0907
1933	0.0086	-0.1770	0.0349	0.4242	0.1678	0.1335	-0.0863	0.1203	-0.1119	-0.0855	0.1125	0.0251	1933	0.5353
1934	0.1064	-0.0325	-0.0002	-0.0252	-0.0737	0.0228	-0.1132	0.0610	-0.0033	-0.0287	0.0941	-0.0012	1934	-0.0160
1935	-0.0412	-0.0342	-0.0287	0.0979	0.0408	0.0698	0.0849	0.0278	0.0255	0.0775	0.0471	0.0392	1935	0.4742
1936	0.0669	0.0222	0.0266	-0.0752	0.0543	0.0330	0.0699	0.0150	0.0030	0.0772	0.0133	-0.0029	1936	0.3368
1937	0.0389	0.0189	-0.0079	-0.0812	-0.0031	-0.0507	0.1042	-0.0485	-0.1406	-0.0983	-0.0868	-0.0459	1937	-0.3523
1938	0.0151	0.0673	-0.2486	0.1446	-0.0330	0.2503	0.0745	-0.0226	0.0164	0.0775	-0.0267	0.0400	1938	0.3114
1939	-0.0673	0.0389	-0.1338	-0.0027	0.0732	-0.0613	0.1105	-0.0647	0.1671	-0.0123	-0.0398	0.0270	1939	-0.0043
1940	-0.0336	0.0133	0.0124	-0.0025	-0.2288	0.0809	0.0339	0.0350	0.0123	0.0422	-0.0316	0.0009	1940	-0.0979
1941	-0.0462	-0.0059	0.0069	-0.0612	0.0182	0.0577	0.0576	0.0009	-0.0069	-0.0657	-0.0285	-0.0407	1941	-0.1164
1942	0.0159	-0.0160	-0.0653	-0.0400	0.0794	0.0218	0.0335	0.0161	0.0287	0.0675	-0.0024	0.0546	1942	0.2002
1943	0.0734	0.0580	0.0542	0.0032	0.0550	0.0220	-0.0529	0.0168	0.0260	-0.0110	-0.0657	0.0614	1943	0.2546
1944	0.0168	0.0039	0.0192	-0.0103	0.0503	0.0539	-0.0195	0.0154	-0.0010	0.0020	0.0130	0.0372	1944	0.1936
1945	0.0156	0.0681	-0.0443	0.0899	0.0192	-0.0009	-0.0183	0.0638	0.0436	0.0319	0.0394	0.0113	1945	0.3599
1946	0.0711	-0.0643	0.0477	0.0390	0.0285	-0.0373	-0.0242	-0.0676	-0.1000	-0.0063	-0.0030	0.0454	1946	-0.0839
1947	0.0252	-0.0079	-0.0152	-0.0365	0.0011	0.0550	0.0378	-0.0206	-0.0117	0.0232	-0.0181	0.0225	1947	0.0518
1948	-0.0386	-0.0395	0.0783	0.0283	0.0870	0.0045	-0.0516	0.0149	-0.0279	0.0706	-0.0965	0.0341	1948	0.0465
1949	0.0030	-0.0304	0.0318	-0.0188	-0.0268	0.0005	0.0641	0.0210	0.0254	0.0331	0.0166	0.0476	1949	0.1750
1950	0.0187	0.0191	0.0060	0.0477	0.0498	-0.0558	0.0109	0.0433	0.0581	0.0081	0.0158	0.0501	1950	0.3016
1951	0.0624	0.0146	-0.0166	0.0496	-0.0311	-0.0239	0.0696	0.0464	0.0001	-0.0119	0.0085	0.0411	1951	0.2219
1952	0.0165	-0.0293	0.0492	-0.0413	0.0330	0.0475	0.0181	-0.0085	-0.0192	0.0006	0.0560	0.0365	1952	0.1644
1953	-0.0065	-0.0120	-0.0230	-0.0253	0.0060	-0.0153	0.0258	-0.0517	0.0018	0.0526	0.0196	0.0040	1953	-0.0276
1954	0.0525	0.0104	0.0317	0.0507	0.0412	0.0025	0.0583	-0.0280	0.0842	-0.0174	0.0902	0.0526	1954	0.5132
1955	0.0189	0.0090	-0.0040	0.0386	0.0041	0.0830	0.0611	-0.0041	0.0113	-0.0302	0.0808	-0.0003	1955	0.2952
1956	-0.0369	0.0393	0.0694	-0.0023	-0.0615	0.0389	0.0507	-0.0344	-0.0457	0.0041	-0.0071	0.0346	1956	0.0400
1957	-0.0426	-0.0287	0.0191	0.0362	0.0411	-0.0020	0.0101	-0.0529	-0.0626	-0.0330	0.0203	-0.0418	1957	-0.1350
1958	0.0416	-0.0153	0.0318	0.0329	0.0201	0.0276	0.0442	0.0171	0.0481	0.0251	0.0273	0.0512	1958	0.4119
1959	0.0032	0.0030	-0.0002	0.0382	0.0217	-0.0047	0.0337	-0.0121	-0.0472	0.0098	0.0160	0.0257	1959	0.0875
1960	-0.0730	0.0118	-0.0157	-0.0180	0.0297	0.0187	-0.0247	0.0300	-0.0605	-0.0029	0.0451	0.0463	1960	-0.0214
1961	0.0625	0.0304	0.0249	0.0033	0.0221	-0.0294	0.0323	0.0228	-0.0200	0.0279	0.0431	0.0028	1961	0.2425
1962	-0.0389	0.0189	-0.0066	-0.0628	-0.0833	-0.0821	0.0624	0.0184	-0.0485	0.0038	0.1064	0.0129	1962	-0.1116
1963	0.0479	-0.0261	0.0346	0.0474	0.0169	-0.0210	-0.0048	0.0509	-0.0124	0.0309	-0.0073	0.0232	1963	0.1909
1964	0.0252	0.0120	0.0133	0.0045	0.0136	0.0147	0.0164	-0.0146	0.0272	0.0067	-0.0024	0.0024	1964	0.1250
1965	0.0315	0.0001	-0.0168	0.0325	-0.0061	-0.0506	0.0116	0.0238	0.0302	0.0257	-0.0066	0.0073	1965	0.0820
1966	0.0024	-0.0166	-0.0243	0.0185	-0.0531	-0.0183	-0.0155	-0.0763	-0.0093	0.0446	0.0055	-0.0038	1966	-0.1415
1967	0.0752	0.0036	0.0369	0.0403	-0.0508	0.0163	0.0435	-0.0100	0.0309	-0.0314	0.0029	0.0244	1967	0.1897
1968	-0.0464	-0.0299	0.0071	0.0787	0.0116	0.0063	-0.0218	0.0121	0.0355	0.0043	0.0486	-0.0443	1968	0.0557
1969	-0.0120	-0.0470	0.0311	0.0174	-0.0022	-0.0590	-0.0637	0.0402	-0.0296	0.0397	-0.0347	-0.0240	1969	-0.1416
1970	-0.0799	0.0521	-0.0027	-0.0935	-0.0597	-0.0537	0.0696	0.0453	0.0292	-0.0143	0.0488	0.0539	1970	-0.0236

* Compound annual return

Table A-16 **Equity Risk Premia**

(continued)

From January 1971 to December 1998

YEAR	JAN	FEB	MAR	APR	MAY	JUN	JUL	AUG	SEP	OCT	NOV	DEC	YEAR	JAN–DEC*
1971	0.0379	0.0107	0.0352	0.0348	-0.0396	-0.0016	-0.0438	0.0364	-0.0092	-0.0439	-0.0011	0.0837	1971	0.0951
1972	0.0165	0.0274	0.0045	0.0028	0.0188	-0.0234	0.0005	0.0361	-0.0070	0.0067	0.0466	0.0093	1972	0.1458
1973	-0.0202	-0.0373	-0.0047	-0.0444	-0.0189	-0.0102	0.0328	-0.0385	0.0345	-0.0062	-0.1132	0.0119	1973	-0.2019
1974	-0.0147	-0.0039	-0.0271	-0.0446	-0.0345	-0.0188	-0.0824	-0.0883	-0.1240	0.1599	-0.0499	-0.0245	1974	-0.3192
1975	0.1186	0.0628	0.0194	0.0447	0.0463	0.0419	-0.0704	-0.0191	-0.0379	0.0578	0.0271	-0.0144	1975	0.2968
1976	0.1147	-0.0091	0.0285	-0.0140	-0.0110	0.0382	-0.0114	-0.0028	0.0202	-0.0245	-0.0049	0.0497	1976	0.1785
1977	-0.0523	-0.0186	-0.0156	-0.0024	-0.0186	0.0433	-0.0192	-0.0176	-0.0043	-0.0462	0.0318	-0.0001	1977	-0.1170
1978	-0.0642	-0.0206	0.0222	0.0812	0.0085	-0.0205	0.0501	0.0283	-0.0109	-0.0952	0.0189	0.0093	1978	-0.0058
1979	0.0342	-0.0355	0.0490	-0.0043	-0.0248	0.0326	0.0033	0.0530	-0.0057	-0.0737	0.0411	0.0096	1979	0.0731
1980	0.0526	-0.0057	-0.1094	0.0300	0.0477	0.0233	0.0620	0.0067	0.0204	0.0091	0.0990	-0.0440	1980	0.1904
1981	-0.0536	0.0100	0.0256	-0.0317	-0.0053	-0.0212	-0.0116	-0.0673	-0.0619	0.0403	0.0331	-0.0349	1981	-0.1710
1982	-0.0241	-0.0599	-0.0156	0.0298	-0.0390	-0.0267	-0.0317	0.1182	0.0059	0.1061	0.0372	0.0105	1982	0.0983
1983	0.0277	0.0197	0.0300	0.0682	-0.0120	0.0313	-0.0384	0.0093	0.0059	-0.0209	0.0162	-0.0133	1983	0.1261
1984	-0.0140	-0.0397	0.0097	-0.0012	-0.0608	0.0145	-0.0223	0.1033	-0.0083	-0.0073	-0.0173	0.0188	1984	-0.0326
1985	0.0699	0.0079	-0.0043	-0.0103	0.0545	0.0103	-0.0088	-0.0115	-0.0379	0.0380	0.0651	0.0399	1985	0.2268
1986	-0.0012	0.0704	0.0492	-0.0175	0.0497	0.0113	-0.0618	0.0699	-0.0863	0.0507	0.0216	-0.0311	1986	0.1159
1987	0.1296	0.0368	0.0224	-0.0132	0.0065	0.0449	0.0450	0.0336	-0.0264	-0.2199	-0.0851	0.0696	1987	-0.0022
1988	0.0396	0.0423	-0.0345	0.0062	0.0027	0.0413	-0.0090	-0.0388	0.0360	0.0211	-0.0198	0.0117	1988	0.0984
1989	0.0664	-0.0308	0.0168	0.0446	0.0321	-0.0124	0.0823	0.0118	-0.0104	-0.0299	0.0138	0.0174	1989	0.2133
1990	-0.0724	0.0072	0.0197	-0.0314	0.0901	-0.0132	-0.0099	-0.0962	-0.0549	-0.0104	0.0584	0.0213	1990	-0.1019
1991	0.0388	0.0665	0.0193	-0.0025	0.0379	-0.0497	0.0417	0.0188	-0.0209	0.0091	-0.0441	0.1101	1991	0.2363
1992	-0.0219	0.0099	-0.0229	0.0258	0.0026	-0.0176	0.0371	-0.0227	0.0089	0.0013	0.0313	0.0102	1992	0.0402
1993	0.0050	0.0113	0.0189	-0.0268	0.0248	0.0008	-0.0071	0.0355	-0.0099	0.0181	-0.0119	0.0100	1993	0.0689
1994	0.0309	-0.0291	-0.0461	0.0103	0.0131	-0.0277	0.0303	0.0369	-0.0277	0.0190	-0.0402	0.0101	1994	-0.0250
1995	0.0218	0.0347	0.0249	0.0245	0.0340	0.0187	0.0286	-0.0020	0.0374	-0.0082	0.0396	0.0136	1995	0.3015
1996	0.0300	0.0057	0.0056	0.0101	0.0215	0.0001	-0.0488	0.0170	0.0516	0.0231	0.0715	-0.0241	1996	0.1698
1997	0.0573	0.0042	-0.0457	0.0552	0.0562	0.0408	0.0748	-0.0595	0.0501	-0.0375	0.0422	0.0124	1997	0.2670
1998	0.0068	0.0679	0.0471	0.0057	-0.0211	0.0364	-0.0146	-0.1482	0.0592	0.0778	0.0574	0.0537	1998	0.2263

* Compound annual return

Table A-17 **Small Stock Premia**

From January 1926 to December 1970

YEAR	JAN	FEB	MAR	APR	MAY	JUN	JUL	AUG	SEP	OCT	NOV	DEC	YEAR	JAN–DEC*
1926	0.0699	-0.0265	-0.0529	-0.0072	-0.0241	-0.0076	-0.0350	0.0008	-0.0246	0.0058	-0.0135	0.0133	1926	-0.1017
1927	0.0498	0.0009	-0.0629	0.0365	0.0120	-0.0237	-0.0145	-0.0659	-0.0386	-0.0166	0.0081	0.0037	1927	-0.1119
1928	0.0523	-0.0112	-0.0514	0.0546	0.0236	-0.0476	-0.0081	-0.0334	0.0615	0.0106	-0.0128	-0.0560	1928	-0.0273
1929	-0.0518	-0.0007	-0.0189	0.0128	-0.1011	-0.0545	-0.0341	-0.1081	-0.0468	-0.0991	-0.0290	-0.0761	1929	-0.4689
1930	0.0615	0.0374	0.0180	-0.0623	-0.0450	-0.0648	-0.0082	-0.0304	-0.0203	-0.0264	0.0061	-0.0495	1930	-0.1764
1931	0.1525	0.1226	-0.0035	-0.1356	-0.0114	0.0349	0.0177	-0.0928	-0.0389	-0.0116	-0.0229	-0.0924	1931	-0.1133
1932	0.1326	-0.0265	-0.0173	-0.0278	0.1284	0.0055	-0.0212	0.2507	-0.1009	-0.0493	-0.0846	-0.1000	1932	0.0305
1933	-0.0168	0.0601	0.0738	0.0548	0.3986	0.1128	0.0341	-0.0251	-0.0537	-0.0417	-0.0425	-0.0193	1933	0.5772
1934	0.2549	0.0505	-0.0012	0.0503	-0.0582	-0.0248	-0.1271	0.0882	-0.0134	0.0394	0.0005	0.0183	1934	0.2604
1935	0.0086	-0.0260	-0.0929	-0.0172	-0.0417	-0.0369	0.0004	0.0258	0.0098	0.0201	0.0896	0.0197	1935	-0.0506
1936	0.2192	0.0370	-0.0197	-0.1129	-0.0258	-0.0546	0.0160	0.0058	0.0509	-0.0129	0.1250	0.0190	1936	0.2306
1937	0.0844	0.0458	0.0199	-0.0947	-0.0385	-0.0715	0.0172	-0.0266	-0.1321	-0.0124	-0.0643	-0.1294	1937	-0.3537
1938	0.0377	-0.0310	-0.1482	0.1161	-0.0537	0.0796	0.0703	-0.0793	-0.0318	0.1261	-0.0427	0.0083	1938	0.0128
1939	-0.0187	-0.0273	-0.1302	0.0169	0.0331	-0.0458	0.1288	-0.1007	0.2975	-0.0277	-0.0683	0.0148	1939	0.0076
1940	0.0358	0.0679	0.0502	0.0681	-0.1796	0.0223	-0.0106	-0.0092	0.0088	0.0117	0.0579	-0.0456	1940	0.0513
1941	0.0512	-0.0230	0.0247	-0.0061	-0.0136	0.0166	0.1500	-0.0070	-0.0404	-0.0016	-0.0217	-0.0831	1941	0.0293
1942	0.1706	0.0087	-0.0061	0.0049	-0.0767	0.0112	0.0386	0.0159	0.0605	0.0383	-0.0491	-0.0129	1942	0.2008
1943	0.1299	0.1274	0.0853	0.0895	0.0572	-0.0299	-0.0588	-0.0171	0.0161	0.0233	-0.0490	0.0588	1943	0.4962
1944	0.0461	0.0252	0.0544	-0.0437	0.0223	0.0799	-0.0108	0.0159	-0.0012	-0.0131	0.0361	0.0477	1944	0.2837
1945	0.0319	0.0305	-0.0440	0.0234	0.0299	0.0862	-0.0383	-0.0080	0.0231	0.0367	0.0746	0.0054	1945	0.2725
1946	0.0791	0.0004	-0.0198	0.0292	0.0295	-0.0096	-0.0298	-0.0187	-0.0673	-0.0058	-0.0114	-0.0080	1946	-0.0387
1947	0.0162	0.0036	-0.0190	-0.0694	-0.0547	-0.0002	0.0393	0.0170	0.0229	0.0043	-0.0130	0.0123	1947	-0.0453
1948	0.0234	-0.0411	0.0179	0.0074	0.0166	-0.0006	-0.0074	-0.0149	-0.0257	-0.0059	-0.0172	-0.0250	1948	-0.0722
1949	0.0142	-0.0191	0.0291	-0.0160	-0.0314	-0.0110	0.0020	0.0036	0.0221	0.0128	-0.0156	0.0195	1949	0.0080
1950	0.0289	0.0021	-0.0106	-0.0071	-0.0242	-0.0242	0.0467	0.0083	-0.0067	-0.0150	0.0151	0.0419	1950	0.0534
1951	0.0182	-0.0095	-0.0326	-0.0136	-0.0033	-0.0308	-0.0315	0.0121	0.0202	-0.0120	-0.0177	-0.0365	1951	-0.1307
1952	0.0010	-0.0018	-0.0312	-0.0122	-0.0301	-0.0208	-0.0082	0.0066	0.0015	-0.0123	-0.0082	-0.0214	1952	-0.1296
1953	0.0460	0.0379	0.0149	-0.0051	0.0064	-0.0357	-0.0118	-0.0134	-0.0296	-0.0235	-0.0076	-0.0316	1953	-0.0555
1954	0.0209	-0.0017	-0.0138	-0.0357	0.0033	0.0055	0.0207	0.0298	-0.0407	0.0239	-0.0119	0.0549	1954	0.0521
1955	0.0004	0.0377	0.0115	-0.0237	0.0022	-0.0506	-0.0525	-0.0003	-0.0020	0.0118	-0.0331	0.0147	1955	-0.0845
1956	0.0311	-0.0130	-0.0261	0.0051	0.0208	-0.0340	-0.0235	0.0200	0.0188	0.0038	0.0104	-0.0320	1956	-0.0213
1957	0.0663	0.0066	-0.0047	-0.0134	-0.0347	0.0069	-0.0189	0.0126	0.0159	-0.0547	-0.0115	-0.0089	1957	-0.0425
1958	0.0632	-0.0029	0.0138	0.0037	0.0172	0.0044	0.0041	0.0248	0.0017	0.0134	0.0206	-0.0211	1958	0.1501
1959	0.0519	0.0245	0.0007	-0.0274	-0.0221	-0.0020	-0.0034	0.0015	0.0013	0.0097	0.0036	0.0030	1959	0.0397
1960	0.0423	-0.0096	-0.0194	-0.0026	-0.0117	0.0126	0.0045	0.0201	-0.0158	-0.0394	-0.0026	-0.0140	1960	-0.0374
1961	0.0253	0.0262	0.0340	0.0076	0.0184	-0.0276	-0.0300	-0.0110	-0.0158	-0.0035	0.0159	0.0033	1961	0.0410
1962	0.0522	-0.0021	0.0103	-0.0182	-0.0215	0.0020	0.0104	0.0080	-0.0203	-0.0434	0.0146	-0.0238	1962	-0.0348
1963	0.0381	0.0280	-0.0214	-0.0180	0.0238	0.0071	0.0055	-0.0017	-0.0067	-0.0099	-0.0061	-0.0302	1963	0.0062
1964	-0.0008	0.0215	0.0053	0.0019	-0.0005	-0.0015	0.0200	0.0090	0.0099	0.0108	0.0006	-0.0167	1964	0.0604
1965	0.0178	0.0358	0.0376	0.0147	-0.0048	-0.0449	0.0297	0.0314	0.0013	0.0275	0.0404	0.0511	1965	0.2606
1966	0.0690	0.0448	0.0013	0.0121	-0.0493	0.0136	0.0109	-0.0382	-0.0111	-0.0573	0.0393	0.0063	1966	0.0339
1967	0.0963	0.0375	0.0198	-0.0159	0.0411	0.0812	0.0461	0.0091	0.0216	-0.0036	0.0051	0.0669	1967	0.4807
1968	0.0605	-0.0460	-0.0216	0.0579	0.0825	-0.0074	-0.0177	0.0200	0.0192	-0.0056	0.0221	0.0484	1968	0.2243
1969	-0.0098	-0.0589	0.0036	0.0162	0.0147	-0.0658	-0.0512	0.0266	-0.0026	0.0145	-0.0268	-0.0520	1969	-0.1809
1970	0.0146	-0.0188	-0.0314	-0.0920	-0.0512	-0.0469	-0.0185	0.0419	0.0714	-0.0615	-0.0378	0.0135	1970	-0.2061

* Compound annual return

Table A-17 **Small Stock Premia**

(continued)

From January 1971 to December 1998

YEAR	JAN	FEB	MAR	APR	MAY	JUN	JUL	AUG	SEP	OCT	NOV	DEC	YEAR	JAN-DEC*
1971	0.1126	0.0174	0.0175	-0.0125	-0.0247	-0.0340	-0.0171	0.0164	-0.0172	-0.0154	-0.0399	0.0246	1971	0.0191
1972	0.0918	-0.0003	-0.0214	0.0072	-0.0401	-0.0102	-0.0448	-0.0197	-0.0314	-0.0279	0.0084	-0.0340	1972	-0.1222
1973	-0.0277	-0.0482	-0.0206	-0.0236	-0.0681	-0.0240	0.0769	-0.0132	0.0622	0.0082	-0.0987	-0.0193	1973	-0.1903
1974	0.1423	-0.0104	0.0146	-0.0094	-0.0535	-0.0019	0.0585	0.0161	0.0585	-0.0510	0.0011	-0.0622	1974	0.0887
1975	0.1347	-0.0364	0.0373	0.0036	0.0147	0.0275	0.0433	-0.0436	0.0151	-0.0646	0.0006	-0.0101	1975	0.1138
1976	0.1326	0.1456	-0.0330	-0.0262	-0.0290	0.0031	0.0114	-0.0304	-0.0139	-0.0003	0.0413	0.0608	1976	0.2708
1977	0.0987	0.0114	0.0252	0.0214	0.0124	0.0284	0.0184	0.0026	0.0092	0.0089	0.0691	0.0033	1977	0.3508
1978	0.0433	0.0517	0.0736	-0.0076	0.0675	-0.0037	0.0118	0.0579	0.0017	-0.1687	0.0460	-0.0004	1978	0.1586
1979	0.0864	0.0002	0.0515	0.0349	0.0206	0.0060	0.0061	0.0137	-0.0368	-0.0534	0.0327	0.0389	1979	0.2113
1980	0.0213	-0.0313	-0.0878	0.0253	0.0178	0.0152	0.0606	0.0467	0.0134	0.0144	-0.0297	-0.0024	1980	0.0563
1981	0.0675	-0.0112	0.0542	0.0889	0.0358	0.0157	-0.0323	-0.0138	-0.0243	0.0203	-0.0158	0.0046	1981	0.1976
1982	-0.0034	0.0228	-0.0026	-0.0030	0.0041	0.0015	0.0204	-0.0505	0.0215	0.0161	0.0327	-0.0040	1982	0.0543
1983	0.0271	0.0441	0.0154	0.0008	0.0926	-0.0032	0.0232	-0.0361	-0.0003	-0.0440	0.0276	-0.0085	1983	0.1400
1984	0.0057	-0.0328	0.0003	-0.0153	0.0014	0.0077	-0.0281	-0.0114	0.0025	-0.0242	-0.0237	-0.0100	1984	-0.1217
1985	0.0270	0.0133	-0.0232	-0.0142	-0.0319	-0.0052	0.0287	-0.0011	-0.0230	-0.0178	-0.0090	0.0003	1985	-0.0567
1986	0.0068	-0.0039	-0.0073	0.0190	-0.0179	-0.0138	-0.0150	-0.0493	0.0287	-0.0199	-0.0280	0.0002	1986	-0.0981
1987	-0.0353	0.0380	-0.0038	-0.0227	-0.0141	-0.0222	-0.0128	-0.0094	0.0142	-0.0977	0.0460	-0.0203	1987	-0.1381
1988	0.0124	0.0277	0.0732	0.0100	-0.0255	0.0141	0.0015	0.0088	-0.0189	-0.0385	-0.0299	0.0209	1988	0.0519
1989	-0.0297	0.0340	0.0119	-0.0225	-0.0038	-0.0148	-0.0451	-0.0070	0.0039	-0.0380	-0.0254	-0.0361	1989	-0.1621
1990	-0.0100	0.0057	0.0102	-0.0019	-0.0377	0.0216	-0.0351	-0.0432	-0.0354	-0.0537	-0.0182	-0.0078	1990	-0.1899
1991	0.0382	0.0370	0.0432	0.0006	-0.0090	-0.0029	-0.0058	0.0025	0.0199	0.0181	0.0133	-0.0486	1991	0.1079
1992	0.1339	0.0320	-0.0054	-0.0674	-0.0068	-0.0380	-0.0032	-0.0027	0.0016	0.0222	0.0530	0.0306	1992	0.1456
1993	0.0467	-0.0311	0.0072	-0.0063	0.0070	-0.0071	0.0214	-0.0040	0.0393	0.0263	-0.0082	0.0070	1993	0.0999
1994	0.0274	0.0254	-0.0012	-0.0069	-0.0172	-0.0015	-0.0142	-0.0067	0.0355	-0.0111	0.0043	-0.0142	1994	0.0178
1995	0.0022	-0.0131	-0.0147	0.0059	-0.0093	0.0325	0.0302	0.0330	-0.0215	-0.0454	-0.0238	0.0053	1995	-0.0216
1996	-0.0305	0.0270	0.0131	0.0691	0.0479	-0.0620	-0.0521	0.0259	-0.0257	-0.0437	-0.0438	0.0408	1996	-0.0443
1997	-0.0189	-0.0285	-0.0077	-0.0824	0.0384	0.0050	-0.0175	0.1128	0.0281	-0.0054	-0.0591	-0.0337	1997	-0.0794
1998	-0.0168	-0.0067	-0.0030	0.0067	-0.0331	-0.0588	-0.0571	-0.0660	-0.0255	-0.0423	0.0143	-0.0307	1998	-0.2791

* Compound annual return

Table A-18 **Bond Default Premia**

From January 1926 to December 1970

YEAR	JAN	FEB	MAR	APR	MAY	JUN	JUL	AUG	SEP	OCT	NOV	DEC	YEAR	JAN-DEC*
1926	-0.0065	-0.0018	0.0043	0.0021	0.0030	-0.0034	0.0053	0.0044	0.0019	-0.0005	-0.0101	-0.0022	1926	-0.0037
1927	-0.0019	-0.0019	-0.0166	0.0060	-0.0118	0.0113	-0.0046	0.0007	0.0131	-0.0043	-0.0029	-0.0003	1927	-0.0136
1928	0.0063	0.0007	-0.0004	0.0018	-0.0001	-0.0065	0.0212	0.0006	0.0071	-0.0073	-0.0039	0.0080	1928	0.0273
1929	0.0134	0.0190	0.0058	-0.0249	0.0210	-0.0154	0.0020	0.0054	0.0006	-0.0298	-0.0249	0.0284	1929	-0.0014
1930	0.0117	-0.0056	0.0054	0.0100	-0.0081	0.0059	0.0021	0.0123	0.0034	0.0018	-0.0054	-0.0020	1930	0.0317
1931	0.0328	-0.0017	-0.0010	-0.0019	-0.0011	0.0048	0.0095	0.0000	0.0274	-0.0034	-0.0216	-0.0068	1931	0.0365
1932	-0.0086	-0.0625	0.0375	-0.0735	0.0301	-0.0074	-0.0418	0.0433	0.0243	0.0091	0.0041	0.0008	1932	-0.0515
1933	0.0393	-0.0272	-0.0049	-0.0063	0.0277	0.0140	0.0178	0.0049	-0.0037	0.0132	-0.0100	0.0374	1933	0.1046
1934	0.0000	0.0064	-0.0010	-0.0021	-0.0041	0.0090	0.0007	0.0167	0.0086	-0.0079	0.0091	-0.0011	1934	0.0347
1935	0.0029	0.0049	0.0002	0.0033	0.0099	0.0020	0.0065	0.0093	-0.0009	-0.0019	0.0059	0.0013	1935	0.0441
1936	0.0027	-0.0027	-0.0024	-0.0009	0.0000	0.0061	-0.0049	-0.0043	0.0098	0.0019	-0.0094	-0.0028	1936	-0.0072
1937	0.0037	-0.0131	0.0310	0.0029	-0.0013	0.0071	-0.0098	0.0088	-0.0020	0.0025	-0.0028	-0.0015	1937	0.0251
1938	-0.0019	-0.0042	-0.0051	-0.0070	-0.0034	0.0090	0.0023	-0.0019	0.0086	-0.0007	0.0059	0.0041	1938	0.0057
1939	-0.0037	-0.0016	-0.0102	-0.0053	-0.0120	0.0062	-0.0119	-0.0195	0.0736	-0.0166	-0.0081	-0.0066	1939	-0.0186
1940	0.0066	-0.0006	-0.0126	-0.0057	0.0287	-0.0134	-0.0031	-0.0021	-0.0018	0.0018	-0.0139	-0.0089	1940	-0.0254
1941	0.0211	-0.0014	-0.0117	-0.0051	0.0022	-0.0003	0.0041	0.0016	0.0060	-0.0105	-0.0065	0.0187	1941	0.0178
1942	-0.0063	-0.0019	-0.0028	0.0035	-0.0055	0.0031	0.0002	-0.0003	0.0017	-0.0018	0.0041	0.0000	1942	-0.0060
1943	0.0016	0.0012	0.0011	0.0001	-0.0002	0.0030	0.0020	-0.0002	-0.0006	-0.0014	-0.0023	0.0031	1943	0.0073
1944	-0.0001	0.0002	0.0027	0.0021	-0.0023	0.0012	-0.0002	0.0007	0.0005	0.0007	0.0024	0.0106	1944	0.0187
1945	-0.0050	-0.0030	-0.0003	-0.0140	-0.0067	-0.0135	0.0076	-0.0022	-0.0022	-0.0072	-0.0092	-0.0060	1945	-0.0601
1946	0.0103	0.0002	0.0024	0.0094	0.0031	-0.0051	0.0028	0.0024	-0.0017	-0.0053	0.0029	-0.0031	1946	0.0183
1947	0.0011	-0.0016	0.0047	0.0057	-0.0013	-0.0006	-0.0042	-0.0151	-0.0088	-0.0062	0.0077	0.0220	1947	0.0029
1948	0.0004	-0.0007	0.0081	-0.0007	-0.0131	0.0001	-0.0031	0.0054	0.0010	0.0017	0.0009	0.0074	1948	0.0071
1949	-0.0043	-0.0011	-0.0067	0.0012	0.0019	-0.0082	0.0065	-0.0073	0.0032	0.0048	0.0000	-0.0196	1949	-0.0295
1950	0.0099	-0.0014	0.0014	-0.0038	-0.0041	0.0048	0.0013	0.0024	0.0034	0.0040	0.0019	0.0007	1950	0.0205
1951	-0.0039	0.0030	-0.0081	0.0054	0.0054	-0.0032	0.0066	0.0015	0.0023	-0.0155	0.0076	0.0120	1951	0.0129
1952	0.0170	-0.0099	-0.0034	-0.0172	0.0065	0.0013	0.0036	0.0134	0.0113	-0.0107	0.0124	-0.0005	1952	0.0233
1953	-0.0092	0.0047	0.0056	-0.0144	0.0119	-0.0111	0.0137	-0.0078	-0.0045	0.0151	-0.0024	-0.0033	1953	-0.0022
1954	0.0034	-0.0041	-0.0019	-0.0136	0.0045	-0.0098	-0.0093	0.0054	0.0050	0.0034	0.0050	-0.0047	1954	-0.0168
1955	0.0148	0.0015	0.0005	-0.0002	-0.0090	0.0106	0.0062	-0.0042	0.0003	-0.0065	0.0015	0.0026	1955	0.0180
1956	0.0021	0.0028	0.0003	-0.0002	-0.0170	-0.0045	0.0118	-0.0022	-0.0037	-0.0051	-0.0069	0.0098	1956	-0.0130
1957	-0.0144	0.0068	0.0074	0.0159	-0.0052	-0.0144	-0.0069	-0.0011	0.0019	0.0074	-0.0211	0.0367	1957	0.0117
1958	0.0185	-0.0107	-0.0147	-0.0023	0.0030	0.0124	0.0129	0.0121	0.0021	-0.0031	-0.0015	0.0125	1958	0.0413
1959	0.0053	0.0009	-0.0099	-0.0056	-0.0109	0.0033	0.0029	-0.0027	-0.0032	0.0014	0.0257	0.0064	1959	0.0132
1960	-0.0005	-0.0074	-0.0089	0.0150	-0.0170	-0.0031	-0.0107	0.0186	-0.0137	0.0036	-0.0004	-0.0170	1960	-0.0414
1961	0.0258	0.0010	0.0009	-0.0228	0.0095	-0.0005	0.0005	0.0020	0.0015	0.0055	0.0048	0.0100	1961	0.0381
1962	0.0094	-0.0050	-0.0100	0.0059	-0.0046	0.0050	0.0095	-0.0043	0.0028	-0.0016	0.0041	-0.0012	1962	0.0099
1963	0.0060	0.0015	0.0017	-0.0039	0.0025	0.0024	-0.0003	0.0014	-0.0027	0.0075	-0.0036	-0.0028	1963	0.0097
1964	0.0101	0.0065	-0.0099	-0.0007	0.0007	-0.0021	0.0044	0.0017	-0.0028	0.0007	-0.0021	0.0058	1964	0.0122
1965	0.0041	-0.0005	-0.0041	-0.0015	-0.0026	-0.0044	-0.0003	0.0007	0.0019	0.0019	0.0005	-0.0072	1965	-0.0116
1966	0.0127	0.0141	-0.0345	0.0076	0.0034	0.0046	-0.0061	-0.0054	-0.0246	0.0032	0.0130	-0.0204	1966	-0.0333
1967	0.0291	0.0020	-0.0079	0.0227	-0.0216	0.0092	-0.0027	0.0078	0.0099	0.0124	-0.0077	-0.0064	1967	0.0466
1968	0.0032	0.0070	0.0015	-0.0175	-0.0011	-0.0106	0.0050	0.0209	0.0050	-0.0028	0.0044	0.0135	1968	0.0284
1969	0.0352	-0.0201	-0.0210	-0.0088	0.0277	-0.0176	-0.0074	0.0049	0.0303	-0.0230	-0.0233	-0.0066	1969	-0.0318
1970	0.0163	-0.0176	0.0023	0.0170	0.0320	-0.0463	0.0229	0.0119	-0.0087	0.0013	-0.0192	0.0460	1970	0.0559

* Compound annual return

Table A-18 **Bond Default Premia**

(continued)

From January 1971 to December 1998

YEAR	JAN	FEB	MAR	APR	MAY	JUN	JUL	AUG	SEP	OCT	NOV	DEC	YEAR	JAN–DEC*
1971	0.0025	-0.0206	-0.0255	0.0048	-0.0155	0.0270	-0.0054	0.0079	-0.0299	0.0113	0.0076	0.0178	1971	-0.0196
1972	0.0031	0.0019	0.0107	0.0008	-0.0105	-0.0003	-0.0182	0.0043	0.0115	-0.0130	0.0022	0.0231	1972	0.0149
1973	0.0276	0.0009	-0.0037	0.0015	0.0066	-0.0035	-0.0045	-0.0034	0.0037	-0.0275	0.0265	-0.0007	1973	0.0227
1974	0.0030	0.0033	-0.0016	-0.0091	-0.0017	-0.0328	-0.0183	-0.0037	-0.0072	0.0377	-0.0173	-0.0242	1974	-0.0711
1975	0.0363	0.0005	0.0021	0.0132	-0.0104	0.0012	0.0057	-0.0108	-0.0028	0.0075	0.0021	0.0050	1975	0.0499
1976	0.0097	-0.0001	0.0001	-0.0033	0.0056	-0.0056	0.0071	0.0019	0.0022	-0.0014	-0.0019	0.0019	1976	0.0162
1977	0.0088	0.0029	0.0003	0.0029	-0.0019	0.0011	0.0066	-0.0061	0.0007	0.0056	-0.0032	0.0064	1977	0.0241
1978	-0.0009	0.0047	0.0063	-0.0018	-0.0050	0.0086	-0.0041	0.0038	0.0058	-0.0005	-0.0054	-0.0003	1978	0.0112
1979	-0.0007	0.0007	-0.0023	0.0061	-0.0032	-0.0041	0.0055	0.0042	-0.0057	-0.0054	-0.0087	-0.0164	1979	-0.0298
1980	0.0104	-0.0208	0.0261	-0.0128	0.0136	-0.0017	0.0049	-0.0014	0.0025	0.0107	-0.0082	-0.0100	1980	0.0124
1981	-0.0015	0.0174	-0.0071	-0.0265	-0.0025	0.0206	-0.0020	0.0043	-0.0055	-0.0284	-0.0125	0.0143	1981	-0.0304
1982	-0.0174	0.0128	0.0073	-0.0034	0.0210	-0.0251	0.0037	0.0052	0.0004	0.0117	0.0203	-0.0198	1982	0.0157
1983	0.0222	-0.0061	0.0167	0.0192	0.0064	-0.0085	0.0033	0.0031	-0.0107	0.0108	-0.0041	0.0026	1983	0.0557
1984	0.0026	0.0006	-0.0080	0.0033	0.0035	0.0049	-0.0100	0.0040	-0.0028	0.0011	0.0093	0.0037	1984	0.0120
1985	-0.0038	0.0126	-0.0124	0.0052	-0.0069	-0.0058	0.0060	0.0001	0.0092	-0.0008	-0.0030	-0.0068	1985	-0.0067
1986	0.0070	-0.0353	-0.0477	0.0097	0.0359	-0.0373	0.0141	-0.0214	0.0406	-0.0097	-0.0033	0.0135	1986	-0.0376
1987	0.0054	-0.0141	0.0139	-0.0030	0.0054	0.0057	0.0060	0.0091	-0.0055	-0.0109	0.0088	0.0046	1987	0.0251
1988	-0.0140	0.0085	0.0122	0.0011	0.0045	0.0010	0.0060	-0.0004	-0.0018	-0.0033	0.0028	-0.0070	1988	0.0094
1989	-0.0001	0.0051	-0.0058	0.0053	-0.0021	-0.0147	-0.0058	0.0098	0.0021	-0.0100	-0.0008	0.0012	1989	-0.0159
1990	0.0157	0.0013	0.0033	0.0011	-0.0029	-0.0014	-0.0005	0.0132	-0.0026	-0.0081	-0.0112	-0.0019	1990	0.0057
1991	0.0019	0.0090	0.0070	-0.0002	0.0039	0.0045	0.0009	-0.0063	-0.0031	-0.0011	0.0024	-0.0137	1991	0.0049
1992	0.0156	0.0045	0.0021	0.0000	0.0011	-0.0043	-0.0086	0.0023	-0.0085	0.0043	0.0059	-0.0018	1992	0.0124
1993	-0.0030	-0.0095	0.0004	-0.0020	-0.0026	-0.0149	-0.0090	-0.0141	0.0038	-0.0045	0.0073	0.0047	1993	-0.0428
1994	-0.0054	0.0171	0.0012	0.0054	0.0021	0.0020	-0.0052	0.0055	0.0068	-0.0026	-0.0048	-0.0004	1994	0.0218
1995	-0.0016	0.0002	0.0004	0.0006	-0.0148	-0.0059	0.0068	-0.0022	-0.0021	-0.0106	-0.0007	-0.0043	1995	-0.0339
1996	0.0025	0.0115	0.0082	0.0005	0.0060	-0.0030	-0.0008	0.0070	-0.0030	-0.0041	-0.0085	0.0072	1996	0.0235
1997	0.0052	0.0023	0.0032	-0.0069	0.0031	-0.0008	-0.0092	0.0080	-0.0087	-0.0145	-0.0046	-0.0021	1997	-0.0251
1998	-0.0062	0.0065	0.0013	0.0027	-0.0015	-0.0111	-0.0016	-0.0359	0.0018	0.0029	0.0172	0.0043	1998	-0.0204

* Compound annual return

Table A-19 **Bond Horizon Premia**

From January 1926 to December 1970

YEAR	JAN	FEB	MAR	APR	MAY	JUN	JUL	AUG	SEP	OCT	NOV	DEC	YEAR	JAN–DEC*
1926	0.0103	0.0036	0.0011	0.0041	0.0013	0.0004	-0.0018	-0.0025	0.0015	0.0070	0.0129	0.0050	1926	0.0436
1927	0.0050	0.0062	0.0223	-0.0030	0.0078	-0.0094	0.0020	0.0048	-0.0003	0.0073	0.0076	0.0049	1927	0.0563
1928	-0.0061	0.0028	0.0016	-0.0026	-0.0109	0.0010	-0.0249	0.0044	-0.0067	0.0116	-0.0035	-0.0002	1928	-0.0334
1929	-0.0124	-0.0192	-0.0177	0.0239	-0.0205	0.0058	-0.0034	-0.0074	-0.0008	0.0335	0.0198	-0.0125	1929	-0.0127
1930	-0.0071	0.0099	0.0048	-0.0037	0.0113	0.0024	0.0015	0.0004	0.0052	0.0027	0.0029	-0.0084	1930	0.0220
1931	-0.0136	0.0081	0.0091	0.0078	0.0136	-0.0004	-0.0048	0.0009	-0.0283	-0.0340	0.0010	-0.0232	1931	-0.0631
1932	0.0011	0.0389	-0.0035	0.0592	-0.0194	0.0063	0.0479	-0.0001	0.0054	-0.0019	0.0030	0.0130	1932	0.1573
1933	0.0147	-0.0256	0.0093	-0.0042	0.0298	0.0047	-0.0019	0.0042	0.0022	-0.0092	-0.0151	-0.0115	1933	-0.0037
1934	0.0252	0.0079	0.0195	0.0125	0.0130	0.0066	0.0039	-0.0119	-0.0146	0.0181	0.0036	0.0111	1934	0.0985
1935	0.0180	0.0090	0.0040	0.0077	-0.0058	0.0091	0.0044	-0.0135	0.0007	0.0060	0.0007	0.0069	1935	0.0481
1936	0.0054	0.0080	0.0105	0.0034	0.0039	0.0018	0.0059	0.0109	-0.0032	0.0004	0.0204	0.0038	1936	0.0732
1937	-0.0014	0.0085	-0.0413	0.0035	0.0046	-0.0021	0.0135	-0.0107	0.0041	0.0041	0.0094	0.0082	1937	-0.0008
1938	0.0057	0.0051	-0.0036	0.0208	0.0044	0.0004	0.0044	0.0000	0.0021	0.0086	-0.0016	0.0080	1938	0.0555
1939	0.0059	0.0079	0.0126	0.0118	0.0170	-0.0028	0.0113	-0.0200	-0.0546	0.0410	0.0162	0.0144	1939	0.0592
1940	-0.0017	0.0027	0.0177	-0.0035	-0.0298	0.0258	0.0051	0.0029	0.0110	0.0031	0.0204	0.0067	1940	0.0608
1941	-0.0200	0.0021	0.0095	0.0130	0.0027	0.0065	0.0019	0.0017	-0.0012	0.0140	-0.0030	-0.0178	1941	0.0087
1942	0.0068	0.0010	0.0091	-0.0030	0.0073	0.0000	0.0015	0.0035	0.0000	0.0021	-0.0038	0.0046	1942	0.0294
1943	0.0030	-0.0008	0.0006	0.0045	0.0048	0.0015	-0.0004	0.0018	0.0008	0.0002	-0.0003	0.0015	1943	0.0173
1944	0.0018	0.0029	0.0018	0.0011	0.0025	0.0005	0.0033	0.0024	0.0012	0.0009	0.0021	0.0040	1944	0.0248
1945	0.0124	0.0074	0.0018	0.0157	0.0053	0.0166	-0.0089	0.0023	0.0051	0.0101	0.0123	0.0191	1945	0.1037
1946	0.0022	0.0029	0.0007	-0.0138	-0.0015	0.0067	-0.0043	-0.0114	-0.0012	0.0071	-0.0057	0.0142	1946	-0.0045
1947	-0.0009	0.0018	0.0017	-0.0040	0.0031	0.0007	0.0059	0.0079	-0.0050	-0.0044	-0.0180	-0.0200	1947	-0.0311
1948	0.0013	0.0039	0.0025	0.0036	0.0133	-0.0093	-0.0029	-0.0007	0.0010	0.0003	0.0072	0.0052	1948	0.0257
1949	0.0072	0.0040	0.0065	0.0002	0.0009	0.0157	0.0025	0.0102	-0.0020	0.0010	0.0013	0.0043	1949	0.0529
1950	-0.0070	0.0013	-0.0001	0.0021	0.0023	-0.0035	0.0046	0.0004	-0.0083	-0.0059	0.0024	0.0005	1950	-0.0112
1951	0.0045	-0.0084	-0.0168	-0.0075	-0.0081	-0.0073	0.0125	0.0085	-0.0092	-0.0005	-0.0147	-0.0073	1951	-0.0534
1952	0.0013	0.0002	0.0100	0.0159	-0.0046	-0.0012	-0.0035	-0.0084	-0.0146	0.0134	-0.0026	-0.0102	1952	-0.0049
1953	-0.0004	-0.0101	-0.0106	-0.0121	-0.0164	0.0204	0.0025	-0.0024	0.0283	0.0062	-0.0057	0.0193	1953	0.0178
1954	0.0078	0.0232	0.0050	0.0095	-0.0092	0.0157	0.0129	-0.0041	-0.0018	-0.0001	-0.0031	0.0056	1954	0.0627
1955	-0.0249	-0.0087	0.0077	-0.0010	0.0059	-0.0086	-0.0112	-0.0012	0.0057	0.0126	-0.0062	0.0019	1955	-0.0282
1956	0.0061	-0.0021	-0.0164	-0.0131	0.0202	0.0007	-0.0230	-0.0203	0.0031	-0.0079	-0.0078	-0.0202	1956	-0.0785
1957	0.0318	0.0001	-0.0047	-0.0246	-0.0048	-0.0204	-0.0070	-0.0023	0.0050	-0.0079	0.0504	0.0282	1957	0.0419
1958	-0.0112	0.0088	0.0093	0.0178	-0.0010	-0.0163	-0.0285	-0.0440	-0.0136	0.0120	0.0109	-0.0203	1958	-0.0752
1959	-0.0101	0.0098	-0.0005	-0.0136	-0.0027	-0.0014	0.0035	-0.0060	-0.0087	0.0120	-0.0144	-0.0192	1959	-0.0506
1960	0.0078	0.0175	0.0247	-0.0189	0.0124	0.0148	0.0354	-0.0084	0.0059	-0.0050	-0.0079	0.0263	1960	0.1083
1961	-0.0126	0.0185	-0.0058	0.0097	-0.0064	-0.0095	0.0016	-0.0052	0.0112	0.0052	-0.0036	-0.0143	1961	-0.0113
1962	-0.0038	0.0083	0.0232	0.0059	0.0022	-0.0095	-0.0135	0.0163	0.0040	0.0058	0.0001	0.0012	1962	0.0404
1963	-0.0026	-0.0015	-0.0014	-0.0037	-0.0002	-0.0003	0.0004	-0.0003	-0.0023	-0.0055	0.0024	-0.0035	1963	-0.0185
1964	-0.0043	-0.0037	0.0006	0.0017	0.0025	0.0038	-0.0022	-0.0008	0.0021	0.0014	-0.0012	-0.0001	1964	-0.0003
1965	0.0012	-0.0016	0.0018	0.0006	-0.0013	0.0012	-0.0009	-0.0046	-0.0065	-0.0004	-0.0097	-0.0110	1965	-0.0310
1966	-0.0141	-0.0284	0.0257	-0.0097	-0.0100	-0.0053	-0.0072	-0.0246	0.0291	0.0182	-0.0188	0.0371	1966	-0.0106
1967	0.0111	-0.0256	0.0158	-0.0323	-0.0072	-0.0338	0.0037	-0.0115	-0.0036	-0.0438	-0.0231	0.0158	1967	-0.1285
1968	0.0286	-0.0072	-0.0249	0.0183	-0.0002	0.0187	0.0240	-0.0045	-0.0144	-0.0175	-0.0310	-0.0404	1968	-0.0520
1969	-0.0257	-0.0004	-0.0036	0.0371	-0.0536	0.0162	0.0026	-0.0119	-0.0590	0.0304	-0.0293	-0.0132	1969	-0.1094
1970	-0.0081	0.0522	-0.0124	-0.0461	-0.0518	0.0426	0.0266	-0.0072	0.0173	-0.0154	0.0742	-0.0126	1970	0.0524

* Compound annual return

Table A-19 **Bond Horizon Premia**

(continued)

From January 1971 to December 1998

YEAR	JAN	FEB	MAR	APR	MAY	JUN	JUL	AUG	SEP	OCT	NOV	DEC	YEAR	JAN–DEC*
1971	0.0466	-0.0196	0.0495	-0.0310	-0.0035	-0.0195	-0.0011	0.0422	0.0166	0.0130	-0.0084	0.0007	1971	0.0847
1972	-0.0092	0.0063	-0.0109	-0.0002	0.0240	-0.0094	0.0184	0.0000	-0.0116	0.0194	0.0188	-0.0266	1972	0.0178
1973	-0.0363	-0.0027	0.0036	-0.0007	-0.0155	-0.0072	-0.0494	0.0319	0.0248	0.0149	-0.0237	-0.0145	1973	-0.0752
1974	-0.0145	-0.0082	-0.0346	-0.0326	0.0047	-0.0016	-0.0099	-0.0290	0.0165	0.0436	0.0240	0.0101	1974	-0.0338
1975	0.0166	0.0088	-0.0307	-0.0225	0.0168	0.0250	-0.0135	-0.0115	-0.0150	0.0417	-0.0149	0.0340	1975	0.0321
1976	0.0043	0.0028	0.0125	-0.0023	-0.0195	0.0163	0.0031	0.0169	0.0101	0.0043	0.0298	0.0286	1976	0.1111
1977	-0.0422	-0.0084	0.0053	0.0033	0.0088	0.0124	-0.0111	0.0153	-0.0072	-0.0142	0.0043	-0.0215	1977	-0.0553
1978	-0.0129	-0.0042	-0.0073	-0.0058	-0.0109	-0.0115	0.0086	0.0161	-0.0167	-0.0266	0.0118	-0.0207	1978	-0.0780
1979	0.0113	-0.0207	0.0048	-0.0190	0.0178	0.0228	-0.0160	-0.0111	-0.0203	-0.0920	0.0211	-0.0038	1979	-0.1052
1980	-0.0814	-0.0551	-0.0430	0.1381	0.0335	0.0296	-0.0526	-0.0492	-0.0334	-0.0355	0.0004	0.0218	1980	-0.1365
1981	-0.0217	-0.0537	0.0260	-0.0618	0.0501	-0.0310	-0.0471	-0.0507	-0.0266	0.0700	0.1290	-0.0793	1981	-0.1120
1982	-0.0034	0.0089	0.0132	0.0258	-0.0071	-0.0316	0.0392	0.0699	0.0564	0.0572	-0.0065	0.0243	1982	0.2697
1983	-0.0375	0.0427	-0.0156	0.0276	-0.0452	-0.0027	-0.0556	-0.0056	0.0425	-0.0206	0.0112	-0.0130	1983	-0.0749
1984	0.0166	-0.0248	-0.0228	-0.0185	-0.0590	0.0074	0.0606	0.0182	0.0254	0.0457	0.0044	0.0026	1984	0.0512
1985	0.0297	-0.0548	0.0244	0.0169	0.0824	0.0086	-0.0241	0.0203	-0.0081	0.0271	0.0338	0.0473	1985	0.2158
1986	-0.0081	0.1087	0.0706	-0.0131	-0.0552	0.0558	-0.0159	0.0451	-0.0543	0.0241	0.0227	-0.0066	1986	0.1730
1987	0.0119	0.0158	-0.0268	-0.0515	-0.0142	0.0050	-0.0223	-0.0211	-0.0412	0.0560	0.0002	0.0126	1987	-0.0776
1988	0.0635	0.0007	-0.0349	-0.0205	-0.0152	0.0318	-0.0219	-0.0002	0.0281	0.0245	-0.0251	0.0046	1988	0.0313
1989	0.0147	-0.0239	0.0055	0.0091	0.0320	0.0476	0.0167	-0.0330	-0.0046	0.0310	0.0009	-0.0067	1989	0.0899
1990	-0.0397	-0.0081	-0.0108	-0.0269	0.0345	0.0167	0.0039	-0.0481	0.0057	0.0146	0.0344	0.0126	1990	-0.0151
1991	0.0078	-0.0017	-0.0006	0.0086	-0.0047	-0.0104	0.0108	0.0293	0.0257	0.0012	0.0043	0.0541	1991	0.1298
1992	-0.0357	0.0023	-0.0127	-0.0017	0.0214	0.0167	0.0366	0.0041	0.0159	-0.0220	-0.0013	0.0217	1992	0.0439
1993	0.0256	0.0331	-0.0004	0.0048	0.0025	0.0422	0.0167	0.0408	-0.0020	0.0074	-0.0283	-0.0003	1993	0.1491
1994	0.0232	-0.0470	-0.0421	-0.0177	-0.0114	-0.0131	0.0335	-0.0122	-0.0366	-0.0063	0.0029	0.0116	1994	-0.1124
1995	0.0230	0.0246	0.0045	0.0124	0.0733	0.0091	-0.0212	0.0189	0.0131	0.0246	0.0206	0.0222	1995	0.2469
1996	-0.0053	-0.0520	-0.0248	-0.0210	-0.0096	0.0162	-0.0027	-0.0180	0.0245	0.0360	0.0309	-0.0301	1996	-0.0583
1997	-0.0124	-0.0033	-0.0294	0.0211	0.0047	0.0157	0.0580	-0.0357	0.0270	0.0297	0.0108	0.0136	1997	0.1007
1998	0.0157	-0.0110	-0.0015	-0.0017	0.0141	0.0186	-0.0079	0.0420	0.0347	-0.0250	0.0066	-0.0069	1998	0.0783

* Compound annual return

Table A-20 **Large Company Stocks: Inflation-Adjusted Total Returns**

From January 1926 to December 1970

YEAR	JAN	FEB	MAR	APR	MAY	JUN	JUL	AUG	SEP	OCT	NOV	DEC	YEAR	JAN-DEC*
1926	0.0000	-0.0349	-0.0522	0.0158	0.0236	0.0536	0.0579	0.0307	0.0193	-0.0320	0.0308	0.0196	1926	0.1331
1927	-0.0118	0.0618	0.0145	0.0201	0.0526	-0.0161	0.0877	0.0576	0.0390	-0.0557	0.0742	0.0298	1927	0.4041
1928	-0.0020	-0.0029	0.1101	0.0325	0.0138	-0.0310	0.0141	0.0782	0.0179	0.0188	0.1313	0.0089	1928	0.4501
1929	0.0604	0.0000	0.0028	0.0216	-0.0419	0.1096	0.0369	0.0986	-0.0458	-0.1973	-0.1229	0.0342	1929	-0.0859
1930	0.0680	0.0299	0.0876	-0.0138	-0.0038	-0.1575	0.0532	0.0203	-0.1335	-0.0800	-0.0008	-0.0571	1930	-0.2008
1931	0.0656	0.1360	-0.0615	-0.0876	-0.1184	0.1547	-0.0701	0.0205	-0.2941	0.0969	-0.0693	-0.1321	1931	-0.3737
1932	-0.0066	0.0721	-0.1116	-0.1940	-0.2082	0.0051	0.3815	0.4041	-0.0297	-0.1284	-0.0368	0.0673	1932	0.0235
1933	0.0244	-0.1642	0.0436	0.4294	0.1652	0.1219	-0.1118	0.1093	-0.1118	-0.0855	0.1127	0.0305	1933	0.5321
1934	0.1013	-0.0395	0.0000	-0.0227	-0.0759	0.0203	-0.1132	0.0584	-0.0180	-0.0214	0.0969	0.0014	1934	-0.0340
1935	-0.0552	-0.0411	-0.0262	0.0874	0.0460	0.0725	0.0903	0.0280	0.0206	0.0777	0.0423	0.0369	1935	0.4339
1936	0.0670	0.0273	0.0318	-0.0751	0.0545	0.0233	0.0649	0.0079	0.0007	0.0800	0.0134	-0.0029	1936	0.3232
1937	0.0316	0.0167	-0.0147	-0.0852	-0.0071	-0.0526	0.0994	-0.0505	-0.1481	-0.0940	-0.0802	-0.0437	1937	-0.3698
1938	0.0295	0.0775	-0.2487	0.1393	-0.0284	0.2503	0.0719	-0.0203	0.0166	0.0827	-0.0250	0.0376	1938	0.3487
1939	-0.0629	0.0440	-0.1318	-0.0003	0.0733	-0.0612	0.1105	-0.0648	0.1451	-0.0076	-0.0398	0.0320	1939	0.0007
1940	-0.0313	0.0060	0.0148	-0.0024	-0.2307	0.0783	0.0365	0.0375	0.0099	0.0422	-0.0316	-0.0038	1940	-0.1064
1941	-0.0463	-0.0060	0.0023	-0.0700	0.0112	0.0385	0.0531	-0.0080	-0.0243	-0.0759	-0.0368	-0.0427	1941	-0.1942
1942	0.0031	-0.0242	-0.0769	-0.0459	0.0685	0.0200	0.0295	0.0102	0.0269	0.0571	-0.0081	0.0466	1942	0.1011
1943	0.0737	0.0562	0.0382	-0.0081	0.0472	0.0242	-0.0453	0.0210	0.0223	-0.0146	-0.0636	0.0597	1943	0.2204
1944	0.0191	0.0061	0.0195	-0.0157	0.0465	0.0522	-0.0248	0.0119	-0.0008	0.0023	0.0133	0.0335	1944	0.1728
1945	0.0158	0.0703	-0.0441	0.0881	0.0119	-0.0099	-0.0199	0.0641	0.0477	0.0322	0.0358	0.0079	1945	0.3343
1946	0.0714	-0.0606	0.0404	0.0336	0.0232	-0.0474	-0.0783	-0.0874	-0.1100	-0.0251	-0.0261	0.0376	1946	-0.2220
1947	0.0255	-0.0061	-0.0359	-0.0363	0.0044	0.0474	0.0288	-0.0305	-0.0341	0.0238	-0.0232	0.0102	1947	-0.0303
1948	-0.0487	-0.0306	0.0824	0.0147	0.0803	-0.0016	-0.0625	0.0116	-0.0276	0.0754	-0.0899	0.0418	1948	0.0272
1949	0.0053	-0.0187	0.0299	-0.0193	-0.0244	0.0000	0.0725	0.0191	0.0220	0.0398	0.0160	0.0545	1949	0.2097
1950	0.0240	0.0228	0.0027	0.0471	0.0465	-0.0601	0.0020	0.0357	0.0519	0.0038	0.0128	0.0372	1950	0.2450
1951	0.0469	0.0038	-0.0194	0.0496	-0.0336	-0.0215	0.0697	0.0478	-0.0051	-0.0154	0.0045	0.0385	1951	0.1714
1952	0.0181	-0.0220	0.0503	-0.0439	0.0330	0.0464	0.0120	-0.0083	-0.0164	0.0008	0.0571	0.0395	1952	0.1733
1953	-0.0024	-0.0056	-0.0237	-0.0249	0.0052	-0.0171	0.0248	-0.0525	0.0022	0.0514	0.0242	0.0065	1953	-0.0160
1954	0.0510	0.0124	0.0338	0.0542	0.0379	0.0018	0.0589	-0.0263	0.0878	-0.0143	0.0896	0.0561	1954	0.5339
1955	0.0197	0.0098	-0.0030	0.0396	0.0055	0.0841	0.0582	0.0000	0.0092	-0.0284	0.0813	0.0040	1955	0.3107
1956	-0.0335	0.0413	0.0697	-0.0017	-0.0640	0.0345	0.0453	-0.0316	-0.0452	0.0005	-0.0050	0.0345	1956	0.0359
1957	-0.0412	-0.0299	0.0190	0.0350	0.0412	-0.0055	0.0083	-0.0516	-0.0613	-0.0302	0.0195	-0.0395	1957	-0.1340
1958	0.0384	-0.0153	0.0256	0.0313	0.0212	0.0267	0.0437	0.0188	0.0501	0.0270	0.0273	0.0548	1958	0.4088
1959	0.0041	0.0060	0.0020	0.0390	0.0228	-0.0068	0.0339	-0.0091	-0.0476	0.0094	0.0186	0.0292	1959	0.1030
1960	-0.0689	0.0136	-0.0123	-0.0216	0.0326	0.0188	-0.0234	0.0317	-0.0600	-0.0052	0.0453	0.0479	1960	-0.0099
1961	0.0645	0.0319	0.0270	0.0051	0.0239	-0.0286	0.0296	0.0254	-0.0205	0.0298	0.0447	0.0046	1961	0.2604
1962	-0.0366	0.0187	-0.0068	-0.0628	-0.0811	-0.0803	0.0629	0.0208	-0.0517	0.0075	0.1086	0.0164	1962	-0.0983
1963	0.0494	-0.0249	0.0359	0.0500	0.0193	-0.0231	-0.0065	0.0535	-0.0097	0.0328	-0.0057	0.0240	1963	0.2081
1964	0.0271	0.0158	0.0154	0.0064	0.0162	0.0156	0.0173	-0.0107	0.0279	0.0085	-0.0017	0.0045	1964	0.1511
1965	0.0345	0.0031	-0.0143	0.0323	-0.0051	-0.0523	0.0137	0.0294	0.0312	0.0278	-0.0052	0.0074	1965	0.1033
1966	0.0062	-0.0193	-0.0236	0.0177	-0.0502	-0.0177	-0.0151	-0.0772	-0.0073	0.0451	0.0095	-0.0008	1966	-0.1298
1967	0.0798	0.0061	0.0388	0.0416	-0.0505	0.0159	0.0416	-0.0099	0.0321	-0.0305	0.0035	0.0247	1967	0.2032
1968	-0.0463	-0.0290	0.0060	0.0802	0.0131	0.0047	-0.0219	0.0135	0.0370	0.0029	0.0491	-0.0429	1968	0.0605
1969	-0.0096	-0.0462	0.0272	0.0163	-0.0002	-0.0603	-0.0630	0.0407	-0.0279	0.0421	-0.0349	-0.0238	1969	-0.1377
1970	-0.0776	0.0530	-0.0022	-0.0945	-0.0588	-0.0531	0.0715	0.0491	0.0294	-0.0148	0.0500	0.0530	1970	-0.0141

* Compound annual return

Table A-20 **Large Company Stocks: Inflation-Adjusted Total Returns**

(continued)

From January 1971 to December 1998

YEAR	JAN	FEB	MAR	APR	MAY	JUN	JUL	AUG	SEP	OCT	NOV	DEC	YEAR	JAN–DEC*
1971	0.0410	0.0124	0.0348	0.0342	-0.0415	-0.0037	-0.0423	0.0387	-0.0064	-0.0419	0.0010	0.0833	1971	0.1060
1972	0.0186	0.0249	0.0056	0.0033	0.0186	-0.0229	-0.0004	0.0375	-0.0075	0.0075	0.0480	0.0099	1972	0.1505
1973	-0.0190	-0.0400	-0.0094	-0.0461	-0.0199	-0.0119	0.0371	-0.0490	0.0385	-0.0078	-0.1147	0.0117	1973	-0.2156
1974	-0.0170	-0.0109	-0.0327	-0.0427	-0.0379	-0.0223	-0.0828	-0.0945	-0.1275	0.1558	-0.0528	-0.0247	1974	-0.3446
1975	0.1201	0.0600	0.0198	0.0440	0.0462	0.0377	-0.0757	-0.0175	-0.0375	0.0572	0.0251	-0.0138	1975	0.2821
1976	0.1172	-0.0082	0.0301	-0.0140	-0.0132	0.0372	-0.0126	-0.0032	0.0205	-0.0245	-0.0038	0.0509	1976	0.1816
1977	-0.0544	-0.0251	-0.0180	-0.0064	-0.0204	0.0406	-0.0194	-0.0170	-0.0038	-0.0441	0.0320	0.0010	1977	-0.1307
1978	-0.0647	-0.0229	0.0206	0.0774	0.0037	-0.0253	0.0484	0.0288	-0.0118	-0.0963	0.0204	0.0117	1978	-0.0226
1979	0.0330	-0.0396	0.0474	-0.0078	-0.0288	0.0314	-0.0020	0.0505	-0.0078	-0.0739	0.0417	0.0086	1979	0.0453
1980	0.0460	-0.0105	-0.1114	0.0313	0.0459	0.0183	0.0667	0.0066	0.0187	0.0098	0.0996	-0.0398	1980	0.1781
1981	-0.0515	0.0103	0.0306	-0.0275	-0.0020	-0.0164	-0.0106	-0.0626	-0.0597	0.0505	0.0411	-0.0293	1981	-0.1271
1982	-0.0198	-0.0542	-0.0049	0.0370	-0.0383	-0.0292	-0.0269	0.1244	0.0093	0.1096	0.0456	0.0215	1982	0.1688
1983	0.0323	0.0257	0.0358	0.0682	-0.0106	0.0347	-0.0352	0.0136	0.0086	-0.0160	0.0216	-0.0074	1983	0.1803
1984	-0.0120	-0.0372	0.0148	0.0020	-0.0562	0.0188	-0.0175	0.1079	-0.0046	0.0001	-0.0101	0.0247	1984	0.0222
1985	0.0748	0.0095	-0.0026	-0.0072	0.0575	0.0128	-0.0041	-0.0083	-0.0351	0.0415	0.0680	0.0441	1985	0.2736
1986	0.0013	0.0791	0.0603	-0.0103	0.0517	0.0116	-0.0572	0.0729	-0.0867	0.0546	0.0247	-0.0273	1986	0.1715
1987	0.1275	0.0373	0.0226	-0.0141	0.0073	0.0456	0.0476	0.0327	-0.0268	-0.2172	-0.0832	0.0741	1987	0.0079
1988	0.0400	0.0443	-0.0344	0.0056	0.0044	0.0420	-0.0082	-0.0372	0.0354	0.0239	-0.0150	0.0164	1988	0.1187
1989	0.0670	-0.0289	0.0177	0.0448	0.0343	-0.0078	0.0872	0.0177	-0.0071	-0.0280	0.0184	0.0220	1989	0.2565
1990	-0.0766	0.0082	0.0207	-0.0262	0.0950	-0.0124	-0.0070	-0.0986	-0.0571	-0.0097	0.0620	0.0274	1990	-0.0874
1991	0.0380	0.0700	0.0223	0.0013	0.0397	-0.0485	0.0453	0.0205	-0.0207	0.0119	-0.0432	0.1135	1991	0.2667
1992	-0.0200	0.0091	-0.0245	0.0276	0.0040	-0.0180	0.0381	-0.0230	0.0086	0.0001	0.0322	0.0138	1992	0.0464
1993	0.0024	0.0100	0.0179	-0.0272	0.0256	0.0019	-0.0047	0.0352	-0.0095	0.0161	-0.0101	0.0123	1993	0.0705
1994	0.0307	-0.0303	-0.0467	0.0116	0.0156	-0.0280	0.0303	0.0365	-0.0267	0.0222	-0.0380	0.0146	1994	-0.0133
1995	0.0219	0.0347	0.0262	0.0257	0.0375	0.0215	0.0333	0.0001	0.0399	-0.0067	0.0447	0.0192	1995	0.3403
1996	0.0284	0.0063	0.0044	0.0108	0.0238	0.0035	-0.0463	0.0193	0.0529	0.0242	0.0739	-0.0196	1996	0.1912
1997	0.0588	0.0049	-0.0440	0.0584	0.0621	0.0433	0.0781	-0.0574	0.0522	-0.0358	0.0469	0.0185	1997	0.3113
1998	0.0092	0.0701	0.0493	0.0082	-0.0190	0.0393	-0.0119	-0.1456	0.0628	0.0787	0.0606	0.0583	1998	0.2654

* Compound annual return

Table A-21 **Small Company Stocks: Inflation-Adjusted Total Returns**

From January 1926 to December 1970

YEAR	JAN	FEB	MAR	APR	MAY	JUN	JUL	AUG	SEP	OCT	NOV	DEC	YEAR	JAN–DEC*
1926	0.0699	-0.0604	-0.1023	0.0084	-0.0010	0.0456	0.0208	0.0315	-0.0058	-0.0264	0.0169	0.0332	1926	0.0179
1927	0.0374	0.0628	-0.0493	0.0573	0.0652	-0.0395	0.0719	-0.0121	-0.0011	-0.0713	0.0829	0.0336	1927	0.2469
1928	0.0502	-0.0141	0.0531	0.0889	0.0377	-0.0771	0.0059	0.0421	0.0806	0.0296	0.1169	-0.0476	1928	0.4106
1929	0.0054	-0.0007	-0.0162	0.0347	-0.1387	0.0492	0.0016	-0.0201	-0.0904	-0.2768	-0.1484	-0.0445	1929	-0.5145
1930	0.1337	0.0685	0.1072	-0.0753	-0.0487	-0.2121	0.0446	-0.0107	-0.1511	-0.1043	0.0054	-0.1038	1930	-0.3418
1931	0.2281	0.2754	-0.0648	-0.2113	-0.1284	0.1950	-0.0536	-0.0742	-0.3216	0.0842	-0.0907	-0.2124	1931	-0.4446
1932	0.1251	0.0437	-0.1270	-0.2164	-0.1065	0.0107	0.3523	0.7561	-0.1277	-0.1713	-0.1183	-0.0395	1932	0.0547
1933	0.0071	-0.1140	0.1206	0.5078	0.6296	0.2484	-0.0816	0.0814	-0.1595	-0.1236	0.0654	0.0106	1933	1.4163
1934	0.3821	0.0090	-0.0012	0.0265	-0.1297	-0.0049	-0.2259	0.1517	-0.0312	0.0172	0.0975	0.0198	1934	0.2175
1935	-0.0470	-0.0661	-0.1167	0.0687	0.0024	0.0330	0.0908	0.0545	0.0306	0.0994	0.1357	0.0573	1935	0.3613
1936	0.3009	0.0654	0.0115	-0.1795	0.0272	-0.0326	0.0820	0.0137	0.0517	0.0661	0.1400	0.0160	1936	0.6283
1937	0.1186	0.0632	0.0048	-0.1718	-0.0453	-0.1203	0.1183	-0.0758	-0.2607	-0.1052	-0.1394	-0.1674	1937	-0.5927
1938	0.0683	0.0441	-0.3600	0.2716	-0.0806	0.3498	0.1472	-0.0980	-0.0157	0.2193	-0.0666	0.0462	1938	0.3659
1939	-0.0805	0.0155	-0.2448	0.0166	0.1088	-0.1042	0.2535	-0.1590	0.4858	-0.0351	-0.1053	0.0472	1939	0.0083
1940	0.0033	0.0743	0.0657	0.0654	-0.3689	0.1024	0.0256	0.0279	0.0188	0.0545	0.0245	-0.0492	1940	-0.0605
1941	0.0025	-0.0288	0.0271	-0.0757	-0.0025	0.0557	0.2110	-0.0150	-0.0638	-0.0774	-0.0577	-0.1223	1941	-0.1706
1942	0.1742	-0.0157	-0.0826	-0.0413	-0.0134	0.0315	0.0693	0.0262	0.0890	0.0976	-0.0567	0.0331	1942	0.3223
1943	0.2132	0.1908	0.1267	0.0807	0.1071	-0.0064	-0.1014	0.0036	0.0388	0.0084	-0.1096	0.1219	1943	0.8260
1944	0.0661	0.0315	0.0749	-0.0587	0.0699	0.1363	-0.0354	0.0280	-0.0020	-0.0108	0.0499	0.0829	1944	0.5055
1945	0.0482	0.1030	-0.0861	0.1136	0.0422	0.0755	-0.0574	0.0557	0.0719	0.0701	0.1131	0.0133	1945	0.6979
1946	0.1562	-0.0602	0.0198	0.0638	0.0534	-0.0565	-0.1057	-0.1045	-0.1699	-0.0308	-0.0373	0.0292	1946	-0.2521
1947	0.0421	-0.0025	-0.0542	-0.1031	-0.0505	0.0472	0.0692	-0.0141	-0.0120	0.0282	-0.0359	0.0227	1947	-0.0742
1948	-0.0264	-0.0704	0.1017	0.0222	0.0982	-0.0022	-0.0694	-0.0035	-0.0526	0.0691	-0.1055	0.0157	1948	-0.0469
1949	0.0196	-0.0374	0.0599	-0.0350	-0.0551	-0.0110	0.0746	0.0228	0.0445	0.0531	0.0002	0.0750	1949	0.2195
1950	0.0536	0.0250	-0.0079	0.0397	0.0212	-0.0829	0.0489	0.0443	0.0449	-0.0113	0.0281	0.0807	1950	0.3115
1951	0.0660	-0.0057	-0.0514	0.0353	-0.0368	-0.0516	0.0360	0.0605	0.0150	-0.0272	-0.0133	0.0006	1951	0.0182
1952	0.0191	-0.0238	0.0175	-0.0555	0.0019	0.0246	0.0036	-0.0018	-0.0149	-0.0115	0.0485	0.0173	1952	0.0213
1953	0.0435	0.0321	-0.0092	-0.0300	0.0116	-0.0522	0.0127	-0.0651	-0.0274	0.0266	0.0164	-0.0253	1953	-0.0707
1954	0.0730	0.0107	0.0196	0.0165	0.0413	0.0073	0.0808	0.0027	0.0436	0.0093	0.0766	0.1140	1954	0.6138
1955	0.0201	0.0479	0.0085	0.0150	0.0078	0.0293	0.0026	-0.0003	0.0072	-0.0170	0.0455	0.0188	1955	0.1999
1956	-0.0035	0.0278	0.0418	0.0034	-0.0445	-0.0006	0.0208	-0.0122	-0.0272	0.0043	0.0053	0.0014	1956	0.0138
1957	0.0224	-0.0235	0.0143	0.0212	0.0051	0.0013	-0.0107	-0.0397	-0.0463	-0.0832	0.0078	-0.0481	1957	-0.1708
1958	0.1040	-0.0181	0.0398	0.0352	0.0387	0.0312	0.0479	0.0440	0.0518	0.0407	0.0484	0.0325	1958	0.6203
1959	0.0562	0.0307	0.0027	0.0105	0.0002	-0.0088	0.0304	-0.0076	-0.0464	0.0192	0.0222	0.0322	1959	0.1468
1960	-0.0295	0.0038	-0.0315	-0.0242	0.0204	0.0317	-0.0189	0.0525	-0.0749	-0.0444	0.0425	0.0332	1960	-0.0470
1961	0.0915	0.0589	0.0619	0.0127	0.0427	-0.0554	-0.0013	0.0142	-0.0360	0.0262	0.0613	0.0079	1961	0.3121
1962	0.0136	0.0165	0.0034	-0.0798	-0.1009	-0.0785	0.0739	0.0289	-0.0710	-0.0363	0.1248	-0.0078	1962	-0.1297
1963	0.0894	0.0023	0.0138	0.0312	0.0436	-0.0162	-0.0011	0.0517	-0.0163	0.0225	-0.0117	-0.0069	1963	0.2156
1964	0.0263	0.0376	0.0208	0.0082	0.0157	0.0141	0.0376	-0.0018	0.0380	0.0194	-0.0011	-0.0122	1964	0.2207
1965	0.0529	0.0390	0.0227	0.0475	-0.0099	-0.0949	0.0437	0.0617	0.0325	0.0561	0.0349	0.0588	1965	0.3908
1966	0.0756	0.0247	-0.0222	0.0301	-0.0971	-0.0043	-0.0043	-0.1125	-0.0184	-0.0147	0.0491	0.0055	1966	-0.1003
1967	0.1838	0.0439	0.0593	0.0250	-0.0115	0.0984	0.0896	-0.0009	0.0544	-0.0340	0.0087	0.0933	1967	0.7815
1968	0.0114	-0.0736	-0.0157	0.1427	0.0967	-0.0028	-0.0392	0.0337	0.0569	-0.0027	0.0724	0.0034	1968	0.2984
1969	-0.0194	-0.1024	0.0309	0.0328	0.0145	-0.1221	-0.1110	0.0684	-0.0305	0.0572	-0.0608	-0.0745	1969	-0.2937
1970	-0.0641	0.0332	-0.0335	-0.1778	-0.1070	-0.0976	0.0517	0.0930	0.1029	-0.0753	0.0103	0.0672	1970	-0.2173

* Compound annual return

Table A-21 **Small Company Stocks: Inflation-Adjusted Total Returns**

(continued)

From January 1971 to December 1998

YEAR	JAN	FEB	MAR	APR	MAY	JUN	JUL	AUG	SEP	OCT	NOV	DEC	YEAR	JAN–DEC*
1971	0.1582	0.0299	0.0529	0.0213	-0.0652	-0.0375	-0.0586	0.0557	-0.0234	-0.0567	-0.0389	0.1099	1971	0.1271
1972	0.1121	0.0246	-0.0159	0.0104	-0.0223	-0.0328	-0.0451	0.0170	-0.0387	-0.0206	0.0567	-0.0244	1972	0.0099
1973	-0.0462	-0.0863	-0.0298	-0.0686	-0.0867	-0.0356	0.1169	-0.0615	0.1031	0.0003	-0.2021	-0.0078	1973	-0.3649
1974	0.1229	-0.0211	-0.0185	-0.0517	-0.0894	-0.0241	-0.0291	-0.0799	-0.0764	0.0969	-0.0518	-0.0853	1974	-0.2865
1975	0.2710	0.0213	0.0578	0.0478	0.0616	0.0662	-0.0356	-0.0603	-0.0230	-0.0111	0.0257	-0.0238	1975	0.4280
1976	0.2654	0.1362	-0.0039	-0.0399	-0.0418	0.0404	-0.0014	-0.0336	0.0063	-0.0248	0.0374	0.1148	1976	0.5015
1977	0.0390	-0.0140	0.0068	0.0149	-0.0083	0.0701	-0.0014	-0.0145	0.0054	-0.0357	0.1032	0.0043	1977	0.1743
1978	-0.0241	0.0276	0.0957	0.0692	0.0714	-0.0290	0.0608	0.0883	-0.0102	-0.2488	0.0673	0.0113	1978	0.1324
1979	0.1222	-0.0395	0.1013	0.0269	-0.0087	0.0375	0.0041	0.0649	-0.0443	-0.1233	0.0758	0.0478	1979	0.2662
1980	0.0683	-0.0415	-0.1894	0.0574	0.0645	0.0338	0.1314	0.0536	0.0323	0.0244	0.0670	-0.0420	1980	0.2445
1981	0.0125	-0.0010	0.0865	0.0589	0.0337	-0.0009	-0.0425	-0.0755	-0.0826	0.0719	0.0247	-0.0248	1981	0.0453
1982	-0.0231	-0.0327	-0.0075	0.0339	-0.0343	-0.0278	-0.0070	0.0676	0.0309	0.1274	0.0797	0.0174	1982	0.2323
1983	0.0603	0.0709	0.0518	0.0690	0.0811	0.0314	-0.0128	-0.0229	0.0083	-0.0593	0.0498	-0.0158	1983	0.3456
1984	-0.0064	-0.0688	0.0151	-0.0133	-0.0549	0.0267	-0.0451	0.0952	-0.0021	-0.0242	-0.0336	0.0144	1984	-0.1022
1985	0.1038	0.0230	-0.0257	-0.0214	0.0238	0.0075	0.0244	-0.0093	-0.0573	0.0229	0.0584	0.0444	1985	0.2013
1986	0.0081	0.0748	0.0525	0.0086	0.0328	-0.0023	-0.0713	0.0200	-0.0605	0.0337	-0.0040	-0.0271	1986	0.0566
1987	0.0877	0.0767	0.0187	-0.0365	-0.0068	0.0224	0.0343	0.0230	-0.0130	-0.2937	-0.0411	0.0523	1987	-0.1313
1988	0.0529	0.0732	0.0363	0.0157	-0.0212	0.0567	-0.0067	-0.0287	0.0159	-0.0156	-0.0445	0.0377	1988	0.1767
1989	0.0352	0.0042	0.0299	0.0212	0.0303	-0.0225	0.0382	0.0106	-0.0032	-0.0649	-0.0075	-0.0150	1989	0.0529
1990	-0.0858	0.0139	0.0312	-0.0281	0.0536	0.0089	-0.0419	-0.1375	-0.0905	-0.0629	0.0427	0.0194	1990	-0.2608
1991	0.0777	0.1097	0.0664	0.0019	0.0304	-0.0513	0.0392	0.0231	-0.0012	0.0302	-0.0304	0.0593	1991	0.4033
1992	0.1112	0.0414	-0.0298	-0.0417	-0.0028	-0.0553	0.0348	-0.0256	0.0102	0.0223	0.0870	0.0448	1992	0.1987
1993	0.0491	-0.0214	0.0253	-0.0333	0.0328	-0.0052	0.0166	0.0310	0.0295	0.0428	-0.0182	0.0194	1993	0.1774
1994	0.0589	-0.0057	-0.0478	0.0046	-0.0019	-0.0295	0.0157	0.0295	0.0078	0.0108	-0.0339	0.0002	1994	0.0042
1995	0.0242	0.0211	0.0111	0.0318	0.0278	0.0547	0.0645	0.0331	0.0175	-0.0518	0.0199	0.0246	1995	0.3113
1996	-0.0030	0.0336	0.0175	0.0806	0.0728	-0.0588	-0.0960	0.0456	0.0258	-0.0206	0.0269	0.0204	1996	0.1384
1997	0.0387	-0.0237	-0.0514	-0.0288	0.1029	0.0485	0.0592	0.0489	0.0817	-0.0410	-0.0149	-0.0159	1997	0.2072
1998	-0.0077	0.0629	0.0462	0.0149	-0.0515	-0.0218	-0.0682	-0.2020	0.0356	0.0331	0.0758	0.0258	1998	-0.0878

* Compound annual return

Table A-22 **Long-Term Corporate Bonds: Inflation-Adjusted Total Returns**

From January 1926 to December 1970

YEAR	JAN	FEB	MAR	APR	MAY	JUN	JUL	AUG	SEP	OCT	NOV	DEC	YEAR	JAN–DEC*
1926	0.0072	0.0083	0.0141	0.0003	0.0100	0.0080	0.0153	0.0102	0.0000	0.0059	0.0019	0.0056	1926	0.0900
1927	0.0133	0.0146	0.0141	0.0055	-0.0088	-0.0052	0.0196	0.0142	0.0090	-0.0003	0.0087	0.0087	1927	0.0973
1928	0.0046	0.0166	0.0041	-0.0006	-0.0136	0.0054	-0.0010	0.0063	-0.0048	0.0103	-0.0017	0.0123	1928	0.0384
1929	0.0063	0.0050	-0.0048	0.0059	-0.0014	-0.0085	-0.0077	-0.0019	0.0053	0.0073	0.0001	0.0251	1929	0.0307
1930	0.0098	0.0111	0.0198	0.0025	0.0117	0.0170	0.0198	0.0198	0.0047	0.0115	0.0070	0.0054	1930	0.1490
1931	0.0353	0.0218	0.0159	0.0132	0.0245	0.0163	0.0074	0.0034	0.0030	-0.0298	-0.0078	-0.0197	1931	0.0848
1932	0.0157	-0.0099	0.0405	-0.0105	0.0255	0.0064	0.0043	0.0565	0.0352	0.0150	0.0124	0.0242	1932	0.2354
1933	0.0711	-0.0373	0.0127	-0.0069	0.0560	0.0083	-0.0124	-0.0009	-0.0014	0.0040	-0.0248	0.0309	1933	0.0982
1934	0.0205	0.0070	0.0187	0.0129	0.0065	0.0133	0.0047	0.0022	-0.0208	0.0177	0.0154	0.0126	1934	0.1158
1935	0.0061	0.0067	0.0067	0.0014	0.0091	0.0137	0.0160	-0.0042	-0.0049	0.0042	0.0020	0.0059	1935	0.0644
1936	0.0082	0.0103	0.0131	0.0026	0.0040	-0.0015	-0.0037	-0.0005	0.0043	0.0049	0.0109	0.0010	1936	0.0547
1937	-0.0047	-0.0070	-0.0184	0.0021	-0.0007	0.0030	-0.0007	-0.0040	-0.0067	0.0113	0.0137	0.0090	1937	-0.0035
1938	0.0179	0.0105	-0.0087	0.0090	0.0057	0.0095	0.0042	0.0005	0.0109	0.0128	0.0061	0.0098	1938	0.0916
1939	0.0070	0.0112	0.0046	0.0088	0.0049	0.0035	-0.0007	-0.0392	-0.0041	0.0286	0.0079	0.0126	1939	0.0446
1940	0.0073	-0.0051	0.0073	-0.0092	-0.0045	0.0097	0.0045	0.0031	0.0068	0.0049	0.0063	-0.0070	1940	0.0241
1941	0.0006	0.0006	-0.0069	-0.0016	-0.0021	-0.0120	0.0017	-0.0056	-0.0129	-0.0076	-0.0180	-0.0016	1941	-0.0637
1942	-0.0122	-0.0093	-0.0063	-0.0056	-0.0083	0.0013	-0.0021	-0.0026	0.0000	-0.0094	-0.0054	-0.0030	1942	-0.0612
1943	0.0049	-0.0014	-0.0136	-0.0067	-0.0029	0.0067	0.0096	0.0058	-0.0033	-0.0047	-0.0004	0.0030	1943	-0.0032
1944	0.0039	0.0053	0.0048	-0.0024	-0.0033	0.0001	-0.0023	-0.0004	0.0019	0.0019	0.0048	0.0111	1944	0.0257
1945	0.0076	0.0065	0.0018	-0.0001	-0.0085	-0.0061	-0.0029	0.0004	0.0069	0.0032	-0.0005	0.0096	1945	0.0178
1946	0.0128	0.0071	-0.0039	-0.0097	-0.0035	-0.0089	-0.0569	-0.0301	-0.0140	-0.0173	-0.0259	0.0034	1946	-0.1391
1947	0.0005	0.0021	-0.0148	0.0020	0.0051	-0.0072	-0.0070	-0.0174	-0.0360	-0.0099	-0.0155	-0.0105	1947	-0.1041
1948	-0.0089	0.0125	0.0144	-0.0103	-0.0062	-0.0152	-0.0174	0.0014	0.0024	0.0065	0.0154	0.0201	1948	0.0139
1949	0.0052	0.0151	-0.0021	0.0009	0.0052	0.0070	0.0170	0.0009	-0.0021	0.0124	0.0007	-0.0089	1949	0.0521
1950	0.0080	0.0035	-0.0021	-0.0022	-0.0050	-0.0033	-0.0029	-0.0045	-0.0107	-0.0062	0.0013	-0.0111	1950	-0.0347
1951	-0.0139	-0.0160	-0.0275	-0.0022	-0.0054	-0.0080	0.0192	0.0114	-0.0121	-0.0195	-0.0111	0.0020	1951	-0.0809
1952	0.0199	-0.0022	0.0076	-0.0042	0.0018	-0.0009	-0.0059	0.0050	-0.0006	0.0026	0.0108	-0.0079	1952	0.0262
1953	-0.0055	0.0010	-0.0058	-0.0260	-0.0055	0.0071	0.0152	-0.0110	0.0240	0.0202	-0.0036	0.0185	1953	0.0277
1954	0.0099	0.0211	0.0051	-0.0009	-0.0079	0.0051	0.0040	0.0030	0.0065	0.0065	0.0013	0.0042	1954	0.0591
1955	-0.0097	-0.0063	0.0092	-0.0001	-0.0018	0.0029	-0.0078	-0.0013	0.0038	0.0078	-0.0042	0.0088	1955	0.0010
1956	0.0117	0.0026	-0.0158	-0.0127	0.0002	-0.0079	-0.0165	-0.0196	0.0000	-0.0165	-0.0126	-0.0106	1956	-0.0941
1957	0.0185	0.0057	0.0026	-0.0102	-0.0099	-0.0379	-0.0157	-0.0021	0.0083	0.0023	0.0275	0.0685	1957	0.0552
1958	0.0040	-0.0020	-0.0115	0.0140	0.0031	-0.0049	-0.0164	-0.0309	-0.0096	0.0107	0.0093	-0.0047	1958	-0.0391
1959	-0.0039	0.0138	-0.0083	-0.0183	-0.0125	-0.0002	0.0066	-0.0057	-0.0122	0.0130	0.0135	-0.0096	1959	-0.0243
1960	0.0118	0.0116	0.0191	-0.0078	-0.0021	0.0118	0.0257	0.0117	-0.0074	-0.0037	-0.0081	0.0104	1960	0.0748
1961	0.0148	0.0210	-0.0029	-0.0116	0.0049	-0.0091	-0.0005	-0.0007	0.0121	0.0127	0.0028	-0.0026	1961	0.0412
1962	0.0080	0.0030	0.0129	0.0120	0.0000	-0.0026	-0.0037	0.0143	0.0034	0.0079	0.0062	0.0034	1962	0.0664
1963	0.0048	0.0012	0.0015	-0.0051	0.0048	-0.0001	-0.0016	0.0035	-0.0023	0.0038	0.0004	-0.0056	1963	0.0054
1964	0.0076	0.0065	-0.0073	0.0029	0.0057	0.0026	0.0030	0.0048	-0.0001	0.0039	-0.0025	0.0077	1964	0.0354
1965	0.0081	0.0009	0.0001	-0.0011	-0.0029	-0.0050	0.0008	0.0015	-0.0036	0.0035	-0.0078	-0.0180	1965	-0.0233
1966	0.0022	-0.0175	-0.0090	-0.0028	-0.0036	-0.0001	-0.0129	-0.0309	0.0057	0.0219	-0.0020	0.0191	1966	-0.0306
1967	0.0450	-0.0211	0.0097	-0.0091	-0.0283	-0.0252	-0.0009	-0.0037	0.0074	-0.0310	-0.0301	0.0097	1967	-0.0776
1968	0.0320	0.0008	-0.0245	0.0019	0.0003	0.0064	0.0292	0.0177	-0.0081	-0.0216	-0.0263	-0.0261	1968	-0.0205
1969	0.0110	-0.0197	-0.0282	0.0268	-0.0254	-0.0029	-0.0040	-0.0065	-0.0288	0.0091	-0.0522	-0.0195	1969	-0.1338
1970	0.0105	0.0346	-0.0097	-0.0309	-0.0206	-0.0051	0.0520	0.0083	0.0087	-0.0146	0.0548	0.0320	1970	0.1221

* Compound annual return

Table A-22 **Long-Term Corporate Bonds: Inflation-Adjusted Total Returns**

(continued)

From January 1971 to December 1998

YEAR	JAN	FEB	MAR	APR	MAY	JUN	JUL	AUG	SEP	OCT	NOV	DEC	YEAR	JAN–DEC*
1971	0.0523	-0.0382	0.0224	-0.0268	-0.0210	0.0049	-0.0050	0.0528	-0.0110	0.0265	0.0013	0.0181	1971	0.0741
1972	-0.0041	0.0058	0.0008	0.0011	0.0130	-0.0092	-0.0010	0.0056	-0.0009	0.0069	0.0225	-0.0035	1972	0.0372
1973	-0.0085	-0.0047	-0.0048	-0.0008	-0.0100	-0.0124	-0.0498	0.0172	0.0325	-0.0146	0.0005	-0.0153	1973	-0.0704
1974	-0.0138	-0.0118	-0.0415	-0.0395	-0.0006	-0.0378	-0.0284	-0.0391	0.0053	0.0793	0.0032	-0.0145	1974	-0.1360
1975	0.0548	0.0066	-0.0284	-0.0102	0.0062	0.0221	-0.0134	-0.0205	-0.0174	0.0489	-0.0148	0.0398	1975	0.0713
1976	0.0164	0.0037	0.0143	-0.0057	-0.0161	0.0096	0.0090	0.0183	0.0126	0.0029	0.0289	0.0317	1976	0.1320
1977	-0.0358	-0.0121	0.0032	0.0021	0.0050	0.0108	-0.0049	0.0097	-0.0060	-0.0065	0.0012	-0.0142	1977	-0.0474
1978	-0.0142	-0.0018	-0.0027	-0.0112	-0.0205	-0.0080	0.0029	0.0205	-0.0118	-0.0283	0.0079	-0.0186	1978	-0.0834
1979	0.0094	-0.0242	0.0010	-0.0164	0.0104	0.0174	-0.0158	-0.0093	-0.0280	-0.0971	0.0127	-0.0211	1979	-0.1543
1980	-0.0777	-0.0791	-0.0203	0.1249	0.0457	0.0228	-0.0437	-0.0506	-0.0326	-0.0244	-0.0073	0.0161	1980	-0.1348
1981	-0.0210	-0.0369	0.0237	-0.0828	0.0508	-0.0062	-0.0481	-0.0418	-0.0297	0.0498	0.1235	-0.0607	1981	-0.0934
1982	-0.0164	0.0279	0.0317	0.0294	0.0145	-0.0583	0.0482	0.0815	0.0605	0.0730	0.0218	0.0150	1982	0.3725
1983	-0.0118	0.0424	0.0065	0.0473	-0.0376	-0.0079	-0.0493	0.0018	0.0340	-0.0051	0.0125	-0.0046	1983	0.0237
1984	0.0213	-0.0217	-0.0257	-0.0121	-0.0511	0.0166	0.0552	0.0264	0.0265	0.0545	0.0212	0.0122	1984	0.1242
1985	0.0305	-0.0412	0.0134	0.0254	0.0780	0.0052	-0.0136	0.0238	0.0040	0.0297	0.0335	0.0443	1985	0.2536
1986	0.0014	0.0782	0.0303	0.0038	-0.0194	0.0168	0.0028	0.0257	-0.0162	0.0180	0.0224	0.0108	1986	0.1851
1987	0.0155	0.0019	-0.0131	-0.0553	-0.0081	0.0113	-0.0139	-0.0130	-0.0469	0.0480	0.0110	0.0215	1987	-0.0448
1988	0.0490	0.0112	-0.0230	-0.0199	-0.0091	0.0335	-0.0153	0.0012	0.0257	0.0239	-0.0177	0.0022	1988	0.0602
1989	0.0151	-0.0170	0.0006	0.0147	0.0320	0.0370	0.0153	-0.0179	0.0008	0.0227	0.0046	-0.0010	1989	0.1107
1990	-0.0291	-0.0059	-0.0065	-0.0206	0.0361	0.0161	0.0063	-0.0381	0.0007	0.0071	0.0262	0.0167	1990	0.0064
1991	0.0090	0.0106	0.0093	0.0123	0.0009	-0.0047	0.0152	0.0245	0.0226	0.0028	0.0077	0.0428	1991	0.1632
1992	-0.0187	0.0060	-0.0123	0.0002	0.0239	0.0120	0.0286	0.0061	0.0070	-0.0191	0.0055	0.0235	1992	0.0631
1993	0.0200	0.0220	-0.0010	0.0024	0.0006	0.0279	0.0100	0.0259	0.0022	0.0010	-0.0195	0.0067	1993	0.1016
1994	0.0174	-0.0319	-0.0416	-0.0110	-0.0069	-0.0115	0.0281	-0.0071	-0.0291	-0.0057	0.0005	0.0157	1994	-0.0822
1995	0.0215	0.0248	0.0062	0.0142	0.0610	0.0059	-0.0101	0.0187	0.0133	0.0152	0.0249	0.0235	1995	0.2406
1996	-0.0044	-0.0404	-0.0181	-0.0198	-0.0014	0.0166	-0.0009	-0.0089	0.0226	0.0328	0.0244	-0.0186	1996	-0.0186
1997	-0.0059	-0.0003	-0.0245	0.0171	0.0134	0.0174	0.0515	-0.0258	0.0201	0.0166	0.0107	0.0176	1997	0.1106
1998	0.0118	-0.0026	0.0019	0.0034	0.0148	0.0103	-0.0068	0.0077	0.0400	-0.0214	0.0270	0.0017	1998	0.0900

* Compound annual return

Table A-23 **Long-Term Government Bonds: Inflation-Adjusted Total Returns**

From January 1926 to December 1970

YEAR	JAN	FEB	MAR	APR	MAY	JUN	JUL	AUG	SEP	OCT	NOV	DEC	YEAR	JAN–DEC*
1926	0.0138	0.0101	0.0098	-0.0018	0.0070	0.0114	0.0100	0.0058	-0.0020	0.0063	0.0122	0.0078	1926	0.0940
1927	0.0151	0.0165	0.0313	-0.0005	0.0031	-0.0163	0.0244	0.0135	-0.0040	0.0040	0.0117	0.0091	1927	0.1124
1928	-0.0017	0.0159	0.0045	-0.0023	-0.0135	0.0120	-0.0217	0.0057	-0.0118	0.0177	0.0023	0.0043	1928	0.0108
1929	-0.0071	-0.0138	-0.0105	0.0316	-0.0220	0.0070	-0.0097	-0.0072	0.0047	0.0382	0.0256	-0.0031	1929	0.0322
1930	-0.0018	0.0169	0.0143	-0.0075	0.0199	0.0111	0.0176	0.0074	0.0013	0.0096	0.0124	0.0074	1930	0.1138
1931	0.0024	0.0236	0.0169	0.0151	0.0256	0.0114	-0.0020	0.0035	-0.0237	-0.0265	0.0141	-0.0130	1931	0.0466
1932	0.0245	0.0561	0.0029	0.0680	-0.0045	0.0139	0.0481	0.0127	0.0107	0.0058	0.0083	0.0234	1932	0.3026
1933	0.0306	-0.0105	0.0177	-0.0006	0.0275	-0.0056	-0.0297	-0.0057	0.0023	-0.0091	-0.0149	-0.0062	1933	-0.0058
1934	0.0205	0.0005	0.0197	0.0151	0.0106	0.0042	0.0040	-0.0143	-0.0291	0.0258	0.0062	0.0138	1934	0.0784
1935	0.0032	0.0018	0.0066	-0.0019	-0.0008	0.0117	0.0095	-0.0133	-0.0040	0.0061	-0.0039	0.0046	1935	0.0194
1936	0.0055	0.0130	0.0156	0.0035	0.0040	-0.0076	0.0012	0.0039	-0.0055	0.0030	0.0205	0.0038	1936	0.0623
1937	-0.0084	0.0063	-0.0479	-0.0008	0.0006	-0.0041	0.0091	-0.0127	-0.0047	0.0088	0.0166	0.0106	1937	-0.0278
1938	0.0199	0.0147	-0.0037	0.0162	0.0092	0.0004	0.0020	0.0024	0.0022	0.0135	0.0002	0.0056	1938	0.0855
1939	0.0107	0.0128	0.0149	0.0142	0.0171	-0.0027	0.0113	-0.0201	-0.0724	0.0459	0.0162	0.0193	1939	0.0645
1940	0.0007	-0.0045	0.0201	-0.0035	-0.0322	0.0234	0.0076	0.0052	0.0086	0.0031	0.0205	0.0019	1940	0.0508
1941	-0.0201	0.0020	0.0048	0.0035	-0.0042	-0.0118	-0.0024	-0.0072	-0.0188	0.0029	-0.0116	-0.0199	1941	-0.0801
1942	-0.0060	-0.0073	-0.0035	-0.0091	-0.0028	-0.0018	-0.0023	-0.0024	-0.0017	-0.0076	-0.0095	-0.0030	1942	-0.0555
1943	0.0033	-0.0025	-0.0146	-0.0068	-0.0026	0.0037	0.0076	0.0059	-0.0028	-0.0033	0.0019	-0.0001	1943	-0.0104
1944	0.0040	0.0051	0.0021	-0.0044	-0.0010	-0.0011	-0.0021	-0.0011	0.0014	0.0012	0.0024	0.0005	1944	0.0069
1945	0.0127	0.0096	0.0021	0.0141	-0.0019	0.0075	-0.0104	0.0026	0.0091	0.0104	0.0088	0.0157	1945	0.0830
1946	0.0025	0.0069	-0.0063	-0.0189	-0.0066	-0.0038	-0.0595	-0.0324	-0.0124	-0.0120	-0.0288	0.0066	1946	-0.1546
1947	-0.0006	0.0037	-0.0194	-0.0037	0.0064	-0.0066	-0.0028	-0.0024	-0.0275	-0.0037	-0.0231	-0.0318	1947	-0.1067
1948	-0.0093	0.0132	0.0063	-0.0096	0.0070	-0.0153	-0.0144	-0.0039	0.0014	0.0048	0.0145	0.0126	1948	0.0067
1949	0.0096	0.0162	0.0046	-0.0003	0.0033	0.0153	0.0104	0.0083	-0.0053	0.0075	0.0007	0.0109	1949	0.0840
1950	-0.0019	0.0050	-0.0034	0.0016	-0.0009	-0.0081	-0.0042	-0.0069	-0.0140	-0.0102	-0.0006	-0.0117	1950	-0.0542
1951	-0.0101	-0.0190	-0.0195	-0.0075	-0.0107	-0.0049	0.0125	0.0099	-0.0143	-0.0041	-0.0186	-0.0098	1951	-0.0926
1952	0.0028	0.0077	0.0111	0.0132	-0.0046	-0.0022	-0.0094	-0.0082	-0.0118	0.0135	-0.0015	-0.0073	1952	0.0027
1953	0.0037	-0.0037	-0.0113	-0.0118	-0.0172	0.0184	0.0014	-0.0032	0.0287	0.0049	-0.0012	0.0219	1953	0.0299
1954	0.0064	0.0252	0.0071	0.0129	-0.0124	0.0150	0.0134	-0.0024	0.0015	0.0031	-0.0037	0.0089	1954	0.0772
1955	-0.0241	-0.0078	0.0087	0.0001	0.0073	-0.0076	-0.0139	0.0029	0.0035	0.0144	-0.0057	0.0062	1955	-0.0166
1956	0.0096	-0.0002	-0.0161	-0.0125	0.0175	-0.0034	-0.0280	-0.0175	0.0037	-0.0115	-0.0057	-0.0202	1956	-0.0821
1957	0.0333	-0.0011	-0.0048	-0.0257	-0.0047	-0.0239	-0.0088	-0.0010	0.0064	-0.0050	0.0496	0.0307	1957	0.0431
1958	-0.0142	0.0089	0.0032	0.0163	0.0001	-0.0171	-0.0289	-0.0424	-0.0117	0.0138	0.0109	-0.0169	1958	-0.0772
1959	-0.0092	0.0129	0.0017	-0.0128	-0.0017	-0.0035	0.0037	-0.0030	-0.0091	0.0116	-0.0119	-0.0159	1959	-0.0370
1960	0.0123	0.0192	0.0282	-0.0225	0.0152	0.0150	0.0368	-0.0067	0.0064	-0.0073	-0.0077	0.0279	1960	0.1212
1961	-0.0107	0.0200	-0.0037	0.0115	-0.0046	-0.0086	-0.0010	-0.0027	0.0107	0.0071	-0.0020	-0.0125	1961	0.0030
1962	-0.0014	0.0081	0.0231	0.0060	0.0046	-0.0076	-0.0131	0.0187	0.0006	0.0095	0.0021	0.0046	1962	0.0559
1963	-0.0012	-0.0003	-0.0002	-0.0012	0.0023	-0.0024	-0.0013	0.0021	0.0004	-0.0037	0.0040	-0.0028	1963	-0.0043
1964	-0.0024	0.0000	0.0026	0.0036	0.0050	0.0047	-0.0014	0.0031	0.0028	0.0032	-0.0005	0.0019	1964	0.0229
1965	0.0040	0.0014	0.0043	0.0004	-0.0004	-0.0006	0.0011	0.0008	-0.0055	0.0017	-0.0083	-0.0109	1965	-0.0119
1966	-0.0104	-0.0311	0.0264	-0.0104	-0.0070	-0.0047	-0.0068	-0.0256	0.0311	0.0187	-0.0148	0.0403	1966	0.0029
1967	0.0154	-0.0231	0.0177	-0.0311	-0.0069	-0.0341	0.0018	-0.0114	-0.0024	-0.0428	-0.0226	0.0162	1967	-0.1186
1968	0.0287	-0.0062	-0.0259	0.0197	0.0014	0.0171	0.0240	-0.0032	-0.0131	-0.0188	-0.0306	-0.0390	1968	-0.0476
1969	-0.0233	0.0004	-0.0073	0.0359	-0.0516	0.0149	0.0034	-0.0114	-0.0574	0.0328	-0.0296	-0.0130	1969	-0.1054
1970	-0.0057	0.0531	-0.0120	-0.0471	-0.0510	0.0432	0.0284	-0.0036	0.0176	-0.0159	0.0755	-0.0134	1970	0.0627

* Compound annual return

Table A-23 **Long-Term Government Bonds: Inflation-Adjusted Total Returns**

(continued)

From January 1971 to December 1998

YEAR	JAN	FEB	MAR	APR	MAY	JUN	JUL	AUG	SEP	OCT	NOV	DEC	YEAR	JAN–DEC*
1971	0.0497	-0.0180	0.0491	-0.0315	-0.0056	-0.0215	0.0005	0.0445	0.0195	0.0150	-0.0063	0.0003	1971	0.0955
1972	-0.0072	0.0039	-0.0098	0.0003	0.0237	-0.0088	0.0175	0.0013	-0.0122	0.0202	0.0202	-0.0260	1972	0.0220
1973	-0.0351	-0.0056	-0.0011	-0.0024	-0.0165	-0.0089	-0.0455	0.0207	0.0287	0.0133	-0.0254	-0.0147	1973	-0.0910
1974	-0.0168	-0.0151	-0.0400	-0.0307	0.0011	-0.0051	-0.0103	-0.0356	0.0126	0.0400	0.0209	0.0099	1974	-0.0699
1975	0.0179	0.0061	-0.0304	-0.0231	0.0167	0.0209	-0.0191	-0.0099	-0.0147	0.0411	-0.0169	0.0347	1975	0.0204
1976	0.0066	0.0037	0.0141	-0.0023	-0.0216	0.0154	0.0019	0.0164	0.0104	0.0043	0.0309	0.0298	1976	0.1140
1977	-0.0443	-0.0150	0.0029	-0.0008	0.0069	0.0097	-0.0114	0.0159	-0.0066	-0.0120	0.0044	-0.0205	1977	-0.0699
1978	-0.0133	-0.0065	-0.0089	-0.0094	-0.0156	-0.0164	0.0071	0.0166	-0.0175	-0.0278	0.0133	-0.0184	1978	-0.0936
1979	0.0102	-0.0249	0.0032	-0.0224	0.0137	0.0216	-0.0212	-0.0134	-0.0224	-0.0922	0.0216	-0.0048	1979	-0.1283
1980	-0.0872	-0.0596	-0.0452	0.1395	0.0317	0.0246	-0.0484	-0.0493	-0.0351	-0.0347	0.0009	0.0263	1980	-0.1454
1981	-0.0195	-0.0534	0.0310	-0.0578	0.0535	-0.0263	-0.0462	-0.0459	-0.0244	0.0806	0.1378	-0.0739	1981	-0.0650
1982	0.0010	0.0150	0.0242	0.0330	-0.0064	-0.0341	0.0444	0.0759	0.0600	0.0605	0.0015	0.0354	1982	0.3513
1983	-0.0332	0.0488	-0.0101	0.0276	-0.0438	0.0005	-0.0525	-0.0013	0.0452	-0.0158	0.0167	-0.0072	1983	-0.0303
1984	0.0187	-0.0223	-0.0179	-0.0154	-0.0544	0.0117	0.0659	0.0224	0.0293	0.0534	0.0118	0.0084	1984	0.1108
1985	0.0344	-0.0532	0.0262	0.0201	0.0855	0.0110	-0.0195	0.0237	-0.0052	0.0306	0.0366	0.0515	1985	0.2621
1986	-0.0056	0.1176	0.0819	-0.0059	-0.0534	0.0562	-0.0111	0.0480	-0.0546	0.0280	0.0258	-0.0027	1986	0.2314
1987	0.0100	0.0162	-0.0266	-0.0524	-0.0135	0.0056	-0.0198	-0.0219	-0.0416	0.0595	0.0022	0.0168	1987	-0.0682
1988	0.0639	0.0026	-0.0348	-0.0210	-0.0135	0.0324	-0.0211	0.0016	0.0276	0.0273	-0.0204	0.0093	1988	0.0503
1989	0.0153	-0.0220	0.0064	0.0093	0.0342	0.0525	0.0213	-0.0274	-0.0013	0.0330	0.0054	-0.0022	1989	0.1287
1990	-0.0441	-0.0071	-0.0098	-0.0217	0.0391	0.0175	0.0068	-0.0506	0.0033	0.0154	0.0379	0.0187	1990	0.0007
1991	0.0070	0.0016	0.0023	0.0125	-0.0029	-0.0092	0.0143	0.0310	0.0258	0.0040	0.0053	0.0573	1991	0.1575
1992	-0.0338	0.0015	-0.0143	0.0002	0.0228	0.0164	0.0376	0.0038	0.0157	-0.0233	-0.0004	0.0253	1992	0.0501
1993	0.0230	0.0318	-0.0014	0.0044	0.0033	0.0434	0.0191	0.0405	-0.0015	0.0055	-0.0265	0.0020	1993	0.1508
1994	0.0229	-0.0482	-0.0428	-0.0164	-0.0089	-0.0134	0.0335	-0.0126	-0.0357	-0.0031	0.0053	0.0161	1994	-0.1017
1995	0.0232	0.0246	0.0058	0.0136	0.0769	0.0119	-0.0168	0.0209	0.0155	0.0261	0.0256	0.0279	1995	0.2841
1996	-0.0069	-0.0513	-0.0260	-0.0203	-0.0073	0.0196	-0.0002	-0.0158	0.0257	0.0371	0.0331	-0.0256	1996	-0.0412
1997	-0.0110	-0.0026	-0.0276	0.0242	0.0103	0.0182	0.0612	-0.0336	0.0290	0.0315	0.0154	0.0197	1997	0.1391
1998	0.0181	-0.0090	0.0006	0.0008	0.0164	0.0216	-0.0052	0.0452	0.0382	-0.0242	0.0097	-0.0026	1998	0.1127

* Compound annual return

Table A-24 Intermediate-Term Government Bonds: Inflation-Adjusted Total Returns

From January 1926 to December 1970

YEAR	JAN	FEB	MAR	APR	MAY	JUN	JUL	AUG	SEP	OCT	NOV	DEC	YEAR	JAN–DEC*
1926	0.0068	0.0069	0.0097	-0.0004	0.0065	0.0102	0.0109	0.0067	-0.0008	0.0016	0.0007	0.0089	1926	0.0697
1927	0.0133	0.0115	0.0096	0.0016	-0.0056	-0.0066	0.0237	0.0115	0.0002	-0.0092	0.0103	0.0057	1927	0.0674
1928	0.0066	0.0094	0.0010	-0.0022	-0.0065	0.0095	-0.0089	0.0031	-0.0050	0.0052	0.0038	0.0032	1928	0.0190
1929	-0.0009	0.0001	0.0044	0.0128	-0.0120	0.0067	-0.0031	0.0014	0.0005	0.0168	0.0200	0.0102	1929	0.0581
1930	-0.0002	0.0133	0.0221	-0.0129	0.0120	0.0202	0.0196	0.0083	0.0002	0.0137	0.0153	0.0169	1930	0.1356
1931	0.0075	0.0249	0.0117	0.0149	0.0230	-0.0106	0.0039	0.0039	-0.0069	-0.0039	0.0163	-0.0069	1931	0.0796
1932	0.0178	0.0272	0.0126	0.0267	0.0055	0.0182	0.0120	0.0249	0.0077	0.0121	0.0082	0.0221	1932	0.2130
1933	0.0140	0.0157	0.0179	0.0084	0.0172	-0.0097	-0.0286	-0.0029	0.0026	-0.0025	0.0027	-0.0204	1933	0.0131
1934	0.0078	-0.0023	0.0189	0.0208	0.0094	0.0065	-0.0024	-0.0117	-0.0283	0.0265	0.0071	0.0150	1934	0.0683
1935	-0.0034	0.0031	0.0150	0.0009	0.0014	0.0138	0.0087	-0.0071	-0.0105	0.0109	-0.0035	0.0096	1935	0.0391
1936	-0.0003	0.0118	0.0080	0.0024	0.0038	-0.0085	-0.0026	-0.0022	-0.0014	0.0049	0.0081	-0.0057	1936	0.0183
1937	-0.0102	-0.0017	-0.0233	0.0000	0.0033	-0.0036	0.0012	-0.0066	-0.0011	0.0078	0.0111	0.0085	1937	-0.0150
1938	0.0227	0.0147	-0.0012	0.0182	0.0070	0.0075	-0.0013	0.0038	-0.0013	0.0142	0.0023	0.0028	1938	0.0927
1939	0.0077	0.0131	0.0105	0.0063	0.0095	0.0002	0.0040	-0.0147	-0.0447	0.0364	0.0074	0.0156	1939	0.0502
1940	0.0010	-0.0036	0.0112	0.0002	-0.0237	0.0162	0.0027	0.0067	0.0024	0.0036	0.0056	-0.0020	1940	0.0199
1941	0.0001	-0.0047	0.0021	-0.0060	-0.0058	-0.0127	-0.0045	-0.0079	-0.0176	-0.0087	-0.0177	-0.0038	1941	-0.0840
1942	-0.0055	-0.0069	-0.0102	-0.0040	-0.0087	-0.0008	-0.0041	-0.0044	-0.0043	-0.0083	-0.0043	-0.0079	1942	-0.0673
1943	0.0039	-0.0006	-0.0134	-0.0092	-0.0020	0.0053	0.0098	0.0041	-0.0024	-0.0021	0.0034	0.0001	1943	-0.0034
1944	0.0030	0.0035	0.0019	-0.0030	-0.0033	-0.0012	-0.0028	-0.0014	0.0011	0.0011	0.0009	-0.0027	1944	-0.0031
1945	0.0052	0.0057	0.0004	-0.0004	-0.0063	-0.0074	-0.0019	0.0016	0.0054	0.0016	-0.0027	-0.0015	1945	-0.0003
1946	0.0039	0.0085	-0.0111	-0.0074	-0.0048	-0.0075	-0.0567	-0.0211	-0.0125	-0.0167	-0.0243	-0.0046	1946	-0.1452
1947	0.0023	0.0021	-0.0190	-0.0013	0.0038	-0.0068	-0.0084	-0.0078	-0.0232	-0.0023	-0.0052	-0.0108	1947	-0.0743
1948	-0.0098	0.0104	0.0046	-0.0122	-0.0017	-0.0078	-0.0125	-0.0045	0.0010	0.0054	0.0090	0.0102	1948	-0.0084
1949	0.0042	0.0124	-0.0003	0.0001	0.0037	0.0036	0.0091	0.0002	-0.0034	0.0062	-0.0012	0.0069	1949	0.0420
1950	0.0038	0.0036	-0.0042	-0.0006	-0.0022	-0.0053	-0.0077	-0.0090	-0.0072	-0.0053	-0.0023	-0.0125	1950	-0.0481
1951	-0.0136	-0.0110	-0.0165	0.0044	-0.0079	0.0063	0.0045	0.0036	-0.0120	-0.0035	-0.0018	-0.0054	1951	-0.0521
1952	0.0038	0.0043	0.0067	0.0016	0.0007	-0.0060	-0.0109	-0.0036	0.0031	0.0054	-0.0006	0.0032	1952	0.0074
1953	0.0023	0.0053	-0.0042	-0.0109	-0.0141	0.0117	0.0030	-0.0033	0.0181	0.0013	0.0051	0.0116	1953	0.0259
1954	0.0040	0.0113	0.0039	0.0068	-0.0110	0.0112	-0.0005	0.0023	0.0005	0.0016	-0.0013	0.0030	1954	0.0320
1955	-0.0032	-0.0052	0.0024	0.0004	0.0001	-0.0036	-0.0108	0.0032	0.0044	0.0072	-0.0066	0.0014	1955	-0.0102
1956	0.0118	0.0003	-0.0113	-0.0014	0.0062	-0.0059	-0.0167	-0.0091	0.0079	-0.0080	-0.0047	-0.0013	1956	-0.0319
1957	0.0225	-0.0049	-0.0006	-0.0137	-0.0041	-0.0165	-0.0062	0.0097	-0.0009	0.0043	0.0359	0.0215	1957	0.0467
1958	-0.0025	0.0127	-0.0017	0.0029	0.0060	-0.0079	-0.0102	-0.0345	-0.0017	0.0002	0.0121	-0.0050	1958	-0.0300
1959	-0.0025	0.0119	-0.0037	-0.0064	-0.0013	-0.0122	0.0011	-0.0067	-0.0015	0.0139	-0.0092	-0.0020	1959	-0.0186
1960	0.0166	0.0060	0.0292	-0.0120	0.0031	0.0194	0.0267	-0.0004	0.0017	-0.0029	-0.0105	0.0210	1960	0.1013
1961	-0.0059	0.0090	0.0037	0.0054	-0.0028	-0.0037	-0.0038	0.0030	0.0056	0.0014	-0.0019	0.0018	1961	0.0117
1962	-0.0045	0.0132	0.0067	0.0002	0.0049	-0.0028	-0.0034	0.0125	-0.0034	0.0062	0.0060	0.0067	1962	0.0429
1963	-0.0040	0.0006	0.0016	0.0030	0.0014	-0.0030	-0.0040	0.0019	0.0014	0.0000	0.0029	-0.0019	1963	-0.0001
1964	0.0022	0.0022	0.0006	0.0022	0.0081	0.0014	0.0006	0.0038	0.0024	0.0022	-0.0025	0.0047	1964	0.0282
1965	0.0042	0.0018	0.0032	-0.0006	0.0014	-0.0004	0.0007	0.0040	-0.0026	-0.0010	-0.0014	-0.0180	1965	-0.0089
1966	0.0003	-0.0145	0.0155	-0.0060	0.0000	-0.0055	-0.0056	-0.0175	0.0195	0.0034	0.0027	0.0212	1966	0.0129
1967	0.0118	-0.0023	0.0163	-0.0109	0.0013	-0.0256	0.0083	-0.0065	-0.0013	-0.0078	-0.0002	-0.0023	1967	-0.0197
1968	0.0106	0.0011	-0.0075	-0.0045	0.0034	0.0108	0.0128	-0.0008	0.0027	-0.0048	-0.0050	-0.0201	1968	-0.0018
1969	0.0058	-0.0051	0.0013	0.0014	-0.0109	-0.0147	0.0037	-0.0063	-0.0344	0.0296	-0.0101	-0.0253	1969	-0.0645
1970	-0.0005	0.0384	0.0035	-0.0267	0.0067	0.0009	0.0117	0.0099	0.0144	0.0043	0.0416	0.0003	1970	0.1078

* Compound annual return

Table A-24

Intermediate-Term Government Bonds: Inflation-Adjusted Total Returns

(continued)

From January 1971 to December 1998

YEAR	JAN	FEB	MAR	APR	MAY	JUN	JUL	AUG	SEP	OCT	NOV	DEC	YEAR	JAN–DEC*
1971	0.0160	0.0207	0.0152	-0.0359	-0.0039	-0.0244	0.0002	0.0325	0.0017	0.0203	0.0036	0.0069	1971	0.0519
1972	0.0097	-0.0034	-0.0002	-0.0010	-0.0016	0.0020	-0.0025	-0.0001	-0.0026	-0.0016	0.0021	0.0160	1972	0.0169
1973	-0.0038	-0.0145	-0.0047	-0.0006	-0.0004	-0.0074	-0.0298	0.0072	0.0220	-0.0031	-0.0009	-0.0025	1973	-0.0385
1974	-0.0077	-0.0092	-0.0321	-0.0207	0.0019	-0.0182	-0.0067	-0.0138	0.0196	0.0023	0.0150	0.0112	1974	-0.0580
1975	0.0008	0.0077	-0.0097	-0.0235	0.0215	-0.0054	-0.0135	-0.0039	-0.0039	0.0303	-0.0070	0.0155	1975	0.0076
1976	0.0032	0.0059	0.0051	0.0074	-0.0203	0.0105	0.0060	0.0141	0.0035	0.0106	0.0292	-0.0003	1976	0.0769
1977	-0.0246	-0.0054	-0.0007	-0.0027	0.0001	0.0036	-0.0043	-0.0031	-0.0023	-0.0087	0.0030	-0.0061	1977	-0.0502
1978	-0.0041	-0.0052	-0.0032	-0.0065	-0.0100	-0.0123	0.0027	0.0028	-0.0013	-0.0191	0.0037	0.0009	1978	-0.0508
1979	-0.0034	-0.0174	0.0016	-0.0081	0.0069	0.0110	-0.0139	-0.0189	-0.0097	-0.0553	0.0268	-0.0018	1979	-0.0813
1980	-0.0274	-0.0768	-0.0001	0.1074	0.0387	-0.0185	-0.0114	-0.0449	-0.0129	-0.0238	-0.0061	0.0085	1980	-0.0755
1981	-0.0049	-0.0335	0.0190	-0.0278	0.0161	-0.0026	-0.0380	-0.0252	0.0062	0.0588	0.0594	-0.0170	1981	0.0047
1982	0.0014	0.0116	0.0053	0.0255	0.0047	-0.0254	0.0406	0.0447	0.0307	0.0502	0.0097	0.0227	1982	0.2428
1983	-0.0017	0.0249	-0.0055	0.0186	-0.0175	-0.0017	-0.0238	0.0047	0.0263	-0.0008	0.0086	0.0034	1983	0.0348
1984	0.0121	-0.0110	-0.0057	-0.0052	-0.0278	0.0066	0.0359	0.0059	0.0153	0.0357	0.0192	0.0137	1984	0.0968
1985	0.0187	-0.0220	0.0122	0.0222	0.0445	0.0077	-0.0061	0.0126	0.0081	0.0131	0.0161	0.0232	1985	0.1596
1986	0.0052	0.0303	0.0386	0.0103	-0.0245	0.0226	0.0154	0.0247	-0.0158	0.0153	0.0103	-0.0002	1986	0.1385
1987	0.0046	0.0020	-0.0076	-0.0296	-0.0067	0.0081	0.0005	-0.0093	-0.0189	0.0272	0.0068	0.0096	1987	-0.0144
1988	0.0289	0.0096	-0.0129	-0.0095	-0.0083	0.0138	-0.0089	-0.0051	0.0127	0.0115	-0.0123	-0.0026	1988	0.0161
1989	0.0071	-0.0092	-0.0008	0.0154	0.0155	0.0299	0.0210	-0.0261	0.0037	0.0188	0.0060	-0.0004	1989	0.0826
1990	-0.0205	-0.0040	-0.0052	-0.0092	0.0238	0.0096	0.0135	-0.0182	0.0010	0.0110	0.0170	0.0161	1990	0.0342
1991	0.0046	0.0033	0.0008	0.0102	0.0030	-0.0052	0.0115	0.0217	0.0171	0.0119	0.0099	0.0258	1991	0.1203
1992	-0.0209	-0.0014	-0.0129	0.0083	0.0207	0.0140	0.0220	0.0121	0.0165	-0.0216	-0.0098	0.0153	1992	0.0417
1993	0.0220	0.0207	0.0008	0.0060	-0.0023	0.0187	0.0005	0.0194	0.0035	-0.0024	-0.0100	0.0032	1993	0.0826
1994	0.0110	-0.0291	-0.0291	-0.0119	-0.0009	-0.0062	0.0142	-0.0015	-0.0185	-0.0030	-0.0083	0.0053	1994	-0.0762
1995	0.0141	0.0194	0.0029	0.0110	0.0348	0.0060	-0.0016	0.0060	0.0044	0.0088	0.0155	0.0101	1995	0.1391
1996	-0.0052	-0.0169	-0.0169	-0.0088	-0.0051	0.0111	0.0005	-0.0024	0.0123	0.0150	0.0130	-0.0078	1996	-0.0118
1997	-0.0007	-0.0029	-0.0139	0.0135	0.0085	0.0089	0.0251	-0.0116	0.0126	0.0125	0.0005	0.0119	1997	0.0657
1998	0.0161	-0.0057	0.0007	0.0043	0.0051	0.0066	0.0014	0.0258	0.0317	0.0016	-0.0098	0.0043	1998	0.0846

* Compound annual return

Table A-25

U.S. Treasury Bills: Inflation-Adjusted Total Returns

From January 1926 to December 1970

YEAR	JAN	FEB	MAR	APR	MAY	JUN	JUL	AUG	SEP	OCT	NOV	DEC	YEAR	JAN–DEC*
1926	0.0034	0.0064	0.0086	-0.0059	0.0057	0.0110	0.0118	0.0083	-0.0035	-0.0006	-0.0007	0.0028	1926	0.0483
1927	0.0101	0.0103	0.0088	0.0025	-0.0047	-0.0069	0.0224	0.0086	-0.0037	-0.0033	0.0040	0.0042	1927	0.0531
1928	0.0045	0.0131	0.0029	0.0003	-0.0026	0.0110	0.0032	0.0013	-0.0051	0.0060	0.0058	0.0045	1928	0.0457
1929	0.0054	0.0055	0.0074	0.0075	-0.0015	0.0013	-0.0064	0.0002	0.0055	0.0046	0.0057	0.0095	1929	0.0454
1930	0.0053	0.0069	0.0094	-0.0038	0.0085	0.0087	0.0161	0.0070	-0.0039	0.0069	0.0095	0.0159	1930	0.0898
1931	0.0162	0.0153	0.0077	0.0072	0.0118	0.0118	0.0028	0.0026	0.0047	0.0078	0.0130	0.0104	1931	0.1171
1932	0.0234	0.0166	0.0064	0.0083	0.0152	0.0076	0.0003	0.0127	0.0053	0.0077	0.0052	0.0103	1932	0.1255
1933	0.0157	0.0155	0.0084	0.0036	-0.0022	-0.0103	-0.0279	-0.0098	0.0002	0.0001	0.0002	0.0053	1933	-0.0021
1934	-0.0046	-0.0073	0.0002	0.0026	-0.0024	-0.0024	0.0001	-0.0024	-0.0147	0.0075	0.0026	0.0026	1934	-0.0183
1935	-0.0146	-0.0071	0.0026	-0.0095	0.0050	0.0026	0.0050	0.0001	-0.0047	0.0001	-0.0046	-0.0023	1935	-0.0273
1936	0.0001	0.0050	0.0051	0.0002	0.0002	-0.0094	-0.0047	-0.0070	-0.0023	0.0026	0.0001	0.0000	1936	-0.0102
1937	-0.0070	-0.0022	-0.0069	-0.0043	-0.0040	-0.0020	-0.0043	-0.0021	-0.0088	0.0048	0.0071	0.0024	1937	-0.0271
1938	0.0141	0.0095	-0.0001	-0.0046	0.0048	0.0000	-0.0024	0.0024	0.0002	0.0049	0.0018	-0.0024	1938	0.0284
1939	0.0047	0.0049	0.0023	0.0024	0.0001	0.0001	0.0000	-0.0001	-0.0189	0.0048	0.0000	0.0048	1939	0.0050
1940	0.0024	-0.0071	0.0024	0.0000	-0.0025	-0.0023	0.0025	0.0023	-0.0024	0.0000	0.0000	-0.0047	1940	-0.0094
1941	-0.0001	-0.0001	-0.0046	-0.0094	-0.0069	-0.0182	-0.0042	-0.0089	-0.0176	-0.0109	-0.0086	-0.0021	1941	-0.0880
1942	-0.0126	-0.0083	-0.0124	-0.0062	-0.0100	-0.0018	-0.0038	-0.0058	-0.0017	-0.0097	-0.0057	-0.0076	1942	-0.0825
1943	0.0003	-0.0017	-0.0152	-0.0112	-0.0074	0.0022	0.0080	0.0042	-0.0036	-0.0035	0.0022	-0.0016	1943	-0.0273
1944	0.0022	0.0022	0.0002	-0.0055	-0.0036	-0.0016	-0.0054	-0.0035	0.0002	0.0003	0.0003	-0.0035	1944	-0.0174
1945	0.0003	0.0021	0.0002	-0.0016	-0.0072	-0.0090	-0.0015	0.0003	0.0040	0.0003	-0.0034	-0.0034	1945	-0.0188
1946	0.0003	0.0040	-0.0070	-0.0052	-0.0051	-0.0105	-0.0554	-0.0212	-0.0111	-0.0189	-0.0232	-0.0075	1946	-0.1507
1947	0.0003	0.0018	-0.0210	0.0003	0.0033	-0.0073	-0.0087	-0.0101	-0.0226	0.0006	-0.0052	-0.0120	1947	-0.0780
1948	-0.0105	0.0093	0.0037	-0.0132	-0.0062	-0.0060	-0.0115	-0.0032	0.0004	0.0045	0.0073	0.0074	1948	-0.0185
1949	0.0023	0.0121	-0.0018	-0.0005	0.0024	-0.0004	0.0079	-0.0019	-0.0033	0.0065	-0.0006	0.0065	1949	0.0296
1950	0.0052	0.0037	-0.0033	-0.0006	-0.0032	-0.0046	-0.0087	-0.0073	-0.0058	-0.0043	-0.0030	-0.0123	1950	-0.0434
1951	-0.0145	-0.0107	-0.0028	0.0000	-0.0026	0.0025	0.0001	0.0013	-0.0052	-0.0035	-0.0040	-0.0026	1951	-0.0414
1952	0.0015	0.0075	0.0011	-0.0026	0.0000	-0.0010	-0.0060	0.0002	0.0029	0.0001	0.0010	0.0029	1952	0.0077
1953	0.0041	0.0064	-0.0007	0.0004	-0.0008	-0.0019	-0.0010	-0.0008	0.0004	-0.0012	0.0045	0.0025	1953	0.0119
1954	-0.0014	0.0019	0.0020	0.0034	-0.0032	-0.0007	0.0005	0.0017	0.0034	0.0032	-0.0006	0.0033	1954	0.0137
1955	0.0008	0.0009	0.0010	0.0010	0.0014	0.0010	-0.0027	0.0041	-0.0021	0.0018	0.0005	0.0043	1955	0.0119
1956	0.0035	0.0019	0.0003	0.0006	-0.0027	-0.0042	-0.0052	0.0029	0.0006	-0.0036	0.0020	0.0000	1956	-0.0039
1957	0.0015	-0.0012	-0.0001	-0.0011	0.0002	-0.0035	-0.0018	0.0013	0.0014	0.0029	-0.0008	0.0024	1957	0.0011
1958	-0.0031	0.0000	-0.0060	-0.0015	0.0011	-0.0009	-0.0005	0.0016	0.0019	0.0018	-0.0001	0.0034	1958	-0.0022
1959	0.0009	0.0030	0.0022	0.0008	0.0010	-0.0021	0.0002	0.0030	-0.0003	-0.0004	0.0026	0.0034	1959	0.0143
1960	0.0045	0.0017	0.0035	-0.0037	0.0027	0.0001	0.0013	0.0017	0.0005	-0.0023	0.0002	0.0016	1960	0.0117
1961	0.0019	0.0014	0.0020	0.0017	0.0018	0.0009	-0.0026	0.0025	-0.0006	0.0019	0.0015	0.0019	1961	0.0144
1962	0.0024	-0.0002	-0.0002	0.0000	0.0024	0.0020	0.0005	0.0023	-0.0034	0.0037	0.0020	0.0034	1962	0.0149
1963	0.0014	0.0012	0.0012	0.0025	0.0024	-0.0021	-0.0017	0.0025	0.0027	0.0018	0.0016	0.0008	1963	0.0144
1964	0.0019	0.0037	0.0020	0.0018	0.0026	0.0009	0.0008	0.0039	0.0006	0.0019	0.0008	0.0020	1964	0.0232
1965	0.0028	0.0030	0.0025	-0.0001	0.0010	-0.0018	0.0020	0.0054	0.0010	0.0021	0.0014	0.0002	1965	0.0197
1966	0.0038	-0.0028	0.0007	-0.0007	0.0031	0.0007	0.0005	-0.0010	0.0020	0.0005	0.0040	0.0030	1966	0.0136
1967	0.0043	0.0026	0.0019	0.0012	0.0003	-0.0004	-0.0019	0.0001	0.0012	0.0010	0.0006	0.0004	1967	0.0113
1968	0.0001	0.0009	-0.0011	0.0014	0.0015	-0.0015	0.0000	0.0013	0.0014	-0.0013	0.0005	0.0014	1968	0.0046
1969	0.0024	0.0009	-0.0037	-0.0011	0.0021	-0.0013	0.0008	0.0005	0.0017	0.0024	-0.0002	0.0002	1969	0.0045
1970	0.0025	0.0009	0.0004	-0.0011	0.0009	0.0006	0.0018	0.0036	0.0002	-0.0005	0.0012	-0.0008	1970	0.0098

* Compound annual return

Table A-25 **U.S. Treasury Bills: Inflation-Adjusted Total Returns**

(continued)

From January 1971 to December 1998

YEAR	JAN	FEB	MAR	APR	MAY	JUN	JUL	AUG	SEP	OCT	NOV	DEC	YEAR	JAN–DEC*
1971	0.0030	0.0016	-0.0004	-0.0006	-0.0020	-0.0020	0.0015	0.0022	0.0029	0.0020	0.0021	-0.0004	1971	0.0099
1972	0.0021	-0.0024	0.0011	0.0005	-0.0002	0.0005	-0.0009	0.0013	-0.0006	0.0008	0.0013	0.0006	1972	0.0041
1973	0.0012	-0.0029	-0.0047	-0.0017	-0.0010	-0.0017	0.0041	-0.0109	0.0038	-0.0016	-0.0017	-0.0002	1973	-0.0172
1974	-0.0024	-0.0070	-0.0057	0.0019	-0.0035	-0.0036	-0.0004	-0.0068	-0.0039	-0.0035	-0.0031	-0.0002	1974	-0.0374
1975	0.0013	-0.0027	0.0003	-0.0007	-0.0001	-0.0040	-0.0057	0.0017	0.0004	-0.0006	-0.0020	0.0006	1975	-0.0113
1976	0.0023	0.0010	0.0016	0.0000	-0.0022	-0.0010	-0.0012	-0.0005	0.0003	0.0000	0.0011	0.0012	1976	0.0026
1977	-0.0021	-0.0067	-0.0024	-0.0041	-0.0018	-0.0026	-0.0002	0.0006	0.0005	0.0022	0.0001	0.0011	1977	-0.0155
1978	-0.0005	-0.0023	-0.0016	-0.0036	-0.0048	-0.0049	-0.0016	0.0005	-0.0009	-0.0012	0.0015	0.0024	1978	-0.0169
1979	-0.0011	-0.0043	-0.0015	-0.0035	-0.0041	-0.0012	-0.0052	-0.0024	-0.0021	-0.0002	0.0005	-0.0010	1979	-0.0259
1980	-0.0063	-0.0048	-0.0023	0.0013	-0.0018	-0.0049	0.0045	-0.0001	-0.0017	0.0008	0.0005	0.0044	1980	-0.0103
1981	0.0022	0.0003	0.0048	0.0043	0.0033	0.0049	0.0010	0.0051	0.0023	0.0099	0.0078	0.0059	1981	0.0530
1982	0.0044	0.0060	0.0109	0.0070	0.0007	-0.0026	0.0050	0.0056	0.0034	0.0032	0.0081	0.0109	1982	0.0642
1983	0.0045	0.0058	0.0056	0.0000	0.0015	0.0033	0.0034	0.0043	0.0026	0.0049	0.0054	0.0059	1983	0.0482
1984	0.0020	0.0025	0.0050	0.0032	0.0049	0.0043	0.0050	0.0041	0.0038	0.0074	0.0073	0.0058	1984	0.0567
1985	0.0046	0.0017	0.0017	0.0031	0.0029	0.0024	0.0047	0.0033	0.0029	0.0034	0.0027	0.0040	1985	0.0381
1986	0.0025	0.0081	0.0106	0.0074	0.0019	0.0003	0.0049	0.0028	-0.0004	0.0037	0.0030	0.0040	1986	0.0498
1987	-0.0019	0.0004	0.0002	-0.0009	0.0008	0.0007	0.0025	-0.0009	-0.0004	0.0034	0.0020	0.0042	1987	0.0101
1988	0.0003	0.0020	0.0001	-0.0005	0.0016	0.0006	0.0008	0.0017	-0.0006	0.0028	0.0048	0.0047	1988	0.0185
1989	0.0005	0.0020	0.0009	0.0002	0.0022	0.0047	0.0045	0.0058	0.0033	0.0020	0.0045	0.0045	1989	0.0356
1990	-0.0046	0.0010	0.0010	0.0053	0.0044	0.0008	0.0029	-0.0026	-0.0024	0.0008	0.0034	0.0060	1990	0.0161
1991	-0.0008	0.0033	0.0029	0.0038	0.0018	0.0012	0.0034	0.0017	0.0002	0.0028	0.0010	0.0031	1991	0.0246
1992	0.0019	-0.0008	-0.0017	0.0018	0.0013	-0.0004	0.0009	-0.0002	-0.0003	-0.0012	0.0009	0.0035	1992	0.0059
1993	-0.0026	-0.0013	-0.0010	-0.0004	0.0008	0.0011	0.0024	-0.0003	0.0005	-0.0019	0.0018	0.0023	1993	0.0014
1994	-0.0002	-0.0013	-0.0007	0.0014	0.0025	-0.0003	0.0000	-0.0004	0.0010	0.0032	0.0023	0.0044	1994	0.0120
1995	0.0001	0.0000	0.0013	0.0011	0.0034	0.0027	0.0045	0.0020	0.0023	0.0014	0.0049	0.0055	1995	0.0298
1996	-0.0016	0.0007	-0.0012	0.0007	0.0023	0.0034	0.0026	0.0022	0.0012	0.0011	0.0022	0.0046	1996	0.0182
1997	0.0013	0.0007	0.0018	0.0031	0.0056	0.0024	0.0030	0.0022	0.0019	0.0017	0.0045	0.0060	1997	0.0349
1998	0.0024	0.0020	0.0021	0.0024	0.0022	0.0029	0.0028	0.0031	0.0033	0.0008	0.0031	0.0044	1998	0.0319

* Compound annual return

STOCKS
BONDS
BILLS
AND
INFLATION

Appendix B: Cumulative Wealth Indices of Basic and Derived Series Returns

December 1925
to
December 1998

Appendix B Cumulative Wealth Indices of Basic and Inflation-Adjusted Series

Basic Series Indices

Inflation-Adjusted Indices

Table B-1 **Large Company Stocks: Total Return Index**

From December 1925 to December 1970

YEAR	JAN	FEB	MAR	APR	MAY	JUN	JUL	AUG	SEP	OCT	NOV	DEC	YR-END	INDEX
1925												1.000	1925	1.000
1926	1.000	0.962	0.906	0.929	0.946	0.989	1.036	1.062	1.089	1.058	1.095	1.116	1926	1.116
1927	1.095	1.154	1.164	1.187	1.259	1.251	1.334	1.403	1.466	1.393	1.493	1.535	1927	1.535
1928	1.529	1.509	1.676	1.733	1.768	1.700	1.724	1.862	1.910	1.942	2.193	2.204	1928	2.204
1929	2.332	2.328	2.325	2.366	2.280	2.540	2.660	2.933	2.794	2.243	1.963	2.018	1929	2.018
1930	2.147	2.203	2.382	2.363	2.340	1.960	2.035	2.064	1.800	1.646	1.631	1.516	1930	1.516
1931	1.592	1.782	1.662	1.506	1.314	1.500	1.392	1.418	0.996	1.085	0.999	0.859	1931	0.859
1932	0.836	0.883	0.781	0.625	0.488	0.487	0.672	0.933	0.900	0.779	0.746	0.789	1932	0.789
1933	0.795	0.654	0.678	0.966	1.129	1.280	1.169	1.310	1.164	1.064	1.184	1.214	1933	1.214
1934	1.344	1.301	1.301	1.268	1.175	1.202	1.066	1.131	1.127	1.095	1.198	1.197	1934	1.197
1935	1.148	1.109	1.077	1.182	1.231	1.317	1.429	1.469	1.507	1.624	1.700	1.767	1935	1.767
1936	1.886	1.928	1.980	1.831	1.931	1.995	2.135	2.167	2.174	2.342	2.374	2.367	1936	2.367
1937	2.459	2.506	2.487	2.286	2.280	2.165	2.391	2.276	1.957	1.765	1.612	1.538	1937	1.538
1938	1.561	1.666	1.252	1.433	1.386	1.733	1.862	1.820	1.850	1.993	1.939	2.016	1938	2.016
1939	1.881	1.954	1.692	1.688	1.811	1.701	1.889	1.766	2.062	2.036	1.955	2.008	1939	2.008
1940	1.941	1.966	1.991	1.986	1.531	1.655	1.712	1.772	1.793	1.869	1.810	1.812	1940	1.812
1941	1.728	1.718	1.730	1.624	1.653	1.749	1.850	1.852	1.839	1.718	1.670	1.602	1941	1.602
1942	1.627	1.602	1.497	1.437	1.552	1.586	1.640	1.666	1.715	1.831	1.827	1.927	1942	1.927
1943	2.070	2.190	2.310	2.318	2.446	2.500	2.368	2.409	2.472	2.446	2.286	2.427	1943	2.427
1944	2.468	2.479	2.527	2.502	2.628	2.771	2.717	2.760	2.758	2.764	2.801	2.906	1944	2.906
1945	2.952	3.154	3.015	3.287	3.351	3.349	3.288	3.499	3.652	3.770	3.919	3.965	1945	3.965
1946	4.248	3.976	4.167	4.330	4.455	4.290	4.188	3.906	3.516	3.495	3.486	3.645	1946	3.645
1947	3.738	3.709	3.654	3.521	3.526	3.721	3.863	3.785	3.743	3.832	3.765	3.853	1947	3.853
1948	3.707	3.563	3.846	3.958	4.305	4.329	4.109	4.174	4.059	4.347	3.929	4.065	1948	4.065
1949	4.081	3.960	4.090	4.017	3.913	3.919	4.174	4.265	4.377	4.526	4.605	4.829	1949	4.829
1950	4.924	5.022	5.057	5.303	5.573	5.267	5.330	5.566	5.895	5.949	6.050	6.360	1950	6.360
1951	6.765	6.871	6.764	7.109	6.896	6.739	7.218	7.563	7.573	7.495	7.567	7.888	1951	7.888
1952	8.030	7.804	8.197	7.867	8.137	8.536	8.703	8.642	8.490	8.507	8.993	9.336	1952	9.336
1953	9.291	9.192	8.997	8.783	8.851	8.732	8.971	8.521	8.551	9.012	9.196	9.244	1953	9.244
1954	9.739	9.848	10.168	10.693	11.139	11.173	11.831	11.506	12.485	12.277	13.393	14.108	1954	14.108
1955	14.387	14.528	14.485	15.059	15.142	16.416	17.437	17.393	17.618	17.118	18.533	18.561	1955	18.561
1956	17.917	18.657	19.982	19.973	18.788	19.557	20.594	19.919	19.043	19.169	19.072	19.778	1956	19.778
1957	18.986	18.485	18.882	19.614	20.472	20.481	20.749	19.701	18.516	17.957	18.372	17.646	1957	17.646
1958	18.431	18.170	18.767	19.400	19.810	20.363	21.277	21.651	22.735	23.348	24.012	25.298	1958	25.298
1959	25.430	25.554	25.605	26.635	27.273	27.213	28.199	27.911	26.674	27.017	27.519	28.322	1959	28.322
1960	26.340	26.729	26.400	25.976	26.821	27.388	26.748	27.596	25.968	25.949	27.154	28.455	1960	28.455
1961	30.291	31.257	32.100	32.262	33.033	32.125	33.223	34.029	33.404	34.401	35.940	36.106	1961	36.106
1962	34.784	35.511	35.349	33.204	30.512	28.061	29.891	30.512	29.092	29.279	32.459	32.954	1962	32.954
1963	34.620	33.794	35.045	36.798	37.510	36.805	36.726	38.692	38.318	39.617	39.435	40.469	1963	40.469
1964	41.612	42.222	42.917	43.238	43.940	44.721	45.592	45.055	46.409	46.856	46.878	47.139	1964	47.139
1965	48.763	48.913	48.264	49.984	49.833	47.477	48.177	49.488	51.140	52.618	52.453	53.008	1965	53.008
1966	53.335	52.634	51.555	52.688	50.096	49.363	48.769	45.234	44.993	47.214	47.662	47.674	1966	47.674
1967	51.478	51.846	53.967	56.325	53.641	54.658	57.215	56.817	58.758	57.136	57.507	59.104	1967	59.104
1968	56.592	55.113	55.718	60.363	61.334	61.980	60.916	61.913	64.387	64.945	68.393	65.642	1968	65.642
1969	65.193	62.414	64.653	66.131	66.303	62.708	59.024	61.705	60.251	63.014	61.141	60.059	1969	60.059
1970	55.594	58.850	59.028	53.779	50.837	48.386	52.026	54.672	56.570	56.019	59.020	62.465	1970	62.465

Table B-1 **Large Company Stocks: Total Return Index**

(continued)

From January 1971 to December 1998

YEAR	JAN	FEB	MAR	APR	MAY	JUN	JUL	AUG	SEP	OCT	NOV	DEC	YR-END	INDEX
1971	65.082	65.998	68.522	71.104	68.491	68.636	65.896	68.612	68.231	65.477	65.650	71.406	1971	71.406
1972	72.791	74.969	75.510	75.940	77.605	76.010	76.287	79.271	78.985	79.828	83.856	84.956	1972	84.956
1973	83.603	80.822	80.807	77.619	76.538	76.144	79.146	76.630	79.813	79.835	71.194	72.500	1973	72.500
1974	71.883	72.017	70.453	67.822	65.974	65.127	60.183	55.197	48.740	56.818	54.273	53.311	1974	53.311
1975	59.983	64.027	65.541	68.773	72.270	75.608	70.628	69.610	67.326	71.613	73.857	73.144	1975	73.144
1976	81.916	81.441	84.095	83.262	82.654	86.185	85.596	85.717	87.830	86.025	85.946	90.584	1976	90.584
1977	86.151	84.849	83.841	83.956	82.699	86.626	85.317	84.186	84.187	80.690	83.675	84.077	1977	84.077
1978	79.062	77.786	79.933	86.888	88.072	86.730	91.583	94.696	94.240	85.847	88.078	89.592	1978	89.592
1979	93.368	90.717	95.934	96.280	94.661	98.541	99.620	105.703	105.970	99.022	104.113	106.113	1979	106.113
1980	112.589	112.934	101.792	106.162	112.130	115.445	123.249	124.865	128.369	130.763	145.085	140.514	1980	140.514
1981	134.359	137.154	142.366	139.333	140.197	139.076	139.173	131.463	124.863	131.456	137.253	133.616	1981	133.616
1982	131.438	124.709	123.960	129.092	125.374	123.193	120.544	135.817	137.311	152.772	159.464	162.223	1982	162.223
1983	167.868	172.233	178.519	192.051	191.052	198.350	192.142	195.408	198.066	195.412	199.965	198.745	1983	198.745
1984	197.453	190.977	194.242	195.583	185.139	189.230	186.524	207.508	207.550	208.089	205.988	211.199	1984	211.199
1985	227.419	230.535	230.950	230.211	244.369	248.254	247.609	246.098	238.199	248.846	266.663	279.117	1985	279.117
1986	280.345	301.679	318.392	314.444	331.707	337.213	318.026	341.814	313.717	331.160	339.637	330.671	1986	330.671
1987	375.080	390.571	401.194	397.664	401.760	421.808	442.814	459.862	449.745	352.960	324.052	347.967	1987	347.967
1988	362.826	379.878	368.406	372.385	375.290	392.703	391.132	378.186	394.221	404.983	399.232	406.458	1988	406.458
1989	435.845	424.993	435.023	457.470	475.860	473.290	515.792	525.747	523.696	511.494	522.133	534.455	1989	534.455
1990	498.594	505.025	518.308	505.505	554.792	550.909	549.146	499.558	474.980	473.222	503.698	517.499	1990	517.499
1991	540.372	579.063	592.845	594.505	619.950	591.618	619.306	633.859	623.464	631.818	606.293	675.592	1991	675.592
1992	663.026	671.513	658.351	677.509	681.168	671.291	698.344	684.237	692.106	694.598	718.006	727.412	1992	727.412
1993	732.722	742.613	758.580	739.994	759.974	762.482	758.898	787.812	781.983	797.857	790.357	800.078	1993	800.078
1994	826.881	804.555	769.557	779.561	792.268	772.699	798.276	830.765	810.744	829.310	798.874	810.538	1994	810.538
1995	831.612	863.878	889.449	915.332	951.488	973.848	1006.227	1008.994	1051.271	1047.591	1093.685	1113.918	1995	1113.918
1996	1152.237	1163.299	1174.466	1191.731	1222.478	1227.490	1172.867	1197.731	1265.044	1299.706	1398.354	1370.946	1996	1370.946
1997	1456.082	1467.876	1406.812	1490.799	1582.334	1652.906	1784.147	1684.948	1777.233	1717.873	1797.411	1828.326	1997	1828.326
1998	1848.621	1981.943	2083.439	2104.398	2068.223	2152.235	2129.313	1821.457	1938.140	2095.788	2222.814	2350.892	1998	2350.892

Table B-2 **Large Company Stocks: Capital Appreciation Index**

From December 1925 to December 1970

YEAR	JAN	FEB	MAR	APR	MAY	JUN	JUL	AUG	SEP	OCT	NOV	DEC	YR-END	INDEX
1925												1.000	1925	1.000
1926	0.998	0.955	0.898	0.918	0.926	0.966	1.009	1.027	1.050	1.017	1.040	1.057	1926	1.057
1927	1.035	1.085	1.092	1.111	1.168	1.158	1.233	1.288	1.343	1.272	1.350	1.384	1927	1.384
1928	1.377	1.353	1.499	1.548	1.567	1.504	1.523	1.636	1.675	1.699	1.903	1.908	1928	1.908
1929	2.017	2.005	2.001	2.033	1.946	2.165	2.263	2.485	2.364	1.893	1.640	1.681	1929	1.681
1930	1.786	1.824	1.970	1.951	1.919	1.603	1.662	1.675	1.457	1.328	1.299	1.202	1930	1.202
1931	1.261	1.405	1.308	1.183	1.020	1.162	1.076	1.086	0.761	0.825	0.745	0.636	1931	0.636
1932	0.618	0.650	0.573	0.457	0.350	0.347	0.478	0.658	0.633	0.545	0.513	0.540	1932	0.540
1933	0.544	0.444	0.458	0.652	0.755	0.855	0.780	0.869	0.770	0.702	0.774	0.792	1933	0.792
1934	0.875	0.843	0.842	0.820	0.753	0.769	0.680	0.717	0.713	0.690	0.748	0.745	1934	0.745
1935	0.713	0.685	0.664	0.727	0.751	0.802	0.868	0.887	0.908	0.976	1.015	1.053	1935	1.053
1936	1.121	1.140	1.169	1.079	1.129	1.163	1.242	1.253	1.255	1.349	1.354	1.346	1936	1.346
1937	1.397	1.418	1.404	1.288	1.274	1.207	1.331	1.257	1.078	0.969	0.871	0.827	1937	0.827
1938	0.838	0.889	0.666	0.760	0.726	0.906	0.972	0.945	0.959	1.032	0.998	1.035	1938	1.035
1939	0.964	0.995	0.861	0.856	0.909	0.851	0.944	0.876	1.020	1.005	0.956	0.979	1939	0.979
1940	0.944	0.951	0.960	0.955	0.726	0.782	0.806	0.828	0.835	0.868	0.832	0.829	1940	0.829
1941	0.789	0.777	0.781	0.730	0.733	0.772	0.814	0.807	0.799	0.745	0.713	0.681	1941	0.681
1942	0.690	0.673	0.628	0.600	0.639	0.650	0.671	0.676	0.694	0.738	0.728	0.766	1942	0.766
1943	0.821	0.862	0.908	0.908	0.949	0.968	0.915	0.925	0.947	0.934	0.864	0.915	1943	0.915
1944	0.929	0.926	0.942	0.930	0.968	1.017	0.996	1.005	1.002	1.002	1.005	1.041	1944	1.041
1945	1.056	1.121	1.069	1.163	1.176	1.172	1.149	1.216	1.266	1.305	1.347	1.361	1945	1.361
1946	1.455	1.354	1.417	1.470	1.503	1.444	1.408	1.305	1.172	1.163	1.150	1.199	1946	1.199
1947	1.227	1.209	1.189	1.143	1.132	1.192	1.235	1.201	1.184	1.209	1.175	1.199	1947	1.199
1948	1.151	1.097	1.182	1.213	1.308	1.312	1.242	1.252	1.214	1.296	1.156	1.191	1948	1.191
1949	1.193	1.146	1.180	1.155	1.112	1.110	1.179	1.193	1.221	1.257	1.259	1.313	1949	1.313
1950	1.336	1.350	1.355	1.416	1.472	1.386	1.398	1.444	1.524	1.531	1.529	1.600	1950	1.600
1951	1.697	1.708	1.677	1.758	1.687	1.643	1.755	1.824	1.823	1.798	1.793	1.863	1951	1.863
1952	1.892	1.823	1.910	1.828	1.870	1.956	1.991	1.962	1.923	1.922	2.011	2.082	1952	2.082
1953	2.067	2.030	1.982	1.929	1.923	1.892	1.940	1.828	1.830	1.923	1.940	1.944	1953	1.944
1954	2.044	2.049	2.111	2.215	2.288	2.289	2.420	2.338	2.532	2.483	2.683	2.820	1954	2.820
1955	2.871	2.881	2.867	2.975	2.971	3.216	3.411	3.384	3.422	3.318	3.567	3.564	1955	3.564
1956	3.434	3.553	3.799	3.792	3.542	3.681	3.871	3.723	3.554	3.572	3.533	3.658	1956	3.658
1957	3.505	3.390	3.457	3.585	3.717	3.712	3.755	3.544	3.324	3.218	3.270	3.134	1957	3.134
1958	3.268	3.201	3.299	3.404	3.455	3.545	3.698	3.742	3.923	4.023	4.113	4.327	1958	4.327
1959	4.343	4.342	4.345	4.513	4.599	4.582	4.742	4.671	4.458	4.508	4.567	4.694	1959	4.694
1960	4.358	4.398	4.337	4.261	4.375	4.461	4.350	4.464	4.194	4.184	4.353	4.554	1960	4.554
1961	4.842	4.972	5.099	5.118	5.216	5.066	5.232	5.335	5.230	5.378	5.589	5.607	1961	5.607
1962	5.395	5.483	5.451	5.113	4.673	4.291	4.563	4.633	4.410	4.429	4.879	4.945	1962	4.945
1963	5.188	5.038	5.217	5.470	5.549	5.437	5.418	5.682	5.619	5.800	5.739	5.879	1963	5.879
1964	6.038	6.097	6.190	6.227	6.299	6.402	6.519	6.413	6.597	6.650	6.616	6.642	1964	6.642
1965	6.862	6.852	6.752	6.984	6.929	6.592	6.681	6.832	7.050	7.243	7.179	7.244	1965	7.244
1966	7.279	7.149	6.993	7.136	6.750	6.641	6.552	6.042	6.000	6.285	6.305	6.295	1966	6.295
1967	6.788	6.801	7.069	7.368	6.981	7.103	7.426	7.339	7.579	7.359	7.367	7.560	1967	7.560
1968	7.229	7.003	7.069	7.648	7.734	7.804	7.660	7.748	8.046	8.104	8.493	8.139	1968	8.139
1969	8.073	7.690	7.955	8.126	8.108	7.658	7.197	7.485	7.298	7.621	7.352	7.210	1969	7.210
1970	6.663	7.014	7.024	6.389	5.999	5.699	6.117	6.389	6.600	6.524	6.834	7.222	1970	7.222

Table B-2

Large Company Stocks: Capital Appreciation Index

(continued)

From January 1971 to December 1998

YEAR	JAN	FEB	MAR	APR	MAY	JUN	JUL	AUG	SEP	OCT	NOV	DEC	YR-END	INDEX
1971	7.514	7.582	7.861	8.147	7.808	7.813	7.491	7.761	7.707	7.385	7.366	8.001	1971	8.001
1972	8.146	8.352	8.401	8.438	8.584	8.397	8.416	8.706	8.664	8.744	9.143	9.252	1972	9.252
1973	9.093	8.752	8.740	8.383	8.225	8.171	8.481	8.170	8.498	8.487	7.520	7.645	1973	7.645
1974	7.568	7.541	7.365	7.078	6.840	6.740	6.215	5.654	4.980	5.792	5.484	5.373	1974	5.373
1975	6.033	6.394	6.533	6.842	7.143	7.460	6.955	6.809	6.573	6.978	7.150	7.068	1975	7.068
1976	7.904	7.814	8.054	7.965	7.851	8.172	8.107	8.065	8.248	8.064	8.002	8.422	1976	8.422
1977	7.996	7.823	7.713	7.715	7.533	7.875	7.747	7.584	7.565	7.237	7.432	7.453	1977	7.453
1978	6.995	6.821	6.991	7.589	7.621	7.487	7.890	8.095	8.036	7.300	7.422	7.532	1978	7.532
1979	7.831	7.545	7.962	7.975	7.765	8.065	8.135	8.567	8.567	7.980	8.320	8.459	1979	8.459
1980	8.947	8.907	8.001	8.330	8.718	8.953	9.535	9.591	9.832	9.989	11.012	10.639	1980	10.639
1981	10.153	10.288	10.658	10.407	10.390	10.285	10.259	9.623	9.105	9.553	9.903	9.605	1981	9.605
1982	9.436	8.865	8.775	9.126	8.769	8.591	8.393	9.367	9.438	10.480	10.858	11.023	1982	11.023
1983	11.388	11.604	11.988	12.886	12.727	13.175	12.741	12.885	13.016	12.818	13.041	12.926	1983	12.926
1984	12.807	12.309	12.475	12.544	11.799	12.005	11.807	13.062	13.017	13.015	12.819	13.106	1984	13.106
1985	14.077	14.198	14.157	14.092	14.854	15.034	14.962	14.783	14.269	14.876	15.844	16.559	1985	16.559
1986	16.598	17.785	18.724	18.460	19.387	19.660	18.506	19.824	18.131	19.123	19.534	18.981	1986	18.981
1987	21.483	22.275	22.864	22.601	22.736	23.825	24.974	25.848	25.222	19.734	18.051	19.366	1987	19.366
1988	20.149	20.991	20.292	20.483	20.548	21.438	21.322	20.499	21.313	21.867	21.454	21.769	1988	21.769
1989	23.317	22.643	23.114	24.272	25.124	24.926	27.129	27.550	27.370	26.680	27.122	27.703	1989	27.703
1990	25.796	26.016	26.648	25.931	28.316	28.065	27.918	25.285	23.991	23.830	25.259	25.886	1990	25.886
1991	26.961	28.774	29.413	29.424	30.559	29.095	30.400	30.998	30.404	30.765	29.413	32.695	1991	32.695
1992	32.045	32.351	31.645	32.528	32.559	31.994	33.254	32.456	32.751	32.820	33.813	34.155	1992	34.155
1993	34.396	34.756	35.406	34.506	35.290	35.317	35.129	36.338	35.975	36.673	36.199	36.565	1993	36.565
1994	37.753	36.619	34.944	35.347	35.785	34.826	35.923	37.273	36.270	37.027	35.565	36.002	1994	36.002
1995	36.876	38.206	39.250	40.348	41.814	42.703	44.060	44.045	45.812	45.583	47.455	48.282	1995	48.282
1996	49.857	50.203	50.600	51.280	52.452	52.570	50.165	51.109	53.878	55.286	59.342	58.066	1996	58.066
1997	61.627	61.992	59.350	62.817	66.496	69.386	74.806	70.509	74.257	71.697	74.893	76.071	1997	76.071
1998	76.844	82.257	86.366	87.149	85.509	88.881	87.849	75.041	79.723	86.124	91.216	96.359	1998	96.359

Table B-3 **Small Company Stocks: Total Return Index**

From December 1925 to December 1970

YEAR	JAN	FEB	MAR	APR	MAY	JUN	JUL	AUG	SEP	OCT	NOV	DEC	YR-END	INDEX
1925												1.000	1925	1.000
1926	1.070	1.001	0.894	0.910	0.904	0.938	0.949	0.973	0.973	0.951	0.971	1.003	1926	1.003
1927	1.032	1.089	1.029	1.088	1.168	1.133	1.191	1.170	1.176	1.098	1.187	1.224	1927	1.224
1928	1.283	1.253	1.319	1.440	1.503	1.376	1.384	1.445	1.574	1.617	1.803	1.710	1928	1.710
1929	1.716	1.712	1.677	1.729	1.498	1.578	1.596	1.569	1.425	1.030	0.876	0.832	1929	0.832
1930	0.939	1.000	1.101	1.024	0.968	0.758	0.781	0.768	0.656	0.584	0.583	0.515	1930	0.515
1931	0.623	0.783	0.727	0.570	0.491	0.581	0.548	0.507	0.342	0.368	0.331	0.259	1931	0.259
1932	0.285	0.293	0.255	0.198	0.175	0.175	0.237	0.411	0.357	0.293	0.257	0.245	1932	0.245
1933	0.243	0.212	0.235	0.354	0.578	0.729	0.689	0.753	0.633	0.555	0.591	0.594	1933	0.594
1934	0.825	0.839	0.838	0.858	0.749	0.747	0.578	0.667	0.656	0.663	0.726	0.738	1934	0.738
1935	0.714	0.672	0.592	0.639	0.637	0.656	0.713	0.751	0.778	0.855	0.976	1.035	1935	1.035
1936	1.346	1.427	1.436	1.179	1.211	1.183	1.286	1.313	1.384	1.472	1.678	1.705	1936	1.705
1937	1.921	2.047	2.072	1.724	1.654	1.458	1.638	1.517	1.132	1.008	0.862	0.716	1937	0.716
1938	0.754	0.780	0.499	0.638	0.584	0.788	0.906	0.815	0.802	0.974	0.907	0.951	1938	0.951
1939	0.870	0.879	0.663	0.672	0.745	0.667	0.837	0.704	1.066	1.023	0.915	0.954	1939	0.954
1940	0.955	1.033	1.099	1.171	0.741	0.818	0.837	0.859	0.877	0.925	0.947	0.905	1940	0.905
1941	0.907	0.881	0.909	0.848	0.852	0.916	1.115	1.108	1.056	0.985	0.936	0.823	1941	0.823
1942	0.979	0.972	0.903	0.872	0.869	0.898	0.964	0.995	1.086	1.204	1.143	1.190	1942	1.190
1943	1.444	1.723	1.971	2.155	2.404	2.384	2.126	2.126	2.217	2.244	1.994	2.242	1943	2.242
1944	2.385	2.456	2.640	2.499	2.684	3.055	2.964	3.059	3.053	3.020	3.170	3.446	1944	3.446
1945	3.612	3.977	3.634	4.055	4.257	4.621	4.364	4.607	4.920	5.265	5.882	5.983	1945	5.983
1946	6.917	6.476	6.653	7.117	7.537	7.189	6.808	6.230	5.232	5.170	5.097	5.287	1946	5.287
1947	5.509	5.487	5.303	4.756	4.502	4.750	5.125	5.106	5.165	5.311	5.150	5.335	1947	5.335
1948	5.254	4.842	5.320	5.515	6.099	6.128	5.774	5.778	5.474	5.828	5.177	5.223	1948	5.223
1949	5.318	5.062	5.380	5.199	4.906	4.859	5.185	5.318	5.578	5.841	5.851	6.254	1949	6.254
1950	6.562	6.706	6.682	6.956	7.134	6.580	6.969	7.338	7.720	7.675	7.922	8.677	1950	8.677
1951	9.398	9.455	9.004	9.334	9.026	8.548	8.867	9.403	9.606	9.392	9.314	9.355	1951	9.355
1952	9.533	9.248	9.410	8.922	8.950	9.193	9.296	9.291	9.142	9.047	9.486	9.638	1952	9.638
1953	10.032	10.302	10.233	9.939	10.079	9.589	9.735	9.123	8.884	9.143	9.258	9.013	1953	9.013
1954	9.694	9.786	9.965	10.104	10.561	10.651	11.512	11.528	12.000	12.082	13.024	14.473	1954	14.473
1955	14.764	15.471	15.602	15.837	15.960	16.428	16.533	16.487	16.667	16.384	17.152	17.431	1955	17.431
1956	17.348	17.830	18.598	18.685	17.942	18.042	18.552	18.303	17.827	18.013	18.108	18.177	1956	18.177
1957	18.607	18.234	18.540	19.000	19.143	19.283	19.167	18.427	17.595	16.131	16.314	15.529	1957	15.529
1958	17.245	16.952	17.750	18.418	19.131	19.752	20.722	21.610	22.730	23.655	24.828	25.605	1958	25.605
1959	27.076	27.875	27.951	28.277	28.315	28.196	29.118	28.863	27.619	28.245	28.873	29.804	1959	29.804
1960	28.891	29.034	28.120	27.594	28.158	29.116	28.565	30.064	27.844	26.728	27.896	28.823	1960	28.823
1961	31.460	33.314	35.376	35.825	37.355	35.326	35.436	35.898	34.682	35.590	37.772	38.072	1961	38.072
1962	38.591	39.314	39.537	36.464	32.786	30.213	32.518	33.458	31.254	30.087	33.842	33.540	1962	33.540
1963	36.580	36.705	37.251	38.412	40.088	39.613	39.744	41.799	41.118	42.090	41.642	41.444	1963	41.444
1964	42.581	44.134	45.099	45.520	46.234	46.985	48.857	48.715	50.676	51.716	51.772	51.193	1964	51.193
1965	53.902	56.003	57.335	60.252	59.782	54.398	56.837	60.220	62.310	65.876	68.319	72.567	1965	72.567
1966	78.051	80.479	78.935	81.645	73.797	73.709	73.617	65.669	64.595	63.902	67.041	67.479	1966	67.479
1967	79.884	83.475	88.606	91.003	90.232	99.411	108.862	109.085	115.244	111.662	112.965	123.870	1967	123.870
1968	125.779	116.861	115.586	132.468	145.698	146.137	141.088	146.266	155.034	155.505	167.388	168.429	1968	168.429
1969	165.634	149.238	155.142	161.265	164.063	144.954	129.449	138.925	135.301	143.552	135.552	126.233	1969	126.233
1970	118.554	123.145	119.641	98.970	88.762	80.519	84.975	93.037	103.140	95.856	97.170	104.226	1970	104.226

Table B-3 **Small Company Stocks: Total Return Index**

(continued)

From January 1971 to December 1998

YEAR	JAN	FEB	MAR	APR	MAY	JUN	JUL	AUG	SEP	OCT	NOV	DEC	YR-END	INDEX
1971	120.820	124.647	131.676	134.923	126.760	122.710	115.802	122.555	119.780	113.180	108.954	121.423	1971	121.423
1972	135.142	139.141	137.144	138.912	136.257	132.100	126.645	129.005	124.506	122.329	129.576	126.807	1972	126.807
1973	121.329	111.635	109.318	102.527	94.211	91.476	102.398	97.837	108.242	109.155	87.737	87.618	1973	87.618
1974	99.238	98.393	97.661	93.129	85.745	84.485	82.637	77.009	71.978	79.629	76.143	70.142	1974	70.142
1975	89.551	92.105	97.799	102.990	109.821	118.053	115.056	108.456	106.488	105.954	109.341	107.189	1975	107.189
1976	135.960	154.854	154.626	149.081	143.698	150.298	150.976	146.592	148.123	145.028	150.881	168.691	1976	168.691
1977	176.275	175.587	177.880	181.941	181.434	195.445	196.028	193.924	195.715	189.249	209.804	211.500	1977	211.500
1978	207.502	214.707	236.868	255.528	276.484	271.254	289.807	317.010	316.002	239.303	256.811	261.120	1978	261.120
1979	295.623	287.279	319.448	331.805	332.955	348.676	354.642	381.457	368.351	325.827	353.796	374.614	1979	374.614
1980	405.926	394.411	324.303	346.795	372.814	389.666	441.224	467.894	487.473	503.725	542.326	523.992	1980	523.992
1981	534.839	539.866	590.776	629.590	656.158	661.145	640.253	596.460	552.739	593.752	610.140	596.717	1981	596.717
1982	585.021	567.705	562.822	584.378	569.886	560.825	559.983	599.070	618.660	699.395	753.878	763.829	1982	763.829
1983	811.793	869.617	915.267	985.448	1071.150	1108.462	1098.662	1077.054	1091.419	1029.455	1082.532	1066.828	1983	1066.828
1984	1065.974	997.219	1014.571	1005.947	953.537	982.143	940.893	1034.794	1037.588	1015.072	980.966	995.680	1984	995.680
1985	1101.123	1131.074	1106.869	1087.609	1117.627	1129.474	1158.840	1150.497	1087.910	1116.304	1185.515	1241.234	1985	1241.234
1986	1255.136	1345.380	1409.555	1418.576	1469.645	1473.466	1368.850	1398.691	1320.504	1366.193	1361.958	1326.275	1986	1326.275
1987	1451.342	1568.756	1605.308	1555.062	1548.997	1590.201	1648.084	1695.384	1681.651	1190.777	1143.503	1202.966	1987	1202.966
1988	1269.850	1366.359	1422.107	1451.829	1425.841	1513.102	1509.320	1472.190	1505.609	1487.090	1422.104	1478.135	1988	1478.135
1989	1537.852	1550.616	1606.128	1650.939	1710.703	1676.318	1744.544	1765.827	1765.827	1659.171	1650.710	1628.590	1989	1628.590
1990	1504.166	1532.294	1588.682	1546.423	1633.178	1656.695	1593.410	1386.904	1271.929	1199.175	1253.138	1277.449	1990	1277.449
1991	1384.882	1539.020	1643.673	1649.261	1704.347	1621.686	1687.688	1731.737	1737.279	1792.350	1742.882	1847.629	1991	1847.629
1992	2056.041	2148.974	2095.465	2011.018	2008.202	1903.977	1974.424	1929.407	1954.682	2005.308	2182.778	2279.039	1992	2279.039
1993	2402.790	2359.540	2427.731	2353.442	2433.930	2424.681	2464.931	2548.492	2629.024	2752.851	2704.676	2757.147	1993	2757.147
1994	2927.539	2920.806	2790.538	2807.281	2803.912	2730.450	2780.690	2874.399	2904.580	2937.983	2842.205	2842.773	1994	2842.773
1995	2923.224	2996.889	3040.344	3147.364	3241.155	3425.253	3646.182	3776.715	3850.361	3662.848	3733.175	3822.398	1995	3822.398
1996	3833.101	3974.542	4065.162	4409.887	4740.188	4464.309	4043.325	4235.787	4359.048	4282.765	4406.109	4495.993	1996	4495.993
1997	4684.825	4588.318	4363.490	4243.058	4676.698	4909.598	5206.628	5471.646	5933.453	5704.421	5616.003	5519.969	1997	5519.969
1998	5487.401	5843.534	6124.608	6227.501	5917.994	5796.084	5407.166	4320.326	4479.746	4639.225	4990.878	5116.648	1998	5116.648

Table B-4 **Long-Term Corporate Bonds: Total Return Index**

From December 1925 to December 1970

YEAR	JAN	FEB	MAR	APR	MAY	JUN	JUL	AUG	SEP	OCT	NOV	DEC	YR-END	INDEX
1925												1.000	1925	1.000
1926	1.007	1.012	1.020	1.030	1.035	1.035	1.041	1.046	1.052	1.062	1.068	1.074	1926	1.074
1927	1.080	1.087	1.096	1.102	1.101	1.106	1.106	1.115	1.132	1.138	1.146	1.154	1927	1.154
1928	1.157	1.165	1.169	1.171	1.162	1.159	1.158	1.168	1.171	1.181	1.177	1.186	1928	1.186
1929	1.192	1.195	1.185	1.187	1.192	1.187	1.189	1.192	1.196	1.204	1.202	1.225	1929	1.225
1930	1.233	1.241	1.259	1.269	1.276	1.290	1.298	1.315	1.329	1.337	1.335	1.323	1930	1.323
1931	1.350	1.359	1.372	1.381	1.400	1.407	1.414	1.416	1.414	1.362	1.337	1.299	1931	1.299
1932	1.292	1.261	1.306	1.283	1.297	1.295	1.301	1.358	1.399	1.409	1.419	1.439	1932	1.439
1933	1.518	1.438	1.445	1.431	1.516	1.544	1.569	1.584	1.582	1.588	1.549	1.588	1933	1.588
1934	1.629	1.653	1.684	1.701	1.717	1.744	1.752	1.760	1.749	1.767	1.790	1.808	1934	1.808
1935	1.846	1.872	1.880	1.901	1.909	1.931	1.952	1.944	1.944	1.952	1.966	1.982	1935	1.982
1936	1.998	2.009	2.026	2.031	2.039	2.056	2.058	2.072	2.086	2.091	2.114	2.116	1936	2.116
1937	2.121	2.111	2.087	2.101	2.110	2.121	2.129	2.125	2.131	2.145	2.159	2.174	1937	2.174
1938	2.182	2.184	2.165	2.195	2.197	2.218	2.233	2.229	2.253	2.271	2.279	2.307	1938	2.307
1939	2.312	2.327	2.332	2.347	2.359	2.367	2.365	2.272	2.307	2.361	2.380	2.399	1939	2.399
1940	2.410	2.415	2.427	2.405	2.400	2.429	2.434	2.436	2.458	2.470	2.486	2.480	1940	2.480
1941	2.482	2.483	2.478	2.497	2.509	2.525	2.541	2.550	2.562	2.570	2.546	2.548	1941	2.548
1942	2.549	2.547	2.563	2.565	2.570	2.579	2.584	2.593	2.598	2.600	2.601	2.614	1942	2.614
1943	2.627	2.628	2.634	2.647	2.659	2.672	2.677	2.682	2.684	2.681	2.675	2.688	1943	2.688
1944	2.693	2.703	2.716	2.725	2.726	2.732	2.741	2.750	2.755	2.761	2.774	2.815	1944	2.815
1945	2.837	2.850	2.855	2.860	2.857	2.866	2.863	2.864	2.873	2.882	2.892	2.930	1945	2.930
1946	2.968	2.978	2.988	2.975	2.981	2.986	2.983	2.956	2.949	2.955	2.947	2.980	1946	2.980
1947	2.982	2.983	3.003	3.009	3.015	3.017	3.023	3.001	2.962	2.933	2.904	2.911	1947	2.911
1948	2.918	2.929	2.963	2.974	2.977	2.952	2.936	2.953	2.960	2.967	2.992	3.031	1948	3.031
1949	3.043	3.054	3.056	3.063	3.075	3.101	3.132	3.143	3.150	3.171	3.178	3.132	1949	3.132
1950	3.143	3.145	3.152	3.150	3.147	3.154	3.176	3.188	3.176	3.173	3.190	3.198	1950	3.198
1951	3.204	3.190	3.114	3.111	3.107	3.078	3.141	3.177	3.159	3.113	3.094	3.112	1951	3.112
1952	3.174	3.147	3.171	3.169	3.179	3.184	3.189	3.209	3.204	3.216	3.251	3.221	1952	3.221
1953	3.196	3.183	3.172	3.094	3.084	3.118	3.173	3.146	3.226	3.299	3.275	3.331	1953	3.331
1954	3.373	3.439	3.453	3.441	3.427	3.448	3.462	3.468	3.482	3.496	3.505	3.511	1954	3.511
1955	3.477	3.455	3.486	3.486	3.480	3.490	3.476	3.462	3.489	3.516	3.505	3.527	1955	3.527
1956	3.564	3.573	3.521	3.481	3.499	3.493	3.460	3.388	3.392	3.357	3.314	3.287	1956	3.287
1957	3.352	3.383	3.400	3.377	3.352	3.244	3.209	3.206	3.236	3.244	3.344	3.573	1957	3.573
1958	3.609	3.606	3.589	3.648	3.659	3.645	3.590	3.475	3.441	3.478	3.515	3.494	1958	3.494
1959	3.484	3.528	3.499	3.439	3.400	3.415	3.445	3.422	3.392	3.447	3.494	3.460	1959	3.460
1960	3.498	3.542	3.610	3.602	3.594	3.645	3.739	3.783	3.759	3.762	3.735	3.774	1960	3.774
1961	3.830	3.911	3.899	3.854	3.873	3.842	3.857	3.850	3.906	3.955	3.966	3.956	1961	3.956
1962	3.988	4.008	4.069	4.127	4.127	4.116	4.110	4.169	4.206	4.234	4.261	4.270	1962	4.270
1963	4.296	4.305	4.317	4.295	4.315	4.334	4.346	4.361	4.351	4.372	4.379	4.364	1963	4.364
1964	4.402	4.426	4.398	4.416	4.441	4.463	4.486	4.502	4.512	4.534	4.533	4.572	1964	4.572
1965	4.609	4.614	4.619	4.629	4.625	4.627	4.635	4.633	4.626	4.647	4.620	4.552	1965	4.552
1966	4.562	4.510	4.483	4.489	4.478	4.491	4.447	4.332	4.366	4.480	4.471	4.560	1966	4.560
1967	4.766	4.670	4.724	4.691	4.572	4.470	4.488	4.485	4.527	4.400	4.280	4.335	1967	4.335
1968	4.491	4.508	4.419	4.440	4.454	4.509	4.662	4.758	4.733	4.658	4.552	4.446	1968	4.446
1969	4.508	4.436	4.347	4.493	4.391	4.406	4.408	4.400	4.292	4.347	4.142	4.086	1969	4.086
1970	4.144	4.310	4.291	4.184	4.115	4.116	4.345	4.388	4.449	4.406	4.664	4.837	1970	4.837

Table B-4 **Long-Term Corporate Bonds: Total Return Index**

(continued)

From January 1971 to December 1998

YEAR	JAN	FEB	MAR	APR	MAY	JUN	JUL	AUG	SEP	OCT	NOV	DEC	YR-END	INDEX
1971	5.095	4.908	5.035	4.916	4.837	4.889	4.876	5.146	5.094	5.238	5.253	5.370	1971	5.370
1972	5.352	5.409	5.422	5.441	5.530	5.493	5.509	5.549	5.566	5.622	5.762	5.760	1972	5.760
1973	5.729	5.742	5.768	5.803	5.780	5.748	5.474	5.669	5.871	5.832	5.878	5.825	1973	5.825
1974	5.795	5.800	5.622	5.430	5.487	5.331	5.218	5.078	5.167	5.624	5.690	5.647	1974	5.647
1975	5.984	6.066	5.916	5.885	5.947	6.128	6.110	6.003	5.927	6.255	6.200	6.474	1975	6.474
1976	6.596	6.636	6.747	6.737	6.667	6.767	6.868	7.027	7.144	7.194	7.424	7.681	1976	7.681
1977	7.448	7.434	7.503	7.579	7.659	7.793	7.789	7.895	7.878	7.848	7.895	7.813	1977	7.813
1978	7.743	7.783	7.815	7.797	7.713	7.731	7.809	8.010	7.971	7.808	7.912	7.807	1978	7.807
1979	7.951	7.849	7.932	7.892	8.072	8.289	8.263	8.269	8.121	7.398	7.563	7.481	1979	7.481
1980	6.998	6.533	6.492	7.386	7.799	8.065	7.719	7.376	7.201	7.086	7.098	7.274	1980	7.274
1981	7.180	6.987	7.204	6.650	7.046	7.062	6.799	6.565	6.434	6.769	7.627	7.185	1981	7.185
1982	7.092	7.313	7.537	7.792	7.983	7.609	8.020	8.691	9.233	9.933	10.133	10.242	1982	10.242
1983	10.146	10.580	10.657	11.241	10.876	10.826	10.334	10.386	10.794	10.767	10.920	10.883	1983	10.883
1984	11.177	10.985	10.727	10.649	10.134	10.336	10.942	11.278	11.632	12.297	12.558	12.718	1984	12.718
1985	13.132	12.642	12.868	13.249	14.336	14.455	14.280	14.651	14.755	15.240	15.804	16.546	1985	16.546
1986	16.620	17.870	18.327	18.357	18.056	18.449	18.506	19.015	18.799	19.154	19.600	19.829	1986	19.829
1987	20.258	20.375	20.198	19.184	19.084	19.380	19.149	19.006	18.204	19.127	19.366	19.776	1987	19.776
1988	20.799	21.086	20.689	20.381	20.265	21.033	20.800	20.912	21.594	22.183	21.808	21.893	1988	21.893
1989	22.335	22.047	22.188	22.661	23.520	24.449	24.884	24.479	24.576	25.255	25.432	25.447	1989	25.447
1990	24.961	24.931	24.903	24.428	25.368	25.916	26.181	25.416	25.647	25.986	26.726	27.173	1990	27.173
1991	27.580	27.914	28.216	28.605	28.717	28.665	29.144	29.945	30.757	30.889	31.216	32.577	1991	32.577
1992	32.014	32.321	32.085	32.136	32.953	33.467	34.497	34.808	35.153	34.604	34.843	35.637	1992	35.637
1993	36.528	37.463	37.557	37.752	37.828	38.936	39.326	40.454	40.628	40.835	40.068	40.336	1993	40.336
1994	41.151	39.974	38.443	38.070	37.834	37.528	38.687	38.567	37.545	37.358	37.425	38.012	1994	38.012
1995	38.985	40.112	40.493	41.202	43.802	44.148	43.702	44.637	45.320	46.158	47.275	48.353	1995	48.353
1996	48.421	46.615	46.009	45.273	45.295	46.074	46.121	45.798	46.984	48.680	49.960	49.031	1996	49.031
1997	48.894	49.031	47.947	48.829	49.454	50.379	53.039	51.766	52.936	53.947	54.492	55.380	1997	55.380
1998	56.139	56.100	56.313	56.611	57.557	58.219	57.893	58.408	60.820	59.664	61.275	61.339	1998	61.339

Table B-5 **Long-Term Government Bonds: Total Return Index**

From December 1925 to December 1970

YEAR	JAN	FEB	MAR	APR	MAY	JUN	JUL	AUG	SEP	OCT	NOV	DEC	YR-END	INDEX
1925												1.000	1925	1.000
1926	1.014	1.020	1.024	1.032	1.034	1.038	1.038	1.038	1.042	1.053	1.069	1.078	1926	1.078
1927	1.086	1.095	1.123	1.122	1.135	1.127	1.132	1.141	1.143	1.154	1.166	1.174	1927	1.174
1928	1.170	1.177	1.182	1.182	1.173	1.178	1.152	1.161	1.156	1.174	1.175	1.175	1928	1.175
1929	1.165	1.146	1.130	1.161	1.142	1.155	1.155	1.151	1.154	1.198	1.226	1.215	1929	1.215
1930	1.208	1.224	1.234	1.232	1.249	1.256	1.260	1.262	1.271	1.276	1.281	1.272	1930	1.272
1931	1.257	1.267	1.280	1.291	1.310	1.311	1.305	1.307	1.270	1.228	1.231	1.204	1931	1.204
1932	1.208	1.258	1.256	1.332	1.307	1.315	1.379	1.379	1.387	1.385	1.389	1.407	1932	1.407
1933	1.428	1.391	1.405	1.400	1.443	1.450	1.447	1.454	1.457	1.444	1.422	1.406	1933	1.406
1934	1.442	1.454	1.483	1.501	1.521	1.531	1.537	1.519	1.497	1.524	1.530	1.547	1934	1.547
1935	1.575	1.590	1.596	1.609	1.600	1.615	1.622	1.600	1.602	1.611	1.613	1.624	1935	1.624
1936	1.633	1.647	1.664	1.670	1.677	1.680	1.690	1.709	1.704	1.705	1.740	1.746	1936	1.746
1937	1.744	1.759	1.687	1.693	1.702	1.699	1.723	1.705	1.712	1.720	1.736	1.750	1937	1.750
1938	1.760	1.770	1.763	1.800	1.808	1.809	1.817	1.817	1.821	1.837	1.833	1.847	1938	1.847
1939	1.858	1.873	1.896	1.919	1.951	1.946	1.968	1.929	1.824	1.898	1.929	1.957	1939	1.957
1940	1.954	1.959	1.994	1.987	1.927	1.977	1.987	1.993	2.015	2.021	2.062	2.076	1940	2.076
1941	2.034	2.039	2.058	2.085	2.090	2.104	2.109	2.113	2.110	2.140	2.133	2.096	1941	2.096
1942	2.110	2.112	2.132	2.126	2.142	2.142	2.146	2.154	2.155	2.160	2.152	2.163	1942	2.163
1943	2.170	2.169	2.171	2.181	2.192	2.196	2.196	2.201	2.203	2.204	2.204	2.208	1943	2.208
1944	2.213	2.220	2.224	2.227	2.234	2.235	2.243	2.249	2.253	2.255	2.261	2.270	1944	2.270
1945	2.299	2.317	2.321	2.358	2.372	2.412	2.391	2.397	2.410	2.435	2.466	2.514	1945	2.514
1946	2.520	2.528	2.531	2.497	2.493	2.511	2.501	2.473	2.471	2.489	2.475	2.511	1946	2.511
1947	2.510	2.515	2.520	2.511	2.519	2.522	2.537	2.558	2.547	2.537	2.493	2.445	1947	2.445
1948	2.450	2.462	2.470	2.481	2.516	2.495	2.490	2.490	2.494	2.496	2.514	2.529	1948	2.529
1949	2.549	2.562	2.581	2.584	2.589	2.632	2.641	2.670	2.667	2.672	2.678	2.692	1949	2.692
1950	2.675	2.681	2.683	2.691	2.700	2.693	2.708	2.712	2.692	2.679	2.689	2.693	1950	2.693
1951	2.709	2.689	2.646	2.630	2.612	2.596	2.632	2.657	2.636	2.639	2.603	2.587	1951	2.587
1952	2.595	2.598	2.627	2.672	2.663	2.664	2.658	2.640	2.606	2.644	2.640	2.617	1952	2.617
1953	2.620	2.598	2.575	2.548	2.510	2.566	2.576	2.574	2.651	2.671	2.658	2.713	1953	2.713
1954	2.737	2.802	2.819	2.848	2.823	2.869	2.908	2.897	2.894	2.896	2.889	2.907	1954	2.907
1955	2.837	2.815	2.840	2.840	2.861	2.839	2.810	2.811	2.832	2.872	2.859	2.870	1955	2.870
1956	2.894	2.893	2.850	2.818	2.881	2.889	2.829	2.776	2.790	2.775	2.759	2.710	1956	2.710
1957	2.803	2.810	2.804	2.741	2.735	2.686	2.675	2.675	2.696	2.682	2.825	2.912	1957	2.912
1958	2.887	2.916	2.946	3.001	3.001	2.953	2.871	2.746	2.714	2.751	2.785	2.734	1958	2.734
1959	2.712	2.744	2.749	2.717	2.715	2.718	2.734	2.723	2.708	2.748	2.716	2.673	1959	2.673
1960	2.702	2.757	2.835	2.787	2.829	2.878	2.984	2.964	2.986	2.978	2.958	3.041	1960	3.041
1961	3.008	3.068	3.057	3.092	3.078	3.055	3.065	3.054	3.093	3.115	3.109	3.070	1961	3.070
1962	3.066	3.098	3.176	3.202	3.217	3.192	3.158	3.217	3.236	3.263	3.270	3.282	1962	3.282
1963	3.281	3.284	3.287	3.283	3.290	3.297	3.307	3.314	3.315	3.307	3.324	3.322	1963	3.322
1964	3.317	3.313	3.326	3.341	3.358	3.381	3.384	3.390	3.407	3.422	3.428	3.438	1964	3.438
1965	3.452	3.457	3.475	3.488	3.494	3.511	3.518	3.514	3.502	3.511	3.490	3.462	1965	3.462
1966	3.427	3.341	3.440	3.418	3.398	3.393	3.380	3.310	3.420	3.498	3.447	3.589	1966	3.589
1967	3.644	3.564	3.634	3.528	3.515	3.405	3.428	3.399	3.398	3.262	3.198	3.259	1967	3.259
1968	3.366	3.355	3.284	3.359	3.373	3.451	3.550	3.549	3.513	3.466	3.373	3.251	1968	3.251
1969	3.184	3.197	3.201	3.337	3.174	3.242	3.267	3.245	3.073	3.185	3.107	3.086	1969	3.086
1970	3.079	3.260	3.238	3.104	2.959	3.103	3.202	3.196	3.269	3.233	3.489	3.460	1970	3.460

Table B-5

Long-Term Government Bonds: Total Return Index

(continued)

From January 1971 to December 1998

YEAR	JAN	FEB	MAR	APR	MAY	JUN	JUL	AUG	SEP	OCT	NOV	DEC	YR-END	INDEX
1971	3.634	3.575	3.763	3.657	3.655	3.597	3.607	3.777	3.854	3.918	3.900	3.917	1971	3.917
1972	3.892	3.927	3.895	3.905	4.011	3.985	4.071	4.082	4.049	4.143	4.237	4.140	1972	4.140
1973	4.007	4.013	4.046	4.064	4.021	4.013	3.839	3.989	4.116	4.205	4.128	4.094	1973	4.094
1974	4.060	4.050	3.932	3.833	3.880	3.897	3.886	3.796	3.890	4.080	4.200	4.272	1974	4.272
1975	4.368	4.426	4.308	4.229	4.319	4.445	4.407	4.377	4.334	4.539	4.490	4.665	1975	4.665
1976	4.707	4.736	4.815	4.824	4.747	4.846	4.884	4.987	5.059	5.102	5.274	5.447	1976	5.447
1977	5.236	5.210	5.257	5.295	5.361	5.449	5.411	5.518	5.502	5.451	5.502	5.410	1977	5.410
1978	5.366	5.368	5.357	5.355	5.323	5.290	5.366	5.483	5.425	5.316	5.416	5.346	1978	5.346
1979	5.448	5.375	5.444	5.383	5.524	5.696	5.647	5.627	5.559	5.091	5.250	5.280	1979	5.280
1980	4.889	4.660	4.514	5.201	5.419	5.613	5.346	5.115	4.982	4.851	4.899	5.071	1980	5.071
1981	5.013	4.795	4.979	4.721	5.015	4.925	4.751	4.568	4.502	4.875	5.562	5.166	1981	5.166
1982	5.189	5.284	5.406	5.608	5.627	5.501	5.777	6.228	6.613	7.033	7.031	7.251	1982	7.251
1983	7.027	7.372	7.303	7.558	7.267	7.295	6.940	6.954	7.305	7.209	7.341	7.298	1983	7.298
1984	7.476	7.343	7.228	7.152	6.782	6.884	7.361	7.557	7.816	8.254	8.352	8.427	1984	8.427
1985	8.734	8.304	8.558	8.766	9.551	9.686	9.512	9.759	9.738	10.067	10.471	11.037	1985	11.037
1986	11.009	12.270	13.215	13.109	12.447	13.210	13.068	13.720	13.034	13.410	13.769	13.745	1986	13.745
1987	13.966	14.247	13.930	13.271	13.132	13.260	13.024	12.810	12.337	13.106	13.154	13.372	1987	13.372
1988	14.263	14.337	13.897	13.675	13.536	14.035	13.797	13.876	14.355	14.796	14.506	14.665	1988	14.665
1989	14.963	14.695	14.875	15.111	15.717	16.582	16.977	16.537	16.569	17.198	17.332	17.322	1989	17.322
1990	16.728	16.686	16.613	16.278	16.954	17.344	17.530	16.796	16.992	17.358	18.056	18.392	1990	18.392
1991	18.632	18.689	18.760	19.023	19.024	18.904	19.202	19.855	20.458	20.569	20.738	21.942	1991	21.942
1992	21.231	21.339	21.140	21.173	21.687	22.121	23.001	23.155	23.584	23.117	23.140	23.709	1992	23.709
1993	24.374	25.237	25.290	25.472	25.591	26.739	27.251	28.433	28.448	28.722	27.979	28.034	1993	28.034
1994	28.755	27.462	26.378	25.981	25.767	25.508	26.435	26.209	25.342	25.280	25.447	25.856	1994	25.856
1995	26.561	27.322	27.572	28.039	30.255	30.675	30.161	30.873	31.413	32.337	33.143	34.044	1995	34.044
1996	34.007	32.366	31.687	31.163	30.994	31.622	31.678	31.237	32.142	33.440	34.612	33.727	1996	33.727
1997	33.459	33.476	32.633	33.465	33.790	34.448	36.603	35.441	36.560	37.807	38.366	39.074	1997	39.074
1998	39.856	39.570	39.668	39.771	40.497	41.421	41.256	43.173	44.876	43.896	44.320	44.178	1998	44.178

Table B-6 Long-Term Government Bonds: Capital Appreciation Index

From December 1925 to December 1970

YEAR	JAN	FEB	MAR	APR	MAY	JUN	JUL	AUG	SEP	OCT	NOV	DEC	YR-END	INDEX
1925												1.000	1925	1.000
1926	1.011	1.014	1.015	1.020	1.018	1.019	1.016	1.013	1.014	1.021	1.034	1.039	1926	1.039
1927	1.044	1.050	1.074	1.070	1.079	1.069	1.071	1.076	1.075	1.083	1.090	1.095	1927	1.095
1928	1.088	1.092	1.094	1.091	1.080	1.081	1.055	1.060	1.053	1.066	1.064	1.061	1928	1.061
1929	1.048	1.029	1.011	1.036	1.016	1.024	1.021	1.014	1.014	1.050	1.072	1.059	1929	1.059
1930	1.050	1.061	1.066	1.062	1.074	1.076	1.077	1.075	1.080	1.081	1.083	1.072	1930	1.072
1931	1.056	1.063	1.071	1.077	1.090	1.087	1.080	1.078	1.045	1.007	1.007	0.982	1931	0.982
1932	0.982	1.019	1.014	1.072	1.049	1.053	1.101	1.098	1.101	1.097	1.097	1.109	1932	1.109
1933	1.122	1.091	1.098	1.092	1.122	1.124	1.120	1.122	1.122	1.108	1.089	1.074	1933	1.074
1934	1.098	1.105	1.123	1.135	1.147	1.152	1.153	1.137	1.118	1.135	1.137	1.146	1934	1.146
1935	1.164	1.173	1.175	1.181	1.172	1.180	1.183	1.164	1.163	1.167	1.166	1.171	1935	1.171
1936	1.175	1.182	1.191	1.193	1.195	1.195	1.199	1.210	1.203	1.201	1.223	1.225	1936	1.225
1937	1.221	1.229	1.176	1.178	1.182	1.176	1.190	1.175	1.177	1.180	1.188	1.195	1937	1.195
1938	1.199	1.203	1.196	1.218	1.221	1.219	1.222	1.219	1.219	1.227	1.222	1.229	1938	1.229
1939	1.233	1.241	1.254	1.266	1.285	1.280	1.292	1.263	1.192	1.238	1.256	1.272	1939	1.272
1940	1.267	1.268	1.288	1.281	1.241	1.270	1.274	1.275	1.287	1.289	1.313	1.319	1940	1.319
1941	1.291	1.291	1.301	1.316	1.317	1.324	1.325	1.325	1.321	1.338	1.332	1.306	1941	1.306
1942	1.312	1.311	1.321	1.314	1.322	1.319	1.319	1.321	1.319	1.319	1.312	1.316	1942	1.316
1943	1.317	1.314	1.313	1.316	1.320	1.320	1.317	1.317	1.316	1.314	1.311	1.311	1943	1.311
1944	1.311	1.312	1.312	1.312	1.312	1.311	1.313	1.314	1.313	1.312	1.312	1.315	1944	1.315
1945	1.329	1.337	1.337	1.356	1.361	1.381	1.367	1.368	1.373	1.384	1.399	1.424	1945	1.424
1946	1.425	1.427	1.427	1.405	1.401	1.408	1.400	1.382	1.378	1.386	1.376	1.393	1946	1.393
1947	1.390	1.390	1.391	1.383	1.385	1.384	1.390	1.399	1.391	1.383	1.357	1.328	1947	1.328
1948	1.328	1.332	1.333	1.337	1.353	1.339	1.333	1.331	1.330	1.328	1.336	1.341	1948	1.341
1949	1.349	1.353	1.360	1.360	1.360	1.380	1.382	1.395	1.391	1.391	1.391	1.396	1949	1.396
1950	1.385	1.386	1.384	1.386	1.388	1.382	1.387	1.387	1.374	1.365	1.367	1.367	1950	1.367
1951	1.372	1.360	1.336	1.325	1.313	1.302	1.317	1.328	1.315	1.313	1.292	1.282	1951	1.282
1952	1.282	1.281	1.293	1.312	1.305	1.302	1.297	1.285	1.266	1.281	1.277	1.263	1952	1.263
1953	1.261	1.248	1.233	1.218	1.197	1.220	1.222	1.218	1.251	1.258	1.248	1.271	1953	1.271
1954	1.280	1.307	1.312	1.322	1.308	1.326	1.341	1.333	1.329	1.327	1.321	1.326	1954	1.326
1955	1.291	1.279	1.287	1.284	1.290	1.277	1.261	1.258	1.265	1.280	1.271	1.272	1955	1.272
1956	1.280	1.277	1.255	1.237	1.262	1.262	1.233	1.207	1.210	1.200	1.189	1.165	1956	1.165
1957	1.202	1.202	1.196	1.166	1.160	1.136	1.127	1.124	1.129	1.120	1.177	1.209	1957	1.209
1958	1.196	1.205	1.214	1.233	1.230	1.207	1.170	1.116	1.100	1.111	1.122	1.098	1958	1.098
1959	1.085	1.095	1.093	1.076	1.072	1.070	1.072	1.064	1.054	1.067	1.050	1.030	1959	1.030
1960	1.038	1.055	1.081	1.059	1.071	1.086	1.122	1.111	1.116	1.109	1.098	1.125	1960	1.125
1961	1.109	1.128	1.121	1.130	1.121	1.109	1.109	1.101	1.112	1.116	1.110	1.093	1961	1.093
1962	1.088	1.095	1.119	1.125	1.126	1.115	1.099	1.115	1.119	1.124	1.123	1.124	1962	1.124
1963	1.120	1.117	1.115	1.110	1.109	1.107	1.107	1.106	1.102	1.096	1.098	1.093	1963	1.093
1964	1.088	1.083	1.083	1.085	1.087	1.090	1.087	1.085	1.087	1.088	1.086	1.085	1964	1.085
1965	1.086	1.084	1.086	1.086	1.085	1.086	1.084	1.079	1.072	1.071	1.060	1.048	1965	1.048
1966	1.033	1.004	1.030	1.019	1.009	1.004	0.996	0.971	1.000	1.019	1.000	1.037	1966	1.037
1967	1.049	1.022	1.038	1.005	0.996	0.961	0.964	0.952	0.947	0.905	0.883	0.896	1967	0.896
1968	0.921	0.914	0.891	0.907	0.907	0.924	0.946	0.942	0.928	0.912	0.883	0.847	1968	0.847
1969	0.825	0.825	0.822	0.853	0.807	0.820	0.822	0.812	0.765	0.788	0.765	0.755	1969	0.755
1970	0.750	0.790	0.780	0.743	0.705	0.734	0.753	0.748	0.761	0.748	0.803	0.792	1970	0.792

Table B-6 **Long-Term Government Bonds: Capital Appreciation Index**

(continued)

From January 1971 to December 1998

YEAR	JAN	FEB	MAR	APR	MAY	JUN	JUL	AUG	SEP	OCT	NOV	DEC	YR-END	INDEX
1971	0.828	0.811	0.849	0.821	0.816	0.799	0.797	0.830	0.843	0.853	0.845	0.844	1971	0.844
1972	0.835	0.838	0.827	0.825	0.843	0.834	0.847	0.846	0.835	0.850	0.865	0.841	1972	0.841
1973	0.810	0.807	0.809	0.808	0.795	0.789	0.750	0.774	0.795	0.807	0.788	0.777	1973	0.777
1974	0.765	0.759	0.733	0.709	0.713	0.712	0.705	0.684	0.696	0.725	0.742	0.750	1974	0.750
1975	0.761	0.767	0.741	0.723	0.733	0.750	0.738	0.728	0.716	0.745	0.732	0.755	1975	0.755
1976	0.757	0.757	0.764	0.761	0.744	0.754	0.755	0.766	0.772	0.774	0.795	0.816	1976	0.816
1977	0.780	0.771	0.773	0.774	0.779	0.787	0.776	0.787	0.780	0.767	0.770	0.752	1977	0.752
1978	0.741	0.737	0.730	0.725	0.715	0.706	0.711	0.721	0.709	0.690	0.698	0.684	1978	0.684
1979	0.692	0.678	0.682	0.669	0.681	0.697	0.686	0.679	0.666	0.604	0.618	0.617	1979	0.617
1980	0.566	0.535	0.512	0.585	0.605	0.621	0.587	0.556	0.537	0.517	0.518	0.530	1980	0.530
1981	0.519	0.492	0.505	0.474	0.499	0.484	0.462	0.439	0.428	0.458	0.518	0.476	1981	0.476
1982	0.473	0.476	0.481	0.494	0.491	0.474	0.492	0.525	0.552	0.582	0.577	0.589	1982	0.589
1983	0.566	0.589	0.578	0.594	0.565	0.563	0.530	0.526	0.547	0.535	0.540	0.532	1983	0.532
1984	0.539	0.524	0.511	0.500	0.469	0.472	0.499	0.507	0.519	0.543	0.544	0.544	1984	0.544
1985	0.558	0.526	0.538	0.545	0.589	0.592	0.576	0.586	0.580	0.594	0.613	0.641	1985	0.641
1986	0.634	0.702	0.751	0.741	0.699	0.737	0.724	0.755	0.713	0.728	0.743	0.737	1986	0.737
1987	0.744	0.755	0.733	0.693	0.682	0.683	0.666	0.650	0.621	0.655	0.652	0.658	1987	0.658
1988	0.697	0.696	0.670	0.654	0.642	0.661	0.645	0.644	0.661	0.676	0.658	0.661	1988	0.661
1989	0.669	0.652	0.655	0.661	0.682	0.715	0.727	0.703	0.700	0.722	0.723	0.718	1989	0.718
1990	0.688	0.681	0.674	0.655	0.677	0.688	0.691	0.657	0.660	0.669	0.691	0.699	1990	0.699
1991	0.703	0.701	0.699	0.703	0.699	0.690	0.695	0.714	0.731	0.730	0.732	0.769	1991	0.769
1992	0.740	0.739	0.727	0.724	0.737	0.747	0.772	0.772	0.782	0.762	0.758	0.772	1992	0.772
1993	0.789	0.813	0.809	0.811	0.810	0.841	0.853	0.885	0.881	0.885	0.858	0.855	1993	0.855
1994	0.872	0.829	0.791	0.775	0.763	0.751	0.774	0.762	0.732	0.726	0.726	0.733	1994	0.733
1995	0.748	0.765	0.767	0.775	0.831	0.838	0.820	0.834	0.845	0.865	0.882	0.901	1995	0.901
1996	0.896	0.848	0.826	0.807	0.798	0.810	0.807	0.791	0.809	0.837	0.862	0.835	1996	0.835
1997	0.824	0.820	0.794	0.810	0.813	0.824	0.871	0.839	0.861	0.885	0.894	0.906	1997	0.906
1998	0.920	0.909	0.907	0.904	0.917	0.933	0.925	0.963	0.997	0.971	0.976	0.968	1998	0.968

Table B-7 **Intermediate-Term Government Bonds: Total Return Index**

From December 1925 to December 1970

YEAR	JAN	FEB	MAR	APR	MAY	JUN	JUL	AUG	SEP	OCT	NOV	DEC	YR-END	INDEX
1925												1.000	1925	1.000
1926	1.007	1.010	1.014	1.023	1.024	1.027	1.028	1.029	1.034	1.040	1.044	1.054	1926	1.054
1927	1.060	1.064	1.068	1.070	1.072	1.075	1.079	1.086	1.092	1.088	1.097	1.101	1927	1.101
1928	1.107	1.106	1.107	1.107	1.106	1.108	1.098	1.104	1.107	1.110	1.112	1.112	1928	1.112
1929	1.108	1.106	1.107	1.117	1.110	1.122	1.129	1.135	1.133	1.153	1.173	1.178	1929	1.178
1930	1.174	1.185	1.204	1.195	1.202	1.219	1.226	1.229	1.236	1.246	1.255	1.258	1930	1.258
1931	1.249	1.261	1.267	1.278	1.293	1.266	1.268	1.270	1.255	1.242	1.248	1.228	1931	1.228
1932	1.224	1.240	1.250	1.274	1.263	1.276	1.292	1.307	1.311	1.317	1.321	1.337	1932	1.337
1933	1.335	1.334	1.348	1.355	1.382	1.383	1.382	1.393	1.396	1.393	1.396	1.361	1933	1.361
1934	1.379	1.386	1.412	1.438	1.455	1.468	1.465	1.451	1.431	1.458	1.465	1.483	1934	1.483
1935	1.500	1.516	1.535	1.552	1.546	1.564	1.570	1.558	1.550	1.566	1.569	1.587	1935	1.587
1936	1.587	1.598	1.603	1.607	1.613	1.615	1.618	1.626	1.628	1.632	1.645	1.636	1936	1.636
1937	1.631	1.632	1.605	1.613	1.625	1.623	1.633	1.626	1.639	1.644	1.651	1.661	1937	1.661
1938	1.676	1.684	1.682	1.721	1.725	1.738	1.740	1.742	1.740	1.756	1.756	1.765	1938	1.765
1939	1.770	1.785	1.799	1.806	1.823	1.823	1.831	1.804	1.756	1.812	1.825	1.845	1939	1.845
1940	1.842	1.849	1.865	1.865	1.825	1.860	1.860	1.868	1.877	1.884	1.894	1.899	1940	1.899
1941	1.900	1.891	1.904	1.910	1.912	1.923	1.923	1.925	1.925	1.930	1.912	1.909	1941	1.909
1942	1.923	1.926	1.930	1.935	1.938	1.940	1.940	1.944	1.939	1.943	1.946	1.946	1942	1.946
1943	1.953	1.956	1.960	1.965	1.976	1.983	1.987	1.987	1.990	1.993	1.996	2.000	1943	2.000
1944	2.003	2.006	2.010	2.015	2.016	2.017	2.023	2.028	2.030	2.033	2.034	2.036	1944	2.036
1945	2.047	2.055	2.056	2.059	2.061	2.065	2.065	2.068	2.072	2.075	2.077	2.082	1945	2.082
1946	2.090	2.100	2.092	2.088	2.089	2.096	2.094	2.094	2.092	2.098	2.096	2.102	1946	2.102
1947	2.107	2.109	2.114	2.111	2.112	2.114	2.115	2.121	2.121	2.116	2.117	2.122	1947	2.122
1948	2.125	2.129	2.132	2.136	2.148	2.146	2.146	2.145	2.147	2.149	2.154	2.161	1948	2.161
1949	2.167	2.169	2.175	2.178	2.183	2.194	2.198	2.205	2.207	2.208	2.208	2.211	1949	2.211
1950	2.210	2.212	2.212	2.213	2.218	2.218	2.223	2.221	2.220	2.221	2.225	2.227	1950	2.227
1951	2.231	2.233	2.205	2.217	2.208	2.219	2.232	2.240	2.227	2.231	2.238	2.235	1951	2.235
1952	2.243	2.239	2.253	2.266	2.270	2.262	2.254	2.249	2.253	2.268	2.267	2.271	1952	2.271
1953	2.271	2.271	2.267	2.246	2.219	2.254	2.266	2.265	2.309	2.317	2.321	2.345	1953	2.345
1954	2.360	2.383	2.390	2.400	2.382	2.412	2.411	2.414	2.409	2.406	2.406	2.407	1954	2.407
1955	2.400	2.387	2.393	2.394	2.394	2.386	2.369	2.370	2.390	2.407	2.394	2.392	1955	2.392
1956	2.417	2.418	2.393	2.393	2.420	2.421	2.398	2.373	2.395	2.390	2.379	2.382	1956	2.382
1957	2.438	2.435	2.439	2.415	2.411	2.385	2.382	2.408	2.408	2.418	2.514	2.568	1957	2.568
1958	2.577	2.613	2.627	2.640	2.656	2.638	2.614	2.521	2.517	2.518	2.551	2.535	1958	2.535
1959	2.532	2.559	2.550	2.536	2.536	2.517	2.525	2.505	2.510	2.554	2.530	2.525	1959	2.525
1960	2.564	2.583	2.658	2.641	2.649	2.707	2.779	2.778	2.786	2.790	2.764	2.822	1960	2.822
1961	2.805	2.831	2.841	2.856	2.848	2.841	2.843	2.848	2.871	2.875	2.869	2.874	1961	2.874
1962	2.861	2.906	2.932	2.939	2.953	2.945	2.941	2.978	2.984	3.000	3.018	3.034	1962	3.034
1963	3.026	3.031	3.039	3.048	3.053	3.057	3.058	3.064	3.068	3.071	3.083	3.084	1963	3.084
1964	3.094	3.098	3.103	3.113	3.138	3.150	3.158	3.167	3.181	3.191	3.190	3.209	1964	3.209
1965	3.222	3.228	3.242	3.250	3.262	3.278	3.283	3.290	3.288	3.288	3.290	3.242	1965	3.242
1966	3.242	3.215	3.275	3.269	3.273	3.265	3.257	3.216	3.286	3.311	3.320	3.394	1966	3.394
1967	3.434	3.429	3.492	3.461	3.476	3.397	3.443	3.430	3.433	3.416	3.425	3.428	1967	3.428
1968	3.478	3.491	3.482	3.477	3.499	3.557	3.620	3.628	3.648	3.651	3.646	3.583	1968	3.583
1969	3.614	3.609	3.644	3.673	3.643	3.613	3.642	3.636	3.527	3.644	3.627	3.557	1969	3.557
1970	3.568	3.724	3.757	3.679	3.720	3.742	3.799	3.843	3.919	3.956	4.134	4.156	1970	4.156

Table B-7

Intermediate-Term Government Bonds: Total Return Index

(continued)

From January 1971 to December 1998

YEAR	JAN	FEB	MAR	APR	MAY	JUN	JUL	AUG	SEP	OCT	NOV	DEC	YR-END	INDEX
1971	4.226	4.321	4.401	4.257	4.262	4.182	4.193	4.340	4.351	4.447	4.470	4.519	1971	4.519
1972	4.567	4.573	4.580	4.586	4.594	4.614	4.621	4.628	4.635	4.642	4.662	4.752	1972	4.752
1973	4.749	4.713	4.735	4.765	4.792	4.790	4.657	4.776	4.895	4.920	4.951	4.971	1973	4.971
1974	4.975	4.993	4.887	4.813	4.876	4.833	4.837	4.831	4.985	5.040	5.159	5.254	1974	5.254
1975	5.282	5.360	5.328	5.229	5.365	5.380	5.363	5.359	5.364	5.561	5.555	5.665	1975	5.665
1976	5.697	5.745	5.788	5.855	5.770	5.862	5.932	6.044	6.089	6.179	6.378	6.394	1976	6.394
1977	6.273	6.303	6.338	6.371	6.407	6.472	6.473	6.478	6.487	6.449	6.499	6.484	1977	6.484
1978	6.492	6.503	6.527	6.543	6.542	6.528	6.592	6.644	6.682	6.608	6.668	6.710	1978	6.710
1979	6.747	6.707	6.783	6.805	6.936	7.079	7.071	7.006	7.010	6.682	6.925	6.985	1979	6.985
1980	6.891	6.449	6.542	7.325	7.684	7.625	7.544	7.252	7.225	7.115	7.136	7.258	1980	7.258
1981	7.281	7.110	7.297	7.140	7.315	7.358	7.160	7.033	7.148	7.585	8.058	7.944	1981	7.944
1982	7.984	8.102	8.137	8.379	8.502	8.387	8.776	9.188	9.486	9.990	10.070	10.256	1982	10.256
1983	10.263	10.522	10.471	10.742	10.611	10.628	10.417	10.501	10.832	10.852	10.964	11.015	1983	11.015
1984	11.211	11.139	11.100	11.097	10.819	10.926	11.355	11.469	11.701	12.149	12.382	12.560	1984	12.560
1985	12.818	12.588	12.798	13.136	13.772	13.922	13.859	14.064	14.222	14.453	14.735	15.113	1985	15.113
1986	15.238	15.657	16.186	16.318	15.968	16.409	16.667	17.109	16.921	17.195	17.389	17.401	1986	17.401
1987	17.587	17.691	17.636	17.205	17.140	17.350	17.394	17.328	17.085	17.596	17.741	17.906	1987	17.906
1988	18.472	18.698	18.537	18.455	18.364	18.698	18.610	18.593	18.957	19.238	19.017	18.999	1988	18.999
1989	19.230	19.133	19.227	19.650	20.067	20.717	21.203	20.682	20.824	21.318	21.497	21.524	1989	21.524
1990	21.299	21.313	21.318	21.154	21.707	22.035	22.418	22.213	22.422	22.804	23.243	23.618	1990	23.618
1991	23.870	23.984	24.039	24.320	24.464	24.409	24.725	25.335	25.881	26.228	26.565	27.270	1991	27.270
1992	26.737	26.796	26.583	26.843	27.438	27.923	28.600	29.029	29.592	29.054	28.810	29.230	1992	29.230
1993	30.021	30.749	30.883	31.156	31.126	31.753	31.769	32.477	32.657	32.714	32.411	32.516	1993	32.516
1994	32.964	32.113	31.286	30.957	30.951	30.863	31.385	31.466	30.968	30.896	30.680	30.843	1994	30.843
1995	31.404	32.140	32.341	32.805	34.014	34.285	34.231	34.525	34.745	35.164	35.687	36.025	1995	36.025
1996	36.048	35.551	35.131	34.955	34.844	35.253	35.340	35.323	35.872	36.527	37.072	36.782	1996	36.782
1997	36.873	36.880	36.460	37.000	37.293	37.671	38.666	38.289	38.867	39.451	39.446	39.864	1997	39.864
1998	40.583	40.426	40.530	40.777	41.062	41.385	41.495	42.619	44.023	44.203	43.772	43.933	1998	43.933

Table B-8 **Intermediate-Term Government Bonds: Capital Appreciation Index**

From December 1925 to December 1970

YEAR	JAN	FEB	MAR	APR	MAY	JUN	JUL	AUG	SEP	OCT	NOV	DEC	YR-END	INDEX
1925												1.000	1925	1.000
1926	1.004	1.004	1.005	1.010	1.008	1.008	1.006	1.004	1.005	1.008	1.009	1.015	1926	1.015
1927	1.018	1.019	1.020	1.018	1.017	1.017	1.019	1.022	1.025	1.018	1.024	1.025	1927	1.025
1928	1.027	1.023	1.022	1.018	1.015	1.013	1.001	1.003	1.002	1.002	1.001	0.997	1928	0.997
1929	0.991	0.985	0.982	0.987	0.978	0.985	0.988	0.990	0.985	0.998	1.013	1.014	1929	1.014
1930	1.007	1.013	1.027	1.017	1.020	1.032	1.034	1.034	1.038	1.043	1.048	1.048	1930	1.048
1931	1.038	1.045	1.048	1.055	1.065	1.040	1.039	1.038	1.023	1.009	1.011	0.991	1931	0.991
1932	0.985	0.994	0.998	1.015	1.002	1.010	1.019	1.029	1.029	1.031	1.032	1.041	1932	1.041
1933	1.037	1.034	1.042	1.045	1.063	1.062	1.059	1.064	1.065	1.060	1.061	1.031	1933	1.031
1934	1.041	1.044	1.061	1.078	1.088	1.096	1.091	1.079	1.061	1.079	1.081	1.092	1934	1.092
1935	1.103	1.112	1.124	1.134	1.129	1.140	1.142	1.132	1.124	1.135	1.134	1.146	1935	1.146
1936	1.144	1.151	1.153	1.154	1.157	1.157	1.158	1.163	1.163	1.164	1.172	1.165	1936	1.165
1937	1.160	1.159	1.139	1.143	1.150	1.147	1.152	1.146	1.154	1.156	1.159	1.165	1937	1.165
1938	1.173	1.177	1.174	1.199	1.200	1.207	1.207	1.207	1.204	1.213	1.211	1.216	1938	1.216
1939	1.218	1.227	1.235	1.239	1.249	1.248	1.252	1.232	1.199	1.235	1.243	1.255	1939	1.255
1940	1.252	1.255	1.265	1.265	1.237	1.259	1.258	1.262	1.267	1.271	1.278	1.280	1940	1.280
1941	1.280	1.273	1.281	1.284	1.285	1.292	1.291	1.292	1.291	1.294	1.281	1.278	1941	1.278
1942	1.287	1.288	1.290	1.292	1.293	1.294	1.293	1.295	1.291	1.293	1.294	1.293	1942	1.293
1943	1.296	1.297	1.297	1.299	1.304	1.307	1.308	1.307	1.307	1.308	1.308	1.309	1943	1.309
1944	1.309	1.309	1.310	1.312	1.311	1.311	1.313	1.314	1.314	1.314	1.314	1.314	1944	1.314
1945	1.319	1.323	1.322	1.323	1.323	1.324	1.323	1.324	1.325	1.325	1.326	1.327	1945	1.327
1946	1.331	1.336	1.330	1.327	1.326	1.329	1.327	1.326	1.324	1.326	1.323	1.326	1946	1.326
1947	1.328	1.327	1.329	1.326	1.326	1.326	1.325	1.327	1.326	1.322	1.321	1.322	1947	1.322
1948	1.322	1.323	1.323	1.324	1.330	1.327	1.325	1.323	1.322	1.322	1.323	1.326	1948	1.326
1949	1.328	1.328	1.329	1.330	1.331	1.336	1.337	1.340	1.340	1.339	1.338	1.338	1949	1.338
1950	1.336	1.336	1.334	1.334	1.335	1.334	1.335	1.333	1.331	1.329	1.330	1.329	1950	1.329
1951	1.330	1.329	1.310	1.315	1.308	1.312	1.317	1.320	1.310	1.310	1.312	1.307	1951	1.307
1952	1.310	1.305	1.311	1.316	1.317	1.310	1.303	1.297	1.297	1.303	1.300	1.300	1952	1.300
1953	1.297	1.295	1.290	1.275	1.257	1.274	1.278	1.274	1.295	1.298	1.297	1.308	1953	1.308
1954	1.314	1.326	1.327	1.331	1.320	1.334	1.332	1.332	1.328	1.325	1.323	1.322	1954	1.322
1955	1.315	1.306	1.307	1.305	1.302	1.295	1.283	1.281	1.288	1.295	1.285	1.281	1955	1.281
1956	1.291	1.289	1.273	1.270	1.281	1.278	1.263	1.246	1.255	1.248	1.239	1.237	1956	1.237
1957	1.262	1.258	1.257	1.240	1.234	1.218	1.212	1.221	1.217	1.219	1.263	1.287	1957	1.287
1958	1.288	1.303	1.307	1.311	1.317	1.305	1.290	1.242	1.236	1.232	1.245	1.233	1958	1.233
1959	1.228	1.237	1.228	1.218	1.214	1.200	1.200	1.186	1.184	1.200	1.184	1.177	1959	1.177
1960	1.190	1.194	1.224	1.213	1.212	1.234	1.263	1.259	1.259	1.257	1.242	1.264	1960	1.264
1961	1.253	1.261	1.262	1.265	1.258	1.251	1.248	1.246	1.252	1.250	1.244	1.243	1961	1.243
1962	1.233	1.248	1.255	1.254	1.257	1.250	1.244	1.255	1.255	1.257	1.261	1.264	1962	1.264
1963	1.257	1.255	1.255	1.255	1.253	1.251	1.247	1.246	1.243	1.240	1.241	1.237	1963	1.237
1964	1.237	1.235	1.233	1.233	1.239	1.239	1.238	1.237	1.239	1.239	1.234	1.237	1964	1.237
1965	1.238	1.237	1.237	1.236	1.237	1.238	1.236	1.234	1.229	1.225	1.221	1.199	1965	1.199
1966	1.194	1.180	1.197	1.190	1.186	1.179	1.171	1.151	1.171	1.174	1.173	1.194	1966	1.194
1967	1.203	1.197	1.214	1.200	1.200	1.168	1.178	1.169	1.165	1.154	1.152	1.148	1967	1.148
1968	1.159	1.158	1.150	1.143	1.145	1.159	1.173	1.171	1.172	1.168	1.162	1.136	1968	1.136
1969	1.140	1.133	1.139	1.141	1.126	1.110	1.113	1.105	1.065	1.093	1.082	1.054	1969	1.054
1970	1.050	1.090	1.092	1.063	1.068	1.068	1.077	1.083	1.098	1.102	1.145	1.145	1970	1.145

Table B-8 **Intermediate-Term Government Bonds: Capital Appreciation Index**

(continued)

From January 1971 to December 1998

YEAR	JAN	FEB	MAR	APR	MAY	JUN	JUL	AUG	SEP	OCT	NOV	DEC	YR-END	INDEX
1971	1.159	1.180	1.197	1.153	1.149	1.121	1.118	1.151	1.149	1.169	1.169	1.177	1971	1.177
1972	1.183	1.180	1.176	1.173	1.169	1.168	1.164	1.160	1.156	1.152	1.151	1.168	1972	1.168
1973	1.161	1.146	1.145	1.146	1.146	1.140	1.101	1.122	1.144	1.143	1.144	1.142	1973	1.142
1974	1.137	1.135	1.105	1.081	1.088	1.072	1.065	1.056	1.083	1.087	1.106	1.120	1974	1.120
1975	1.119	1.129	1.116	1.088	1.110	1.106	1.095	1.088	1.081	1.114	1.106	1.121	1975	1.121
1976	1.121	1.124	1.125	1.131	1.109	1.119	1.125	1.139	1.142	1.152	1.183	1.180	1976	1.180
1977	1.151	1.151	1.151	1.151	1.151	1.156	1.150	1.144	1.140	1.126	1.128	1.119	1977	1.119
1978	1.113	1.109	1.105	1.101	1.093	1.084	1.087	1.088	1.087	1.067	1.069	1.069	1978	1.069
1979	1.066	1.053	1.057	1.052	1.064	1.079	1.069	1.052	1.045	0.987	1.015	1.015	1979	1.015
1980	0.992	0.920	0.924	1.025	1.067	1.051	1.031	0.983	0.970	0.946	0.940	0.946	1980	0.946
1981	0.939	0.908	0.921	0.892	0.904	0.898	0.864	0.838	0.841	0.881	0.926	0.903	1981	0.903
1982	0.897	0.902	0.894	0.911	0.915	0.892	0.923	0.956	0.978	1.021	1.021	1.031	1982	1.031
1983	1.023	1.041	1.027	1.045	1.023	1.016	0.988	0.986	1.007	1.000	1.001	0.997	1983	0.997
1984	1.005	0.990	0.977	0.967	0.933	0.932	0.958	0.958	0.968	0.994	1.004	1.009	1984	1.009
1985	1.021	0.994	1.002	1.019	1.059	1.063	1.049	1.056	1.059	1.068	1.081	1.100	1985	1.100
1986	1.101	1.124	1.155	1.157	1.125	1.149	1.160	1.184	1.164	1.176	1.183	1.177	1986	1.177
1987	1.183	1.184	1.173	1.138	1.126	1.132	1.127	1.116	1.092	1.117	1.118	1.121	1987	1.121
1988	1.149	1.156	1.138	1.126	1.112	1.125	1.112	1.103	1.116	1.125	1.105	1.096	1988	1.096
1989	1.100	1.088	1.085	1.101	1.115	1.144	1.163	1.127	1.128	1.146	1.149	1.143	1989	1.143
1990	1.123	1.117	1.109	1.093	1.113	1.122	1.134	1.116	1.119	1.130	1.144	1.155	1990	1.155
1991	1.160	1.158	1.154	1.160	1.159	1.150	1.156	1.178	1.196	1.205	1.214	1.240	1991	1.240
1992	1.209	1.206	1.189	1.193	1.213	1.228	1.251	1.263	1.282	1.253	1.236	1.248	1992	1.248
1993	1.275	1.301	1.300	1.305	1.299	1.318	1.314	1.337	1.339	1.336	1.318	1.317	1993	1.317
1994	1.329	1.290	1.250	1.231	1.224	1.213	1.227	1.223	1.197	1.187	1.171	1.170	1994	1.170
1995	1.184	1.205	1.205	1.216	1.253	1.257	1.249	1.253	1.255	1.264	1.277	1.283	1995	1.283
1996	1.278	1.255	1.235	1.222	1.212	1.220	1.216	1.209	1.221	1.237	1.249	1.233	1996	1.233
1997	1.230	1.225	1.204	1.215	1.218	1.224	1.250	1.232	1.244	1.256	1.251	1.257	1997	1.257
1998	1.274	1.264	1.261	1.263	1.266	1.270	1.267	1.296	1.333	1.334	1.316	1.316	1998	1.316

Table B-9 **U.S. Treasury Bills: Total Return Index**

From December 1925 to December 1970

YEAR	JAN	FEB	MAR	APR	MAY	JUN	JUL	AUG	SEP	OCT	NOV	DEC	YR-END	INDEX
1925												1.000	1925	1.000
1926	1.003	1.006	1.009	1.013	1.013	1.016	1.018	1.021	1.023	1.027	1.030	1.033	1926	1.033
1927	1.035	1.038	1.041	1.044	1.047	1.049	1.053	1.055	1.058	1.060	1.063	1.065	1927	1.065
1928	1.068	1.071	1.074	1.077	1.080	1.084	1.087	1.091	1.093	1.098	1.102	1.103	1928	1.103
1929	1.107	1.111	1.114	1.118	1.123	1.129	1.133	1.137	1.141	1.147	1.151	1.155	1929	1.155
1930	1.157	1.160	1.164	1.167	1.170	1.173	1.175	1.176	1.179	1.180	1.181	1.183	1930	1.183
1931	1.185	1.185	1.187	1.188	1.189	1.190	1.190	1.191	1.191	1.192	1.194	1.196	1931	1.196
1932	1.198	1.201	1.203	1.205	1.205	1.206	1.206	1.206	1.207	1.207	1.207	1.207	1932	1.207
1933	1.207	1.207	1.208	1.209	1.209	1.210	1.210	1.210	1.210	1.210	1.211	1.211	1933	1.211
1934	1.211	1.212	1.212	1.212	1.212	1.212	1.212	1.212	1.212	1.213	1.213	1.213	1934	1.213
1935	1.213	1.213	1.213	1.213	1.214	1.214	1.214	1.214	1.214	1.214	1.215	1.215	1935	1.215
1936	1.215	1.215	1.215	1.216	1.216	1.216	1.216	1.216	1.217	1.217	1.217	1.217	1936	1.217
1937	1.217	1.217	1.218	1.218	1.219	1.219	1.219	1.220	1.220	1.220	1.221	1.221	1937	1.221
1938	1.221	1.221	1.221	1.221	1.221	1.221	1.221	1.221	1.221	1.221	1.221	1.221	1938	1.221
1939	1.220	1.221	1.220	1.220	1.220	1.221	1.221	1.221	1.221	1.221	1.221	1.221	1939	1.221
1940	1.221	1.221	1.221	1.221	1.221	1.221	1.221	1.221	1.221	1.221	1.221	1.221	1940	1.221
1941	1.221	1.221	1.221	1.221	1.221	1.221	1.221	1.221	1.221	1.221	1.221	1.222	1941	1.222
1942	1.222	1.222	1.222	1.222	1.222	1.223	1.223	1.223	1.224	1.224	1.225	1.225	1942	1.225
1943	1.225	1.226	1.226	1.226	1.227	1.227	1.227	1.228	1.228	1.228	1.229	1.229	1943	1.229
1944	1.229	1.230	1.230	1.230	1.231	1.231	1.231	1.232	1.232	1.233	1.233	1.233	1944	1.233
1945	1.233	1.234	1.234	1.234	1.235	1.235	1.235	1.236	1.236	1.237	1.237	1.237	1945	1.237
1946	1.238	1.238	1.238	1.239	1.239	1.239	1.240	1.240	1.240	1.241	1.241	1.242	1946	1.242
1947	1.242	1.242	1.243	1.243	1.243	1.244	1.244	1.244	1.245	1.246	1.247	1.248	1947	1.248
1948	1.249	1.250	1.251	1.252	1.253	1.254	1.255	1.256	1.256	1.257	1.257	1.258	1948	1.258
1949	1.259	1.260	1.262	1.263	1.264	1.265	1.266	1.267	1.269	1.270	1.271	1.272	1949	1.272
1950	1.273	1.274	1.275	1.276	1.278	1.279	1.280	1.281	1.283	1.284	1.286	1.287	1950	1.287
1951	1.289	1.290	1.291	1.293	1.295	1.296	1.298	1.300	1.301	1.303	1.305	1.306	1951	1.306
1952	1.308	1.310	1.311	1.313	1.314	1.316	1.318	1.320	1.322	1.324	1.326	1.328	1952	1.328
1953	1.330	1.332	1.334	1.337	1.339	1.341	1.343	1.345	1.348	1.349	1.350	1.352	1953	1.352
1954	1.354	1.355	1.356	1.357	1.357	1.358	1.359	1.360	1.361	1.362	1.363	1.364	1954	1.364
1955	1.365	1.366	1.367	1.369	1.371	1.372	1.373	1.376	1.378	1.380	1.383	1.385	1955	1.385
1956	1.388	1.391	1.393	1.396	1.399	1.402	1.405	1.407	1.410	1.413	1.416	1.419	1956	1.419
1957	1.423	1.426	1.430	1.433	1.437	1.441	1.445	1.448	1.452	1.456	1.460	1.464	1957	1.464
1958	1.468	1.470	1.471	1.472	1.474	1.474	1.475	1.476	1.479	1.481	1.483	1.486	1958	1.486
1959	1.489	1.492	1.496	1.499	1.502	1.505	1.509	1.512	1.517	1.521	1.525	1.530	1959	1.530
1960	1.535	1.540	1.545	1.548	1.552	1.556	1.558	1.561	1.563	1.567	1.569	1.571	1960	1.571
1961	1.574	1.576	1.579	1.582	1.585	1.588	1.591	1.593	1.596	1.599	1.601	1.604	1961	1.604
1962	1.608	1.612	1.615	1.618	1.622	1.626	1.630	1.634	1.637	1.641	1.645	1.648	1962	1.648
1963	1.652	1.656	1.660	1.664	1.668	1.672	1.677	1.681	1.685	1.690	1.695	1.700	1963	1.700
1964	1.705	1.709	1.715	1.720	1.724	1.729	1.734	1.739	1.744	1.749	1.754	1.760	1964	1.760
1965	1.765	1.770	1.776	1.782	1.787	1.794	1.799	1.805	1.811	1.817	1.823	1.829	1965	1.829
1966	1.836	1.842	1.849	1.856	1.863	1.870	1.877	1.885	1.892	1.901	1.908	1.916	1966	1.916
1967	1.924	1.931	1.939	1.945	1.951	1.957	1.963	1.969	1.975	1.983	1.990	1.997	1967	1.997
1968	2.005	2.012	2.020	2.029	2.038	2.046	2.056	2.065	2.074	2.083	2.092	2.101	1968	2.101
1969	2.112	2.121	2.131	2.143	2.153	2.164	2.175	2.186	2.200	2.213	2.225	2.239	1969	2.239
1970	2.252	2.266	2.279	2.291	2.303	2.316	2.328	2.341	2.353	2.364	2.375	2.385	1970	2.385

Table B-9 **U.S. Treasury Bills: Total Return Index**

(continued)

From January 1971 to December 1998

YEAR	JAN	FEB	MAR	APR	MAY	JUN	JUL	AUG	SEP	OCT	NOV	DEC	YR-END	INDEX
1971	2.394	2.402	2.409	2.416	2.423	2.432	2.442	2.453	2.462	2.471	2.480	2.490	1971	2.490
1972	2.497	2.503	2.510	2.517	2.525	2.532	2.540	2.547	2.556	2.566	2.575	2.585	1972	2.585
1973	2.596	2.607	2.619	2.633	2.646	2.660	2.677	2.695	2.714	2.732	2.747	2.764	1973	2.764
1974	2.782	2.798	2.813	2.835	2.856	2.873	2.893	2.911	2.934	2.949	2.965	2.986	1974	2.986
1975	3.003	3.016	3.028	3.042	3.055	3.067	3.082	3.097	3.113	3.131	3.144	3.159	1975	3.159
1976	3.174	3.184	3.197	3.210	3.222	3.237	3.252	3.265	3.280	3.293	3.306	3.319	1976	3.319
1977	3.331	3.343	3.356	3.368	3.381	3.394	3.408	3.423	3.438	3.455	3.472	3.489	1977	3.489
1978	3.506	3.522	3.541	3.560	3.578	3.597	3.618	3.638	3.660	3.685	3.711	3.740	1978	3.740
1979	3.769	3.796	3.827	3.858	3.889	3.921	3.951	3.981	4.014	4.049	4.089	4.128	1979	4.128
1980	4.161	4.198	4.248	4.302	4.336	4.363	4.386	4.414	4.447	4.489	4.532	4.592	1980	4.592
1981	4.639	4.689	4.746	4.797	4.852	4.917	4.978	5.042	5.105	5.166	5.221	5.267	1981	5.267
1982	5.309	5.358	5.411	5.472	5.530	5.583	5.641	5.684	5.713	5.747	5.783	5.822	1982	5.822
1983	5.862	5.899	5.936	5.978	6.020	6.060	6.105	6.151	6.198	6.245	6.289	6.335	1983	6.335
1984	6.383	6.428	6.475	6.528	6.579	6.629	6.683	6.738	6.796	6.864	6.914	6.959	1984	6.959
1985	7.004	7.044	7.088	7.138	7.186	7.225	7.271	7.311	7.355	7.403	7.448	7.496	1985	7.496
1986	7.538	7.578	7.623	7.663	7.700	7.741	7.781	7.817	7.852	7.889	7.919	7.958	1986	7.958
1987	7.991	8.025	8.063	8.099	8.129	8.169	8.206	8.245	8.282	8.331	8.360	8.393	1987	8.393
1988	8.418	8.456	8.493	8.532	8.576	8.617	8.661	8.712	8.766	8.819	8.869	8.926	1988	8.926
1989	8.975	9.030	9.090	9.152	9.224	9.289	9.354	9.423	9.485	9.549	9.614	9.673	1989	9.673
1990	9.728	9.783	9.846	9.914	9.981	10.043	10.111	10.178	10.238	10.308	10.366	10.429	1990	10.429
1991	10.483	10.533	10.579	10.635	10.685	10.730	10.782	10.832	10.881	10.928	10.970	11.012	1991	11.012
1992	11.049	11.081	11.118	11.154	11.185	11.221	11.255	11.285	11.314	11.340	11.366	11.398	1992	11.398
1993	11.425	11.450	11.479	11.506	11.531	11.561	11.588	11.617	11.647	11.673	11.702	11.728	1993	11.728
1994	11.758	11.783	11.814	11.846	11.884	11.921	11.954	11.998	12.042	12.088	12.132	12.186	1994	12.186
1995	12.237	12.286	12.342	12.397	12.464	12.522	12.579	12.638	12.692	12.752	12.806	12.868	1995	12.868
1996	12.923	12.974	13.025	13.084	13.140	13.192	13.252	13.306	13.365	13.421	13.476	13.538	1996	13.538
1997	13.599	13.652	13.710	13.769	13.837	13.888	13.948	14.005	14.067	14.127	14.182	14.250	1997	14.250
1998	14.311	14.367	14.423	14.485	14.544	14.603	14.662	14.725	14.792	14.840	14.886	14.942	1998	14.942

Table B-10 **Inflation Index**

From December 1925 to December 1970

YEAR	JAN	FEB	MAR	APR	MAY	JUN	JUL	AUG	SEP	OCT	NOV	DEC	YR-END	INDEX
1925												1.000	1925	1.000
1926	1.000	0.996	0.991	1.000	0.994	0.987	0.978	0.972	0.978	0.981	0.985	0.985	1926	0.985
1927	0.978	0.970	0.965	0.965	0.972	0.981	0.963	0.957	0.963	0.968	0.966	0.965	1927	0.965
1928	0.963	0.953	0.953	0.955	0.961	0.953	0.953	0.955	0.963	0.961	0.959	0.955	1928	0.955
1929	0.953	0.952	0.948	0.944	0.950	0.953	0.963	0.966	0.965	0.965	0.963	0.957	1929	0.957
1930	0.953	0.950	0.944	0.950	0.944	0.939	0.926	0.920	0.926	0.920	0.912	0.899	1930	0.899
1931	0.886	0.873	0.868	0.862	0.853	0.844	0.842	0.840	0.836	0.831	0.821	0.814	1931	0.814
1932	0.797	0.786	0.782	0.777	0.765	0.760	0.760	0.750	0.747	0.741	0.737	0.730	1932	0.730
1933	0.719	0.708	0.702	0.700	0.702	0.709	0.730	0.737	0.737	0.737	0.737	0.734	1933	0.734
1934	0.737	0.743	0.743	0.741	0.743	0.745	0.745	0.747	0.758	0.752	0.750	0.749	1934	0.749
1935	0.760	0.765	0.764	0.771	0.767	0.765	0.762	0.762	0.765	0.765	0.769	0.771	1935	0.771
1936	0.771	0.767	0.764	0.764	0.764	0.771	0.775	0.780	0.782	0.780	0.780	0.780	1936	0.780
1937	0.786	0.788	0.793	0.797	0.801	0.803	0.806	0.808	0.816	0.812	0.806	0.804	1937	0.804
1938	0.793	0.786	0.786	0.790	0.786	0.786	0.788	0.786	0.786	0.782	0.780	0.782	1938	0.782
1939	0.778	0.775	0.773	0.771	0.771	0.771	0.771	0.771	0.786	0.782	0.782	0.778	1939	0.778
1940	0.777	0.782	0.780	0.780	0.782	0.784	0.782	0.780	0.782	0.782	0.782	0.786	1940	0.786
1941	0.786	0.786	0.790	0.797	0.803	0.818	0.821	0.829	0.844	0.853	0.860	0.862	1941	0.862
1942	0.873	0.881	0.892	0.898	0.907	0.909	0.912	0.918	0.920	0.929	0.935	0.942	1942	0.942
1943	0.942	0.944	0.959	0.970	0.978	0.976	0.968	0.965	0.968	0.972	0.970	0.972	1943	0.972
1944	0.970	0.968	0.968	0.974	0.978	0.980	0.985	0.989	0.989	0.989	0.989	0.993	1944	0.993
1945	0.993	0.991	0.991	0.993	1.000	1.009	1.011	1.011	1.007	1.007	1.011	1.015	1945	1.015
1946	1.015	1.011	1.019	1.024	1.030	1.041	1.102	1.127	1.140	1.162	1.190	1.199	1946	1.199
1947	1.199	1.197	1.223	1.223	1.220	1.229	1.240	1.253	1.283	1.283	1.291	1.307	1947	1.307
1948	1.322	1.311	1.307	1.326	1.335	1.345	1.361	1.367	1.367	1.361	1.352	1.343	1948	1.343
1949	1.341	1.326	1.330	1.331	1.330	1.331	1.322	1.326	1.331	1.324	1.326	1.318	1949	1.318
1950	1.313	1.309	1.315	1.317	1.322	1.330	1.343	1.354	1.363	1.371	1.376	1.395	1950	1.395
1951	1.417	1.434	1.439	1.441	1.447	1.445	1.447	1.447	1.456	1.464	1.471	1.477	1951	1.477
1952	1.477	1.467	1.467	1.473	1.475	1.479	1.490	1.492	1.490	1.492	1.492	1.490	1952	1.490
1953	1.486	1.479	1.482	1.484	1.488	1.493	1.497	1.501	1.503	1.507	1.501	1.499	1953	1.499
1954	1.503	1.501	1.499	1.495	1.501	1.503	1.503	1.501	1.497	1.493	1.495	1.492	1954	1.492
1955	1.492	1.492	1.492	1.492	1.492	1.492	1.497	1.493	1.499	1.499	1.501	1.497	1955	1.497
1956	1.495	1.495	1.497	1.499	1.507	1.516	1.527	1.525	1.527	1.536	1.536	1.540	1956	1.540
1957	1.542	1.547	1.551	1.557	1.561	1.570	1.577	1.579	1.581	1.581	1.587	1.587	1957	1.587
1958	1.596	1.598	1.609	1.613	1.613	1.615	1.616	1.615	1.615	1.615	1.616	1.615	1958	1.615
1959	1.616	1.615	1.615	1.616	1.618	1.626	1.629	1.628	1.633	1.639	1.639	1.639	1959	1.639
1960	1.637	1.639	1.639	1.648	1.648	1.652	1.652	1.652	1.654	1.661	1.663	1.663	1960	1.663
1961	1.663	1.663	1.663	1.663	1.663	1.665	1.672	1.670	1.674	1.674	1.674	1.674	1961	1.674
1962	1.674	1.678	1.682	1.685	1.685	1.685	1.689	1.689	1.698	1.696	1.696	1.695	1962	1.695
1963	1.696	1.698	1.700	1.700	1.700	1.708	1.715	1.715	1.715	1.717	1.719	1.723	1963	1.723
1964	1.724	1.723	1.724	1.726	1.726	1.730	1.734	1.732	1.736	1.737	1.741	1.743	1964	1.743
1965	1.743	1.743	1.745	1.750	1.754	1.764	1.765	1.762	1.765	1.767	1.771	1.777	1965	1.777
1966	1.777	1.788	1.793	1.801	1.803	1.808	1.814	1.823	1.827	1.834	1.834	1.836	1966	1.836
1967	1.836	1.838	1.842	1.845	1.851	1.857	1.866	1.872	1.875	1.881	1.886	1.892	1967	1.892
1968	1.899	1.905	1.914	1.920	1.926	1.937	1.946	1.952	1.957	1.968	1.976	1.981	1968	1.981
1969	1.987	1.994	2.011	2.024	2.030	2.043	2.052	2.061	2.071	2.078	2.089	2.102	1969	2.102
1970	2.110	2.121	2.132	2.145	2.155	2.166	2.173	2.177	2.188	2.199	2.207	2.218	1970	2.218

Table B-10 **Inflation Index**

(continued)

From January 1971 to December 1998

YEAR	JAN	FEB	MAR	APR	MAY	JUN	JUL	AUG	SEP	OCT	NOV	DEC	YR-END	INDEX
1971	2.220	2.223	2.231	2.238	2.250	2.263	2.268	2.274	2.276	2.279	2.283	2.292	1971	2.292
1972	2.294	2.305	2.309	2.315	2.322	2.328	2.337	2.341	2.350	2.358	2.363	2.371	1972	2.371
1973	2.378	2.395	2.417	2.434	2.449	2.466	2.471	2.516	2.523	2.544	2.562	2.579	1973	2.579
1974	2.602	2.635	2.665	2.680	2.710	2.736	2.756	2.791	2.825	2.849	2.873	2.894	1974	2.894
1975	2.907	2.927	2.939	2.953	2.967	2.991	3.022	3.032	3.047	3.065	3.084	3.097	1975	3.097
1976	3.104	3.112	3.119	3.132	3.151	3.168	3.186	3.201	3.214	3.227	3.237	3.246	1976	3.246
1977	3.264	3.298	3.318	3.345	3.363	3.386	3.400	3.413	3.426	3.436	3.453	3.466	1977	3.466
1978	3.484	3.508	3.533	3.564	3.600	3.637	3.663	3.682	3.708	3.737	3.758	3.778	1978	3.778
1979	3.812	3.857	3.894	3.939	3.987	4.024	4.076	4.117	4.160	4.197	4.237	4.281	1979	4.281
1980	4.343	4.402	4.466	4.516	4.561	4.611	4.615	4.644	4.687	4.728	4.771	4.812	1980	4.812
1981	4.851	4.901	4.937	4.968	5.009	5.052	5.110	5.149	5.201	5.212	5.227	5.242	1981	5.242
1982	5.261	5.278	5.272	5.294	5.346	5.412	5.441	5.453	5.462	5.477	5.467	5.445	1982	5.445
1983	5.458	5.460	5.464	5.503	5.533	5.551	5.574	5.592	5.620	5.635	5.644	5.652	1983	5.652
1984	5.683	5.710	5.723	5.750	5.767	5.786	5.805	5.829	5.857	5.872	5.872	5.875	1984	5.875
1985	5.886	5.911	5.937	5.961	5.983	6.002	6.011	6.024	6.043	6.061	6.082	6.097	1985	6.097
1986	6.115	6.099	6.071	6.058	6.076	6.106	6.108	6.119	6.149	6.155	6.160	6.166	1986	6.166
1987	6.203	6.227	6.255	6.289	6.307	6.333	6.346	6.382	6.413	6.430	6.439	6.438	1987	6.438
1988	6.454	6.471	6.499	6.532	6.555	6.583	6.610	6.638	6.683	6.705	6.711	6.722	1988	6.722
1989	6.756	6.783	6.822	6.867	6.906	6.923	6.940	6.951	6.973	7.007	7.023	7.034	1989	7.034
1990	7.107	7.140	7.180	7.191	7.207	7.246	7.274	7.341	7.403	7.447	7.464	7.464	1990	7.464
1991	7.509	7.520	7.531	7.542	7.564	7.587	7.598	7.620	7.654	7.665	7.687	7.693	1991	7.693
1992	7.704	7.732	7.771	7.782	7.793	7.821	7.838	7.860	7.882	7.910	7.921	7.916	1992	7.916
1993	7.955	7.983	8.011	8.033	8.044	8.055	8.055	8.078	8.094	8.128	8.133	8.133	1993	8.133
1994	8.156	8.184	8.212	8.223	8.228	8.256	8.278	8.312	8.334	8.340	8.351	8.351	1994	8.351
1995	8.384	8.418	8.446	8.474	8.490	8.507	8.507	8.530	8.546	8.574	8.569	8.563	1995	8.563
1996	8.613	8.641	8.686	8.719	8.736	8.741	8.758	8.775	8.803	8.831	8.847	8.847	1996	8.847
1997	8.875	8.903	8.926	8.937	8.931	8.942	8.953	8.970	8.993	9.015	9.009	8.998	1997	8.998
1998	9.015	9.032	9.048	9.065	9.082	9.093	9.104	9.115	9.126	9.149	9.149	9.143	1998	9.143

Table B-11 **Large Company Stocks: Inflation-Adjusted Total Return Index**

From December 1925 to December 1970

YEAR	JAN	FEB	MAR	APR	MAY	JUN	JUL	AUG	SEP	OCT	NOV	DEC	YR-END	INDEX
1925												1.000	1925	1.000
1926	1.000	0.965	0.915	0.929	0.951	1.002	1.060	1.093	1.114	1.078	1.111	1.133	1926	1.133
1927	1.120	1.189	1.206	1.230	1.295	1.274	1.386	1.466	1.523	1.438	1.545	1.591	1927	1.591
1928	1.588	1.583	1.757	1.815	1.840	1.783	1.808	1.949	1.984	2.021	2.287	2.307	1928	2.307
1929	2.446	2.446	2.453	2.506	2.401	2.664	2.763	3.035	2.896	2.325	2.039	2.109	1929	2.109
1930	2.252	2.320	2.523	2.488	2.479	2.088	2.199	2.244	1.944	1.789	1.788	1.685	1930	1.685
1931	1.796	2.040	1.915	1.747	1.540	1.779	1.654	1.688	1.191	1.307	1.216	1.056	1931	1.056
1932	1.049	1.124	0.999	0.805	0.637	0.641	0.885	1.243	1.206	1.051	1.012	1.080	1932	1.080
1933	1.107	0.925	0.965	1.380	1.608	1.804	1.602	1.777	1.578	1.443	1.606	1.655	1933	1.655
1934	1.823	1.751	1.751	1.711	1.581	1.613	1.431	1.514	1.487	1.455	1.596	1.599	1934	1.599
1935	1.511	1.449	1.410	1.534	1.604	1.721	1.876	1.929	1.968	2.121	2.211	2.292	1935	2.292
1936	2.446	2.513	2.593	2.398	2.529	2.588	2.756	2.778	2.780	3.002	3.042	3.033	1936	3.033
1937	3.129	3.182	3.135	2.868	2.847	2.697	2.966	2.816	2.399	2.173	1.999	1.912	1937	1.912
1938	1.968	2.120	1.593	1.815	1.764	2.205	2.363	2.315	2.354	2.549	2.485	2.578	1938	2.578
1939	2.416	2.522	2.190	2.189	2.350	2.206	2.450	2.291	2.623	2.603	2.500	2.580	1939	2.580
1940	2.499	2.514	2.551	2.545	1.958	2.111	2.188	2.270	2.293	2.390	2.314	2.305	1940	2.305
1941	2.199	2.186	2.191	2.037	2.060	2.139	2.253	2.235	2.180	2.015	1.941	1.858	1941	1.858
1942	1.863	1.818	1.679	1.601	1.711	1.745	1.797	1.815	1.864	1.970	1.955	2.046	1942	2.046
1943	2.196	2.320	2.408	2.389	2.501	2.562	2.446	2.497	2.553	2.516	2.356	2.496	1943	2.496
1944	2.544	2.560	2.610	2.569	2.688	2.829	2.758	2.791	2.789	2.796	2.833	2.928	1944	2.928
1945	2.974	3.183	3.043	3.311	3.351	3.318	3.252	3.460	3.625	3.742	3.876	3.907	1945	3.907
1946	4.186	3.932	4.091	4.228	4.326	4.121	3.799	3.467	3.085	3.008	2.929	3.039	1946	3.039
1947	3.117	3.098	2.986	2.878	2.891	3.028	3.115	3.020	2.917	2.987	2.917	2.947	1947	2.947
1948	2.804	2.718	2.942	2.985	3.225	3.219	3.018	3.053	2.969	3.193	2.906	3.027	1948	3.027
1949	3.044	2.987	3.076	3.017	2.943	2.943	3.157	3.217	3.287	3.418	3.473	3.662	1949	3.662
1950	3.750	3.836	3.846	4.028	4.215	3.961	3.969	4.111	4.325	4.341	4.396	4.560	1950	4.560
1951	4.774	4.792	4.699	4.932	4.766	4.664	4.989	5.227	5.200	5.121	5.143	5.341	1951	5.341
1952	5.438	5.318	5.586	5.341	5.517	5.773	5.842	5.794	5.699	5.703	6.029	6.267	1952	6.267
1953	6.252	6.217	6.069	5.918	5.949	5.847	5.992	5.677	5.690	5.982	6.127	6.166	1953	6.166
1954	6.481	6.561	6.783	7.151	7.421	7.435	7.873	7.666	8.339	8.220	8.956	9.458	1954	9.458
1955	9.645	9.740	9.711	10.096	10.152	11.006	11.646	11.646	11.753	11.419	12.348	12.397	1955	12.397
1956	11.982	12.476	13.346	13.324	12.471	12.902	13.487	13.060	12.471	12.477	12.414	12.843	1956	12.843
1957	12.313	11.945	12.173	12.599	13.119	13.046	13.155	12.475	11.711	11.358	11.580	11.122	1957	11.122
1958	11.549	11.372	11.664	12.029	12.284	12.612	13.163	13.410	14.081	14.461	14.855	15.669	1958	15.669
1959	15.733	15.828	15.859	16.478	16.854	16.739	17.306	17.149	16.333	16.486	16.793	17.283	1959	17.283
1960	16.092	16.311	16.110	15.761	16.275	16.581	16.194	16.707	15.704	15.622	16.329	17.111	1960	17.111
1961	18.215	18.796	19.303	19.401	19.864	19.296	19.867	20.372	19.953	20.549	21.468	21.567	1961	21.567
1962	20.777	21.165	21.022	19.702	18.105	16.650	17.697	18.065	17.130	17.259	19.133	19.447	1962	19.447
1963	20.407	19.899	20.613	21.644	22.062	21.553	21.413	22.560	22.342	23.074	22.943	23.494	1963	23.494
1964	24.131	24.512	24.888	25.047	25.454	25.851	26.297	26.015	26.740	26.968	26.923	27.044	1964	27.044
1965	27.976	28.062	27.660	28.555	28.408	26.922	27.290	28.092	28.968	29.774	29.618	29.838	1965	29.838
1966	30.022	29.442	28.749	29.259	27.791	27.299	26.888	24.811	24.629	25.740	25.984	25.964	1966	25.964
1967	28.036	28.208	29.303	30.521	28.979	29.440	30.663	30.359	31.334	30.378	30.485	31.239	1967	31.239
1968	29.794	28.930	29.105	31.440	31.853	32.003	31.303	31.725	32.898	32.995	34.615	33.129	1968	33.129
1969	32.810	31.295	32.147	32.670	32.665	30.697	28.762	29.932	29.096	30.321	29.263	28.567	1969	28.567
1970	26.349	27.746	27.684	25.069	23.595	22.342	23.940	25.114	25.854	25.472	26.746	28.164	1970	28.164

Table B-11 **Large Company Stocks: Inflation-Adjusted Total Return Index**

(continued)

From January 1971 to December 1998

YEAR	JAN	FEB	MAR	APR	MAY	JUN	JUL	AUG	SEP	OCT	NOV	DEC	YR-END	INDEX
1971	29.319	29.682	30.715	31.766	30.447	30.335	29.052	30.176	29.984	28.726	28.755	31.149	1971	31.149
1972	31.728	32.519	32.701	32.807	33.419	32.654	32.642	33.865	33.609	33.861	35.485	35.837	1972	35.837
1973	35.156	33.749	33.431	31.891	31.255	30.883	32.028	30.459	31.630	31.384	27.784	28.110	1973	28.110
1974	27.631	27.331	26.438	25.309	24.349	23.807	21.836	19.774	17.253	19.942	18.888	18.422	1974	18.422
1975	20.634	21.872	22.304	23.285	24.362	25.281	23.368	22.961	22.099	23.363	23.950	23.619	1975	23.619
1976	26.388	26.172	26.960	26.582	26.232	27.208	26.864	26.777	27.326	26.656	26.555	27.908	1976	27.908
1977	26.391	25.728	25.265	25.102	24.590	25.587	25.090	24.663	24.570	23.485	24.236	24.260	1977	24.260
1978	22.692	22.171	22.627	24.377	24.467	23.847	25.002	25.722	25.418	22.969	23.438	23.712	1978	23.712
1979	24.493	23.522	24.637	24.445	23.742	24.487	24.438	25.673	25.473	23.591	24.575	24.786	1979	24.786
1980	25.926	25.654	22.795	23.509	24.587	25.038	26.709	26.885	27.387	27.656	30.410	29.201	1980	29.201
1981	27.697	27.983	28.838	28.044	27.987	27.528	27.236	25.532	24.007	25.220	26.257	25.489	1981	25.489
1982	24.985	23.630	23.513	24.383	23.450	22.765	22.153	24.909	25.140	27.895	29.166	29.792	1982	29.792
1983	30.756	31.544	32.674	34.900	34.532	35.731	34.474	34.943	35.242	34.678	35.427	35.165	1983	35.165
1984	34.742	33.449	33.943	34.011	32.102	32.706	32.134	35.601	35.438	35.440	35.082	35.947	1984	35.947
1985	38.634	39.003	38.902	38.620	40.842	41.363	41.192	40.852	39.419	41.054	43.845	45.781	1985	45.781
1986	45.842	49.466	52.447	51.908	54.590	55.226	52.068	55.862	51.020	53.808	55.135	53.631	1986	53.631
1987	60.468	62.721	64.139	63.236	63.698	66.602	69.775	72.059	70.126	54.892	50.323	54.053	1987	54.053
1988	56.215	58.704	56.687	57.006	57.255	59.658	59.168	56.970	58.988	60.397	59.490	60.466	1988	60.466
1989	64.517	62.652	63.763	66.618	68.904	68.366	74.326	75.638	75.102	73.002	74.343	75.977	1989	75.977
1990	70.155	70.727	72.193	70.300	76.975	76.025	75.491	68.048	64.164	63.543	67.484	69.333	1990	69.333
1991	71.967	77.005	78.721	78.825	81.956	77.981	81.510	83.181	81.459	82.431	78.871	87.822	1991	87.822
1992	86.064	86.851	84.721	87.061	87.406	85.832	89.100	87.052	87.804	87.809	90.641	91.893	1992	91.893
1993	92.109	93.027	94.696	92.119	94.475	94.656	94.211	97.530	96.608	98.163	97.174	98.369	1993	98.369
1994	101.386	98.313	93.717	94.806	96.286	93.591	96.428	99.948	97.279	99.440	95.662	97.059	1994	97.059
1995	99.185	102.624	105.312	108.020	112.066	114.474	118.285	118.295	123.010	122.180	127.639	130.085	1995	130.085
1996	133.776	134.624	135.218	136.679	139.937	140.421	133.916	136.494	143.708	147.180	158.051	154.953	1996	154.953
1997	164.059	164.869	157.616	166.817	177.170	184.841	199.269	187.838	197.635	190.561	199.507	203.190	1997	203.190
1998	205.064	219.446	230.257	232.144	227.733	236.693	233.885	199.825	212.366	229.080	242.965	257.121	1998	257.121

Table B-12 **Small Company Stocks: Inflation-Adjusted Total Return Index**

From December 1925 to December 1970

YEAR	JAN	FEB	MAR	APR	MAY	JUN	JUL	AUG	SEP	OCT	NOV	DEC	YR-END	INDEX
1925												1.000	1925	1.000
1926	1.070	1.005	0.902	0.910	0.909	0.951	0.970	1.001	0.995	0.969	0.985	1.018	1926	1.018
1927	1.056	1.122	1.067	1.128	1.202	1.154	1.237	1.222	1.221	1.134	1.228	1.269	1927	1.269
1928	1.333	1.314	1.384	1.507	1.564	1.443	1.452	1.513	1.635	1.683	1.880	1.790	1928	1.790
1929	1.800	1.799	1.770	1.831	1.577	1.655	1.657	1.624	1.477	1.068	0.910	0.869	1929	0.869
1930	0.985	1.053	1.166	1.078	1.026	0.808	0.844	0.835	0.709	0.635	0.638	0.572	1930	0.572
1931	0.703	0.896	0.838	0.661	0.576	0.688	0.651	0.603	0.409	0.444	0.403	0.318	1931	0.318
1932	0.357	0.373	0.326	0.255	0.228	0.230	0.312	0.547	0.477	0.396	0.349	0.335	1932	0.335
1933	0.337	0.299	0.335	0.505	0.823	1.028	0.944	1.021	0.858	0.752	0.801	0.810	1933	0.810
1934	1.119	1.129	1.128	1.158	1.008	1.003	0.776	0.894	0.866	0.881	0.967	0.986	1934	0.986
1935	0.939	0.877	0.775	0.828	0.830	0.858	0.936	0.986	1.017	1.118	1.269	1.342	1935	1.342
1936	1.746	1.860	1.881	1.544	1.586	1.534	1.660	1.683	1.770	1.887	2.151	2.185	1936	2.185
1937	2.445	2.599	2.612	2.163	2.065	1.817	2.031	1.878	1.388	1.242	1.069	0.890	1937	0.890
1938	0.951	0.993	0.635	0.808	0.743	1.003	1.150	1.037	1.021	1.245	1.162	1.216	1938	1.216
1939	1.118	1.135	0.857	0.872	0.966	0.866	1.085	0.913	1.356	1.308	1.171	1.226	1939	1.226
1940	1.230	1.321	1.408	1.500	0.947	1.044	1.071	1.100	1.121	1.182	1.211	1.152	1940	1.152
1941	1.154	1.121	1.151	1.064	1.062	1.121	1.357	1.337	1.252	1.155	1.088	0.955	1941	0.955
1942	1.121	1.104	1.013	0.971	0.958	0.988	1.057	1.084	1.181	1.296	1.222	1.263	1942	1.263
1943	1.532	1.824	2.056	2.221	2.459	2.444	2.196	2.204	2.289	2.308	2.055	2.306	1943	2.306
1944	2.459	2.536	2.726	2.566	2.745	3.119	3.009	3.093	3.087	3.054	3.206	3.472	1944	3.472
1945	3.639	4.014	3.668	4.085	4.257	4.579	4.316	4.556	4.884	5.226	5.817	5.895	1945	5.895
1946	6.815	6.405	6.532	6.948	7.319	6.906	6.176	5.530	4.591	4.449	4.283	4.409	1946	4.409
1947	4.594	4.582	4.334	3.887	3.691	3.865	4.133	4.074	4.026	4.139	3.991	4.081	1947	4.081
1948	3.973	3.694	4.069	4.160	4.568	4.558	4.242	4.227	4.005	4.281	3.830	3.890	1948	3.890
1949	3.966	3.818	4.046	3.905	3.690	3.649	3.921	4.011	4.189	4.412	4.413	4.744	1949	4.744
1950	4.998	5.123	5.082	5.284	5.395	4.948	5.190	5.420	5.664	5.600	5.757	6.221	1950	6.221
1951	6.632	6.594	6.255	6.476	6.238	5.916	6.128	6.499	6.596	6.417	6.331	6.335	1951	6.335
1952	6.456	6.302	6.413	6.057	6.068	6.217	6.240	6.229	6.136	6.066	6.359	6.469	1952	6.469
1953	6.751	6.967	6.903	6.696	6.774	6.421	6.502	6.078	5.912	6.069	6.168	6.012	1953	6.012
1954	6.451	6.520	6.647	6.757	7.036	7.088	7.660	7.681	8.015	8.090	8.709	9.703	1954	9.703
1955	9.898	10.372	10.460	10.617	10.700	11.014	11.043	11.039	11.118	10.930	11.427	11.642	1955	11.642
1956	11.602	11.924	12.422	12.464	11.909	11.902	12.149	12.001	11.674	11.725	11.787	11.803	1956	11.803
1957	12.067	11.783	11.952	12.205	12.267	12.284	12.152	11.669	11.129	10.203	10.282	9.788	1957	9.788
1958	10.806	10.610	11.032	11.421	11.863	12.234	12.820	13.385	14.078	14.651	15.360	15.859	1958	15.859
1959	16.751	17.265	17.312	17.494	17.497	17.344	17.870	17.734	16.911	17.236	17.619	18.187	1959	18.187
1960	17.650	17.717	17.159	16.744	17.086	17.627	17.293	18.201	16.838	16.091	16.775	17.333	1960	17.333
1961	18.918	20.033	21.273	21.543	22.463	21.219	21.191	21.491	20.717	21.259	22.562	22.741	1961	22.741
1962	23.052	23.431	23.512	21.637	19.454	17.927	19.252	19.809	18.403	17.735	19.948	19.792	1962	19.792
1963	21.562	21.613	21.910	22.593	23.579	23.198	23.173	24.371	23.974	24.514	24.227	24.060	1963	24.060
1964	24.693	25.622	26.154	26.369	26.783	27.159	28.181	28.129	29.198	29.766	29.734	29.370	1964	29.370
1965	30.924	32.130	32.859	34.420	34.079	30.846	32.196	34.184	35.296	37.276	38.577	40.848	1965	40.848
1966	43.934	45.018	44.016	45.339	40.939	40.763	40.587	36.021	35.359	34.838	36.549	36.751	1966	36.751
1967	43.507	45.416	48.111	49.313	48.747	53.544	58.342	58.287	61.456	59.369	59.883	65.471	1967	65.471
1968	66.219	61.343	60.379	68.997	75.667	75.457	72.502	74.947	79.213	79.003	84.719	85.005	1968	85.005
1969	83.360	74.828	77.140	79.668	80.827	70.957	63.080	67.392	65.339	69.075	64.876	60.042	1969	60.042
1970	56.190	58.058	56.111	46.134	41.197	37.178	39.102	42.738	47.137	43.586	44.034	46.993	1970	46.993

Table B-12 **Small Company Stocks: Inflation-Adjusted Total Return Index**

(continued)

From January 1971 to December 1998

YEAR	JAN	FEB	MAR	APR	MAY	JUN	JUL	AUG	SEP	OCT	NOV	DEC	YR-END	INDEX
1971	54.430	56.060	59.023	60.277	56.349	54.235	51.055	53.900	52.637	49.655	47.723	52.968	1971	52.968
1972	58.905	60.354	59.392	60.012	58.677	56.750	54.190	55.112	52.979	51.888	54.832	53.492	1972	53.492
1973	51.020	46.616	45.226	42.124	38.472	37.102	41.437	38.888	42.897	42.911	34.240	33.971	1973	33.971
1974	38.146	37.340	36.648	34.753	31.646	30.884	29.984	27.587	25.479	27.948	26.499	24.238	1974	24.238
1975	30.806	31.463	33.281	34.871	37.020	39.473	38.068	35.774	34.953	34.567	35.456	34.612	1975	34.612
1976	43.797	49.764	49.572	47.596	45.606	47.448	47.384	45.794	46.084	44.939	46.618	51.971	1976	51.971
1977	53.998	53.241	53.603	54.400	53.948	57.730	57.649	56.812	57.118	55.082	60.768	61.029	1977	61.029
1978	59.555	61.198	67.052	71.691	76.808	74.584	79.118	86.107	85.229	64.028	68.338	69.108	1978	69.108
1979	77.552	74.489	82.038	84.245	83.510	86.644	86.999	92.646	88.542	77.625	83.511	87.502	1979	87.502
1980	93.474	89.593	72.623	76.795	81.748	84.511	95.616	100.745	104.001	106.537	113.672	108.894	1980	108.894
1981	110.252	110.147	119.670	126.719	130.987	130.863	125.296	115.840	106.272	113.913	116.723	113.831	1981	113.831
1982	111.205	107.571	106.759	110.380	106.592	103.634	102.912	109.870	113.269	127.702	137.885	140.278	1982	140.278
1983	148.731	159.271	167.517	179.081	193.606	199.678	197.119	192.599	194.198	182.688	191.790	188.759	1983	188.759
1984	187.557	174.659	177.293	174.932	165.336	169.748	162.097	177.534	177.164	172.880	167.071	169.470	1984	169.470
1985	187.061	191.362	186.444	182.456	186.792	188.188	192.782	190.980	180.034	184.165	194.925	203.588	1985	203.588
1986	205.241	220.603	232.189	234.177	241.864	241.310	224.110	228.584	214.754	221.983	221.094	215.106	1986	215.106
1987	233.977	251.922	256.641	247.283	245.591	251.086	259.691	265.663	262.211	185.188	177.578	186.867	1987	186.867
1988	196.745	211.150	218.822	222.250	217.529	229.864	228.322	221.769	225.289	221.777	211.909	219.893	1988	219.893
1989	227.643	228.589	235.417	240.412	247.707	242.141	251.389	254.047	253.234	236.802	235.033	231.516	1989	231.516
1990	211.646	214.593	221.280	215.060	226.597	228.622	219.045	188.919	171.821	161.022	167.891	171.148	1990	171.148
1991	184.439	204.663	218.256	218.674	225.311	213.753	222.126	227.256	226.986	233.841	226.727	240.179	1991	240.179
1992	266.884	277.941	269.658	258.420	257.689	243.443	251.912	245.469	247.981	253.506	275.553	287.908	1992	287.908
1993	302.051	295.578	303.061	292.971	302.571	301.003	306.000	315.500	324.796	338.694	332.538	338.990	1993	338.990
1994	358.954	356.908	339.832	341.407	340.766	330.717	335.894	345.816	348.511	352.283	340.343	340.412	1994	340.412
1995	348.648	356.012	359.982	371.427	381.741	402.630	428.600	442.783	450.533	427.198	435.683	446.387	1995	446.387
1996	445.027	459.959	468.029	505.769	542.610	510.704	461.661	482.713	495.186	484.984	498.007	508.167	1996	508.167
1997	527.846	515.353	488.875	474.789	523.639	549.030	581.521	609.980	659.821	632.782	623.360	613.460	1997	613.460
1998	608.708	647.012	676.879	686.980	651.634	637.428	593.927	473.967	490.856	507.090	545.528	559.616	1998	559.616

Table B-13 **Long-Term Corporate Bonds: Inflation-Adjusted Total Return Index**

From December 1925 to December 1970

YEAR	JAN	FEB	MAR	APR	MAY	JUN	JUL	AUG	SEP	OCT	NOV	DEC	YR-END	INDEX
1925												1.000	1925	1.000
1926	1.007	1.016	1.030	1.030	1.040	1.049	1.065	1.076	1.076	1.082	1.084	1.090	1926	1.090
1927	1.104	1.121	1.136	1.143	1.133	1.127	1.149	1.165	1.176	1.175	1.186	1.196	1927	1.196
1928	1.202	1.222	1.227	1.226	1.209	1.216	1.215	1.222	1.216	1.229	1.227	1.242	1928	1.242
1929	1.250	1.256	1.250	1.257	1.255	1.245	1.235	1.233	1.239	1.249	1.249	1.280	1929	1.280
1930	1.293	1.307	1.333	1.336	1.352	1.375	1.402	1.430	1.436	1.453	1.463	1.471	1930	1.471
1931	1.523	1.556	1.581	1.602	1.641	1.668	1.680	1.686	1.691	1.640	1.628	1.596	1931	1.596
1932	1.621	1.605	1.670	1.652	1.694	1.705	1.712	1.809	1.873	1.901	1.925	1.971	1932	1.971
1933	2.111	2.033	2.058	2.044	2.159	2.177	2.150	2.148	2.145	2.153	2.100	2.165	1933	2.165
1934	2.209	2.225	2.266	2.296	2.310	2.341	2.352	2.357	2.308	2.349	2.385	2.415	1934	2.415
1935	2.430	2.446	2.463	2.466	2.489	2.523	2.563	2.553	2.540	2.551	2.556	2.571	1935	2.571
1936	2.592	2.619	2.653	2.660	2.671	2.666	2.657	2.655	2.667	2.680	2.709	2.712	1936	2.712
1937	2.699	2.680	2.631	2.636	2.635	2.642	2.640	2.630	2.612	2.642	2.678	2.702	1937	2.702
1938	2.751	2.780	2.755	2.780	2.796	2.823	2.835	2.836	2.867	2.904	2.921	2.950	1938	2.950
1939	2.970	3.004	3.018	3.044	3.059	3.070	3.068	2.948	2.935	3.019	3.043	3.082	1939	3.082
1940	3.104	3.088	3.111	3.082	3.068	3.098	3.112	3.122	3.143	3.158	3.178	3.156	1940	3.156
1941	3.158	3.160	3.138	3.133	3.126	3.089	3.094	3.077	3.037	3.014	2.960	2.955	1941	2.955
1942	2.919	2.892	2.874	2.858	2.834	2.838	2.832	2.824	2.824	2.798	2.783	2.774	1942	2.774
1943	2.788	2.784	2.746	2.728	2.720	2.738	2.765	2.781	2.771	2.758	2.757	2.765	1943	2.765
1944	2.776	2.791	2.804	2.798	2.788	2.789	2.782	2.781	2.787	2.792	2.805	2.836	1944	2.836
1945	2.858	2.876	2.882	2.881	2.857	2.840	2.831	2.832	2.852	2.861	2.860	2.887	1945	2.887
1946	2.924	2.945	2.933	2.905	2.894	2.869	2.706	2.624	2.587	2.543	2.477	2.485	1946	2.485
1947	2.487	2.492	2.455	2.460	2.472	2.454	2.437	2.395	2.309	2.286	2.250	2.227	1947	2.227
1948	2.207	2.234	2.266	2.243	2.229	2.195	2.157	2.160	2.165	2.179	2.213	2.258	1948	2.258
1949	2.269	2.304	2.299	2.301	2.313	2.329	2.369	2.371	2.366	2.395	2.397	2.375	1949	2.375
1950	2.394	2.403	2.398	2.392	2.380	2.372	2.366	2.355	2.330	2.315	2.318	2.293	1950	2.293
1951	2.261	2.225	2.163	2.159	2.147	2.130	2.171	2.195	2.169	2.127	2.103	2.107	1951	2.107
1952	2.149	2.144	2.161	2.152	2.156	2.154	2.141	2.152	2.150	2.156	2.179	2.162	1952	2.162
1953	2.150	2.153	2.140	2.084	2.073	2.088	2.119	2.096	2.146	2.190	2.182	2.222	1953	2.222
1954	2.244	2.291	2.303	2.301	2.283	2.294	2.304	2.311	2.326	2.341	2.344	2.354	1954	2.354
1955	2.331	2.316	2.337	2.337	2.333	2.340	2.321	2.318	2.327	2.345	2.335	2.356	1955	2.356
1956	2.383	2.390	2.352	2.322	2.322	2.304	2.266	2.221	2.221	2.185	2.157	2.134	1956	2.134
1957	2.174	2.186	2.192	2.170	2.148	2.067	2.034	2.030	2.047	2.052	2.108	2.252	1957	2.252
1958	2.261	2.257	2.231	2.262	2.269	2.258	2.221	2.152	2.131	2.154	2.174	2.164	1958	2.164
1959	2.156	2.185	2.167	2.128	2.101	2.100	2.114	2.102	2.077	2.104	2.132	2.112	1959	2.112
1960	2.137	2.162	2.203	2.186	2.181	2.207	2.264	2.290	2.273	2.265	2.246	2.270	1960	2.270
1961	2.303	2.352	2.345	2.318	2.329	2.308	2.307	2.305	2.333	2.363	2.369	2.363	1961	2.363
1962	2.382	2.389	2.420	2.449	2.449	2.442	2.433	2.468	2.476	2.496	2.511	2.520	1962	2.520
1963	2.532	2.535	2.539	2.526	2.538	2.538	2.534	2.543	2.537	2.547	2.548	2.534	1963	2.534
1964	2.553	2.569	2.551	2.558	2.573	2.580	2.587	2.600	2.600	2.610	2.603	2.623	1964	2.623
1965	2.645	2.647	2.647	2.644	2.637	2.623	2.626	2.630	2.620	2.629	2.609	2.562	1965	2.562
1966	2.568	2.523	2.500	2.493	2.484	2.484	2.452	2.376	2.390	2.442	2.437	2.484	1966	2.484
1967	2.595	2.541	2.565	2.542	2.470	2.408	2.405	2.396	2.414	2.339	2.269	2.291	1967	2.291
1968	2.364	2.366	2.308	2.313	2.313	2.328	2.396	2.438	2.418	2.366	2.304	2.244	1968	2.244
1969	2.269	2.224	2.161	2.220	2.163	2.157	2.148	2.134	2.073	2.092	1.982	1.944	1969	1.944
1970	1.964	2.032	2.012	1.950	1.910	1.900	1.999	2.016	2.033	2.004	2.113	2.181	1970	2.181

Table B-13

Long-Term Corporate Bonds: Inflation-Adjusted Total Return Index

(continued)

From January 1971 to December 1998

YEAR	JAN	FEB	MAR	APR	MAY	JUN	JUL	AUG	SEP	OCT	NOV	DEC	YR-END	INDEX
1971	2.295	2.207	2.257	2.196	2.150	2.161	2.150	2.263	2.238	2.298	2.301	2.343	1971	2.343
1972	2.333	2.346	2.348	2.351	2.381	2.360	2.357	2.370	2.368	2.385	2.438	2.430	1972	2.430
1973	2.409	2.398	2.386	2.384	2.360	2.331	2.215	2.253	2.327	2.293	2.294	2.259	1973	2.259
1974	2.227	2.201	2.110	2.026	2.025	1.949	1.893	1.819	1.829	1.974	1.980	1.951	1974	1.951
1975	2.058	2.072	2.013	1.993	2.005	2.049	2.022	1.980	1.946	2.041	2.010	2.091	1975	2.091
1976	2.125	2.133	2.163	2.151	2.116	2.136	2.156	2.195	2.223	2.229	2.294	2.366	1976	2.366
1977	2.282	2.254	2.261	2.266	2.277	2.302	2.291	2.313	2.299	2.284	2.287	2.254	1977	2.254
1978	2.222	2.218	2.212	2.188	2.143	2.126	2.132	2.176	2.150	2.089	2.105	2.066	1978	2.066
1979	2.086	2.035	2.037	2.004	2.024	2.060	2.027	2.008	1.952	1.763	1.785	1.747	1979	1.747
1980	1.611	1.484	1.454	1.635	1.710	1.749	1.673	1.588	1.536	1.499	1.488	1.512	1980	1.512
1981	1.480	1.425	1.459	1.338	1.407	1.398	1.331	1.275	1.237	1.299	1.459	1.371	1981	1.371
1982	1.348	1.386	1.430	1.472	1.493	1.406	1.474	1.594	1.690	1.814	1.853	1.881	1982	1.881
1983	1.859	1.938	1.950	2.043	1.966	1.950	1.854	1.857	1.921	1.911	1.935	1.926	1983	1.926
1984	1.967	1.924	1.874	1.852	1.757	1.786	1.885	1.935	1.986	2.094	2.139	2.165	1984	2.165
1985	2.231	2.139	2.168	2.223	2.396	2.408	2.376	2.432	2.442	2.514	2.599	2.714	1985	2.714
1986	2.718	2.930	3.019	3.030	2.971	3.021	3.030	3.108	3.057	3.112	3.182	3.216	1986	3.216
1987	3.266	3.272	3.229	3.051	3.026	3.060	3.017	2.978	2.838	2.975	3.007	3.072	1987	3.072
1988	3.222	3.258	3.184	3.120	3.092	3.195	3.146	3.150	3.231	3.308	3.250	3.257	1988	3.257
1989	3.306	3.250	3.252	3.300	3.406	3.532	3.586	3.522	3.524	3.604	3.621	3.617	1989	3.617
1990	3.512	3.491	3.469	3.397	3.520	3.576	3.599	3.462	3.465	3.489	3.581	3.641	1990	3.641
1991	3.673	3.712	3.747	3.793	3.796	3.778	3.836	3.930	4.019	4.030	4.061	4.235	1991	4.235
1992	4.156	4.180	4.129	4.130	4.228	4.279	4.401	4.428	4.460	4.375	4.399	4.502	1992	4.502
1993	4.592	4.693	4.688	4.700	4.703	4.834	4.882	5.008	5.019	5.024	4.926	4.959	1993	4.959
1994	5.046	4.885	4.682	4.630	4.598	4.545	4.673	4.640	4.505	4.479	4.481	4.552	1994	4.552
1995	4.650	4.765	4.794	4.862	5.159	5.189	5.137	5.233	5.303	5.383	5.517	5.647	1995	5.647
1996	5.622	5.395	5.297	5.192	5.185	5.271	5.266	5.219	5.337	5.513	5.647	5.542	1996	5.542
1997	5.509	5.507	5.372	5.464	5.537	5.634	5.924	5.771	5.887	5.984	6.048	6.155	1997	6.155
1998	6.227	6.212	6.224	6.245	6.338	6.403	6.359	6.408	6.664	6.522	6.698	6.709	1998	6.709

Table B-14 **Long-Term Government Bonds: Inflation-Adjusted Total Return Index**

From December 1925 to December 1970

YEAR	JAN	FEB	MAR	APR	MAY	JUN	JUL	AUG	SEP	OCT	NOV	DEC	YR-END	INDEX
1925												1.000	1925	1.000
1926	1.014	1.024	1.034	1.032	1.039	1.051	1.062	1.068	1.066	1.072	1.086	1.094	1926	1.094
1927	1.111	1.129	1.164	1.164	1.167	1.148	1.176	1.192	1.187	1.192	1.206	1.217	1927	1.217
1928	1.215	1.234	1.240	1.237	1.220	1.235	1.208	1.215	1.201	1.222	1.225	1.230	1928	1.230
1929	1.221	1.205	1.192	1.230	1.203	1.211	1.199	1.191	1.196	1.242	1.274	1.270	1929	1.270
1930	1.267	1.289	1.307	1.297	1.323	1.338	1.362	1.372	1.373	1.387	1.404	1.414	1930	1.414
1931	1.418	1.451	1.476	1.498	1.536	1.554	1.551	1.556	1.519	1.479	1.500	1.480	1931	1.480
1932	1.516	1.601	1.606	1.715	1.708	1.731	1.815	1.838	1.857	1.868	1.884	1.928	1932	1.928
1933	1.987	1.966	2.001	2.000	2.055	2.043	1.983	1.971	1.976	1.958	1.929	1.917	1933	1.917
1934	1.956	1.957	1.996	2.026	2.047	2.056	2.064	2.034	1.975	2.026	2.039	2.067	1934	2.067
1935	2.073	2.077	2.091	2.087	2.085	2.110	2.130	2.101	2.093	2.105	2.097	2.107	1935	2.107
1936	2.119	2.146	2.180	2.187	2.196	2.179	2.182	2.190	2.178	2.185	2.230	2.238	1936	2.238
1937	2.219	2.233	2.126	2.125	2.126	2.117	2.137	2.109	2.100	2.118	2.153	2.176	1937	2.176
1938	2.219	2.252	2.244	2.280	2.301	2.302	2.306	2.312	2.317	2.348	2.349	2.362	1938	2.362
1939	2.387	2.418	2.454	2.489	2.531	2.524	2.553	2.502	2.321	2.427	2.467	2.514	1939	2.514
1940	2.516	2.505	2.555	2.546	2.464	2.522	2.541	2.554	2.576	2.584	2.637	2.642	1940	2.642
1941	2.589	2.594	2.607	2.616	2.605	2.574	2.568	2.549	2.501	2.509	2.480	2.430	1941	2.430
1942	2.416	2.398	2.390	2.368	2.361	2.357	2.352	2.346	2.342	2.324	2.302	2.295	1942	2.295
1943	2.303	2.297	2.264	2.248	2.242	2.251	2.268	2.281	2.275	2.267	2.272	2.271	1943	2.271
1944	2.281	2.292	2.297	2.287	2.285	2.282	2.277	2.275	2.278	2.281	2.286	2.287	1944	2.287
1945	2.316	2.338	2.343	2.376	2.372	2.390	2.365	2.371	2.392	2.417	2.439	2.477	1945	2.477
1946	2.483	2.500	2.485	2.438	2.421	2.412	2.269	2.195	2.168	2.142	2.080	2.094	1946	2.094
1947	2.093	2.100	2.060	2.052	2.065	2.052	2.046	2.041	1.985	1.978	1.932	1.871	1947	1.871
1948	1.853	1.878	1.890	1.871	1.885	1.856	1.829	1.822	1.824	1.833	1.860	1.883	1948	1.883
1949	1.901	1.932	1.941	1.940	1.947	1.977	1.997	2.014	2.003	2.018	2.020	2.042	1949	2.042
1950	2.038	2.048	2.041	2.044	2.042	2.026	2.017	2.003	1.975	1.955	1.954	1.931	1950	1.931
1951	1.911	1.875	1.838	1.825	1.805	1.796	1.819	1.837	1.810	1.803	1.769	1.752	1951	1.752
1952	1.757	1.771	1.790	1.814	1.806	1.802	1.784	1.770	1.749	1.773	1.770	1.757	1952	1.757
1953	1.763	1.757	1.737	1.717	1.687	1.718	1.721	1.715	1.764	1.773	1.771	1.809	1953	1.809
1954	1.821	1.867	1.880	1.905	1.881	1.909	1.935	1.930	1.933	1.939	1.932	1.949	1954	1.949
1955	1.902	1.887	1.904	1.904	1.918	1.903	1.877	1.882	1.889	1.916	1.905	1.917	1955	1.917
1956	1.935	1.935	1.904	1.880	1.913	1.906	1.853	1.820	1.827	1.806	1.796	1.759	1956	1.759
1957	1.818	1.816	1.807	1.761	1.753	1.711	1.696	1.694	1.705	1.696	1.781	1.835	1957	1.835
1958	1.809	1.825	1.831	1.861	1.861	1.829	1.776	1.701	1.681	1.704	1.723	1.694	1958	1.694
1959	1.678	1.700	1.702	1.681	1.678	1.672	1.678	1.673	1.658	1.677	1.657	1.631	1959	1.631
1960	1.651	1.683	1.730	1.691	1.717	1.743	1.807	1.794	1.806	1.793	1.779	1.829	1960	1.829
1961	1.809	1.845	1.838	1.859	1.851	1.835	1.833	1.828	1.848	1.861	1.857	1.834	1961	1.834
1962	1.831	1.846	1.889	1.900	1.909	1.894	1.870	1.905	1.906	1.924	1.928	1.937	1962	1.937
1963	1.934	1.934	1.933	1.931	1.935	1.931	1.928	1.932	1.933	1.926	1.934	1.928	1963	1.928
1964	1.924	1.924	1.929	1.936	1.945	1.954	1.952	1.958	1.963	1.970	1.969	1.972	1964	1.972
1965	1.980	1.983	1.992	1.993	1.992	1.991	1.993	1.995	1.984	1.987	1.970	1.949	1965	1.949
1966	1.929	1.869	1.918	1.898	1.885	1.876	1.864	1.816	1.872	1.907	1.879	1.955	1966	1.955
1967	1.985	1.939	1.973	1.912	1.899	1.834	1.837	1.816	1.812	1.734	1.695	1.723	1967	1.723
1968	1.772	1.761	1.716	1.749	1.752	1.782	1.824	1.819	1.795	1.761	1.707	1.641	1968	1.641
1969	1.602	1.603	1.591	1.649	1.563	1.587	1.592	1.574	1.484	1.532	1.487	1.468	1969	1.468
1970	1.460	1.537	1.519	1.447	1.373	1.433	1.473	1.468	1.494	1.470	1.581	1.560	1970	1.560

Table B-14

Long-Term Government Bonds: Inflation-Adjusted Total Return Index

(continued)

From January 1971 to December 1998

YEAR	JAN	FEB	MAR	APR	MAY	JUN	JUL	AUG	SEP	OCT	NOV	DEC	YR-END	INDEX
1971	1.637	1.608	1.687	1.634	1.625	1.590	1.590	1.661	1.694	1.719	1.708	1.709	1971	1.709
1972	1.697	1.703	1.687	1.687	1.727	1.712	1.742	1.744	1.723	1.758	1.793	1.746	1972	1.746
1973	1.685	1.676	1.674	1.670	1.642	1.628	1.554	1.586	1.631	1.653	1.611	1.587	1973	1.587
1974	1.561	1.537	1.476	1.430	1.432	1.425	1.410	1.360	1.377	1.432	1.462	1.476	1974	1.476
1975	1.503	1.512	1.466	1.432	1.456	1.486	1.458	1.444	1.422	1.481	1.456	1.506	1975	1.506
1976	1.516	1.522	1.544	1.540	1.507	1.530	1.533	1.558	1.574	1.581	1.630	1.678	1976	1.678
1977	1.604	1.580	1.584	1.583	1.594	1.610	1.591	1.617	1.606	1.587	1.594	1.561	1977	1.561
1978	1.540	1.530	1.516	1.502	1.479	1.455	1.465	1.489	1.463	1.422	1.441	1.415	1978	1.415
1979	1.429	1.394	1.398	1.367	1.385	1.415	1.385	1.367	1.336	1.213	1.239	1.233	1979	1.233
1980	1.126	1.059	1.011	1.152	1.188	1.217	1.159	1.101	1.063	1.026	1.027	1.054	1980	1.054
1981	1.033	0.978	1.009	0.950	1.001	0.975	0.930	0.887	0.866	0.935	1.064	0.985	1981	0.985
1982	0.986	1.001	1.025	1.059	1.052	1.017	1.062	1.142	1.211	1.284	1.286	1.332	1982	1.332
1983	1.287	1.350	1.337	1.374	1.313	1.314	1.245	1.244	1.300	1.279	1.301	1.291	1983	1.291
1984	1.315	1.286	1.263	1.244	1.176	1.190	1.268	1.297	1.335	1.406	1.422	1.434	1984	1.434
1985	1.484	1.405	1.442	1.471	1.596	1.614	1.582	1.620	1.612	1.661	1.722	1.810	1985	1.810
1986	1.800	2.012	2.177	2.164	2.048	2.163	2.139	2.242	2.120	2.179	2.235	2.229	1986	2.229
1987	2.251	2.288	2.227	2.110	2.082	2.094	2.052	2.007	1.924	2.038	2.043	2.077	1987	2.077
1988	2.210	2.216	2.138	2.093	2.065	2.132	2.087	2.090	2.148	2.207	2.162	2.182	1988	2.182
1989	2.215	2.166	2.180	2.201	2.276	2.395	2.446	2.379	2.376	2.455	2.468	2.462	1989	2.462
1990	2.354	2.337	2.314	2.264	2.352	2.394	2.410	2.288	2.295	2.331	2.419	2.464	1990	2.464
1991	2.481	2.485	2.491	2.522	2.515	2.492	2.527	2.606	2.673	2.684	2.698	2.852	1991	2.852
1992	2.756	2.760	2.720	2.721	2.783	2.828	2.935	2.946	2.992	2.922	2.921	2.995	1992	2.995
1993	3.064	3.161	3.157	3.171	3.181	3.319	3.383	3.520	3.515	3.534	3.440	3.447	1993	3.447
1994	3.526	3.356	3.212	3.160	3.132	3.090	3.193	3.153	3.041	3.031	3.047	3.096	1994	3.096
1995	3.168	3.246	3.265	3.309	3.563	3.606	3.545	3.620	3.676	3.771	3.868	3.976	1995	3.976
1996	3.948	3.746	3.648	3.574	3.548	3.617	3.617	3.560	3.651	3.787	3.912	3.812	1996	3.812
1997	3.770	3.760	3.656	3.745	3.783	3.852	4.088	3.951	4.066	4.194	4.259	4.342	1997	4.342
1998	4.421	4.381	4.384	4.387	4.459	4.555	4.532	4.736	4.917	4.798	4.844	4.832	1998	4.832

Table B-15 **Intermediate-Term Government Bonds: Inflation-Adjusted Total Return Index**

From December 1925 to December 1970

YEAR	JAN	FEB	MAR	APR	MAY	JUN	JUL	AUG	SEP	OCT	NOV	DEC	YR-END	INDEX
1925												1.000	1925	1.000
1926	1.007	1.014	1.024	1.023	1.030	1.040	1.052	1.059	1.058	1.060	1.060	1.070	1926	1.070
1927	1.084	1.096	1.107	1.109	1.103	1.095	1.121	1.134	1.134	1.124	1.135	1.142	1927	1.142
1928	1.149	1.160	1.161	1.159	1.151	1.162	1.152	1.155	1.150	1.155	1.160	1.164	1928	1.164
1929	1.163	1.163	1.168	1.183	1.169	1.176	1.173	1.174	1.175	1.195	1.219	1.231	1929	1.231
1930	1.231	1.247	1.275	1.258	1.274	1.299	1.325	1.336	1.336	1.354	1.375	1.398	1930	1.398
1931	1.409	1.444	1.461	1.482	1.516	1.500	1.506	1.512	1.501	1.496	1.520	1.509	1931	1.509
1932	1.536	1.578	1.598	1.641	1.650	1.680	1.700	1.742	1.756	1.777	1.791	1.831	1932	1.831
1933	1.857	1.886	1.920	1.936	1.969	1.950	1.894	1.888	1.893	1.889	1.894	1.855	1933	1.855
1934	1.870	1.865	1.901	1.940	1.958	1.971	1.966	1.944	1.888	1.939	1.952	1.982	1934	1.982
1935	1.975	1.981	2.011	2.013	2.015	2.043	2.061	2.046	2.025	2.047	2.040	2.059	1935	2.059
1936	2.058	2.083	2.099	2.104	2.112	2.094	2.089	2.084	2.082	2.092	2.109	2.097	1936	2.097
1937	2.075	2.072	2.023	2.023	2.030	2.023	2.025	2.012	2.010	2.025	2.048	2.065	1937	2.065
1938	2.112	2.143	2.140	2.179	2.195	2.211	2.208	2.217	2.214	2.245	2.250	2.257	1938	2.257
1939	2.274	2.304	2.328	2.342	2.365	2.365	2.374	2.340	2.235	2.316	2.334	2.370	1939	2.370
1940	2.372	2.364	2.390	2.391	2.334	2.372	2.378	2.394	2.400	2.408	2.422	2.417	1940	2.417
1941	2.417	2.406	2.411	2.397	2.383	2.352	2.342	2.323	2.282	2.262	2.222	2.214	1941	2.214
1942	2.202	2.187	2.164	2.156	2.137	2.135	2.126	2.117	2.108	2.090	2.081	2.065	1942	2.065
1943	2.073	2.072	2.044	2.025	2.021	2.032	2.052	2.060	2.055	2.051	2.058	2.058	1943	2.058
1944	2.064	2.071	2.075	2.069	2.062	2.060	2.054	2.051	2.053	2.056	2.057	2.052	1944	2.052
1945	2.062	2.074	2.075	2.074	2.061	2.046	2.042	2.045	2.056	2.060	2.054	2.051	1945	2.051
1946	2.059	2.077	2.054	2.038	2.028	2.013	1.899	1.859	1.836	1.805	1.761	1.753	1946	1.753
1947	1.757	1.761	1.728	1.725	1.732	1.720	1.706	1.692	1.653	1.649	1.641	1.623	1947	1.623
1948	1.607	1.624	1.631	1.611	1.609	1.596	1.576	1.569	1.571	1.579	1.593	1.609	1948	1.609
1949	1.616	1.636	1.636	1.636	1.642	1.648	1.663	1.663	1.657	1.668	1.666	1.677	1949	1.677
1950	1.683	1.689	1.682	1.681	1.677	1.669	1.656	1.641	1.629	1.620	1.617	1.596	1950	1.596
1951	1.575	1.557	1.532	1.538	1.526	1.536	1.543	1.548	1.529	1.524	1.521	1.513	1951	1.513
1952	1.519	1.525	1.536	1.538	1.539	1.530	1.513	1.508	1.512	1.520	1.520	1.524	1952	1.524
1953	1.528	1.536	1.530	1.513	1.492	1.509	1.514	1.509	1.536	1.538	1.546	1.564	1953	1.564
1954	1.570	1.588	1.594	1.605	1.587	1.605	1.604	1.608	1.609	1.611	1.609	1.614	1954	1.614
1955	1.609	1.600	1.604	1.605	1.605	1.599	1.582	1.587	1.594	1.606	1.595	1.597	1955	1.597
1956	1.616	1.617	1.599	1.596	1.606	1.597	1.570	1.556	1.568	1.556	1.548	1.547	1956	1.547
1957	1.581	1.574	1.573	1.551	1.545	1.519	1.510	1.525	1.523	1.530	1.585	1.619	1957	1.619
1958	1.615	1.635	1.632	1.637	1.647	1.634	1.617	1.562	1.559	1.559	1.578	1.570	1958	1.570
1959	1.566	1.585	1.579	1.569	1.567	1.548	1.550	1.539	1.537	1.558	1.544	1.541	1959	1.541
1960	1.567	1.576	1.622	1.602	1.608	1.639	1.682	1.682	1.685	1.680	1.662	1.697	1960	1.697
1961	1.687	1.702	1.709	1.718	1.713	1.707	1.700	1.705	1.715	1.717	1.714	1.717	1961	1.717
1962	1.709	1.732	1.743	1.744	1.752	1.748	1.742	1.763	1.757	1.768	1.779	1.791	1962	1.791
1963	1.784	1.785	1.788	1.793	1.795	1.790	1.783	1.786	1.789	1.789	1.794	1.790	1963	1.790
1964	1.794	1.799	1.800	1.804	1.818	1.821	1.822	1.829	1.833	1.837	1.832	1.841	1964	1.841
1965	1.849	1.852	1.858	1.857	1.859	1.859	1.860	1.867	1.863	1.861	1.858	1.825	1965	1.825
1966	1.825	1.799	1.827	1.816	1.816	1.806	1.796	1.764	1.799	1.805	1.810	1.848	1966	1.848
1967	1.870	1.866	1.896	1.875	1.878	1.830	1.845	1.833	1.831	1.816	1.816	1.812	1967	1.812
1968	1.831	1.833	1.819	1.811	1.817	1.837	1.860	1.859	1.864	1.855	1.846	1.808	1968	1.808
1969	1.819	1.810	1.812	1.815	1.795	1.768	1.775	1.764	1.703	1.753	1.736	1.692	1969	1.692
1970	1.691	1.756	1.762	1.715	1.726	1.728	1.748	1.765	1.791	1.799	1.873	1.874	1970	1.874

Table B-15 **Intermediate-Term Government Bonds: Inflation-Adjusted Total Return Index**

(continued)

From January 1971 to December 1998

YEAR	JAN	FEB	MAR	APR	MAY	JUN	JUL	AUG	SEP	OCT	NOV	DEC	YR-END	INDEX
1971	1.904	1.943	1.973	1.902	1.895	1.848	1.849	1.909	1.912	1.951	1.958	1.971	1971	1.971
1972	1.990	1.984	1.983	1.981	1.978	1.982	1.977	1.977	1.972	1.969	1.973	2.005	1972	2.005
1973	1.997	1.968	1.959	1.958	1.957	1.943	1.885	1.898	1.940	1.934	1.932	1.927	1973	1.927
1974	1.912	1.895	1.834	1.796	1.799	1.767	1.755	1.731	1.765	1.769	1.795	1.815	1974	1.815
1975	1.817	1.831	1.813	1.770	1.808	1.799	1.775	1.768	1.761	1.814	1.801	1.829	1975	1.829
1976	1.835	1.846	1.856	1.869	1.831	1.851	1.862	1.888	1.895	1.915	1.971	1.970	1976	1.970
1977	1.922	1.911	1.910	1.905	1.905	1.912	1.904	1.898	1.893	1.877	1.882	1.871	1977	1.871
1978	1.863	1.854	1.848	1.836	1.817	1.795	1.800	1.805	1.802	1.768	1.774	1.776	1978	1.776
1979	1.770	1.739	1.742	1.728	1.740	1.759	1.735	1.702	1.685	1.592	1.635	1.632	1979	1.632
1980	1.587	1.465	1.465	1.622	1.685	1.654	1.635	1.562	1.541	1.505	1.496	1.508	1980	1.508
1981	1.501	1.451	1.478	1.437	1.460	1.456	1.401	1.366	1.374	1.455	1.542	1.515	1981	1.515
1982	1.518	1.535	1.543	1.583	1.590	1.550	1.613	1.685	1.737	1.824	1.842	1.884	1982	1.884
1983	1.880	1.927	1.916	1.952	1.918	1.915	1.869	1.878	1.927	1.926	1.942	1.949	1983	1.949
1984	1.973	1.951	1.940	1.930	1.876	1.888	1.956	1.968	1.998	2.069	2.109	2.138	1984	2.138
1985	2.178	2.130	2.156	2.204	2.302	2.320	2.305	2.335	2.354	2.384	2.423	2.479	1985	2.479
1986	2.492	2.567	2.666	2.694	2.628	2.687	2.729	2.796	2.752	2.794	2.823	2.822	1986	2.822
1987	2.835	2.841	2.819	2.736	2.718	2.740	2.741	2.715	2.664	2.736	2.755	2.782	1987	2.782
1988	2.862	2.889	2.852	2.825	2.802	2.840	2.815	2.801	2.837	2.869	2.834	2.826	1988	2.826
1989	2.847	2.820	2.818	2.861	2.906	2.993	3.055	2.975	2.986	3.043	3.061	3.060	1989	3.060
1990	2.997	2.985	2.969	2.942	3.012	3.041	3.082	3.026	3.029	3.062	3.114	3.164	1990	3.164
1991	3.179	3.189	3.192	3.225	3.234	3.217	3.254	3.325	3.382	3.422	3.456	3.545	1991	3.545
1992	3.471	3.466	3.421	3.449	3.521	3.570	3.649	3.693	3.754	3.673	3.637	3.693	1992	3.693
1993	3.774	3.852	3.855	3.878	3.869	3.942	3.944	4.021	4.035	4.025	3.985	3.998	1993	3.998
1994	4.042	3.924	3.810	3.765	3.762	3.738	3.791	3.786	3.716	3.705	3.674	3.693	1994	3.693
1995	3.746	3.818	3.829	3.871	4.006	4.030	4.024	4.048	4.066	4.101	4.165	4.207	1995	4.207
1996	4.185	4.114	4.045	4.009	3.989	4.033	4.035	4.025	4.075	4.136	4.190	4.157	1996	4.157
1997	4.155	4.142	4.085	4.140	4.176	4.213	4.319	4.268	4.322	4.376	4.378	4.430	1997	4.430
1998	4.502	4.476	4.479	4.498	4.521	4.551	4.558	4.676	4.824	4.832	4.784	4.805	1998	4.805

Table B-16 **U.S. Treasury Bills: Inflation-Adjusted Total Return Index**

From December 1925 to December 1970

YEAR	JAN	FEB	MAR	APR	MAY	JUN	JUL	AUG	SEP	OCT	NOV	DEC	YR-END	INDEX
1925												1.000	1925	1.000
1926	1.003	1.010	1.019	1.013	1.018	1.030	1.042	1.050	1.047	1.046	1.045	1.048	1926	1.048
1927	1.059	1.070	1.079	1.082	1.077	1.069	1.093	1.103	1.099	1.095	1.099	1.104	1927	1.104
1928	1.109	1.123	1.127	1.127	1.124	1.136	1.140	1.142	1.136	1.143	1.149	1.154	1928	1.154
1929	1.161	1.167	1.176	1.185	1.183	1.184	1.177	1.177	1.183	1.189	1.195	1.207	1929	1.207
1930	1.213	1.222	1.233	1.228	1.239	1.250	1.270	1.279	1.274	1.283	1.295	1.315	1930	1.315
1931	1.337	1.357	1.368	1.377	1.394	1.410	1.414	1.418	1.424	1.435	1.454	1.469	1931	1.469
1932	1.504	1.529	1.538	1.551	1.575	1.587	1.587	1.607	1.616	1.628	1.637	1.654	1932	1.654
1933	1.680	1.706	1.720	1.726	1.722	1.705	1.657	1.641	1.641	1.641	1.642	1.650	1933	1.650
1934	1.643	1.631	1.631	1.635	1.631	1.627	1.627	1.623	1.600	1.612	1.616	1.620	1934	1.620
1935	1.596	1.585	1.589	1.574	1.582	1.586	1.594	1.594	1.586	1.587	1.579	1.576	1935	1.576
1936	1.576	1.584	1.592	1.592	1.592	1.577	1.570	1.559	1.556	1.560	1.560	1.560	1936	1.560
1937	1.549	1.545	1.535	1.528	1.522	1.519	1.512	1.509	1.496	1.503	1.514	1.517	1937	1.517
1938	1.539	1.554	1.553	1.546	1.554	1.554	1.550	1.554	1.554	1.561	1.564	1.561	1938	1.561
1939	1.568	1.576	1.579	1.583	1.583	1.583	1.583	1.583	1.553	1.561	1.561	1.568	1939	1.568
1940	1.572	1.561	1.565	1.565	1.561	1.557	1.561	1.565	1.561	1.561	1.561	1.554	1940	1.554
1941	1.553	1.553	1.546	1.532	1.521	1.493	1.487	1.474	1.448	1.432	1.420	1.417	1941	1.417
1942	1.399	1.387	1.370	1.362	1.348	1.346	1.340	1.333	1.330	1.317	1.310	1.300	1942	1.300
1943	1.300	1.298	1.278	1.264	1.255	1.257	1.267	1.273	1.268	1.264	1.266	1.264	1943	1.264
1944	1.267	1.270	1.270	1.263	1.259	1.257	1.250	1.246	1.246	1.246	1.247	1.242	1944	1.242
1945	1.243	1.245	1.246	1.244	1.235	1.224	1.222	1.222	1.227	1.227	1.223	1.219	1945	1.219
1946	1.219	1.224	1.216	1.209	1.203	1.191	1.125	1.101	1.088	1.068	1.043	1.035	1946	1.035
1947	1.036	1.038	1.016	1.016	1.019	1.012	1.003	0.993	0.971	0.971	0.966	0.955	1947	0.955
1948	0.944	0.953	0.957	0.944	0.938	0.933	0.922	0.919	0.919	0.923	0.930	0.937	1948	0.937
1949	0.939	0.951	0.949	0.948	0.951	0.950	0.958	0.956	0.953	0.959	0.958	0.965	1949	0.965
1950	0.970	0.973	0.970	0.969	0.966	0.962	0.954	0.947	0.941	0.937	0.934	0.923	1950	0.923
1951	0.909	0.900	0.897	0.897	0.895	0.897	0.897	0.898	0.894	0.890	0.887	0.885	1951	0.885
1952	0.886	0.893	0.894	0.891	0.891	0.890	0.885	0.885	0.888	0.888	0.889	0.891	1952	0.891
1953	0.895	0.901	0.900	0.901	0.900	0.898	0.897	0.896	0.897	0.896	0.900	0.902	1953	0.902
1954	0.901	0.902	0.904	0.907	0.904	0.904	0.904	0.906	0.909	0.912	0.911	0.914	1954	0.914
1955	0.915	0.916	0.917	0.918	0.919	0.920	0.917	0.921	0.919	0.921	0.921	0.925	1955	0.925
1956	0.928	0.930	0.930	0.931	0.929	0.925	0.920	0.923	0.923	0.920	0.922	0.922	1956	0.922
1957	0.923	0.922	0.922	0.921	0.921	0.918	0.916	0.917	0.918	0.921	0.920	0.923	1957	0.923
1958	0.920	0.920	0.914	0.913	0.914	0.913	0.913	0.914	0.916	0.918	0.918	0.921	1958	0.921
1959	0.921	0.924	0.926	0.927	0.928	0.926	0.926	0.929	0.929	0.928	0.931	0.934	1959	0.934
1960	0.938	0.940	0.943	0.939	0.942	0.942	0.943	0.945	0.945	0.943	0.943	0.945	1960	0.945
1961	0.947	0.948	0.950	0.951	0.953	0.954	0.951	0.954	0.953	0.955	0.957	0.958	1961	0.958
1962	0.961	0.961	0.960	0.960	0.963	0.965	0.965	0.967	0.964	0.967	0.969	0.973	1962	0.973
1963	0.974	0.975	0.976	0.979	0.981	0.979	0.978	0.980	0.983	0.984	0.986	0.987	1963	0.987
1964	0.989	0.992	0.994	0.996	0.999	1.000	1.000	1.004	1.005	1.007	1.008	1.010	1964	1.010
1965	1.012	1.015	1.018	1.018	1.019	1.017	1.019	1.025	1.026	1.028	1.029	1.029	1965	1.029
1966	1.033	1.030	1.031	1.030	1.034	1.034	1.035	1.034	1.036	1.036	1.040	1.043	1966	1.043
1967	1.048	1.051	1.053	1.054	1.054	1.054	1.052	1.052	1.053	1.054	1.055	1.055	1967	1.055
1968	1.055	1.056	1.055	1.057	1.058	1.057	1.057	1.058	1.060	1.058	1.059	1.060	1968	1.060
1969	1.063	1.064	1.060	1.058	1.061	1.059	1.060	1.061	1.062	1.065	1.065	1.065	1969	1.065
1970	1.068	1.068	1.069	1.068	1.069	1.069	1.071	1.075	1.075	1.075	1.076	1.075	1970	1.075

Table B-16 **U.S. Treasury Bills: Inflation-Adjusted Total Return Index**

(continued)

From January 1971 to December 1998

YEAR	JAN	FEB	MAR	APR	MAY	JUN	JUL	AUG	SEP	OCT	NOV	DEC	YR-END	INDEX
1971	1.079	1.080	1.080	1.079	1.077	1.075	1.077	1.079	1.082	1.084	1.086	1.086	1971	1.086
1972	1.088	1.086	1.087	1.087	1.087	1.088	1.087	1.088	1.088	1.088	1.090	1.091	1972	1.091
1973	1.092	1.089	1.084	1.082	1.081	1.079	1.083	1.071	1.076	1.074	1.072	1.072	1973	1.072
1974	1.069	1.062	1.056	1.058	1.054	1.050	1.050	1.043	1.039	1.035	1.032	1.032	1974	1.032
1975	1.033	1.030	1.031	1.030	1.030	1.026	1.020	1.022	1.022	1.021	1.019	1.020	1975	1.020
1976	1.022	1.023	1.025	1.025	1.023	1.022	1.021	1.020	1.020	1.020	1.021	1.023	1976	1.023
1977	1.020	1.014	1.011	1.007	1.005	1.003	1.002	1.003	1.003	1.006	1.006	1.007	1977	1.007
1978	1.006	1.004	1.002	0.999	0.994	0.989	0.988	0.988	0.987	0.986	0.987	0.990	1978	0.990
1979	0.989	0.984	0.983	0.979	0.975	0.974	0.969	0.967	0.965	0.965	0.965	0.964	1979	0.964
1980	0.958	0.954	0.951	0.953	0.951	0.946	0.950	0.950	0.949	0.950	0.950	0.954	1980	0.954
1981	0.956	0.957	0.961	0.965	0.969	0.973	0.974	0.979	0.981	0.991	0.999	1.005	1981	1.005
1982	1.009	1.015	1.026	1.034	1.034	1.032	1.037	1.042	1.046	1.049	1.058	1.069	1982	1.069
1983	1.074	1.080	1.086	1.086	1.088	1.092	1.095	1.100	1.103	1.108	1.114	1.121	1983	1.121
1984	1.123	1.126	1.132	1.135	1.141	1.146	1.151	1.156	1.160	1.169	1.178	1.184	1984	1.184
1985	1.190	1.192	1.194	1.198	1.201	1.204	1.210	1.214	1.217	1.221	1.225	1.230	1985	1.230
1986	1.233	1.243	1.256	1.265	1.267	1.268	1.274	1.277	1.277	1.282	1.286	1.291	1986	1.291
1987	1.288	1.289	1.289	1.288	1.289	1.290	1.293	1.292	1.291	1.296	1.298	1.304	1987	1.304
1988	1.304	1.307	1.307	1.306	1.308	1.309	1.310	1.312	1.312	1.315	1.322	1.328	1988	1.328
1989	1.329	1.331	1.332	1.333	1.336	1.342	1.348	1.356	1.360	1.363	1.369	1.375	1989	1.375
1990	1.369	1.370	1.371	1.379	1.385	1.386	1.390	1.386	1.383	1.384	1.389	1.397	1990	1.397
1991	1.396	1.401	1.405	1.410	1.413	1.414	1.419	1.421	1.422	1.426	1.427	1.431	1991	1.431
1992	1.434	1.433	1.431	1.433	1.435	1.435	1.436	1.436	1.435	1.434	1.435	1.440	1992	1.440
1993	1.436	1.434	1.433	1.432	1.433	1.435	1.439	1.438	1.439	1.436	1.439	1.442	1993	1.442
1994	1.442	1.440	1.439	1.441	1.444	1.444	1.444	1.443	1.445	1.449	1.453	1.459	1994	1.459
1995	1.459	1.459	1.461	1.463	1.468	1.472	1.479	1.482	1.485	1.487	1.494	1.503	1995	1.503
1996	1.500	1.501	1.500	1.501	1.504	1.509	1.513	1.516	1.518	1.520	1.523	1.530	1996	1.530
1997	1.532	1.533	1.536	1.541	1.549	1.553	1.558	1.561	1.564	1.567	1.574	1.584	1997	1.584
1998	1.587	1.591	1.594	1.598	1.601	1.606	1.610	1.615	1.621	1.622	1.627	1.634	1998	1.634

STOCKS
BONDS
BILLS
AND
INFLATION

Appendix C: Rates of Return for All Yearly Holding Periods

1926 to 1998

Appendix C Rates of Return for all Yearly Holding Periods: 1926–1998

Basic Series: Total Rates of Return for all Holding Periods

Each table in this section consists of five pages.

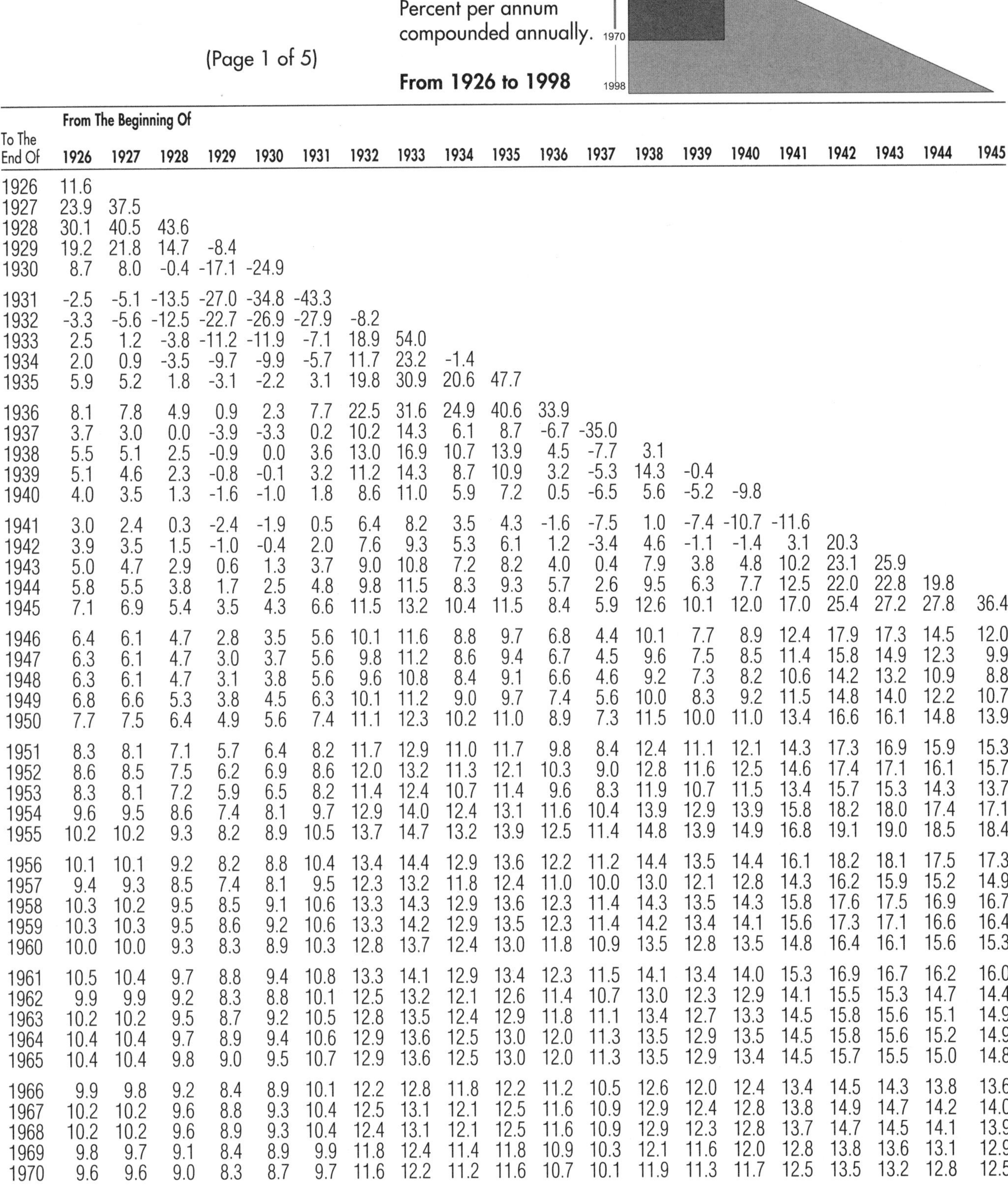

Table C-1

Large Company Stocks Total Returns

(Page 1 of 5)

Rates of Return for all holding periods.

Percent per annum compounded annually.

From 1926 to 1998

To The End Of	From The Beginning Of 1926	1927	1928	1929	1930	1931	1932	1933	1934	1935	1936	1937	1938	1939	1940	1941	1942	1943	1944	1945
1926	11.6																			
1927	23.9	37.5																		
1928	30.1	40.5	43.6																	
1929	19.2	21.8	14.7	-8.4																
1930	8.7	8.0	-0.4	-17.1	-24.9															
1931	-2.5	-5.1	-13.5	-27.0	-34.8	-43.3														
1932	-3.3	-5.6	-12.5	-22.7	-26.9	-27.9	-8.2													
1933	2.5	1.2	-3.8	-11.2	-11.9	-7.1	18.9	54.0												
1934	2.0	0.9	-3.5	-9.7	-9.9	-5.7	11.7	23.2	-1.4											
1935	5.9	5.2	1.8	-3.1	-2.2	3.1	19.8	30.9	20.6	47.7										
1936	8.1	7.8	4.9	0.9	2.3	7.7	22.5	31.6	24.9	40.6	33.9									
1937	3.7	3.0	0.0	-3.9	-3.3	0.2	10.2	14.3	6.1	8.7	-6.7	-35.0								
1938	5.5	5.1	2.5	-0.9	0.0	3.6	13.0	16.9	10.7	13.9	4.5	-7.7	3.1							
1939	5.1	4.6	2.3	-0.8	-0.1	3.2	11.2	14.3	8.7	10.9	3.2	-5.3	14.3	-0.4						
1940	4.0	3.5	1.3	-1.6	-1.0	1.8	8.6	11.0	5.9	7.2	0.5	-6.5	5.6	-5.2	-9.8					
1941	3.0	2.4	0.3	-2.4	-1.9	0.5	6.4	8.2	3.5	4.3	-1.6	-7.5	1.0	-7.4	-10.7	-11.6				
1942	3.9	3.5	1.5	-1.0	-0.4	2.0	7.6	9.3	5.3	6.1	1.2	-3.4	4.6	-1.1	-1.4	3.1	20.3			
1943	5.0	4.7	2.9	0.6	1.3	3.7	9.0	10.8	7.2	8.2	4.0	0.4	7.9	3.8	4.8	10.2	23.1	25.9		
1944	5.8	5.5	3.8	1.7	2.5	4.8	9.8	11.5	8.3	9.3	5.7	2.6	9.5	6.3	7.7	12.5	22.0	22.8	19.8	
1945	7.1	6.9	5.4	3.5	4.3	6.6	11.5	13.2	10.4	11.5	8.4	5.9	12.6	10.1	12.0	17.0	25.4	27.2	27.8	36.4
1946	6.4	6.1	4.7	2.8	3.5	5.6	10.1	11.6	8.8	9.7	6.8	4.4	10.1	7.7	8.9	12.4	17.9	17.3	14.5	12.0
1947	6.3	6.1	4.7	3.0	3.7	5.6	9.8	11.2	8.6	9.4	6.7	4.5	9.6	7.5	8.5	11.4	15.8	14.9	12.3	9.9
1948	6.3	6.1	4.7	3.1	3.8	5.6	9.6	10.8	8.4	9.1	6.6	4.6	9.2	7.3	8.2	10.6	14.2	13.2	10.9	8.8
1949	6.8	6.6	5.3	3.8	4.5	6.3	10.1	11.2	9.0	9.7	7.4	5.6	10.0	8.3	9.2	11.5	14.8	14.0	12.2	10.7
1950	7.7	7.5	6.4	4.9	5.6	7.4	11.1	12.3	10.2	11.0	8.9	7.3	11.5	10.0	11.0	13.4	16.6	16.1	14.8	13.9
1951	8.3	8.1	7.1	5.7	6.4	8.2	11.7	12.9	11.0	11.7	9.8	8.4	12.4	11.1	12.1	14.3	17.3	16.9	15.9	15.3
1952	8.6	8.5	7.5	6.2	6.9	8.6	12.0	13.2	11.3	12.1	10.3	9.0	12.8	11.6	12.5	14.6	17.4	17.1	16.1	15.7
1953	8.3	8.1	7.2	5.9	6.5	8.2	11.4	12.4	10.7	11.4	9.6	8.3	11.9	10.7	11.5	13.4	15.7	15.3	14.3	13.7
1954	9.6	9.5	8.6	7.4	8.1	9.7	12.9	14.0	12.4	13.1	11.6	10.4	13.9	12.9	13.9	15.8	18.2	18.0	17.4	17.1
1955	10.2	10.2	9.3	8.2	8.9	10.5	13.7	14.7	13.2	13.9	12.5	11.4	14.8	13.9	14.9	16.8	19.1	19.0	18.5	18.4
1956	10.1	10.1	9.2	8.2	8.8	10.4	13.4	14.4	12.9	13.6	12.2	11.2	14.4	13.5	14.4	16.1	18.2	18.1	17.5	17.3
1957	9.4	9.3	8.5	7.4	8.1	9.5	12.3	13.2	11.8	12.4	11.0	10.0	13.0	12.1	12.8	14.3	16.2	15.9	15.2	14.9
1958	10.3	10.2	9.5	8.5	9.1	10.6	13.3	14.3	12.9	13.6	12.3	11.4	14.3	13.5	14.3	15.8	17.6	17.5	16.9	16.7
1959	10.3	10.3	9.5	8.6	9.2	10.6	13.3	14.2	12.9	13.5	12.3	11.4	14.2	13.4	14.1	15.6	17.3	17.1	16.6	16.4
1960	10.0	10.0	9.3	8.3	8.9	10.3	12.8	13.7	12.4	13.0	11.8	10.9	13.5	12.8	13.5	14.8	16.4	16.1	15.6	15.3
1961	10.5	10.4	9.7	8.8	9.4	10.8	13.3	14.1	12.9	13.4	12.3	11.5	14.1	13.4	14.0	15.3	16.9	16.7	16.2	16.0
1962	9.9	9.9	9.2	8.3	8.8	10.1	12.5	13.2	12.1	12.6	11.4	10.7	13.0	12.3	12.9	14.1	15.5	15.3	14.7	14.4
1963	10.2	10.2	9.5	8.7	9.2	10.5	12.8	13.5	12.4	12.9	11.8	11.1	13.4	12.7	13.3	14.5	15.8	15.6	15.1	14.9
1964	10.4	10.4	9.7	8.9	9.4	10.6	12.9	13.6	12.5	13.0	12.0	11.3	13.5	12.9	13.5	14.5	15.8	15.6	15.2	14.9
1965	10.4	10.4	9.8	9.0	9.5	10.7	12.9	13.6	12.5	13.0	12.0	11.3	13.5	12.9	13.4	14.5	15.7	15.5	15.0	14.8
1966	9.9	9.8	9.2	8.4	8.9	10.1	12.2	12.8	11.8	12.2	11.2	10.5	12.6	12.0	12.4	13.4	14.5	14.3	13.8	13.6
1967	10.2	10.2	9.6	8.8	9.3	10.4	12.5	13.1	12.1	12.5	11.6	10.9	12.9	12.4	12.8	13.8	14.9	14.7	14.2	14.0
1968	10.2	10.2	9.6	8.9	9.3	10.4	12.4	13.1	12.1	12.5	11.6	10.9	12.9	12.3	12.8	13.7	14.7	14.5	14.1	13.9
1969	9.8	9.7	9.1	8.4	8.9	9.9	11.8	12.4	11.4	11.8	10.9	10.3	12.1	11.6	12.0	12.8	13.8	13.6	13.1	12.9
1970	9.6	9.6	9.0	8.3	8.7	9.7	11.6	12.2	11.2	11.6	10.7	10.1	11.9	11.3	11.7	12.5	13.5	13.2	12.8	12.5

Table C-1

Large Company Stocks Total Returns

(Page 2 of 5)

Rates of Return for all holding periods.

Percent per annum compounded annually.

From 1926 to 1998

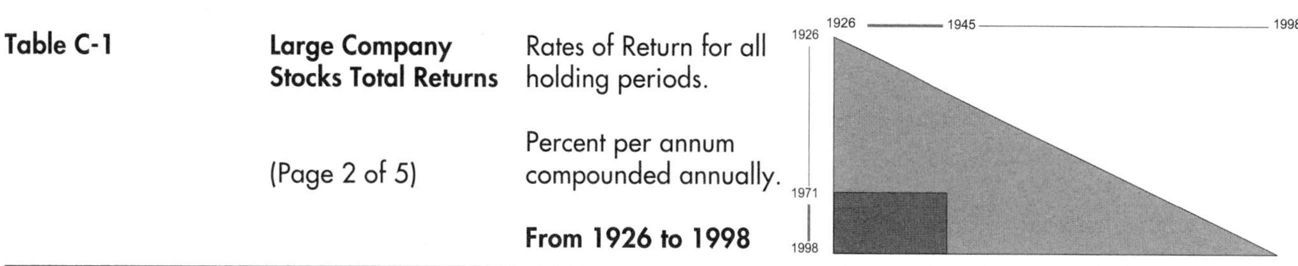

To The End Of	From The Beginning Of 1926	1927	1928	1929	1930	1931	1932	1933	1934	1935	1936	1937	1938	1939	1940	1941	1942	1943	1944	1945
1971	9.7	9.7	9.1	8.4	8.9	9.9	11.7	12.2	11.3	11.7	10.8	10.2	11.9	11.4	11.8	12.6	13.5	13.3	12.8	12.6
1972	9.9	9.9	9.3	8.7	9.1	10.1	11.9	12.4	11.5	11.9	11.0	10.5	12.1	11.6	12.0	12.8	13.7	13.5	13.0	12.8
1973	9.3	9.3	8.7	8.1	8.5	9.4	11.1	11.7	10.8	11.1	10.3	9.7	11.3	10.8	11.1	11.8	12.7	12.4	12.0	11.7
1974	8.5	8.4	7.8	7.2	7.5	8.4	10.1	10.6	9.7	10.0	9.1	8.5	10.1	9.5	9.8	10.5	11.2	10.9	10.5	10.2
1975	9.0	8.9	8.4	7.7	8.1	9.0	10.6	11.1	10.2	10.6	9.8	9.2	10.7	10.2	10.5	11.1	11.9	11.6	11.2	11.0
1976	9.2	9.2	8.7	8.0	8.4	9.3	10.9	11.4	10.5	10.9	10.1	9.5	11.0	10.5	10.8	11.5	12.2	12.0	11.6	11.3
1977	8.9	8.8	8.3	7.7	8.1	8.9	10.5	10.9	10.1	10.4	9.6	9.1	10.5	10.0	10.3	10.9	11.6	11.4	11.0	10.7
1978	8.9	8.8	8.3	7.7	8.0	8.9	10.4	10.8	10.0	10.3	9.6	9.0	10.4	9.9	10.2	10.8	11.5	11.3	10.9	10.6
1979	9.0	9.0	8.5	7.9	8.2	9.1	10.6	11.0	10.2	10.5	9.8	9.2	10.6	10.1	10.4	11.0	11.7	11.4	11.1	10.8
1980	9.4	9.4	8.9	8.3	8.7	9.5	11.0	11.4	10.6	10.9	10.2	9.7	11.1	10.6	10.9	11.5	12.2	11.9	11.6	11.4
1981	9.1	9.1	8.6	8.1	8.4	9.2	10.6	11.0	10.3	10.6	9.9	9.4	10.7	10.2	10.5	11.1	11.7	11.5	11.1	10.9
1982	9.3	9.3	8.8	8.3	8.6	9.4	10.8	11.2	10.5	10.8	10.1	9.6	10.9	10.5	10.8	11.3	11.9	11.7	11.4	11.2
1983	9.6	9.5	9.1	8.5	8.9	9.6	11.0	11.5	10.7	11.0	10.3	9.9	11.1	10.7	11.0	11.5	12.2	12.0	11.6	11.4
1984	9.5	9.5	9.0	8.5	8.8	9.6	10.9	11.3	10.6	10.9	10.3	9.8	11.0	10.6	10.9	11.4	12.0	11.8	11.5	11.3
1985	9.8	9.8	9.4	8.9	9.2	9.9	11.3	11.7	11.0	11.3	10.7	10.2	11.4	11.1	11.3	11.8	12.4	12.3	12.0	11.8
1986	10.0	9.9	9.5	9.0	9.4	10.1	11.4	11.8	11.2	11.4	10.8	10.4	11.6	11.2	11.5	12.0	12.6	12.4	12.1	11.9
1987	9.9	9.9	9.5	9.0	9.3	10.0	11.3	11.7	11.0	11.3	10.7	10.3	11.5	11.1	11.3	11.8	12.4	12.2	11.9	11.8
1988	10.0	10.0	9.6	9.1	9.4	10.1	11.4	11.8	11.1	11.4	10.8	10.4	11.6	11.2	11.4	11.9	12.5	12.3	12.1	11.9
1989	10.3	10.3	9.9	9.4	9.7	10.5	11.7	12.1	11.5	11.7	11.2	10.8	11.9	11.6	11.8	12.3	12.9	12.7	12.4	12.3
1990	10.1	10.1	9.7	9.2	9.5	10.2	11.5	11.8	11.2	11.4	10.9	10.5	11.6	11.3	11.5	12.0	12.5	12.4	12.1	11.9
1991	10.4	10.4	10.0	9.5	9.8	10.5	11.8	12.1	11.5	11.8	11.2	10.8	11.9	11.6	11.8	12.3	12.9	12.7	12.4	12.3
1992	10.3	10.3	9.9	9.5	9.8	10.5	11.7	12.1	11.4	11.7	11.1	10.8	11.8	11.5	11.8	12.2	12.7	12.6	12.3	12.2
1993	10.3	10.3	9.9	9.5	9.8	10.5	11.7	12.0	11.4	11.7	11.1	10.8	11.8	11.5	11.7	12.2	12.7	12.5	12.3	12.1
1994	10.2	10.2	9.8	9.4	9.7	10.3	11.5	11.8	11.3	11.5	10.9	10.6	11.6	11.3	11.5	12.0	12.5	12.3	12.1	11.9
1995	10.5	10.5	10.2	9.7	10.0	10.7	11.9	12.2	11.6	11.9	11.3	11.0	12.0	11.7	11.9	12.4	12.9	12.7	12.5	12.4
1996	10.7	10.7	10.3	9.9	10.2	10.9	12.0	12.4	11.8	12.0	11.5	11.2	12.2	11.9	12.1	12.6	13.1	12.9	12.7	12.6
1997	11.0	11.0	10.6	10.2	10.5	11.2	12.3	12.7	12.1	12.3	11.8	11.5	12.5	12.2	12.5	12.9	13.4	13.3	13.1	12.9
1998	11.2	11.2	10.9	10.5	10.8	11.4	12.5	12.9	12.3	12.6	12.1	11.8	12.8	12.5	12.7	13.2	13.6	13.5	13.3	13.2

Table C-1 **Large Company Stocks Total Returns**

(Page 3 of 5)

Rates of Return for all holding periods.

Percent per annum compounded annually.

From 1926 to 1998

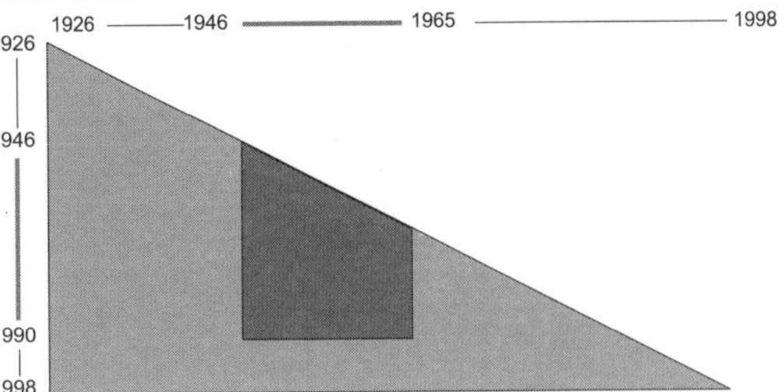

To The End Of	From The Beginning Of 1946	1947	1948	1949	1950	1951	1952	1953	1954	1955	1956	1957	1958	1959	1960	1961	1962	1963	1964	1965
1946	-8.1																			
1947	-1.4	5.7																		
1948	0.8	5.6	5.5																	
1949	5.1	9.8	11.9	18.8																
1950	9.9	14.9	18.2	25.1	31.7															
1951	12.1	16.7	19.6	24.7	27.8	24.0														
1952	13.0	17.0	19.4	23.1	24.6	21.2	18.4													
1953	11.2	14.2	15.7	17.9	17.6	13.3	8.3	-1.0												
1954	15.1	18.4	20.4	23.0	23.9	22.0	21.4	22.9	52.6											
1955	16.7	19.8	21.7	24.2	25.2	23.9	23.9	25.7	41.7	31.6										
1956	15.7	18.4	19.9	21.9	22.3	20.8	20.2	20.6	28.9	18.4	6.6									
1957	13.2	15.4	16.4	17.7	17.6	15.7	14.4	13.6	17.5	7.7	-2.5	-10.8								
1958	15.3	17.5	18.7	20.1	20.2	18.8	18.1	18.1	22.3	15.7	10.9	13.1	43.4							
1959	15.1	17.1	18.1	19.3	19.4	18.1	17.3	17.2	20.5	15.0	11.1	12.7	26.7	12.0						
1960	14.0	15.8	16.6	17.6	17.5	16.2	15.3	14.9	17.4	12.4	8.9	9.5	17.3	6.1	0.5					
1961	14.8	16.5	17.3	18.3	18.3	17.1	16.4	16.2	18.6	14.4	11.7	12.8	19.6	12.6	12.9	26.9				
1962	13.3	14.8	15.4	16.1	15.9	14.7	13.9	13.4	15.2	11.2	8.5	8.9	13.3	6.8	5.2	7.6	-8.7			
1963	13.8	15.2	15.8	16.6	16.4	15.3	14.6	14.3	15.9	12.4	10.2	10.8	14.8	9.9	9.3	12.5	5.9	22.8		
1964	13.9	15.3	15.9	16.6	16.4	15.4	14.7	14.4	16.0	12.8	10.9	11.5	15.1	10.9	10.7	13.5	9.3	19.6	16.5	
1965	13.8	15.1	15.7	16.3	16.2	15.2	14.6	14.3	15.7	12.8	11.1	11.6	14.7	11.1	11.0	13.2	10.1	17.2	14.4	12.5
1966	12.6	13.7	14.2	14.7	14.4	13.4	12.7	12.4	13.4	10.7	9.0	9.2	11.7	8.2	7.7	9.0	5.7	9.7	5.6	0.6
1967	13.1	14.2	14.6	15.1	14.9	14.0	13.4	13.1	14.2	11.6	10.1	10.5	12.8	9.9	9.6	11.0	8.6	12.4	9.9	7.8
1968	13.0	14.0	14.5	14.9	14.7	13.8	13.3	13.0	14.0	11.6	10.2	10.5	12.7	10.0	9.8	11.0	8.9	12.2	10.2	8.6
1969	12.0	13.0	13.3	13.7	13.4	12.5	11.9	11.6	12.4	10.1	8.7	8.9	10.7	8.2	7.8	8.7	6.6	9.0	6.8	5.0
1970	11.7	12.6	12.9	13.2	13.0	12.1	11.5	11.1	11.9	9.7	8.4	8.6	10.2	7.8	7.5	8.2	6.3	8.3	6.4	4.8
1971	11.8	12.6	12.9	13.3	13.0	12.2	11.6	11.3	12.0	10.0	8.8	8.9	10.5	8.3	8.0	8.0	7.1	9.0	7.4	6.1
1972	12.0	12.9	13.2	13.5	13.3	12.5	12.0	11.7	12.4	10.5	9.4	9.5	11.0	9.0	8.8	9.5	8.1	9.9	8.6	7.6
1973	10.9	11.7	11.9	12.2	11.9	11.2	10.6	10.3	10.8	9.0	7.9	7.9	9.2	7.3	6.9	7.5	6.0	7.4	6.0	4.9
1974	9.4	10.1	10.2	10.4	10.1	9.3	8.7	8.2	8.7	6.9	5.7	5.7	6.7	4.8	4.3	4.6	3.0	4.1	2.5	1.2
1975	10.2	10.9	11.1	11.3	11.0	10.3	9.7	9.4	9.9	8.2	7.1	7.1	8.2	6.4	6.1	6.5	5.2	6.3	5.1	4.1
1976	10.6	11.3	11.5	11.7	11.5	10.8	10.3	9.9	10.4	8.8	7.8	7.9	9.0	7.3	7.1	7.5	6.3	7.5	6.4	5.6
1977	10.0	10.7	10.8	11.0	10.7	10.0	9.5	9.2	9.6	8.1	7.1	7.1	8.1	6.5	6.2	6.6	5.4	6.4	5.4	4.6
1978	9.9	10.5	10.7	10.9	10.6	9.9	9.4	9.1	9.5	8.0	7.1	7.1	8.0	6.5	6.2	6.6	5.5	6.5	5.4	4.7
1979	10.2	10.8	10.9	11.1	10.8	10.2	9.7	9.4	9.8	8.4	7.5	7.6	8.5	7.1	6.8	7.2	6.2	7.1	6.2	5.6
1980	10.7	11.3	11.5	11.7	11.5	10.9	10.4	10.2	10.6	9.2	8.4	8.5	9.4	8.1	7.9	8.3	7.4	8.4	7.6	7.1
1981	10.3	10.8	11.0	11.2	10.9	10.3	9.9	9.6	10.0	8.7	7.9	7.9	8.8	7.5	7.3	7.6	6.8	7.6	6.9	6.3
1982	10.6	11.1	11.3	11.5	11.2	10.7	10.2	10.0	10.4	9.1	8.4	8.4	9.3	8.1	7.9	8.2	7.4	8.3	7.6	7.1
1983	10.9	11.4	11.6	11.8	11.6	11.0	10.6	10.4	10.8	9.6	8.8	8.9	9.8	8.6	8.5	8.8	8.1	8.9	8.3	7.9
1984	10.7	11.3	11.4	11.6	11.4	10.9	10.5	10.2	10.6	9.4	8.7	8.8	9.6	8.5	8.4	8.7	8.0	8.8	8.2	7.8
1985	11.2	11.8	11.9	12.1	11.9	11.4	11.1	10.8	11.2	10.1	9.5	9.6	10.4	9.3	9.2	9.6	8.9	9.7	9.2	8.8
1986	11.4	11.9	12.1	12.3	12.1	11.6	11.3	11.1	11.4	10.4	9.7	9.8	10.6	9.6	9.5	9.9	9.3	10.1	9.6	9.3
1987	11.2	11.8	11.9	12.1	11.9	11.4	11.1	10.9	11.3	10.2	9.6	9.7	10.4	9.5	9.4	9.7	9.1	9.9	9.4	9.1
1988	11.4	11.9	12.0	12.2	12.0	11.6	11.2	11.1	11.4	10.4	9.8	9.9	10.6	9.7	9.6	10.0	9.4	10.1	9.7	9.4
1989	11.8	12.3	12.5	12.6	12.5	12.0	11.7	11.6	11.9	10.9	10.4	10.5	11.2	10.3	10.3	10.6	10.1	10.9	10.4	10.2
1990	11.4	11.9	12.1	12.2	12.1	11.6	11.3	11.1	11.5	10.5	10.0	10.1	10.8	9.9	9.8	10.2	9.6	10.3	9.9	9.7

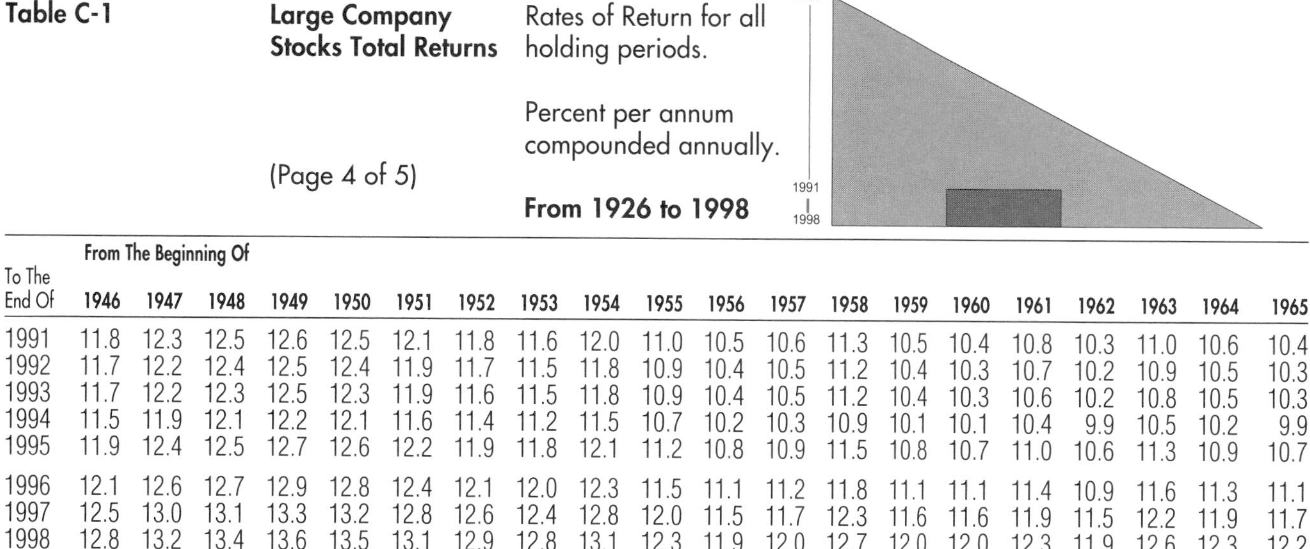

Table C-1

Large Company Stocks Total Returns

(Page 4 of 5)

Rates of Return for all holding periods.

Percent per annum compounded annually.

From 1926 to 1998

To The End Of	From The Beginning Of 1946	1947	1948	1949	1950	1951	1952	1953	1954	1955	1956	1957	1958	1959	1960	1961	1962	1963	1964	1965
1991	11.8	12.3	12.5	12.6	12.5	12.1	11.8	11.6	12.0	11.0	10.5	10.6	11.3	10.5	10.4	10.8	10.3	11.0	10.6	10.4
1992	11.7	12.2	12.4	12.5	12.4	11.9	11.7	11.5	11.8	10.9	10.4	10.5	11.2	10.4	10.3	10.7	10.2	10.9	10.5	10.3
1993	11.7	12.2	12.3	12.5	12.3	11.9	11.6	11.5	11.8	10.9	10.4	10.5	11.2	10.4	10.3	10.6	10.2	10.8	10.5	10.3
1994	11.5	11.9	12.1	12.2	12.1	11.6	11.4	11.2	11.5	10.7	10.2	10.3	10.9	10.1	10.1	10.4	9.9	10.5	10.2	9.9
1995	11.9	12.4	12.5	12.7	12.6	12.2	11.9	11.8	12.1	11.2	10.8	10.9	11.5	10.8	10.7	11.0	10.6	11.3	10.9	10.7
1996	12.1	12.6	12.7	12.9	12.8	12.4	12.1	12.0	12.3	11.5	11.1	11.2	11.8	11.1	11.1	11.4	10.9	11.6	11.3	11.1
1997	12.5	13.0	13.1	13.3	13.2	12.8	12.6	12.4	12.8	12.0	11.5	11.7	12.3	11.6	11.6	11.9	11.5	12.2	11.9	11.7
1998	12.8	13.2	13.4	13.6	13.5	13.1	12.9	12.8	13.1	12.3	11.9	12.0	12.7	12.0	12.0	12.3	11.9	12.6	12.3	12.2

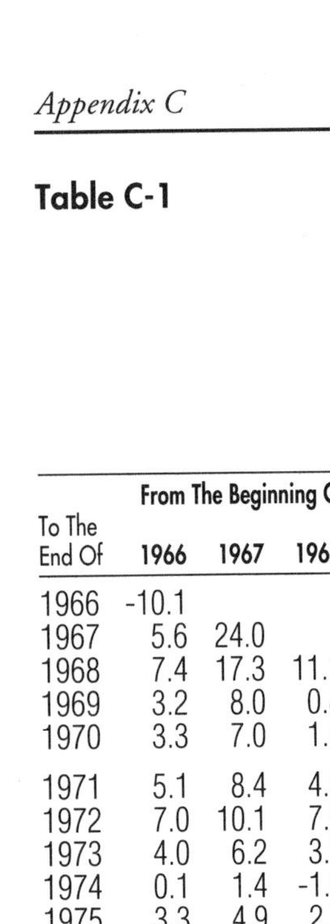

Table C-1

Large Company Stocks Total Returns

(Page 5 of 5)

Rates of Return for all holding periods.

Percent per annum compounded annually.

From 1926 to 1998

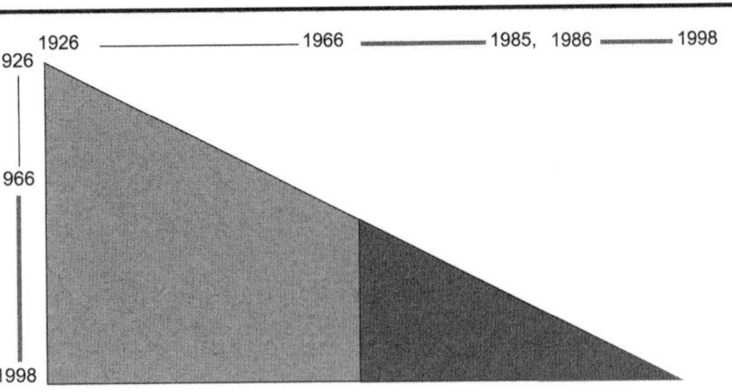

To The End Of	From The Beginning Of 1966	1967	1968	1969	1970	1971	1972	1973	1974	1975	1976	1977	1978	1979	1980	1981	1982	1983	1984	1985
1966	-10.1																			
1967	5.6	24.0																		
1968	7.4	17.3	11.1																	
1969	3.2	8.0	0.8	-8.5																
1970	3.3	7.0	1.9	-2.4	4.0															
1971	5.1	8.4	4.8	2.8	9.0	14.3														
1972	7.0	10.1	7.5	6.7	12.3	16.6	19.0													
1973	4.0	6.2	3.5	2.0	4.8	5.1	0.8	-14.7												
1974	0.1	1.4	-1.5	-3.4	-2.4	-3.9	-9.3	-20.8	-26.5											
1975	3.3	4.9	2.7	1.6	3.3	3.2	0.6	-4.9	0.4	37.2										
1976	5.0	6.6	4.9	4.1	6.0	6.4	4.9	1.6	7.7	30.4	23.8									
1977	3.9	5.3	3.6	2.8	4.3	4.3	2.8	-0.2	3.8	16.4	7.2	-7.2								
1978	4.1	5.4	3.9	3.2	4.5	4.6	3.3	0.9	4.3	13.9	7.0	-0.5	6.6							
1979	5.1	6.3	5.0	4.5	5.9	6.1	5.1	3.2	6.6	14.8	9.7	5.4	12.3	18.4						
1980	6.7	8.0	6.9	6.5	8.0	8.4	7.8	6.5	9.9	17.5	13.9	11.6	18.7	25.2	32.4					
1981	5.9	7.1	6.0	5.6	6.9	7.2	6.5	5.2	7.9	14.0	10.6	8.1	12.3	14.3	12.2	-4.9				
1982	6.8	8.0	7.0	6.7	7.9	8.3	7.7	6.7	9.4	14.9	12.1	10.2	14.0	16.0	15.2	7.4	21.4			
1983	7.6	8.8	7.9	7.7	8.9	9.3	8.9	8.0	10.6	15.7	13.3	11.9	15.4	17.3	17.0	12.3	22.0	22.5		
1984	7.5	8.6	7.8	7.6	8.7	9.1	8.7	7.9	10.2	14.8	12.5	11.2	14.1	15.4	14.8	10.7	16.5	14.1	6.3	
1985	8.7	9.7	9.0	8.9	10.1	10.5	10.2	9.6	11.9	16.2	14.3	13.3	16.2	17.6	17.5	14.7	20.2	19.8	18.5	32.2
1986	9.1	10.2	9.5	9.4	10.6	11.0	10.8	10.2	12.4	16.4	14.7	13.8	16.4	17.7	17.6	15.3	19.9	19.5	18.5	25.1
1987	8.9	9.9	9.3	9.2	10.3	10.6	10.4	9.9	11.9	15.5	13.9	13.0	15.3	16.3	16.0	13.8	17.3	16.5	15.0	18.1
1988	9.3	10.2	9.6	9.5	10.6	11.0	10.8	10.3	12.2	15.6	14.1	13.3	15.4	16.3	16.1	14.2	17.2	16.5	15.4	17.8
1989	10.1	11.1	10.5	10.5	11.5	12.0	11.8	11.4	13.3	16.6	15.3	14.6	16.7	17.6	17.5	16.0	18.9	18.6	17.9	20.4
1990	9.5	10.4	9.9	9.8	10.8	11.2	11.0	10.6	12.3	15.3	13.9	13.3	15.0	15.7	15.5	13.9	16.2	15.6	14.6	16.1
1991	10.3	11.2	10.7	10.7	11.6	12.0	11.9	11.5	13.2	16.1	14.9	14.3	16.0	16.8	16.7	15.3	17.6	17.2	16.5	18.1
1992	10.2	11.1	10.6	10.5	11.5	11.8	11.7	11.3	12.9	15.6	14.5	13.9	15.5	16.1	16.0	14.7	16.7	16.2	15.5	16.7
1993	10.2	11.0	10.5	10.5	11.4	11.7	11.6	11.3	12.8	15.3	14.2	13.7	15.1	15.7	15.5	14.3	16.1	15.6	14.9	16.0
1994	9.9	10.6	10.2	10.1	11.0	11.3	11.1	10.8	12.2	14.6	13.5	12.9	14.3	14.8	14.5	13.3	14.9	14.3	13.6	14.4
1995	10.7	11.5	11.1	11.1	11.9	12.2	12.1	11.8	13.2	15.6	14.6	14.1	15.4	16.0	15.8	14.8	16.4	16.0	15.4	16.3
1996	11.1	11.8	11.5	11.5	12.3	12.6	12.5	12.3	13.6	15.9	15.0	14.6	15.8	16.4	16.2	15.3	16.8	16.5	16.0	16.9
1997	11.7	12.5	12.1	12.2	13.0	13.3	13.3	13.1	14.4	16.6	15.8	15.4	16.6	17.2	17.1	16.3	17.8	17.5	17.2	18.1
1998	12.2	13.0	12.6	12.7	13.5	13.8	13.8	13.6	14.9	17.1	16.3	16.0	17.2	17.7	17.7	16.9	18.4	18.2	17.9	18.8

To The End Of	From The Beginning Of 1986	1987	1988	1989	1990	1991	1992	1993	1994	1995	1996	1997	1998
1986	18.5												
1987	11.7	5.2											
1988	13.3	10.9	16.8										
1989	17.6	17.4	23.9	31.5									
1990	13.1	11.8	14.1	12.8	-3.2								
1991	15.9	15.4	18.0	18.5	12.4	30.5							
1992	14.7	14.0	15.9	15.7	10.8	18.6	7.7						
1993	14.1	13.5	14.9	14.5	10.6	15.6	8.8	10.0					
1994	12.6	11.9	12.8	12.2	8.7	11.9	6.3	5.6	1.3				
1995	14.8	14.4	15.7	15.5	13.0	16.6	13.3	15.3	18.0	37.4			
1996	15.6	15.3	16.5	16.4	14.4	17.6	15.2	17.2	19.7	30.1	23.1		
1997	17.0	16.8	18.0	18.2	16.6	19.8	18.0	20.2	23.0	31.1	28.1	33.4	
1998	17.8	17.8	19.0	19.2	17.9	20.8	19.5	21.6	24.1	30.5	28.3	31.0	28.6

Table C-2

Small Company Stocks Total Returns

(Page 1 of 5)

Rates of Return for all holding periods.

Percent per annum compounded annually.

From 1926 to 1998

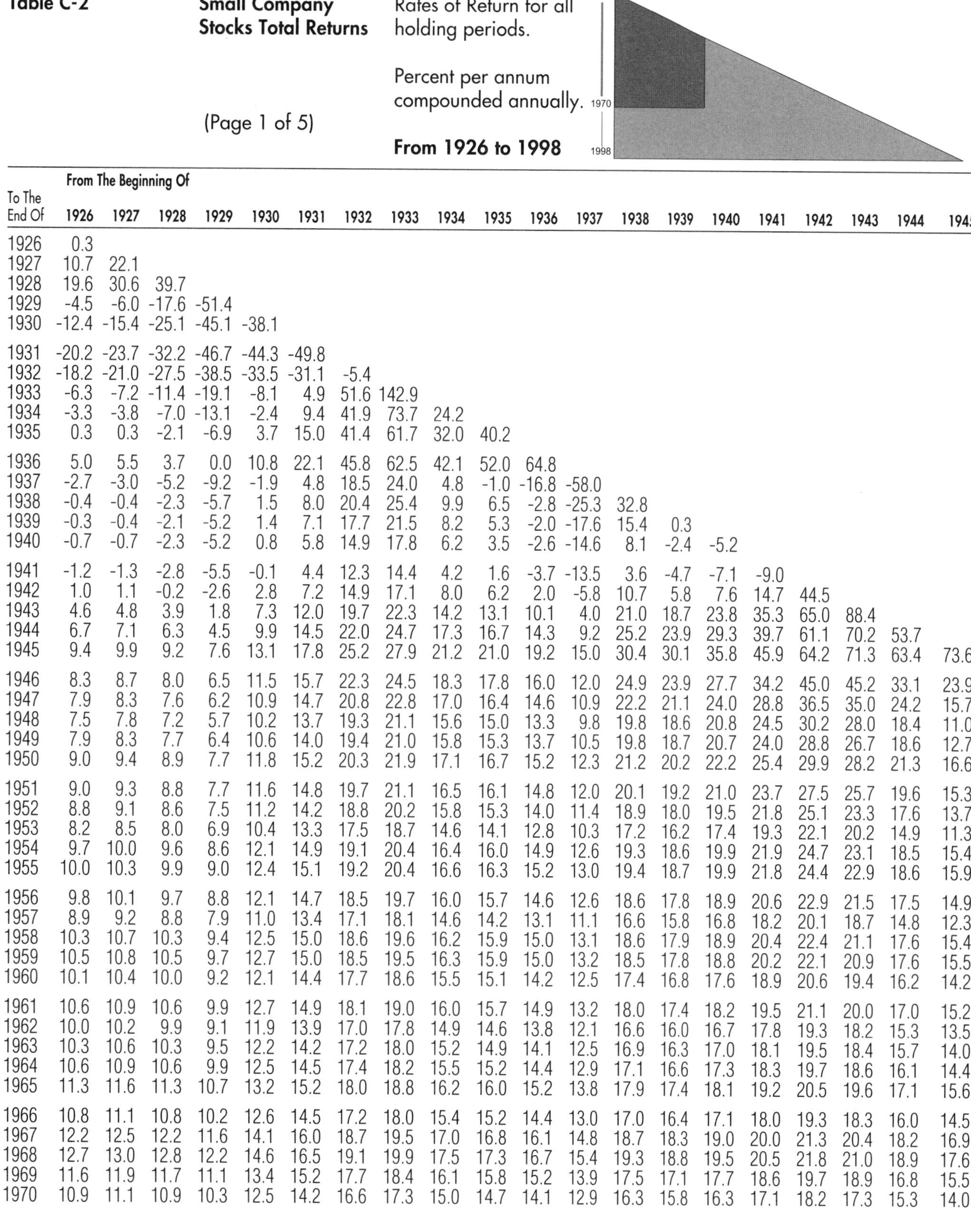

From The Beginning Of

To The End Of	1926	1927	1928	1929	1930	1931	1932	1933	1934	1935	1936	1937	1938	1939	1940	1941	1942	1943	1944	1945
1926	0.3																			
1927	10.7	22.1																		
1928	19.6	30.6	39.7																	
1929	-4.5	-6.0	-17.6	-51.4																
1930	-12.4	-15.4	-25.1	-45.1	-38.1															
1931	-20.2	-23.7	-32.2	-46.7	-44.3	-49.8														
1932	-18.2	-21.0	-27.5	-38.5	-33.5	-31.1	-5.4													
1933	-6.3	-7.2	-11.4	-19.1	-8.1	4.9	51.6	142.9												
1934	-3.3	-3.8	-7.0	-13.1	-2.4	9.4	41.9	73.7	24.2											
1935	0.3	0.3	-2.1	-6.9	3.7	15.0	41.4	61.7	32.0	40.2										
1936	5.0	5.5	3.7	0.0	10.8	22.1	45.8	62.5	42.1	52.0	64.8									
1937	-2.7	-3.0	-5.2	-9.2	-1.9	4.8	18.5	24.0	4.8	-1.0	-16.8	-58.0								
1938	-0.4	-0.4	-2.3	-5.7	1.5	8.0	20.4	25.4	9.9	6.5	-2.8	-25.3	32.8							
1939	-0.3	-0.4	-2.1	-5.2	1.4	7.1	17.7	21.5	8.2	5.3	-2.0	-17.6	15.4	0.3						
1940	-0.7	-0.7	-2.3	-5.2	0.8	5.8	14.9	17.8	6.2	3.5	-2.6	-14.6	8.1	-2.4	-5.2					
1941	-1.2	-1.3	-2.8	-5.5	-0.1	4.4	12.3	14.4	4.2	1.6	-3.7	-13.5	3.6	-4.7	-7.1	-9.0				
1942	1.0	1.1	-0.2	-2.6	2.8	7.2	14.9	17.1	8.0	6.2	2.0	-5.8	10.7	5.8	7.6	14.7	44.5			
1943	4.6	4.8	3.9	1.8	7.3	12.0	19.7	22.3	14.2	13.1	10.1	4.0	21.0	18.7	23.8	35.3	65.0	88.4		
1944	6.7	7.1	6.3	4.5	9.9	14.5	22.0	24.7	17.3	16.7	14.3	9.2	25.2	23.9	29.3	39.7	61.1	70.2	53.7	
1945	9.4	9.9	9.2	7.6	13.1	17.8	25.2	27.9	21.2	21.0	19.2	15.0	30.4	30.1	35.8	45.9	64.2	71.3	63.4	73.6
1946	8.3	8.7	8.0	6.5	11.5	15.7	22.3	24.5	18.3	17.8	16.0	12.0	24.9	23.9	27.7	34.2	45.0	45.2	33.1	23.9
1947	7.9	8.3	7.6	6.2	10.9	14.7	20.8	22.8	17.0	16.4	14.6	10.9	22.2	21.1	24.0	28.8	36.5	35.0	24.2	15.7
1948	7.5	7.8	7.2	5.7	10.2	13.7	19.3	21.1	15.6	15.0	13.3	9.8	19.8	18.6	20.8	24.5	30.2	28.0	18.4	11.0
1949	7.9	8.3	7.7	6.4	10.6	14.0	19.4	21.0	15.8	15.3	13.7	10.5	19.8	18.7	20.7	24.0	28.8	26.7	18.6	12.7
1950	9.0	9.4	8.9	7.7	11.8	15.2	20.3	21.9	17.1	16.7	15.2	12.3	21.2	20.2	22.2	25.4	29.9	28.2	21.3	16.6
1951	9.0	9.3	8.8	7.7	11.6	14.8	19.7	21.1	16.5	16.1	14.8	12.0	20.1	19.2	21.0	23.7	27.5	25.7	19.6	15.3
1952	8.8	9.1	8.6	7.5	11.2	14.2	18.8	20.2	15.8	15.3	14.0	11.4	18.9	18.0	19.5	21.8	25.1	23.3	17.6	13.7
1953	8.2	8.5	8.0	6.9	10.4	13.3	17.5	18.7	14.6	14.1	12.8	10.3	17.2	16.2	17.4	19.3	22.1	20.2	14.9	11.3
1954	9.7	10.0	9.6	8.6	12.1	14.9	19.1	20.4	16.4	16.0	14.9	12.6	19.3	18.6	19.9	21.9	24.7	23.1	18.5	15.4
1955	10.0	10.3	9.9	9.0	12.4	15.1	19.2	20.4	16.6	16.3	15.2	13.0	19.4	18.7	19.9	21.8	24.4	22.9	18.6	15.9
1956	9.8	10.1	9.7	8.8	12.1	14.7	18.5	19.7	16.0	15.7	14.6	12.6	18.6	17.8	18.9	20.6	22.9	21.5	17.5	14.9
1957	8.9	9.2	8.8	7.9	11.0	13.4	17.1	18.1	14.6	14.2	13.1	11.1	16.6	15.8	16.8	18.2	20.1	18.7	14.8	12.3
1958	10.3	10.7	10.3	9.4	12.5	15.0	18.6	19.6	16.2	15.9	15.0	13.1	18.6	17.9	18.9	20.4	22.4	21.1	17.6	15.4
1959	10.5	10.8	10.5	9.7	12.7	15.0	18.5	19.5	16.3	15.9	15.0	13.2	18.5	17.8	18.8	20.2	22.1	20.9	17.6	15.5
1960	10.1	10.4	10.0	9.2	12.1	14.4	17.7	18.6	15.5	15.1	14.2	12.5	17.4	16.8	17.6	18.9	20.6	19.4	16.2	14.2
1961	10.6	10.9	10.6	9.9	12.7	14.9	18.1	19.0	16.0	15.7	14.9	13.2	18.0	17.4	18.2	19.5	21.1	20.0	17.0	15.2
1962	10.0	10.2	9.9	9.1	11.9	13.9	17.0	17.8	14.9	14.6	13.8	12.1	16.6	16.0	16.7	17.8	19.3	18.2	15.3	13.5
1963	10.3	10.6	10.3	9.5	12.2	14.2	17.2	18.0	15.2	14.9	14.1	12.5	16.9	16.3	17.0	18.1	19.5	18.4	15.7	14.0
1964	10.6	10.9	10.6	9.9	12.5	14.5	17.4	18.2	15.5	15.2	14.4	12.9	17.1	16.6	17.3	18.3	19.7	18.6	16.1	14.4
1965	11.3	11.6	11.3	10.7	13.2	15.2	18.0	18.8	16.2	16.0	15.2	13.8	17.9	17.4	18.1	19.2	20.5	19.6	17.1	15.6
1966	10.8	11.1	10.8	10.2	12.6	14.5	17.2	18.0	15.4	15.2	14.4	13.0	17.0	16.4	17.1	18.0	19.3	18.3	16.0	14.5
1967	12.2	12.5	12.2	11.6	14.1	16.0	18.7	19.5	17.0	16.8	16.1	14.8	18.7	18.3	19.0	20.0	21.3	20.4	18.2	16.9
1968	12.7	13.0	12.8	12.2	14.6	16.5	19.1	19.9	17.5	17.3	16.7	15.4	19.3	18.8	19.5	20.5	21.8	21.0	18.9	17.6
1969	11.6	11.9	11.7	11.1	13.4	15.2	17.7	18.4	16.1	15.8	15.2	13.9	17.5	17.1	17.7	18.6	19.7	18.9	16.8	15.5
1970	10.9	11.1	10.9	10.3	12.5	14.2	16.6	17.3	15.0	14.7	14.1	12.9	16.3	15.8	16.3	17.1	18.2	17.3	15.3	14.0

Table C-2 **Small Company Stocks Total Returns**

(Page 2 of 5)

Rates of Return for all holding periods.

Percent per annum compounded annually.

From 1926 to 1998

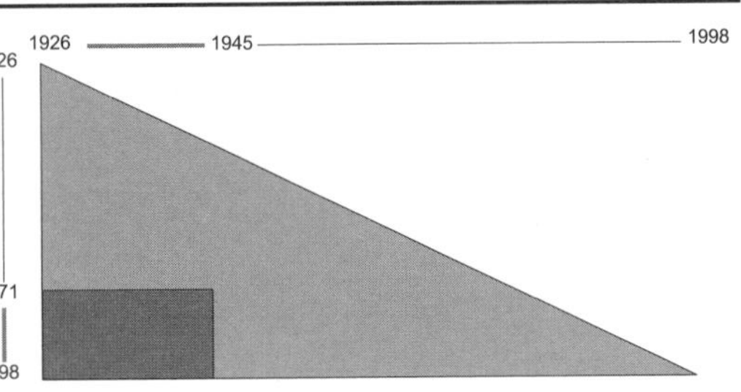

To The End Of	From The Beginning Of 1926	1927	1928	1929	1930	1931	1932	1933	1934	1935	1936	1937	1938	1939	1940	1941	1942	1943	1944	1945
1971	11.0	11.2	11.0	10.4	12.6	14.3	16.6	17.3	15.0	14.8	14.2	13.0	16.3	15.8	16.4	17.1	18.1	17.3	15.3	14.1
1972	10.9	11.1	10.9	10.3	12.4	14.0	16.3	16.9	14.7	14.5	13.9	12.7	15.9	15.5	16.0	16.7	17.6	16.8	14.9	13.7
1973	9.8	10.0	9.7	9.1	11.2	12.7	14.9	15.4	13.3	13.0	12.4	11.2	14.3	13.8	14.2	14.9	15.7	14.9	13.0	11.8
1974	9.1	9.3	9.0	8.4	10.4	11.8	13.9	14.4	12.3	12.1	11.4	10.3	13.2	12.7	13.1	13.7	14.4	13.6	11.7	10.6
1975	9.8	10.0	9.8	9.2	11.1	12.6	14.7	15.2	13.2	12.9	12.3	11.2	14.1	13.6	14.0	14.6	15.4	14.6	12.8	11.7
1976	10.6	10.8	10.6	10.0	12.0	13.4	15.5	16.0	14.0	13.8	13.2	12.2	15.0	14.6	15.0	15.6	16.4	15.7	14.0	12.9
1977	10.8	11.1	10.9	10.3	12.2	13.7	15.7	16.2	14.3	14.1	13.5	12.5	15.3	14.9	15.3	15.9	16.7	16.0	14.3	13.3
1978	11.1	11.3	11.1	10.6	12.4	13.9	15.9	16.4	14.5	14.3	13.7	12.7	15.5	15.1	15.5	16.1	16.8	16.2	14.6	13.6
1979	11.6	11.8	11.6	11.1	13.0	14.4	16.4	16.9	15.0	14.8	14.3	13.4	16.1	15.7	16.1	16.7	17.5	16.8	15.3	14.3
1980	12.1	12.3	12.1	11.6	13.5	14.9	16.8	17.3	15.5	15.3	14.8	13.9	16.6	16.2	16.6	17.2	18.0	17.4	15.9	15.0
1981	12.1	12.3	12.1	11.7	13.5	14.8	16.8	17.3	15.5	15.3	14.8	13.9	16.5	16.2	16.6	17.2	17.9	17.3	15.8	14.9
1982	12.4	12.6	12.4	12.0	13.7	15.1	17.0	17.5	15.7	15.6	15.1	14.2	16.8	16.4	16.8	17.4	18.1	17.5	16.1	15.3
1983	12.8	13.0	12.9	12.4	14.2	15.5	17.4	17.9	16.2	16.0	15.6	14.7	17.2	16.9	17.3	17.9	18.6	18.0	16.7	15.8
1984	12.4	12.6	12.5	12.0	13.8	15.0	16.9	17.3	15.7	15.5	15.0	14.2	16.6	16.3	16.7	17.3	17.9	17.4	16.0	15.2
1985	12.6	12.8	12.7	12.3	13.9	15.2	17.0	17.5	15.8	15.7	15.2	14.4	16.8	16.5	16.9	17.4	18.1	17.5	16.2	15.4
1986	12.5	12.7	12.6	12.2	13.8	15.1	16.8	17.3	15.7	15.5	15.1	14.2	16.6	16.3	16.6	17.2	17.8	17.3	16.0	15.2
1987	12.1	12.3	12.2	11.8	13.4	14.6	16.3	16.7	15.1	15.0	14.5	13.7	16.0	15.7	16.0	16.5	17.2	16.6	15.4	14.6
1988	12.3	12.5	12.3	11.9	13.5	14.7	16.4	16.8	15.3	15.1	14.7	13.9	16.1	15.8	16.2	16.7	17.3	16.8	15.5	14.8
1989	12.2	12.5	12.3	11.9	13.5	14.6	16.3	16.7	15.2	15.0	14.6	13.8	16.0	15.7	16.0	16.5	17.1	16.6	15.4	14.7
1990	11.6	11.8	11.7	11.3	12.8	13.9	15.5	15.9	14.4	14.2	13.8	13.0	15.2	14.9	15.2	15.6	16.2	15.6	14.5	13.7
1991	12.1	12.3	12.1	11.7	13.2	14.4	15.9	16.3	14.9	14.7	14.3	13.5	15.7	15.4	15.7	16.1	16.7	16.2	15.0	14.3
1992	12.2	12.4	12.3	11.9	13.4	14.5	16.1	16.5	15.0	14.9	14.5	13.7	15.8	15.5	15.8	16.3	16.8	16.3	15.2	14.5
1993	12.4	12.5	12.4	12.0	13.5	14.6	16.1	16.5	15.1	15.0	14.6	13.8	15.9	15.6	15.9	16.3	16.9	16.4	15.3	14.6
1994	12.2	12.4	12.3	11.9	13.3	14.4	15.9	16.3	14.9	14.8	14.4	13.6	15.6	15.4	15.7	16.1	16.6	16.1	15.0	14.4
1995	12.5	12.7	12.6	12.2	13.6	14.7	16.2	16.6	15.2	15.1	14.7	14.0	15.9	15.7	16.0	16.4	16.9	16.5	15.4	14.7
1996	12.6	12.8	12.6	12.3	13.7	14.7	16.2	16.6	15.2	15.1	14.7	14.0	16.0	15.7	16.0	16.4	16.9	16.5	15.4	14.8
1997	12.7	12.9	12.8	12.4	13.8	14.9	16.3	16.7	15.3	15.2	14.8	14.2	16.1	15.8	16.1	16.5	17.0	16.6	15.6	14.9
1998	12.4	12.6	12.5	12.1	13.5	14.5	15.9	16.3	15.0	14.8	14.5	13.8	15.7	15.4	15.7	16.1	16.6	16.1	15.1	14.5

Table C-2 **Small Company Stocks Total Returns**

(Page 3 of 5)

Rates of Return for all holding periods.

Percent per annum compounded annually.

From 1926 to 1998

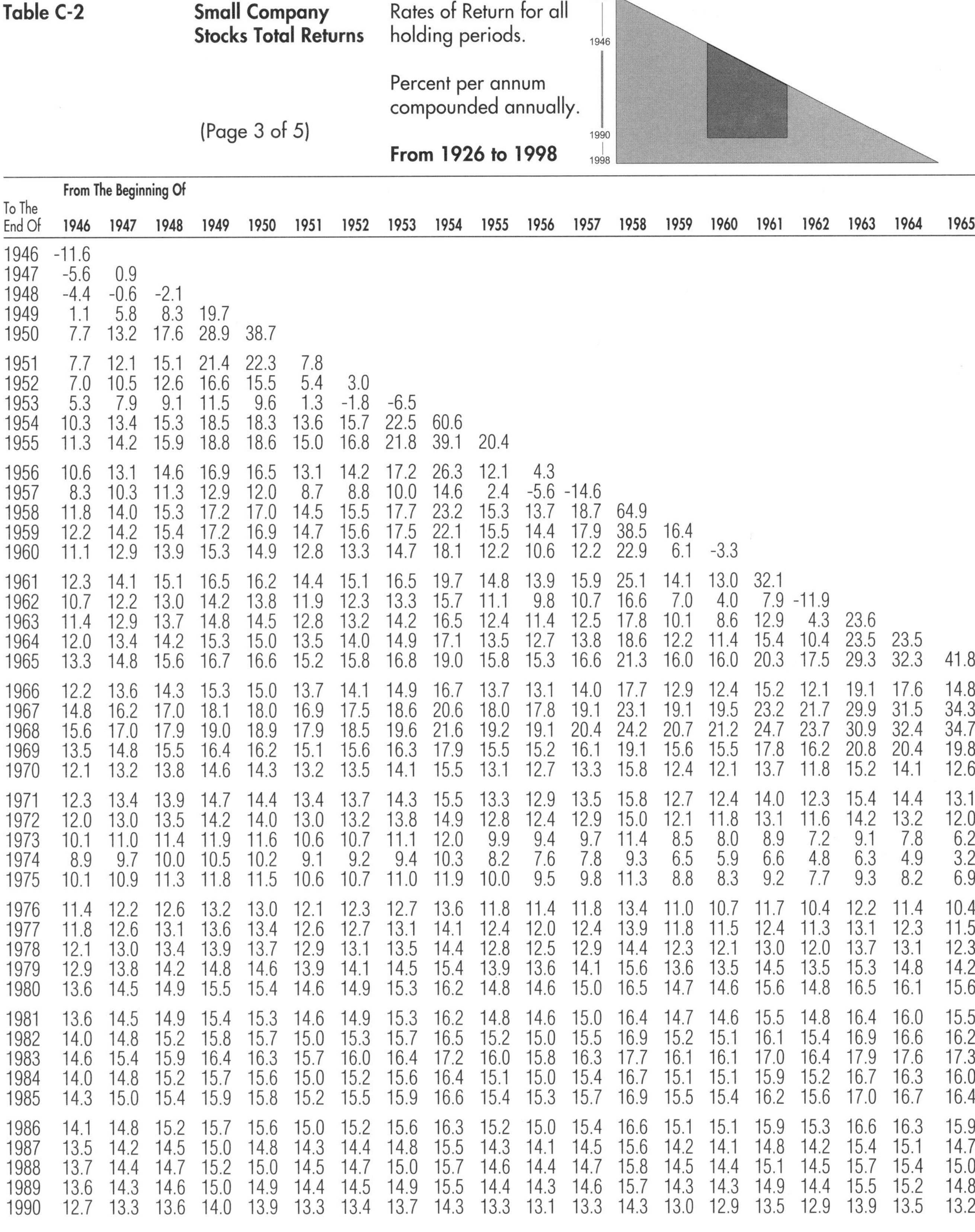

To The End Of	From The Beginning Of 1946	1947	1948	1949	1950	1951	1952	1953	1954	1955	1956	1957	1958	1959	1960	1961	1962	1963	1964	1965
1946	-11.6																			
1947	-5.6	0.9																		
1948	-4.4	-0.6	-2.1																	
1949	1.1	5.8	8.3	19.7																
1950	7.7	13.2	17.6	28.9	38.7															
1951	7.7	12.1	15.1	21.4	22.3	7.8														
1952	7.0	10.5	12.6	16.6	15.5	5.4	3.0													
1953	5.3	7.9	9.1	11.5	9.6	1.3	-1.8	-6.5												
1954	10.3	13.4	15.3	18.5	18.3	13.6	15.7	22.5	60.6											
1955	11.3	14.2	15.9	18.8	18.6	15.0	16.8	21.8	39.1	20.4										
1956	10.6	13.1	14.6	16.9	16.5	13.1	14.2	17.2	26.3	12.1	4.3									
1957	8.3	10.3	11.3	12.9	12.0	8.7	8.8	10.0	14.6	2.4	-5.6	-14.6								
1958	11.8	14.0	15.3	17.2	17.0	14.5	15.5	17.7	23.2	15.3	13.7	18.7	64.9							
1959	12.2	14.2	15.4	17.2	16.9	14.7	15.6	17.5	22.1	15.5	14.4	17.9	38.5	16.4						
1960	11.1	12.9	13.9	15.3	14.9	12.8	13.3	14.7	18.1	12.2	10.6	12.2	22.9	6.1	-3.3					
1961	12.3	14.1	15.1	16.5	16.2	14.4	15.1	16.5	19.7	14.8	13.9	15.9	25.1	14.1	13.0	32.1				
1962	10.7	12.2	13.0	14.2	13.8	11.9	12.3	13.3	15.7	11.1	9.8	10.7	16.6	7.0	4.0	7.9	-11.9			
1963	11.4	12.9	13.7	14.8	14.5	12.8	13.2	14.2	16.5	12.4	11.4	12.5	17.8	10.1	8.6	12.9	4.3	23.6		
1964	12.0	13.4	14.2	15.3	15.0	13.5	14.0	14.9	17.1	13.5	12.7	13.8	18.6	12.2	11.4	15.4	10.4	23.5	23.5	
1965	13.3	14.8	15.6	16.7	16.6	15.2	15.8	16.8	19.0	15.8	15.3	16.6	21.3	16.0	16.0	20.3	17.5	29.3	32.3	41.8
1966	12.2	13.6	14.3	15.3	15.0	13.7	14.1	14.9	16.7	13.7	13.1	14.0	17.7	12.9	12.4	15.2	12.1	19.1	17.6	14.8
1967	14.8	16.2	17.0	18.1	18.0	16.9	17.5	18.6	20.6	18.0	17.8	19.1	23.1	19.1	19.5	23.2	21.7	29.9	31.5	34.3
1968	15.6	17.0	17.9	19.0	18.9	17.9	18.5	19.6	21.6	19.2	19.1	20.4	24.2	20.7	21.2	24.7	23.7	30.9	32.4	34.7
1969	13.5	14.8	15.5	16.4	16.2	15.1	15.6	16.3	17.9	15.5	15.2	16.1	19.1	15.6	15.5	17.8	16.2	20.8	20.4	19.8
1970	12.1	13.2	13.8	14.6	14.3	13.2	13.5	14.1	15.5	13.1	12.7	13.3	15.8	12.4	12.1	13.7	11.8	15.2	14.1	12.6
1971	12.3	13.4	13.9	14.7	14.4	13.4	13.7	14.3	15.5	13.3	12.9	13.5	15.8	12.7	12.4	14.0	12.3	15.4	14.4	13.1
1972	12.0	13.0	13.5	14.2	14.0	13.0	13.2	13.8	14.9	12.8	12.4	12.9	15.0	12.1	11.8	13.1	11.6	14.2	13.2	12.0
1973	10.1	11.0	11.4	11.9	11.6	10.6	10.7	11.1	12.0	9.9	9.4	9.7	11.4	8.5	8.0	8.9	7.2	9.1	7.8	6.2
1974	8.9	9.7	10.0	10.5	10.2	9.1	9.2	9.4	10.3	8.2	7.6	7.8	9.3	6.5	5.9	6.6	4.8	6.3	4.9	3.2
1975	10.1	10.9	11.3	11.8	11.5	10.6	10.7	11.0	11.9	10.0	9.5	9.8	11.3	8.8	8.3	9.2	7.7	9.3	8.2	6.9
1976	11.4	12.2	12.6	13.2	13.0	12.1	12.3	12.7	13.6	11.8	11.4	11.8	13.4	11.0	10.7	11.7	10.4	12.2	11.4	10.4
1977	11.8	12.6	13.1	13.6	13.4	12.6	12.7	13.1	14.1	12.4	12.0	12.4	13.9	11.8	11.5	12.4	11.3	13.1	12.3	11.5
1978	12.1	13.0	13.4	13.9	13.7	12.9	13.1	13.5	14.4	12.8	12.5	12.9	14.4	12.3	12.1	13.0	12.0	13.7	13.1	12.3
1979	12.9	13.8	14.2	14.8	14.6	13.9	14.1	14.5	15.4	13.9	13.6	14.1	15.6	13.6	13.5	14.5	13.5	15.3	14.8	14.2
1980	13.6	14.5	14.9	15.5	15.4	14.6	14.9	15.3	16.2	14.8	14.6	15.0	16.5	14.7	14.6	15.6	14.8	16.5	16.1	15.6
1981	13.6	14.5	14.9	15.4	15.3	14.6	14.9	15.3	16.2	14.8	14.6	15.0	16.4	14.7	14.6	15.5	14.8	16.4	16.0	15.5
1982	14.0	14.8	15.2	15.8	15.7	15.0	15.3	15.7	16.5	15.2	15.0	15.5	16.9	15.2	15.1	16.1	15.4	16.9	16.6	16.2
1983	14.6	15.4	15.9	16.4	16.3	15.7	16.0	16.4	17.2	16.0	15.8	16.3	17.7	16.1	16.1	17.0	16.4	17.9	17.6	17.3
1984	14.0	14.8	15.2	15.7	15.6	15.0	15.2	15.6	16.4	15.1	15.0	15.4	16.7	15.1	15.1	15.9	15.2	16.7	16.3	16.0
1985	14.3	15.0	15.4	15.9	15.8	15.2	15.5	15.9	16.6	15.4	15.3	15.7	16.9	15.5	15.4	16.2	15.6	17.0	16.7	16.4
1986	14.1	14.8	15.2	15.7	15.6	15.0	15.2	15.6	16.3	15.2	15.0	15.4	16.6	15.1	15.1	15.9	15.3	16.6	16.3	15.9
1987	13.5	14.2	14.5	15.0	14.8	14.3	14.4	14.8	15.5	14.3	14.1	14.5	15.6	14.2	14.1	14.8	14.2	15.4	15.1	14.7
1988	13.7	14.4	14.7	15.2	15.0	14.5	14.7	15.0	15.7	14.6	14.4	14.7	15.8	14.5	14.4	15.1	14.5	15.7	15.4	15.0
1989	13.6	14.3	14.6	15.0	14.9	14.4	14.5	14.9	15.5	14.4	14.3	14.6	15.7	14.3	14.3	14.9	14.4	15.5	15.2	14.8
1990	12.7	13.3	13.6	14.0	13.9	13.3	13.4	13.7	14.3	13.3	13.1	13.3	14.3	13.0	12.9	13.5	12.9	13.9	13.5	13.2

Table C-2 **Small Company Stocks Total Returns**

Rates of Return for all holding periods.

Percent per annum compounded annually.

(Page 4 of 5)

From 1926 to 1998

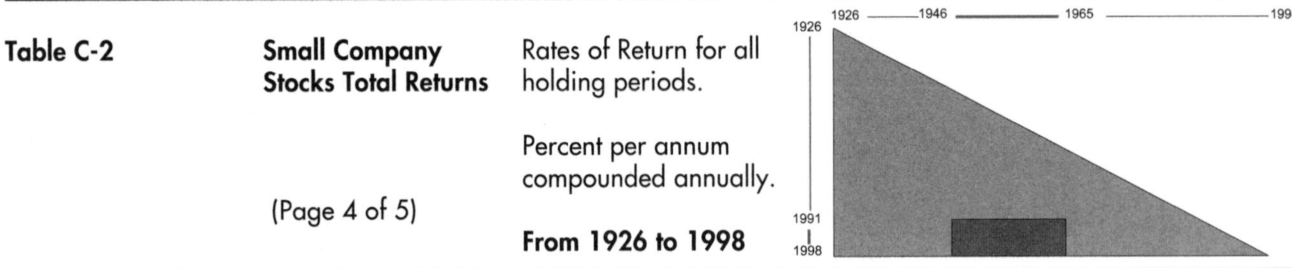

To The End Of	From The Beginning Of 1946	1947	1948	1949	1950	1951	1952	1953	1954	1955	1956	1957	1958	1959	1960	1961	1962	1963	1964	1965
1991	13.3	13.9	14.2	14.6	14.5	14.0	14.1	14.4	15.0	14.0	13.8	14.1	15.1	13.8	13.8	14.4	13.8	14.8	14.5	14.2
1992	13.5	14.1	14.4	14.8	14.7	14.2	14.3	14.6	15.2	14.2	14.1	14.4	15.3	14.1	14.0	14.6	14.1	15.1	14.8	14.5
1993	13.6	14.2	14.5	14.9	14.8	14.3	14.5	14.8	15.4	14.4	14.3	14.5	15.5	14.3	14.2	14.8	14.3	15.3	15.0	14.7
1994	13.4	14.0	14.3	14.7	14.6	14.1	14.2	14.5	15.1	14.1	14.0	14.2	15.1	14.0	13.9	14.5	14.0	14.9	14.6	14.3
1995	13.8	14.4	14.7	15.1	15.0	14.5	14.6	14.9	15.5	14.6	14.4	14.7	15.6	14.5	14.4	15.0	14.5	15.4	15.2	14.9
1996	13.9	14.4	14.7	15.1	15.0	14.6	14.7	15.0	15.5	14.6	14.5	14.8	15.6	14.6	14.5	15.1	14.6	15.5	15.3	15.0
1997	14.0	14.6	14.9	15.3	15.2	14.7	14.9	15.2	15.7	14.8	14.7	15.0	15.8	14.8	14.7	15.3	14.8	15.7	15.5	15.2
1998	13.6	14.1	14.4	14.8	14.7	14.2	14.4	14.6	15.1	14.3	14.1	14.4	15.2	14.2	14.1	14.6	14.2	15.0	14.8	14.5

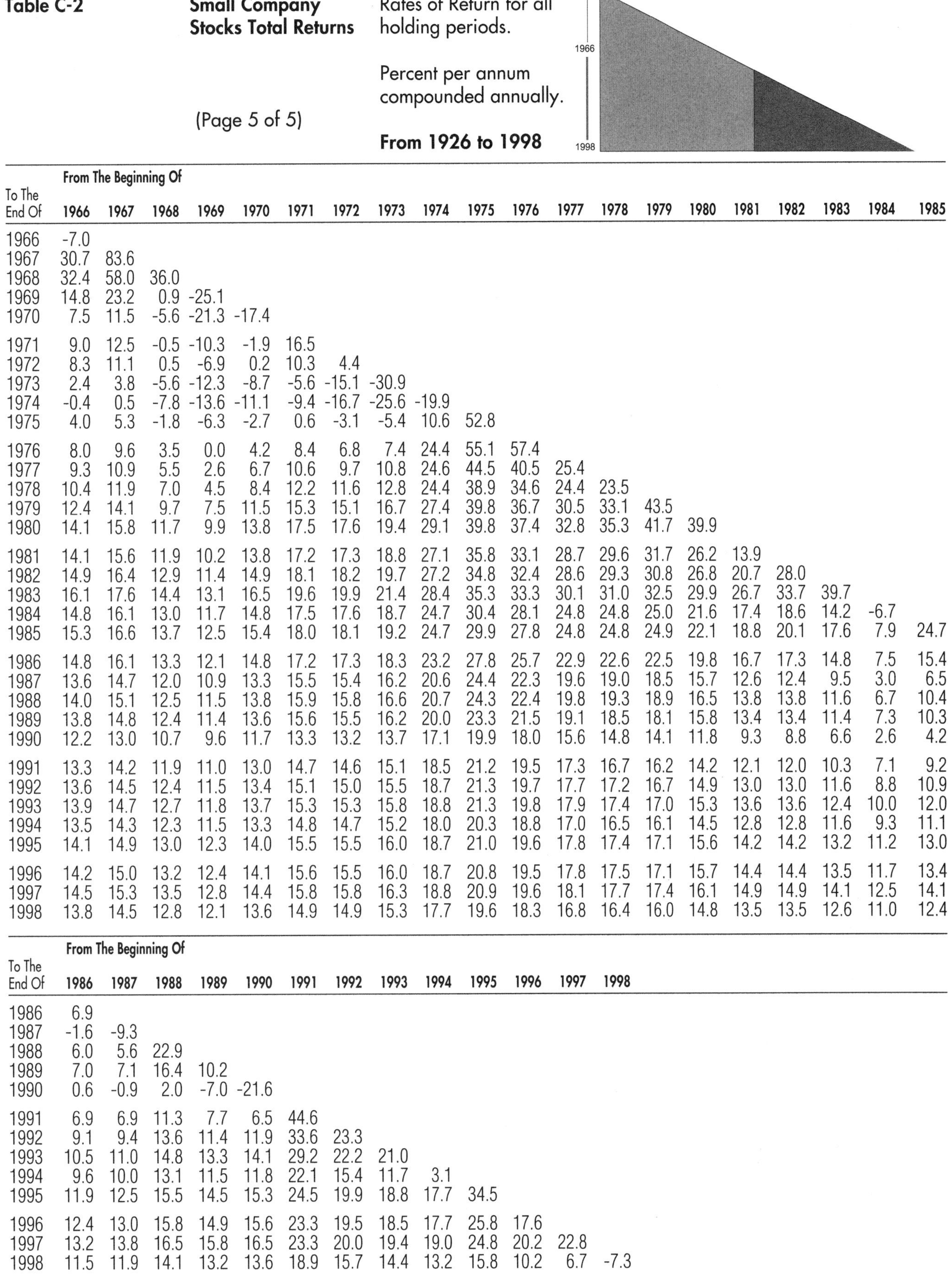

Table C-2

Small Company Stocks Total Returns

(Page 5 of 5)

Rates of Return for all holding periods.

Percent per annum compounded annually.

From 1926 to 1998

To The End Of	From The Beginning Of 1966	1967	1968	1969	1970	1971	1972	1973	1974	1975	1976	1977	1978	1979	1980	1981	1982	1983	1984	1985
1966	-7.0																			
1967	30.7	83.6																		
1968	32.4	58.0	36.0																	
1969	14.8	23.2	0.9	-25.1																
1970	7.5	11.5	-5.6	-21.3	-17.4															
1971	9.0	12.5	-0.5	-10.3	-1.9	16.5														
1972	8.3	11.1	0.5	-6.9	0.2	10.3	4.4													
1973	2.4	3.8	-5.6	-12.3	-8.7	-5.6	-15.1	-30.9												
1974	-0.4	0.5	-7.8	-13.6	-11.1	-9.4	-16.7	-25.6	-19.9											
1975	4.0	5.3	-1.8	-6.3	-2.7	0.6	-3.1	-5.4	10.6	52.8										
1976	8.0	9.6	3.5	0.0	4.2	8.4	6.8	7.4	24.4	55.1	57.4									
1977	9.3	10.9	5.5	2.6	6.7	10.6	9.7	10.8	24.6	44.5	40.5	25.4								
1978	10.4	11.9	7.0	4.5	8.4	12.2	11.6	12.8	24.4	38.9	34.6	24.4	23.5							
1979	12.4	14.1	9.7	7.5	11.5	15.3	15.1	16.7	27.4	39.8	36.7	30.5	33.1	43.5						
1980	14.1	15.8	11.7	9.9	13.8	17.5	17.6	19.4	29.1	39.8	37.4	32.8	35.3	41.7	39.9					
1981	14.1	15.6	11.9	10.2	13.8	17.2	17.3	18.8	27.1	35.8	33.1	28.7	29.6	31.7	26.2	13.9				
1982	14.9	16.4	12.9	11.4	14.9	18.1	18.2	19.7	27.2	34.8	32.4	28.6	29.3	30.8	26.8	20.7	28.0			
1983	16.1	17.6	14.4	13.1	16.5	19.6	19.9	21.4	28.4	35.3	33.3	30.1	31.0	32.5	29.9	26.7	33.7	39.7		
1984	14.8	16.1	13.0	11.7	14.8	17.5	17.6	18.7	24.7	30.4	28.1	24.8	24.8	25.0	21.6	17.4	18.6	14.2	-6.7	
1985	15.3	16.6	13.7	12.5	15.4	18.0	18.1	19.2	24.7	29.9	27.8	24.8	24.8	24.9	22.1	18.8	20.1	17.6	7.9	24.7
1986	14.8	16.1	13.3	12.1	14.8	17.2	17.3	18.3	23.2	27.8	25.7	22.9	22.6	22.5	19.8	16.7	17.3	14.8	7.5	15.4
1987	13.6	14.7	12.0	10.9	13.3	15.5	15.4	16.2	20.6	24.4	22.3	19.6	19.0	18.5	15.7	12.6	12.4	9.5	3.0	6.5
1988	14.0	15.1	12.5	11.5	13.8	15.9	15.8	16.6	20.7	24.3	22.4	19.8	19.3	18.9	16.5	13.8	13.8	11.6	6.7	10.4
1989	13.8	14.8	12.4	11.4	13.6	15.6	15.5	16.2	20.0	23.3	21.5	19.1	18.5	18.1	15.8	13.4	13.4	11.4	7.3	10.3
1990	12.2	13.0	10.7	9.6	11.7	13.3	13.2	13.7	17.1	19.9	18.0	15.6	14.8	14.1	11.8	9.3	8.8	6.6	2.6	4.2
1991	13.3	14.2	11.9	11.0	13.0	14.7	14.6	15.1	18.5	21.2	19.5	17.3	16.7	16.2	14.2	12.1	12.0	10.3	7.1	9.2
1992	13.6	14.5	12.4	11.5	13.4	15.1	15.0	15.5	18.7	21.3	19.7	17.7	17.2	16.7	14.9	13.0	13.0	11.6	8.8	10.9
1993	13.9	14.7	12.7	11.8	13.7	15.3	15.3	15.8	18.8	21.3	19.8	17.9	17.4	17.0	15.3	13.6	13.6	12.4	10.0	12.0
1994	13.5	14.3	12.3	11.5	13.3	14.8	14.7	15.2	18.0	20.3	18.8	17.0	16.5	16.1	14.5	12.8	12.8	11.6	9.3	11.1
1995	14.1	14.9	13.0	12.3	14.0	15.5	15.5	16.0	18.7	21.0	19.6	17.8	17.4	17.1	15.6	14.2	14.2	13.2	11.2	13.0
1996	14.2	15.0	13.2	12.4	14.1	15.6	15.5	16.0	18.7	20.8	19.5	17.8	17.5	17.1	15.7	14.4	14.4	13.5	11.7	13.4
1997	14.5	15.3	13.5	12.8	14.4	15.8	15.8	16.3	18.8	20.9	19.6	18.1	17.7	17.4	16.1	14.9	14.9	14.1	12.5	14.1
1998	13.8	14.5	12.8	12.1	13.6	14.9	14.9	15.3	17.7	19.6	18.3	16.8	16.4	16.0	14.8	13.5	13.5	12.6	11.0	12.4

To The End Of	From The Beginning Of 1986	1987	1988	1989	1990	1991	1992	1993	1994	1995	1996	1997	1998
1986	6.9												
1987	-1.6	-9.3											
1988	6.0	5.6	22.9										
1989	7.0	7.1	16.4	10.2									
1990	0.6	-0.9	2.0	-7.0	-21.6								
1991	6.9	6.9	11.3	7.7	6.5	44.6							
1992	9.1	9.4	13.6	11.4	11.9	33.6	23.3						
1993	10.5	11.0	14.8	13.3	14.1	29.2	22.2	21.0					
1994	9.6	10.0	13.1	11.5	11.8	22.1	15.4	11.7	3.1				
1995	11.9	12.5	15.5	14.5	15.3	24.5	19.9	18.8	17.7	34.5			
1996	12.4	13.0	15.8	14.9	15.6	23.3	19.5	18.5	17.7	25.8	17.6		
1997	13.2	13.8	16.5	15.8	16.5	23.3	20.0	19.4	19.0	24.8	20.2	22.8	
1998	11.5	11.9	14.1	13.2	13.6	18.9	15.7	14.4	13.2	15.8	10.2	6.7	-7.3

Table C-3

Long-Term Corporate Bonds Total Returns

(Page 1 of 5)

Rates of Return for all holding periods.

Percent per annum compounded annually.

From 1926 to 1998

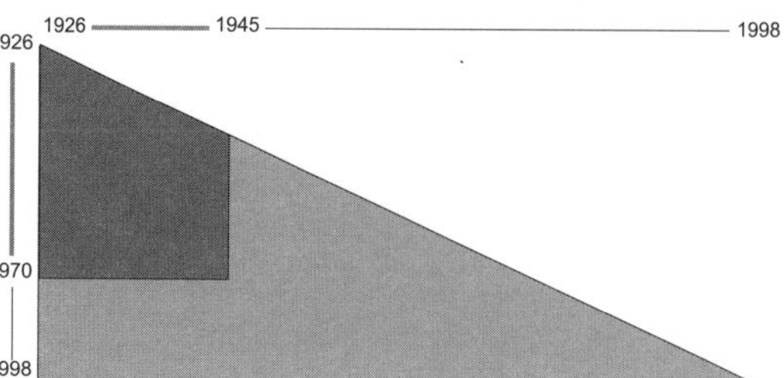

To The End Of	From The Beginning Of 1926	1927	1928	1929	1930	1931	1932	1933	1934	1935	1936	1937	1938	1939	1940	1941	1942	1943	1944	1945
1926	7.4																			
1927	7.4	7.4																		
1928	5.9	5.1	2.8																	
1929	5.2	4.5	3.1	3.3																
1930	5.8	5.4	4.7	5.6	8.0															
1931	4.4	3.9	3.0	3.1	2.9	-1.9														
1932	5.3	5.0	4.5	4.9	5.5	4.3	10.8													
1933	6.0	5.8	5.5	6.0	6.7	6.3	10.6	10.4												
1934	6.8	6.7	6.6	7.3	8.1	8.1	11.7	12.1	13.8											
1935	7.1	7.0	7.0	7.6	8.3	8.4	11.2	11.3	11.7	9.6										
1936	7.1	7.0	7.0	7.5	8.1	8.1	10.3	10.1	10.0	8.2	6.7									
1937	6.7	6.6	6.5	7.0	7.4	7.4	9.0	8.6	8.2	6.3	4.7	2.7								
1938	6.6	6.6	6.5	6.9	7.3	7.2	8.6	8.2	7.8	6.3	5.2	4.4	6.1							
1939	6.4	6.4	6.3	6.6	6.9	6.8	8.0	7.6	7.1	5.8	4.9	4.3	5.0	4.0						
1940	6.2	6.2	6.1	6.3	6.6	6.5	7.5	7.0	6.6	5.4	4.6	4.1	4.5	3.7	3.4					
1941	6.0	5.9	5.8	6.1	6.3	6.1	7.0	6.6	6.1	5.0	4.3	3.8	4.0	3.4	3.1	2.7				
1942	5.8	5.7	5.6	5.8	6.0	5.8	6.6	6.2	5.7	4.7	4.0	3.6	3.8	3.2	2.9	2.7	2.6			
1943	5.6	5.5	5.4	5.6	5.8	5.6	6.3	5.8	5.4	4.5	3.9	3.5	3.6	3.1	2.9	2.7	2.7	2.8		
1944	5.6	5.5	5.4	5.5	5.7	5.5	6.1	5.8	5.3	4.5	4.0	3.6	3.8	3.4	3.3	3.2	3.4	3.8	4.7	
1945	5.5	5.4	5.3	5.5	5.6	5.4	6.0	5.6	5.2	4.5	4.0	3.7	3.8	3.5	3.4	3.4	3.6	3.9	4.4	4.1
1946	5.3	5.2	5.1	5.3	5.4	5.2	5.7	5.3	5.0	4.3	3.8	3.5	3.6	3.3	3.2	3.1	3.2	3.3	3.5	2.9
1947	5.0	4.9	4.7	4.8	4.9	4.7	5.2	4.8	4.4	3.7	3.3	2.9	3.0	2.6	2.4	2.3	2.2	2.2	2.0	1.1
1948	4.9	4.8	4.7	4.8	4.9	4.7	5.1	4.8	4.4	3.8	3.3	3.0	3.1	2.8	2.6	2.5	2.5	2.5	2.4	1.9
1949	4.9	4.8	4.6	4.7	4.8	4.6	5.0	4.7	4.3	3.7	3.3	3.1	3.1	2.8	2.7	2.6	2.6	2.6	2.6	2.2
1950	4.8	4.7	4.5	4.6	4.7	4.5	4.9	4.5	4.2	3.6	3.2	3.0	3.0	2.8	2.6	2.6	2.6	2.6	2.5	2.1
1951	4.5	4.3	4.2	4.3	4.3	4.2	4.5	4.1	3.8	3.2	2.9	2.6	2.6	2.3	2.2	2.1	2.0	2.0	1.8	1.4
1952	4.4	4.3	4.2	4.2	4.3	4.1	4.4	4.1	3.8	3.3	2.9	2.7	2.7	2.4	2.3	2.2	2.2	2.1	2.0	1.7
1953	4.4	4.3	4.2	4.2	4.3	4.1	4.4	4.1	3.8	3.3	2.9	2.7	2.7	2.5	2.4	2.3	2.3	2.2	2.2	1.9
1954	4.4	4.3	4.2	4.3	4.3	4.2	4.4	4.1	3.8	3.4	3.1	2.9	2.9	2.7	2.6	2.5	2.5	2.5	2.5	2.2
1955	4.3	4.2	4.1	4.1	4.2	4.0	4.3	4.0	3.7	3.2	2.9	2.7	2.7	2.5	2.4	2.4	2.4	2.3	2.3	2.1
1956	3.9	3.8	3.7	3.7	3.7	3.6	3.8	3.5	3.2	2.8	2.4	2.2	2.2	2.0	1.9	1.8	1.7	1.6	1.6	1.3
1957	4.1	4.0	3.8	3.9	3.9	3.7	4.0	3.7	3.4	3.0	2.7	2.5	2.5	2.3	2.2	2.2	2.1	2.1	2.1	1.9
1958	3.9	3.8	3.6	3.7	3.7	3.5	3.7	3.5	3.2	2.8	2.5	2.3	2.3	2.1	2.0	1.9	1.9	1.8	1.8	1.6
1959	3.7	3.6	3.5	3.5	3.5	3.4	3.6	3.3	3.0	2.6	2.3	2.2	2.1	1.9	1.8	1.8	1.7	1.7	1.6	1.4
1960	3.9	3.8	3.7	3.7	3.7	3.6	3.7	3.5	3.3	2.9	2.6	2.4	2.4	2.3	2.2	2.1	2.1	2.1	2.0	1.8
1961	3.9	3.8	3.7	3.7	3.7	3.6	3.8	3.5	3.3	2.9	2.7	2.5	2.5	2.4	2.3	2.2	2.2	2.2	2.2	2.0
1962	4.0	3.9	3.8	3.8	3.9	3.7	3.9	3.7	3.5	3.1	2.9	2.7	2.7	2.6	2.5	2.5	2.5	2.5	2.5	2.3
1963	4.0	3.9	3.8	3.8	3.8	3.7	3.9	3.6	3.4	3.1	2.9	2.7	2.7	2.6	2.5	2.5	2.5	2.5	2.5	2.3
1964	4.0	3.9	3.8	3.8	3.8	3.7	3.9	3.7	3.5	3.1	2.9	2.8	2.8	2.7	2.6	2.6	2.6	2.6	2.6	2.5
1965	3.9	3.8	3.7	3.7	3.7	3.6	3.8	3.6	3.3	3.0	2.8	2.7	2.7	2.5	2.5	2.5	2.4	2.4	2.4	2.3
1966	3.8	3.7	3.6	3.6	3.6	3.5	3.7	3.5	3.2	2.9	2.7	2.6	2.6	2.5	2.4	2.4	2.4	2.3	2.3	2.2
1967	3.6	3.5	3.4	3.4	3.4	3.3	3.4	3.2	3.0	2.7	2.5	2.3	2.3	2.2	2.1	2.1	2.1	2.0	2.0	1.9
1968	3.5	3.4	3.3	3.4	3.4	3.2	3.4	3.2	3.0	2.7	2.5	2.3	2.3	2.2	2.2	2.1	2.1	2.1	2.0	1.9
1969	3.3	3.2	3.1	3.1	3.1	2.9	3.1	2.9	2.7	2.4	2.2	2.0	2.0	1.9	1.8	1.7	1.7	1.7	1.6	1.5
1970	3.6	3.5	3.4	3.4	3.4	3.3	3.4	3.2	3.1	2.8	2.6	2.5	2.5	2.3	2.3	2.3	2.2	2.2	2.2	2.1

Table C-3

Long-Term Corporate Bonds Total Returns

(Page 2 of 5)

Rates of Return for all holding periods.

Percent per annum compounded annually.

From 1926 to 1998

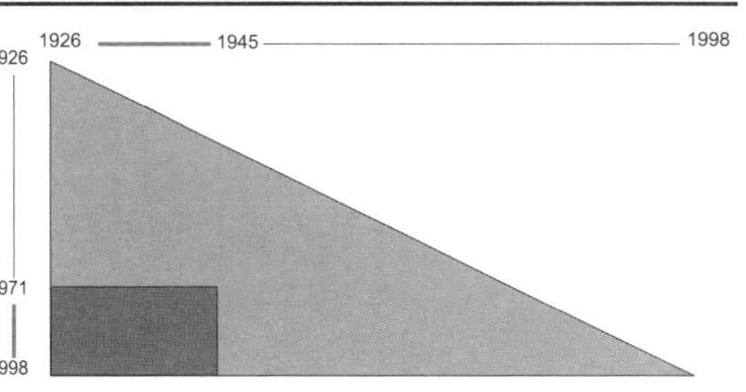

To The End Of	From The Beginning Of 1926	1927	1928	1929	1930	1931	1932	1933	1934	1935	1936	1937	1938	1939	1940	1941	1942	1943	1944	1945
1971	3.7	3.6	3.6	3.6	3.6	3.5	3.6	3.4	3.3	3.0	2.8	2.7	2.7	2.6	2.6	2.5	2.5	2.5	2.5	2.4
1972	3.8	3.7	3.6	3.7	3.7	3.6	3.7	3.5	3.4	3.1	2.9	2.8	2.8	2.7	2.7	2.7	2.7	2.7	2.7	2.6
1973	3.7	3.7	3.6	3.6	3.6	3.5	3.6	3.5	3.3	3.0	2.9	2.8	2.8	2.7	2.6	2.6	2.6	2.6	2.6	2.5
1974	3.6	3.5	3.4	3.4	3.5	3.4	3.5	3.3	3.1	2.9	2.7	2.6	2.6	2.5	2.5	2.4	2.4	2.4	2.4	2.3
1975	3.8	3.7	3.7	3.7	3.7	3.6	3.7	3.6	3.4	3.2	3.0	2.9	2.9	2.8	2.8	2.8	2.8	2.8	2.8	2.7
1976	4.1	4.0	3.9	4.0	4.0	3.9	4.0	3.9	3.7	3.5	3.4	3.3	3.3	3.2	3.2	3.2	3.2	3.2	3.2	3.2
1977	4.0	4.0	3.9	3.9	3.9	3.9	4.0	3.8	3.7	3.5	3.3	3.2	3.2	3.2	3.2	3.1	3.2	3.2	3.2	3.1
1978	4.0	3.9	3.8	3.8	3.9	3.8	3.9	3.7	3.6	3.4	3.2	3.2	3.2	3.1	3.1	3.1	3.1	3.1	3.1	3.0
1979	3.8	3.7	3.7	3.7	3.7	3.6	3.7	3.6	3.4	3.2	3.1	3.0	3.0	2.9	2.9	2.9	2.9	2.9	2.9	2.8
1980	3.7	3.6	3.5	3.5	3.6	3.5	3.6	3.4	3.3	3.1	2.9	2.8	2.8	2.8	2.7	2.7	2.7	2.7	2.7	2.7
1981	3.6	3.5	3.4	3.5	3.5	3.4	3.5	3.3	3.2	3.0	2.8	2.8	2.8	2.7	2.6	2.6	2.6	2.6	2.6	2.6
1982	4.2	4.1	4.1	4.1	4.1	4.0	4.1	4.0	3.9	3.7	3.6	3.5	3.5	3.4	3.4	3.4	3.5	3.5	3.5	3.5
1983	4.2	4.1	4.1	4.1	4.1	4.1	4.2	4.0	3.9	3.7	3.6	3.5	3.6	3.5	3.5	3.5	3.5	3.5	3.6	3.5
1984	4.4	4.4	4.3	4.3	4.3	4.3	4.4	4.3	4.2	4.0	3.9	3.8	3.8	3.8	3.8	3.8	3.8	3.8	3.9	3.8
1985	4.8	4.7	4.7	4.7	4.8	4.7	4.8	4.7	4.6	4.4	4.3	4.3	4.3	4.3	4.3	4.3	4.3	4.4	4.4	4.4
1986	5.0	5.0	4.9	5.0	5.0	5.0	5.1	5.0	4.9	4.7	4.6	4.6	4.6	4.6	4.6	4.6	4.7	4.7	4.8	4.8
1987	4.9	4.9	4.8	4.9	4.9	4.9	5.0	4.9	4.8	4.6	4.5	4.5	4.5	4.5	4.5	4.5	4.6	4.6	4.6	4.6
1988	5.0	5.0	4.9	5.0	5.0	5.0	5.1	5.0	4.9	4.7	4.6	4.6	4.6	4.6	4.6	4.6	4.7	4.7	4.8	4.8
1989	5.2	5.2	5.1	5.2	5.2	5.1	5.3	5.2	5.1	4.9	4.8	4.8	4.8	4.8	4.8	4.9	4.9	5.0	5.0	5.0
1990	5.2	5.2	5.1	5.2	5.2	5.2	5.3	5.2	5.1	5.0	4.9	4.8	4.9	4.9	4.9	4.9	4.9	5.0	5.0	5.1
1991	5.4	5.4	5.4	5.4	5.4	5.4	5.5	5.4	5.3	5.2	5.1	5.1	5.1	5.1	5.1	5.2	5.2	5.3	5.3	5.3
1992	5.5	5.4	5.4	5.5	5.5	5.5	5.6	5.5	5.4	5.3	5.2	5.2	5.2	5.2	5.2	5.3	5.3	5.4	5.4	5.4
1993	5.6	5.6	5.5	5.6	5.6	5.6	5.7	5.6	5.5	5.4	5.3	5.3	5.4	5.3	5.4	5.4	5.5	5.5	5.6	5.6
1994	5.4	5.4	5.4	5.4	5.4	5.4	5.5	5.4	5.3	5.2	5.1	5.1	5.1	5.1	5.2	5.2	5.2	5.3	5.3	5.3
1995	5.7	5.7	5.6	5.7	5.7	5.7	5.8	5.7	5.7	5.5	5.5	5.4	5.5	5.5	5.5	5.5	5.6	5.7	5.7	5.7
1996	5.6	5.6	5.6	5.6	5.7	5.6	5.7	5.7	5.6	5.5	5.4	5.4	5.4	5.4	5.4	5.5	5.5	5.6	5.6	5.6
1997	5.7	5.7	5.7	5.7	5.8	5.7	5.9	5.8	5.7	5.6	5.5	5.5	5.5	5.5	5.6	5.6	5.7	5.7	5.8	5.8
1998	5.8	5.8	5.8	5.8	5.8	5.8	5.9	5.9	5.8	5.7	5.6	5.6	5.6	5.6	5.6	5.7	5.7	5.8	5.9	5.9

Table C-3

Long-Term Corporate Bonds Total Returns

(Page 3 of 5)

Rates of Return for all holding periods.

Percent per annum compounded annually.

From 1926 to 1998

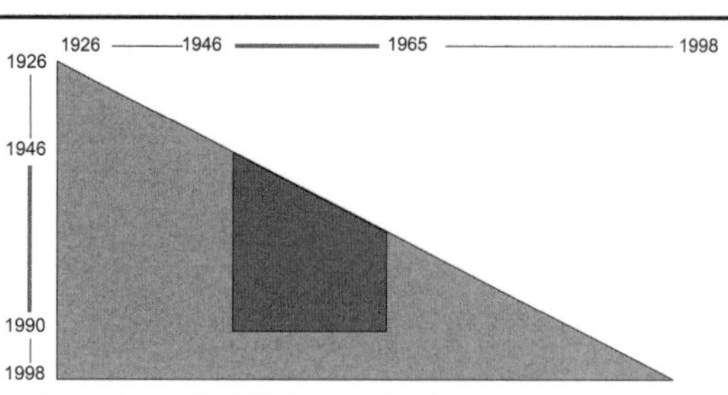

To The End Of	From The Beginning Of 1946	1947	1948	1949	1950	1951	1952	1953	1954	1955	1956	1957	1958	1959	1960	1961	1962	1963	1964	1965
1946	1.7																			
1947	-0.3	-2.3																		
1948	1.1	0.8	4.1																	
1949	1.7	1.7	3.7	3.3																
1950	1.8	1.8	3.2	2.7	2.1															
1951	1.0	0.9	1.7	0.9	-0.3	-2.7														
1952	1.4	1.3	2.0	1.5	0.9	0.4	3.5													
1953	1.6	1.6	2.3	1.9	1.6	1.4	3.5	3.4												
1954	2.0	2.1	2.7	2.5	2.3	2.4	4.1	4.4	5.4											
1955	1.9	1.9	2.4	2.2	2.0	2.0	3.2	3.1	2.9	0.5										
1956	1.1	1.0	1.4	1.0	0.7	0.5	1.1	0.5	-0.4	-3.2	-6.8									
1957	1.7	1.7	2.1	1.8	1.7	1.6	2.3	2.1	1.8	0.6	0.7	8.7								
1958	1.4	1.3	1.7	1.4	1.2	1.1	1.7	1.4	1.0	-0.1	-0.3	3.1	-2.2							
1959	1.2	1.2	1.5	1.2	1.0	0.9	1.3	1.0	0.6	-0.3	-0.5	1.7	-1.6	-1.0						
1960	1.7	1.7	2.0	1.8	1.7	1.7	2.2	2.0	1.8	1.2	1.4	3.5	1.8	3.9	9.1					
1961	1.9	1.9	2.2	2.1	2.0	2.0	2.4	2.3	2.2	1.7	1.9	3.8	2.6	4.2	6.9	4.8				
1962	2.2	2.3	2.6	2.5	2.4	2.4	2.9	2.9	2.8	2.5	2.8	4.5	3.6	5.1	7.3	6.4	7.9			
1963	2.2	2.3	2.6	2.5	2.4	2.4	2.9	2.8	2.7	2.4	2.7	4.1	3.4	4.5	6.0	5.0	5.0	2.2		
1964	2.4	2.4	2.7	2.6	2.6	2.6	3.0	3.0	2.9	2.7	2.9	4.2	3.6	4.6	5.7	4.9	4.9	3.5	4.8	
1965	2.2	2.3	2.5	2.4	2.4	2.4	2.8	2.7	2.6	2.4	2.6	3.7	3.1	3.8	4.7	3.8	3.6	2.1	2.1	-0.5
1966	2.1	2.1	2.4	2.3	2.2	2.2	2.6	2.5	2.4	2.2	2.4	3.3	2.7	3.4	4.0	3.2	2.9	1.7	1.5	-0.1
1967	1.8	1.8	2.0	1.9	1.8	1.8	2.1	2.0	1.9	1.6	1.7	2.5	1.9	2.4	2.9	2.0	1.5	0.3	-0.2	-1.8
1968	1.8	1.8	2.0	1.9	1.9	1.8	2.1	2.0	1.9	1.7	1.8	2.5	2.0	2.4	2.8	2.1	1.7	0.7	0.4	-0.7
1969	1.4	1.4	1.6	1.4	1.3	1.3	1.5	1.4	1.3	1.0	1.1	1.7	1.1	1.4	1.7	0.9	0.4	-0.6	-1.1	-2.2
1970	2.0	2.0	2.2	2.1	2.1	2.1	2.3	2.3	2.2	2.0	2.1	2.8	2.4	2.7	3.1	2.5	2.3	1.6	1.5	0.9
1971	2.4	2.4	2.6	2.5	2.5	2.5	2.8	2.7	2.7	2.5	2.7	3.3	3.0	3.4	3.7	3.3	3.1	2.6	2.6	2.3
1972	2.5	2.6	2.8	2.7	2.7	2.7	3.0	2.9	2.9	2.8	2.9	3.6	3.2	3.6	4.0	3.6	3.5	3.0	3.1	2.9
1973	2.5	2.5	2.7	2.6	2.6	2.6	2.9	2.9	2.8	2.7	2.8	3.4	3.1	3.5	3.8	3.4	3.3	2.9	2.9	2.7
1974	2.3	2.3	2.5	2.4	2.4	2.4	2.6	2.6	2.5	2.4	2.5	3.1	2.7	3.0	3.3	2.9	2.8	2.4	2.4	2.1
1975	2.7	2.7	2.9	2.9	2.8	2.9	3.1	3.1	3.1	3.0	3.1	3.6	3.4	3.7	4.0	3.7	3.6	3.3	3.3	3.2
1976	3.2	3.2	3.4	3.4	3.4	3.4	3.7	3.7	3.7	3.6	3.8	4.3	4.1	4.5	4.8	4.5	4.5	4.3	4.4	4.4
1977	3.1	3.2	3.3	3.3	3.3	3.4	3.6	3.6	3.6	3.5	3.7	4.2	4.0	4.3	4.6	4.4	4.3	4.1	4.2	4.2
1978	3.0	3.1	3.2	3.2	3.2	3.2	3.5	3.5	3.5	3.4	3.5	4.0	3.8	4.1	4.4	4.1	4.1	3.8	4.0	3.9
1979	2.8	2.8	3.0	3.0	2.9	3.0	3.2	3.2	3.2	3.1	3.2	3.6	3.4	3.7	3.9	3.7	3.6	3.4	3.4	3.3
1980	2.6	2.7	2.8	2.8	2.8	2.8	3.0	3.0	2.9	2.8	2.9	3.4	3.1	3.4	3.6	3.3	3.3	3.0	3.1	2.9
1981	2.5	2.5	2.7	2.6	2.6	2.6	2.8	2.8	2.8	2.7	2.8	3.2	3.0	3.2	3.4	3.1	3.0	2.8	2.8	2.7
1982	3.4	3.5	3.7	3.6	3.7	3.7	3.9	3.9	3.9	3.9	4.0	4.5	4.3	4.6	4.8	4.6	4.6	4.5	4.6	4.6
1983	3.5	3.6	3.7	3.7	3.7	3.8	4.0	4.0	4.0	4.0	4.1	4.5	4.4	4.6	4.9	4.7	4.7	4.6	4.7	4.7
1984	3.8	3.9	4.1	4.1	4.1	4.1	4.4	4.4	4.4	4.4	4.5	5.0	4.8	5.1	5.3	5.2	5.2	5.1	5.2	5.2
1985	4.4	4.5	4.7	4.7	4.7	4.8	5.0	5.1	5.1	5.1	5.3	5.7	5.6	5.9	6.2	6.1	6.1	6.1	6.2	6.3
1986	4.8	4.9	5.0	5.1	5.1	5.2	5.4	5.5	5.6	5.6	5.7	6.2	6.1	6.4	6.7	6.6	6.7	6.6	6.8	6.9
1987	4.7	4.7	4.9	4.9	5.0	5.0	5.3	5.3	5.4	5.4	5.5	6.0	5.9	6.2	6.4	6.3	6.4	6.3	6.5	6.6
1988	4.8	4.9	5.0	5.1	5.1	5.2	5.4	5.5	5.5	5.5	5.7	6.1	6.0	6.3	6.6	6.5	6.5	6.5	6.7	6.7
1989	5.0	5.1	5.3	5.3	5.4	5.5	5.7	5.7	5.8	5.8	6.0	6.4	6.3	6.6	6.9	6.8	6.9	6.8	7.0	7.1
1990	5.1	5.2	5.3	5.4	5.4	5.5	5.7	5.8	5.8	5.8	6.0	6.4	6.3	6.6	6.9	6.8	6.9	6.8	7.0	7.1

Table C-3

Long-Term Corporate Bonds Total Returns

(Page 4 of 5)

Rates of Return for all holding periods.

Percent per annum compounded annually.

From 1926 to 1998

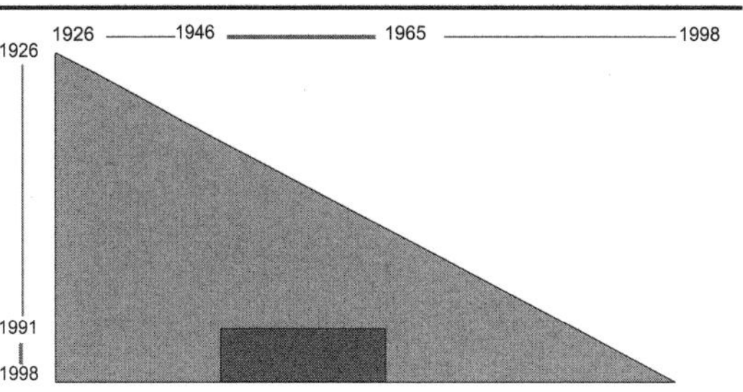

To The End Of	From The Beginning Of 1946	1947	1948	1949	1950	1951	1952	1953	1954	1955	1956	1957	1958	1959	1960	1961	1962	1963	1964	1965
1991	5.4	5.5	5.6	5.7	5.7	5.8	6.0	6.1	6.2	6.2	6.4	6.8	6.7	7.0	7.3	7.2	7.3	7.3	7.4	7.5
1992	5.5	5.5	5.7	5.8	5.8	5.9	6.1	6.2	6.3	6.3	6.5	6.8	6.8	7.1	7.3	7.3	7.3	7.3	7.5	7.6
1993	5.6	5.7	5.9	5.9	6.0	6.1	6.3	6.4	6.4	6.5	6.6	7.0	7.0	7.2	7.5	7.4	7.5	7.5	7.7	7.8
1994	5.4	5.4	5.6	5.7	5.7	5.8	6.0	6.1	6.1	6.1	6.3	6.7	6.6	6.9	7.1	7.0	7.1	7.1	7.2	7.3
1995	5.8	5.9	6.0	6.1	6.1	6.2	6.4	6.5	6.6	6.6	6.8	7.1	7.1	7.4	7.6	7.6	7.6	7.6	7.8	7.9
1996	5.7	5.8	5.9	6.0	6.0	6.1	6.3	6.4	6.5	6.5	6.6	7.0	6.9	7.2	7.4	7.4	7.5	7.4	7.6	7.7
1997	5.8	5.9	6.1	6.1	6.2	6.3	6.5	6.5	6.6	6.6	6.8	7.1	7.1	7.3	7.6	7.5	7.6	7.6	7.8	7.9
1998	5.9	6.0	6.2	6.2	6.3	6.3	6.5	6.6	6.7	6.7	6.9	7.2	7.2	7.4	7.7	7.6	7.7	7.7	7.8	7.9

Table C-3

Long-Term Corporate Bonds Total Returns

(Page 5 of 5)

Rates of Return for all holding periods.

Percent per annum compounded annually.

From 1926 to 1998

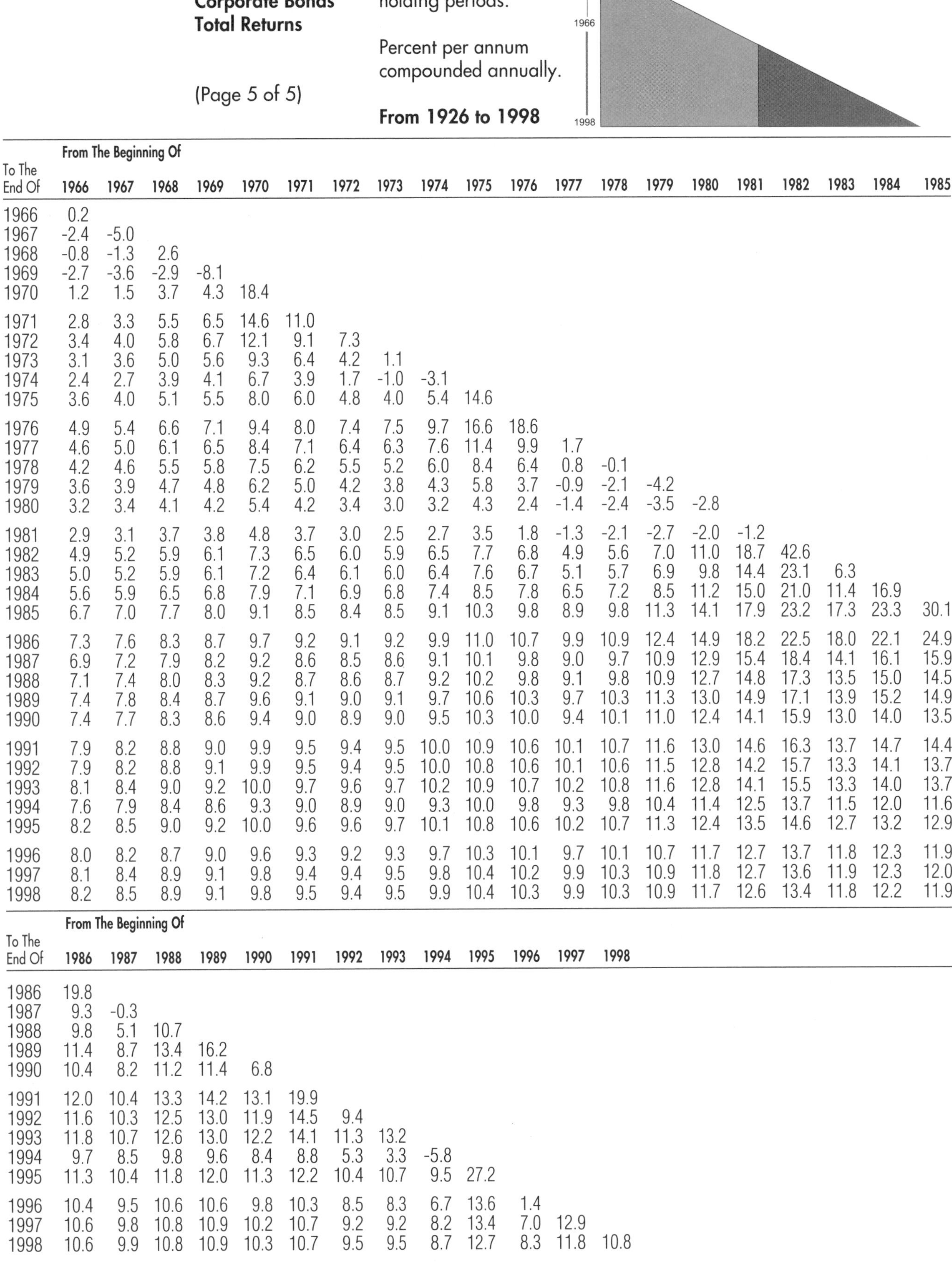

To The End Of	From The Beginning Of 1966	1967	1968	1969	1970	1971	1972	1973	1974	1975	1976	1977	1978	1979	1980	1981	1982	1983	1984	1985
1966	0.2																			
1967	-2.4	-5.0																		
1968	-0.8	-1.3	2.6																	
1969	-2.7	-3.6	-2.9	-8.1																
1970	1.2	1.5	3.7	4.3	18.4															
1971	2.8	3.3	5.5	6.5	14.6	11.0														
1972	3.4	4.0	5.8	6.7	12.1	9.1	7.3													
1973	3.1	3.6	5.0	5.6	9.3	6.4	4.2	1.1												
1974	2.4	2.7	3.9	4.1	6.7	3.9	1.7	-1.0	-3.1											
1975	3.6	4.0	5.1	5.5	8.0	6.0	4.8	4.0	5.4	14.6										
1976	4.9	5.4	6.6	7.1	9.4	8.0	7.4	7.5	9.7	16.6	18.6									
1977	4.6	5.0	6.1	6.5	8.4	7.1	6.4	6.3	7.6	11.4	9.9	1.7								
1978	4.2	4.6	5.5	5.8	7.5	6.2	5.5	5.2	6.0	8.4	6.4	0.8	-0.1							
1979	3.6	3.9	4.7	4.8	6.2	5.0	4.2	3.8	4.3	5.8	3.7	-0.9	-2.1	-4.2						
1980	3.2	3.4	4.1	4.2	5.4	4.2	3.4	3.0	3.2	4.3	2.4	-1.4	-2.4	-3.5	-2.8					
1981	2.9	3.1	3.7	3.8	4.8	3.7	3.0	2.5	2.7	3.5	1.8	-1.3	-2.1	-2.7	-2.0	-1.2				
1982	4.9	5.2	5.9	6.1	7.3	6.5	6.0	5.9	6.5	7.7	6.8	4.9	5.6	7.0	11.0	18.7	42.6			
1983	5.0	5.2	5.9	6.1	7.2	6.4	6.1	6.0	6.4	7.6	6.7	5.1	5.7	6.9	9.8	14.4	23.1	6.3		
1984	5.6	5.9	6.5	6.8	7.9	7.1	6.9	6.8	7.4	8.5	7.8	6.5	7.2	8.5	11.2	15.0	21.0	11.4	16.9	
1985	6.7	7.0	7.7	8.0	9.1	8.5	8.4	8.5	9.1	10.3	9.8	8.9	9.8	11.3	14.1	17.9	23.2	17.3	23.3	30.1
1986	7.3	7.6	8.3	8.7	9.7	9.2	9.1	9.2	9.9	11.0	10.7	9.9	10.9	12.4	14.9	18.2	22.5	18.0	22.1	24.9
1987	6.9	7.2	7.9	8.2	9.2	8.6	8.5	8.6	9.1	10.1	9.8	9.0	9.7	10.9	12.9	15.4	18.4	14.1	16.1	15.9
1988	7.1	7.4	8.0	8.3	9.2	8.7	8.6	8.7	9.2	10.2	9.8	9.1	9.8	10.9	12.7	14.8	17.3	13.5	15.0	14.5
1989	7.4	7.8	8.4	8.7	9.6	9.1	9.0	9.1	9.7	10.6	10.3	9.7	10.3	11.3	13.0	14.9	17.1	13.9	15.2	14.9
1990	7.4	7.7	8.3	8.6	9.4	9.0	8.9	9.0	9.5	10.3	10.0	9.4	10.1	11.0	12.4	14.1	15.9	13.0	14.0	13.5
1991	7.9	8.2	8.8	9.0	9.9	9.5	9.4	9.5	10.0	10.9	10.6	10.1	10.7	11.6	13.0	14.6	16.3	13.7	14.7	14.4
1992	7.9	8.2	8.8	9.1	9.9	9.5	9.4	9.5	10.0	10.8	10.6	10.1	10.6	11.5	12.8	14.2	15.7	13.3	14.1	13.7
1993	8.1	8.4	9.0	9.2	10.0	9.7	9.6	9.7	10.2	10.9	10.7	10.2	10.8	11.6	12.8	14.1	15.5	13.3	14.0	13.7
1994	7.6	7.9	8.4	8.6	9.3	9.0	8.9	9.0	9.3	10.0	9.8	9.3	9.8	10.4	11.4	12.5	13.7	11.5	12.0	11.6
1995	8.2	8.5	9.0	9.2	10.0	9.6	9.6	9.7	10.1	10.8	10.6	10.2	10.7	11.3	12.4	13.5	14.6	12.7	13.2	12.9
1996	8.0	8.2	8.7	9.0	9.6	9.3	9.2	9.3	9.7	10.3	10.1	9.7	10.1	10.7	11.7	12.7	13.7	11.8	12.3	11.9
1997	8.1	8.4	8.9	9.1	9.8	9.4	9.4	9.5	9.8	10.4	10.2	9.9	10.3	10.9	11.8	12.7	13.6	11.9	12.3	12.0
1998	8.2	8.5	8.9	9.1	9.8	9.5	9.4	9.5	9.9	10.4	10.3	9.9	10.3	10.9	11.7	12.6	13.4	11.8	12.2	11.9

To The End Of	From The Beginning Of 1986	1987	1988	1989	1990	1991	1992	1993	1994	1995	1996	1997	1998
1986	19.8												
1987	9.3	-0.3											
1988	9.8	5.1	10.7										
1989	11.4	8.7	13.4	16.2									
1990	10.4	8.2	11.2	11.4	6.8								
1991	12.0	10.4	13.3	14.2	13.1	19.9							
1992	11.6	10.3	12.5	13.0	11.9	14.5	9.4						
1993	11.8	10.7	12.6	13.0	12.2	14.1	11.3	13.2					
1994	9.7	8.5	9.8	9.6	8.4	8.8	5.3	3.3	-5.8				
1995	11.3	10.4	11.8	12.0	11.3	12.2	10.4	10.7	9.5	27.2			
1996	10.4	9.5	10.6	10.6	9.8	10.3	8.5	8.3	6.7	13.6	1.4		
1997	10.6	9.8	10.8	10.9	10.2	10.7	9.2	9.2	8.2	13.4	7.0	12.9	
1998	10.6	9.9	10.8	10.9	10.3	10.7	9.5	9.5	8.7	12.7	8.3	11.8	10.8

Table C-4

Long-Term Government Bonds Total Returns

(Page 1 of 5)

Rates of Return for all holding periods.

Percent per annum compounded annually.

From 1926 to 1998

To The End Of	From The Beginning Of 1926	1927	1928	1929	1930	1931	1932	1933	1934	1935	1936	1937	1938	1939	1940	1941	1942	1943	1944	1945
1926	7.8																			
1927	8.3	8.9																		
1928	5.5	4.4	0.1																	
1929	5.0	4.1	1.7	3.4																
1930	4.9	4.2	2.7	4.0	4.7															
1931	3.1	2.2	0.6	0.8	-0.5	-5.3														
1932	5.0	4.5	3.7	4.6	5.0	5.2	16.8													
1933	4.4	3.9	3.1	3.7	3.7	3.4	8.1	-0.1												
1934	5.0	4.6	4.0	4.7	4.9	5.0	8.7	4.9	10.0											
1935	5.0	4.7	4.1	4.7	5.0	5.0	7.8	4.9	7.5	5.0										
1936	5.2	4.9	4.5	5.1	5.3	5.4	7.7	5.5	7.5	6.2	7.5									
1937	4.8	4.5	4.1	4.5	4.7	4.7	6.4	4.5	5.6	4.2	3.8	0.2								
1938	4.8	4.6	4.2	4.6	4.8	4.8	6.3	4.6	5.6	4.5	4.4	2.8	5.5							
1939	4.9	4.7	4.4	4.7	4.9	4.9	6.3	4.8	5.7	4.8	4.8	3.9	5.7	5.9						
1940	5.0	4.8	4.5	4.9	5.0	5.0	6.2	5.0	5.7	5.0	5.0	4.4	5.9	6.0	6.1					
1941	4.7	4.5	4.2	4.5	4.6	4.6	5.7	4.5	5.1	4.4	4.3	3.7	4.6	4.3	3.5	0.9				
1942	4.6	4.5	4.2	4.5	4.5	4.5	5.5	4.4	4.9	4.3	4.2	3.6	4.3	4.0	3.4	2.1	3.2			
1943	4.5	4.3	4.0	4.3	4.4	4.3	5.2	4.2	4.6	4.0	3.9	3.4	3.9	3.6	3.1	2.1	2.6	2.1		
1944	4.4	4.2	4.0	4.2	4.3	4.2	5.0	4.1	4.5	3.9	3.8	3.3	3.8	3.5	3.0	2.3	2.7	2.4	2.8	
1945	4.7	4.6	4.3	4.6	4.6	4.6	5.4	4.6	5.0	4.5	4.5	4.1	4.6	4.5	4.3	3.9	4.7	5.1	6.7	10.7
1946	4.5	4.3	4.1	4.3	4.4	4.3	5.0	4.2	4.6	4.1	4.0	3.7	4.1	3.9	3.6	3.2	3.7	3.8	4.4	5.2
1947	4.1	4.0	3.7	3.9	4.0	3.9	4.5	3.8	4.0	3.6	3.5	3.1	3.4	3.2	2.8	2.4	2.6	2.5	2.6	2.5
1948	4.1	4.0	3.7	3.9	3.9	3.9	4.5	3.7	4.0	3.6	3.5	3.1	3.4	3.2	2.9	2.5	2.7	2.6	2.7	2.7
1949	4.2	4.1	3.8	4.0	4.1	4.0	4.6	3.9	4.1	3.8	3.7	3.4	3.7	3.5	3.2	2.9	3.2	3.2	3.4	3.5
1950	4.0	3.9	3.7	3.8	3.9	3.8	4.3	3.7	3.9	3.5	3.4	3.1	3.4	3.2	2.9	2.6	2.8	2.8	2.9	2.9
1951	3.7	3.6	3.3	3.5	3.5	3.4	3.9	3.3	3.4	3.1	3.0	2.7	2.8	2.6	2.4	2.0	2.1	2.0	2.0	1.9
1952	3.6	3.5	3.3	3.4	3.4	3.3	3.8	3.2	3.3	3.0	2.8	2.6	2.7	2.5	2.3	1.9	2.0	1.9	1.9	1.8
1953	3.6	3.5	3.3	3.4	3.4	3.3	3.8	3.2	3.3	3.0	2.9	2.6	2.8	2.6	2.4	2.1	2.2	2.1	2.1	2.0
1954	3.7	3.6	3.4	3.5	3.6	3.5	3.9	3.4	3.5	3.2	3.1	2.9	3.0	2.9	2.7	2.4	2.6	2.5	2.5	2.5
1955	3.6	3.4	3.2	3.4	3.4	3.3	3.7	3.1	3.3	3.0	2.9	2.6	2.8	2.6	2.4	2.2	2.3	2.2	2.2	2.2
1956	3.3	3.1	2.9	3.0	3.0	3.0	3.3	2.8	2.9	2.6	2.5	2.2	2.3	2.2	1.9	1.7	1.7	1.6	1.6	1.5
1957	3.4	3.3	3.1	3.2	3.2	3.1	3.5	3.0	3.1	2.8	2.7	2.5	2.6	2.4	2.2	2.0	2.1	2.0	2.0	1.9
1958	3.1	3.0	2.8	2.9	2.8	2.8	3.1	2.6	2.7	2.4	2.3	2.1	2.1	2.0	1.8	1.5	1.6	1.5	1.4	1.3
1959	2.9	2.8	2.6	2.7	2.7	2.6	2.9	2.4	2.5	2.2	2.1	1.9	1.9	1.8	1.6	1.3	1.4	1.3	1.2	1.1
1960	3.2	3.1	2.9	3.0	3.0	2.9	3.2	2.8	2.9	2.6	2.5	2.3	2.4	2.3	2.1	1.9	2.0	1.9	1.9	1.8
1961	3.2	3.0	2.9	3.0	2.9	2.9	3.2	2.7	2.8	2.6	2.5	2.3	2.4	2.2	2.1	1.9	1.9	1.9	1.8	1.8
1962	3.3	3.1	3.0	3.1	3.1	3.0	3.3	2.9	3.0	2.7	2.6	2.5	2.5	2.4	2.3	2.1	2.2	2.1	2.1	2.1
1963	3.2	3.1	2.9	3.0	3.0	3.0	3.2	2.8	2.9	2.7	2.6	2.4	2.5	2.4	2.2	2.1	2.1	2.1	2.1	2.0
1964	3.2	3.1	2.9	3.0	3.0	3.0	3.2	2.8	2.9	2.7	2.6	2.4	2.5	2.4	2.3	2.1	2.2	2.1	2.1	2.1
1965	3.2	3.0	2.9	3.0	3.0	2.9	3.2	2.8	2.9	2.6	2.6	2.4	2.5	2.4	2.2	2.1	2.1	2.1	2.1	2.0
1966	3.2	3.1	2.9	3.0	3.0	2.9	3.2	2.8	2.9	2.7	2.6	2.4	2.5	2.4	2.3	2.1	2.2	2.1	2.1	2.1
1967	2.9	2.7	2.6	2.7	2.6	2.6	2.8	2.4	2.5	2.3	2.2	2.0	2.1	2.0	1.8	1.7	1.7	1.7	1.6	1.6
1968	2.8	2.7	2.5	2.6	2.6	2.5	2.7	2.4	2.4	2.2	2.1	2.0	2.0	1.9	1.8	1.6	1.6	1.6	1.6	1.5
1969	2.6	2.5	2.3	2.4	2.4	2.3	2.5	2.1	2.2	2.0	1.9	1.7	1.8	1.7	1.5	1.4	1.4	1.3	1.3	1.2
1970	2.8	2.7	2.5	2.6	2.6	2.5	2.7	2.4	2.5	2.3	2.2	2.0	2.1	2.0	1.9	1.7	1.7	1.7	1.7	1.6

Table C-4

Long-Term Government Bonds Total Returns

(Page 2 of 5)

Rates of Return for all holding periods.

Percent per annum compounded annually.

From 1926 to 1998

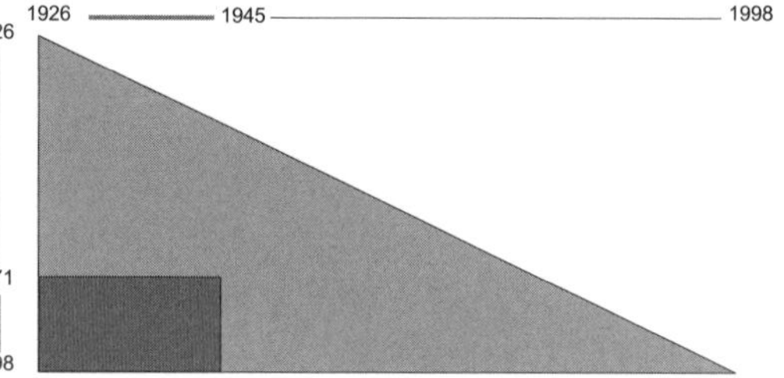

From The Beginning Of

To The End Of	1926	1927	1928	1929	1930	1931	1932	1933	1934	1935	1936	1937	1938	1939	1940	1941	1942	1943	1944	1945
1971	3.0	2.9	2.8	2.8	2.8	2.8	3.0	2.7	2.7	2.5	2.5	2.3	2.4	2.3	2.2	2.1	2.1	2.1	2.1	2.0
1972	3.1	3.0	2.8	2.9	2.9	2.8	3.1	2.7	2.8	2.6	2.6	2.4	2.5	2.4	2.3	2.2	2.2	2.2	2.2	2.2
1973	3.0	2.9	2.8	2.8	2.8	2.8	3.0	2.6	2.7	2.5	2.5	2.3	2.4	2.3	2.2	2.1	2.1	2.1	2.1	2.1
1974	3.0	2.9	2.8	2.8	2.8	2.8	3.0	2.7	2.7	2.6	2.5	2.4	2.4	2.4	2.3	2.1	2.2	2.2	2.2	2.1
1975	3.1	3.0	2.9	3.0	3.0	2.9	3.1	2.8	2.9	2.7	2.7	2.6	2.6	2.5	2.4	2.3	2.4	2.4	2.4	2.4
1976	3.4	3.3	3.2	3.2	3.2	3.2	3.4	3.1	3.2	3.0	3.0	2.9	3.0	2.9	2.8	2.7	2.8	2.8	2.8	2.8
1977	3.3	3.2	3.1	3.2	3.2	3.1	3.3	3.0	3.1	3.0	2.9	2.8	2.9	2.8	2.7	2.6	2.7	2.7	2.7	2.7
1978	3.2	3.1	3.0	3.1	3.1	3.0	3.2	2.9	3.0	2.9	2.8	2.7	2.8	2.7	2.6	2.5	2.6	2.5	2.6	2.6
1979	3.1	3.0	2.9	3.0	3.0	2.9	3.1	2.9	2.9	2.8	2.7	2.6	2.7	2.6	2.5	2.4	2.5	2.4	2.5	2.4
1980	3.0	2.9	2.8	2.9	2.8	2.8	3.0	2.7	2.8	2.6	2.6	2.5	2.5	2.4	2.3	2.3	2.3	2.3	2.3	2.3
1981	3.0	2.9	2.8	2.8	2.8	2.8	3.0	2.7	2.7	2.6	2.5	2.4	2.5	2.4	2.3	2.2	2.3	2.3	2.3	2.2
1982	3.5	3.5	3.4	3.4	3.4	3.4	3.6	3.3	3.4	3.3	3.2	3.1	3.2	3.2	3.1	3.0	3.1	3.1	3.1	3.1
1983	3.5	3.4	3.3	3.4	3.4	3.4	3.5	3.3	3.3	3.2	3.2	3.1	3.2	3.1	3.0	3.0	3.0	3.0	3.0	3.0
1984	3.7	3.6	3.5	3.6	3.6	3.6	3.7	3.5	3.6	3.4	3.4	3.3	3.4	3.4	3.3	3.2	3.3	3.3	3.3	3.3
1985	4.1	4.0	3.9	4.0	4.0	4.0	4.2	4.0	4.0	3.9	3.9	3.8	3.9	3.9	3.8	3.8	3.8	3.9	3.9	3.9
1986	4.4	4.3	4.3	4.3	4.3	4.3	4.5	4.3	4.4	4.3	4.3	4.2	4.3	4.3	4.2	4.2	4.3	4.3	4.3	4.4
1987	4.3	4.2	4.1	4.2	4.2	4.2	4.4	4.2	4.3	4.2	4.1	4.1	4.2	4.1	4.1	4.0	4.1	4.1	4.2	4.2
1988	4.4	4.3	4.2	4.3	4.3	4.3	4.5	4.3	4.4	4.3	4.2	4.2	4.3	4.2	4.2	4.2	4.2	4.2	4.3	4.3
1989	4.6	4.5	4.4	4.5	4.5	4.5	4.7	4.5	4.6	4.5	4.5	4.4	4.5	4.5	4.5	4.4	4.5	4.5	4.6	4.6
1990	4.6	4.5	4.5	4.5	4.6	4.6	4.7	4.5	4.6	4.5	4.5	4.5	4.5	4.5	4.5	4.5	4.5	4.6	4.6	4.7
1991	4.8	4.7	4.7	4.8	4.8	4.8	5.0	4.8	4.9	4.8	4.8	4.7	4.8	4.8	4.8	4.7	4.8	4.8	4.9	4.9
1992	4.8	4.8	4.7	4.8	4.8	4.8	5.0	4.8	4.9	4.8	4.8	4.8	4.9	4.8	4.8	4.8	4.9	4.9	5.0	5.0
1993	5.0	5.0	4.9	5.0	5.0	5.0	5.2	5.0	5.1	5.0	5.0	5.0	5.1	5.1	5.1	5.0	5.1	5.2	5.2	5.3
1994	4.8	4.8	4.7	4.8	4.8	4.8	5.0	4.8	4.9	4.8	4.8	4.8	4.8	4.8	4.8	4.8	4.9	4.9	4.9	5.0
1995	5.2	5.1	5.1	5.2	5.2	5.2	5.4	5.2	5.3	5.2	5.2	5.2	5.3	5.2	5.2	5.2	5.3	5.3	5.4	5.5
1996	5.1	5.0	5.0	5.1	5.1	5.1	5.3	5.1	5.2	5.1	5.1	5.1	5.1	5.1	5.1	5.1	5.2	5.2	5.3	5.3
1997	5.2	5.2	5.1	5.2	5.2	5.2	5.4	5.2	5.3	5.3	5.3	5.2	5.3	5.3	5.3	5.3	5.4	5.4	5.5	5.5
1998	5.3	5.3	5.2	5.3	5.3	5.4	5.5	5.4	5.4	5.4	5.4	5.3	5.4	5.4	5.4	5.4	5.5	5.5	5.6	5.7

Table C-4 **Long-Term Government Bonds Total Returns**

(Page 3 of 5)

Rates of Return for all holding periods.

Percent per annum compounded annually.

From 1926 to 1998

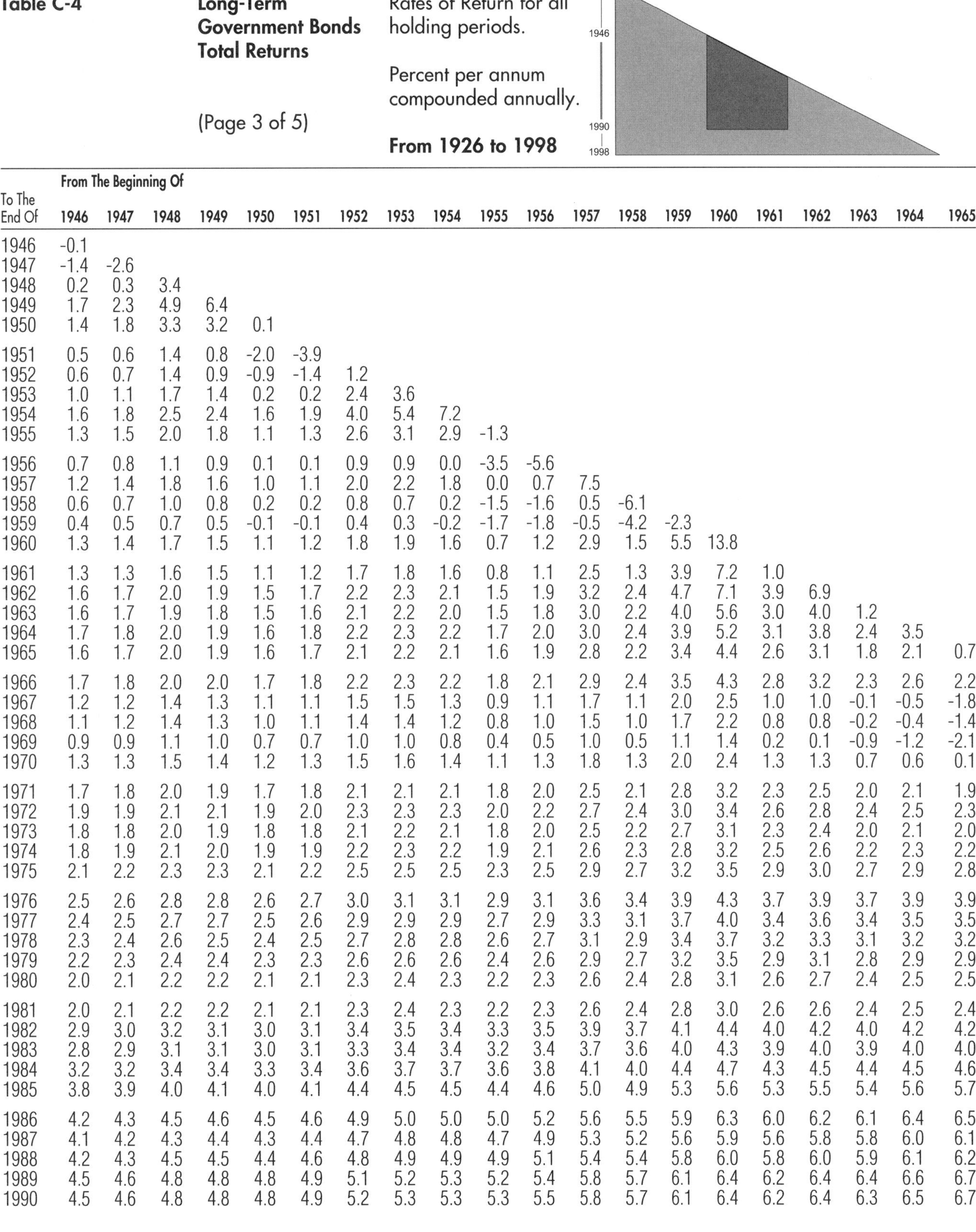

To The End Of	From The Beginning Of 1946	1947	1948	1949	1950	1951	1952	1953	1954	1955	1956	1957	1958	1959	1960	1961	1962	1963	1964	1965
1946	-0.1																			
1947	-1.4	-2.6																		
1948	0.2	0.3	3.4																	
1949	1.7	2.3	4.9	6.4																
1950	1.4	1.8	3.3	3.2	0.1															
1951	0.5	0.6	1.4	0.8	-2.0	-3.9														
1952	0.6	0.7	1.4	0.9	-0.9	-1.4	1.2													
1953	1.0	1.1	1.7	1.4	0.2	0.2	2.4	3.6												
1954	1.6	1.8	2.5	2.4	1.6	1.9	4.0	5.4	7.2											
1955	1.3	1.5	2.0	1.8	1.1	1.3	2.6	3.1	2.9	-1.3										
1956	0.7	0.8	1.1	0.9	0.1	0.1	0.9	0.9	0.0	-3.5	-5.6									
1957	1.2	1.4	1.8	1.6	1.0	1.1	2.0	2.2	1.8	0.0	0.7	7.5								
1958	0.6	0.7	1.0	0.8	0.2	0.2	0.8	0.7	0.2	-1.5	-1.6	0.5	-6.1							
1959	0.4	0.5	0.7	0.5	-0.1	-0.1	0.4	0.3	-0.2	-1.7	-1.8	-0.5	-4.2	-2.3						
1960	1.3	1.4	1.7	1.5	1.1	1.2	1.8	1.9	1.6	0.7	1.2	2.9	1.5	5.5	13.8					
1961	1.3	1.3	1.6	1.5	1.1	1.2	1.7	1.8	1.6	0.8	1.1	2.5	1.3	3.9	7.2	1.0				
1962	1.6	1.7	2.0	1.9	1.5	1.7	2.2	2.3	2.1	1.5	1.9	3.2	2.4	4.7	7.1	3.9	6.9			
1963	1.6	1.7	1.9	1.8	1.5	1.6	2.1	2.2	2.0	1.5	1.8	3.0	2.2	4.0	5.6	3.0	4.0	1.2		
1964	1.7	1.8	2.0	1.9	1.6	1.8	2.2	2.3	2.2	1.7	2.0	3.0	2.4	3.9	5.2	3.1	3.8	2.4	3.5	
1965	1.6	1.7	2.0	1.9	1.6	1.7	2.1	2.2	2.1	1.6	1.9	2.8	2.2	3.4	4.4	2.6	3.1	1.8	2.1	0.7
1966	1.7	1.8	2.0	2.0	1.7	1.8	2.2	2.3	2.2	1.8	2.1	2.9	2.4	3.5	4.3	2.8	3.2	2.3	2.6	2.2
1967	1.2	1.2	1.4	1.3	1.1	1.1	1.5	1.5	1.3	0.9	1.1	1.7	1.1	2.0	2.5	1.0	1.0	-0.1	-0.5	-1.8
1968	1.1	1.2	1.4	1.3	1.0	1.1	1.4	1.4	1.2	0.8	1.0	1.5	1.0	1.7	2.2	0.8	0.8	-0.2	-0.4	-1.4
1969	0.9	0.9	1.1	1.0	0.7	0.7	1.0	1.0	0.8	0.4	0.5	1.0	0.5	1.1	1.4	0.2	0.1	-0.9	-1.2	-2.1
1970	1.3	1.3	1.5	1.4	1.2	1.3	1.5	1.6	1.4	1.1	1.3	1.8	1.3	2.0	2.4	1.3	1.3	0.7	0.6	0.1
1971	1.7	1.8	2.0	1.9	1.7	1.8	2.1	2.1	2.1	1.8	2.0	2.5	2.1	2.8	3.2	2.3	2.5	2.0	2.1	1.9
1972	1.9	1.9	2.1	2.1	1.9	2.0	2.3	2.3	2.3	2.0	2.2	2.7	2.4	3.0	3.4	2.6	2.8	2.4	2.5	2.3
1973	1.8	1.8	2.0	1.9	1.8	1.8	2.1	2.2	2.1	1.8	2.0	2.5	2.2	2.7	3.1	2.3	2.4	2.0	2.1	2.0
1974	1.8	1.9	2.1	2.0	1.9	1.9	2.2	2.3	2.2	1.9	2.1	2.6	2.3	2.8	3.2	2.5	2.6	2.2	2.3	2.2
1975	2.1	2.2	2.3	2.3	2.1	2.2	2.5	2.5	2.5	2.3	2.5	2.9	2.7	3.2	3.5	2.9	3.0	2.7	2.9	2.8
1976	2.5	2.6	2.8	2.8	2.6	2.7	3.0	3.1	3.1	2.9	3.1	3.6	3.4	3.9	4.3	3.7	3.9	3.7	3.9	3.9
1977	2.4	2.5	2.7	2.7	2.5	2.6	2.9	2.9	2.9	2.7	2.9	3.3	3.1	3.7	4.0	3.4	3.6	3.4	3.5	3.5
1978	2.3	2.4	2.6	2.5	2.4	2.5	2.7	2.8	2.8	2.6	2.7	3.1	2.9	3.4	3.7	3.2	3.3	3.1	3.2	3.2
1979	2.2	2.3	2.4	2.4	2.3	2.3	2.6	2.6	2.6	2.4	2.6	2.9	2.7	3.2	3.5	2.9	3.1	2.8	2.9	2.9
1980	2.0	2.1	2.2	2.2	2.1	2.1	2.3	2.4	2.3	2.2	2.3	2.6	2.4	2.8	3.1	2.6	2.7	2.4	2.5	2.5
1981	2.0	2.1	2.2	2.2	2.1	2.1	2.3	2.4	2.3	2.2	2.3	2.6	2.4	2.8	3.0	2.6	2.6	2.4	2.5	2.4
1982	2.9	3.0	3.2	3.1	3.0	3.1	3.4	3.5	3.4	3.3	3.5	3.9	3.7	4.1	4.4	4.0	4.2	4.0	4.2	4.2
1983	2.8	2.9	3.1	3.1	3.0	3.1	3.3	3.4	3.4	3.2	3.4	3.7	3.6	4.0	4.3	3.9	4.0	3.9	4.0	4.0
1984	3.2	3.2	3.4	3.4	3.3	3.4	3.6	3.7	3.7	3.6	3.8	4.1	4.0	4.4	4.7	4.3	4.5	4.4	4.5	4.6
1985	3.8	3.9	4.0	4.1	4.0	4.1	4.4	4.5	4.5	4.4	4.6	5.0	4.9	5.3	5.6	5.3	5.5	5.4	5.6	5.7
1986	4.2	4.3	4.5	4.6	4.5	4.6	4.9	5.0	5.0	5.0	5.2	5.6	5.5	5.9	6.3	6.0	6.2	6.1	6.4	6.5
1987	4.1	4.2	4.3	4.4	4.3	4.4	4.7	4.8	4.8	4.7	4.9	5.3	5.2	5.6	5.9	5.6	5.8	5.8	6.0	6.1
1988	4.2	4.3	4.5	4.5	4.4	4.6	4.8	4.9	4.9	4.9	5.1	5.4	5.4	5.8	6.0	5.8	6.0	5.9	6.1	6.2
1989	4.5	4.6	4.8	4.8	4.8	4.9	5.1	5.2	5.3	5.2	5.4	5.8	5.7	6.1	6.4	6.2	6.4	6.4	6.6	6.7
1990	4.5	4.6	4.8	4.8	4.8	4.9	5.2	5.3	5.3	5.3	5.5	5.8	5.7	6.1	6.4	6.2	6.4	6.3	6.5	6.7

Table C-4 **Long-Term Government Bonds Total Returns**

(Page 4 of 5)

Rates of Return for all holding periods.

Percent per annum compounded annually.

From 1926 to 1998

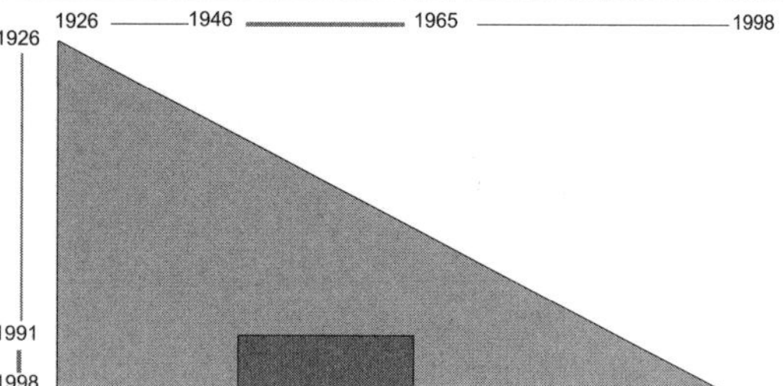

To The End Of	From The Beginning Of 1946	1947	1948	1949	1950	1951	1952	1953	1954	1955	1956	1957	1958	1959	1960	1961	1962	1963	1964	1965
1991	4.8	4.9	5.1	5.2	5.1	5.2	5.5	5.6	5.7	5.6	5.8	6.2	6.1	6.5	6.8	6.6	6.8	6.8	7.0	7.1
1992	4.9	5.0	5.2	5.2	5.2	5.3	5.6	5.7	5.7	5.7	5.9	6.2	6.2	6.6	6.8	6.6	6.8	6.8	7.0	7.1
1993	5.2	5.3	5.4	5.5	5.5	5.6	5.8	6.0	6.0	6.0	6.2	6.5	6.5	6.9	7.2	7.0	7.2	7.2	7.4	7.5
1994	4.9	5.0	5.1	5.2	5.2	5.3	5.5	5.6	5.7	5.6	5.8	6.1	6.1	6.4	6.7	6.5	6.7	6.7	6.8	7.0
1995	5.3	5.5	5.6	5.7	5.7	5.8	6.0	6.1	6.2	6.2	6.4	6.7	6.7	7.1	7.3	7.1	7.3	7.3	7.5	7.7
1996	5.2	5.3	5.5	5.5	5.5	5.6	5.9	6.0	6.0	6.0	6.2	6.5	6.5	6.8	7.1	6.9	7.1	7.1	7.3	7.4
1997	5.4	5.5	5.7	5.7	5.7	5.9	6.1	6.2	6.3	6.2	6.4	6.7	6.7	7.1	7.3	7.1	7.3	7.3	7.5	7.6
1998	5.6	5.7	5.8	5.9	5.9	6.0	6.2	6.3	6.4	6.4	6.6	6.9	6.9	7.2	7.5	7.3	7.5	7.5	7.7	7.8

Table C-4

Long-Term Government Bonds Total Returns

(Page 5 of 5)

Rates of Return for all holding periods.

Percent per annum compounded annually.

From 1926 to 1998

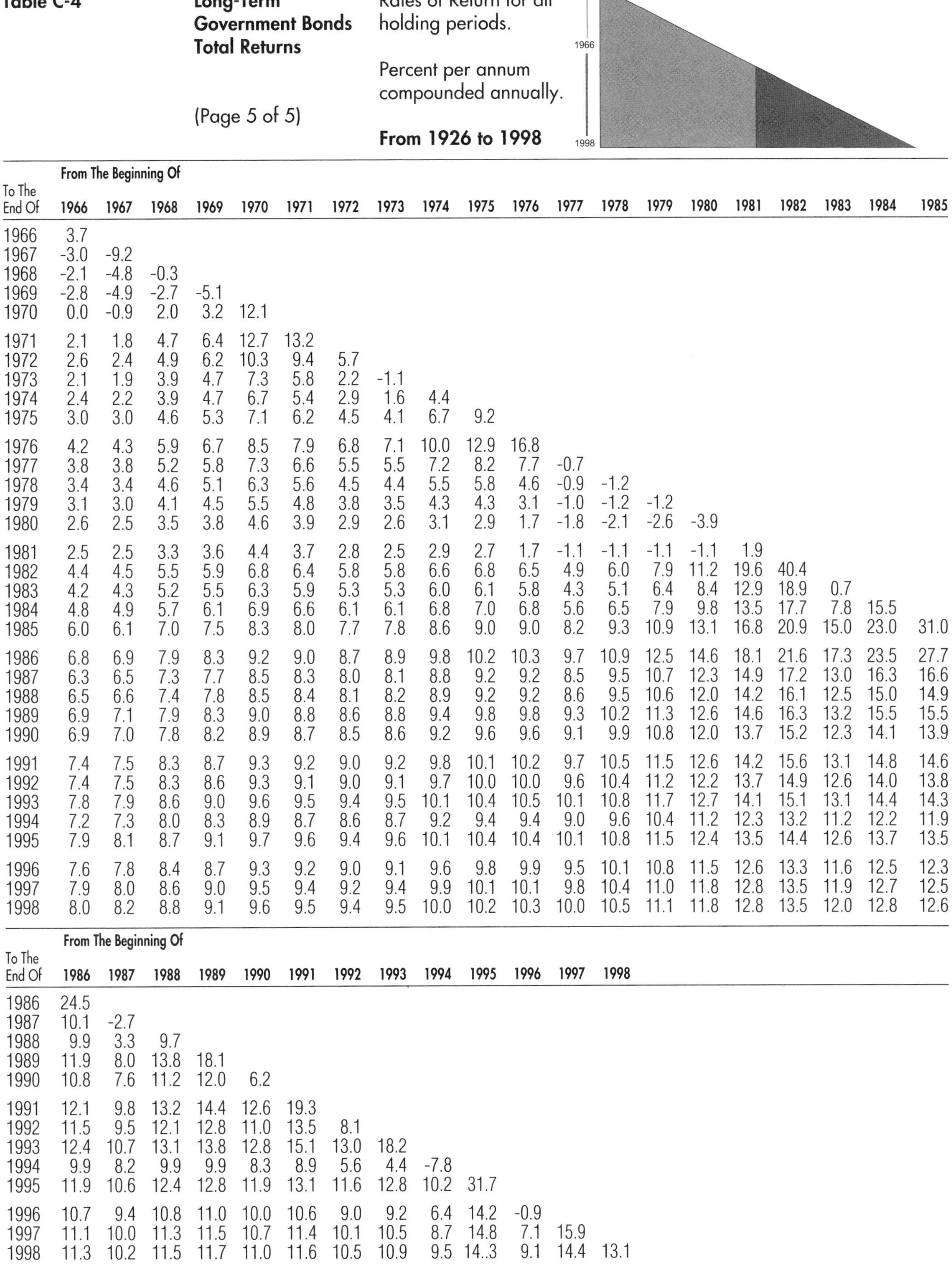

To The End Of	From The Beginning Of 1966	1967	1968	1969	1970	1971	1972	1973	1974	1975	1976	1977	1978	1979	1980	1981	1982	1983	1984	1985
1966	3.7																			
1967	-3.0	-9.2																		
1968	-2.1	-4.8	-0.3																	
1969	-2.8	-4.9	-2.7	-5.1																
1970	0.0	-0.9	2.0	3.2	12.1															
1971	2.1	1.8	4.7	6.4	12.7	13.2														
1972	2.6	2.4	4.9	6.2	10.3	9.4	5.7													
1973	2.1	1.9	3.9	4.7	7.3	5.8	2.2	-1.1												
1974	2.4	2.2	3.9	4.7	6.7	5.4	2.9	1.6	4.4											
1975	3.0	3.0	4.6	5.3	7.1	6.2	4.5	4.1	6.7	9.2										
1976	4.2	4.3	5.9	6.7	8.5	7.9	6.8	7.1	10.0	12.9	16.8									
1977	3.8	3.8	5.2	5.8	7.3	6.6	5.5	5.5	7.2	8.2	7.7	-0.7								
1978	3.4	3.4	4.6	5.1	6.3	5.6	4.5	4.4	5.5	5.8	4.6	-0.9	-1.2							
1979	3.1	3.0	4.1	4.5	5.5	4.8	3.8	3.5	4.3	4.3	3.1	-1.0	-1.2	-1.2						
1980	2.6	2.5	3.5	3.8	4.6	3.9	2.9	2.6	3.1	2.9	1.7	-1.8	-2.1	-2.6	-3.9					
1981	2.5	2.5	3.3	3.6	4.4	3.7	2.8	2.5	2.9	2.7	1.7	-1.1	-1.1	-1.1	-1.1	1.9				
1982	4.4	4.5	5.5	5.9	6.8	6.4	5.8	5.8	6.6	6.8	6.5	4.9	6.0	7.9	11.2	19.6	40.4			
1983	4.2	4.3	5.2	5.5	6.3	5.9	5.3	5.3	6.0	6.1	5.8	4.3	5.1	6.4	8.4	12.9	18.9	0.7		
1984	4.8	4.9	5.7	6.1	6.9	6.6	6.1	6.1	6.8	7.0	6.8	5.6	6.5	7.9	9.8	13.5	17.7	7.8	15.5	
1985	6.0	6.1	7.0	7.5	8.3	8.0	7.7	7.8	8.6	9.0	9.0	8.2	9.3	10.9	13.1	16.8	20.9	15.0	23.0	31.0
1986	6.8	6.9	7.9	8.3	9.2	9.0	8.7	8.9	9.8	10.2	10.3	9.7	10.9	12.5	14.6	18.1	21.6	17.3	23.5	27.7
1987	6.3	6.5	7.3	7.7	8.5	8.3	8.0	8.1	8.8	9.2	9.2	8.5	9.5	10.7	12.3	14.9	17.2	13.0	16.3	16.6
1988	6.5	6.6	7.4	7.8	8.5	8.4	8.1	8.2	8.9	9.2	9.2	8.6	9.5	10.6	12.0	14.2	16.1	12.5	15.0	14.9
1989	6.9	7.1	7.9	8.3	9.0	8.8	8.6	8.8	9.4	9.8	9.8	9.3	10.2	11.3	12.6	14.6	16.3	13.2	15.5	15.5
1990	6.9	7.0	7.8	8.2	8.9	8.7	8.5	8.6	9.2	9.6	9.6	9.1	9.9	10.8	12.0	13.7	15.2	12.3	14.1	13.9
1991	7.4	7.5	8.3	8.7	9.3	9.2	9.0	9.2	9.8	10.1	10.2	9.7	10.5	11.5	12.6	14.2	15.6	13.1	14.8	14.6
1992	7.4	7.5	8.3	8.6	9.3	9.1	9.0	9.1	9.7	10.0	10.0	9.6	10.4	11.2	12.2	13.7	14.9	12.6	14.0	13.8
1993	7.8	7.9	8.6	9.0	9.6	9.5	9.4	9.5	10.1	10.4	10.5	10.1	10.8	11.7	12.7	14.1	15.1	13.1	14.4	14.3
1994	7.2	7.3	8.0	8.3	8.9	8.7	8.6	8.7	9.2	9.4	9.4	9.0	9.6	10.4	11.2	12.3	13.2	11.2	12.2	11.9
1995	7.9	8.1	8.7	9.1	9.7	9.6	9.4	9.6	10.1	10.4	10.4	10.1	10.8	11.5	12.4	13.5	14.4	12.6	13.7	13.5
1996	7.6	7.8	8.4	8.7	9.3	9.2	9.0	9.1	9.6	9.8	9.9	9.5	10.1	10.8	11.5	12.6	13.3	11.6	12.5	12.3
1997	7.9	8.0	8.6	9.0	9.5	9.4	9.2	9.4	9.9	10.1	10.1	9.8	10.4	11.0	11.8	12.8	13.5	11.9	12.7	12.5
1998	8.0	8.2	8.8	9.1	9.6	9.5	9.4	9.5	10.0	10.2	10.3	10.0	10.5	11.1	11.8	12.8	13.5	12.0	12.8	12.6

To The End Of	From The Beginning Of 1986	1987	1988	1989	1990	1991	1992	1993	1994	1995	1996	1997	1998
1986	24.5												
1987	10.1	-2.7											
1988	9.9	3.3	9.7										
1989	11.9	8.0	13.8	18.1									
1990	10.8	7.6	11.2	12.0	6.2								
1991	12.1	9.8	13.2	14.4	12.6	19.3							
1992	11.5	9.5	12.1	12.8	11.0	13.5	8.1						
1993	12.4	10.7	13.1	13.8	12.8	15.1	13.0	18.2					
1994	9.9	8.2	9.9	9.9	8.3	8.9	5.6	4.4	-7.8				
1995	11.9	10.6	12.4	12.8	11.9	13.1	11.6	12.8	10.2	31.7			
1996	10.7	9.4	10.8	11.0	10.0	10.6	9.0	9.2	6.4	14.2	-0.9		
1997	11.1	10.0	11.3	11.5	10.7	11.4	10.1	10.5	8.7	14.8	7.1	15.9	
1998	11.3	10.2	11.5	11.7	11.0	11.6	10.5	10.9	9.5	14..3	9.1	14.4	13.1

Table C-5

Intermediate-Term Government Bonds Total Returns

(Page 1 of 5)

Rates of Return for all holding periods.

Percent per annum compounded annually.

From 1926 to 1998

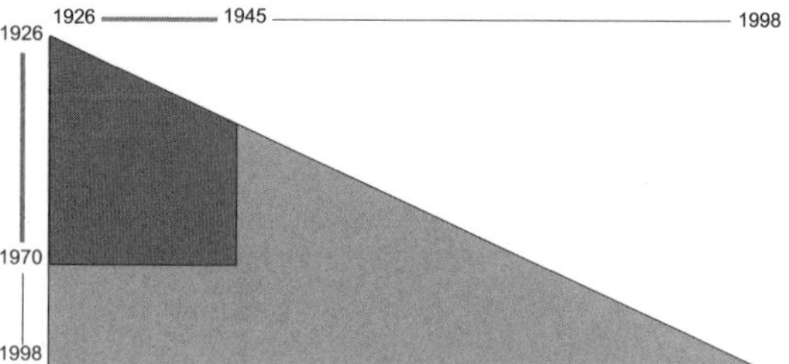

To The End Of	From The Beginning Of 1926	1927	1928	1929	1930	1931	1932	1933	1934	1935	1936	1937	1938	1939	1940	1941	1942	1943	1944	1945
1926	5.4																			
1927	4.9	4.5																		
1928	3.6	2.7	0.9																	
1929	4.2	3.8	3.4	6.0																
1930	4.7	4.5	4.5	6.4	6.7															
1931	3.5	3.1	2.8	3.4	2.1	-2.3														
1932	4.2	4.0	3.9	4.7	4.3	3.1	8.8													
1933	3.9	3.7	3.6	4.1	3.7	2.7	5.3	1.8												
1934	4.5	4.4	4.3	4.9	4.7	4.2	6.5	5.4	9.0											
1935	4.7	4.7	4.7	5.2	5.1	4.8	6.6	5.9	8.0	7.0										
1936	4.6	4.5	4.5	4.9	4.8	4.5	5.9	5.2	6.3	5.0	3.1									
1937	4.3	4.2	4.2	4.6	4.4	4.1	5.2	4.4	5.1	3.8	2.3	1.6								
1938	4.5	4.4	4.4	4.7	4.6	4.3	5.3	4.7	5.3	4.4	3.6	3.9	6.2							
1939	4.5	4.4	4.4	4.7	4.6	4.3	5.2	4.7	5.2	4.5	3.8	4.1	5.4	4.5						
1940	4.4	4.3	4.3	4.6	4.4	4.2	5.0	4.5	4.9	4.2	3.7	3.8	4.6	3.7	3.0					
1941	4.1	4.0	4.0	4.2	4.1	3.9	4.5	4.0	4.3	3.7	3.1	3.1	3.5	2.6	1.7	0.5				
1942	4.0	3.9	3.9	4.1	3.9	3.7	4.3	3.8	4.1	3.4	3.0	2.9	3.2	2.5	1.8	1.2	1.9			
1943	3.9	3.8	3.8	4.0	3.9	3.6	4.1	3.7	3.9	3.4	2.9	2.9	3.1	2.5	2.0	1.7	2.4	2.8		
1944	3.8	3.7	3.7	3.9	3.7	3.5	4.0	3.6	3.7	3.2	2.8	2.8	2.9	2.4	2.0	1.8	2.2	2.3	1.8	
1945	3.7	3.6	3.6	3.8	3.6	3.4	3.8	3.5	3.6	3.1	2.7	2.7	2.9	2.4	2.0	1.8	2.2	2.3	2.0	2.2
1946	3.6	3.5	3.5	3.6	3.5	3.3	3.6	3.3	3.4	2.9	2.6	2.5	2.7	2.2	1.9	1.7	2.0	2.0	1.7	1.6
1947	3.5	3.4	3.3	3.5	3.3	3.1	3.5	3.1	3.2	2.8	2.4	2.4	2.5	2.1	1.8	1.6	1.8	1.7	1.5	1.4
1948	3.4	3.3	3.3	3.4	3.2	3.1	3.4	3.0	3.1	2.7	2.4	2.3	2.4	2.0	1.8	1.6	1.8	1.8	1.6	1.5
1949	3.4	3.3	3.2	3.3	3.2	3.0	3.3	3.0	3.1	2.7	2.4	2.3	2.4	2.1	1.8	1.7	1.9	1.8	1.7	1.7
1950	3.3	3.2	3.1	3.2	3.1	2.9	3.2	2.9	2.9	2.6	2.3	2.2	2.3	2.0	1.7	1.6	1.7	1.7	1.5	1.5
1951	3.1	3.1	3.0	3.1	3.0	2.8	3.0	2.7	2.8	2.4	2.2	2.1	2.1	1.8	1.6	1.5	1.6	1.5	1.4	1.3
1952	3.1	3.0	2.9	3.0	2.9	2.7	3.0	2.7	2.7	2.4	2.1	2.1	2.1	1.8	1.6	1.5	1.6	1.6	1.4	1.4
1953	3.1	3.0	2.9	3.0	2.9	2.7	3.0	2.7	2.8	2.4	2.2	2.1	2.2	1.9	1.7	1.6	1.7	1.7	1.6	1.6
1954	3.1	3.0	2.9	3.0	2.9	2.7	3.0	2.7	2.8	2.5	2.2	2.2	2.2	2.0	1.8	1.7	1.8	1.8	1.7	1.7
1955	2.9	2.9	2.8	2.9	2.8	2.6	2.8	2.6	2.6	2.3	2.1	2.0	2.0	1.8	1.6	1.5	1.6	1.6	1.5	1.5
1956	2.8	2.8	2.7	2.8	2.6	2.5	2.7	2.4	2.5	2.2	2.0	1.9	1.9	1.7	1.5	1.4	1.5	1.5	1.4	1.3
1957	3.0	2.9	2.9	2.9	2.8	2.7	2.9	2.6	2.7	2.4	2.2	2.2	2.2	2.0	1.9	1.8	1.9	1.9	1.8	1.8
1958	2.9	2.8	2.7	2.8	2.7	2.5	2.7	2.5	2.5	2.3	2.1	2.0	2.0	1.8	1.7	1.6	1.7	1.7	1.6	1.6
1959	2.8	2.7	2.6	2.7	2.6	2.4	2.6	2.4	2.4	2.2	2.0	1.9	1.9	1.7	1.6	1.5	1.6	1.5	1.5	1.4
1960	3.0	2.9	2.9	3.0	2.9	2.7	2.9	2.7	2.7	2.5	2.3	2.3	2.3	2.2	2.0	2.0	2.1	2.1	2.0	2.1
1961	3.0	2.9	2.9	2.9	2.8	2.7	2.9	2.7	2.7	2.5	2.3	2.3	2.3	2.1	2.0	2.0	2.1	2.1	2.0	2.0
1962	3.0	3.0	2.9	3.0	2.9	2.8	3.0	2.8	2.8	2.6	2.4	2.4	2.4	2.3	2.2	2.2	2.2	2.2	2.2	2.2
1963	3.0	2.9	2.9	3.0	2.9	2.8	2.9	2.7	2.8	2.6	2.4	2.4	2.4	2.3	2.2	2.1	2.2	2.2	2.2	2.2
1964	3.0	3.0	2.9	3.0	2.9	2.8	3.0	2.8	2.8	2.6	2.5	2.4	2.5	2.3	2.2	2.2	2.3	2.3	2.3	2.3
1965	3.0	2.9	2.9	2.9	2.9	2.7	2.9	2.7	2.7	2.6	2.4	2.4	2.4	2.3	2.2	2.2	2.2	2.2	2.2	2.2
1966	3.0	3.0	2.9	3.0	2.9	2.8	2.9	2.8	2.8	2.6	2.5	2.5	2.5	2.4	2.3	2.3	2.3	2.3	2.3	2.3
1967	3.0	2.9	2.9	2.9	2.8	2.7	2.9	2.7	2.8	2.6	2.4	2.4	2.4	2.3	2.2	2.2	2.3	2.3	2.3	2.3
1968	3.0	3.0	2.9	3.0	2.9	2.8	2.9	2.8	2.8	2.6	2.5	2.5	2.5	2.4	2.3	2.3	2.4	2.4	2.4	2.4
1969	2.9	2.9	2.8	2.9	2.8	2.7	2.8	2.7	2.7	2.5	2.4	2.4	2.4	2.3	2.2	2.2	2.2	2.3	2.2	2.3
1970	3.2	3.2	3.1	3.2	3.1	3.0	3.2	3.0	3.1	2.9	2.8	2.8	2.8	2.7	2.7	2.6	2.7	2.7	2.7	2.8

Table C-5

Intermediate-Term Government Bonds Total Returns

(Page 2 of 5)

Rates of Return for all holding periods.

Percent per annum compounded annually.

From 1926 to 1998

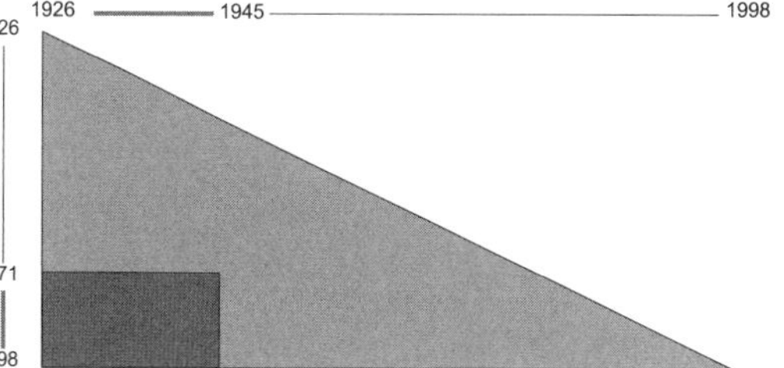

To The End Of	From The Beginning Of 1926	1927	1928	1929	1930	1931	1932	1933	1934	1935	1936	1937	1938	1939	1940	1941	1942	1943	1944	1945
1971	3.3	3.3	3.3	3.3	3.3	3.2	3.3	3.2	3.2	3.1	2.9	2.9	3.0	2.9	2.8	2.8	2.9	2.9	3.0	3.0
1972	3.4	3.3	3.3	3.4	3.3	3.2	3.4	3.2	3.3	3.1	3.0	3.0	3.0	3.0	2.9	2.9	3.0	3.0	3.0	3.1
1973	3.4	3.4	3.3	3.4	3.3	3.2	3.4	3.3	3.3	3.1	3.0	3.0	3.1	3.0	3.0	3.0	3.0	3.1	3.1	3.1
1974	3.4	3.4	3.4	3.4	3.4	3.3	3.4	3.3	3.3	3.2	3.1	3.1	3.2	3.1	3.0	3.0	3.1	3.2	3.2	3.2
1975	3.5	3.5	3.5	3.5	3.5	3.4	3.5	3.4	3.5	3.3	3.2	3.2	3.3	3.2	3.2	3.2	3.3	3.3	3.3	3.4
1976	3.7	3.7	3.7	3.7	3.7	3.6	3.7	3.6	3.7	3.5	3.5	3.5	3.5	3.4	3.4	3.4	3.5	3.6	3.6	3.6
1977	3.7	3.6	3.6	3.7	3.6	3.6	3.7	3.6	3.6	3.5	3.4	3.4	3.5	3.4	3.4	3.4	3.5	3.5	3.5	3.6
1978	3.7	3.6	3.6	3.7	3.6	3.6	3.7	3.6	3.6	3.5	3.4	3.4	3.5	3.4	3.4	3.4	3.5	3.5	3.5	3.6
1979	3.7	3.6	3.6	3.7	3.6	3.6	3.7	3.6	3.6	3.5	3.4	3.4	3.5	3.4	3.4	3.4	3.5	3.5	3.5	3.6
1980	3.7	3.6	3.6	3.7	3.6	3.6	3.7	3.6	3.6	3.5	3.4	3.4	3.5	3.4	3.4	3.4	3.5	3.5	3.5	3.6
1981	3.8	3.7	3.7	3.8	3.7	3.7	3.8	3.7	3.7	3.6	3.6	3.6	3.6	3.6	3.5	3.6	3.6	3.7	3.7	3.7
1982	4.2	4.1	4.1	4.2	4.2	4.1	4.2	4.2	4.2	4.1	4.0	4.1	4.1	4.1	4.1	4.1	4.2	4.2	4.3	4.3
1983	4.2	4.2	4.2	4.3	4.2	4.2	4.3	4.2	4.3	4.2	4.1	4.1	4.2	4.2	4.1	4.2	4.3	4.3	4.4	4.4
1984	4.4	4.4	4.4	4.4	4.4	4.4	4.5	4.4	4.5	4.4	4.3	4.3	4.4	4.4	4.4	4.4	4.5	4.5	4.6	4.7
1985	4.6	4.6	4.6	4.7	4.7	4.6	4.8	4.7	4.7	4.7	4.6	4.6	4.7	4.7	4.7	4.7	4.8	4.9	4.9	5.0
1986	4.8	4.8	4.8	4.9	4.8	4.8	4.9	4.9	4.9	4.8	4.8	4.8	4.9	4.9	4.9	4.9	5.0	5.1	5.2	5.2
1987	4.8	4.8	4.8	4.8	4.8	4.8	4.9	4.8	4.9	4.8	4.8	4.8	4.9	4.8	4.8	4.9	5.0	5.1	5.1	5.2
1988	4.8	4.8	4.8	4.8	4.8	4.8	4.9	4.9	4.9	4.8	4.8	4.8	4.9	4.9	4.9	4.9	5.0	5.1	5.1	5.2
1989	4.9	4.9	4.9	5.0	5.0	4.9	5.1	5.0	5.1	5.0	4.9	5.0	5.0	5.0	5.0	5.1	5.2	5.2	5.3	5.4
1990	5.0	5.0	5.0	5.1	5.0	5.0	5.1	5.1	5.1	5.1	5.0	5.1	5.1	5.1	5.1	5.2	5.3	5.3	5.4	5.5
1991	5.1	5.1	5.1	5.2	5.2	5.2	5.3	5.2	5.3	5.2	5.2	5.2	5.3	5.3	5.3	5.4	5.5	5.5	5.6	5.7
1992	5.2	5.2	5.2	5.2	5.2	5.2	5.3	5.3	5.3	5.3	5.2	5.3	5.4	5.3	5.4	5.4	5.5	5.6	5.6	5.7
1993	5.3	5.3	5.3	5.3	5.3	5.3	5.4	5.4	5.4	5.4	5.3	5.4	5.5	5.4	5.5	5.5	5.6	5.7	5.7	5.8
1994	5.1	5.1	5.1	5.2	5.2	5.1	5.2	5.2	5.2	5.2	5.2	5.2	5.3	5.2	5.3	5.3	5.4	5.5	5.5	5.6
1995	5.3	5.3	5.3	5.3	5.3	5.3	5.4	5.4	5.4	5.4	5.3	5.4	5.4	5.4	5.5	5.5	5.6	5.7	5.7	5.8
1996	5.2	5.2	5.2	5.3	5.3	5.2	5.4	5.3	5.4	5.3	5.3	5.3	5.4	5.4	5.4	5.4	5.5	5.6	5.6	5.7
1997	5.3	5.3	5.3	5.3	5.3	5.3	5.4	5.4	5.4	5.4	5.3	5.4	5.4	5.4	5.4	5.5	5.6	5.6	5.7	5.8
1998	5.3	5.3	5.3	5.4	5.4	5.4	5.5	5.4	5.5	5.4	5.4	5.5	5.5	5.5	5.5	5.6	5.7	5.7	5.8	5.9

Table C-5

Intermediate-Term Government Bonds Total Returns

(Page 3 of 5)

Rates of Return for all holding periods.

Percent per annum compounded annually.

From 1926 to 1998

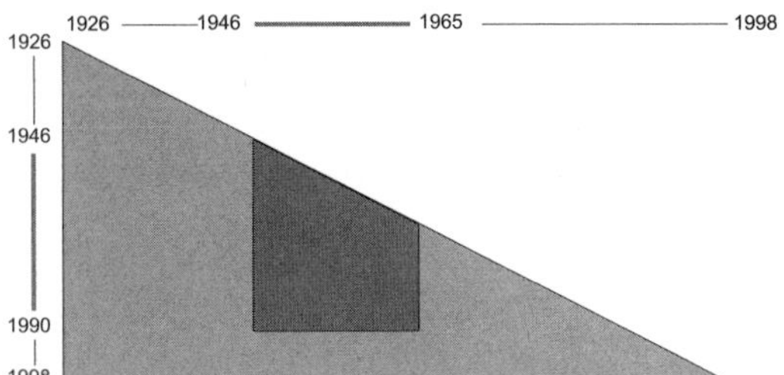

To The End Of	From The Beginning Of 1946	1947	1948	1949	1950	1951	1952	1953	1954	1955	1956	1957	1958	1959	1960	1961	1962	1963	1964	1965
1946	1.0																			
1947	1.0	0.9																		
1948	1.3	1.4	1.8																	
1949	1.5	1.7	2.1	2.3																
1950	1.4	1.4	1.6	1.5	0.7															
1951	1.2	1.2	1.3	1.1	0.5	0.4														
1952	1.3	1.3	1.4	1.3	0.9	1.0	1.6													
1953	1.5	1.6	1.7	1.6	1.5	1.7	2.4	3.2												
1954	1.6	1.7	1.8	1.8	1.7	2.0	2.5	3.0	2.7											
1955	1.4	1.4	1.5	1.5	1.3	1.4	1.7	1.7	1.0	-0.7										
1956	1.2	1.3	1.3	1.2	1.1	1.1	1.3	1.2	0.5	-0.5	-0.4									
1957	1.8	1.8	1.9	1.9	1.9	2.1	2.3	2.5	2.3	2.2	3.6	7.8								
1958	1.5	1.6	1.6	1.6	1.5	1.6	1.8	1.9	1.6	1.3	2.0	3.2	-1.3							
1959	1.4	1.4	1.5	1.4	1.3	1.4	1.5	1.5	1.2	1.0	1.4	2.0	-0.8	-0.4						
1960	2.1	2.1	2.2	2.3	2.2	2.4	2.6	2.8	2.7	2.7	3.4	4.3	3.2	5.5	11.8					
1961	2.0	2.1	2.2	2.2	2.2	2.3	2.5	2.7	2.6	2.6	3.1	3.8	2.9	4.3	6.7	1.8				
1962	2.2	2.3	2.4	2.5	2.5	2.6	2.8	2.9	2.9	2.9	3.5	4.1	3.4	4.6	6.3	3.7	5.6			
1963	2.2	2.3	2.4	2.4	2.4	2.5	2.7	2.8	2.8	2.8	3.2	3.8	3.1	4.0	5.1	3.0	3.6	1.6		
1964	2.3	2.4	2.5	2.5	2.5	2.6	2.8	2.9	2.9	2.9	3.3	3.8	3.2	4.0	4.9	3.3	3.7	2.8	4.0	
1965	2.2	2.3	2.4	2.4	2.4	2.5	2.7	2.8	2.7	2.7	3.1	3.5	3.0	3.6	4.2	2.8	3.1	2.2	2.5	1.0
1966	2.4	2.4	2.5	2.5	2.6	2.7	2.8	2.9	2.9	2.9	3.2	3.6	3.1	3.7	4.3	3.1	3.4	2.8	3.2	2.8
1967	2.3	2.4	2.4	2.5	2.5	2.6	2.7	2.8	2.8	2.8	3.0	3.4	2.9	3.4	3.9	2.8	3.0	2.5	2.7	2.2
1968	2.4	2.5	2.5	2.6	2.6	2.7	2.8	2.9	2.9	2.9	3.2	3.5	3.1	3.5	4.0	3.0	3.2	2.8	3.0	2.8
1969	2.3	2.3	2.4	2.4	2.4	2.5	2.6	2.7	2.6	2.6	2.9	3.1	2.8	3.1	3.5	2.6	2.7	2.3	2.4	2.1
1970	2.8	2.9	3.0	3.0	3.1	3.2	3.3	3.4	3.4	3.5	3.8	4.1	3.8	4.2	4.6	3.9	4.2	4.0	4.4	4.4
1971	3.0	3.1	3.2	3.3	3.3	3.4	3.6	3.7	3.7	3.8	4.1	4.4	4.1	4.5	5.0	4.4	4.6	4.5	4.9	5.0
1972	3.1	3.2	3.3	3.3	3.4	3.5	3.7	3.8	3.8	3.9	4.1	4.4	4.2	4.6	5.0	4.4	4.7	4.6	4.9	5.0
1973	3.2	3.2	3.3	3.4	3.4	3.6	3.7	3.8	3.8	3.9	4.1	4.4	4.2	4.6	5.0	4.5	4.7	4.6	4.9	5.0
1974	3.2	3.3	3.4	3.5	3.5	3.6	3.8	3.9	3.9	4.0	4.2	4.5	4.3	4.7	5.0	4.5	4.7	4.7	5.0	5.1
1975	3.4	3.5	3.6	3.6	3.7	3.8	4.0	4.1	4.1	4.2	4.4	4.7	4.5	4.8	5.2	4.8	5.0	4.9	5.2	5.3
1976	3.7	3.8	3.9	4.0	4.0	4.1	4.3	4.4	4.5	4.5	4.8	5.1	4.9	5.3	5.6	5.2	5.5	5.5	5.8	5.9
1977	3.6	3.7	3.8	3.9	3.9	4.0	4.2	4.3	4.3	4.4	4.6	4.9	4.7	5.1	5.4	5.0	5.2	5.2	5.5	5.6
1978	3.6	3.7	3.8	3.8	3.9	4.0	4.2	4.3	4.3	4.4	4.6	4.8	4.7	5.0	5.3	4.9	5.1	5.1	5.3	5.4
1979	3.6	3.7	3.8	3.9	3.9	4.0	4.2	4.2	4.3	4.4	4.6	4.8	4.7	4.9	5.2	4.9	5.1	5.0	5.2	5.3
1980	3.6	3.7	3.8	3.9	3.9	4.0	4.1	4.2	4.3	4.3	4.5	4.8	4.6	4.9	5.2	4.8	5.0	5.0	5.2	5.2
1981	3.8	3.9	4.0	4.0	4.1	4.2	4.3	4.4	4.5	4.5	4.7	4.9	4.8	5.1	5.3	5.1	5.2	5.2	5.4	5.5
1982	4.4	4.5	4.6	4.7	4.8	4.9	5.0	5.2	5.2	5.3	5.5	5.8	5.7	6.0	6.3	6.0	6.2	6.3	6.5	6.7
1983	4.5	4.6	4.7	4.8	4.8	5.0	5.1	5.2	5.3	5.4	5.6	5.8	5.8	6.1	6.3	6.1	6.3	6.3	6.6	6.7
1984	4.7	4.8	4.9	5.0	5.1	5.2	5.4	5.5	5.6	5.7	5.9	6.1	6.1	6.3	6.6	6.4	6.6	6.7	6.9	7.1
1985	5.1	5.2	5.3	5.4	5.5	5.6	5.8	5.9	6.0	6.1	6.3	6.6	6.5	6.8	7.1	6.9	7.2	7.2	7.5	7.7
1986	5.3	5.4	5.5	5.6	5.7	5.9	6.0	6.2	6.3	6.4	6.6	6.9	6.8	7.1	7.4	7.2	7.5	7.5	7.8	8.0
1987	5.3	5.4	5.5	5.6	5.7	5.8	6.0	6.1	6.2	6.3	6.5	6.7	6.7	7.0	7.2	7.1	7.3	7.4	7.6	7.8
1988	5.3	5.4	5.5	5.6	5.7	5.8	6.0	6.1	6.2	6.3	6.5	6.7	6.7	6.9	7.2	7.0	7.2	7.3	7.5	7.7
1989	5.5	5.6	5.7	5.8	5.9	6.0	6.1	6.3	6.4	6.5	6.7	6.9	6.9	7.1	7.4	7.3	7.5	7.5	7.8	7.9
1990	5.5	5.7	5.8	5.9	5.9	6.1	6.2	6.4	6.4	6.5	6.8	7.0	7.0	7.2	7.5	7.3	7.5	7.6	7.8	8.0

Table C-5

Intermediate-Term Government Bonds Total Returns

(Page 4 of 5)

Rates of Return for all holding periods.

Percent per annum compounded annually.

From 1926 to 1998

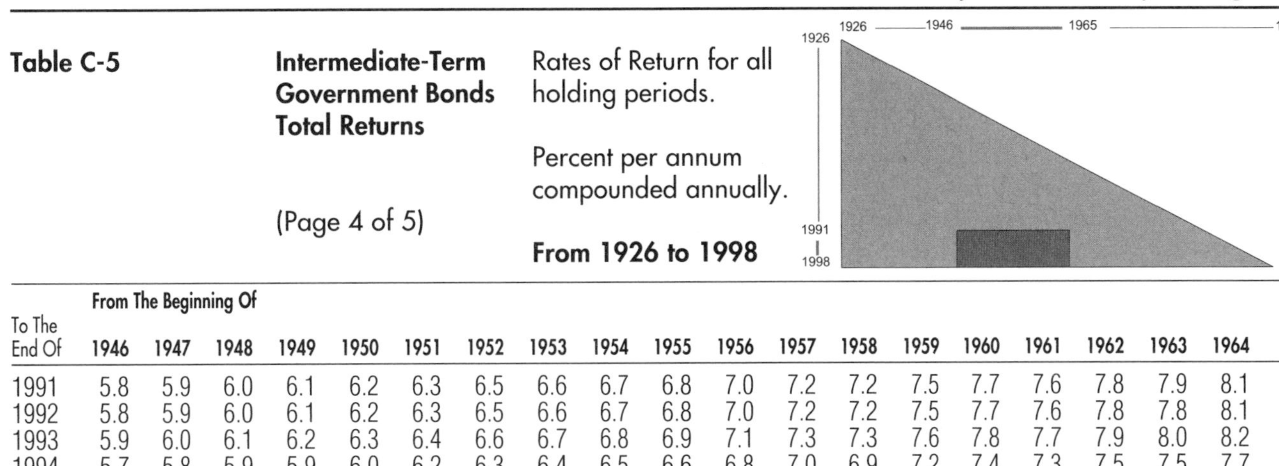

To The End Of	From The Beginning Of 1946	1947	1948	1949	1950	1951	1952	1953	1954	1955	1956	1957	1958	1959	1960	1961	1962	1963	1964	1965
1991	5.8	5.9	6.0	6.1	6.2	6.3	6.5	6.6	6.7	6.8	7.0	7.2	7.2	7.5	7.7	7.6	7.8	7.9	8.1	8.2
1992	5.8	5.9	6.0	6.1	6.2	6.3	6.5	6.6	6.7	6.8	7.0	7.2	7.2	7.5	7.7	7.6	7.8	7.8	8.1	8.2
1993	5.9	6.0	6.1	6.2	6.3	6.4	6.6	6.7	6.8	6.9	7.1	7.3	7.3	7.6	7.8	7.7	7.9	8.0	8.2	8.3
1994	5.7	5.8	5.9	5.9	6.0	6.2	6.3	6.4	6.5	6.6	6.8	7.0	6.9	7.2	7.4	7.3	7.5	7.5	7.7	7.8
1995	5.9	6.0	6.1	6.2	6.3	6.4	6.5	6.6	6.7	6.8	7.0	7.2	7.2	7.4	7.7	7.5	7.7	7.8	8.0	8.1
1996	5.8	5.9	6.0	6.1	6.2	6.3	6.4	6.5	6.6	6.7	6.9	7.1	7.1	7.3	7.5	7.4	7.6	7.6	7.8	7.9
1997	5.8	5.9	6.0	6.1	6.2	6.3	6.5	6.6	6.7	6.7	6.9	7.1	7.1	7.3	7.5	7.4	7.6	7.6	7.8	7.9
1998	5.9	6.0	6.1	6.2	6.3	6.4	6.5	6.7	6.7	6.8	7.0	7.2	7.2	7.4	7.6	7.5	7.6	7.7	7.9	8.0

Table C-5

Intermediate-Term Government Bonds Total Returns

(Page 5 of 5)

Rates of Return for all holding periods.

Percent per annum compounded annually.

From 1926 to 1998

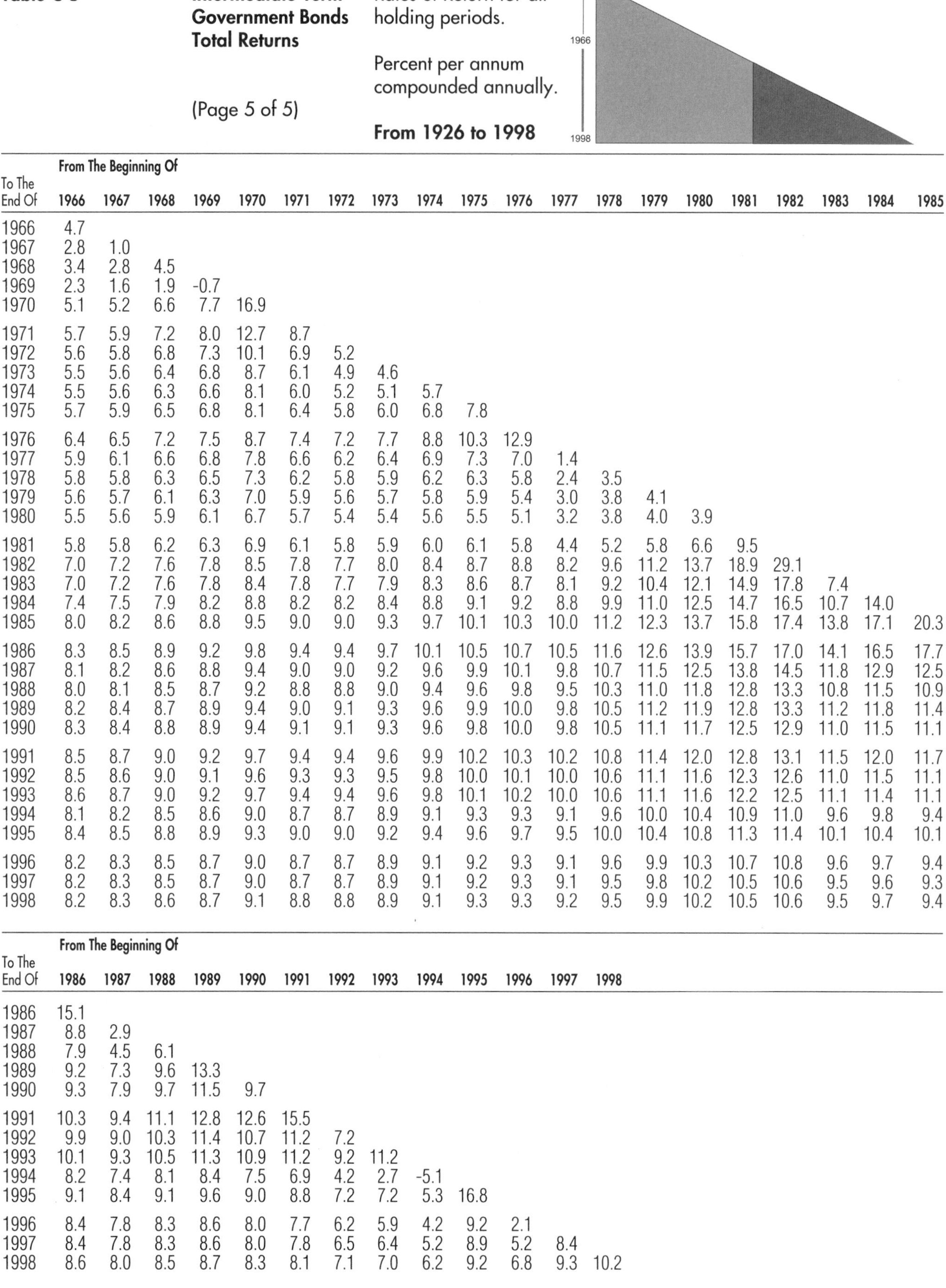

To The End Of	From The Beginning Of 1966	1967	1968	1969	1970	1971	1972	1973	1974	1975	1976	1977	1978	1979	1980	1981	1982	1983	1984	1985
1966	4.7																			
1967	2.8	1.0																		
1968	3.4	2.8	4.5																	
1969	2.3	1.6	1.9	-0.7																
1970	5.1	5.2	6.6	7.7	16.9															
1971	5.7	5.9	7.2	8.0	12.7	8.7														
1972	5.6	5.8	6.8	7.3	10.1	6.9	5.2													
1973	5.5	5.6	6.4	6.8	8.7	6.1	4.9	4.6												
1974	5.5	5.6	6.3	6.6	8.1	6.0	5.2	5.1	5.7											
1975	5.7	5.9	6.5	6.8	8.1	6.4	5.8	6.0	6.8	7.8										
1976	6.4	6.5	7.2	7.5	8.7	7.4	7.2	7.7	8.8	10.3	12.9									
1977	5.9	6.1	6.6	6.8	7.8	6.6	6.2	6.4	6.9	7.3	7.0	1.4								
1978	5.8	5.8	6.3	6.5	7.3	6.2	5.8	5.9	6.2	6.3	5.8	2.4	3.5							
1979	5.6	5.7	6.1	6.3	7.0	5.9	5.6	5.7	5.8	5.9	5.4	3.0	3.8	4.1						
1980	5.5	5.6	5.9	6.1	6.7	5.7	5.4	5.4	5.6	5.5	5.1	3.2	3.8	4.0	3.9					
1981	5.8	5.8	6.2	6.3	6.9	6.1	5.8	5.9	6.0	6.1	5.8	4.4	5.2	5.8	6.6	9.5				
1982	7.0	7.2	7.6	7.8	8.5	7.8	7.7	8.0	8.4	8.7	8.8	8.2	9.6	11.2	13.7	18.9	29.1			
1983	7.0	7.2	7.6	7.8	8.4	7.8	7.7	7.9	8.3	8.6	8.7	8.1	9.2	10.4	12.1	14.9	17.8	7.4		
1984	7.4	7.5	7.9	8.2	8.8	8.2	8.2	8.4	8.8	9.1	9.2	8.8	9.9	11.0	12.5	14.7	16.5	10.7	14.0	
1985	8.0	8.2	8.6	8.8	9.5	9.0	9.0	9.3	9.7	10.1	10.3	10.0	11.2	12.3	13.7	15.8	17.4	13.8	17.1	20.3
1986	8.3	8.5	8.9	9.2	9.8	9.4	9.4	9.7	10.1	10.5	10.7	10.5	11.6	12.6	13.9	15.7	17.0	14.1	16.5	17.7
1987	8.1	8.2	8.6	8.8	9.4	9.0	9.0	9.2	9.6	9.9	10.1	9.8	10.7	11.5	12.5	13.8	14.5	11.8	12.9	12.5
1988	8.0	8.1	8.5	8.7	9.2	8.8	8.8	9.0	9.4	9.6	9.8	9.5	10.3	11.0	11.8	12.8	13.3	10.8	11.5	10.9
1989	8.2	8.4	8.7	8.9	9.4	9.0	9.1	9.3	9.6	9.9	10.0	9.8	10.5	11.2	11.9	12.8	13.3	11.2	11.8	11.4
1990	8.3	8.4	8.8	8.9	9.4	9.1	9.1	9.3	9.6	9.8	10.0	9.8	10.5	11.1	11.7	12.5	12.9	11.0	11.5	11.1
1991	8.5	8.7	9.0	9.2	9.7	9.4	9.4	9.6	9.9	10.2	10.3	10.2	10.8	11.4	12.0	12.8	13.1	11.5	12.0	11.7
1992	8.5	8.6	9.0	9.1	9.6	9.3	9.3	9.5	9.8	10.0	10.1	10.0	10.6	11.1	11.6	12.3	12.6	11.0	11.5	11.1
1993	8.6	8.7	9.0	9.2	9.7	9.4	9.4	9.6	9.8	10.1	10.2	10.0	10.6	11.1	11.6	12.2	12.5	11.1	11.4	11.1
1994	8.1	8.2	8.5	8.6	9.0	8.7	8.7	8.9	9.1	9.3	9.3	9.1	9.6	10.0	10.4	10.9	11.0	9.6	9.8	9.4
1995	8.4	8.5	8.8	8.9	9.3	9.0	9.0	9.2	9.4	9.6	9.7	9.5	10.0	10.4	10.8	11.3	11.4	10.1	10.4	10.1
1996	8.2	8.3	8.5	8.7	9.0	8.7	8.7	8.9	9.1	9.2	9.3	9.1	9.6	9.9	10.3	10.7	10.8	9.6	9.7	9.4
1997	8.2	8.3	8.5	8.7	9.0	8.7	8.7	8.9	9.1	9.2	9.3	9.1	9.5	9.8	10.2	10.5	10.6	9.5	9.6	9.3
1998	8.2	8.3	8.6	8.7	9.1	8.8	8.8	8.9	9.1	9.3	9.3	9.2	9.5	9.9	10.2	10.5	10.6	9.5	9.7	9.4

To The End Of	From The Beginning Of 1986	1987	1988	1989	1990	1991	1992	1993	1994	1995	1996	1997	1998
1986	15.1												
1987	8.8	2.9											
1988	7.9	4.5	6.1										
1989	9.2	7.3	9.6	13.3									
1990	9.3	7.9	9.7	11.5	9.7								
1991	10.3	9.4	11.1	12.8	12.6	15.5							
1992	9.9	9.0	10.3	11.4	10.7	11.2	7.2						
1993	10.1	9.3	10.5	11.3	10.9	11.2	9.2	11.2					
1994	8.2	7.4	8.1	8.4	7.5	6.9	4.2	2.7	-5.1				
1995	9.1	8.4	9.1	9.6	9.0	8.8	7.2	7.2	5.3	16.8			
1996	8.4	7.8	8.3	8.6	8.0	7.7	6.2	5.9	4.2	9.2	2.1		
1997	8.4	7.8	8.3	8.6	8.0	7.8	6.5	6.4	5.2	8.9	5.2	8.4	
1998	8.6	8.0	8.5	8.7	8.3	8.1	7.1	7.0	6.2	9.2	6.8	9.3	10.2

Table C-6 | **U.S. Treasury Bills Total Returns** | (Page 1 of 5)

Rates of Return for all holding periods.

Percent per annum compounded annually.

From 1926 to 1998

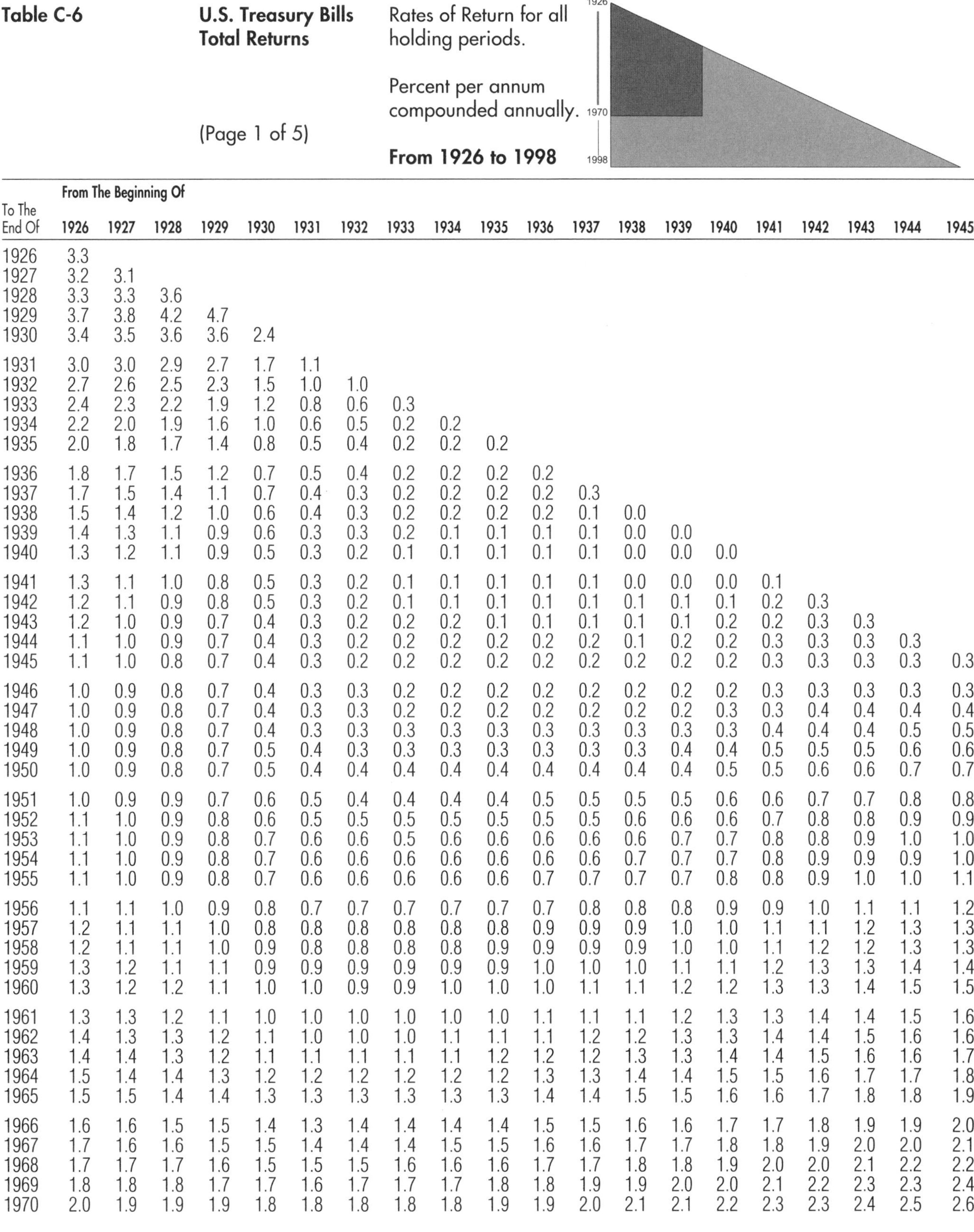

To The End Of	From The Beginning Of 1926	1927	1928	1929	1930	1931	1932	1933	1934	1935	1936	1937	1938	1939	1940	1941	1942	1943	1944	1945
1926	3.3																			
1927	3.2	3.1																		
1928	3.3	3.3	3.6																	
1929	3.7	3.8	4.2	4.7																
1930	3.4	3.5	3.6	3.6	2.4															
1931	3.0	3.0	2.9	2.7	1.7	1.1														
1932	2.7	2.6	2.5	2.3	1.5	1.0	1.0													
1933	2.4	2.3	2.2	1.9	1.2	0.8	0.6	0.3												
1934	2.2	2.0	1.9	1.6	1.0	0.6	0.5	0.2	0.2											
1935	2.0	1.8	1.7	1.4	0.8	0.5	0.4	0.2	0.2	0.2										
1936	1.8	1.7	1.5	1.2	0.7	0.5	0.4	0.2	0.2	0.2	0.2									
1937	1.7	1.5	1.4	1.1	0.7	0.4	0.3	0.2	0.2	0.2	0.2	0.3								
1938	1.5	1.4	1.2	1.0	0.6	0.4	0.3	0.2	0.2	0.2	0.2	0.1	0.0							
1939	1.4	1.3	1.1	0.9	0.6	0.3	0.3	0.2	0.1	0.1	0.1	0.1	0.0	0.0						
1940	1.3	1.2	1.1	0.9	0.5	0.3	0.2	0.1	0.1	0.1	0.1	0.1	0.0	0.0	0.0					
1941	1.3	1.1	1.0	0.8	0.5	0.3	0.2	0.1	0.1	0.1	0.1	0.1	0.0	0.0	0.0	0.1				
1942	1.2	1.1	0.9	0.8	0.5	0.3	0.2	0.1	0.1	0.1	0.1	0.1	0.1	0.1	0.1	0.2	0.3			
1943	1.2	1.0	0.9	0.7	0.4	0.3	0.2	0.2	0.2	0.1	0.1	0.1	0.1	0.1	0.2	0.2	0.3	0.3		
1944	1.1	1.0	0.9	0.7	0.4	0.3	0.2	0.2	0.2	0.2	0.2	0.2	0.1	0.2	0.2	0.3	0.3	0.3	0.3	
1945	1.1	1.0	0.8	0.7	0.4	0.3	0.2	0.2	0.2	0.2	0.2	0.2	0.2	0.2	0.2	0.3	0.3	0.3	0.3	0.3
1946	1.0	0.9	0.8	0.7	0.4	0.3	0.3	0.2	0.2	0.2	0.2	0.2	0.2	0.2	0.2	0.3	0.3	0.3	0.3	0.3
1947	1.0	0.9	0.8	0.7	0.4	0.3	0.3	0.2	0.2	0.2	0.2	0.2	0.2	0.2	0.3	0.3	0.4	0.4	0.4	0.4
1948	1.0	0.9	0.8	0.7	0.4	0.3	0.3	0.3	0.3	0.3	0.3	0.3	0.3	0.3	0.3	0.4	0.4	0.4	0.5	0.5
1949	1.0	0.9	0.8	0.7	0.5	0.4	0.3	0.3	0.3	0.3	0.3	0.3	0.3	0.4	0.4	0.5	0.5	0.5	0.6	0.6
1950	1.0	0.9	0.8	0.7	0.5	0.4	0.4	0.4	0.4	0.4	0.4	0.4	0.4	0.4	0.5	0.5	0.6	0.6	0.7	0.7
1951	1.0	0.9	0.9	0.7	0.6	0.5	0.4	0.4	0.4	0.4	0.5	0.5	0.5	0.5	0.6	0.6	0.7	0.7	0.8	0.8
1952	1.1	1.0	0.9	0.8	0.6	0.5	0.5	0.5	0.5	0.5	0.5	0.5	0.6	0.6	0.6	0.7	0.8	0.8	0.9	0.9
1953	1.1	1.0	0.9	0.8	0.7	0.6	0.6	0.5	0.6	0.6	0.6	0.6	0.6	0.7	0.7	0.8	0.8	0.9	1.0	1.0
1954	1.1	1.0	0.9	0.8	0.7	0.6	0.6	0.6	0.6	0.6	0.6	0.6	0.7	0.7	0.7	0.8	0.9	0.9	0.9	1.0
1955	1.1	1.0	0.9	0.8	0.7	0.6	0.6	0.6	0.6	0.6	0.7	0.7	0.7	0.7	0.8	0.8	0.9	1.0	1.0	1.1
1956	1.1	1.1	1.0	0.9	0.8	0.7	0.7	0.7	0.7	0.7	0.7	0.8	0.8	0.8	0.9	0.9	1.0	1.1	1.1	1.2
1957	1.2	1.1	1.1	1.0	0.8	0.8	0.8	0.8	0.8	0.8	0.9	0.9	0.9	1.0	1.0	1.1	1.1	1.2	1.3	1.3
1958	1.2	1.1	1.1	1.0	0.9	0.8	0.8	0.8	0.8	0.9	0.9	0.9	0.9	1.0	1.0	1.1	1.2	1.2	1.3	1.3
1959	1.3	1.2	1.1	1.1	0.9	0.9	0.9	0.9	0.9	0.9	1.0	1.0	1.0	1.1	1.1	1.2	1.3	1.3	1.4	1.4
1960	1.3	1.2	1.2	1.1	1.0	1.0	0.9	0.9	1.0	1.0	1.0	1.1	1.1	1.2	1.2	1.3	1.3	1.4	1.5	1.5
1961	1.3	1.3	1.2	1.1	1.0	1.0	1.0	1.0	1.0	1.0	1.1	1.1	1.1	1.2	1.3	1.3	1.4	1.4	1.5	1.6
1962	1.4	1.3	1.3	1.2	1.1	1.0	1.0	1.0	1.1	1.1	1.1	1.2	1.2	1.3	1.3	1.4	1.4	1.5	1.6	1.6
1963	1.4	1.4	1.3	1.2	1.1	1.1	1.1	1.1	1.1	1.2	1.2	1.2	1.3	1.3	1.4	1.4	1.5	1.6	1.6	1.7
1964	1.5	1.4	1.4	1.3	1.2	1.2	1.2	1.2	1.2	1.2	1.3	1.3	1.4	1.4	1.5	1.5	1.6	1.7	1.7	1.8
1965	1.5	1.5	1.4	1.4	1.3	1.3	1.3	1.3	1.3	1.3	1.4	1.4	1.5	1.5	1.6	1.6	1.7	1.8	1.8	1.9
1966	1.6	1.6	1.5	1.5	1.4	1.3	1.4	1.4	1.4	1.4	1.5	1.5	1.6	1.6	1.7	1.7	1.8	1.9	1.9	2.0
1967	1.7	1.6	1.6	1.5	1.5	1.4	1.4	1.4	1.5	1.5	1.6	1.6	1.7	1.7	1.8	1.8	1.9	2.0	2.0	2.1
1968	1.7	1.7	1.7	1.6	1.5	1.5	1.5	1.6	1.6	1.6	1.7	1.7	1.8	1.8	1.9	2.0	2.0	2.1	2.2	2.2
1969	1.8	1.8	1.8	1.7	1.7	1.6	1.7	1.7	1.7	1.8	1.8	1.9	1.9	2.0	2.0	2.1	2.2	2.3	2.3	2.4
1970	2.0	1.9	1.9	1.9	1.8	1.8	1.8	1.8	1.8	1.9	1.9	2.0	2.1	2.1	2.2	2.3	2.3	2.4	2.5	2.6

Table C-6 | **U.S. Treasury Bills Total Returns** | Rates of Return for all holding periods.

Percent per annum compounded annually.

(Page 2 of 5)

From 1926 to 1998

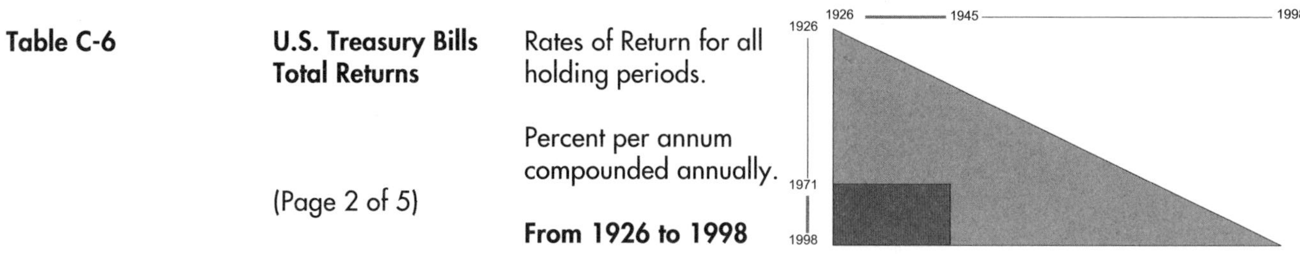

To The End Of	From The Beginning Of 1926	1927	1928	1929	1930	1931	1932	1933	1934	1935	1936	1937	1938	1939	1940	1941	1942	1943	1944	1945
1971	2.0	2.0	1.9	1.9	1.8	1.8	1.9	1.9	1.9	2.0	2.0	2.1	2.1	2.2	2.3	2.3	2.4	2.5	2.6	2.6
1972	2.0	2.0	2.0	2.0	1.9	1.9	1.9	1.9	2.0	2.0	2.1	2.1	2.2	2.2	2.3	2.4	2.4	2.5	2.6	2.7
1973	2.1	2.1	2.1	2.1	2.0	2.0	2.0	2.0	2.1	2.1	2.2	2.2	2.3	2.4	2.4	2.5	2.6	2.7	2.7	2.8
1974	2.3	2.2	2.2	2.2	2.1	2.1	2.2	2.2	2.2	2.3	2.3	2.4	2.4	2.5	2.6	2.7	2.7	2.8	2.9	3.0
1975	2.3	2.3	2.3	2.3	2.2	2.2	2.2	2.3	2.3	2.4	2.4	2.5	2.5	2.6	2.7	2.8	2.8	2.9	3.0	3.1
1976	2.4	2.4	2.3	2.3	2.3	2.3	2.3	2.3	2.4	2.4	2.5	2.5	2.6	2.7	2.7	2.8	2.9	3.0	3.1	3.1
1977	2.4	2.4	2.4	2.4	2.3	2.3	2.4	2.4	2.4	2.5	2.5	2.6	2.7	2.7	2.8	2.9	3.0	3.0	3.1	3.2
1978	2.5	2.5	2.5	2.5	2.4	2.4	2.5	2.5	2.5	2.6	2.6	2.7	2.8	2.8	2.9	3.0	3.1	3.1	3.2	3.3
1979	2.7	2.6	2.6	2.6	2.6	2.6	2.6	2.7	2.7	2.8	2.8	2.9	2.9	3.0	3.1	3.2	3.3	3.3	3.4	3.5
1980	2.8	2.8	2.8	2.8	2.7	2.7	2.8	2.8	2.9	2.9	3.0	3.1	3.1	3.2	3.3	3.4	3.5	3.5	3.6	3.7
1981	3.0	3.0	3.0	3.0	3.0	3.0	3.0	3.1	3.1	3.2	3.2	3.3	3.4	3.5	3.5	3.6	3.7	3.8	3.9	4.0
1982	3.1	3.1	3.1	3.1	3.1	3.1	3.2	3.2	3.3	3.3	3.4	3.5	3.5	3.6	3.7	3.8	3.9	4.0	4.1	4.2
1983	3.2	3.2	3.2	3.2	3.2	3.2	3.3	3.3	3.4	3.4	3.5	3.6	3.6	3.7	3.8	3.9	4.0	4.1	4.2	4.3
1984	3.3	3.3	3.3	3.3	3.3	3.3	3.4	3.4	3.5	3.6	3.6	3.7	3.8	3.9	3.9	4.0	4.1	4.2	4.3	4.4
1985	3.4	3.4	3.4	3.4	3.4	3.4	3.5	3.5	3.6	3.6	3.7	3.8	3.9	3.9	4.0	4.1	4.2	4.3	4.4	4.5
1986	3.5	3.5	3.5	3.5	3.4	3.5	3.5	3.6	3.6	3.7	3.8	3.8	3.9	4.0	4.1	4.2	4.3	4.3	4.4	4.5
1987	3.5	3.5	3.5	3.5	3.5	3.5	3.5	3.6	3.7	3.7	3.8	3.9	3.9	4.0	4.1	4.2	4.3	4.4	4.5	4.6
1988	3.5	3.5	3.5	3.5	3.5	3.5	3.6	3.6	3.7	3.8	3.8	3.9	4.0	4.1	4.1	4.2	4.3	4.4	4.5	4.6
1989	3.6	3.6	3.6	3.6	3.6	3.6	3.7	3.7	3.8	3.8	3.9	4.0	4.1	4.1	4.2	4.3	4.4	4.5	4.6	4.7
1990	3.7	3.7	3.7	3.7	3.7	3.7	3.7	3.8	3.8	3.9	4.0	4.1	4.1	4.2	4.3	4.4	4.5	4.6	4.7	4.8
1991	3.7	3.7	3.7	3.7	3.7	3.7	3.8	3.8	3.9	3.9	4.0	4.1	4.2	4.2	4.3	4.4	4.5	4.6	4.7	4.8
1992	3.7	3.7	3.7	3.7	3.7	3.7	3.8	3.8	3.9	3.9	4.0	4.1	4.1	4.2	4.3	4.4	4.5	4.6	4.7	4.7
1993	3.7	3.7	3.7	3.7	3.7	3.7	3.8	3.8	3.9	3.9	4.0	4.1	4.1	4.2	4.3	4.4	4.4	4.5	4.6	4.7
1994	3.7	3.7	3.7	3.7	3.7	3.7	3.8	3.8	3.9	3.9	4.0	4.1	4.1	4.2	4.3	4.4	4.4	4.5	4.6	4.7
1995	3.7	3.7	3.7	3.7	3.7	3.7	3.8	3.8	3.9	3.9	4.0	4.1	4.1	4.2	4.3	4.4	4.5	4.5	4.6	4.7
1996	3.7	3.7	3.8	3.8	3.7	3.8	3.8	3.8	3.9	4.0	4.0	4.1	4.2	4.2	4.3	4.4	4.5	4.5	4.6	4.7
1997	3.8	3.8	3.8	3.8	3.8	3.8	3.8	3.9	3.9	4.0	4.1	4.1	4.2	4.3	4.3	4.4	4.5	4.6	4.6	4.7
1998	3.8	3.8	3.8	3.8	3.8	3.8	3.8	3.9	3.9	4.0	4.1	4.1	4.2	4.3	4.3	4.4	4.5	4.6	4.6	4.7

Table C-6

U.S. Treasury Bills Total Returns

(Page 3 of 5)

Rates of Return for all holding periods.

Percent per annum compounded annually.

From 1926 to 1998

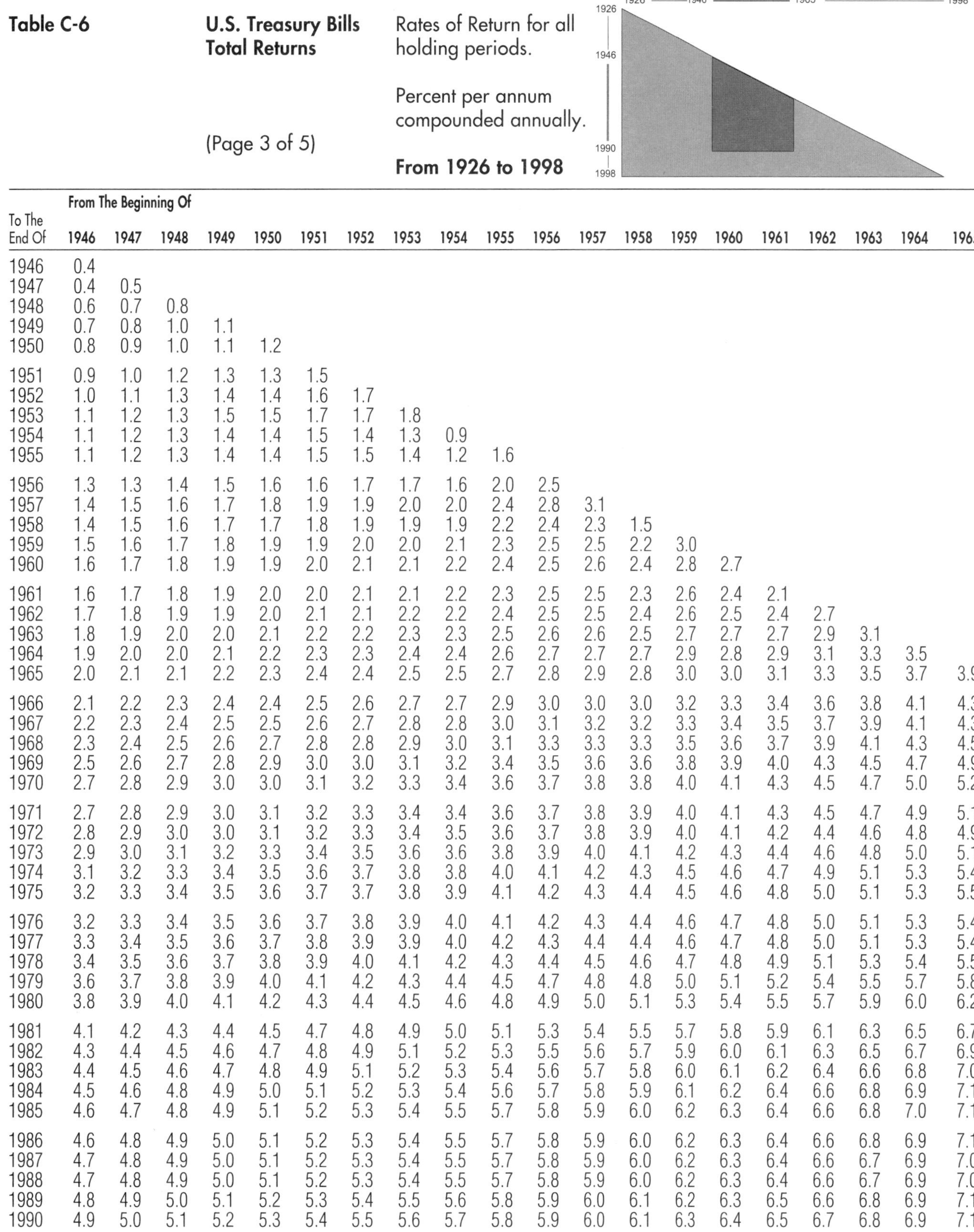

To The End Of	From The Beginning Of 1946	1947	1948	1949	1950	1951	1952	1953	1954	1955	1956	1957	1958	1959	1960	1961	1962	1963	1964	1965
1946	0.4																			
1947	0.4	0.5																		
1948	0.6	0.7	0.8																	
1949	0.7	0.8	1.0	1.1																
1950	0.8	0.9	1.0	1.1	1.2															
1951	0.9	1.0	1.2	1.3	1.3	1.5														
1952	1.0	1.1	1.3	1.4	1.4	1.6	1.7													
1953	1.1	1.2	1.3	1.5	1.5	1.7	1.7	1.8												
1954	1.1	1.2	1.3	1.4	1.4	1.5	1.4	1.3	0.9											
1955	1.1	1.2	1.3	1.4	1.4	1.5	1.5	1.4	1.2	1.6										
1956	1.3	1.3	1.4	1.5	1.6	1.6	1.7	1.7	1.6	2.0	2.5									
1957	1.4	1.5	1.6	1.7	1.8	1.9	1.9	2.0	2.0	2.4	2.8	3.1								
1958	1.4	1.5	1.6	1.7	1.7	1.8	1.9	1.9	1.9	2.2	2.4	2.3	1.5							
1959	1.5	1.6	1.7	1.8	1.9	1.9	2.0	2.0	2.1	2.3	2.5	2.5	2.2	3.0						
1960	1.6	1.7	1.8	1.9	1.9	2.0	2.1	2.1	2.2	2.4	2.5	2.6	2.4	2.8	2.7					
1961	1.6	1.7	1.8	1.9	2.0	2.0	2.1	2.1	2.2	2.3	2.5	2.5	2.3	2.6	2.4	2.1				
1962	1.7	1.8	1.9	1.9	2.0	2.1	2.1	2.2	2.2	2.4	2.5	2.5	2.4	2.6	2.5	2.4	2.7			
1963	1.8	1.9	2.0	2.0	2.1	2.2	2.2	2.3	2.3	2.5	2.6	2.6	2.5	2.7	2.7	2.7	2.9	3.1		
1964	1.9	2.0	2.0	2.1	2.2	2.3	2.3	2.4	2.4	2.6	2.7	2.7	2.7	2.9	2.8	2.9	3.1	3.3	3.5	
1965	2.0	2.1	2.1	2.2	2.3	2.4	2.4	2.5	2.5	2.7	2.8	2.9	2.8	3.0	3.0	3.1	3.3	3.5	3.7	3.9
1966	2.1	2.2	2.3	2.4	2.4	2.5	2.6	2.7	2.7	2.9	3.0	3.0	3.0	3.2	3.3	3.4	3.6	3.8	4.1	4.3
1967	2.2	2.3	2.4	2.5	2.5	2.6	2.7	2.8	2.8	3.0	3.1	3.2	3.2	3.3	3.4	3.5	3.7	3.9	4.1	4.3
1968	2.3	2.4	2.5	2.6	2.7	2.8	2.8	2.9	3.0	3.1	3.3	3.3	3.3	3.5	3.6	3.7	3.9	4.1	4.3	4.5
1969	2.5	2.6	2.7	2.8	2.9	3.0	3.0	3.1	3.2	3.4	3.5	3.6	3.6	3.8	3.9	4.0	4.3	4.5	4.7	4.9
1970	2.7	2.8	2.9	3.0	3.0	3.1	3.2	3.3	3.4	3.6	3.7	3.8	3.8	4.0	4.1	4.3	4.5	4.7	5.0	5.2
1971	2.7	2.8	2.9	3.0	3.1	3.2	3.3	3.4	3.4	3.6	3.7	3.8	3.9	4.0	4.1	4.3	4.5	4.7	4.9	5.1
1972	2.8	2.9	3.0	3.0	3.1	3.2	3.3	3.4	3.5	3.6	3.7	3.8	3.9	4.0	4.1	4.2	4.4	4.6	4.8	4.9
1973	2.9	3.0	3.1	3.2	3.3	3.4	3.5	3.6	3.6	3.8	3.9	4.0	4.1	4.2	4.3	4.4	4.6	4.8	5.0	5.1
1974	3.1	3.2	3.3	3.4	3.5	3.6	3.7	3.8	3.8	4.0	4.1	4.2	4.3	4.5	4.6	4.7	4.9	5.1	5.3	5.4
1975	3.2	3.3	3.4	3.5	3.6	3.7	3.7	3.8	3.9	4.1	4.2	4.3	4.4	4.5	4.6	4.8	5.0	5.1	5.3	5.5
1976	3.2	3.3	3.4	3.5	3.6	3.7	3.8	3.9	4.0	4.1	4.2	4.3	4.4	4.6	4.7	4.8	5.0	5.1	5.3	5.4
1977	3.3	3.4	3.5	3.6	3.7	3.8	3.9	3.9	4.0	4.2	4.3	4.4	4.4	4.6	4.7	4.8	5.0	5.1	5.3	5.4
1978	3.4	3.5	3.6	3.7	3.8	3.9	4.0	4.1	4.2	4.3	4.4	4.5	4.6	4.7	4.8	4.9	5.1	5.3	5.4	5.5
1979	3.6	3.7	3.8	3.9	4.0	4.1	4.2	4.3	4.4	4.5	4.7	4.8	4.8	5.0	5.1	5.2	5.4	5.5	5.7	5.8
1980	3.8	3.9	4.0	4.1	4.2	4.3	4.4	4.5	4.6	4.8	4.9	5.0	5.1	5.3	5.4	5.5	5.7	5.9	6.0	6.2
1981	4.1	4.2	4.3	4.4	4.5	4.7	4.8	4.9	5.0	5.1	5.3	5.4	5.5	5.7	5.8	5.9	6.1	6.3	6.5	6.7
1982	4.3	4.4	4.5	4.6	4.7	4.8	4.9	5.1	5.2	5.3	5.5	5.6	5.7	5.9	6.0	6.1	6.3	6.5	6.7	6.9
1983	4.4	4.5	4.6	4.7	4.8	4.9	5.1	5.2	5.3	5.4	5.6	5.7	5.8	6.0	6.1	6.2	6.4	6.6	6.8	7.0
1984	4.5	4.6	4.8	4.9	5.0	5.1	5.2	5.3	5.4	5.6	5.7	5.8	5.9	6.1	6.2	6.4	6.6	6.8	6.9	7.1
1985	4.6	4.7	4.8	4.9	5.1	5.2	5.3	5.4	5.5	5.7	5.8	5.9	6.0	6.2	6.3	6.4	6.6	6.8	7.0	7.1
1986	4.6	4.8	4.9	5.0	5.1	5.2	5.3	5.4	5.5	5.7	5.8	5.9	6.0	6.2	6.3	6.4	6.6	6.8	6.9	7.1
1987	4.7	4.8	4.9	5.0	5.1	5.2	5.3	5.4	5.5	5.7	5.8	5.9	6.0	6.2	6.3	6.4	6.6	6.7	6.9	7.0
1988	4.7	4.8	4.9	5.0	5.1	5.2	5.3	5.4	5.5	5.7	5.8	5.9	6.0	6.2	6.3	6.4	6.6	6.7	6.9	7.0
1989	4.8	4.9	5.0	5.1	5.2	5.3	5.4	5.5	5.6	5.8	5.9	6.0	6.1	6.2	6.3	6.5	6.6	6.8	6.9	7.1
1990	4.9	5.0	5.1	5.2	5.3	5.4	5.5	5.6	5.7	5.8	5.9	6.0	6.1	6.3	6.4	6.5	6.7	6.8	6.9	7.1

Table C-6

U.S. Treasury Bills Total Returns

(Page 4 of 5)

Rates of Return for all holding periods.

Percent per annum compounded annually.

From 1926 to 1998

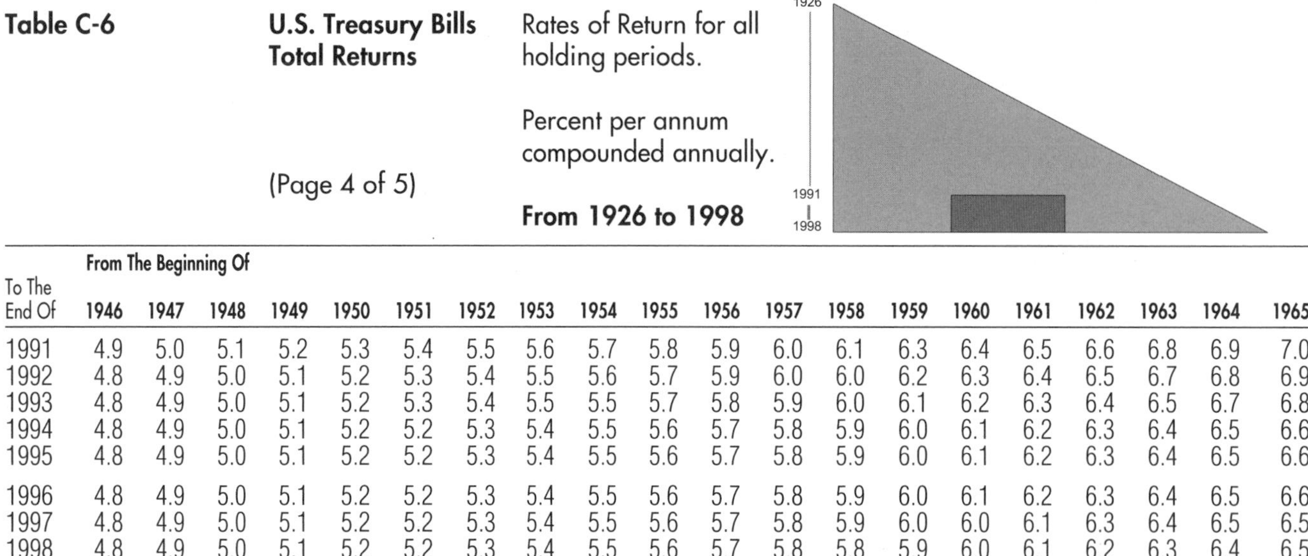

To The End Of	From The Beginning Of 1946	1947	1948	1949	1950	1951	1952	1953	1954	1955	1956	1957	1958	1959	1960	1961	1962	1963	1964	1965
1991	4.9	5.0	5.1	5.2	5.3	5.4	5.5	5.6	5.7	5.8	5.9	6.0	6.1	6.3	6.4	6.5	6.6	6.8	6.9	7.0
1992	4.8	4.9	5.0	5.1	5.2	5.3	5.4	5.5	5.6	5.7	5.9	6.0	6.0	6.2	6.3	6.4	6.5	6.7	6.8	6.9
1993	4.8	4.9	5.0	5.1	5.2	5.3	5.4	5.5	5.5	5.7	5.8	5.9	6.0	6.1	6.2	6.3	6.4	6.5	6.7	6.8
1994	4.8	4.9	5.0	5.1	5.2	5.2	5.3	5.4	5.5	5.6	5.7	5.8	5.9	6.0	6.1	6.2	6.3	6.4	6.5	6.6
1995	4.8	4.9	5.0	5.1	5.2	5.2	5.3	5.4	5.5	5.6	5.7	5.8	5.9	6.0	6.1	6.2	6.3	6.4	6.5	6.6
1996	4.8	4.9	5.0	5.1	5.2	5.2	5.3	5.4	5.5	5.6	5.7	5.8	5.9	6.0	6.1	6.2	6.3	6.4	6.5	6.6
1997	4.8	4.9	5.0	5.1	5.2	5.2	5.3	5.4	5.5	5.6	5.7	5.8	5.9	6.0	6.0	6.1	6.3	6.4	6.5	6.5
1998	4.8	4.9	5.0	5.1	5.2	5.2	5.3	5.4	5.5	5.6	5.7	5.8	5.8	5.9	6.0	6.1	6.2	6.3	6.4	6.5

Table C-6

U.S. Treasury Bills Total Returns

(Page 5 of 5)

Rates of Return for all holding periods.

Percent per annum compounded annually.

From 1926 to 1998

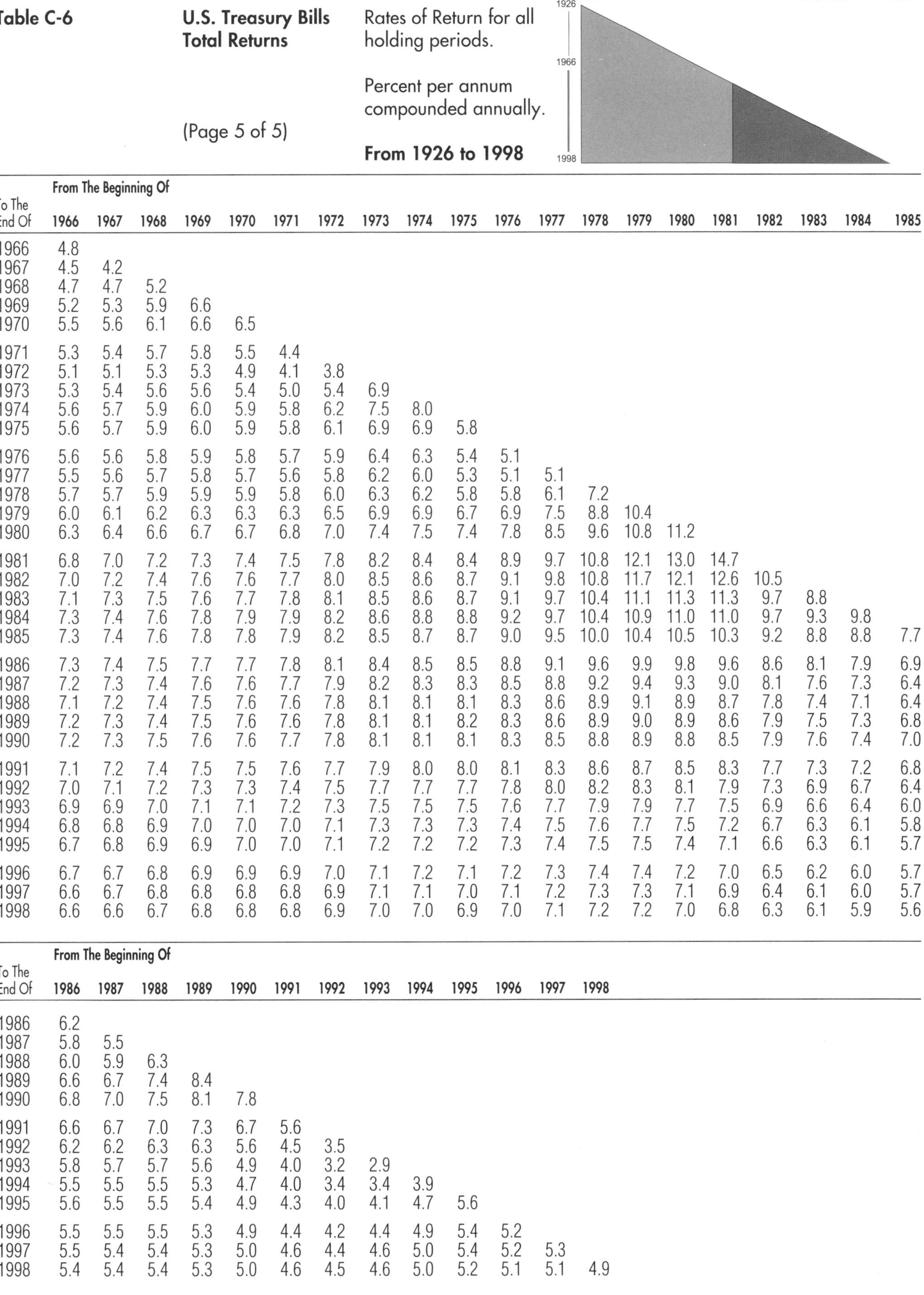

To The End Of	From The Beginning Of 1966	1967	1968	1969	1970	1971	1972	1973	1974	1975	1976	1977	1978	1979	1980	1981	1982	1983	1984	1985
1966	4.8																			
1967	4.5	4.2																		
1968	4.7	4.7	5.2																	
1969	5.2	5.3	5.9	6.6																
1970	5.5	5.6	6.1	6.6	6.5															
1971	5.3	5.4	5.7	5.8	5.5	4.4														
1972	5.1	5.1	5.3	5.3	4.9	4.1	3.8													
1973	5.3	5.4	5.6	5.6	5.4	5.0	5.4	6.9												
1974	5.6	5.7	5.9	6.0	5.9	5.8	6.2	7.5	8.0											
1975	5.6	5.7	5.9	6.0	5.9	5.8	6.1	6.9	6.9	5.8										
1976	5.6	5.6	5.8	5.9	5.8	5.7	5.9	6.4	6.3	5.4	5.1									
1977	5.5	5.6	5.7	5.8	5.7	5.6	5.8	6.2	6.0	5.3	5.1	5.1								
1978	5.7	5.7	5.9	5.9	5.9	5.8	6.0	6.3	6.2	5.8	5.8	6.1	7.2							
1979	6.0	6.1	6.2	6.3	6.3	6.3	6.5	6.9	6.9	6.7	6.9	7.5	8.8	10.4						
1980	6.3	6.4	6.6	6.7	6.7	6.8	7.0	7.4	7.5	7.4	7.8	8.5	9.6	10.8	11.2					
1981	6.8	7.0	7.2	7.3	7.4	7.5	7.8	8.2	8.4	8.4	8.9	9.7	10.8	12.1	13.0	14.7				
1982	7.0	7.2	7.4	7.6	7.6	7.7	8.0	8.5	8.6	8.7	9.1	9.8	10.8	11.7	12.1	12.6	10.5			
1983	7.1	7.3	7.5	7.6	7.7	7.8	8.1	8.5	8.6	8.7	9.1	9.7	10.4	11.1	11.3	11.3	9.7	8.8		
1984	7.3	7.4	7.6	7.8	7.9	7.9	8.2	8.6	8.8	8.8	9.2	9.7	10.4	10.9	11.0	11.0	9.7	9.3	9.8	
1985	7.3	7.4	7.6	7.8	7.8	7.9	8.2	8.5	8.7	8.7	9.0	9.5	10.0	10.4	10.5	10.3	9.2	8.8	8.8	7.7
1986	7.3	7.4	7.5	7.7	7.7	7.8	8.1	8.4	8.5	8.5	8.8	9.1	9.6	9.9	9.8	9.6	8.6	8.1	7.9	6.9
1987	7.2	7.3	7.4	7.6	7.6	7.7	7.9	8.2	8.3	8.3	8.5	8.8	9.2	9.4	9.3	9.0	8.1	7.6	7.3	6.4
1988	7.1	7.2	7.4	7.5	7.6	7.6	7.8	8.1	8.1	8.1	8.3	8.6	8.9	9.1	8.9	8.7	7.8	7.4	7.1	6.4
1989	7.2	7.3	7.4	7.5	7.6	7.6	7.8	8.1	8.1	8.2	8.3	8.6	8.9	9.0	8.9	8.6	7.9	7.5	7.3	6.8
1990	7.2	7.3	7.5	7.6	7.6	7.7	7.8	8.1	8.1	8.1	8.3	8.5	8.8	8.9	8.8	8.5	7.9	7.6	7.4	7.0
1991	7.1	7.2	7.4	7.5	7.5	7.6	7.7	7.9	8.0	8.0	8.1	8.3	8.6	8.7	8.5	8.3	7.7	7.3	7.2	6.8
1992	7.0	7.1	7.2	7.3	7.3	7.4	7.5	7.7	7.7	7.7	7.8	8.0	8.2	8.3	8.1	7.9	7.3	6.9	6.7	6.4
1993	6.9	6.9	7.0	7.1	7.1	7.2	7.3	7.5	7.5	7.5	7.6	7.7	7.9	7.9	7.7	7.5	6.9	6.6	6.4	6.0
1994	6.8	6.8	6.9	7.0	7.0	7.0	7.1	7.3	7.3	7.3	7.4	7.5	7.6	7.7	7.5	7.2	6.7	6.3	6.1	5.8
1995	6.7	6.8	6.9	6.9	7.0	7.0	7.1	7.2	7.2	7.2	7.3	7.4	7.5	7.5	7.4	7.1	6.6	6.3	6.1	5.7
1996	6.7	6.7	6.8	6.9	6.9	6.9	7.0	7.1	7.2	7.1	7.2	7.3	7.4	7.4	7.2	7.0	6.5	6.2	6.0	5.7
1997	6.6	6.7	6.8	6.8	6.8	6.8	6.9	7.1	7.1	7.0	7.1	7.2	7.3	7.3	7.1	6.9	6.4	6.1	6.0	5.7
1998	6.6	6.6	6.7	6.8	6.8	6.8	6.9	7.0	7.0	6.9	7.0	7.1	7.2	7.2	7.0	6.8	6.3	6.1	5.9	5.6

To The End Of	From The Beginning Of 1986	1987	1988	1989	1990	1991	1992	1993	1994	1995	1996	1997	1998
1986	6.2												
1987	5.8	5.5											
1988	6.0	5.9	6.3										
1989	6.6	6.7	7.4	8.4									
1990	6.8	7.0	7.5	8.1	7.8								
1991	6.6	6.7	7.0	7.3	6.7	5.6							
1992	6.2	6.2	6.3	6.3	5.6	4.5	3.5						
1993	5.8	5.7	5.7	5.6	4.9	4.0	3.2	2.9					
1994	5.5	5.5	5.5	5.3	4.7	4.0	3.4	3.4	3.9				
1995	5.6	5.5	5.5	5.4	4.9	4.3	4.0	4.1	4.7	5.6			
1996	5.5	5.5	5.5	5.3	4.9	4.4	4.2	4.4	4.9	5.4	5.2		
1997	5.5	5.4	5.4	5.3	5.0	4.6	4.4	4.6	5.0	5.4	5.2	5.3	
1998	5.4	5.4	5.4	5.3	5.0	4.6	4.5	4.6	5.0	5.2	5.1	5.1	4.9

Table C-7 **Inflation**

(Page 1 of 5)

Rates of Return for all holding periods.

Percent per annum compounded annually.

From 1926 to 1998

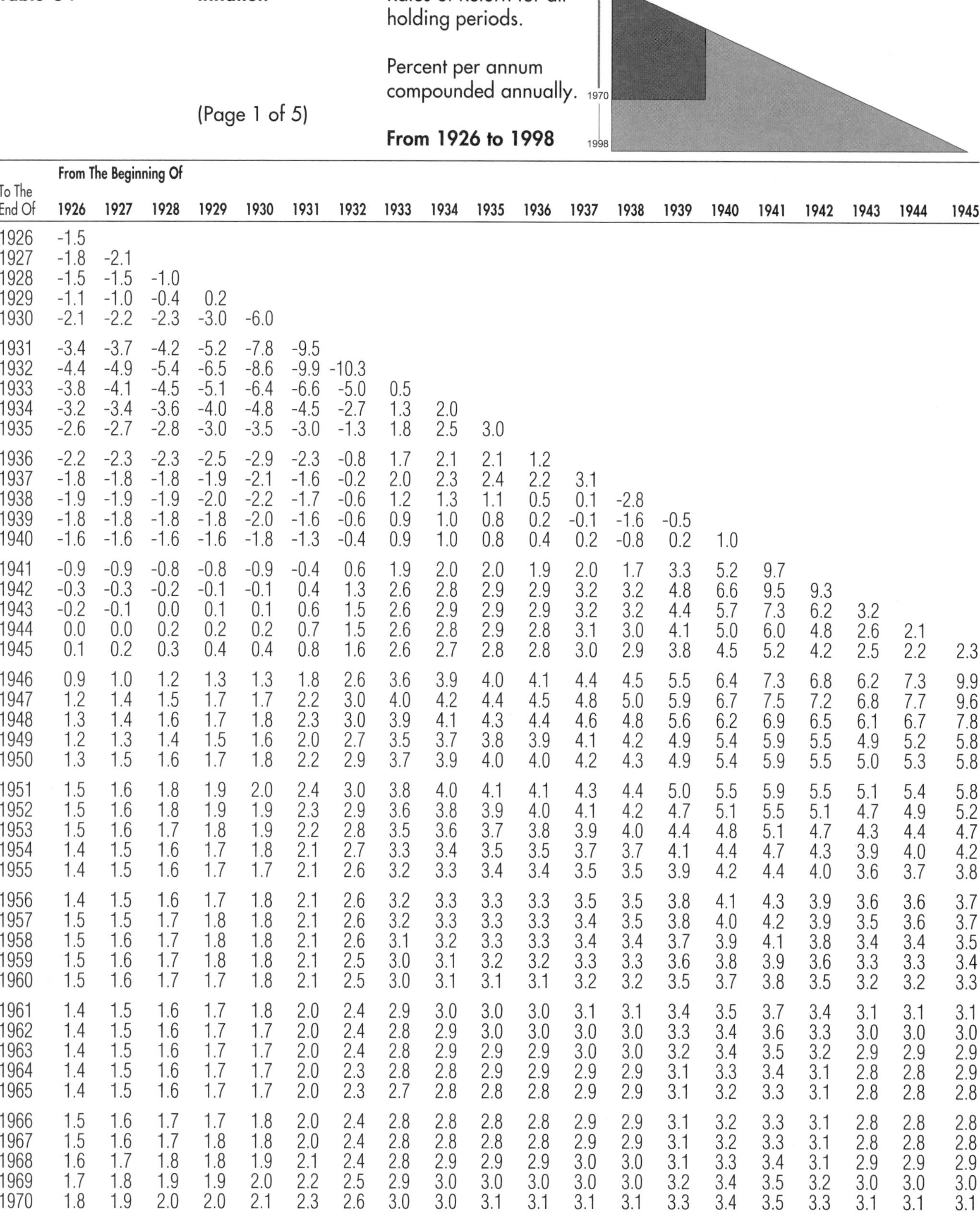

To The End Of	From The Beginning Of 1926	1927	1928	1929	1930	1931	1932	1933	1934	1935	1936	1937	1938	1939	1940	1941	1942	1943	1944	1945
1926	-1.5																			
1927	-1.8	-2.1																		
1928	-1.5	-1.5	-1.0																	
1929	-1.1	-1.0	-0.4	0.2																
1930	-2.1	-2.2	-2.3	-3.0	-6.0															
1931	-3.4	-3.7	-4.2	-5.2	-7.8	-9.5														
1932	-4.4	-4.9	-5.4	-6.5	-8.6	-9.9	-10.3													
1933	-3.8	-4.1	-4.5	-5.1	-6.4	-6.6	-5.0	0.5												
1934	-3.2	-3.4	-3.6	-4.0	-4.8	-4.5	-2.7	1.3	2.0											
1935	-2.6	-2.7	-2.8	-3.0	-3.5	-3.0	-1.3	1.8	2.5	3.0										
1936	-2.2	-2.3	-2.3	-2.5	-2.9	-2.3	-0.8	1.7	2.1	2.1	1.2									
1937	-1.8	-1.8	-1.8	-1.9	-2.1	-1.6	-0.2	2.0	2.3	2.4	2.2	3.1								
1938	-1.9	-1.9	-1.9	-2.0	-2.2	-1.7	-0.6	1.2	1.3	1.1	0.5	0.1	-2.8							
1939	-1.8	-1.8	-1.8	-1.8	-2.0	-1.6	-0.6	0.9	1.0	0.8	0.2	-0.1	-1.6	-0.5						
1940	-1.6	-1.6	-1.6	-1.6	-1.8	-1.3	-0.4	0.9	1.0	0.8	0.4	0.2	-0.8	0.2	1.0					
1941	-0.9	-0.9	-0.8	-0.8	-0.9	-0.4	0.6	1.9	2.0	2.0	1.9	2.0	1.7	3.3	5.2	9.7				
1942	-0.3	-0.3	-0.2	-0.1	-0.1	0.4	1.3	2.6	2.8	2.9	2.9	3.2	3.2	4.8	6.6	9.5	9.3			
1943	-0.2	-0.1	0.0	0.1	0.1	0.6	1.5	2.6	2.9	2.9	2.9	3.2	3.2	4.4	5.7	7.3	6.2	3.2		
1944	0.0	0.0	0.2	0.2	0.2	0.7	1.5	2.6	2.8	2.9	2.8	3.1	3.0	4.1	5.0	6.0	4.8	2.6	2.1	
1945	0.1	0.2	0.3	0.4	0.4	0.8	1.6	2.6	2.7	2.8	2.8	3.0	2.9	3.8	4.5	5.2	4.2	2.5	2.2	2.3
1946	0.9	1.0	1.2	1.3	1.3	1.8	2.6	3.6	3.9	4.0	4.1	4.4	4.5	5.5	6.4	7.3	6.8	6.2	7.3	9.9
1947	1.2	1.4	1.5	1.7	1.7	2.2	3.0	4.0	4.2	4.4	4.5	4.8	5.0	5.9	6.7	7.5	7.2	6.8	7.7	9.6
1948	1.3	1.4	1.6	1.7	1.8	2.3	3.0	3.9	4.1	4.3	4.4	4.6	4.8	5.6	6.2	6.9	6.5	6.1	6.7	7.8
1949	1.2	1.3	1.4	1.5	1.6	2.0	2.7	3.5	3.7	3.8	3.9	4.1	4.2	4.9	5.4	5.9	5.5	4.9	5.2	5.8
1950	1.3	1.5	1.6	1.7	1.8	2.2	2.9	3.7	3.9	4.0	4.0	4.2	4.3	4.9	5.4	5.9	5.5	5.0	5.3	5.8
1951	1.5	1.6	1.8	1.9	2.0	2.4	3.0	3.8	4.0	4.1	4.1	4.3	4.4	5.0	5.5	5.9	5.5	5.1	5.4	5.8
1952	1.5	1.6	1.8	1.9	1.9	2.3	2.9	3.6	3.8	3.9	4.0	4.1	4.2	4.7	5.1	5.5	5.1	4.7	4.9	5.2
1953	1.5	1.6	1.7	1.8	1.9	2.2	2.8	3.5	3.6	3.7	3.8	3.9	4.0	4.4	4.8	5.1	4.7	4.3	4.4	4.7
1954	1.4	1.5	1.6	1.7	1.8	2.1	2.7	3.3	3.4	3.5	3.5	3.7	3.7	4.1	4.4	4.7	4.3	3.9	4.0	4.2
1955	1.4	1.5	1.6	1.7	1.7	2.1	2.6	3.2	3.3	3.4	3.4	3.5	3.5	3.9	4.2	4.4	4.0	3.6	3.7	3.8
1956	1.4	1.5	1.6	1.7	1.8	2.1	2.6	3.2	3.3	3.3	3.3	3.5	3.5	3.8	4.1	4.3	3.9	3.6	3.6	3.7
1957	1.5	1.5	1.7	1.8	1.8	2.1	2.6	3.2	3.3	3.3	3.3	3.4	3.5	3.8	4.0	4.2	3.9	3.5	3.6	3.7
1958	1.5	1.6	1.7	1.8	1.8	2.1	2.6	3.1	3.2	3.3	3.3	3.4	3.4	3.7	3.9	4.1	3.8	3.4	3.4	3.5
1959	1.5	1.6	1.7	1.8	1.8	2.1	2.5	3.0	3.1	3.2	3.2	3.3	3.3	3.6	3.8	3.9	3.6	3.3	3.3	3.4
1960	1.5	1.6	1.7	1.7	1.8	2.1	2.5	3.0	3.1	3.1	3.1	3.2	3.2	3.5	3.7	3.8	3.5	3.2	3.2	3.3
1961	1.4	1.5	1.6	1.7	1.8	2.0	2.4	2.9	3.0	3.0	3.0	3.1	3.1	3.4	3.5	3.7	3.4	3.1	3.1	3.1
1962	1.4	1.5	1.6	1.7	1.7	2.0	2.4	2.8	2.9	3.0	3.0	3.0	3.0	3.3	3.4	3.6	3.3	3.0	3.0	3.0
1963	1.4	1.5	1.6	1.7	1.7	2.0	2.4	2.8	2.9	2.9	2.9	3.0	3.0	3.2	3.4	3.5	3.2	2.9	2.9	2.9
1964	1.4	1.5	1.6	1.7	1.7	2.0	2.3	2.8	2.8	2.9	2.9	2.9	2.9	3.1	3.3	3.4	3.1	2.8	2.8	2.9
1965	1.4	1.5	1.6	1.7	1.7	2.0	2.3	2.7	2.8	2.8	2.8	2.9	2.9	3.1	3.2	3.3	3.1	2.8	2.8	2.8
1966	1.5	1.6	1.7	1.7	1.8	2.0	2.4	2.8	2.8	2.8	2.8	2.9	2.9	3.1	3.2	3.3	3.1	2.8	2.8	2.8
1967	1.5	1.6	1.7	1.8	1.8	2.0	2.4	2.8	2.8	2.8	2.8	2.9	2.9	3.1	3.2	3.3	3.1	2.8	2.8	2.8
1968	1.6	1.7	1.8	1.8	1.9	2.1	2.4	2.8	2.9	2.9	2.9	3.0	3.0	3.1	3.3	3.4	3.1	2.9	2.9	2.9
1969	1.7	1.8	1.9	1.9	2.0	2.2	2.5	2.9	3.0	3.0	3.0	3.0	3.0	3.2	3.4	3.5	3.2	3.0	3.0	3.0
1970	1.8	1.9	2.0	2.0	2.1	2.3	2.6	3.0	3.0	3.1	3.1	3.1	3.1	3.3	3.4	3.5	3.3	3.1	3.1	3.1

Table C-7 **Inflation**

Rates of Return for all holding periods.

Percent per annum compounded annually.

(Page 2 of 5)

From 1926 to 1998

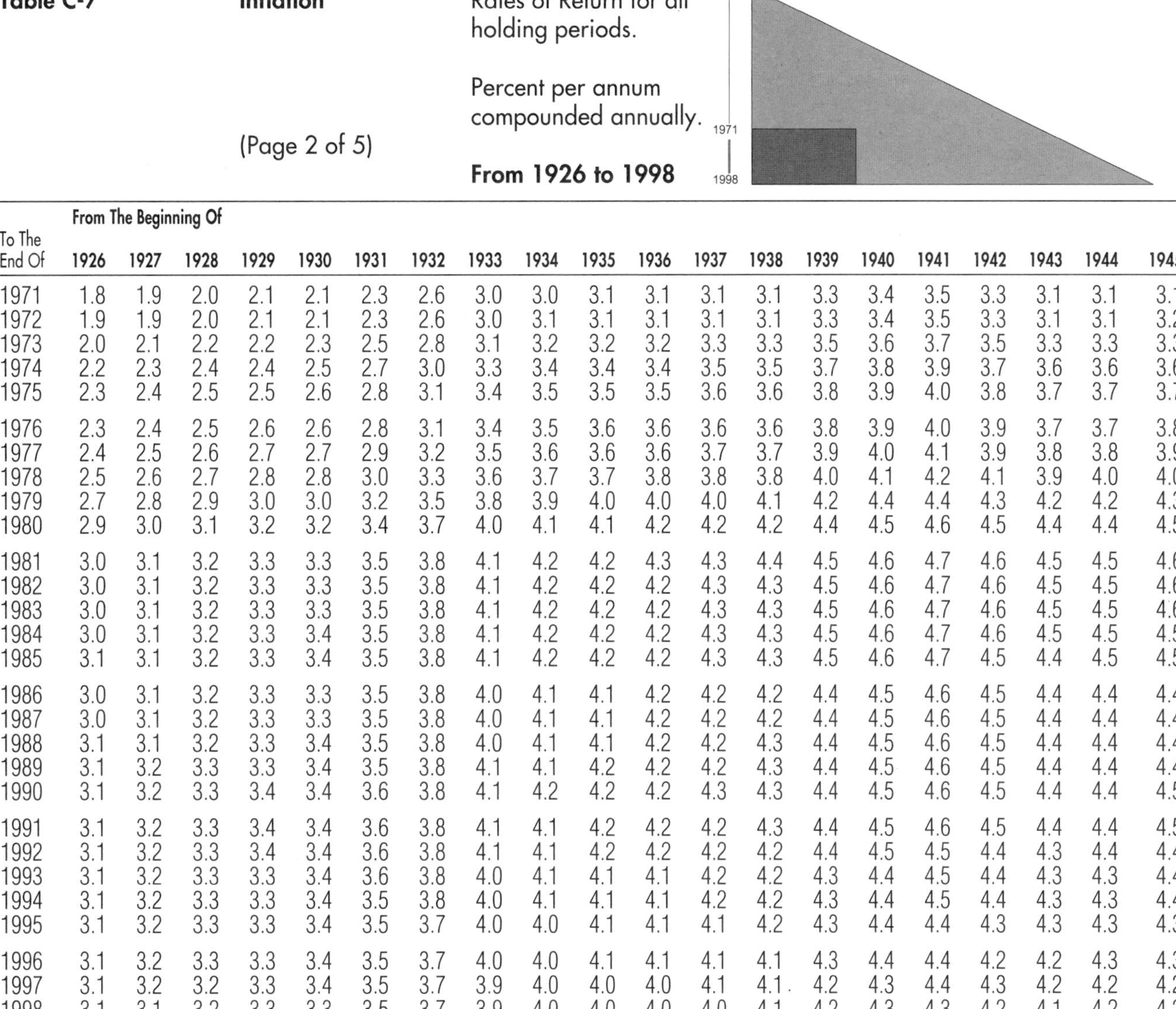

To The End Of	From The Beginning Of 1926	1927	1928	1929	1930	1931	1932	1933	1934	1935	1936	1937	1938	1939	1940	1941	1942	1943	1944	1945
1971	1.8	1.9	2.0	2.1	2.1	2.3	2.6	3.0	3.0	3.1	3.1	3.1	3.1	3.3	3.4	3.5	3.3	3.1	3.1	3.1
1972	1.9	1.9	2.0	2.1	2.1	2.3	2.6	3.0	3.1	3.1	3.1	3.1	3.1	3.3	3.4	3.5	3.3	3.1	3.1	3.2
1973	2.0	2.1	2.2	2.2	2.3	2.5	2.8	3.1	3.2	3.2	3.2	3.3	3.3	3.5	3.6	3.7	3.5	3.3	3.3	3.3
1974	2.2	2.3	2.4	2.4	2.5	2.7	3.0	3.3	3.4	3.4	3.4	3.5	3.5	3.7	3.8	3.9	3.7	3.6	3.6	3.6
1975	2.3	2.4	2.5	2.5	2.6	2.8	3.1	3.4	3.5	3.5	3.5	3.6	3.6	3.8	3.9	4.0	3.8	3.7	3.7	3.7
1976	2.3	2.4	2.5	2.6	2.6	2.8	3.1	3.4	3.5	3.6	3.6	3.6	3.6	3.8	3.9	4.0	3.9	3.7	3.7	3.8
1977	2.4	2.5	2.6	2.7	2.7	2.9	3.2	3.5	3.6	3.6	3.6	3.7	3.7	3.9	4.0	4.1	3.9	3.8	3.8	3.9
1978	2.5	2.6	2.7	2.8	2.8	3.0	3.3	3.6	3.7	3.7	3.8	3.8	3.8	4.0	4.1	4.2	4.1	3.9	4.0	4.0
1979	2.7	2.8	2.9	3.0	3.0	3.2	3.5	3.8	3.9	4.0	4.0	4.0	4.1	4.2	4.4	4.4	4.3	4.2	4.2	4.3
1980	2.9	3.0	3.1	3.2	3.2	3.4	3.7	4.0	4.1	4.1	4.2	4.2	4.2	4.4	4.5	4.6	4.5	4.4	4.4	4.5
1981	3.0	3.1	3.2	3.3	3.3	3.5	3.8	4.1	4.2	4.2	4.3	4.3	4.4	4.5	4.6	4.7	4.6	4.5	4.5	4.6
1982	3.0	3.1	3.2	3.3	3.3	3.5	3.8	4.1	4.2	4.2	4.2	4.3	4.3	4.5	4.6	4.7	4.6	4.5	4.5	4.6
1983	3.0	3.1	3.2	3.3	3.3	3.5	3.8	4.1	4.2	4.2	4.2	4.3	4.3	4.5	4.6	4.7	4.6	4.5	4.5	4.6
1984	3.0	3.1	3.2	3.3	3.4	3.5	3.8	4.1	4.2	4.2	4.2	4.3	4.3	4.5	4.6	4.7	4.6	4.5	4.5	4.5
1985	3.1	3.1	3.2	3.3	3.4	3.5	3.8	4.1	4.2	4.2	4.2	4.3	4.3	4.5	4.6	4.7	4.5	4.4	4.5	4.5
1986	3.0	3.1	3.2	3.3	3.3	3.5	3.8	4.0	4.1	4.1	4.2	4.2	4.2	4.4	4.5	4.6	4.5	4.4	4.4	4.4
1987	3.0	3.1	3.2	3.3	3.3	3.5	3.8	4.0	4.1	4.1	4.2	4.2	4.2	4.4	4.5	4.6	4.5	4.4	4.4	4.4
1988	3.1	3.1	3.2	3.3	3.4	3.5	3.8	4.0	4.1	4.1	4.2	4.2	4.3	4.4	4.5	4.6	4.5	4.4	4.4	4.4
1989	3.1	3.2	3.3	3.3	3.4	3.5	3.8	4.1	4.1	4.2	4.2	4.2	4.3	4.4	4.5	4.6	4.5	4.4	4.4	4.4
1990	3.1	3.2	3.3	3.4	3.4	3.6	3.8	4.1	4.2	4.2	4.2	4.3	4.3	4.4	4.5	4.6	4.5	4.4	4.4	4.5
1991	3.1	3.2	3.3	3.4	3.4	3.6	3.8	4.1	4.1	4.2	4.2	4.2	4.3	4.4	4.5	4.6	4.5	4.4	4.4	4.5
1992	3.1	3.2	3.3	3.4	3.4	3.6	3.8	4.1	4.1	4.2	4.2	4.2	4.2	4.4	4.5	4.5	4.4	4.3	4.4	4.4
1993	3.1	3.2	3.3	3.3	3.4	3.6	3.8	4.0	4.1	4.1	4.1	4.2	4.2	4.3	4.4	4.5	4.4	4.3	4.3	4.4
1994	3.1	3.2	3.3	3.3	3.4	3.5	3.8	4.0	4.1	4.1	4.1	4.2	4.2	4.3	4.4	4.5	4.4	4.3	4.3	4.4
1995	3.1	3.2	3.3	3.3	3.4	3.5	3.7	4.0	4.0	4.1	4.1	4.1	4.2	4.3	4.4	4.4	4.3	4.3	4.3	4.3
1996	3.1	3.2	3.3	3.3	3.4	3.5	3.7	4.0	4.0	4.1	4.1	4.1	4.1	4.3	4.4	4.4	4.2	4.2	4.3	4.3
1997	3.1	3.2	3.2	3.3	3.4	3.5	3.7	3.9	4.0	4.0	4.0	4.1	4.1	4.2	4.3	4.4	4.3	4.2	4.2	4.2
1998	3.1	3.1	3.2	3.3	3.3	3.5	3.7	3.9	4.0	4.0	4.0	4.0	4.1	4.2	4.3	4.3	4.2	4.1	4.2	4.2

Table C-7 **Inflation**

(Page 3 of 5)

Rates of Return for all holding periods.

Percent per annum compounded annually.

From 1926 to 1998

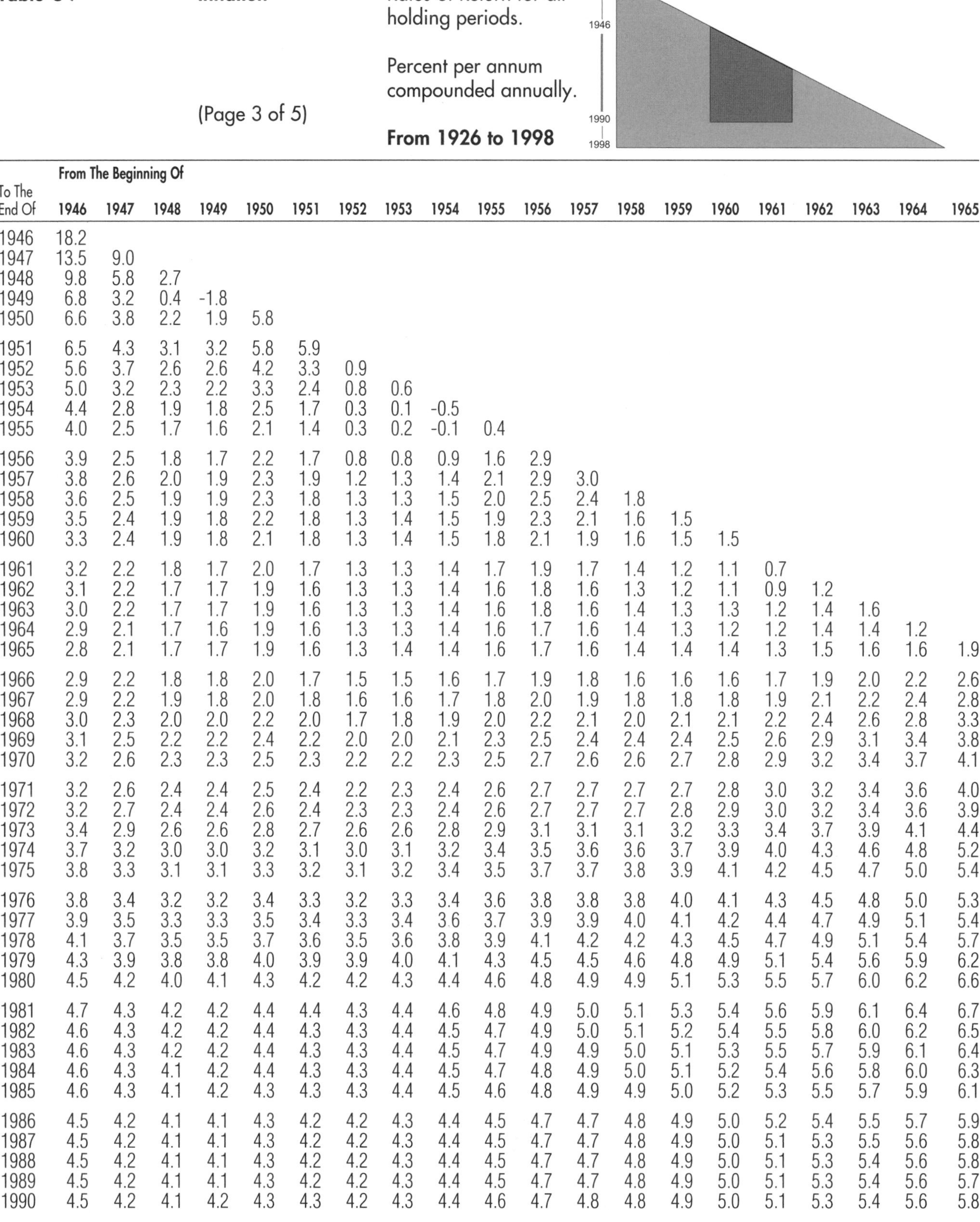

To The End Of	From The Beginning Of 1946	1947	1948	1949	1950	1951	1952	1953	1954	1955	1956	1957	1958	1959	1960	1961	1962	1963	1964	1965
1946	18.2																			
1947	13.5	9.0																		
1948	9.8	5.8	2.7																	
1949	6.8	3.2	0.4	-1.8																
1950	6.6	3.8	2.2	1.9	5.8															
1951	6.5	4.3	3.1	3.2	5.8	5.9														
1952	5.6	3.7	2.6	2.6	4.2	3.3	0.9													
1953	5.0	3.2	2.3	2.2	3.3	2.4	0.8	0.6												
1954	4.4	2.8	1.9	1.8	2.5	1.7	0.3	0.1	-0.5											
1955	4.0	2.5	1.7	1.6	2.1	1.4	0.3	0.2	-0.1	0.4										
1956	3.9	2.5	1.8	1.7	2.2	1.7	0.8	0.8	0.9	1.6	2.9									
1957	3.8	2.6	2.0	1.9	2.3	1.9	1.2	1.3	1.4	2.1	2.9	3.0								
1958	3.6	2.5	1.9	1.9	2.3	1.8	1.3	1.3	1.5	2.0	2.5	2.4	1.8							
1959	3.5	2.4	1.9	1.8	2.2	1.8	1.3	1.4	1.5	1.9	2.3	2.1	1.6	1.5						
1960	3.3	2.4	1.9	1.8	2.1	1.8	1.3	1.4	1.5	1.8	2.1	1.9	1.6	1.5	1.5					
1961	3.2	2.2	1.8	1.7	2.0	1.7	1.3	1.3	1.4	1.7	1.9	1.7	1.4	1.2	1.1	0.7				
1962	3.1	2.2	1.7	1.7	1.9	1.6	1.3	1.3	1.4	1.6	1.8	1.6	1.3	1.2	1.1	0.9	1.2			
1963	3.0	2.2	1.7	1.7	1.9	1.6	1.3	1.3	1.4	1.6	1.8	1.6	1.4	1.3	1.3	1.2	1.4	1.6		
1964	2.9	2.1	1.7	1.6	1.9	1.6	1.3	1.3	1.4	1.6	1.7	1.6	1.4	1.3	1.2	1.2	1.4	1.4	1.2	
1965	2.8	2.1	1.7	1.7	1.9	1.6	1.3	1.4	1.4	1.6	1.7	1.6	1.4	1.4	1.4	1.3	1.5	1.6	1.6	1.9
1966	2.9	2.2	1.8	1.8	2.0	1.7	1.5	1.5	1.6	1.7	1.9	1.8	1.6	1.6	1.6	1.7	1.9	2.0	2.2	2.6
1967	2.9	2.2	1.9	1.8	2.0	1.8	1.6	1.6	1.7	1.8	2.0	1.9	1.8	1.8	1.8	1.9	2.1	2.2	2.4	2.8
1968	3.0	2.3	2.0	2.0	2.2	2.0	1.7	1.8	1.9	2.0	2.2	2.1	2.0	2.1	2.1	2.2	2.4	2.6	2.8	3.3
1969	3.1	2.5	2.2	2.2	2.4	2.2	2.0	2.0	2.1	2.3	2.5	2.4	2.4	2.4	2.5	2.6	2.9	3.1	3.4	3.8
1970	3.2	2.6	2.3	2.3	2.5	2.3	2.2	2.2	2.3	2.5	2.7	2.6	2.6	2.7	2.8	2.9	3.2	3.4	3.7	4.1
1971	3.2	2.6	2.4	2.4	2.5	2.4	2.2	2.3	2.4	2.6	2.7	2.7	2.7	2.7	2.8	3.0	3.2	3.4	3.6	4.0
1972	3.2	2.7	2.4	2.4	2.6	2.4	2.3	2.3	2.4	2.6	2.7	2.7	2.7	2.8	2.9	3.0	3.2	3.4	3.6	3.9
1973	3.4	2.9	2.6	2.6	2.8	2.7	2.6	2.6	2.8	2.9	3.1	3.1	3.1	3.2	3.3	3.4	3.7	3.9	4.1	4.4
1974	3.7	3.2	3.0	3.0	3.2	3.1	3.0	3.1	3.2	3.4	3.5	3.6	3.6	3.7	3.9	4.0	4.3	4.6	4.8	5.2
1975	3.8	3.3	3.1	3.1	3.3	3.2	3.1	3.2	3.4	3.5	3.7	3.7	3.8	3.9	4.1	4.2	4.5	4.7	5.0	5.4
1976	3.8	3.4	3.2	3.2	3.4	3.3	3.2	3.3	3.4	3.6	3.8	3.8	3.8	4.0	4.1	4.3	4.5	4.8	5.0	5.3
1977	3.9	3.5	3.3	3.3	3.5	3.4	3.3	3.4	3.6	3.7	3.9	3.9	4.0	4.1	4.2	4.4	4.7	4.9	5.1	5.4
1978	4.1	3.7	3.5	3.5	3.7	3.6	3.5	3.6	3.8	3.9	4.1	4.2	4.2	4.3	4.5	4.7	4.9	5.1	5.4	5.7
1979	4.3	3.9	3.8	3.8	4.0	3.9	3.9	4.0	4.1	4.3	4.5	4.5	4.6	4.8	4.9	5.1	5.4	5.6	5.9	6.2
1980	4.5	4.2	4.0	4.1	4.3	4.2	4.2	4.3	4.4	4.6	4.8	4.9	4.9	5.1	5.3	5.5	5.7	6.0	6.2	6.6
1981	4.7	4.3	4.2	4.2	4.4	4.4	4.3	4.4	4.6	4.8	4.9	5.0	5.1	5.3	5.4	5.6	5.9	6.1	6.4	6.7
1982	4.6	4.3	4.2	4.2	4.4	4.3	4.3	4.4	4.5	4.7	4.9	5.0	5.1	5.2	5.4	5.5	5.8	6.0	6.2	6.5
1983	4.6	4.3	4.2	4.2	4.4	4.3	4.3	4.4	4.5	4.7	4.9	4.9	5.0	5.1	5.3	5.5	5.7	5.9	6.1	6.4
1984	4.6	4.3	4.1	4.2	4.4	4.3	4.3	4.4	4.5	4.7	4.8	4.9	5.0	5.1	5.2	5.4	5.6	5.8	6.0	6.3
1985	4.6	4.3	4.1	4.2	4.3	4.3	4.3	4.4	4.5	4.6	4.8	4.9	4.9	5.0	5.2	5.3	5.5	5.7	5.9	6.1
1986	4.5	4.2	4.1	4.1	4.3	4.2	4.2	4.3	4.4	4.5	4.7	4.7	4.8	4.9	5.0	5.2	5.4	5.5	5.7	5.9
1987	4.5	4.2	4.1	4.1	4.3	4.2	4.2	4.3	4.4	4.5	4.7	4.7	4.8	4.9	5.0	5.1	5.3	5.5	5.6	5.8
1988	4.5	4.2	4.1	4.1	4.3	4.2	4.2	4.3	4.4	4.5	4.7	4.7	4.8	4.9	5.0	5.1	5.3	5.4	5.6	5.8
1989	4.5	4.2	4.1	4.1	4.3	4.2	4.2	4.3	4.4	4.5	4.7	4.7	4.8	4.9	5.0	5.1	5.3	5.4	5.6	5.7
1990	4.5	4.2	4.1	4.2	4.3	4.3	4.2	4.3	4.4	4.6	4.7	4.8	4.8	4.9	5.0	5.1	5.3	5.4	5.6	5.8

Table C-7 **Inflation**

(Page 4 of 5)

Rates of Return for all holding periods.

Percent per annum compounded annually.

From 1926 to 1998

1926 1946 1965 1998
1926
1991
1998

To The End Of	From The Beginning Of 1946	1947	1948	1949	1950	1951	1952	1953	1954	1955	1956	1957	1958	1959	1960	1961	1962	1963	1964	1965
1991	4.5	4.2	4.1	4.1	4.3	4.3	4.2	4.3	4.4	4.5	4.7	4.7	4.8	4.8	5.0	5.1	5.2	5.4	5.5	5.7
1992	4.5	4.2	4.1	4.1	4.3	4.2	4.2	4.3	4.4	4.5	4.6	4.7	4.7	4.8	4.9	5.0	5.1	5.3	5.4	5.6
1993	4.4	4.2	4.1	4.1	4.2	4.2	4.1	4.2	4.3	4.4	4.6	4.6	4.6	4.7	4.8	4.9	5.1	5.2	5.3	5.5
1994	4.4	4.1	4.0	4.1	4.2	4.2	4.1	4.2	4.3	4.4	4.5	4.5	4.6	4.7	4.8	4.9	5.0	5.1	5.2	5.4
1995	4.4	4.1	4.0	4.0	4.2	4.1	4.1	4.2	4.2	4.4	4.5	4.5	4.5	4.6	4.7	4.8	4.9	5.0	5.1	5.3
1996	4.3	4.1	4.0	4.0	4.1	4.1	4.1	4.1	4.2	4.3	4.4	4.5	4.5	4.6	4.7	4.8	4.9	5.0	5.1	5.2
1997	4.3	4.0	3.9	4.0	4.1	4.0	4.0	4.1	4.2	4.3	4.4	4.4	4.4	4.5	4.6	4.7	4.8	4.9	5.0	5.1
1998	4.2	4.0	3.9	3.9	4.0	4.0	4.0	4.0	4.1	4.2	4.3	4.3	4.4	4.4	4.5	4.6	4.7	4.8	4.9	5.0

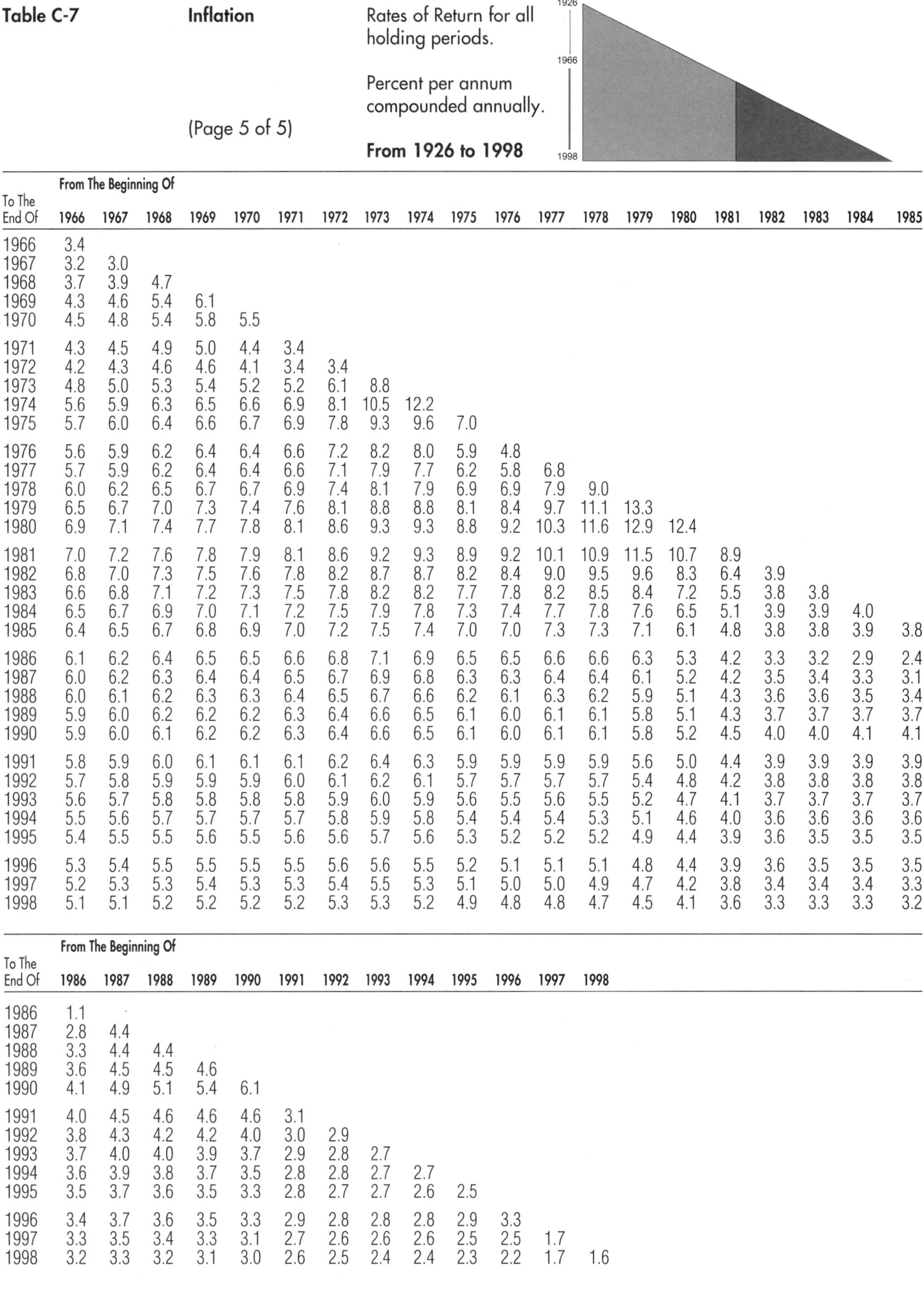

Table C-7 **Inflation**

(Page 5 of 5)

Rates of Return for all holding periods.

Percent per annum compounded annually.

From 1926 to 1998

To The End Of	From The Beginning Of 1966	1967	1968	1969	1970	1971	1972	1973	1974	1975	1976	1977	1978	1979	1980	1981	1982	1983	1984	1985
1966	3.4																			
1967	3.2	3.0																		
1968	3.7	3.9	4.7																	
1969	4.3	4.6	5.4	6.1																
1970	4.5	4.8	5.4	5.8	5.5															
1971	4.3	4.5	4.9	5.0	4.4	3.4														
1972	4.2	4.3	4.6	4.6	4.1	3.4	3.4													
1973	4.8	5.0	5.3	5.4	5.2	5.2	6.1	8.8												
1974	5.6	5.9	6.3	6.5	6.6	6.9	8.1	10.5	12.2											
1975	5.7	6.0	6.4	6.6	6.7	6.9	7.8	9.3	9.6	7.0										
1976	5.6	5.9	6.2	6.4	6.4	6.6	7.2	8.2	8.0	5.9	4.8									
1977	5.7	5.9	6.2	6.4	6.4	6.6	7.1	7.9	7.7	6.2	5.8	6.8								
1978	6.0	6.2	6.5	6.7	6.7	6.9	7.4	8.1	7.9	6.9	6.9	7.9	9.0							
1979	6.5	6.7	7.0	7.3	7.4	7.6	8.1	8.8	8.8	8.1	8.4	9.7	11.1	13.3						
1980	6.9	7.1	7.4	7.7	7.8	8.1	8.6	9.3	9.3	8.8	9.2	10.3	11.6	12.9	12.4					
1981	7.0	7.2	7.6	7.8	7.9	8.1	8.6	9.2	9.3	8.9	9.2	10.1	10.9	11.5	10.7	8.9				
1982	6.8	7.0	7.3	7.5	7.6	7.8	8.2	8.7	8.7	8.2	8.4	9.0	9.5	9.6	8.3	6.4	3.9			
1983	6.6	6.8	7.1	7.2	7.3	7.5	7.8	8.2	8.2	7.7	7.8	8.2	8.5	8.4	7.2	5.5	3.8	3.8		
1984	6.5	6.7	6.9	7.0	7.1	7.2	7.5	7.9	7.8	7.3	7.4	7.7	7.8	7.6	6.5	5.1	3.9	3.9	4.0	
1985	6.4	6.5	6.7	6.8	6.9	7.0	7.2	7.5	7.4	7.0	7.0	7.3	7.3	7.1	6.1	4.8	3.8	3.8	3.9	3.8
1986	6.1	6.2	6.4	6.5	6.5	6.6	6.8	7.1	6.9	6.5	6.5	6.6	6.6	6.3	5.3	4.2	3.3	3.2	2.9	2.4
1987	6.0	6.2	6.3	6.4	6.4	6.5	6.7	6.9	6.8	6.3	6.3	6.4	6.4	6.1	5.2	4.2	3.5	3.4	3.3	3.1
1988	6.0	6.1	6.2	6.3	6.3	6.4	6.5	6.7	6.6	6.2	6.1	6.3	6.2	5.9	5.1	4.3	3.6	3.6	3.5	3.4
1989	5.9	6.0	6.2	6.2	6.2	6.3	6.4	6.6	6.5	6.1	6.0	6.1	6.1	5.8	5.1	4.3	3.7	3.7	3.7	3.7
1990	5.9	6.0	6.1	6.2	6.2	6.3	6.4	6.6	6.5	6.1	6.0	6.1	6.1	5.8	5.2	4.5	4.0	4.0	4.1	4.1
1991	5.8	5.9	6.0	6.1	6.1	6.1	6.2	6.4	6.3	5.9	5.9	5.9	5.9	5.6	5.0	4.4	3.9	3.9	3.9	3.9
1992	5.7	5.8	5.9	5.9	5.9	6.0	6.1	6.2	6.1	5.7	5.7	5.7	5.7	5.4	4.8	4.2	3.8	3.8	3.8	3.8
1993	5.6	5.7	5.8	5.8	5.8	5.8	5.9	6.0	5.9	5.6	5.5	5.6	5.5	5.2	4.7	4.1	3.7	3.7	3.7	3.7
1994	5.5	5.6	5.7	5.7	5.7	5.7	5.8	5.9	5.8	5.4	5.4	5.4	5.3	5.1	4.6	4.0	3.6	3.6	3.6	3.6
1995	5.4	5.5	5.5	5.6	5.5	5.6	5.6	5.7	5.6	5.3	5.2	5.2	5.2	4.9	4.4	3.9	3.6	3.5	3.5	3.5
1996	5.3	5.4	5.5	5.5	5.5	5.5	5.6	5.6	5.5	5.2	5.1	5.1	5.1	4.8	4.4	3.9	3.6	3.5	3.5	3.5
1997	5.2	5.3	5.3	5.4	5.3	5.3	5.4	5.5	5.3	5.1	5.0	5.0	4.9	4.7	4.2	3.8	3.4	3.4	3.4	3.3
1998	5.1	5.1	5.2	5.2	5.2	5.2	5.3	5.3	5.2	4.9	4.8	4.8	4.7	4.5	4.1	3.6	3.3	3.3	3.3	3.2

To The End Of	From The Beginning Of 1986	1987	1988	1989	1990	1991	1992	1993	1994	1995	1996	1997	1998
1986	1.1												
1987	2.8	4.4											
1988	3.3	4.4	4.4										
1989	3.6	4.5	4.5	4.6									
1990	4.1	4.9	5.1	5.4	6.1								
1991	4.0	4.5	4.6	4.6	4.6	3.1							
1992	3.8	4.3	4.2	4.2	4.0	3.0	2.9						
1993	3.7	4.0	4.0	3.9	3.7	2.9	2.8	2.7					
1994	3.6	3.9	3.8	3.7	3.5	2.8	2.8	2.7	2.7				
1995	3.5	3.7	3.6	3.5	3.3	2.8	2.7	2.7	2.6	2.5			
1996	3.4	3.7	3.6	3.5	3.3	2.9	2.8	2.8	2.8	2.9	3.3		
1997	3.3	3.5	3.4	3.3	3.1	2.7	2.6	2.6	2.6	2.5	2.5	1.7	
1998	3.2	3.3	3.2	3.1	3.0	2.6	2.5	2.4	2.4	2.3	2.2	1.7	1.6

STOCKS
BONDS
BILLS
AND
INFLATION

Glossary

Glossary

American Stock Exchange (AMEX) One of the largest stock exchanges in the U.S. Securities traded on this exchange are generally of small to medium-size companies.

Arbitrage Pricing Theory (APT) A model in which multiple betas and multiple risk premia are used to generate the expected return of a security.

Arithmetic Mean Return A simple average of a series of returns.

Asset Class A grouping of securities with similar characteristics and properties. As a group, these securities will tend to react in a specific way to economic factors (e.g., stocks, bonds, and real estate are all asset classes).

Basic Series The seven primary time series representing Stocks, Bonds, Bills and Inflation: large company stocks, small company stocks, long-term corporate bonds, long-term government bonds, intermediate-term government bonds, U.S. Treasury bills, and inflation.

Beta The systematic risk of a security as estimated by regressing the security's returns against the market portfolio's returns. The slope of the regression is beta.

Callable Bonds Bonds that the issuer has the right to redeem (or call) prior to maturity at a specified price.

Capital Appreciation Return The component of total return which results from the price change of an asset class over a given period.

Capital Asset Pricing Model (CAPM) A model in which the cost of capital for any security or portfolio of securities equals the riskless rate plus a risk premium that is proportionate to the amount of systematic risk of the security or portfolio.

Convexity The property of a bond that its price does not change in proportion to changes in its yield. A bond with positive convexity will rise in price faster than the rate at which yields decline, and will fall in price slower that the rate at which yields rise.

Correlation Coefficient The degree of association or strength between two variables. A value of +1 indicates a perfectly positive relationship, -1 indicates a perfectly inverse relationship, and 0 indicates no relationship between the variables.

Cost of Capital The discount rate which should be used to derive the present value of an asset's future cash flows.

Coupon The periodic interest payment on a bond.

Decile One of 10 portfolios formed by ranking a set of securities by some criteria and dividing them into 10 equally populated subsets. The New York Stock Exchange market capitalization deciles are formed by ranking the stocks traded on the Exchange by their market capitalization.

Derived Series The components or elemental parts of the returns of the seven primary Stocks, Bonds, Bills, and Inflation asset classes. The two categories of derived series are: risk premia, or payoffs for taking various types of risk, and inflation-adjusted asset returns.

Discount Rate The rate used to convert a series of future cash flows to a single present value.

Duration (Macauley Duration) The weighted average term-to-maturity of a security's cash flows. The weights are the present values of each cash flow as a percentage of the present value of all cash flows.

Efficient Frontier The set of portfolios that provides the highest expected returns for their respective risk levels. The efficient frontier is calculated for a given set of assets with estimates of expected return and standard deviation for each asset, and a correlation coefficient for each pair of asset returns.

Geometric Mean Return The compound rate of return. The geometric mean of a return series is a measure of the actual average performance of a portfolio over a given time period.

Histogram A bar graph in which the frequency of occurrence for each class of data is represented by the relative height of the bars.

Income Return The component of total return which results from a periodic cash flow, such as dividends.

Index Value The cumulative value of returns on a dollar amount invested. It is used when measuring investment performance and computing returns over non-calendar periods.

Inflation The rate of change in consumer prices. The Consumer Price Index for All Urban Consumers (CPI-U), not seasonally adjusted, is used to measure inflation. Prior to January 1978, the CPI (as compared with CPI-U) was used. Both inflation measures are constructed by the U.S. Department of Labor, Bureau of Labor Statistics, Washington.

Inflation-Adjusted Returns Asset class returns in real terms. The inflation-adjusted return of an asset is calculated by geometrically subtracting inflation from the asset's nominal return.

Intermediate-Term Government Bonds A one-bond portfolio with a maturity near 5 years.

Large Company Stocks The Standard and Poor's 500 Stock Composite Index® (S&P 500).

Logarithmic Scale A scale in which equal percentage changes are represented by equal distances.

Lognormal Distribution The distribution of a random variable whose natural logarithm is normally distributed. A lognormal distribution is skewed so that a higher proportion of possible returns exceed the expected value versus falling short of the expected value. In the lognormal forecasting model, one plus the total return has a lognormal distribution.

Long-Term Corporate Bonds Salomon Brothers long-term, high-grade corporate bond total return index.

Long-Term Government Bonds A one-bond portfolio with a maturity near 20 years.

Low-cap Stocks The portfolio of stocks comprised of the 6-8th deciles of the New York Stock Exchange.

Market Capitalization The current market price of a security determined by the most recently recorded trade multiplied by the number of issues outstanding of that security. For equities, market capitalization is computed by taking the share price of a stock times the number of shares outstanding.

Mean-Variance Optimization (MVO) The process of identifying portfolios that have the highest possible return for a given level of risk or the lowest possible risk for a given return. The inputs for MVO are return, standard deviation, and the correlation coefficients of returns for each pair of asset classes.

Micro-cap Stocks The portfolio of stocks comprised of the 9-10th deciles of the New York Stock Exchange.

Mid-cap Stocks The portfolio of stocks comprised of the 3-5th deciles of the New York Stock Exchange.

National Association of Securities Dealers Automated Quotation System (NASDAQ) A computerized system showing current bid and asked prices for stocks traded on the Over-the-Counter market, as well as some New York Stock Exchange listed stocks.

New York Stock Exchange (NYSE) The largest and oldest stock exchange in the United States, founded in 1792.

Over-the-Counter Market (OTC) A market in which assets are not traded on an organized exchange like the New York Stock Exchange, but rather through various dealers or market makers who are linked electronically.

Quintile One of 5 portfolios formed by ranking a set of securities by some criteria and dividing them into 5 equally populated subsets. The micro-cap stocks are a market capitalization quintile.

Return see **Total Return**

Risk The extent to which an investment is subject to uncertainty. Risk may be measured by standard deviation.

Riskless Rate of Return The return on a riskless investment; it is the rate of return an investor can obtain without taking market risk.

Risk Premium The reward which investors require to accept the uncertain outcomes associated with securities. The size of the risk premium will depend upon the type and extent of the risk.

Rolling Period Returns A series of overlapping contiguous periods of returns defined by the frequency of the data under examination. In examining 5-year rolling periods of returns for annual data that starts in 1970, the first rolling period would be 1970–1974, the second rolling period would be 1971–1975, the third rolling period would be 1972–1976, etc.

Serial Correlation (Autocorrelation) The degree to which the return of a given series is related from period to period. A serial correlation near +1 or -1 indicates that returns are predictable from one period to the next; a serial correlation near zero indicates returns are random or unpredictable.

Small Company Stocks A portfolio of stocks represented by the fifth capitalization quintile of stocks on the NYSE for 1926–1981 and the performance of the Dimensional Fund Advisors (DFA) Small Company Fund thereafter.

Standard Deviation A measure of the dispersion of returns of an asset, or the extent to which returns vary from the arithmetic mean. It represents the volatility or risk of an asset. The greater the degree of dispersion, the greater the risk associated with the asset.

Systematic Risk The risk that is unavoidable according to CAPM. It is the risk that is common to all risky securities and cannot be eliminated through diversification. The amount of an asset's systematic risk is measured by its beta.

Total Return A measure of performance of an asset class over a designated time period. It is comprised of income return, reinvestment of income return and capital appreciation return components.

Treasury Bills A one-bill portfolio containing, at the beginning of each month, the bill having the shortest maturity not less than one month.

Unsystematic Risk The portion of total risk specific to an individual security that can be avoided through diversification.

Volatility The extent to which an asset's returns fluctuate from period to period.

Yield The yield to maturity is the internal rate of return that equates the bond's price with the stream of cash flows promised to the bondholder. The yield on a stock is the percentage rate of return paid in dividends.

STOCKS
BONDS
BILLS
AND
INFLATION

Index

Index

M

N

O

IBBOTSON INVESTMENT TOOLS + RESOURCES

SBBI Report Subscriptions

Receive the most up-to-date data available when you subscribe to our SBBI reports on a monthly, quarterly or semi-annual basis. These reports feature:

- Updated returns and index values available on a monthly basis for six U.S. asset classes plus inflation.
- Inflation-adjusted returns and index values plus other derived series.
- The Stocks, Bonds, Bills, and Inflation index graph updated every quarter.
- Market commentary on a semi-annual basis.
- Prompt delivery of time-sensitive market data via fax.

All report subscriptions include a 1999 Yearbook and can begin at any time throughout the year. Current Yearbook subscribers can call our sales department for information on upgrade pricing.

SBBI Yearbook with 11 Monthly Reports (Best Value!) \$695
SBBI Yearbook 3 Quarterly Reports \$280
SBBI Yearbook with Semi-Annual Report \$160

The Cost of Capital Center Web Site

Visit Ibbotson's enhanced valuation web site, The Cost of Capital Center, where you can conveniently purchase cost of capital information online. Located at **http://valuation.ibbotson.com**, the site enables you to purchase Cost of Capital Quarterly analysis on over 300 industries, purchase individual company betas from the Beta Book database of 5,000 companies, and purchase risk premia and company tax rate reports.

1999 Cost of Capital Quarterly™ Yearbook

Providing data on over 300 industries, Cost of Capital Quarterly (CCQ™) is an invaluable reference for anyone performing discounted cash flow analysis. CCQ contains critical statistics you need to analyze corporations and industries and includes:

- Five separate measures of cost of equity.
- Weighted average cost of capital.
- Detailed statistics for sales, profitability, capitalization, beta, equity returns, and capital structure.

Published annually, the CCQ Yearbook is updated with data through March 1999. For the most frequent data available, subscribe to the CCQ Yearbook with quarterly updates.

1999 CCQ Yearbook with 3 Quarterly Updates \$995
1999 Cost of Capital Quarterly Yearbook \$395
(Shipped in June)

Stocks, Bonds, Bills, and Inflation® Valuation Edition 1999 Yearbook

Created specifically for business valuation professionals, this new addition to Ibbotson Associates' data publication series discusses many cost of capital issues in great detail and includes:

- Alternative methods of calculating equity risk premia, size premia and beta.
- An easy-to-understand analysis of the CAPM, Fama-French 3-factor model, and the build-up approach.
- Calculations of risk premia for any time period.

With easy to follow graphs and examples that illustrate the analysis, this publication provides a critical look at new developments in cost of capital estimation.

SBBI: Valuation Edition 1999 Yearbook \$120

Ibbotson Beta Book

The Beta Book is an invaluable resource for modeling stock performance and accurately pricing securities. With data on 5,000 companies, the book provides statistics critical for calculating cost of equity with the CAPM and the Fama-French 3-factor model. Employing the most current methods, the Beta Book contains traditional 60-month levered beta calculations, unlevered betas, betas for thinly traded securities, and betas adjusted toward peer group averages. Published semi-annually, the First Edition provides data through December 1998 and the Second Edition provides data through June 1999.

1999 First Edition \$625 *(Shipped in February)*
1999 Second Edition \$625 *(Shipped in August)*
Both Editions \$1,000

Ibbotson Sales Builder™ Presentation System

The Sales Builder Presentation System features Ibbotson charts and presentations packaged three ways–as a complete Asset Allocation Library, 11 different Sales Builder Presentation Modules or individual images of our 10 most popular graphs. Presentations are available in Microsoft PowerPoint format or as 8 1/2" x 11" laminated prints.

Sales Builder Asset Allocation Library \$800
Sales Builder Presentation Module \$100 each
Sales Builder Individual Image \$25 each

IBBOTSON INVESTMENT TOOLS + RESOURCES
(continued)

Ibbotson Software + Data

We have developed a line of software that allows you to discover, understand and present the tradeoffs that must be considered when working towards the right balance between risk and reward for your clients.

Ibbotson Analyst™

Analyst is designed to help you look at the historical behavior of a variety of asset classes. You can use Analyst to examine past market performance from as early as 1926 by creating graphs, charts and tables of statistical data. Choose from a wide selection of Ibbotson data or import your own. Included with Analyst is the Stocks, Bonds, Bills, and Inflation (SBBI) data module, with 29 historical data series on U.S. asset classes from 1926 to the present. Series are updated monthly via our web site, **www.ibbotson.com**.

First year subscription $1,050

Ibbotson Portfolio Strategist™

To help build better portfolios for you clients, Portfolio Strategist helps determine the asset mix that offers the best chance of achieving the highest return for a given level of risk. You can also evaluate investor behavior using Ibbotson's risk-tolerance questionnaire, and take into account your client's needs and objectives, constraints, and tax situation in order to recommend the appropriate range of optimal portfolios.

First year subscription $1,050

Ibbotson Fund Strategist®

Selecting mutual funds to implement an asset allocation policy can be difficult, especially when you encounter outdated or abbreviated holdings, changing managers and objectives, and most importantly, drifting or mislabeled styles. Fund Strategist simplifies the process by helping you monitor the behavior of mutual funds using returns-based style-analysis. Featuring analysis on over 4,000 of the largest U.S. mutual funds, the Fund Strategist analysis results are presented in a concise, fact sheet-style format.

First year subscription $600

Ibbotson EnCorr™

Designed for money managers, plan sponsors and consultants, the EnCorr software system embodies sophisticated investment concepts within an easy-to-use framework. EnCorr is a modular system that integrates historical data analysis, strategic asset allocation, forecasting, style analysis, performance measurement, portfolio attribution and a wide array of statistical and graphical analyses into one family.

Prices begin at $2,000

For more information or to request a product catalog, call **800 758 3557** or visit our web site at **www.ibbotson.com**.

2000 YEARBOOK ORDER FORM

To Order

Call: 800 758 3557
Fax: 312 616 0404
Web: **www.ibbotson.com**
Mail: Ibbotson Associates
225 North Michigan Avenue
Suite 700
Chicago, Illinois 60601-7676
Attn: Order Processing

Item	Price	Quantity	Total
SBBI 2000 Yearbook (PB001-00)	$100		
SBBI 2000 Yearbook and **Semi-Annual** Report	$160		
SBBI 2000 Yearbook and **Quarterly** Reports	$280		
SBBI 2000 Yearbook and **Monthly** Reports	$695		
		Merchandise Total	
		Add applicable sales tax (NY, TX, IL)	
		Shipping and Handling	$10
		Special delivery surcharge (see table at left)	
		Total Amount	

code=ROMC

For delivery outside the United States and Canada, please **add $30**.

For an extra charge, we can expedite delivery by Federal Express to most U.S. and Canadian destinations.

Overnight delivery **add $25** Express delivery (2-day) **add $15**

Name

Company

Street Address Suite/Floor

City State Zip

Phone Number

PAYMENT METHOD

○ Check enclosed, payable to: **Ibbotson Associates** (in U.S. dollars)
○ MasterCard
○ American Express
○ Visa

Card Number

Expiration Date

Signature of Authorized Buyer

IbbotsonAssociates